# GLIDER
# PILOTS
## AT
# ARNHEM

# GLIDER
# PILOTS
## AT
# ARNHEM

### MIKE PETERS
#### and
### LUUK BUIST

Pen & Sword
**MILITARY**

First published in Great Britain in 2009 by
PEN & SWORD MILITARY
An imprint of
Pen & Sword Books Ltd
47 Church Street
Barnsley
South Yorkshire
S70 2AS

Copyright © Mike Peters, 2009

ISBN 978 1 84415 763 1

A CIP catalogue record for this book is
available from the British Library

Printed and bound in England
By CPI

Pen & Sword Books Ltd incorporates the Imprints of Pen & Sword Aviation,
Pen & Sword Family History, Pen & Sword Maritime, Pen & Sword Military, Wharncliffe
Local History, Pen & Sword Select, Pen & Sword Military Classics, Leo Cooper,
Remember When, Seaforth Publishing and Frontline Publishing

For a complete list of Pen & Sword titles please contact
PEN & SWORD BOOKS LIMITED
47 Church Street, Barnsley, South Yorkshire, S70 2AS, England
E-mail: enquiries@pen-and-sword.co.uk

Website: www.pen-and-sword.co.uk

# Contents

# Maps/Forms

# Foreword

## By Brigadier M.D.K. Dauncey DSO DL

I can think of no stronger partnership than that of my long-standing friends Mike Peters and Luuk Buist, who have produced this fascinating account, *Glider Pilots at Arnhem*. I did not take part in the airborne landing on Sicily or in Normandy and only achieved an average grading on my Second Pilot's Flying Course. So the offer from Mike to write this foreword was not just a huge surprise but also a great honour. The book, which is unique, has surpassed all my expectations. When the proofs arrived, they were too exciting not to read straight away, which I did far into the night!

Good luck always plays a major role in war. It certainly led to the widely differing escapades of the glider pilots in the battle. The first lift, on 17 September 1944, was a trouble-free armada as regards the flight and landings which came as a complete surprise to the enemy. However successive lifts came under increasing pressure as the week wore on, with the German anti-aircraft batteries, enemy fighters and ground troops all ready and waiting for the arrival of our gliders, aircraft and paratroops. On Thursday afternoon, 21 September 1944, a resupply mission to Arnhem was mounted by 190 Squadron RAF. Out of the ten Short's Stirlings that took off from RAF Fairford bound for Arnhem, only three returned to England. Not one of the surviving aircraft landed undamaged. They all flew straight and level over the planned Dropping Zone, disregarding the deafening flak. It was heart-breaking to watch such outstanding bravery by our aircrews and air despatchers.

By this time there was a shortage of glider pilots in England, as about 90 per cent of the Regiment had already taken part in the landings at Arnhem. Staff Sergeant Roy Howard, who successfully landed his glider in Normandy in the dramatic coup de main attack on the Orne Bridges, found that the sixteen gliders flying from RAF Keevil had composite crews drawn from A, B, D and E Squadrons. He only met his second pilot Sgt Davey for the first time on the day of the flight and was never to see him again after that eventful day.

When the Airborne troops under Lieutenant Colonel John Frost at the bridge had finally been overwhelmed, a divisional bridgehead was formed. Known as the perimeter, it was loosely centred on Divisional Headquarters at the Hartenstein Hotel in the north and the Royal Artillery gun line near Oosterbeek Church to the south. The aim was to hold this bridgehead until the arrival of XXX Corps. After the landings, the glider pilots were to be withdrawn to England to prepare for further airborne operations. Instead they were ordered to remain with 1st British Airborne Division. They proved to be invaluable reinforcements, and as this book will show so vividly they took a full part in every aspect of the battle from the first landings to the final withdrawal over the river. Here the glider pilots organized and taped the withdrawal for the Division. The glider pilots were known as 'Total Soldiers'; this is the kernel of this unique book.

Trevor Francis and his wife Meg are old friends. Shortly after the first lift landings, we were told to remain with the Light Regiment RA near Oosterbeek Church as a protective infantry screen. However Trevor wanted to do more. He became a gun number with one of the 75mm Pack Howitzer guns of the light regiment and fought as a member of a gun crew throughout the week. Sadly one of his last duties was to help the crew to cast the gun's breech block into a deep ditch nearby, this last act of defiance rendering the gun useless to the enemy.

I have always felt that as infantryman we compared favourably with our enemy counterparts, who were shy of us. There was no shouting on our part – it was unnecessary as all airborne soldiers got on so well. My commander, Major Bob Croot, OC of G Squadron, had the wonderful knack of always being with us when things 'hotted' up. Also Lieutenant Colonel Iain Murray, who used to take the trouble and the risk to come and see us from Divisional HQ; it made such a difference to feel that he had our interests at heart.

Finally I would like to end this foreword by expressing my gratitude to the Dutch people for all of their kindness and help both during and after the battle. Their courage, support and generosity were unbounded. They will never accept that we caused them so many hardships and losses; they merely say 'you gave us hope'. What wonderful friends. No wonder we keep returning to Arnhem and Oosterbeek to see them, their children and their grandchildren year after year.

This is a superb read and unique in that the idea has never been used before. So heartiest congratulations to Mike and Luuk on producing such a splendid account of the 'Glider Pilots at Arnhem' which will always be enjoyed and appreciated.


Mike Dauncey
Uley, Glos

# Acknowledgements

It has been my ambition to tell the story of the men of the Glider Pilot Regiment and their role in the Battle of Arnhem for many years. I promised my many friends in the GPRA that one day I would collate all of their memories of Arnhem into a single book focussed on their exploits – an aspiration shared with my good friend and fellow honorary GPRA member, Luuk Buist. Without Luuk's co-operation and assistance I could not have written such a comprehensive account of the events surrounding the GPR in September 1944. Researching a battle that took place in Holland when you are located in England has its own practical problems, even if it is as well documented as Arnhem. Luuk has unselfishly shared his intimate knowledge of the battlefield, and has given me unrestricted access to his extensive archives and his unique database of 1,250 veteran names collated during thirty years of personal research. I must also single out his hard work producing and formatting all the maps and photographs. We both hope that the result of our joint efforts has produced a worthy and enduring tribute to the men of the Glider Pilot Regiment.

There are many other people to thank for helping us to achieve our aim. First of all, two friends and fellow battlefield guides, accomplished authors Jon Cooksey and Tim Saunders. Two years ago they both persuaded me that I could write and encouraged me to start working on this book. Once the book was underway, further encouragement came from other battlefield guides, Bob Hilton, Bob Darby and Major John Greenacre AAC. They have all freely shared their extensive knowledge of Arnhem and Airborne Forces with me. Thanks are due as well to Major Steve Elsey AAC, firstly for his research activities at the Museum of Army Flying, and also for suggesting that Luuk and I combine our efforts to produce this book. Steve and Arthur Shackleton are both responsible for the resulting partnership. Luuk would also like to acknowledge the support and inspiration provided by his good friends, glider pilot veteran John McGeough and John Howes for his hard work in the National Archives. Assistance was given too by Niall Cherry and the Friends of the Airborne Museum Hartenstein.

In Holland, Dutch historians Geert Maassen and Phillip Reinders added their support and extensive knowledge of the battle. In Oosterbeek, the Kremer family's permission to publish their unique photographs is a valuable contribution that is greatly appreciated. I was further assisted in England in my own research by Steve Wright, Scott Revell (Defending Arnhem), Mark Hickman (Pegasus Archive), Sarah Hayes, Mark Hone and Thomas Buttress. Numerous members of the Glider Pilot Regiment Association offered their personal memories and pictures. They are too numerous to name and some have sadly passed away, but I must thank those that follow for their generosity. The GPRA support was spearheaded by David Brook, editor of *The Eagle* magazine. Permission to use the diaries of Major Ian Toler was freely given by Celia Toler on behalf of the Toler family. Candy Gibson gave her permission to use her father's (SSgt R. Gibson) account of his experiences. The Foreword to the book was written by a true gentleman and a great ambassador for the GPR, Brigadier Mike Dauncey DSO – thank you, sir. Glider pilots and other Arnhem veterans who must be thanked are: L.M. Affolter, H.N. Andrews, R.F. Ashby, W. Ashworth, A. Baldwin, G.

Barton, G.S. Baylis, W. Blanthorn, P.J. Bond, E.W. Browne, K.W. Bryant, R.W. Cardy, A.G. Chapman, M. Clayton, S. Dadd, R. Dance, S. Dodd, R. Driver, L.J. Frater, O. Frazer, G. Freeman, H. Gibbons, W.D. Gordon, R. Grant, B.J.F. Haller, S. Hann, B. Harget, C.A. Harman, W.F. Harrison, D. Hartley, M. Herridge, G. Higgins, W. Holcroft, J.M. Hooper, P. Jackson, J.H. Jenkins, R.O. Johnson, A.F. Johnston, G.H. Kilbryde, M. Leaver, C. Lyne, P.J. Mahoney, A.S. Maughan, A. Midgeley, G.W. Milburn, A.E. Mills, W. Mullett, B. Murdoch, G.H.E. Nye, F.E. Otto, T. Owen, P. Pauwels (NL), T. Pearce, E.J. Peters (Border), F.C. Ponsford, M.J. Potter (RE), G.F. Pyne, N.T. Ramsden, A. Richards, A.A. Rigby, R.D. Rose, B. Shipley, W. Simpson (RAF), D. Smithson, F. Sullivan, G.B. Tapping, R.K. Taylor, B.A. Tomblin, B. Vincent, G. Voller, N.H. Walton, C.R. Watkinson, L.L. Weeden, E.C. Wedgbury, J.A.B. Wetherall, A. Williams, P. Wood.

The accounts of the men delivered into battle by the GPR are, of course, vital to completing this story. The respective regimental museums were all supportive, and particular acknowledgements are due to Stuart Eastwood of the KOBR Museum and the staff of the KOSB Museum. I cannot draw these acknowledgements to a close without mentioning 'Chaz' Lloyd who took me and a minibus full of young AAC soldiers on our first visit to Arnhem in 1984. I was already interested in the GPR then but the battlefield tour we undertook that weekend away from Germany really triggered an insatiable appetite in me for military history and battlefields. Henry Wilson, Bobby Gainher and everybody at Pen & Sword deserve a mention for their patience and encouragement, particularly when I was away in Afghanistan. Finally Luuk and I must thank our wives Astrid and Karen for their support, encouragement and most importantly their never-ending patience over the past two years. Our family and friends also deserve recognition for their continued interest and in some cases practical help proofreading draft chapters. I hope I have not forgotten anybody – if I have it is entirely unintentional.

Mike Peters
Little Stonham
Suffolk

# Introduction

## *'A' Tag*

**10 May 1940**

Out of the subdued grey light of dawn a loose formation of small shark-like gliders packed with assault troops cast off from their tugs. Immediately they began a rapid descent toward a landing zone. Their rapid approach onto their objective was almost silent until they landed literally on top of their respective targets. Now in the midst of a largely unsuspecting garrison, at the controls of one of the small drab-coloured gliders was a German glider pilot, Feldwebel (Sergeant) Heiner Lange:

> I was being shot at as I approached the fort by machine gun fire and it was a fireworks that I did not enjoy! I rolled the aircraft a bit to get through. It was strange to see tracer bullets seemingly coming straight at me, only for them to go on past at the last moment to the left and the right. But they gave me an advantage, as I knew exactly where I had to go. That was where the anti-aircraft fire was coming from that was where I had to go … I came in so low that with the left wing strut I tore a machine gun out of its pit and then I halted next to another machine gun position. The crew were just standing there with the glider above them. It was an absolute egg of a landing as we glider pilots say!
>
> Then I opened the cockpit, undid my belt, climbed onto the edge of the transport glider and jumped into the shallow machine-gun pit where the four Belgian gunners were cowering. I had my pistol in my right hand and my dagger in my left. I must have made a fearful sort of impression, as they immediately put up their hands.

So on the day designated by Hitler as *'A' Tag*, the shocked defenders of Eben Emael witnessed the birth of a new weapon of war – the Assault Glider. What followed over the next few hours was Operation GRANITE, an audacious German glider assault on the Belgian fortress of Eben Emael. The state-of-the-art fortress was reputed to be the most expensive and well constructed in the world to date. The glider had made the dramatic transition from an unproven concept to a new and potent weapon of war. It is the rapid neutralization and capture of what was thought to have been a near impregnable fortress that is commonly believed to have triggered the birth of a British glider force. The Prime Minister, Winston Churchill, along with most of the General Staff had been both stunned and impressed by Germany's blitzkrieg of Western Europe. One of the most dynamic components of the blitzkrieg onslaught was the use of airborne forces. The landings in Norway, the parachute assault on The Hague in Holland and the successful glider *coup de main* on Eben Emael during 1940 had particularly caught the Prime Minister's attention. The fortress complex at Eben Emael was the lynch pin of Belgium's defences. The fort was garrisoned by 1,200 well-trained troops, and had been intended to act as an unassailable obstacle blocking the path of any invading army. The fort's powerful guns were encased in concrete and surrounded by well-sited machine-gun posts, anti-tank guns and anti-aircraft positions. German planners had predicted casualties of up to 6,000 men if they attempted to capture the fort using conventional tactics.

The *Fallschirmjaeger* of *Sturmgruppe Granit* were landed silently and with pinpoint accuracy on top of the gun turrets in nine small DFS 230 Assault Gliders. The 78-strong force used specially developed shaped demolition charges to neutralize the guns and paralyse the defences. The attack coincided with another three glider-borne *coup de main* attacks that secured three key road bridges over the Albert Canal. The raid on Eben Emael was a phenomenal success that was achieved at the relatively light cost of six German casualties. Winston Churchill wasted no time in issuing directions on the subject of airborne forces; on 22 June he issued one of his famous minutes ordering the creation of a British airborne capability:

> We ought to have a corps of at least 5,000 parachute troops, including a proportion of Australians, New Zealanders and Canadians, together with some trustworthy people from Norway and France. I see more difficulty in selecting and employing Danes, Dutch and Belgians. I hear something is being done already to form such a corps, but only I believe on a very small scale. Advantage must be taken of the summer to train these forces, who can, none the less, play their part meanwhile as shock troops in home defences. Pray let me have a note from the War Office on the subject.[1]

The successful execution of Operation Granite guaranteed the inclusion of some form of glider-borne force within Churchill's new 'Airborne Corps'.

The volunteers who subsequently joined the Glider Pilot Regiment were forged over a very short period of time into a totally unique body of fighting men. A body of men that was to gain the dual distinction of being both the shortest-lived regiment in British Army history and the unit that accrued the highest casualty rate per head. By September 1944, just prior to the Battle of Arnhem, the Glider Pilot Regiment had reached the peak of its strength and capabilities. Formed in February 1942, the Glider Pilot Regiment was blooded in battle in the skies over Sicily in July 1943. It went on to figure prominently in the airborne landings that secured the eastern flank of the Allied landings in Normandy. Proven in battle and expanding at a steady rate, the glider pilots seemed capable of any task set before them. Buoyed by the success of Normandy, they were ready to undertake any operation presented to them. Finally, after a frustrating series of cancelled operations, they received orders for the greatest airborne operation of all. Operation MARKET GARDEN, the Allied plan to use three airborne divisions consecutively with the ultimate objective of securing a crossing over the River Rhine. The outcome of that operation is well known even to those with only a passing interest in military history. What is less well known is the part played in the battle of Arnhem by the men of the Glider Pilot Regiment. The aim of this book is to tell the story of those men who fought alongside their comrades in the 1st British Airborne Division at Arnhem. They flew into battle proudly wearing the coveted Army Flying Badge and the Red Beret. The regiments motto 'Nothing is Impossible' had been vindicated in Sicily and in Normandy. The fighting in and around Nijmegen, Arnhem and Oosterbeek would put these brave men and their motto to the test. This book is a tribute to all of the men of the Glider Pilot Regiment who fought in Holland. It is particularly dedicated to those brave men who paid the ultimate price for their endeavours.

**Notes**

1     NA, CAB 120/262, Churchill to War Office, 22 June 1940.

# CHAPTER 1

# Genesis

*'The Glider Pilot Regiment is part of the Army Air Corps and will have the honour of delivering men, guns, vehicles and even tanks right into the heart of the forthcoming battle ... not only will you have to be a top rate pilot, but also able to fight efficiently after landing.'*

In September 1939, nine months before the skilful execution of Operation GRANITE by German airborne forces, a conference had taken place at the British Air Ministry in London. The need for gliders and trained military pilots to fly them had been agreed. The initial concept involved the use of Army Co-operation Squadrons to assist in the training of the fledgling force. The training syllabus required the volunteer aviators to complete three solo sorties prior to moving on to a dedicated Glider Training School. Three solo flights is a pathetic amount of landings for a military pilot, so it can only be assumed that there was a plan for some form of continuation training. The gliders available at the time were little more than sail planes – a far more comprehensive course would be required to handle the heavier military glider that would be required for airborne landings. Further development of the concept was interrupted by the German Blitzkrieg campaign launched in the summer of 1940. The battle to save France and Belgium from the German military juggernaut drew the Army Co-operation Squadrons over to France away from their training role. Their deployment and the resulting losses of aircraft and instructors during the campaign delayed the formation of the new training depots until December 1940. In spite of the delays research had continued into what exactly an airborne force would comprise and how it would be equipped. A Central Landing School was established at Ringway Airport near Manchester. Squadron Leader Louis Strange DSO MC DFC & Bar was appointed commanding officer and he arrived at Ringway on 21 June 1940 on the official formation of the CLS. He was joined by Squadron Leader Jack Benham as chief instructor, development of equipment and techniques. The senior army officer at the School was to be Major John Rock who was to play a significant role in the development of the fledgling Glider Pilot Regiment.

The first gliding school was eventually established at Haddenham (renamed RAF Thame), near Aylesbury, in March 1941. The school was commanded by Squadron Leader H.E. Hervey MC and the training staff comprised pilots from all three services who had flown gliders as a hobby before the war. As there were no true military gliders available to equip the school, the first students were taught to glide using civilian sail planes. The sail planes had been donated or requisitioned from all over the country, ironically a number of them being of German manufacture. Prior to glider training each student pilot was required to undergo elementary flying training at Royal Air Force flying schools, where they learnt to fly in the iconic De Havilland Tiger Moth and the Miles Magister trainer. At the end of this powered-aircraft phase of their training, each student was expected to have accumulated an average of 130 flying hours in his log book. The Tiger Moth was also employed as a tug aircraft at the glider schools.

Although small in scale the conceptual development of a British glider force appeared to make good initial progress. On 26 September 1940, a demonstration was mounted using two First World War vintage Avro 504 trainers towing two of the civilian sail planes. This was followed in October by a night-flying sortie using four sail planes. Later in the same month, sixty-six men from No. 2 Commando, who had declared some previous flying experience, were selected for training as 'Glider Coxswains'. When the new Glider Wing was officially established in December 1940, with its army pilots included in its order of battle, the new unit immediately created controversy. The decision was not welcomed in some quarters. On 11 December 1940, Air Marshal Sir Arthur Harris AFC made the following sceptical statement that was to become infamous within the GPR:

> The idea that semi-skilled, unpicked personnel (infantry corporals have, I believe, even been suggested) could with a maximum of training be entrusted with the piloting of these troop carriers is fantastic. Their operation is the equivalent to forced landing the largest sized aircraft without engine aid – than which there is no higher test of piloting skill.[1]

The Army General Staff did not share the Air Marshal's opinion; they believed that an experienced soldier who was trained to fly had clear advantages. Countering with the following argument:

> The glider coxswain [pilot] on touching down will be the only man present who will know exactly where the landing has been made and in which direction the troops should go. He has the best forward view, he is highly trained in map reading and studying ground from the air, and he will have noted the lie of the land to the objective. Even if only a Corporal, he will be the one to lead the other 23 officers and men to the right place.[2]

The need for an airborne force of any size or composition was the subject of fierce and protracted inter-service debate and correspondence. Many within the RAF were loathe to squander valuable crews, aircraft and resources on the development of a capability that might never be used. The wrangling hindered any real progress towards the creation of the 'Airborne Corps' envisaged by Winston Churchill in his original minute and the woeful lack of progress was made evident to the Prime Minister in the spring of 1941. Winston Churchill came to inspect progress personally on 26 April 1941, accompanied by Mrs Churchill, US Ambassador Averill Harriman, Major General Hastings Lionel Ismay CB DSO and Air Marshal Sir Arthur Sheridan Barratt CB CMG MC. A combined demonstration was staged by the now renamed Central Landing Establishment and the Parachute Training School involving a formation of six Whitleys dropping forty paratroops and their equipment on Ringway. The parachute drop was accompanied by an equally small formation landing of five single-seat gliders and a demonstration by the newly delivered eight-seat Hotspur troop-carrying glider. Churchill's inspection of the exercise troops included a section of Free French personnel. The Prime Minister addressed the PTS members and he was said to be reasonably satisfied with the progress made in difficult circumstances. Only a month later the argument for British airborne forces received support from a most unexpected quarter – the Germans.

On 20 May 1941, the Germans mounted a huge airborne operation to capture the Mediterranean island of Crete. The massed landings using over 3,000 paratroops and glider-borne infantry overwhelmed a much larger British and Commonwealth garrison, and placed the strategically important island under German occupation. Yet another German airborne success reinvigorated Churchill's determination that Britain must at least achieve parity in airborne forces with the Germans. He called for immediate action and it was agreed that the Army would supply glider pilots, with the RAF taking responsibility for qualifying them. To counter any problems which might arise at parent units with personnel on detached duties, it was also decided to form a new Army Air Corps with two autonomous regiments: the Glider Pilot Regiment and the Parachute Regiment.

It was some weeks later, in June 1941, that the first deliveries of production variants of a purpose-built British military glider began. The General Aircraft Ltd Hotspur was a relatively small assault glider that was designed to carry a section of infantry into battle. It was never used in action but after some initial production teething problems it proved to be an ideal training aircraft. The birth of military gliding and the training of soldiers to fly were regarded by many as a dangerous novelty. Such a degree of suspicion and wariness existed at the time that whenever gliding was in progress at Thame airfield a 10-mile exclusion zone was advertised to other airfields.

In August 1941, the Air Ministry finally acceded and agreed that glider pilots should be fighting soldiers. They further agreed that they could be officers or NCOs and that they would be seconded to the RAF for training. The decision was also taken to formalize the training of glider pilots by the creation of Elementary Flying Training Schools that would train army pilots. In late 1941, the War Office approved the formation of an Army Air Corps, and within the new corps, the Glider Pilot Regiment. The next step was to recruit the soldiers required and notices began to appear in unit orderly rooms all over England:

THE AIRBORNE FORCES OF THE BRITISH ARMY CONSIST OF PARACHUTE TROOPS AND GLIDER-BORNE TROOPS OF ALL ARMS OF THE SERVICE.

Officers and men in any Regiment or Corps (except RAC), who are medically fit, may apply for transfer to a parachute or glider-borne unit of the Airborne Forces ... A limited number of officers and other ranks are urgently required for training as glider pilots. Applications for transfer or further information should be made to unit headquarters.

In December of the same year, the RAF's Flying Training Command was directed to administer the training of ab-initio army students on powered aircraft. There was, however, an initial delay due to a lack of students as the Army was unable to provide them. The first students for the new course would not be available until January 1942. The new regiment officially came into being on 24 February 1942, and sufficient progress was made the same month for Major John Frost to lead 'C' Company of 2nd Battalion of the Parachute Regiment in a successful raid on occupied France. The use of paratroops to attack the German radar station at Bruneval was a significant milestone in the development of airborne forces. Further progress was made when the Glider Pilot Regiment depot was opened at Tilshead Camp on Salisbury Plain in Wiltshire. The pilots, who were all volunteers, had to pass the Royal Air Force selection boards for standard aircrews. During that first year, when the Regiment had little idea of its employment, it was structured on the traditional infantry model. The new units were to be formed around companies and grouped into battalions. The first Commanding Officer of the new regiment was Lieutenant Colonel John Rock, a Royal Engineer officer with staff experience. Rock had been the Army liaison officer at Ringway, and had written a series of papers on the strategic and tactical employment of parachute forces. He had also 'staffed' a number of ideas for the development of specialist clothing and equipment for the new force. As the Regiment's first commander he was among the students that would learn to fly under the new system. The Regiment would need sub-unit commanders and its own staff officers to lead the freshly trained glider pilots. In advance of the first intakes, the 'Officers' Course' formed up at 16 EFTS at Burnaston on New Year's Day 1942.

The officers' course comprised Regular Army captains and majors who had been selected to form the command structure of the Glider Pilot Regiment. Each of the eight student pilots had been personally selected by Major General 'Boy' Browning, the commander of a very new British formation – the 1st Airborne Division. Assisted by two staff officers, 'Boy' Browning had interviewed thirty candidates before choosing the eight for the course. After the results of the selection board had been published, an amendment was issued. The post of Second in Command had been offered to Major Willoughby of the Highland Light Infantry, although this was subsequently withdrawn and the post was given to Major George Chatterton, a former RAF pilot and infantry officer. As Second in Command of the Regiment his responsibilities included training and the running of the Tilshead Depot. Previous experience as a fighter pilot and later as an infantryman in France had given Major Chatterton very clear views on the skills and qualities every glider pilot would require. This extract from the opening address delivered by him to new intakes of recruits gives some indication of the priorities he set for his depot staff and the potential recruits in their charge:

> The Glider Pilot Regiment is established from volunteers of all regiments, which have grown out of the traditions heretofore mentioned. It is the most unusual unit ever conceived by the British Army. A soldier who will pilot an aircraft, and then fight in the battle, a task indeed.
>
> It must start from nothing, and weld its own name. However, let it not fail to see that within its ranks are the material and tradition of years. This being so, it must set itself the highest standards of spiritual endeavour. From the parade ground to the air, let it only be in the highest rank. Let the Esprit de Corps be second to none, and the bearing and discipline of all be that which can only be admired. Let manners, and humour and sympathy predominate, and above all, let loyalty to all be the mainstay of the regiment. Let there be no limits to the ambition of its material feats.
>
> With every kind of weapon will the regiment fight, and let the traditions and experiences of the Royal Air Force be its standard as airmen.[3]

The basic principles outlined in the opening address were formalized in the training notes produced by George Chatterton when he later became the Commanding Officer of the Regiment:

> There is no doubt, that, to produce the type of advanced soldier necessary for the Glider Pilot, a good grounding is essential, and is in the early stages that the character and faith in the Regiment is born.
>
> Operational Commanders have found that a well disciplined, well trained, and smart Glider Pilot is an asset, whereas a stubborn and casual type is definitely a liability, both in the air and on the ground. A great deal of individual initiative is required in order that the complex situations and varying operational tasks may be faced and successfully overcome. A weakness in morale can mean disaster to the individual and to all concerned.
>
> It is therefore suggested that the Glider Pilot must have the following simple principles instilled, both during his progress from the Regimental Depot and to the Glider Training School.

Recognition of the high standard that will constantly be required.

Importance of bearing, saluting and drill.

Highest standard of knowledge of Infantry weapons.

Full appreciation of the responsibility of his rank.

The vital importance of the ground subjects taught by the RAF.

That the Regiment will only tolerate men of the highest principles and ideals.

The instructors who would 'instil' these standards in the trainee pilots were drawn almost exclusively from the Household Division's brigade of Foot Guards. Major Chatterton had been attached to the Grenadier Guards during the Dunkirk campaign. The bearing and discipline of the Guards warrant officers and sergeants made a deep impression on him. He had been able to persuade 'Boy' Browning, who was also a 'Grenadier', to use his influence to secure instructors for the new depot from the Household Division. The resulting level of discipline and 'bullshit' at Tilshead was therefore not what many of the new GPR recruits had anticipated when they volunteered to fly. A large number were 'RTU'd' – 'Returned To Unit' – by the training staff or voluntarily withdrew their papers and left the depot. Many glider pilots still have vivid memories of the intensive training regime that they underwent at the camp out on Salisbury Plain, not all of them pleasant. Each potential glider pilot developed his own survival strategy to ensure that he progressed beyond Tilshead. Corporal Joe Michie had left the Worcestershire Regiment to join his new regiment and had no intention of falling at the first hurdle. The Londoner arrived for training in Wiltshire in December 1942 with the simplest of plans: 'I knew that if you shut up and did everything you were told – no matter what – you would get through. I knew what this meant when RSM Jim Cowley arrived having been away sick, bellowing "Make way for a soldier!" Were his tunic buttons really sewn on with wire?'[4]

The opening of the depot was followed in May 1942 with the formulation of plans to train and maintain a force of 1,200 glider pilots to support airborne operations. The pace of the expansion programme was maintained with the opening of three new Glider Training Schools by the end of July 1943. A Heavy Glider Conversion Unit at RAF Brize Norton was also opened to introduce glider pilots to the intricacies of handling the Horsa and later the Hamilcar.

Corporal Trevor Francis was among the first volunteers for the new course. Trevor had enlisted in the Territorials in 1939, and had served in the Duke of Lancaster's Own Yeomanry until eventually his unit had given up its horses and been absorbed into the mechanized ranks of the Royal Artillery. Trevor had always wanted to fly – at sixteen he had failed to persuade his father to allow him to join the Royal Air Force. The formation of the Glider Pilot Regiment offered him an opportunity to realize his ambition to fly and to escape his life in the Artillery. Trevor arrived at a snow-covered Tilshead camp in late February 1942. The next six weeks were spent undergoing the extremely tough training implemented by the new regiment's Second in Command, Major George Chatterton. Trevor's impression was that the sole aim of the regime was to encourage him and his comrades to opt for the easier option of a 'Return To Unit' chit and a train warrant. Many did fall by the wayside but for Trevor and the majority of those that were destined to wear the Army Flying Badge, the desire to fly was irrepressible. Trevor Francis survived Tilshead and moved on to undergo elementary flying training at Burnaston Aerodrome near Derby.

The contrast between Tilshead and Burnaston could not be starker. Having endured the Spartan intensity of the training on Salisbury Plain, life in elementary flying school was almost luxurious. The class room syllabus included all of the staples required to form the foundations of flying training. Students were introduced to the complexities of the theory of flight, meteorology, map reading, Morse code and the slightly 'dicey' art of manually starting an aircraft engine by swinging the propeller. The weeks of effort at Tilshead were all justified at Burnaston when the course was finally introduced to their first aircraft, the monoplane Miles Magister. Trevor Francis described this initial flying phase of his training as 'heaven'. He was paired up with his flying instructor, Pilot

Officer 'Slow Roll' Booth. The nickname was apt as it was rare to fly with him without executing that particular aerobatic manoeuvre. Trevor learnt quickly to tighten his straps in the cockpit whenever he heard the phrase 'I want to wave goodbye to my girlfriend'. The phrase was normally followed by the aircraft flying inverted alongside a train at about one-hundred feet. With the Pilot Officer's girlfriend waving from her carriage window, the Magister would fly along on a parallel track upside down!

The greatest psychological hurdle for most student pilots is successfully flying solo for the first time. For Trevor this happened very suddenly as he accumulated the grand total of seven and a half hours of dual flying in the Magister. Having successfully flown solo all appeared to be going well for him until the next day. While flying 'circuits and bumps' around the Burnaston circuit he ran into problems:

> I suddenly found that I could not touch down without bouncing about fifty feet in the air. Finally, after trying for an hour, covered in sweat, my approach was too far up the field. I tried again, but with the flaps down and full throttle I skimmed the hedge heading for the trees, which this time I could not fly over, so tried banking between two of them. The right wing hit a tree at about a height of seventy feet and snapped off whilst the plane spun around like a boomerang, I vaguely remembered spinning around the house then seeing circular pans (roof tiles) and brick towers, one of which took the left wing off at a height of about ten feet, immediately the fuselage spun in a circle, one of the towers taking it off just behind me. What was left dived into the ground with the engine still at full throttle and being forced into the front pilot's seat.[5]

A shaken but uninjured Trevor climbed out of the wreckage to the sound of approaching ambulance sirens. There was a downside to his good fortune – the crash site was in the middle of the station sewerage farm! After twenty-four hours in the medical centre the unfortunate Trevor emerged expecting to find himself returned to the relative monotony of life in a gun battery, but was to be pleasantly surprised:

> I walked to the crew room only to find Pilot Officer Booth waiting on the door step. His only comment was 'Well you might have phoned me and told me you were in the shit!' Pointing to a plane he said 'Get in' and off I went with Pilot Officer Booth, giving a flying display of just about everything that can be done with an aircraft. He landed and got out, said 'Off you go, circuits and bumps', which went like a dream, leaving me uncertain about what had caused my accident in the first place.[6]

The new structure of the training experienced by Trevor and his fellow students had a number of benefits. The most obvious advantage of placing training under the control of Flying Training Command was the continuity gained by centralising the process under a single chain of command. The improved control of equipment, personnel and aircraft resulted in a reduction of the length of the gliding course from eleven weeks down to eight, with students logging more flying hours than under the old method, despite the fact the course was three weeks shorter. Once established the Glider Schools were staffed and equipped to train a course of sixty-six pilots in three weeks. Each student pilot would work a five and a half day week and make an average of thirty-three day landings during the course. The grass strips used by the schools became exceptionally active airfields; a single course would rapidly log over 2,000 landings in their three weeks of training. The tug pilots would log an identical number of take-offs and landings, an average of 180 sorties per day from each airfield.

Corporal Johnny Wetherall remembers progressing through the training programme with the sole aim of becoming a qualified glider pilot:

> The initial flying was carried out on a small powered aircraft, in my case a Tiger Moth, and it was exhilarating to be able to do aerobatics in these things after first passing out solo. Passing the powered-aircraft course meant moving on and learning to fly small gliders. The training gliders were Hotspurs, which carried two pilots and five fully equipped soldiers when necessary. These gliders were towed into the sky behind powered aircraft and then released into free flight from there to journey to the airfield and land.
>
> Passing out on these so-called small gliders meant a move to the real operational gliders, in my case the Horsa, which was as big as any other aircraft in use at the time and they were capable of carrying twenty-eight fully equipped soldiers, or a combination of Jeeps, guns or trailers … there was a lot of practice flying early in 1944 in preparation for Airborne operations in Europe and this used to become boring in stages, so to liven up proceedings we would ask the tug pilot if he noted some Italian prisoners of war working on haystacks below … we would go in, flying low and he would pass on one side of the haystack and we in the glider would pass on the other side. With the tow rope dangling between us, the object was to try and knock the haystack makers off.[7]

On completion of their flying training and conversion to heavy gliders at Brize Norton, the newly qualified glider pilots were posted to 'Battle School' to develop their infantry skills prior to joining their first unit. Many of the volunteers were regular soldiers who had seen active service with the BEF in France. Others had served in the Territorial Army prior to the outbreak of war. The total soldier concept required every pilot to be able to fight on the battlefield immediately after emerging from the cockpit of his glider. The Regiment established battle schools to hone the skills and tactics required to turn the newly qualified pilots into the total soldier envisaged by Major George Chatterton. The first of these new facilities was Southbourne Battle School which came into being in Bournemouth during the winter of 1942. The headquarters of the school was located in the Overcliffe Hotel which also doubled up as a barracks; the Warrant Officer's and Sergeants' Mess was set up in Crawford's Café.

The training staff for the battle school comprised glider pilots who had previously served as sergeants in infantry battalions. Staff Sergeant Ken Barratt was appointed as the senior instructor and tasked with establishing the school. The first officer to command the school was Captain Hamilton O'Malley of the Irish Guards. The syllabus was designed to produce glider pilots who could use every British infantry weapon and a number of German weapons. Much time was spent practising the art of fighting in buildings, described at the time as 'street fighting', skills that would be put to great use by glider pilots on the streets of Arnhem and Oosterbeek later in the war.

The 'Total Soldier' ethos was further enhanced during this phase of training, with glider pilots expected to fight as individuals or as formed bodies of troops. The need for this capability was outlined in the Glider Pilot Regiment training pamphlet and included this description of the qualities required of the GPR Staff Sergeant: 'He must be a soldier of the highest type, fully trained in all methods of warfare, confident to take on anything, anytime, and be constantly ready to use his initiative, from being an ordinary rifleman, to commanding a platoon.'

One of the roles envisaged for gliders from the outset was the carriage of heavy weapons and vehicles onto the battlefield. If glider pilots were to be of use after landing this equipment, Major Chatterton's view was that they had to be trained to operate it. Clear direction was also available from the training pamphlet formulated on the subject:

> The Glider Pilots load may be Anti-Tank Guns, Machine Guns, Mortars, Light Artillery – it

may be tanks, carriers, or wireless. Here again the Glider Pilot will train as the unit requires, and must be able to operate his load. This calls for complicated, specialist and individual training – all Glider Pilots will have attended courses in their squadrons.

Further to direction on individual training the role of the Regiment after landing its loads of troops and stores was also explained:

> The Glider Pilot Regiment once landed will be generally concentrated as a Light Infantry Regiment, its task being mainly a defensive one. All commanders and Other Ranks must be prepared to fight as Battalion, Company, and Platoon. Therefore squadrons will constantly train as a normal Infantry Company – from individual to company training. The Regiment will be practised in the field as a two Battalion Brigade, and must be prepared to fight as such.

In October 1942 a tragic event occurred that was to change the character and the direction of the Regiment. As a result of injuries incurred in a flying accident during a night flying exercise at Shrewton on 27 September, Lieutenant Colonel John Rock died on 8 October in Tidworth Hospital. The immensely popular Royal Engineer was replaced in command by his Second in Command, the newly promoted Lieutenant Colonel George Chatterton. The 'Total Soldier' concept became the foundation stone that the Glider Pilot Regiments would be built on. The intent of the new Commanding Officer is captured in another extract from one of his opening addresses: 'We will forge this regiment as a weapon of attack ... Not only will we be trained as pilots, but in all we do ... I shall be quite ruthless ... Only the best will be tolerated. If you do not like it, you can go back whence you came.'

With the selection and training process for the glider pilots taking shape, the need for gliders increased. The Hotspur would never see action but remained the mainstay of the glider training schools. In November 1942, Britain's first glider operation was mounted using the newly introduced Horsa glider. The Horsa was designed to meet a specification issued in October 1940 for a glider that could carry twenty-five fully equipped troops into battle. By January 1941, Air Speed Limited were already assembling jigs in preparation to meet an initial order for 440 Horsas. Production got underway in August 1941 and the glider that was destined to be the principal British assault glider was cleared for daylight operations from June 1942; within months the Horsa was also cleared for night operations. It is testament to its design and its builders that it was only modified once during its service history.

From the outset the vulnerability of lightly armed airborne forces to armoured counter-attacks and heavy weapons was realized. In October 1940, a specification was also issued for a larger glider that could deliver large anti-tank guns or a light tank onto the battlefield. The development and production of a glider that was as large as a four-engined bomber was controversial. Even Lieutenant Colonel Rock advocated adapting loads for carriage by the relatively smaller Horsa; he believed that any glider built to meet this specification would be ungainly and vulnerable to ground fire. The aircraft that emerged as a result of the heavy glider specification was christened the 'Hamilcar'. It would never be produced in the numbers that the Horsa was but it did play a significant part in the landings in Normandy and Arnhem. It was also used successfully on Operation VARSITY – the Rhine crossing in March 1945.

The first operation undertaken by the GPR, Operation FRESHMAN, ended in disaster. On 19 November 1942, two Horsas towed by Halifax bombers took off from RAF Wick in Scotland. Their mission was to attack the German heavy water plant at Vermork in southern Norway. The plant was playing a pivotal role in the Nazi programme to develop an atomic bomb.

The first glider combination to take off was a Horsa flown by Staff Sergeant Malcolm Strathdee and Sergeant Peter Doig. The tug was piloted by Squadron Leader Wilkinson. They took off at 1745 hours from Wick. The second combination Horsa tug took off at 1800 hours. Pilot Officer Norman Davies and Pilot Officer Herbert Fraser, both of the Royal Australian Air Force, were at the controls of the second glider. The second Halifax was flown by Flight Lieutenant Arthur Parkinson, Royal Canadian Air Force.

Each glider carried fifteen Sappers of the 9th Field Company and 261 Field Park Company, Royal Engineers, under the command of Lieutenant David Methven GM. What was already an intimidating prospect was further complicated by the relative inexperience of all those on board the gliders. The distance to the landing zone, the inadequate mapping of the landing zone area and the poor weather conditions at that time of year increased the already significant risks. The weather on the night chosen was bad over Scotland but promised to improve over Norway. The first combination decided to fly over the cloud all the way. The second combination decided to fly below the cloud until nearing the coast, and then climb in the better weather nearer the target. For some reason the low-flying Halifax flew into a mountain at Helleland, Rogaland, killing its crew; the glider was cast off and made a very heavy landing approximately 2.5 kilometres north-east of Lensmannsgard, 400-500 metres north-west of Gasetjern, some 4 kilometres north of where the towing Halifax crashed, killing and injuring most of its occupants.

Meanwhile the first combination approached the Norwegian coast at 10,000 feet, the weather improved but it was unable to find the landing zone. With fuel running low, the Halifax turned for home with the glider still in tow. On crossing the coast the combination ran into heavy cloud and icing, the air became very bumpy and the tow parted. The glider crash-landed at Fylgjesdal near Lysefjord, but the lead Halifax, flown by Squadron Leader Wilkinson, returned safely to Wick. The survivors of both gliders were captured and almost immediately fell into the hands of the Gestapo. The four glider pilots and twenty-one of their passengers are buried in Stavanger (Eiganes) Churchyard, Norway. Five passengers are buried in Oslo Western Civil Cemetery and four have no known graves. The crew of the second Halifax are buried in Helleland Churchyard.

It was the summer of 1943 before Britain was ready to mount its first large-scale airborne operation, when the Regiment would receive its baptism of fire in the Mediterranean theatre. The 1st Airborne Division under command of Major General George Hopkinson OBE MC was to be used en masse for the first time since its formation. The Airlanding Brigade and its gliders were to be given a chance to prove their worth in action as part of the invasion of the Italian island of Sicily. Operation LADBROKE would be launched from airfields in North Africa with the object of seizing key points in advance of seaborne landings. The 1st Battalion, The Glider Pilot Regiment, as it was then named, had been shipped to North Africa to prepare for the invasion of Sicily. Once in North Africa they encountered a series of logistic problems, extremes of weather and a dire shortage of aircraft. Eventually the shortfall in gliders was met by the loan of 500 American CG4A Waco gliders. Totally different in concept to the British Horsa, the Hadrian (the British designation for the Waco) was smaller, lighter and handled more like a sail plane on landing.

The American gliders were located at La Senia Airfield near Oran, still in the packing crates in which they had been shipped from America. Assembly of the Waco was beyond the knowledge and skill of the British pilots, who would require American technical assistance. Lieutenant Colonel George Chatterton had to approach his American counterparts to request the loan of aircraft fitters, flying instructors and even tug aircraft. Initial assistance materialized in the form of a two USAF aircraft fitters who taught two officers and fifty men of the 1st Battalion to assemble the gliders from scratch. In May, an ad-hoc production line steadily swung into action, manned by Chatterton's men under the supervision of the American fitters. The assembly line worked day and night in temperatures that reached 100 degrees Fahrenheit, living and sleeping in the empty packing cases left over after assembly. All of their working day was spent working in the open on the dust-blown airfield. As soon as the first gliders were assembled at the end of May, a small group of American instructors began to convert their British opposite numbers onto their new aircraft at Froha Airfield. Flying the Waco was such a huge contrast compared to the Horsa that the British pilots either loved it or absolutely hated it. Most accrued the grand total of four hours day flying and one hour at night. The majority disliked the aluminium, tubular-framed American glider – although renamed the Hadrian by the Air Ministry, it was christened the 'Whacko' by those who flew it.

Lieutenant Colonel Chatterton was very aware of the need to ensure that the Airlanding and Parachute Brigades each had their own anti-tank capability immediately after landing. He also had concerns about the suitability of the Waco for the *coup de main* landing envisaged on the Ponte Grande Bridge as it did not carry enough troops. He quickly reached the conclusion that he needed forty Horsa gliders to augment his force of Wacos. The request resulted in Operation TURKEY BUZZARD, a series of long-range aerial delivery flights between England and North Africa. A trial was staged in the UK to prove that Halifax tugs would have the necessary range to tow a Horsa glider the 1,400 miles to Sale (Rabat) Airfield in Morocco; they would then be towed on overland to their jump-off airfields in Algeria and Tunisia. The trial conducted by 295 Squadron RAF was successful and specially modified Halifax tugs were prepared for the task. The RAF called the long-range mission Operation BEGGAR.

The events of the night of 9 July 1943 can only be described as close to catastrophic for the Glider Pilot Regiment and the 1st Airlanding Brigade. The formation of 144 tug-glider combinations began taking off from Tunisian airfields at 1900 hours. After taking off in a sandstorm and after a difficult flight against the prevailing winds they finally approached Sicily in darkness. The darkness and winds had resulted in a number of the inexperienced American tug crews breaking formation after becoming disorientated. As the poor visibility and significant headwinds made it difficult for the remaining tugs and gliders to formate correctly, the formation became looser and looser until a number of aircraft lost the formation totally and became separated. The dispersal of the formation was compounded further when Italian anti-aircraft batteries opened fire. The crews of the American tug aircraft were flying on their first combat mission and lacked experience of flying in these conditions. Their aircraft also lacked armour plating and self-sealing fuel tanks – what followed are a series of events that remain contentious today. A number of the tug pilots elected to turn back to North Africa with their gliders in tow. Others, unaware of their position, simply released their gliders over the sea and headed for their home airfield, abandoning the glider to its fate. Many of the gliders were released miles out to sea, at low altitude, flying into a headwind making it impossible for them to make landfall. Seventy-three gliders ditched in the sea where they floated for a while, in some cases for hours. Those that landed within sight of Italian positions suffered the added ordeal of being swept by machine-gun fire as they clung onto the wings of their gliders. The sea and enemy fire claimed the lives of 326 men of the 1st Airlanding Brigade that night; 1,730 men had boarded gliders in North Africa. Amid the chaos of the landing many demonstrated exactly the qualities expected of them during their training. Staff Sergeant John Ainsworth was awarded the Military Medal in recognition of his bravery after ditching in the sea:

> This Staff Sergeant was forced to land his aircraft far out in the sea when attacking Sicily. Having seen that his crew were provided with life saving jackets and that all had been extricated from the water logged part of the glider, he swam ashore 3 miles distant. Armed with nothing but a fighting knife he killed two sentries and with the rifle of the second

continued fighting throughout the battle. The leadership and courage of this SSgt Pilot was in the best traditions of the service.[8]

Lieutenant Colonel Chatterton was at the controls of his own glider that night, carrying Brigadier 'Pip' Hicks, the commander of the 1st Airlanding Brigade and a number of his staff officers. When he reached the release point, he was, like the majority of his pilots, in a desperate situation with limited options. He had reached the release point but in the darkness and still could not see the coastline. Having cast off from his tug and begun his descent toward Sicily, he reached two hundred feet at which point he could discern what appeared to be a cliff face looming rapidly out of the night. It was directly in his glide path. As he fought desperately to gain some height and clear the cliffs, his Waco was hit by flak. The glider crashed into the sea about a hundred yards from the shore. Having floated for a very short time very shortly it began to fill with sea water. Luckily all of the glider's crew and passengers survived the crash and managed to swim to shore.

On reaching land the bedraggled group met a roving SAS patrol and joined them in attacking a series of enemy strongpoints on the cliffs. When dawn broke the joint force had accumulated a haul of 150 prisoners as a result of their nocturnal exploits. In spite of the disastrous start to the Airborne landing the men of the Glider Pilot Regiment and the Airlanding Brigade had fought extremely well. In recognition of his efforts to prepare the Glider Pilot Regiment for the invasion, Lieutenant Colonel George Chatterton was later awarded the Distinguished Service Order:

> On the night 9/10th July Lieutenant Colonel Chatterton led the 1st Battalion The Glider Pilot Regiment into action in a difficult operation involving a landing by moonlight in Sicily. The Regiment, organised and trained by this officer, performed a hazardous and difficult task with great distinction. He himself landed his glider under the most trying and exhausting circumstances without damage to the crew. By his personal disregard for his own safety at all times Lieutenant Colonel Chatterton set an example of courage and determination which, together with his outstanding leadership, enabled the 1st Battalion The Glider Pilot Regiment to carry out its first airborne operation with such distinction and gallantry.

The situation for the fifty-six gliders that had actually made it to shore was little better than those that had been ditched in the sea. The dispersal of the tug formation resulted in the landings being spread over a huge area, in some cases a distance of 30 miles from their intended LZ. The glider pilots and their passengers attempted to carry out their orders but the majority became involved in independent skirmishes with Italian troops until they linked up with advancing Eighth Army units. Operation LADBROKE was a disastrous start in operational terms for the Airlanding Brigade, and the Glider Pilot Regiment in particular. The 1st Battalion had managed to deploy 297 pilots on the landing, including twenty-four American volunteer pilots. Fifty-seven British pilots were killed on the operation and five of their American comrades. Despite the failings in the planning and execution of the plan, what had been proven was the ethos of the total soldier in the former and the aggressive fighting spirit of both. Lieutenant Frank Barclay was another member of the Regiment decorated after Sicily – part of the citation for his the Military Cross read:

> Lieutenant Barclay was the first pilot of his glider in this total glider borne operation. He made a successful landing against great odds, crashing [?] forward laden with his passengers to move forward for the assault on the Syracuse bridge. Lieutenant Barclay led the platoon which he had landed from his landing area to the bridge and showed great courage and leadership. Though the bridge was counter attacked several times this party

held on until relieved and Lieutenant Barclay must be given a great deal of credit for the success of this operation.

Only forty-eight hours after the Syracuse landings a second glider operation was mounted. Operation FUSTIAN was launched with the intent of capturing the Primasole Bridge across the River Simeto and Gornalunga Canal. The operation was a *coup de main* landing that if successful would secure a crossing point for an armoured thrust toward the town of Catania. The eight Waco and eleven Horsa gliders were towed to Sicily by RAF tugs, while the parachute element of the operation were carried in American C47 transports from US 51st Troop Carrier Command. Only four gliders reached their objective intact, delivering three 6-pounder anti-tank guns with their attendant Jeeps. The bridge was secured at 0430 hours by a force of fifty men. Three hours later Brigadier Gerald Lathbury arrived to reinforce the bridge after scraping together a force of 100 men. By midday, with minimal ammunition, the defenders now numbering 250 were driven back by an Italian counter-attack. The bridge was lost until first light on 16 July when it was retaken with the assistance of British armour and infantry.

The period after the liberation of Sicily was acutely frustrating for the men of 1st Battalion GPR. They were initially confined to a transit camp amid concerns that they would vent their anger over the loss of so many comrades on their American tug pilots. Brigadier 'Shan' Hackett remembered the level of anger felt by the glider pilots:

> Glider pilots who were recovered from the sea came back looking for tug pilots' throats to cut. I saw no option but to confine them to camp until after the American parade for the award of decorations for gallantry, by which time the admirable qualities always to be found in glider pilots had reasserted themselves and calm was restored.[9]

There then followed a frustrating five-month period of non-flying limbo spent in Italy as reserve infantry. The feelings of neglect were not helped by news of a reorganization of the Regiment. The combat-proven 1st Battalion was renamed as 2 Wing GPR and the newly formed 2nd Battalion in England had been given the title of 1 Wing GPR. The veterans of Sicily were far from impressed with what they perceived to be a slight on their reputation. Eventually orders were received for the new 2 Wing GPR to be recovered by sea to England. They embarked at Taranto on Christmas Eve 1943 and docked in Liverpool later in January 1944.

The return of the Sicilian veterans coincided with the formal reorganization of the Glider Pilot Regiment. The two battalions were formally retitled as wings. Each of the wings was made up of squadrons. Four squadrons were grouped under 1 Wing GPR commanded by Lieutenant Colonel Iain Murray MC. Lieutenant Colonel John Place was appointed to command 2 Wing GPR which comprised three squadrons. Each of the squadrons was made up of three to five flights of forty-four pilots. Wherever possible each squadron was located at the same airfield as its attendant RAF tug squadron. It was intended that the two units would over time build a close working relationship and an understanding of each other's requirements on operations. The reorganization was timely as the summer of 1944 would bring another airborne operation – Operation OVERLORD, the Allied invasion of Europe, was looming on the horizon and airborne forces were destined to play a critical role in the operation's success. This time the Glider Pilot Regiment would not be carrying their old friends from the 1st Airlanding Brigade, as they began training with the airlanding battalions of the 6th Airlanding Brigade.

The newly formed brigade had been formed around two airlanding battalions that originated from the 1st Airlanding Brigade. It was part of Britain's second airborne formation, the 6th Airborne Division. The 1st Battalion, The Royal Ulster Rifles and the 2nd Battalion, The Oxfordshire and

Buckinghamshire Light Infantry been left behind in England when the 1st Airborne Division sailed for North Africa and Sicily. The Brigade had been augmented by the addition of the initially untrained 12th Battalion, The Devonshire Regiment. The selection of Normandy as the landing site for the invasion set in train a lengthy period of intensive planning for what would be 6th Airborne Division's first operation. The 6th Airlanding Brigade was given a pivotal role in the plan formulated by Major General Richard 'Windy' Gale MC, the commander of 6th Airborne Division. The initial objective set for 6th Airborne was to capture and secure the key bridges over the Caen River and its parallel canal. Control of the bridges would help secure the Allied Armies' eastern flank, protecting the vulnerable landing beaches from German armoured counter-attacks.

The initial concept of the landing used only the 3rd Parachute Brigade drop and capture of the bridges at Bénouville and Ranville. The 2nd Battalion, The Ox & Bucks Light Infantry were initially ordered to allocate a company to seize each bridge by glider *coup de main*. As the plan developed further it was decided to bring the whole of 6th Airborne Division into play. The 6th Airlanding Brigade was given the task of securing the bridges while the 3rd Parachute Brigade switched its attention to the capture of the high ground east of Ranville. The plan changed again when reconnaissance photographs confirmed intelligence from the local area that the Germans were covering the area around the bridges with anti-glider poles fitted with mines. The presence of these poles achieved their aim and the plan was adapted again. With the option of a large-scale glider landing denied to him, Richard Gale decided to add the 5th Parachute Brigade to his plan – they would drop in with the first wave and secure the bridges. The gliders of the 6th Airlanding Brigade would come in after the parachute drop as part of the second wave on the night of D-Day. It was intended that the poles would be cleared by then allowing the gliders to land safely.

There was one element of the Airlanding Brigade that remained an indispensable element of the plan – Major John Howard and 'D' Company of the 2nd Battalion, The Ox & Bucks Light Infantry, reinforced by two platoons of 'B' Company. The reinforced company and the crews of their six Horsa gliders remained focussed on seizing the bridges in a dramatic *coup de main* landing. They and their glider pilots would have the distinction of being the first British troops to land in Normandy. The operation to capture the bridges was code-named DEADSTICK and was a spectacular success with light casualties. A larger and more complex operation involving three 'B' Squadron gliders was mounted by 9th Parachute Battalion to capture and neutralize the gun battery emplaced at Merville. The operation was plagued with problems resulting in the assault force being scattered over a wide area. Not all of the three gliders reached the objective and many of the paratroops were drowned in marshes on landing. Instead of the complete battalion assaulting the guns only 150 lightly equipped paratroops and sappers stormed the German battery. As a result of their bravery the guns at Merville did little to interfere with landings on the nearby British and Canadian beaches. Controversy still surrounds the execution and outcome of the Merville operation, however there can be no doubt about the courage of the men who attacked the heavily fortified German battery that night.

Later, on 6 June 1944, two large-scale glider landings took place. The first was Operation TONGA, a massed landing involving ninety-two Horsa gliders. The daylight landing delivered anti-tank guns to screen the newly secured bridgehead from German armour. Later the same day, before dark, Operation MALLARD took place. Twenty-nine Hamilcars and 229 Horsas delivered the bulk of the 6th Airlanding Brigade onto Norman soil. The Hamilcars of 'C' Squadron GPR made their operational debut carrying the Tetrach light tanks of 6th Airborne Division's Armoured Reconnaissance Regiment. This was the first ever landing of armour in such force by glider in history. When measured against the disastrous events of Sicily less than a year before, the

Normandy landings were deemed to be a great success. Lieutenant Colonel Iain Murray commanded 1 Wing GPR during the operation. He had taken off from RAF Harwell during the early hours of 6 June with his co-pilot Lieutenant Brian Bottomley. His Horsa carried Brigadier The Honourable Hugh Kindersley, his Jeep and a handful of staff from Headquarters 6th Airlanding Brigade. Also on board was the Australian War Correspondent Chester Wilmot, who recorded a running commentary during the flight on a tape recorder. Their landing was eventful as one of the anti-glider obstacles on the landing zone ripped off the tip of the left wing, and another collided with the cockpit head-on. Fortunately the pole was loose and was immediately torn from the ground on impact. Lieutenant Colonel Murray deducted that the poorly fixed pole had been planted by a reluctant Frenchman, forced to work by the Germans. He was awarded the Distinguished Service Order for his efforts.

Lieutenant Colonel Murray led his Glider Pilots who landed in the Caen area on the morning of the 6th June 1944. He showed great courage and leadership and complete disregard for his own safety. Through his personal example and leadership, the pilots of his Glider Pilot Regiment successfully landed the 6th Airborne Division although faced with intense anti-aircraft fire and mortar fire on the landing zone. He also had to make his landing in poor visibility by night.[10]

The success of the Normandy landings inevitably shaped the thinking of the GPR hierarchy on future operations. The following is an extract from Lieutenant Colonel Murray's report on Operation OVERLORD:

The following comments are forwarded for consideration:

(1)    The white stripes on gliders were of great value for picking out gliders already landed. If these markings are dispensed with in future something of the same nature on upper surfaces of wings is most desirable.

(2)    The green hollophane lights were excellent but the red air sea rescue lights were not seen by all pilots.

(3)    Differential brakes are essential when landing on L.Zs. which have posts erected.

From experience of this operation the following changes of equipment are suggested:-

(i)    2 trained snipers per section with sniper rifles fitted with telescopic sights.

(ii)   Rucksacks in place of present web equipment.

(iii)  Torches are not needed in operations as each glider has one as part of its equipment.

(iv)   One jeep is required for Wing HQ if the Glider Pilot force is in more than one locality.

(v)    In the place of T.S.M. [Thompson] guns it is suggested that each section should have two Mark V Sten guns.

With the exception of the above, the equipment was most satisfactory. The morale of the men was very high, especially those forming part of gun crews.

Major John Royle added further comment and suggestions regarding the training and equipping of glider pilots. The majority would be implemented prior to the Arnhem landings later the same year:

> The morale and conduct of the men was excellent at all times. Movement and battle drill was fast and efficient. Digging-in was completed well on time.
>
> It is suggested that one of the best roles for Glider Pilots on the ground is neutralizing or destroying snipers, who, in this operation, were a constant source of irritation. The best method of dealing with snipers is by means of snipers. It is therefore suggested that each section has two trained snipers with sniper's rifles and telescopic sights, and two extra men with Mk. V. Stens instead of rifles. I have already spoken to Major Harding [Quartermaster] about this.[11]

The painful lessons of the Sicily landings appeared to be have been learned by everybody involved in British Airborne forces. The overhaul of the Glider Pilot Regiment and the development of its partnership with the dedicated tug squadrons of 38 Group RAF had been subjected to the ultimate test and passed with flying colours. With its reputation significantly enhanced and more trainee glider pilots progressing through the now refined training system, the outlook appeared promising for the Regiment. Normandy had dramatically changed the view of many of the Regiment's doubters in the RAF. Air Marshal Sir Trafford Leigh Mallory's post-war comment on the *coup de main* landings that resulted in the capture of Pegasus and Horsa bridges gives a hint of the change in perception at the time. When asked his opinion on the glider landings he described them as 'one of the most outstanding flying achievements of the war'.

After a protracted and costly gestation the men of the Glider Pilot Regiment and the gliders they flew had evolved into a battle-winning combination. The new and unique regiment was now firmly established in the British Army order of battle.

## Notes

1    Otway, Lieutenant Colonel T., *Airborne Forces*, London, Imperial War Museum, 1990, p. 35.

2    NA, AIR 32/2, CLE paper, 14 November 1940.

3    IWM, Papers of Brigadier A.G. Walch OBE, opening address by Colonel Chatterton to GPR recruits, undated.

4    Michie, SSgt J., 20 Flt, 'B' Sqn GPR, by permission of *The Eagle*.

5    Francis, SSgt T., 20 Flt, 'B' Sqn GPR, by permission of *The Eagle*.

6    Francis, SSgt T., 20 Flt, 'B' Sqn GPR, by permission of *The Eagle*.

7    Wetherall, Sergeant J., 16 Flt, 'F' Sqn GPR, by permission of *The Eagle*.

8    NA MM Citation, SSgt J. Ainsworth, 1 Bn GPR, July 1943.

9    Hackett, Lieutenant General J.W., *'Shan' Hackett*, Barnsley, Pen and Sword Ltd, 2003.

10   NA, DSO Citation, Lieutenant Colonel I. Murray GPR.

11   Royle, Major J.P., 1 Wing, GPR, report on Operation OVERLORD, 10 June 1944.

# CHAPTER 2

# A Long Summer of Frustration

*'By September 1944 my division was battle hungry to a degree which only those who have commanded large forces of trained soldiers can fully comprehend.'*

The success of the airborne landings in Normandy proved that the terrible lessons of the Sicily debacle had been learned, and that Colonel George Chatterton's drive to co-locate the Glider Pilot Regiment (GPR) squadrons, with their respective tug units, on RAF stations, had been sound. The decision to withdraw the two GPR wings from their respective Airborne Divisions and their realignment under Browning's Airborne Corps headquarters and Chatterton's direct command, had also proved to be well founded.

In contrast to Sicily, the Normandy operations had been extremely successful; the *coup de main* landings on Pegasus and Horsa bridges were heralded far and wide as outstanding feats of airmanship. The larger-scale tactical landings around Ranville on the eastern flank of the Allied amphibious landings were also completed in textbook manner with limited casualties. The majority of glider pilots were back in England within days, some returning home so quickly that they were barracked by civilians for being on the 'wrong' side of the Channel. As the Normandy campaign developed, a series of reinforcement or blocking operations were planned. The 1st British Airborne Division and 1 Polish Independent Parachute Brigade Group were held in reserve in the UK, and went through a repeated cycle of planning, preparation, and rehearsal for fifteen operations. The frustration and stress of being out of the battle and then pitched into the frenzy of nugatory planning against a deadline soon began to affect morale.

The majority of these operations included the use of gliders and the small staffs at GPR Wing and Squadron headquarters were fully engaged in this planning. Even before the long-awaited Normandy breakout was achieved, there was a continual cycle of planning – cancellation – planning – cancellation. The volume of staff work and logistical effort was immense, and each time the respective operations were about to be mounted participating troops would be placed in isolation. This isolation and preparation for battle imposed its own unique pressures on glider pilot and infantryman alike.

The preparation for these airborne operations were, of course, linked to the progress of the fighting on the ground. A general outline of the scope and size of these operations is listed below.

The first five operations were to be mounted in direct support of the Normandy landings:

1.  Operation TUXEDO – Planned before D-Day, a contingency plan requiring 4 Parachute Brigade to remain at 4 hours' notice to drop in support of any of the amphibious landings.

2.   Operation WASTAGE – Again a pre-planned operation that was in fact an enhanced TUXEDO using the 1st British Airborne Division.

3.   Operation REINFORCEMENT –1st British Airborne Division to be dropped near St Sauveur-le-Vicomte on the western flank of the Normandy Bridgehead to support 82nd US Airborne Division. (The above operations were cancelled on 10 June 1944.)

4.   Operation WILD OATS –1st British Airborne Division blocking possible German withdrawal to the west of Caen – this would have resulted in the Division being dropped onto Caen's Carpiquet Airfield. The field was at the time held by the formidable 12th SS Panzer Division; the outcome of such a drop against such determined and well-trained troops could only have been disastrous. The operation was planned to start at 13 June and finally cancelled on 17 June.

5.   Operation BENEFICIARY –1st British Airborne Division to support US XX Corps in the capture of the port of St Malo. The Operation order included direction for the Horsa gliders of the GPR to deliver the 1st Air Landing Brigade onto the beach. This operation was planned to start on 3 July and was finally cancelled on 15 July.

Montgomery had forecast that the Normandy campaign would probably last ninety days; few political commentators or military critics had that amount of patience. The fighting on the ground had become almost as attritional in nature as the trench warfare of the Western Front, with a horrific casualty rate to match. Pressure mounted on Montgomery to take Caen and break out of the lodgement, and yet more airborne operations were planned to break the deadlock.

6.   Operation LUCKY STRIKE –1st British Airborne Division is to seize the Seine crossings in the area of Rouen. This operation never progressed beyond the planning stage.

7.   Operation SWORD HILT –1st British Airborne Division was to cut off the port of Brest and seize and destroy the Morlaix viaduct. The planning for this operation started on 20 July and the operation was cancelled on 29 July.

8.   Operation HANDS UP –1st British Airborne Division were to seize Vannes Airfield in Brittany, in support of Patton's Third US Army. The planning started on 15 July and the operation was cancelled on 15 August.

As with all the previously planned operations, either the tactical situation on the ground changed or the ground forces overran the airborne objectives. On the other hand, the metrological forecasts were poor and the windows of opportunity were missed, or the weather was just too bad on the day, with the result that the troops were stood down at the last possible moment. From July 1944 onwards, a series of larger-scale airborne operations to break out of Normandy or the Cherbourg peninsula were planned and subsequently cancelled.

By August 1944, the British and American armies had finally broken out from Normandy and Cherbourg, and were pushing hard toward Paris and Brussels. Further airborne operations were first planned and then cancelled just as quickly as the Allied ground forces drove ever eastward. At this point the First Allied Airborne Army was established (8 August 1944) and British, Polish

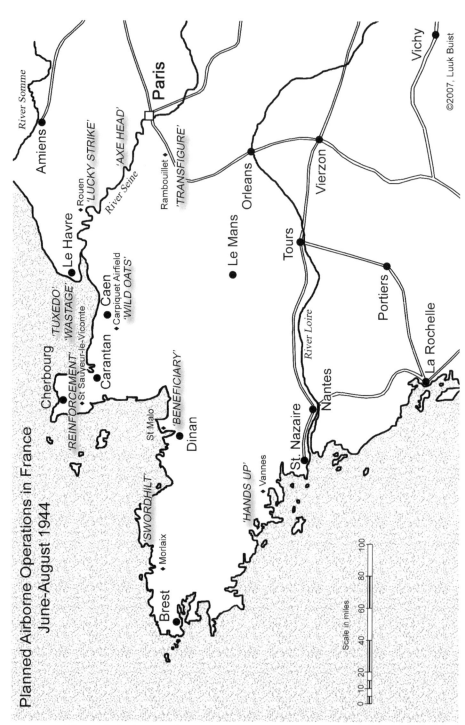

Planned Airborne Operations in France, June–August 1944

and American airborne formations were grouped together under a single chain of command. This is reflected in the composition of the forces that were selected for operations:

9.   Operation TRANSFIGURE –   1st British Airborne Division, 1 Polish Independent Parachute Brigade Group, 101st US Airborne Division, 878th US Airborne Aviation Engineer Battalion and 52nd British (Lowland) Division were to land in the Rambouillet-St Arnoult area to close the gap between Paris and Orleans. The 52nd (Lowland) Division had, until the summer of 1944, been trained as a mountain warfare formation, however, it was quickly retrained as an airportable unit that could follow on by air transport and reinforce airborne troops. The planning for this operation on 17 August started on 3 August and by 16.00 hours on the 17th the operation was cancelled.

10.   Operation AXE HEAD –1st British Airborne Division, 1 Polish Independent Parachute Brigade Group, 101st US Airborne Division, 878th US Airborne Aviation Engineer Battalion and 52nd British (Lowland) Division were to seize and hold bridgeheads over the River Seine in advance of Montgomery's 21st Army Group. The planning started on the 17th and by 19 August the operation was cancelled.

11.   Operation BOXER –1st British Airborne Division, 1 Polish Independent Parachute Brigade Group, 101st US Airborne Division, 878th US Airborne Aviation Engineer Battalion and 52nd British (Lowland) Division were to seize the port of Boulogne, attack V1 rocket launch sites and draw German forces away from the main front. The planning for Operation BOXER started on 17 August and was cancelled on the 26th.


The troops of the 1st British Airborne Division were particularly justified in their frustration; the bulk of the formation had not seen action since 1943. The Division had been held back in reserve because of cancelled operations throughout the Normandy campaign, while its sister formation, the 6th Airborne Division had played a significant and well-publicized role on the eastern flank of the landings. The Glider Pilot Regiment had taken part in the initial landings, but they too were beginning to show signs of frustration. The perceived morale problem was thought significant enough for Browning to issue a divisional circular on 14 August, shortly after Operation TRANSFIGURE was cancelled. The general tone was sympathetic and stressed that he understood the feeling of irritation and disappointment among all ranks, but they could rest assured that they were being held back for the *decisive blow*.

The River Seine was crossed without airborne assistance, fourteen days ahead of schedule on 26 August 1944. Amidst the prevailing optimism, Montgomery, and his staff began to formalize their argument for a concentrated strike into the heartland of the German Ruhr. Eisenhower was still advocating an advance on a broad front to the Rhine. With the Seine now behind them and Paris liberated, the cycle of nugatory planning was once again set in motion.

A statement from Major General Roy Urquhart commander of the 1st British Airborne Division, gives a clear insight into the underlying mood of his division and his staff:

By September 1944 my division was battle hungry to a degree which Only those who have commanded large forces of trained soldiers can fully comprehend. In fact, there were already signs of that dangerous mixture of boredom and cynicism creeping into our daily lives. We were ready for anything.[1]

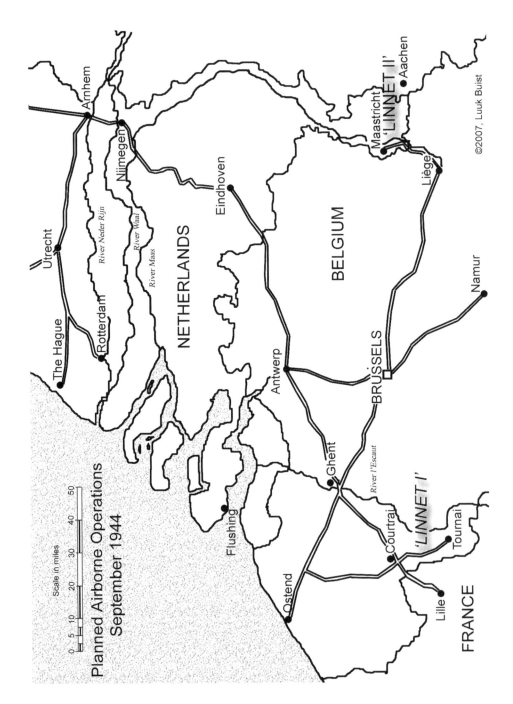

*Planned Airborne Operations, September 1944*

Montgomery began to focus his efforts on a drive out of France and into Belgium. The newly established First Allied Airborne Army (FAAA), under the American Lieutenant General Lewis H. Brereton, again figured in the thoughts of the 21st Army Group staff. The next round of planning generated Operation Linnet and Linnet 2:

12.     Operation LINNET - I British Airborne Corps (1st British Airborne Division, 1 Polish Independent Parachute Brigade Group, 82nd and 101st US Airborne Divisions, 878th US Airborne Aviation Engineer Battalion and the 52nd British (Lowland) Division). This force was to be landed in the Lille-Tournai area in Belgium, seize the Escaut crossings for the Second Army and block the German retreat. The capture of a bridgehead and the major roads running north-east from France into Belgium would cut off large numbers of German troops and push the Allied front into Belgium.

The Operation Order for LINNET was issued on 25 August with a D-Day of Sunday, 3 September; the time-frame for preparation was tight but achievable. Work got underway at pace, Major Ian Toler was commanding B Squadron GPR in the August of 1944. He recorded the events of the days leading up to 'LINNET' in his diary, the following extracts give an insight into the thoughts of a glider pilot right up to the final minutes before take-off on a combat operation:

Wednesday, 30th August 1944 I am on forty-eight hours leave. John Neale [2i/c B Sqn] rings me up in the morning and tells me I am to return at once. Flight Lieutenant Halpin meets me at Cramage with an Albemarle. On returning to Brize Norton I am informed we must be ready for an operation which may take place on Saturday, September 2nd. All personnel are recalled from leave and loading will start on the morrow.[2]

Thursday, 31st August 1944

Loading and preparations continue.

Friday, 1st September 1944

Briefing for Operation LINNET commences. This is a landing of the Airborne Army in the Lille, Tournai, Courtrai, Renaix area. The 'run up' is from Arras and we go over much of the ground which I covered in 1940. We are to land astride the railway at Berchem, North West Renaix. We are to carry two companies and the Headquarters of the 2nd Battalion, the South Staffordshire Regiment, and the 1st Airlanding Anti Tank Battery, Royal Artillery (my old battery) on the first lift. I am taking Colonel McCardie [Lieutenant Colonel W.D.H. McCardie, CO 2 S Staffords] in my glider which will be the leading one from RAF Brize Norton. It was to have contained a platoon of A Company but Colonel McCardie altered it as he wanted to fly with me. We are in 'Place Force' under Colonel Place [Lieutenant Colonel J. W. Place, CO 2 Wing GPR] and are to defend Quaremont.

Saturday, 2nd September 1944

Briefing and loading have been completed, and having contacted 'Boy' Wilson [Major B.A. Wilson MC, OC 21st Independent Parachute Company] regarding the landing aids, all is now set for take off in the early hours of Sunday morning. It will be a dark take off and not so easy. It has rained hard yesterday and today the ground is very soft. Gliders may easily get bogged. We have a drink in the bar and I go up to my room to fold my maps and mark in the route and check over my personal equipment. Now that it has come to the time I am undoubtedly feeling a nasty feeling in my stomach. What will it be like to going into action

23

in a glider for the first time? What will the 'Flak' be like? What of the opposition on the ground when we get there? All these thoughts flash through my mind. I write a last letter to my wife. This is the second letter I have written since D Day but somehow feel that this one may get to the post. Then just as I have completed my preparations the Tannoy gives out the message 'Night flying tonight is cancelled' – this is the code for postponement. Relief and disappointment both surge up together. I go down to the bar to confirm that the message is correct and find it in uproar. This must be the thirteenth op since D-Day.

The weather had prevented LINNET from being launched, the early part of September 1944 being particularly poor. The signal cancelling LINNET had been transmitted from General Brereton's Headquarters at 18.12 hours on Saturday, 2 September. Once again the weather and friendly ground forces had prevented the Airborne Army from joining the battle on mainland Europe; Brereton's signal bears more than a hint of disappointment:

> Weather requires delay in mounting LINNET tomorrow. Second Army will be in area by time airborne can land. Have talked to Chief of Staff Northern Group Armies and stated in my opinion Linnet should be cancelled.

While Major Toler and his squadron were preparing for LINNET, events on the ground were once again outpacing the planners at the FAAA HQ. On 3 September, Charleroi and Mons were liberated by Allied troops; the next day the larger cities of Brussels and Antwerp were also taken. There was now some concern that the Allied Airborne Army was beginning to develop into an expensive drain on highly trained man power, aircraft, and resources.

Brereton was determined to get his airborne army into the battle and now suggested a further operation to seize crossings over the Meuse. He stated that he could mount such an operation with thirty-six hours' notice. He also stressed that if the ground forces continued to maintain their current rate of advance that this would be the last strategic objective within range of his current airfields. This new operation was similar in concept to LINNET, but it had to be mounted deeper into occupied territory, Holland was now the objective of the Brereton FAAA:

13.   Operation LINNET 2 – I British Airborne Corps was given the task of seizing the Meuse crossings between Maastricht and Liege for the First US Army. The 1st British Airborne Division was allocated the specific task of seizing the high ground at Mont L' Enclus inclusive of the crossroads at Kerkhove. The Division, with 1 Polish Independent Parachute Brigade Group under command, was also to capture Courtrai, or at least the major roads around it, and an airfield to the west.

The planning of LINNET 2 had taken place on the back of LINNET; D-Day was scheduled for 4 September. The bulk of the stores and equipment from LINNET were to remain in situ, as were the troops and aircraft. This created a stagnant pause as commanders were rebriefed for the new operation. There was an inevitable feeling of frustration building among the troops confined to their airfields all over England. The scale of LINNET 2 was impressive: two separate landings would take place on D-Day. The initial landing would comprise of 1,533 aircraft, 358 of which would be British gliders, the second landing would include a further 307 British gliders among its total of 1,313 aircraft. The first gliders and paratroops were scheduled to land at 08.24 hours with the second landing arriving at 18.30 hours.

The GPR would be almost totally committed to this operation; a total of 665 gliders would be launched with every available glider pilot in action on the first day of the operation. There were to be two further reinforcement lifts and parachute resupply drops on D+1, but the bulk of the fighting echelons would be on the ground by last light on D-Day.

Major Toler's diary is once again an ideal barometer of the mood of the GPR at the time – his entry for the Sunday morning, after LINNET was cancelled and LINNET 2 was in embryo form, is revealing. The pace of the planning is evident and the shifting of objectives is hectic, all the more so when the level of communications technology then in service is taken into account.

3 September 1944

No further information in the morning so I go to church. Just after I have come out there is a frantic 'flap'. The station is to move to Manston today, ready to operate from tomorrow. This is almost an impossible undertaking at such short notice but we get down to it and are ready to take off at 14.00 hours. However, word comes through from Group to hold hard and not to move at present.

Major Toler was subsequently informed that LINNET was cancelled as the landing zones had once again been overrun by ground forces, and planning was already underway for a new operation:

In the evening I am called to Harwell for briefing on another operation. I arrive there at 7 o'clock and find we are to wait until Colonel Chatterton arrives from Eastcote. The bar is well attended and we have dinner and wait. Several continue in the bar. Colonel Chatterton does not arrive until 10 o'clock by which time several are well away. The Intelligence Officers are taken away to get the maps ready and at 11 o'clock the squadron commanders go to the operations room to be briefed. The operation has not got a name and details are very sketchy. We are to land by the Maastricht and Liege bridges and it is likely that D-Day will be tomorrow, and in addition Brize Norton aircraft will have to operate from Manston.

All is complete and we are about to disperse when the telephone rings. The Colonel answers it and at first cannot hear. At last the message gets through – the operation is cancelled once again!

Everyone breaks down and we laugh and laugh and laugh. Frank Davies starts and his laugh is infectious. We are told there is another operation planned and we are to disperse to our respective aerodromes.

The requirement for B Squadron to move from RAF Brize Norton to RAF Manston was entirely due to the location of the tug aircraft of 296 and 297 Squadrons RAF which were equipped with Albemarle aircraft. The Albemarle did not have sufficient range to complete the round trip into Holland and back, so B Squadron would have to be forward based for any future operation.

The cancellation order for LINNET 2 was received at unit level at roughly 23.00 hours on the evening of Sunday, 3 September. A signal was sent from Headquarters Airborne Troops early on the morning of Monday 4 September:

Cancel repeat cancel Operation discussed today. 82nd and 101st Airborne Divs return to billets and revert command 18 US Corps. Following units still under command British Airborne Corps, remain in present locations ready for another operation Wednesday, 6th September.

Corps HQ, 1st British Airborne Div, 1 Polish Parachute Brigade, 2 Airlanding Lt AA Bty, 878 Airborne Aviation Engineer Battalion, AFDAG, 52 Div remains under command with possibility inclusion in new operation. All parachute aircraft to be unloaded early

Monday 4 Sept. Airlift new operation follows earliest possible. Planning staffs definitely required 18.00 Hrs Monday 4 Sept. At Moor Park, all informed.

There was to be no let-up in pace. A new operation was being planned and a second older operation was being run in tandem with it. The older operation had been in the wings since early September – it was Operation 14:

14.     Operation INFATUATE – I British Airborne Corps was to assist in the cutting of the Scheldt estuary. This action would further hasten the opening of the port of Antwerp and threaten the rear of the German Fifteenth Army in the south-west of Holland.

There were concerns about the feasibility of INFATUATE, due to the poor landing zones and the concentration of German anti-aircraft batteries. It was, however, still a live plan and remained so until 4 April 1945.

The continual preparation and loading was also having a detrimental affect on the morale of the glider-borne infantry, who were to be carried in the aircraft of the GPR.

Lance Corporal Albert Blockwell of the 7th Battalion, King's Own Scottish Borderers (7/KOSB), recorded his own experiences of September 1944; his entries illustrate the tempo of life for the men in that battalion:

We were on another short leave at the time, when suddenly we were recalled back to camp. We thought, 'This is it again!' When we reached Woodhall we found all the seaborne party were loaded up and ready to move. They moved off the following morning and we never saw them again … We came to two conclusions, either we were going to a base in France or else there was another 'flap on' – we were all for going for a base in France.

Well, down to Keevil again we went, same thing again, load up, briefing – and then the whole show was cancelled. The morale of the boys was dropping a bit after all these cancellations so we were sent on leave again to cheer us up and then back again to the drome.[3]

While Lance Corporal Blockwell suffered the frustration of yet another cancellation, the movement of B Squadron to RAF Manston was underway, soon after the cancellation of LINNET 2. Staff Sergeant Jim Hooper was tasked to ferry a squadron Horsa over to the Kent airfield from RAF Brize Norton:

Accordingly, on Tuesday 5 September, with my 2nd pilot Sergeant P Johnson and carrying airborne troopers of 13 Platoon, 2/S Staffords, I flew glider No. RN 829. On take off bound for Manston, the undercarriage of the Armstrong Whitworth Albemarle towing aircraft flown by Flight Sergeant E J Flavell retracted causing it to belly land at the end of the runway, but without injury to pilot or crew. I took action to avoid the crashed aircraft, but hit obstacles past the end of the runway before coming to a halt with a badly damaged glider at the edge of the airfield. Although badly shaken there were no serious injuries to either glider pilots or to the troops.

The following day, 6 September, I took off in replacement glider No. RN 606, with Sergeant Johnson and troopers of 13 Platoon, behind an Albemarle piloted by Flying Officer W H McCutcheon of The Royal Canadian Air Force. The take off was successful but after 20 minutes flying time and at a height of about 2,000ft the tow rope broke loose to the rear of the Albemarle. I hastily selected a place to land and ordered Sergeant Johnson to pull the release lever to free the rope and made a near perfect touch down. Almost simultaneously, the rope caught in trees then tightened making the glider start to cart wheel but then checked causing the fuselage to break in two aft of the main plane. Injuries to pilots and passengers were not serious but for the second day running, I was surveying a wrecked glider wondering if I could get 13 Platoon and myself to Manston?

Two days later, the Army, taking no chances, transported the 'unlucky 13' Platoon to Manston by road and flew me there as a passenger in another glider![4]

Even as the crews and passengers of the airlanding brigade were unloading their gliders again, planning was well advanced for Operation FIFTEEN. The concept would be familiar, airborne forces landing in front of the advancing 21st Army Group deeper into enemy-held territory. Familiarity, they say, does breed contempt and often leads to the making of false assumptions – which was the case within Browning's airborne headquarters in early September 1944. The seeds of failure at Arnhem were planted weeks before amongst the ashes of LINNET 2.

**Notes**

1      Urquhart, Major General, *Arnhem*, London, Cassell & Co Ltd, 1958, p. 18.

2      Toler, Major, *Harvest of Ten Years*, Arnhem Airborne Museum, 1988, pp. 103-20.

3      Blackwell, Albert, *Diary of a Red* Devil, Solihull, Helion and Company Ltd., 2005, p. 88.

4      Correspondence with the author, September 2007.

# CHAPTER 3

# Operation COMET

*'I must admit privately I thought we were about to go
on a suicide mission.'*

After the cancellation of LINNET 2, the 1st British Airborne Division and 1st Polish Independent Parachute Brigade Group were immediately locked into planning for another large-scale airborne operation. The new operation would be the fifteenth planned by Browning's headquarters since the Normandy landings. Code-named COMET, it was similar in concept to its recent predecessors, requiring airborne landings ahead of 21st Army Group.

Three major obstacles in Holland barred Montgomery's route to a suitable jumping-off point for his desired thrust into Germany. Like hurdles on a racecourse, they ran in series: the River Maas (Grave), the River Waal (Nijmegen) and the lower Rhine (Arnhem). Seizing bridgeheads over these major rivers and other minor but still significant obstacles, was immediately identified as an ideal task for Browning's Airborne Corps.

Initial planning for the new operation used the successful landings in Normandy as its template; the assault would take place under cover of night. It was hoped that the combination of darkness, glider-borne *coup de main* parties and the element of surprise would enable the crossings of the three rivers to be seized intact. Concurrently, large-scale parachute drops and further waves of gliders would land on less hazardous drop zones (DZs) and landing zones (LZs) before moving in to reinforce the previously secured bridgeheads.

General Urquhart gave a detailed briefing and issued his 'Op' Order for Operation FIFTEEN to his commanders at RAF Cottesmore on 6 September. While his divisional staff may have been fully engaged in planning FIFTEEN, there is no doubt that further down the chain of command an unhealthy level of scepticism was developing. The diary entry of Lieutenant Alec Johnston of E Squadron for the same day leaves the reader in no doubt of his outlook on life at the time:

> A thoroughly cynical and brassed off regiment of glider pilots heard reports of a proposed landing in Holland. But as over six months had dragged by since anyone had seen leave, they were viewed with a jaundiced eye.
>
> Nevertheless, the following day the briefing huts were busy, destination Arnhem in Holland, take off 4 am the next morning. A day of hectic coming and going ensued, at teatime the take off was brought forward to 3.15 am, which meant breakfast at 2.30 am, a ridiculous hour at which to eat, no matter what the meal is called.[1]

The war diary for HQ 1st British Airborne Division states that FIFTEEN was officially designated 'COMET' at 0120 hours on 7 September, which is an unusual time to record such a change. It is most likely that this was the date and time that the signal informing units of the name change was released. The commanders attending Urquhart's briefing at RAF Cottesmore had already been made aware of the code name when they received their written confirmatory orders.

The majority of troops participating in the scramble to prepare for COMET were unaware of the disagreement between their most senior commanders over how best to launch their final assault on what appeared to be a mortally wounded foe. There were numerous problems affecting the Allied armies that were now at the limit of their logistical supply chain – the Normandy beaches were now over 300 miles to their rear. All the combat supplies, the lifeblood of a modern army, were being transported forward almost entirely by road as the rail network had been devastated by pre-invasion Allied bombing. With many of the major French ports still in German hands, the Allies were struggling to sustain their offensive across an ever-widening front over increasingly longer distances.

General Eisenhower, Supreme Commander Allied Expeditionary Force, had delegated operational command of the landings in Normandy and subsequent breakout from the beachheads to the more experienced Montgomery. This command relationship changed on 1 September 1944 when Eisenhower's headquarters opened in Normandy and assumed direct command of the Allied Expeditionary Force. Montgomery was promoted to the rank of Field Marshal on the same day and continued in command of the now largely Anglo-Canadian 21st Army Group. Montgomery found it difficult to hand over the reins of command at what he considered a critical phase of the campaign. He had a clear vision of what was required to end the war in Europe, writing to Eisenhower on 4 September, shortly after the capture of Antwerp and Louvain, he outlined his reasoning for a single thrust to Berlin:

I would like to put before you certain aspects of future operations and give you my views.

1. I consider we have now reached a stage where one really powerful and full-blooded thrust toward Berlin is likely to get there and thus end the German war.

2. We have not enough maintenance resources for two full-blooded thrusts.

3. The selected thrust must have all the maintenance resources it needs without any qualification and any other operation must do the best with what is left over.

4. There are only two possible thrusts: one via the Ruhr and the other via Metz and the Saar.

5. In my opinion the thrust likely to give the best and the quickest results is the northern one via the Ruhr.

6. Time is vital and the decision regarding the selected thrust must be made at once and para 3. above will then apply.

7. If we attempt a compromise solution and split our maintenance resources so that neither thrust is full-blooded we will prolong the war.

8. I consider the problem viewed as above is very simple and clear cut.

9. The matter is of such vital importance that I feel sure you will agree that a decision on the above lines is required at once. If you are coming this way perhaps you would look in and discuss it. If so delighted to see you at lunch tomorrow. Do not feel I can leave this battle just at the present.[2]

The sense of urgency is obvious in Montgomery's tone; he knew that Britain was struggling to sustain its armies on three fronts. The pool of manpower was beginning to run dry at home and divisions were being broken up to reinforce those already deployed overseas. The continuing bombardment of southern England by Hitler's V1 flying bombs from the Channel coast had placed added pressure on him to overrun their launch sites as soon as possible. This moral factor was to be further compounded on 8 September when the first of the longer-range, more powerful and invulnerable V2 rockets hit Chiswick in west London. The launch sites for this new and more capable terror weapon were believed to be located in western Holland, which now needed to be cleared as soon as possible.

There were also a number of strategic reasons that made Montgomery's plan to strike out for Arnhem a sound one. A bridgehead over the lower Rhine would enable the Allies to launch an offensive on the Ruhr, the industrial heart of Nazi Germany. If this operation did succeed and Allied armour thrust into the Ruhr and beyond, it would deal the German war machine a mortal blow, 65 per cent of Germany's steel and 53 per cent of its coal was still being produced on the Ruhr itself, with more being taken from occupied Holland and Belgium.

Montgomery et al. believed that by threatening the powerhouse of Hitler's Reich he would draw what was left of the German Army in the West into a final battle on the north German plain that only he could win. The need to protect the Ruhr would take priority over the remainder of the western front and force the German High Command to weaken its defences in other areas and leave them vulnerable to attack by the American armies further to the south. This strategy was viewed as the only course acceptable to the British – the need to finish the war was immediate and pressing. The British economy was war weary and close to breaking point, and this, coupled with the dwindling reserves of troops, placed ever-increasing pressure on the government and in turn Montgomery to strike out for Berlin and final victory. British Intelligence predicted that if successful this plan would end the war within six months. Montgomery presented a typically logical and concise argument for his proposed strategy and, in essence, he was correct. Eisenhower knew he could not logistically sustain his current broad front strategy; he would have to focus his efforts and, most importantly, his combat supplies behind one of his Army Groups, or distribute them to keep all his armies advancing, albeit more slowly and on a broad front.

Eisenhower had the unenviable task of controlling his numerous Allied commanders and placating his and their political masters. The prospect of diverting the bulk of his logistical supplies to support a British and Canadian offensive at the expense of the more numerous American armies was not a politically practical one. The wrangling between the two men carried on for days as Montgomery continually prodded his American superior with signals, letters and telegrams trying to manoeuvre him into making a decision. If the unceasing pressure from the British Field Marshal was not enough for Eisenhower, he also had the aspirations of his own chain of command in Washington DC to contend with. The Chief of the US General staff, General George C. Marshall, viewed the successful use of the Allied Airborne Army as the ideal method of dramatically shortening the war. Marshall was supported in Washington by the commander of the United States Air Force, General 'Hap' Arnold, both men wishing to see their belief in large-scale airborne operations vindicated. The technical resources tied up in supporting the Airborne Army were extensive, as an example the US IX Troop Carrier Command fielded close to 1,300 transport aircraft. The airborne divisions themselves were highly capable and the product of exhaustive and realistic training; they were drawn from the cream of Allied manpower. The investment of such high-quality troops and scarce logistic assets had been the subject of controversy since the formation of airborne formations in both the UK and the US. Should the war come to a close without their employment, it would surely be seen as a flawed experiment that had wasted precious time and resources. In early September 1944, the German Army appeared to be collapsing in dramatic style, so that the opportunity for the Airborne Army to emerge from the war as a battle-proven concept appeared to be slipping away.

Montgomery's staff were still working on COMET when Eisenhower made a decision that would shape events over the coming weeks: he placed the newly formed First Allied Airborne Army under command of Montgomery's 21st Army Group headquarters. The order was effective from 4 September 1944, the planning for COMET too far advanced at this stage to consider amendment to incorporate the newly available American and British divisions that constituted the Airborne Army. Operation COMET remained active but only the 1st British Airborne Division was thought to be sufficiently briefed and prepared to actually mount the operation within the required time-frame.

The plan for COMET was exceptionally bold and imaginative in concept; it was also far more ambitious than any previous airborne operation attempted by the Allies. The apparent state of disarray of the German forces across the majority of the western front presented what seemed to be an excellent opportunity to land Montgomery's desired blow on an already reeling opponent. The operation would involve the whole of the 1st British Airborne Division, including 1 Polish Independent Parachute Brigade Group; they were to seize bridges ahead of an armoured thrust by Second Army spearheaded by Lieutenant General Brian Horrocks and his XXX Corps. The tanks would force a 60-mile corridor from their start line in Belgium, through German territory, linking up the bridgeheads seized by the airborne brigades 60 miles to Arnhem on the lower Rhine.

Each of the brigades within the 1st British Airborne Division were allocated separate river crossings as their objectives: 4 Parachute Brigade was to land at Grave; 1 Airlanding Brigade would seize Nijmegen accompanied by Urquhart's Divisional Headquarters; and 1 Parachute Brigade was given the most distant objective, the bridge at Arnhem. D-Day for COMET was set for 8 September. The Allied Intelligence picture at the time was generally optimistic but there were indications that German resistance was beginning to toughen in front of British Second Army. The German ability to regroup shattered units in very quick time was by now renowned; among those being reorganized were the *Kampfgruppen* from the Hermann Göring Division, which had been reinforced with surplus Luftwaffe personnel and thrown in to bolster the German resistance. The level of training and equipment given varied considerably but they were committed to battle regardless of consequence. Regimental commander, Oberstleutnant [Lieutenant Colonel] Fritz Fullriede, wrote in his diary:

8 Sep. The enemy is already over the Albert canal at Beeringen. On order from General Student's Para High command that all air force troops were to be taken under command, I despatched the II Abteilung on the road before Harderwijk post-haste to Eindhoven.

The entry for 10 September is emotional, bitter and has a cynical tone that carries more weight when we consider that Fullriede was a combat veteran and holder of the Knight's Cross:

10 Sep. The II Abteilung following a successful attack, after being inserted in the wrong place, and stabbed in the back by its neighbours, was surrounded by strong forces in Hechtel and following a three day battle practically wiped out, only a few stragglers and tanks returned.

Almost all the tanks, armoured artillery, anti tank guns and flak elements were lost. All due to the mistakes of our joke of a high command.[3]

While Fullriede and the rest of the German military wrestled with their own problems in Holland, the British were still trying to find a way to maintain their momentum in the Low Countries and keep the Germans off balance. However, the optimism among senior British planners for the prospects of success for COMET was not shared among the rank and file of the Glider Pilot Regiment. Staff Sergeant Arthur Shackleton was a pilot serving with B Squadron at Brize Norton; he had not flown on the Normandy operations and was keen to fly on his first operation.

Arthur had been designated as the Squadron Commander's co-pilot. Along with the other B Squadron pilots, he attended the squadron orders group for COMET given by Major Ian Toler at Manston on 7 September:

> I remember Major Toler briefing us on Comet quite clearly; we were grouped around a blackboard as he pointed out Eindhoven, Nijmegen and Arnhem and the front line of our ground troops. Then he proceeded to explain the plan in detail and our role in it, we were to land the South Staffs at Groesbeek and then get to Nijmegen Bridge.
>
> There were a few seconds of stunned silence immediately broken by a loud gasp around the room followed by some very colourful language. As he explained how far behind enemy lines we would be there were some very straight questions and a number of doubts raised. Major Toler stated that these were our orders and we must carry them out regardless. I must admit privately I thought we were about to go on a suicide mission.[4]

The 2nd Battalion South Staffords Outline Operation Order for COMET lays out the plan in concise detail and highlights a significant change to the original concept for the mission; the majority of the landings would take place in daylight. The levels of moonlight for much of September 1944 were too low for a night operation. The key details as briefed to participating troops are outlined in the extract below:

1.     1 Airborne Div, with under command the Polish Para Brigade, is to secure the bridges over the RHINE at ARNHEM [Grid] 747767, over the WAAL at NIJMEGEN [Grid ] 715633, over the MAAS at GRAVE [Grid] 620543. The object of the task is to hold the route into GERMANY for 2nd Army, directed on HAMM.

2.     Bridges are to be secured against demolition in the first place by Coup-de-Main parties of 1 Airlanding Bde landing at 080430 as follows:

(a)     ARNHEM Bridge, Coy 2 S. Staffords (A Coy – Major Lane)

(b)     NIJMEGEN Bridge, Coy 7 KOSB (A Coy – Major Buchanan)

(c)     GRAVE Bridge, Coy 1 Border

3.     The first lift of the main body is to land at about 080900 and take over the bridges as follows:

(a)     ARNHEM Bridge – 1 Para Bde

(b)     NIJMEGEN Bridge – 1 Airlanding Bde

(c)     GRAVE Bridge – 4 Para Bde (later to be relieved by Polish Para Bde) Coup de Main parties to rejoin units on relief.

4.     1 Airlanding Brigade is to land and move to NIJMEGEN as shown on the trace at Appendix A.

5.     Additional troops under command:

(a)     Coup de Main Party (A Coy) – Detachment of 9 Field Coy RE

(b)     Field Ambulance Section.

Intention

6.      2 S. Staffords will occupy the Railway Bridge [Grid] 705653 at NIJMEGEN and be prepared to reinforce 7 KOSB at Bridge 715633.[5]

The whole document is riddled with clues to the pace that this operation had been formulated at and how sketchy the intelligence picture was. An example is the intent to impose a curfew on Nijmegen as quickly as possible after landing could only suggest that little opposition was expected in and around the town itself. A Dutch liaison officer was to accompany the Staffords and assist them in arresting known German sympathizers and agents. The direction for the *coup de main* troops to move back to their parent units after the main body arrived would seem to suggest that the corridor between the bridgeheads would be secure and that these companies could be spared from defending the newly secured bridges.

The weather on 7 September was particularly bad, heavy rain settled in for the day and life at RAF Manston in particular was unpleasant. The disruption of the move from RAF Brize Norton had a detrimental effect on the usually slick routine of B Squadron and the Albemarle tugs of 296 and 297 Squadrons RAF. Major Toler captures the mood and provides an accurate description of 7 September in his diary:

> It rains very heavily today, all the tents leak, and the cinema leaks and everything is wet. We have to move the troops under cover, anywhere, in the NAAFI and the church, all over the place. The ground where the gliders are parked becomes a bog and it is almost impossible to move the length of a towrope.
>
> Main briefing is in the afternoon and we are due to take off the following morning in the dark again. Operations make a mistake in the crew lists once again and this adds to the chaos. Marshalling is left until very late and by the evening it is in such a mess that it is doubtful that it can be sorted out. The Station Commander is nearly berserk. Then about Eight o'clock we hear that it is postponed nearly twenty-four hours. For once, this is probably just as well as it is doubtful if we could have made the take off under the existing conditions.

Ever the professional and with classic British reserve, Major Toler recounts his understanding of COMET with only a hint of the concerns that are clearly playing on his mind. These concerns could not be passed on to the men under his command:

> The operation consists, as far as I can make out, of the British Airborne Division only, landing at Arnhem, Nijmegen and Grave, to hold the bridges over the rivers at these places until the British 2nd Army could advance and take over. Three Coup de Main parties had been organised to drop at each bridge as on the Orne bridges on D-Day; but in this case, there appeared to have been no preparation of the crews, which took place three months before the Normandy invasion. We were to land near GROESBEEK and advance with the South Staffords into Nijmegen and take over the bridges from the coup de main party. Just now, we received an intelligence summary, which suggested that the high ground overlooking our LZ might be an enemy strong point. This did not improve our peace of mind.

The possible presence of a German strongpoint overlooking the Groesbeek landing zone was later to play a significant part in the planning of Operation MARKET. The securing of the heights was given precedence over the capture of the Nijmegen Bridge, arguments still rage as to whether this was a tactically sound decision.

The war diary of 7th Battalion King's Own Scottish Borderers reveals the intent to fit the COMET *coup de main* Horsa gliders with arrestor parachutes to dramatically reduce their landing run on the objective. This technical innovation had been successfully used on Operation DEADSTICK, the capture of Pegasus and Horsa Bridges over the Orne River and Canal:

7 KOSB War Diary entries

6th September 1944

Place: Keevil

1030 – An 'O' Gp was held and the CO gave out the Bn's plans for operation 'COMET'. Briefing of Coys continued until 1500 hrs when the Bn less 'A' Coy prepared to move to the airfields.

Place: Blakehill Farm

1600 – The remainder of the Bn at KEEVIL moved in two groups, the larger one to DOWN AMPNEY and the other to BLAKEHILL FARM. Final arrangements were made there to emplane by 0400 hrs on the 7th Sept. Meanwhile 'A' Coy were at HARWELL where they were to emplane by 0100 hrs and land in the dark about 0430 hrs on the 7th Sept. The landing was so arranged that they were to be released between 6,000 and 7,000 feet and to glide several miles to enable them to make a very close approach to the bridge at NIJMEGEN. To assist them in landing in a confined space a parachute was attached to each glider to enable them to pull up quickly on touching down.

The use of *coup de main* gliders to capture the Orne bridges was an unqualified success but it had taken close to three months to train the specially selected pilots and assault infantry for the task. The period of preparation for COMET was dramatically shorter – there would be no detailed collective or even individual training. Colonel George Chatterton, Commander Glider Pilots, however, did plan to utilize the experience gained on the Orne mission. Staff Sergeant Jim Wallwork, who flew the lead glider of the mission to seize Pegasus Bridge, recounted his feelings when selected at short notice for what was now a dawn *coup de main* operation on Nijmegen Bridge:

You say it is strange that expertise generated during the Dead stick training was not used in the next Op. But it almost was, about two weeks before the actual assault [Op MARKET], I with SSgt Stan Pearson as my 2ic were scheduled to land six Horsas at night beside the bridge [Nijmegen]. The other five [crews] had no training but were to follow us and land on the mud flats against the bridge.
Our load was KOSB commanded by Major Buchanan of the Whiskey family whose main interest was that several bottles of his brew, secured in the glider, were not damaged on arrival. Pearson and I knew from the start that we would arrive alone and decided to surrender as soon as possible and call it a day! I didn't tell anyone of course which was as well since it was cancelled, we all returned to our squadrons.[6]

Even while Jim Wallwork, Ian Toler and Arthur Shackleton were all having their personal doubts about COMET and their own respective parts in it, the plan was again changing. The low moonlight levels prevented any form of massed airborne landing and introduced a significant risk that the *coup de main* parties would be separated from each other, lost or even as had happened during the Normandy landings, land on the wrong objective. There was also the significant threat posed by the German air-defence system that had been developed to counter the RAF night-bombing offensive;

this was by now a finely tuned and integrated network that regularly inflicted significant attrition on RAF bomber formations. This operation would take place within sight of the Reichswald and in very close proximity to Germany itself. The prospect of the highly potent Luftwaffe night fighter force loose among the massed streams of transport aircraft and gliders was unthinkable. The Allied air force commanders believed that a daylight operation supported by large numbers of escort fighters, preceded by waves of ground-attack aircraft to neutralize German anti-aircraft positions, stood the greatest chance of success.

Even as the plan for COMET was distributed and orders were being formulated at unit level, one key component was still not in place. There was still doubt as to the level of anti-aircraft defences around the objectives, so the use of *coup de main* gliders was still to be agreed by air force planners; at 2035 hours on the evening of 5 September, a signal sent from HQ Air Troops (Browning's Airborne Corps headquarters) to 21st Army Group, read:

> In view of complete lack of LZs and DZs near bridges after study of maps and photos on my return here consider it essential to land Coup de Main glider parties on each bridge night 7/8 Sept. Then next bring in first main lift airborne force early daylight 8 Sept otherwise surprise impossible. Must warn you strong protest against the latter has been lodged with Air C in C [Commander-in-Chief] and Americans. Please confirm that if protest overruled timings are suitable.

The reply to the signal from 21st Army Group was succinct: 'Ref 0845 of 052035. Air C in C has overruled protest.'[7]

The operation was to be mounted in daylight; this contravened all accepted airborne doctrine of the day and was certainly deemed high risk. There had been successful daylight glider landings during the Normandy landings, although these were follow-on landings behind friendly lines. The operation had gained a momentum of its own with preparations and briefings continuing at pace as the glider squadrons and the rest of the 1st British Airborne Division raced to meet yet another deadline.

There was a central briefing at RAF Harwell for eighteen *coup de main* crews given by Colonel Chatterton himself. 'A' Squadron's war diary records the briefing as taking place at 1530 hours on 6 September, followed at 1730 hours by a further briefing for the all squadron commanders and their intelligence officers. This was the first time that the chosen crews had the opportunity to discuss their respective missions with the infantrymen and engineers they would carry into battle – a process that is known in today's military as 'hot planning'. As mentioned in Major Toler's diary, they would receive a day's grace on the evening of 7 September, when the operation was delayed twenty-four hours.

The war diary of 2nd Battalion the South Staffords provides an insight into the torturous daily routine running up to the eventual cancellation of COMET. Following the previous fourteen cancellations and months of training this period was unbearably frustrating for all concerned, being confined to the airfield and allowed no outside communication.


7 Sept 1944

Place: Manston

After a night of heavy rain, most of the troops were compelled to evacuate their tents for drier accommodation. The rain continued until well after mid-day, rather dampening everyone's spirits. The CO [Commanding Officer] and IO [Intelligence Officer] arrived at

1615 hrs, with details of operation. General briefing of officers at 1700 hrs. Coy Comds special briefing after, then down to NCOs and men. Rather hurriedly carried out. At 2230 hrs news received that operation was postponed 24 hrs. Ground bogged. Unable to marshal gliders and tugs.

8 Sep 1944

Place: Manston

2100 – Operation postponed for 24 hrs.

The 24 hrs cancellation proved rather a blessing. The Coy Comds were able to brief their men thoroughly, and altogether get a really good idea of the job on hand. Everyone seemed well keyed up for the Op. However, at approx 1700 hrs new gen came in through Bde, which rather upset our plans. CO in consultation at Bde 2100 hrs, operation postponed for tactical reasons. Another night's undisturbed sleep.

9 Sept 1944

Place: Manston

2115 – Operation postponed for 48 hrs. No official reason given. All heavy loads ordered to be unloaded on Sunday, starting at 1330 hrs for 2nd lift. Reloading to start at same time Monday.

A rather quiet morning. Everyone seemed to think further postponement likely. A rather mild surprise at 1215. Six gliders and crews were to go up in the afternoon for testing a new take off system. The new system worked beautifully. No complaints anywhere. At 0915 hrs word received official postponement for yet another 48 hrs. Tactical reasons.

10 Sept 1944

Place: Manston

1615 – Operation COMET cancelled. Operation 16 brewing up. Camp unsealed, men went to Oxford in our transport.

Another quiet morning. 'O' Gp conference 1030 hrs. Church Parade 1100 hrs. Word received late afternoon (official) 'operation scrubbed'. 1730 hrs – Bn allowed out of camp. Not many took advantage. Reason – financial difficulties, plenty of foreign currency, no English money.

Sergeant Godfrey Freeman was a glider pilot with 19 Flight, B Squadron at RAF Manston with the South Staffords. He gives an excellent summary of the cumulative affect of the continual mental roller coaster of continually preparing for battle then being stood down:

We did not have to wait long before another operation was planned, and once again, the glowingly familiar preparations took place. We attended briefings, saw that our loads were evenly and properly made fast, drew G1098 kit, mixed with our airlanding passengers and held ourselves in a state of readiness.

The one night we went to bed, with a prospect of a ten o'clock take off in the morning. At breakfast time, however, word came round again that that there had been a postponement of forty-eight hours, so we drifted back to our barrack rooms, partially unpacked what was necessary for washing and shaving. We cleaned our weapons and prepared to wait for the time stipulated.

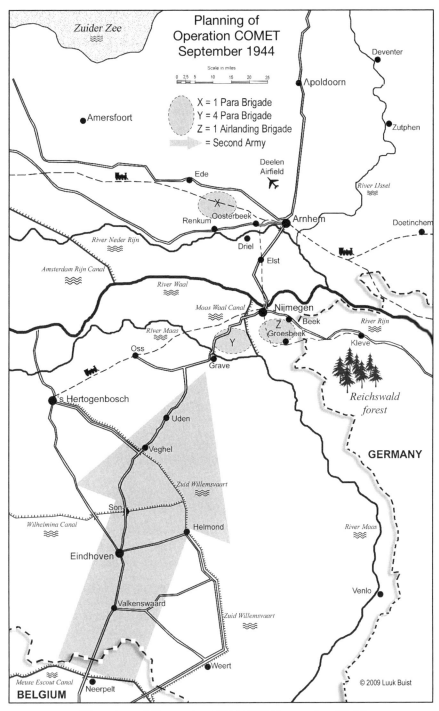

*Planning of Operation COMET, September 1944*

At the end of that time word came round again that the operation had been postponed for a further forty-eight hours, so we unloaded the gliders to take the strain off the undercarriage legs and loaded them again twenty four hours before the start was due. Then word came round that the operation was cancelled. We unloaded again, and the airlanding force dispersed.

It definitely affected morale although it did not quite break it. It is a devastating thing to be 'psyched up' ready for action, take off when the moment comes, then straight to grips with the enemy without anymore to do.

It is doubly devastating to be psyched up then told to hold off for forty-eight hours, and finally to be told the whole operation has been cancelled. I do not wish to make too much of a song and dance about it, but the general effect, when the Market Garden or Arnhem operation was announced, was that few of us believed it would actually happen ... that much at any rate morale was affected.

We studied the usual maps and photographs, went through the same routines of drawing G1098 kit and loading gliders. Then waited for the cancellation or postponement, which, according to what now seemed to be the normal pattern of events came through forty-eight hours before the projected start of the operation.

Twenty-four hours later, we would be told to unload our gliders, twenty-four hours after that we would re load them. Because we were now going to take off from RAF Manston in Kent, to allow a greater fuel margin for the tugs to make the outward and return journey ... with rather bad grace we did so, in due course we arrived, still only half believing the operation was still actually going to take place.[8]

The war diary for 2 Wing, the Glider Pilot Regiment is less emotional but describes the same effect on the pilots of the wing:

8th to 14th September 1944

Place: Broadwell

During this period, operations were continually being planned, postponed, and then cancelled. Owing to the swift advances of the Allied Armies, it proved exceedingly difficult to time an Airborne Operation exactly. As a result, all pilots of 2 Wing were almost continually on tenterhooks, planning and preparing for an operation, finding it postponed, sometimes 2 or 3 times, and eventually suffering the disappointment of having it cancelled.

This planning fatigue appears to have been endemic right through the command structure of the 1st British Airborne Division by the time COMET collapsed and went the same way as its fourteen predecessors. This quote from Major General Roy Urquhart is brutally honest:

By the time we went on Market Garden we couldn't have cared less. I mean I really shouldn't admit that, but we really couldn't ... we became callous. Every operation was planned to the best of our ability in every way. But we got so bored, and the troops were more bored than we were ... We had approached the state of mind when we weren't thinking as hard about the risks as we possibly had done earlier.[9]

**Notes**

1   Lieutenant Alec Johnston, 'E' Sqn GPR, correspondence with Luuk Buist, 1991.

2   Montgomery, Field Marshal, *Memoirs*, Barnsley, Pen & Sword Books Ltd, 2005, p. 271.

3   Kershaw, Robert J., *It Never Snows In September*, Ian Allan Publishing, Hersham, 2005, p. 26.

4   SSgt Arthur Shackleton, 'B' Sqn GPR, interview with the author, March 2007.

5   Outline Op Order 2 Bn South Staffords (WO 171/1375) dated 6 September 1944.

6   Wallwork, SSgt Jim, 'C' Sqn GPR, correspondence with Major Steve Elsey, January 2006.

7   Signal Ref 0845 5 September 1944, HQ Air Troops – 21st Army Group.

8   Freeman, Sergeant G., 'B' Sqn GPR, correspondence with Luuk Buist, 1991.

9   Harclerode, Peter, *Arnhem: A Tragedy of Errors*, Caxton Publishing Group, London

# CHAPTER 4

# Operation MARKET

*'George, it's too late. It has all been decided.'*

The decision to postpone COMET was probably made by Montgomery much earlier than the officially recorded date of 10 September 1944. Montgomery remained absolutely convinced that his combined armoured and airborne thrust over the Rhine and into the Ruhr was the 'silver bullet' that would bring about the collapse of Hitler's Western defences.

Determined as he was to engineer a British and Canadian breakout of Belgium, he recognized that he could not contemplate even the most limited of offensives without Eisenhower's political and practical support. Without unrestricted access to the Allies overstretched supply chain, his audacious plan was not viable.

The command relationship between both men was however distant in both geographical and personal terms; Eisenhower and Montgomery were truly poles apart. The former lacked battlefield command experience, but was adept at managing the eclectic group of Allied commanders that were placed under him. He also acted as the interface between the politicians, both at home in the US and the UK, and his coalition of generals. His strength rested in his tact and diplomacy, not his grasp of the dynamics of command at the level of his subordinate generals, on a day-to-day basis.

Montgomery, on the other hand, was a proven field commander of some renown, but was regarded by most as prickly and arrogant. This view was particularly strong among the American commanders, who disliked his pithy and arrogant manner when dealing with them and, it seemed, in all other matters.

The distance between the headquarters of both commanders was also significant; Eisenhower was located 400 miles behind the front line on the west side of the Cherbourg peninsula, and had no direct telephone or radio links with any of his army group commanders. The primary method of communication between the respective headquarters was by signal – at best an erratic and unreliable system that frequently delivered only portions of messages or failed to deliver signals completely.

At the time COMET was being formulated he was physically hindered by a knee injury that greatly restricted his movement and therefore prevented him travelling to visit his subordinate commanders.

Eisenhower did regain enough mobility to board his personal aircraft and fly to Melsbroek Airfield near Brussels on 10 September 1944 to meet Montgomery; he could not, however, leave the aircraft, so the meeting took place on board. It was during this meeting that Montgomery's brisk manner came to the fore, and he pushed hard for sole claim on the combat supplies required to sustain his northern thrust into the Reich.

While Montgomery was characteristically forthright in manner from the outset and treated Eisenhower at best as a less-experienced equal, the American showed great restraint, only gently reprimanding the British Field Marshal. Patting Montgomery on the knee, he gently chided his subordinate with the words, 'Steady Monty; you can't speak to me like that. I'm your boss.' Montgomery was astute enough to realize he had overstepped the mark with his superior and the remainder of the meeting was conducted in a less aggressive manner.

Montgomery then surprised Eisenhower by outlining his plan for an enhanced COMET, using the bulk of First Allied Airborne Army to seize objectives along an airborne corridor (Op MARKET) ahead of a 60-mile armoured thrust by British Second Army (Op GARDEN). In effect, a complete airborne division would now seize each of the bridgeheads currently allocated to individual British brigades. Eisenhower was genuinely surprised by the scale and audacity of Montgomery's plan, as it was out of character for the reserved Englishman to advocate such a bold and imaginative course of action, but it had great appeal to the Supreme Commander, both strategically and politically.

The Airborne Army could now be gainfully employed in what was a dynamic joint operation, vindicating the substantial investment made in it by British and American commanders.

Eisenhower agreed to support Montgomery's plan as far as the securing of a crossing over the Rhine, always maintaining that he intended to review the support given to Montgomery's plan at that point. He immediately authorized the use of Brereton's First Allied Airborne Allied Army and agreed in principle to the operation becoming the main effort for the Allies; Montgomery would get the precious combat supplies he needed at the expense of the American armies to the south. Inevitably there were problems with this and Montgomery had to raise the issue again with Eisenhower to secure his supplies.

Anticipating Eisenhower's acquiescence, Montgomery had Lieutenant General 'Boy' Browning waiting at the airfield for his orders and directed General Miles Dempsey, the commander of Second Army, to give the airborne commander a full briefing on the outcome of the meeting and the clearance for the inclusion of the American airborne divisions on the new operation. Browning then left Brussels by air, landing back in England at 1430 hours, and then headed for Headquarters First Allied Airborne Army at Sunninghill Park near Ascot.

On arrival, he briefed Brereton on the concept and outline of the new operation. By early evening both he and his American superior had briefed the key officers of the Airborne Army on Operation MARKET GARDEN and what their respective roles in the largest airborne landing in history were to be. The initial planning conference understandably carried on into, and used up most of the next day, as vital details were hammered out.

Brereton had immediately appointed Browning, already his deputy commander, as the ground commander of all airborne troops committed to the new operation. This decision was logical, given Brereton's air force background and lack of experience in ground operations, added to which was the fact that the overall command of MARKET GARDEN rested with the British. The repercussions of this decision were, however, to have a direct effect on the operation at the lowest level. Browning was determined to take part in the battle himself and made the decision to deploy with a tactical headquarters by glider to Nijmegen.

The plan for MARKET had to be developed as quickly as possible to allow commanders to digest its implications for them and then give detailed orders to the troops under their command.

The operation order for COMET was the obvious starting point for the new plan; but this had been planned in haste and would require significant revision to incorporate the complexities of delivering the 35,000 men of First Allied Airborne Army to their drop and landing zones.

Airborne forces are used to short-notice changes and planning under pressure, and there were standard load configurations and well-practised operating procedures that would speed the planning process. It would be these standard operating procedures which would give the MARKET planners a realistic chance of adapting the COMET plan within the very short time frame available to them.

The Air Movement Staff Table drafted for LINNET, which had generally remained extant for COMET, was retained again wherever possible. The intent was to minimize disruption to the troops and aircraft still massed at mounting airfields all over England.

Troops and loads remained with the same aircraft and crews, and with few exceptions were earmarked for departure from the same airfields. The problems faced by the airborne staff were, however, of little concern to the men destined to implement the plans they wrestled with. The priorities of life, as always, were of an entirely different nature for the soldier in the lower echelons of the command chain.

Sergeant Godfrey Freeman had moved south with 'B' Sqn GPR from RAF Brize Norton to RAF Manston in Kent. He and his comrades found themselves in the midst of organized chaos:

> To say that RAF Manston was nearly overwhelmed by our presence would be to put it mildly. The Glider Pilot Regiment made up a small contingent compared with the Airlanding Anti-Tank Batteries, Airborne Infantry, Medical Corps and a whole host of other units who had gathered there for take off. There was hardly a nook or cranny, including the chapel, which wasn't taken over for temporary sleeping accommodation. Then there were the ground crews for two squadrons of tugs, all the cooks, orderly room staff, and batmen, as well as a strong contingent of WAAFs who had contrived to come along.
>
> In spite of all this the station coped magnificently, and at the same time continued to operate a Maori Fighter Squadron flying Typhoons and Tempests, a jet Meteor squadron, which was then very secret and always surrounded at dispersal by an armed guard, as well as maintaining a twenty four hour readiness for any aircraft in distress returning from 'the other side'. There was the biggest graveyard of crashed aircraft I have ever seen containing almost every known type of aircraft then flying, and a small canteen, which served 'char and wads', situated near the crash truck and fire-engine post, and about a hundred yards or so from the main runway.
>
> Around the walls of this canteen were graffiti and cartoons, depicting a whole range of near miss, dodgy landings, by damaged aircraft, and soon another was added to the collection which depicted a Horsa glider in free flight. Underneath it was the simple inscription: The Glider Pilot Regiment – 50 Engineless landings in one day!
>
> Now came the most trying time of all, the time of waiting. For two or three days we were at a loose end, and there were few of us who did not take the opportunity of treating each day as though it were our last. I don't know where the beer came from, but come it did, and went as rapidly. The more adventurous among us went into Margate or Ramsgate to exchange the foreign currency in our escape packs for sterling, and thence into the pubs. These escape packs, besides containing money also included sweets, chewing gum, Horlicks tablets, a hacksaw blade, some fishing tackle, maps, condensed rations and an escape compass.
>
> To cash the currency meant that we would have to answer for it if the operation did not come off, but as things turned out, that eventually did not transpire. In any case, the currency was French, and we were due to land in Holland, so it would not have helped us much anyway.[1]

Well away from the confusion of Manston and the other airfields, Brereton's staff quickly allocated objectives and the troops to task to seize and hold them. Over the course of the conference at Sunninghill Park the MARKET phase of Montgomery's plan was formulated, D-Day was still not set but the situation on the ground in Holland could require its launch in less than a week.

Time was limited further by the need for the airborne troops to receive and digest aerial

Pen & Sword Books
FREEPOST SF5
47 Church Street
BARNSLEY
South Yorkshire
S70 2BR

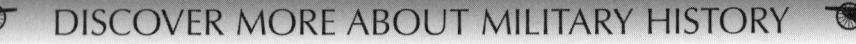

photographs and maps of their respective landing zones and subsequent objectives. A window of seventy-two hours prior to landing was judged to be the irreducible minimum for the mission-planning process to be successfully completed by the participating units. This reduced the time available to the Airborne Army Headquarters yet further.

As a direct result of this rigid constraint Brereton made a fateful, but entirely logical decision: once the plan was completed and the Operation Order issued it could not be changed. There were simply too many variables and interacting moving parts involved to tamper with it once it was set.

The circulation of even the smallest amendment to the orders was thought to be unachievable; MARKET would be launched on the timetable agreed at Sunninghill Park. There could be no modification of the plan once the conference dispersed and the operations orders were issued.

The Sunninghill Park meeting went on into the evening of the 10th, putting flesh onto the bones of Montgomery's concept of MARKET. Objectives were agreed and allocated to the airborne divisions; British and Polish airborne formations were now concentrated on the Arnhem bridgehead. After some discussion about which of the American divisions should be given Nijmegen as its objective, the more experienced and battle-hardened 82nd Airborne was allocated the task.

There were also sound practical and logistic reasons why this made sense: whereas the 82nd would be required to mount its operations from airfields centred on the Lincolnshire town of Grantham, its sister division, the 101st Airborne, was based around southern England.

If the 82nd had been tasked to attack Eindhoven and the 101st Nijmegen, their respective transport aircraft streams would have had to cross each other en route to Holland. The decision was taken to separate the routes, thereby minimizing risk of collision and confusion, and the objectives were allocated accordingly. This decision also ensured that the least-experienced American airborne division was relieved by advancing British armour first.

The 101st Airborne Division was commanded by Major General Maxwell Taylor. His 'Screaming Eagles' had incurred significant casualties in the Normandy campaign and it now contained a large number of replacement troops who were viewed as relatively untried. Its intended objectives beyond Eindhoven required it to stretch itself northwards over a narrow corridor 30 miles in length.

Maxwell Taylor was unhappy with the planned dispersal of his division and the effect it would have on his ability to hold the corridor against German counter-attack. He voiced his concerns from the outset during a meeting with the man responsible for Operation MARKET, General Miles Dempsey, the commander of British Second Army. On 12 September, the two generals agreed that the original objective of securing Eindhoven itself after landing, while concurrently clearing and holding a lengthy section of corridor, was beyond the capability of a single division. The meeting resulted in a more realistic, but still sizeable, objective for the 'Screaming Eagles' to secure – the corridor was reduced but even so it was still 16 miles long.

British tanks and infantry would race through Eindhoven without 101st Division support and then travel along Taylor's 16-mile corridor toward Nijmegen. By the conclusion of the meeting he was content that he would have adequate British armour and artillery to support his division and that his task was achievable.

The Nijmegen-Grave objective was viewed as a tougher nut to crack than Eindhoven, and it was handed to Major General James Gavin's 82nd Airborne Division. At thirty-seven, Gavin was the youngest divisional commander in the US Army; known as 'Slim Jim' to his men he was both tough and dynamic. Gavin and his 'All-American' division, who were veterans of Sicily, Italy and the Normandy landings, understood the intricacies and pitfalls of large-scale airborne operations from bitter experience. He quickly concluded that the key to the success of his division's mission was the capture of a hump of high ground 2 miles to the south-east of Nijmegen, known as the Groesbeek

Heights. This was vital ground. At 300 feet in height, the feature was the only significant high ground for miles; possession of it would allow him or indeed the Germans to dominate the landing zones and the roads into Nijmegen. His division's landing zones had been overrun by German troops during the Normandy landings, causing immense problems, and Gavin was determined this would not be replayed in Holland.

The town of Nijmegen itself had a population of 82,000, and was thought to have a strong garrison supported by at least twenty-two heavy anti-aircraft guns and over eighty lighter artillery pieces. Gavin elected, with Browning's approval, to land close to the heights and secure them and his landing zones against German counter- attack; he would seize the bridges over the Maas at Grave and secure the smaller canal bridges between that objective and Nijmegen itself. The main bridge over the Waal in Nijmegen would then be taken with support from British armour, artillery and heavy infantry.

The highway bridge that spanned the lower Rhine at Arnhem was the prize at the end of the airborne corridor; the task of seizing and holding it and two other less significant crossings fell to Major General Roy Urquhart's 1st British Airborne Division. They would be supported by the 1st Polish Independent Parachute Brigade Group, a task that required the use of every glider pilot that the Glider Pilot Regiment could muster.

General Brereton appointed Major General Paul L. Williams, the commander of the United States Army Air Force IX Troop Carrier Command, as the overall commander of the air operation that would deliver the three airborne divisions. He was well known to British and American Airborne commanders for his 'can do' attitude and professional abilities; his opinion carried weight and was trusted by all.

General Williams's British counter part was the equally capable and highly regarded Air-Vice Marshal Leslie Hollinghurst commanding 38 Group, Royal Air Force. He would also coordinate 46 Group, Royal Air Force and 130 USAAF Dakota aircraft, all of which would be employed carrying Urquhart's 1st Airborne Division to Arnhem.

The formulation of an Air Movement Order on this scale would have been a complex and demanding task at any time – three months of briefings and conferences had been required to coordinate the Normandy landings. The Air Movement Orders for MARKET had to be completed and in circulation in less than three days, during which Brereton, Williams and Hollinghurst were faced with some difficult decisions.

The first decision taken by Brereton was that the landings would take place in daylight – this was not without precedent but it also carried its own risks. The aerial armada required to carry this huge airborne force would present a target of unprecedented size to the Luftwaffe in broad daylight and in close proximity to its homeland defences.

General Williams had overseen the successful parachute and glider landings during the Allied invasion of Southern France; he therefore argued that the benefits of day landings outweighed the huge risks of navigating to objectives and landing on them in darkness.

The British were well versed in night landings and initially advocated landing in darkness on D-Day at least. They had used navigation beams from their radar Gee system to guide the air transport streams onto their objectives on both flanks of the Normandy landings, although the technique had limited success.

Technology was also used to produce a ground-to-air link for the Normandy operation. As the transports approached the DZs, pathfinders transmitted homing signals from the objective using Eureka transmitters, whose signal could be received in the incoming aircraft on Rebecca equipment.

The MARKET objectives, however, were beyond the effective range of the Gee system, so accurate guidance could not be guaranteed in darkness.

The Germans had also made technological progress. Their anti-aircraft defence system was radar controlled, making its night fighters and guns as effective in darkness as by day. The airmen among their planning staff successfully argued that it could totally disrupt any concentrated formation of slow-moving transport aircraft.

By day, however, the air supremacy maintained by the Allies would allow them to destroy any anti-aircraft emplacement that engaged the MARKET air formations within minutes. The likelihood of the embattled German day fighter force being able to penetrate the Allied fighter escort was considered minimal.

The American airborne landings in Normandy, and to a lesser degree the British, had suffered from serious problems with navigation and dispersion, scattering paratroops and gliders over wide areas. The resulting confusion, coupled with German counter-attacks had seriously hampered American airborne abilities for days after D-Day.

Eisenhower himself had voiced concerns about the navigational abilities of the American transport crews, who had had far less time to accumulate experience than their British counterparts. The General's concerns were shared lower down the American chain of command – the paratroopers of the 82nd US Airborne Division joked about their countrymen's abilities with typical black military humour stating 'we always use blind pilots'.

The moon light levels forecast for the week of 17 September onwards made debate about the merits of day versus night landings academic, as they were well below practicable levels for massed parachuting or gliding.

The lack of moonlight above all else was the deciding factor. The need for the airborne divisions to arrive over their objectives en masse without incident and to subsequently land without interference confirmed the decision – it had to be a daylight operation.

The allocation of aircraft to the ground formations was the next thorny issue that had to be considered, for even with the huge transport fleet he had at his disposal General Brereton could only plan on lifting a maximum of 16,500 men in a single lift. A series of consecutive lifts would have to be mounted to carry all 35,000 troops over to Holland.

The allocation of resources and transport lift was considered in detail on 11 September at headquarters IX Troop Carrier Command at Eastcote, the meeting beginning at 0900 hours. The Air Force and Airborne planners each approached the meeting with differing priorities. Whereas the airmen had planned routes in outline as well as departure airfields and transit times, the soldiers attended to ensure tactically sound drop and landing zones were selected for their troops and to secure as much air- lift capacity for their respective formations as possible.

There was then, and still is today, the tradition of a 'bun fight' at this point as each organization attempted to ensure it got what it considered to be essential to the smooth running of its facet of the operation.

Despite the conflicting priorities of the airmen and their airborne associates, the Eastcote conference progressed well with D-Day set for 17 September and an H-Hour of 1300 hours local time (two hours ahead of Greenwich Mean Time) was decided upon.

The planners could now work backwards from that point in time and formulate their Air Movement Staff Table – the fine detail of who, when, how and where would they land?

During the conference the need to get the bulk of the airborne divisions onto their respective drop and landing zones on D-Day was debated at length, being seen as critical to the success of MARKET by airborne commanders. While the shortfall in lift capacity prevented a single mass lift, the feasibility of a double lift on D-Day was explored.

Air-Vice Marshal Hollinghurst was prepared to mount consecutive lifts. He argued that there was adequate time to turn around crews and aircraft, provided that the first wave took off in pre-dawn darkness and returned for an afternoon sortie onto the same objectives.

Major General Williams, however, was reluctant to let his American crews fly the first lift in darkness; he also had concerns about aircrew fatigue induced by two consecutive combat sorties in a single day.

The recent reinforcement of his command with large numbers of new aircraft had not been matched with a corresponding increase in aircraft mechanics and refuellers. He only had about half the number required to sustain his fleet, should his aircraft encounter effective 'flak' and return with battle damage. He was therefore not convinced that he had the capacity to turn his squadrons around in time for a second lift on the same day.

Another key planning consideration was German flak dispositions. Intelligence summaries for COMET had not rated the anti-aircraft defences around Arnhem as particularly significant. The concept for COMET had included potential *coup de main* landings on the bridges under cover of darkness, followed by a brigade landing against what was at the time perceived to be a disorganized enemy. All of the assaulting troops would have been on the ground on the first day with the advantage of surprise behind them; MARKET would be a very different proposition.

The German front line was stabilizing and the anti-aircraft threat now loomed large; the defences around the Luftwaffe airfield at Deelen to the north of Arnhem and protecting the town itself were thought potent enough to deter a landing in close proximity to the airfield or the bridge.

The flak along the whole of the selected air route for MARKET would have to be suppressed by ground-attack aircraft, requiring time and daylight. A pre-dawn lift would leave no time for the tactical air forces to execute this vital task. The Allies greatest advantage would potentially be wasted and any second wave would have to fly over a fully alerted and relatively intact air-defence system. The ever-present variable of the British weather had also to be considered – early mist, fog and rain was a real possibility in September 1944. Disruption by weather at just a few of the airfields would cause chaos to the marshalling of the columns of transport aircraft charged with delivering the airborne army to Holland.

The tactical air forces that would be tasked with clearing a path through the German air defences were based on the Continent, and so were spared the nuances of the weather in southern England; they would therefore be able to continue their mission unhindered by English fog and rain.

A later H-Hour would also allow XXX Corps more time to drive its ground attack through Eindhoven and give the ground-attack formations freedom to manoeuvre over their targets, without the complication of avoiding inbound air transport streams.

Logic, therefore, suggested that a pre-dawn lift was not viable for logistic, meteorological and tactical reasons, whereas a later H-Hour would ensure optimum conditions on the objectives for both air and ground forces. General Williams ruled it out of consideration, together with a subsequent lift later in the day. With hindsight, this has been portrayed by commentators to be a catastrophic error. However, tempered with the intelligence available to him on the day and the predicted rate that Second Army was to project XXX Corps along the 60-mile corridor to Arnhem, it does appear to be a not unreasonable decision.

The delivery of the Airborne Army would now be spread over three consecutive days, as the application of the 'bottom-up' principle to the air plan created clear disparities in lift allocation between the airborne divisions.

Only Maxwell Taylor's 101st US Airborne Division would be delivered complete on D-Day. Gavin's 82nd Division would require a second wave on 18 September and Urquhart's 1st British Airborne was to be delivered to Arnhem over three days.

It was assumed that the loss of the element of surprise on the second and third days would be mitigated by the rapid advance of XXX Corps, linking the airborne bridgeheads together within forty-eight hours.

The staggered arrival of his division did, however, create a tactical and logistic problem for Major General Urquhart that would not have presented itself if the lift capacity had been adequate to deliver everybody on D-Day.

1st British Airborne Division landing and drop zones for the subsequent lifts would have to be secured and defended until they were complete in Arnhem on the third day. This would tie down vital infantry battalions that would be better used seizing and holding the Arnhem bridges and their environs. The use of glider pilots was considered for this task, indeed it was a role that they were trained in, but they were considered too vital an asset to be wasted in this manner. It was intended that they would be kept as a reserve and recovered back to England as quickly as possible for use on future operations.

During the afternoon conference of 11 September, the matter of landing zones had been discussed at length. When Urquhart and his staff pressed for landing zones as close as possible to the bridges and on both sides of the river, this request and a bid to resurrect *coup de main* landings was quashed by Air-Vice Marshal Hollinghurst.

The thinking of the Royal Air Force planners was shaped by the intelligence assessments of German flak dispositions in and around Arnhem and Deelen airfield to the north, the vulnerability of slow-moving, heavily laden transport aircraft and glider-tug combinations being foremost in their thoughts.

There were thought to be forty-four heavy anti-aircraft guns around Arnhem, supported by 112 lighter-calibre weapons. The perceived threat was compounded further by reports from RAF Bomber Command crews of flak being encountered from the area as they returned from raids on the Ruhr valley. Air reconnaissance sorties also identified vehicle-based mobile flak batteries whose locations were impossible to predict; these were supplemented with flak units mounted on barges that could roam around the canals and rivers.

The threat posed by German anti-aircraft fire, particularly around Deelen airfield, therefore dominated the thought process of the RAF planners, and as they had primacy over Major General Urquhart and his staff until they were physically on the ground, it was the avoidance of flak that ultimately selected the landing zones for 1st British Airborne Division.

Any proposition of a landing close to the bridges was made even less attractive when the ground close to the Arnhem bridges was assessed from aerial photographs. The photo interpretation resulted in the landing zone being classified as polder land – boggy, reclaimed land interlaced with ditches and prone to flooding that was unsuitable for glider or parachute landings.

After the initial landings the assessment was found to be totally incorrect – the ground, though not ideal, would have taken gliders with little risk.

The exclusion of a *coup de main* mission due to unsuitable ground remains a matter of controversy, as elements of the Polish Brigade were scheduled to land on the same ground during the third lift.

The option of a *coup de main* landing on the main highway bridge at Arnhem was thought viable by Commander Glider Pilots, Colonel George Chatterton. He had advocated company sized coup de main glider landings for COMET and still argued for such a landing close to the highway bridge for MARKET. Peter Harclerode quotes Chatterton some forty years after the battle in his book Arnhem: A Tragedy of Errors:

> I went to see General Browning and suggested to him that we were landing too far away but he said that it was out of our hands. It was an RAF decision because they said that the bridge was so well defended by anti-aircraft guns that they wished to keep their tugs away from it. I nevertheless suggested that my pilots could land their gliders near the bridge and although

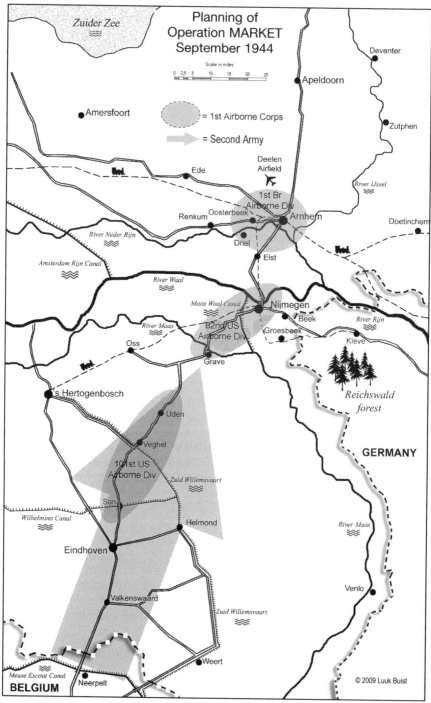

Planning of
Operation MARKET
September 1944

Scale in miles
0  2.5  5    10    15    20    25

= 1st Airborne Corps

= Second Army

*Zuider Zee*

Amersfoort

Deventer

Apeldoorn

Zutphen

Deelen
Airfield

Ede

*River IJssel*

1st Br
Airborne Div

Renkum  Oosterbeek    Arnhem

*River Neder Rijn*

Doetinchem

Driel

*Amsterdam Rijn Canal*

Elst

*River Waal*

*Maas Waal Canal*

Nijmegen

Beek

*River Rijn*

82nd US
Airborne Div

Groesbeek

*River Maas*

Kleve

Oss

Grave

*Reichswald
forest*

's Hertogenbosch

Uden

Veghel

**GERMANY**

101st US
Airborne Div

*Zuid Willemsvaart*

Son

Helmond

*Wilhelmina Canal*

*River Maas*

Eindhoven

Valkenswaard

Venlo

*Zuid Willemsvaart*

Weert

*Meuse Escout Canal*

© 2009 Luuk Buist

**BELGIUM**  Neerpelt

*Planning of Operation MARKET, September 1944*

there would be more casualties on landing due to the size and unevenness of the enclosures, it would surely be preferable to landing miles away.

When General Browning said that no doubt there would be more tugs shot down this way, I suggested that this could be avoided by a remote release, so allowing the tugs to turn back for home well before the bridge. He replied, George it's too late. It has all been decided.[2]

Colonel Chatterton is also recorded as saying that he had been called a murderer and an assassin at the time for suggesting the *coup de main* landing and that nobody else saw the need for such an attack.[3]

The reliance on flawed photo interpretation of the potential landing sites close to the bridge, supported with similarly inaccurate information from the Dutch resistance about marshy ground conditions, made the case for dismissing a *coup de main* overwhelming.

The case for abandonment was further strengthened by the assumption that any glider-borne force attempting to storm and hold the highway bridge would be overlooked from buildings and high ground on the northern bank of the river. This would give German defenders a tactical advantage over any assaulting troops landing on the proposed landing zone. The *coup de main* force would undoubtedly find itself exposed to machine-gun and artillery fire from well-sited German defenders.

There would be no direct glider assault on any of the Arnhem bridges. General Urquhart would have to look elsewhere for landing zones that were acceptable to the RAF planners.

The LZs and DZs used for MARKET were selected by Urquhart himself from the limited options offered to him by the air planners. With any hope of seizing his objectives using the preferred airborne combination of surprise, speed and overwhelming violence denied to his division, he had to look for other ways to maximize the firepower of his lightly equipped force.

The staggered delivery of his troops in three lifts on separate days presented him with the added complication of defending the LZs and DZs beyond D-Day.

A conventional airborne operation with a single landing close to the objective would ideally have resulted in the perimeter held by the airborne troops encompassing the LZ, or in the troops moving off to secure the objective and having no subsequent requirement for the original zones. Any resupply or reinforcement would come by parachute drop directly into the new perimeter.

The capture of an enemy airfield would provide the ideal staging area for subsequent reinforcement – 52nd (Lowland) Division had been re-roled for this purpose and was designated for this task within MARKET.

The capture of Deelen airfield was intended soon after XXX Corps reached Arnhem, whereupon 52nd (Lowland) Division would be flown in to reinforce the corps, supported by specialist American engineer units who would further expand the newly captured airfield for Allied use.

General Urquhart selected a total of five LZs and DZs that were technically suited for their respective purposes. The areas chosen comprised open heathland and large expanses of well-established farmland; both types of ground would accept large numbers of parachute troops or gliders with minimal casualties.

The dimensions of the Landing Zones were generous, which would reduce the risk of the paratroops and gliders being scattered. This would improve Urquhart's chances of concentrating his division quickly and forming them up into their respective battalion groups, which would go some way toward compensating for the vetoing of a more direct but high-risk *coup de main* attack.

There were, however, significant drawbacks to the selected LZs: they were all between 6 and 8 miles away from the highway bridge in Arnhem itself. By the time the first British troops landed on Dutch soil, the German troops in and around Arnhem would be alerted and racing to their defensive positions.

Even the fittest airborne soldier could not expect to extract himself from the organized chaos of the landings, orientate himself and reach the bridge in much less than two hours.

The LZs were dissected by the railway line running south-east to north-west from Arnhem to Utrecht, the glider LZs designated Love (L) and Sugar (S) being north of the railway line. To the south of the railway was also LZ Yoke (Y) on Ginkel Heath. Renkum Heath was south of the railway line and was neatly divided by a minor road running north to south; the dual-purpose LZ and DZ X-Ray (X) was sited on the western side of the road. Across the road on the eastern side sat LZ Zebra (Z).

There was an additional DZ selected for use later in the operation, DZ King (K), whch was on the southern bank of the Rhine close to the town. This was to be used by 1st Independent Polish Parachute Brigade Group on the third day of the operation; it was assumed the German anti-aircraft threat would be neutralized by this stage.

A Supply Dropping Point (SDP) was sited within the intended divisional perimeter, to allow parachute resupply to take place throughout the operation. This SDP, designated Victor (V), was on the north-west outskirts of Arnhem itself.

By midday on 12 September, the air delivery of First Allied Airborne Army had been formulated and agreed in broad terms, so that detailed planning could now get underway. There would be two routes used for the duration of the operation, designated Northern and Southern Routes respectively.

The Northern Route would primarily serve the Arnhem and Nijmegen lifts and was very close in configuration to that proposed for COMET. It was viewed as simpler to follow, aircraft departing on a more or less straight line, however, it did involve a transit over 80 miles of occupied territory. The margin of error created by changing course, or dog legging over the sea where there were no visual markers, was thought too great for many of the less experienced tug crews; the advantage of a straight-line transit over the sea was essential on both routes.

Aircraft on this route would depart the English coast at Aldeburgh in Suffolk, and then track in a straight line for 94 miles over the North Sea. Landfall would be made at the island of Schouwen, off the coast of Holland. The plot for the route followed the 18-mile length of the island to its south-eastern point, where the route changed heading for 52 miles over German-occupied territory. At the end of this overland leg, the crews would confirm their position against a group of prominent major road junctions south of s'Hertogenbosch and then turn north for 25 miles to Nijmegen or 35 miles to Arnhem.

Intelligence summaries suggested that there were only isolated concentrations of flak deployed close to the route and that they could easily be dealt with by ground- attack aircraft. The lack of concentrated flak on the northern route made it particularly alluring to the Air Transport commanders.

The Southern Route would be used concurrently to get the 101st Airborne Division from its airfields in the south of England to Eindhoven. The mounting airfields for General Maxwell Taylor's troops were much closer to the English coast and their objectives and, therefore, they would have a shorter flight than the northern lift.

The southern formation cut across the Thames estuary from RAF Bradwell Bay in Essex to North Foreland, giving the London Air Defence Zone a wide berth. Having reached North Foreland, the route then tracked east for 150 miles over the sea until landfall on the Belgian coast. The aircraft stream carried on heading east until the Albert Canal was identified; the route then took a turn to the north-east for 30 miles where the Eindhoven LZs lay.

With the air routes established in principle, the allocation of transport aircraft could get underway in earnest. The decision was taken from the outset to prioritize lift capacity on a 'bottom to top' principle (Eindhoven-Nijmegen-Arnhem). In effect the initial lifts would be configured to favour the divisions closest to the GARDEN forces – if they failed to seize their bridges or to hold their length of corridor, the capture of the prized bridges over the Rhine at Arnhem would be pointless.

Although the ultimate objective of the entire operation was the Arnhem crossings, on D-Day they would receive the lowest priority in terms of air transport.

Major General Urquhart and his American counterparts wanted every available aircraft they could squeeze out of Brereton and Williams, but despite each of their respective best efforts, none of the divisional commanders were successful in securing any significant increase in their quota of transport aircraft.

It was at this point that Lieutenant General Browning's controversial decision to deploy his headquarters on the operation began to affect the operational conduct of MARKET GARDEN.

The headquarters of First Allied Airborne Army was never conceived as a field-deployable organization, nor in fact was the British Airborne Corps headquarters. Neither organization had the equipment, training, radios or staff to operate as a tactical headquarters that could provide command and control in the field to the divisions that it administered in England.

During the week leading up to 17 September, frantic preparations took place in order to produce a corps headquarters that could effectively support Browning and his staff. The prospect of the war ending without taking part in a major airborne operation was just too much for 'Boy' Browning and many of his staff officers, who viewed this great airborne invasion of Holland as potentially their last chance of action before the end of hostilities.

The lift requirement for this new and untried headquarters would deny 1st British Airborne Division thirty-two precious Horsa gliders from Major Stewart Griffiths' Harwell-based A Squadron, and six Hadrian gliders from 'X' Flight were also detailed to lift elements of the headquarters from Manston, under command of Lieutenant Peter Clarke.

The British division would start D-Day with 480 aircraft, 320 of which would be glider-tug combinations. This gave Urquhart 110 transport aircraft less than the 101st US Division, and roughly forty less than the 82nd US Division.

**Notes**

1    Freeman, Sgt G., 'B' Sqn GPR, correspondence with Luuk Buist, 1991.

2    Chatterton, Colonel, GPR, in Harclerode, Arnhem, Tragedy of Errors, Caxton, London, 1994, p. 51.

3    Chatterton, Colonel, GPR, in Ryan, Cornelius, A Bridge Too Far, Coronet, Aylesbury, 1974.

4    878th (US) Airborne Aviation Engineer Battalion (10 x Hamilcar and 147 (US) Waco gliders).

# CHAPTER 5

# Preparation for Battle

*'It was a town called Arnhem in Holland, the principle*
*objective being a great bridge spanning the River Rhine.'*

In spite of all of the challenges and unknown variables he was confronted with, Major General Urquhart managed to formulate his initial plan for the seizing of the Arnhem bridges by 12 September. He had returned to his own headquarters at Moor Park Golf Club in Hertfordshire on the evening of 11 September and spent three hours in his command caravan pouring over maps and aerial photographs of the area, wrestling with the constraints placed on him by the air commanders. Finally, he settled on the only viable course of action available to him: he would use the landing zones spread 4 to 8 miles from his main objective in Arnhem.

Despite his dissatisfaction with the refusal of the Air Staff to consider mounting a *coup de main* operation close to his objective, Roy Urquhart could see some advantages to a daylight landing on the wide open heathland and fields outside Arnhem. The risk of his division being scattered across the Dutch countryside and subsequently being delayed in rallying and mounting the operation would be dramatically reduced by the combination of good weather, daylight and the use of landing and drop zones that were technically ideal for the purpose. Once he had made his decision, and the concept of his plan was clear in his mind, he briefed his divisional staff officers and set them to work producing the detailed operation orders that had to be distributed the next day. The work went on into the night and through the morning of 12 September. The completed Operation Order was typed and copied for distribution, just in time for Roy Urquhart's 'Orders Group' later the same day. The brigade commanders, accompanied by a few key staff officers from the divisional staff, gathered at Moor Park to receive their orders at 1700 hours.

D-Day for Operation MARKET GARDEN remained set at 17 September; the operation would begin with the drop of the 'Pathfinders' of the 21st Independent Parachute Company, lead by Major 'Boy' Wilson MC, one of the early pioneers of British Airborne forces, who at the age of forty-five was the oldest parachutist in the Division. Urquhart himself had a high opinion of the pathfinders and described them later as a 'group of highly intelligent and battle crusted men'. In his own account of MARKET GARDEN, entitled *Arnhem*, he recounted his first meeting with Boy Wilson soon after he took command of the 1st British Airborne Division:

> I recalled my first meeting with Wilson soon after I took command. Modestly built, he oozed a confidence and assertiveness out of proportion to his size which compelled me to remark: 'Ah Wilson I understand you bounce off everybody.' 'Sir,' he replied formally and without diffidence, 'I have an independent unit and I'm considered rather independent.'[1]

Twenty-five of 'Boy' Wilson's 180-man company were Jewish refugees of German or Austrian origin, whose families had escaped Europe and persecution by the Nazis. They had later enlisted to hit back at Hitler, their bi-lingual knowledge having an obvious appeal to an organization such as the pathfinders. Another small group of these determined young men had been unsuccessful in their bid to be selected by the Glider Pilot Regiment, they would fight at Arnhem as pathfinders.

Three strong platoons of Wilson's pathfinders were to be dropped from twelve RAF Stirling bombers flying ahead of the main force, the transport element following on the second lift by Horsa. Once on the ground they were tasked to mark quickly DZ 'X' and LZs 'S' and 'Z' for immediate use that day; they would use a combination of well-practised methods to achieve their aim.

A chain of Eureka homing beacons would guide the streams of transport aircraft across England and over the Channel and liberated Belgium, then on to their respective dropping and landing areas. On approaching the area of their respective dropping and glider-release points, coloured marker panels would give visual identification of each LZ or DZ. The incoming pilots and paratroops would then make use of coloured smoke markers that would identify rally points from the air and on the ground; these would be lit by the pathfinders once the landing was imminent. The smoke would also give the glider pilots and paratroops indication of the wind direction as they made their respective descents. An approach into the oncoming wind is the preferred option for gliders and powered aircraft, as it reduces the length of 'run on' after landing, thereby reducing the size of the landing zone required.

The pathfinders would drop in advance of the first lift, commencing their drop at 1240 hours. They would then have approximately twenty minutes on the ground to complete their vital task before the first gliders carrying the bulk of the 1st Airlanding Brigade would cast off from their tugs, and begin their descents onto their designated LZs. The glider-borne infantry of Brigadier Philip 'Pip' Hicks DSO MC were given the immediate responsibility of securing the DZs and LZs that the 1st British Airborne Division would depend on to expand the bridgehead of the first day.

Brigadier Hicks was the oldest man in the 1st British Airborne Division and was due to celebrate his forty-ninth birthday during the Battle of Arnhem. A veteran of the 1940 campaign in France, he had commanded the Airlanding Brigade in Sicily and Italy. 'Pip' Hicks was well known to the Glider Pilot Regiment. During the Sicily landings of July 1943 he had been a passenger in Colonel George Chatterton's glider. Like the majority of those taking part in the disastrous airborne phase of the invasion, the glider had been cast off too early and forced to ditch in the Mediterranean in darkness. Despite the gradually sinking glider being illuminated by Italian searchlights and swept by machine-gun fire, he had managed to swim ashore minus most of his equipment and join the fight on land. As a result of his leadership and bravery that night and over the following days while commanding the scattered remnants of his brigade, he was awarded the Distinguished Service Order (DSO).

Literally following in the slipstream of the last glider-tug combinations of the Airlanding Brigade would be 143 Dakota transport aircraft of the American IX Troop Carrier Command, carrying Brigadier Gerald 'Legs' Lathbury DSO and his 1st Parachute Brigade. The paratroops of Lathbury's brigade were to land on DZ 'X', their objective to secure the railway bridge, the pontoon bridge and the main highway bridge in Arnhem.

It was Brigadier Lathbury who, during the initial planning discussions, had suggested that the Division's Reconnaissance Squadron should be used to dash ahead of his advancing troops in their recce Jeeps to conduct a vehicle-mounted *coup de main* on the highway bridge. The 1st Airborne Reconnaissance Squadron was commanded by Major 'Freddie' Gough MC; its modified Jeeps, armed with twin Vickers 'K' machine guns, would be carried to Arnhem by twenty-two Horsa gliders.

Urquhart's intent was that by last light on D-Day, Lathbury and his parachute battalions would have made best use of the element of surprise to speed march on three separate routes through and around the town of Oosterbeek. Once clear of the small town they would race down into Arnhem, capturing the railway and pontoon bridges. With these tasks complete they would arrive on Arnhem Bridge to relieve Gough's Reconnaissance Squadron on the main objective.

While this was in progress Brigadier Hicks and his glider-borne battalions would dig in and consolidate their hold on the DZs and LZs, in preparation for the arrival of the second lift the next day.

The main body of the first lift would include 358 glider-tug combinations, all Arnhem bound less thirty-two Horsa gliders from 'A' Squadron and six Hadrian gliders from Lieutenant Peter 'Peggy' Clark's 'X' Flight, allocated to carry Browning's corps headquarters, which was to be landed near Nijmegen on LZ 'N'. The main body of the glider lift destined for Arnhem would be split into two distinct groups landing on separate landing zones. LZ 'S' was allocated for gliders carrying Brigadier Hicks and the tactical headquarters of 1st Airlanding Brigade, while the majority of the 173 Horsa gliders designated to land alongside Hicks on LZ 'S' were loaded with the airlanding infantry of his brigade.

Each of 'Pip' Hicks's three glider battalions were identical in organization, established strength and equipment, although they did maintain their own unique regimental character. Two of his regiments were pre-war Regular Army battalions. 1st Battalion, The Border Regiment and 2nd Battalion, The South Staffordshire Regiment had both become airlanding battalions in October 1941, when 31st (Independent) Infantry Brigade was converted from the mountain warfare role and retitled 1st Airlanding Brigade. During those early days there had also been two other battalions within the brigade: 1st Battalion, The Royal Ulster Rifles and 2nd Battalion, The Oxford and Buckinghamshire Light Infantry; both left the 1st Airborne Division when the newly established 6th Airborne Division formed in April 1943.

The glider-borne airlanding battalions differed in character to their Parachute Regiment comrades in that, although the early airlanding battalions were technically volunteers, the process of volunteering differed dramatically from that undertaken by individuals joining the parachute battalions in 1944. The Border Regiment had approached the problem in classic British military style. Sergeant Joe Hardy was the Signal Platoon Sergeant in September 1941:

> All Airborne soldiers were supposedly volunteers – it was judged to be a risky business. The way in which they had us volunteer was to announce that in future the battalion was to be designated an airborne unit, and those men that did not want to take part in airborne operations should report to the Orderly Room and apply to be transferred to other units. We had one man in the battalion who had the guts to say he did not want to fly; he was transferred out, and the rest of us were deemed to have volunteered.[2]

'The Borders' history records a further thirty soldiers being classed as unsuitable for the airborne role and leaving the Battalion over the Christmas of 1941. There was, however, a small incentive to serve in an airlanding battalion: a shilling a day above that paid to an infantryman in a conventional line battalion, although this daily bonus was still half the amount paid to parachutists for carrying out their specialist role. This deficiency in pay was a frequent cause of contention between the two groups. This occasionally triggered contact of a more physical nature when the two elements encountered each other in public houses close to their respective barracks.

The character of the two regular battalions was further shaped after conversion by intensive airborne training and a series of demanding exercises designed to hone their newly developed skills. The first use of the 1st British Airborne Division, including the airlanding brigade and its gliders, came during the invasion of Sicily in July 1943. Casualties among both battalions and their attached glider pilots were extremely high, indeed the brigade reported over 300 personnel drowned after ditching in the Mediterranean.

The third and least experienced airlanding battalion was the 7th (Galloway) Battalion, The King's Own Scottish Borderers, which had started the war as a Territorial Army battalion and had spent much of the war to date employed on garrison duties. They were in the Scottish Isles and then later moved south to guard the East Anglian port of Lowestoft and its naval base. The order to convert 'The KOSB' to a glider-borne battalion came in December 1943, the requirement for airlanding infantrymen to be volunteers having long expired. This battalion was converted en masse and had to make the transition to airborne status rapidly, the methods used to screen the soldiers already serving in the battalion being classic British Army.

The Company Sergeant Major (CSM) of D Company, Warrant Officer Jimmy Swanston recounts how he shed the unfit and undesirable men from his company by devising his own selection process:

> A weeding out process started and for my own company this turned out to be satisfactory. The method was an easy one. I marched the men one by one to the Medical Officer. I was to stand just behind the man to be examined and then I would just nod yes or no to the doctor. This resulting in a positive or negative check. I am sure some never understood why they were turned down.[3]

This 'weeding' inevitably produced an infantry company or battalion which now had the desired standard physical fitness and was hopefully free of any ill-disciplined elements; it did however now need reinforcement. The glamour of wearing parachute wings and the incentive of higher pay made the parachute units much more attractive to potential volunteers, whereas the glider battalions had to look elsewhere to reconstitute their ranks. Inevitably the regiments concerned drew suitable replacements from their own training depots, a large number of these soldiers 'posted in' being 'young soldiers' fresh from training who had been too young for overseas service and who had been held back in depots, while older comrades were released to front-line battalions. During 1944, there had also been a steady trickle of soldiers volunteering to leave the airlanding battalions for the glamour and 'jump' pay of the Parachute Regiment. The combination of heavy casualties in Sicily, the transfers to parachute units and the influx of replacement 'young soldiers' lowered the average age of the infantry soldier in the airlanding brigade in comparison to the parachute brigades.

The Airlanding Brigade was equipped and manned to add weight and firepower to the lightly equipped airborne division, each of the glider battalions being significantly larger than a parachute battalion. The 806 officers and men were organised in sixteen 27-man platoons (a Horsa load), grouped into four rifle companies. The airlanding battalion order of battle also included a large and powerful Support Company, fielding three times as many 3-inch mortar tubes (12) than a parachute battalion, two medium machine gun platoons, as well as two integral 6-pounder anti-tank gun platoons with four guns each. This relative abundance of support weapons made the glider battalions the ideal choice to defend the landing zones. The landing of a single airlanding battalion required sixty-two Horsa gliders and a single Hamilcar, the latter carrying the battalion's two Bren carriers.

In comparison, the fully manned parachute battalion organized its 556 paratroops in nine large platoons under three rifle companies, and did not possess its own Anti-Tank Platoon. The support echelon included: its Regimental Aid Post and a small number of Jeeps which were carried in seven or eight Horsas. The Battalion's two Bren carriers were normally used to support its Mortar Platoon and its Medium Machine Gun Platoon, and travelled in a single Hamilcar. The rifle companies and the Regimental Headquarters would all be dropped onto the battlefield by parachute.

Also listed in the air movement table for the first glider lift onto LZ 'S' were: seven Horsas, carrying medics of 181, Airlanding Field Ambulance Royal Army Medical Corps and two 'F' Squadron Horsas lifting support platoons from 250 (Airborne) Light Composite Company, Royal Army Service Corps from RAF Broadwell.

The southern boundary of LZ 'S' butted against a steep embankment that carried the main railway line from Arnhem to Utrecht. Just over the other side of this sizeable feature was Renkum Heath, another area of open heathland designated as LZ 'Z'. This second, larger landing zone ran south away from the embankment and the small town of Wolfheze. Access between the two landing zones was possible by way of a minor road that crossed over the railway line and through the embankment, using a level crossing close to the Wolfheze railway station.

LZ 'Z' would be the destination of a further 154 Horsa and thirteen Hamilcar gliders, delivering the weight of Roy Urquhart's divisional troops and some of the units that were key components of his plan. Most notably this lift included the twenty-two 'C' Squadron Horsas crammed with the thirty-nine Jeeps of Gough's Airborne Reconnaissance Squadron, as well as their motorcycles, trailers and even two 20-millimetre Polsten anti-aircraft guns.

Another sixteen 'D' Squadron Horsas taking off from Keevil would be carrying Sappers of 9th (Airborne) Field Company, Royal Engineers, an element of which would support Gough's hastily formed strike force with a further four Jeeps. In all it was intended that a combined total of thirty-five Jeeps would form up as quickly as possible after landing and mount the *coup de main* assault.

General Urquhart and elements of his staff remained sceptical of the predictions of paper-thin German resistance and the loading of the air movement table reflected this. As well as infantry, the first glider lift would include the bulk of his artillery in the form of 1st Airlanding Light Regiment, Royal Artillery less one battery of its rugged 75mm pack howitzers that would arrive with the second lift. The howitzers would be the Division's only integral artillery, until the advance of XXX Corps brought the considerable artillery resources of Second Army in range. A total of fifty-seven Horsas would be required to deliver all twent-four of the vital light guns, their ammunition and their Jeeps onto the landing zone.

The threat of German armour remained prominent in Roy Urquhart's thoughts. He was aware that the parachute battalions, in particular, carried only the lightest anti-tank weapons and were vulnerable to attack from even the most outdated German armour. The Division possessed its own much more capable anti-armour capability in the form of over forty 6- and 17-pounder anti-tank guns shared between two Airlanding Anti-Tank Batteries. A number of these guns were attached to the 1st Parachute Brigade to give them an adequate anti-tank capability.

The 1st Airlanding Anti-Tank Battery, Royal Artillery would be flown in on D-Day with sixteen 6-pounders and eight of the highly potent 17-pounders. Both calibres of anti-tank gun had long barrels and required a Jeep or tractor unit to move them over all but the shortest distances. In order to reduce the risk of separation in flight, both halves of the combination had to be flown together. The resulting load, combined with ready-use ammunition and crew, required a Horsa glider for each 6-pounder and its attendant Jeep. The larger and much heavier 17-pounder gun, with its Morris tractor unit, could only be carried by the giant 'C' Squadron Hamilcars, flown from Tarant Rushton.

As with all matters 'airborne', delivering these vital guns to Arnhem was not straightforward and there were special considerations to be made when loading a 6-pounder into the fuselage of a Horsa. Private Alexander 'Sandy' Masterton, the 'number two' on 'Scimitar Hill' – a 6-pounder gun in one of 1st Border, anti-tank platoons, explains:

> As the loader, I flew with the gun and the jeep, which were securely held by chains and quick release shackles to metal channels bolted to the floor of the glider. The gun was hitched to the jeep ready to be towed out of the glider and the jeep was laden with stores, equipment, petrol and six pounder shells, which were strapped in boxes to the bonnet and on top of the front bumper. Had the glider been hit by small arms fire or flak, then results would have been spectacular to say the least. The gun and jeep were loaded in by ramps through the large door on the port side of the glider behind the cockpit. The jeep was loaded first, then the gun, which

was man handled into place. There was very little clearance within the fuselage so the operation proved somewhat difficult. As the steering wheel of the jeep would strike against the frames of the glider, it was removed by releasing the butterfly nut that held it in place and lay on the passenger seat. The two steel loading ramps were carried in the glider and were fixed down to prevent movement.[4]

Once the lift was complete, and troops and loads were clear of the gliders, men of the Glider Pilot Regiment were to regroup into their respective squadrons ready to fight as formed units in the infantry role. 1 Wing GPR, under Lieutenant Colonel Iain Murray DSO MC, was to protect Urquhart's tactical headquarters and act as divisional reserve. Lieutenant Colonel John Place and the pilots of 2 Wing GPR were to remain under command of Headquarters 1st Airlanding Brigade.

There were notable exceptions to these instructions – those pilots carrying the guns of the anti-tank batteries of the Royal Artillery were instructed to remain with their loads and accompany them until relieved. This included those crews from 'B' Squadron, who were carrying the 6-pounder anti-tank guns detached to support the parachute battalions. They would follow the guns and act as local defence for them, until the order to regroup at their squadron headquarters was received.

A similar mission was given to the glider pilots who carried the light guns of 1st Airlanding Light Regiment, Royal Artillery. These pilots were also to act as close defence for their precious loads after landing.

Captain Angus Low GPR, who commanded 20 Flight of 'B' Squadron under Major Ian Toler, was to receive one of the most unusual orders of the entire operation. Wing headquarters had directed Ian Toler to detach one of the flights from his squadron shortly after landing outside Arnhem and despatch it back down the airborne corridor to Nijmegen. The journey of 22 miles was to be made by whatever means available. Once there, they were to reinforce 'A' Squadron and assist them in their role of defending General Browning's corps headquarters.

The last of the gliders were due to be on the ground by 1400 hours, by which time Brigadier Lathbury and his 1st Parachute Brigade would begin dropping from American C47 Dakota transport aircraft on an area of open heath and ploughed fields adjacent to LZ 'Z'. Their destination was a large open area of Renkum Heath designated as DZ 'X'. The drop zone was also south of the railway embankment and ran parallel to LZ 'Z', away from the railway line to the south, until its boundary just short of the outskirts of the village of Heelsum and the minor road that ran through it. A small advance party from 4th Parachute Brigade would also jump in with Gerald Lathbury's brigade on D day.

Brigadier Lathbury had a very strong airborne pedigree, having been involved with British airborne forces since their earliest days. He had extensive experience in parachute operations, and had also worked as a staff officer in the Air Directorate of the War Ministry. His technical knowledge of airborne doctrine and tactics was enhanced by a reputation for bravery and courage under fire. He had commanded the 1st Parachute Brigade during the Sicily landings where he had miraculously survived a parachute drop from one hundred feet by landing in darkness in a recently ploughed field. Having gained his bearings he found that the brigade had been scattered and he was 1½ miles away from his intended drop zone. He set out for his objective, the Primisole Bridge, collecting small groups of paratroops as he progressed. Although less than a third of 1st Parachute Brigade were available to mount the assault on the bridge, they did so and successfully secured it. It was then that the brigade was subjected to determined counter-arracks mounted by German airborne troops. Gerald Lathbury was wounded by a grenade when splinters were lodged in his back and legs, but despite his wounds he continued to command his brigade. His part in the Primisole Bridge action was recognized with the award of the DSO.

In September 1944, Brigadier Lathbury was the natural choice as Roy Urquhart's deputy and played a significant role advising his superior in the formulation of the 1st Airborne Division plan that was now being delivered at Moor Park. Like their commander, 1st Parachute Brigade could trace their lineage back to the earliest days of British airborne history. They were the original 'Red Devils', christened with that nickname by respectful German opponents during the hard-fought Tunisian campaign of winter 1942. After the mountains of North Africa, they had jumped into Sicily and later fought in the Italian campaign. They then returned to England to prepare for the Normandy invasion, although to their frustration they had been held in reserve and played no part in the landings. The reserve role had not been well received by these battle-hardened troops and they were desperate to get back into battle.

Each of the parachute battalions would require thirty-four C47 Dakotas to carry its rifle companies, flying from the American airfields at Barkston Heath and Saltby. The heavy equipment, Jeeps and some ammunition would be deployed by glider. The Brigade Headquarters and its three subordinate battalion headquarters would fly from Keevil using twenty 'D' Squadron Horsas to carry a total of thirty-eight Jeeps, staff officers, signallers and medics. Each of the parachute battalions was also allocated a single 'C' Squadron Hamilcar to carry two Universal 'Bren' carriers.

The 1st Parachute Brigade viewed themselves as an elite formation that should be the spearhead of the Division, and as such viewed the key task of seizing the Arnhem Bridges as exactly the type of mission to which they were best suited. Gerald Lathbury had formulated a plan that was designed to ensure his parachute battalions reached their respective objectives quickly, with minimum hindrance. He realized speed was of the essence and that his troops must rally on the drop zone, before following on after 'Freddie' Gough's Jeep force as quickly as possible.

The three parachute battalions would take separate routes away from the drop zone and move as rapidly as possible into Arnhem on a broad front. One of the planning assumptions made by Brigadier Lathbury and his staff, based on intelligence reports, was that resistance immediately after their landing would be light. Any German troops who did react quickly enough to oppose them would be of low quality. The lightly equipped but aggressive paratroops should be able to forge through to their objectives without too much trouble. In fact, the brigade staff were more concerned with the prospect of the battalions becoming entangled with each other en route and slowing each other down. In order to avoid this potential congestion, the brigade orders outlined a separate approach route for each of the three battalions.

The plan outlined at the briefing detailed 2nd Parachute Battalion, commanded by Lieutenant Colonel John Frost DSO MC, as the right-hand battalion, following route Lion away from the drop zone through Heelsum and down onto the north bank of the Rhine. He was then to move quickly along the river bank, detaching his 'C' Company, under Major 'Dickie' Dover MC, to seize the railway bridge (code name 'Charing Cross'). The successful capture of the railway bridge would give John Frost a foothold on the southern river bank and allow 'C' Company to move in parallel to the rest of the Battalion on the opposite bank. The main bridge (code name 'Waterloo') could now be attacked in textbook fashion from both ends.

Further along the river bank, and just half a mile short of the main road bridge, was a floating pontoon bridge (code name 'Putney') that had been constructed by the Germans. This bridge had a centre section that could be removed to allow barges to pass through it. The task of securing this less substantial, but tactically important, crossing was given by John Frost to Major 'Doug' Crawley MC & Bar and the men of 'B' Company. The intent was similar to that of 'C' Company: the capture of the crossing followed by an attack on the southern foot of the main bridge. The remainder of John Frost's men would push further on along the northern bank on Route 'Lion', with the objective of taking the north side of the bridge.

As John Frost and his battalion dashed along the river bank, securing the secondary crossings as they went, the 3rd Parachute Battalion would also be on the move. They would be led by Lieutenant Colonel John Fitch and would be the centre battalion, moving alongside 2nd Battalion, keeping station on their left flank. They had a longer and more urban route, taking them through Heelsum, Oosterbeek and finally into Arnhem. Their route was code-named 'Tiger' and used the wider and straighter Utrecht-Arnhem road. They would make best speed to reach the road bridge, in order to reinforce John Frost's battalion around the bridgehead.

Brigadier Lathbury gave his last battalion, 1st Parachute Battalion, the left flank position with the objective of securing high ground to the north of Arnhem itself. The Battalion was required to move along route Leopard, which ran roughly parallel to the Utrecht-Arnhem railway line. The Commanding Officer, Lieutenant Colonel David Dobie DSO, was directed to detach one rifle company from his force to act as the Brigade reserve.

The scheduling of the second lift on D+1 was more problematical than the first day's operation; ideally it should have arrived over the Arnhem landing zones as early as possible on the morning of Monday, 18 September, although the timing of its arrival would be dictated by first light, and of course the weather.

The lift would deliver the balance of Brigadier Hicks's Airlanding Brigade and Brigadier Shan Hackett's 4th Parachute Brigade complete. Whereas the D-Day lift could be delayed in favour of better weather, once those troops were committed and on the ground in Holland, the second lift had to follow on at all costs. Without reinforcement the first wave of the 1st British Airborne Division would inevitably be isolated and destroyed by the now alerted Germans. Roy Urquhart's intent was to compensate for the staggered delivery of his division by reinforcing the newly established bridgehead with the second lift as early on that Monday morning as humanly possible.

The glider component of the lift would total 274 glider-tug combinations carrying units that had been overspilled from the first lift. This would include the remaining pack howitzer battery from the 1st Airlanding Light Regiment, RA and the remaining troop of 6-pounder anti-tank guns from the 1st Airlanding Anti-Tank Battery, RA, which had also not made it onto the staff table for the first lift. In addition, there would be two companies of the South Staffords, displaced from the first lift in order to provide tugs for the lift of General Browning's Corps Headquarters.

As well as the infantry required to bring 'Pip' Hicks's brigade up to full fighting strength, the second lift also included the 2nd (Oban) Airlanding Anti-Tank Battery, RA, comprising two troops of 6-pounder guns and two troops of the heavier 17-pounders. The 229 gliders required to lift the artillery and 4th Parachute Brigade's support echelons, including fifteen Hamilcars, were to land on 1st Parachute Brigade's old DZ 'X' which would be redesignated as LZ 'X' for the second lift.

The Hamilcars would deliver eight 17-pounders and their Morris tractors, two Bren carriers for each of the 4th Parachute Brigade battalions and a further two carriers for the South Staffords. Three Hamilcars were included in the lift to carry 'bulk stores' such as ammunition, engineer stores and other heavy supplies. The completion of the Airlanding Brigade lift plan would utilize sixty-eight gliders from the second lift's total, which would fly into LZ 'S'. The South Staffords formed the core of the airlanding infantry included in the second lift, although a small final increment of troops from Brigadier Hicks's two other battalions were also to be landed on LZ 'S'. The balance of the 1st Battalion, The Border Regiment and 7th Battalion, The King's Own Scottish Borderers would be landing concurrently with elements of 181 Airlanding Field Ambulance, RAMC and troops from the brigade support echelon.

The parachute element of the second lift comprised 'Shan' Hackett's brigade in its entirety; they would jump on D+1 onto DZ 'Y'. Their target was north of the railway embankment on Ginkel Heath and, although ideal for parachuting, the heath was a mile to the east of LZ 'S' and furthest away from Arnhem. At the core of his brigade were 10th, 11th and 156th Parachute Battalions. The brigade support elements would also jump as part of the second lift, with engineers from the 4th Parachute Squadron, Royal Engineers and the medics of 133rd Parachute Field Ambulance, RAMC completing Hackett's force. The Brigade was similar in its configuration to its sister parachute formation. It did however drop more of its troops by parachute, the 'Q' elements deployed by parachute rather than going by glider. The battalion support weapons were also grouped in a separate company with its own headquarters rather than under Headquarter Company as in 1st Parachute Brigade.

Brigadier John 'Shan' Hackett was known as a professional soldier to the core; originally a cavalryman he had seen action in Syria and North Africa. In both theatres he had been wounded in action, as a consequence of which he had developed a healthy respect for the capabilities of the German Army. What the short Irishman lacked in physical stature he more than compensated with in intellect, decisiveness and drive. He had raised 4th Parachute Brigade in the Middle East and forged it into a capable airborne unit. He knew his brigade and his men well. The men of his brigade were nearly all regular soldiers who took great pride in their commander and in their brigade.

Hackett had raised doubts about the viability of Operation COMET but he had been less critical of the proposed plan for MARKET GARDEN. He, like many other officers in the 1st British Airborne Division, felt that the repeated cancellation of airborne operations was having a detrimental effect on the morale of the Division. With this in mind he prepared his brigade for the landing in Holland. The battalions within the 4th Parachute Brigade were formed from volunteers recruited from regular units. The 10th and 11th Parachute Battalions had been raised in North Africa where they were later joined by the 156th Battalion, which was raised in India. The Brigade was given the task of marching from DZ 'Y', the furthest away from Arnhem, into the town. Once clear of the drop zone Brigadier Hackett and his battalions were ordered to reinforce 1st Parachute Brigade and establish defensive positions to the north and north-west of Arnhem.

The safe arrival of 4th Parachute Brigade and their departure from DZ 'Y' would allow Brigadier 'Pip' Hicks to release two airlanding battalions from protecting the landing zones. The two airlanding battalions were to redeploy toward the village of Oosterbeek and establish a defensive line that would become the western side of the new perimeter. The third airlanding battalion would maintain a defensive perimeter around LZ 'L' for a further twenty-four hours. The third lift on D+2 would then deliver the Polish Brigade Group onto DZ 'K' south of the river and close to Arnhem Bridge. The thirty-five gliders of the third lift carrying Polish heavy equipment, vehicles and anti-tank guns would land on LZ 'L' to the north of the river.

When all of this activity was complete the airlanding battalion would withdraw to the western side of the Arnhem perimeter rejoining its sister battalions. Once reorganized after their drop, the Polish Brigade Group were assigned responsibility for the eastern flank of the perimeter protecting the Arnhem Bridge. If all went to plan the 18-mile perimeter would be complete on the evening of D+2 and XXX Corps tanks would be close at hand. At this stage the 1st Parachute Brigade would form a Divisional reserve inside the newly formed perimeter. The Glider Pilot Regiment was to be incorporated as part of the reserve force.

The 1st Polish Parachute Brigade Group was commanded by Major General Stanislaw Sosabowski. The 52-year-old Pole was a highly experienced officer who had fought against the Russians as a corporal in the Austrian Army during the First World War. Equal in rank but not seniority to Urquhart, he had been vocal in his criticism of Operation COMET. Although friendly with 'Shan' Hackett, his relations with some of the other British commanders were strained. The outspoken Pole also had doubts about the Arnhem operation but kept them to himself in the belief that he was unpopular enough. He did however see the capture of a Rhine crossing as a worthy objective for his exiled Polish troops. It had been agreed that this would be the Poles' final operation. After Arnhem they would be looking for an opportunity to return to their homeland.

Sosabowski was unhappy about the separation of the two elements of his brigade to the north and south of the river, although he grudgingly accepted that there was no alternative in the short time frame and set about preparing his men for their landing on D+2.

After General Urquhart's 'O' group, the onward transmission of the Operation MARKET plan and its component orders was impressive even by modern standards. Brigade commanders issued their own orders on 14 September; at unit level all officers were briefed the next day. All troops were confined to their barracks and airfields and isolated from the outside world prior to mass briefings on 16 September. The orders, maps and aerial photographs were rapidly disseminated to units and airfields all over southern England. Staff Sergeant Wally Holcroft was at RAF Blakehill Farm on 15 September; like most glider pilots he was bored with kicking his heels. The mood at Blakehill Farm was similar to that across most of the GPR squadrons – one of uncertainty as to whether the waiting would ever end. Indeed, it seemed doubtful that he and the rest of 14 Flight would ever take off on a real operation. But his frustration was about to end – 'F' Squadron, including Lieutenant Aubrey Pickwoad's 14 Flight, were about to receive new orders that would instantly change their mood:

> I was standing in the doorway of my Nissen hut, Lieutenant Pickwoad was walking towards me carrying a large roll of maps. When he saw me he called out 'Here's your chance at last Holcroft', and waved the roll of maps in the air. I laughed thinking he was joking, but later that day he called a Squadron parade in the Squadron Office. When we all arrived Lieutenant Pickwoad unrolled the maps and gave us two each. On the wall were pinned various photographs. We crushed round them eagerly to learn the venue of the prospective 'operation'.
>
> It was a town called Arnhem in Holland, the principle objective being a great bridge spanning the River Rhine … After Lieutenant Pickwoad had given us all the information he could, together with a warning about security, we dispersed to discuss the matter among ourselves. I didn't like the look of the operation, nor did my friend Mick Hall. George Hogg, however, Mick's second pilot, and a regular soldier, was all for it and hoped it would not suffer the fate of the previously planned 'Ops' and be cancelled.[5]

In accordance with the 1st British Airborne Division standard practice all ranks were briefed on the whole divisional plan. This ensured that in the event of a scattered drop or aircraft being shot down the mission could still be executed by those that made it to the objective. In the case of MARKET GARDEN exposure to the wider picture did cause concern among some of the experienced veterans in the division. Of particular concern was the distance that XXX Corps was expected to drive through German lines to reach Arnhem. At the conclusion of his own orders group, Brigadier 'Shan' Hackett asked his senior officers to remain behind. He had these final sage and prophetic words for them: 'You can forget all that. Your hardest fighting will not be defending the northern sector of Arnhem perimeter, but trying to get there.'[6]

FORM B GLIDER.

PART II.

Exercise/Operation ~~LINNET~~ MARKET

Date 17·09·44 . Unit 7 KOSB

GLIDER NUMBER 267 TUG AIRCRAFT NUMBER _____

| NUMBER. | RANK. | NAME (or) ITEM OF EQUIPMENT. | | SEAT-NUMBER (or) Bulkhead number (Port or starboard to be stated). | | | | WEIGHT. | REMARKS. |
|---|---|---|---|---|---|---|---|---|---|
| | | | | LOAD STN | P | S | AFT. | | |
| | | HANDCART N°1 | | 17 | | | | 417 | |
| | | N°2 | | 22 | | | | 417 | |
| | | 2 LT M/Gs | | 19 | | | | 260 | |
| | | 2 FDG CYCLES | | 30 | | | | 66 | |
| | | 2 MK 5 BICYCLES | | 19 | | | | 90 | |
| | | CAMERAMAN | | 32 | | | | 210 | PIGTAIL H.D...N... |
| 7402778 | Pte | DUDOY | | 32 | | 3 | | 210 | |
| 3191749 | PTE | DOYLE | ? | | 4 | | | 210 | |
| 90195 | NASR | DINWIDDIE | GM | | 5 | | | 210 | |
| 14212449 | LCPL | LOTHIAN | T | | | 6 | | 210 | |
| | | | | | 1 | | | 210 | |
| | Pte | | J | | | 8? | | 210 | |
| 1559280 | PTE | TIMPSON | J | | 7 | | | 210 | |
| 14410841 | PTE | DEVLIN | J. | | | 10 | | 210 | |
| 1569280 | PTE | FAIRHALL | R | | 11 | | | 210 | |
| 3190240 | PTE | McINALLY | J | | | 20 | | 210 | |
| 3715903 | LSGT | ASHMORE | R | | 21 | | | 210 | |
| 14334138 | PTE | WILCOX | | | | 22 | | 210 | |
| 14211071 | PTE | COLQUHOUN | J | | 23 | | | 210 | |
| 3187599 | CSM | BUCHANAN | W | | | 24 | | 210 | |
| 14376151 | PTE | HARWOOD | A | | 25 | | | 210 | |
| 3059292 | Pte | SKELTON | T. | | | | 26 | 210 | |
| 14412767 | PTE | CHRISTIE | A | | | | 27 | 210 | |
| 142053/2 | PTE | CAMPBELL | J | | | | 28 | 210 | |
| 5052832 | LSGT | HOOPER | F | | | 29 | | 210 | |
| 14211481 | PTE | McMORROW | T. | | | 30 | | 210 | |
| 3190824 | Tpr | McEWAN | P.J. | | | 31 | | 210 | |
| 1763063 | PTE | SIMPSON | S | | | 8 | | | |
| | | 2 Chandolts | | | | | | 420 | |
| | | EQPT | | | | | | 350 | |
| | | | | | | | | 6480 | |

DELETE THOSE NOT APPLICABLE.
(1) The following seats to be removed 12 - 16 incl
(2) All seats to be left in position.
(3) Freight carrying only.

Signed _____ (Senior Passenger).

Load Checked _____ (Glider Pilot).

Countersigned _____ (Tug Pilot).

*Form 'B' (Manifest) for Chalk Number 267 –*
*a Horsa carrying troops and equipment for 7th Bn KOSB.*
Note the crossings out at the head of the page; the name changes but the load remains extant.

**Notes**

1       Urquhart, Major General R., *Arnhem*, Barnsley, Pen and Sword Ltd, 2008, p. 28.

2       Hardy, Sergeant J., Border, 'When Dragons Flew', p. 30, by permission of The Border Regiment Museum.

3       Swanston, WO2 J., KOSB, *Diary of a Red Devil*, Solihull, Helion Ltd, 2005, p. 63.

4       Masterton, Private A., Border, 'When Dragons Flew', p. 105, by permission of The Border Regiment Museum.

5       Holcroft, SSgt W., 14 Flight, 'F' Sqn GPR, 'No medals for Lt Pickwoad', September 1945.

6       Hackett, Brigadier J., Comd 4 Para Bde, *'Shan' Hackett*, Barnsley, Pen and Sword Ltd, 2003, p. 101

# CHAPTER 6

# D-Day – The First Lift

*'A glider quickly smashes, for it is made only of plywood.'*

**Sunday, 17 September 1944**

The Glider Pilot Regiment would be fully committed to the operation, as across England over 1,330 pilots drawn from both GPR Wings prepared over 650 gliders and their own personal equipment for D-Day and the subsequent lifts.

Weather, of course, is a critical factor that must be considered prior to any flight – indeed it has even more significance to the pilot of a non-powered aircraft whose focus is sharpened by the fact that he will only get one attempt at landing. The Metrological Office predictions were optimistic for Sunday morning, the forecast being for low ground mist at first light. The morning sun was expected to have burnt any residue mist off all of the Operation MARKET airfields by 0900 hours at the latest. The 'Met' for the landing zones was not quite as perfect as the English weather, with some haze and cloud anticipated en route and traces of cloud predicted over the landing zones themselves. Overall the outlook for D-Day was close to ideal, which, given the time of year, seemed to bode well.

One of the many pre-flight checks required was the calculation of the effect of the load on their individual glider's centre of gravity and consequently its handling. If the 'C of G' was incorrectly calculated prior to take-off the miscalculation could result in the glider crashing. Many hours were spent training glider pilots to make this calculation and they were also provided with a complicated set of scales, known as the 'CG and Weight Determinator'.

This apparatus included numerous weights to replicate every possible type of load, complimented with a complex series of charts and tables to decipher the results. There are very few glider pilots who have ever professed to have fully understood this overcomplicated instrument; some deny ever having seen one. Most employed a far more rudimentary method of establishing that the 'C of G' for their glider was within limits prior to take-off. Staff Sergeant 'Eddie' Edwards of 'A' Squadron explains the less scientific procedure that was favoured by most GPR pilots:

> One had to be careful about positioning the load so that the centre of gravity was correct. This means that the load must be evenly distributed along the cargo area, according to the weight of each item. If it is not then the backside or nose of the glider will be too heavy, which in turn causes cold sweats amongst the pilots when taking off.
>
> Originally, we were taught to position loads correctly by means of a cutaway model of a glider, with weights representing various items of gear, but this proved too tedious, so some bright spark came up with a better idea than this official method. After loading … If the two pilots swung on the tail section, the nose wheel should just lift off the ground. It worked, and any minor errors could be corrected by the trim control in the cockpit once in flight.[1]

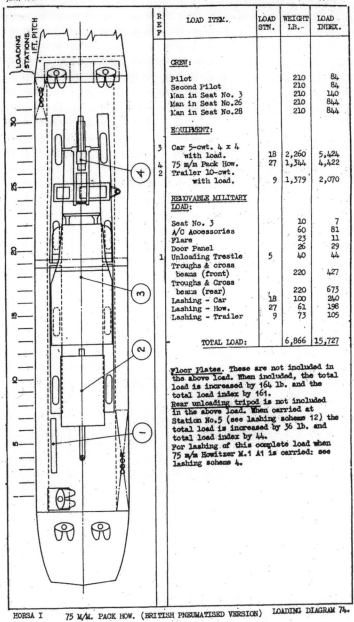

| REF | LOAD ITEM. | LOAD STN. | WEIGHT LB.- | LOAD INDEX. |
|---|---|---|---|---|
| | CREW: | | | |
| | Pilot | | 210 | 84 |
| | Second Pilot | | 210 | 84 |
| | Man in Seat No. 3 | | 210 | 140 |
| | Man in Seat No.26 | | 210 | 844 |
| | Man in Seat No.28 | | 210 | 844 |
| | EQUIPMENT: | | | |
| 3 | Car 5-cwt. 4 x 4 with load. | 18 | 2,260 | 5,424 |
| 4 | 75 m/m Pack How. | 27 | 1,344 | 4,422 |
| 2 | Trailer 10-cwt. with load. | 9 | 1,379 | 2,070 |
| | REMOVABLE MILITARY LOAD: | | | |
| | Seat No. 3 | | 10 | 7 |
| | A/C Accessories | | 60 | 81 |
| | Flare | | 23 | 11 |
| | Door Panel | | 26 | 29 |
| 1 | Unloading Trestle | 5 | 40 | 44 |
| | Troughs & cross beams (front) | | 220 | 427 |
| | Troughs & Cross beams (rear) | | 220 | 673 |
| | Lashing – Car | 18 | 100 | 240 |
| | Lashing – How. | 27 | 61 | 198 |
| | Lashing – Trailer | 9 | 73 | 105 |
| | TOTAL LOAD: | | 6,866 | 15,727 |

Floor Plates. These are not included in the above load. When included, the total load is increased by 164 lb. and the total load index by 161.
Rear unloading tripod is not included in the above load. When carried at Station No.5 (see lashing scheme 12) the total load is increased by 36 lb. and total load index by 44.
For lashing of this complete load when 75 m/m Howitzer M.1 A1 is carried: see lashing scheme 4.

HORSA I    75 M/M. PACK HOW. (BRITISH PNEUMATISED VERSION)    LOADING DIAGRAM 74.

Two pilots; 3 men; Car, 5 cwt, 4 x 4 Willys or Ford,with load; O.Q.F. 75 m.m. pack How. on carriage M.I. (British version); Trailer, 10 cwt, 2 wheeled, Airborne, with load.

*The loading diagram for the 75mm Pack Howitzer and its attendant Jeep and trailer loaded with Gunners in a Horsa.*

65

The tug crews of 38 and 46 Groups of the Royal Air Force were located on the same airfields as their comrades in the GPR squadrons that they were charged to deliver intact to Holland. The aircraft available to 38 Group included the Short Stirling, Handley Page Halifax and the Albemarle, spread across five airfields. All eight squadrons of the Group were to be used in support of Lieutenant Colonel Iain Murray's 1 Wing GPR. The six squadrons of 46 Group were equipped with C47 Dakotas operating from three airfields from which all of Lieutenant Colonel John Place's 2 Wing GPR would take off. The only exception to this policy was 'C' Squadron which, although part of 2 Wing, would be towed by 38 Group Halifaxes. The Hamilcar was too hefty a load for the twin-engined Dakota, requiring the four-engined power of a Halifax to get it airborne. No British gliders would be towed by American-flown tugs; conversely, the only British parachutists dropped by the RAF would be 'Boy' Wilson's Pathfinder Company.

The RAF tug pilots and their aircrew shared the concerns and emotions of the glider pilots. Flying Officer R.N. Bassarab was the Operations Officer of 299 Squadron RAF, which operated Short Stirlings from RAF Keevil. His squadron was co-located with 'D' Squadron GPR, both units having already been through preparations and briefings for three separate operations during the preceding weeks. He gives a detailed account of the pre-operation activity in his squadron on the run-up to Sunday's lift; no doubt the pattern was very similar in all of the tug squadrons:

> Three times the crews and glider pilots trooped into the briefing room, observing a red tape strung over the map of Europe indicating the routes to be flown, listening to estimation of enemy fighters and flak opposition, and complete details as to navigation, weather reports, runways, maintenance, and job to be done on reaching the Landing Zone (LZ). Each time the operation was cancelled and the pent up anxiety and energy yet received another set back. The normal reaction was to have a few (pints) and retire early for yet another day.
>
> Finally on Saturday … the camp was sealed, everyone concerned proceeded to the briefing room at 1400 hrs and Group Captain Troop gave the fourth preview of the Airborne Operation in hand.
>
> Details for further operations were carefully arranged, the Navigators again made their flight plans, checked courses and distances, made notes of Radar aids to be given and rechecked with other Navigators. The Bomb Aimers drew in tracks noted flak positions and all prominent features. The pilots checked their petrol loads, carefully gone over by their Squadron Commanding Officer. The ground crews worked feverishly on all aircraft checking every last detail and the Radar chaps checked all sets giving a final OK. Lastly the gunners changed their ammunition so that it would include daylight tracer and tested their guns for harmonisation and firepower. The glider pilots had a separate brief as to the detail of the jobs they were to do, now the preliminaries were over the stage was set.[2]

Well before the morning mist had cleared, all over southern and eastern England aircrew and the troops of the three airborne divisions were waking to the realization that this time the 'Op' was on. After months of anticipation and frustration they really were finally going to leave England behind them and fly into battle.

Padre George Pare, the Chaplain to 1 Wing Glider Pilot Regiment describes his first waking moments early that Sunday morning and his conversation with his 'batman', Private Hardy:

> 'Time to get up, sir … Nice morning… but, a bit cool … Here's your cup of tea … I'll just give your boots another rub. Anything else you want, sir?'
>
> I put aside the pretence of sleeping, and sat up. I was in an uncomfortable Nissen hut which had been my abode for the one night at Fairford aerodrome. 'Is it still on, Hardy?' 'Still

on, sir? Is what still on? The maddening questions that one can be asked when there is only one question which can be 'on'.

'Oh, you mean the Op, sir?' Oh yes. At any rate, I think so. Everybody is getting up ... and I haven't heard it's been cancelled this time. Here's your hot water. By the look of the weather I think you'll have a good trip. Wish I was coming with you, sir.' 'Yes, I wish you were' ... I sipped the tea.

I celebrated the Holy Communion service in one of the huts for men who wished to receive the Sacrament – a moving service for none knew if it would be his last.

After breakfast, I checked my kit, then climbed into a truck and was driven to the tow path. The huge Horsa gliders were drawn up in massive array on one side, and the powerful four-engined Stirlings on the other. With mixed feelings we saw the first Stirlings take off their Pathfinder parachute contingent, whose task was to mark the landing zone for the gliders.

I was still surprised as we had had so many cancellations. We were really to go after all. I was sorry that I had not left my other kit properly packed. However we should be back within a few days and my things should be safe.[3]

George Pare clearly believed he would be back on English soil within days – not a case of a clergyman being over optimistic, as the value placed on GPR pilots was such that they were extracted from the battle area as quickly as possible. The majority of the GPR pilots who had taken part in the Normandy operations had made their way safely back to England via the beaches within a matter of days. They had practised the recovery procedure across terrain and distances in Oxfordshire remarkably similar to the countryside around their eventual landing zones in the Ranville and Bénouville area of Normandy during Exercise Candid in May 1944.[4]

Contingency plans for 'follow-on' landings to reinforce the existing bridgeheads established by the 6th Airborne Division with the 1st Airborne Division were already in existence before D-Day. Although there were enough airborne troops, tug aircraft and gliders to carry out a second operation on a divisional scale there were not enough GPR pilots to fly a second lift. Consequently every glider pilot landing in Normandy had but one aim once he had delivered his glider and load safely to its destination in France – get back to England.

Their orders were to use the pass they had been issued and make their way back to the nearest beachhead against the flow of British and Canadian troops. Once at the beachhead they were given a high priority for return passage back across the Channel and onward transport back to their squadron airfield. The Operation Order for MARKET also made provision for the speedy recovery of GPR pilots as soon as practically possible after the relief of 1st Airborne Division by XXX Corps.

While Padre Pare busied himself at RAF Fairford, Sergeant Brian Tomblin was with 'E' Squadron at RAF Down Ampney also readying himself for the flight to Arnhem; he too expected to return from Holland within days of the landing but like all good soldiers he was ensuring he was suitably equipped if all did not go according to plan:

We woke early on Sunday, the 17th September (the anniversary of the Battle of Britain) – still no cancellation, so we shrugged our shoulders and thought 'Well if it is on, let's get it over with and get home for next week-end, like we did from Normandy'.

Everybody's kit had been checked, double checked, and packed. Our weapons and ammunition had been cleaned and inspected with meticulous care – always in our mind was the embarrassing danger of the Sten and Bren guns jamming at the wrong time. Our escape kits of miniature saws, button compasses and silk maps had been sewn into the linings of our battle-dress, and syringes of morphia had been issued. Personal belongings had been packed and stored.

We pored over many enlarged maps and aerial photographs, so much so that it seemed one only had to close one's eyes to visualise the sandy woody countryside west of Arnhem, and it seemed odd that I had never heard of the place before that week.[5]

As the morning progressed the routine practised on numerous training flights and airborne exercises took over. Tug crews and their GPR partners adhered to the timings outlined to them by their respective squadron and flight commanders. Flying Officer Bassarab had the extra responsibility of being the Squadron Ops Officer. He gives a detailed description of the final hours at RAF Keevil that give a real insight into the tension at the Wiltshire airfield as the combinations of Stirling crews from 299 Squadron RAF and 'D' Squadron GPR moved out to the runway and the lines of waiting aircraft:

I found all the crews dressed and ready for breakfast by 7 o'clock. Tension was high and that ticklish sensation in the pit of the stomach was rather annoying.

At 8 am a final navigation briefing was held to ensure each navigator of having the proper information – no chances were being taken. Wind direction, wind speed, tracks, distances and times were double checked until the Station Navigation Officer was completely satisfied. The general buzz soon subsided and crews dispersed to their various flights. In the flight rooms airmen emptied pockets of all but essential articles. Mae Wests donned, and parachutes harnesses buckled up or slung over a shoulder. Flight vans made numerous trips until all were at their proper positions …

The scene now shifts to the end of the runway … fifty Stirlings lined up either side of the runway with a corresponding number of Horsa gliders marshalled in such a manner to form a combination, each combination hitched by a tow rope lying inconspicuously on the ground. Ground crews making last minute checks and chatting with the aircrew giving assurance that all would be well. Here and there motor cycles cruised along the line passing out last minute instructions. And of course the good natured banter among the glider pilots and aircrew, each assuring each other of a good ride with wishes for an early and safe return to England. Engines roared along the stretch of runway as tests were made of maximum power, then cutting out as each pilot completed his checks. By 10 am most crews had emplaned and a heavy roar of motors filled the area.[6]

The morning followed a similar pattern for the pilots of both GPR Wings. Staff Sergeant Wally Holcroft, who was at RAF Blakehill Farm with 'F' Squadron, wrote an account that not only captures the mood of the time but also the bond of trust between the GPR pilots who were paired together as crews and their relationship with the Airlanding Brigade troops they were to carry into battle:

We were told to parade in the RAF briefing room at 0830 hrs on Sunday morning … When we arrived we found everything in readiness, tables were laid out to accommodate each glider crew and his respective Tug crew. The first words of the briefing officer were 'The Ops are on'. I looked at Norman Hartford my co-pilot, he grinned. We were scheduled to take off at 10 am. After receiving the latest weather reports and other relevant information, Hartford and I decided to walk down to our glider and give it a final check. Before we left the briefing room we had another look at the maps and pictures of the landing zone. I got it firmly fixed in my mind.

Hartford and I were lucky, we were taking in our glider twenty-eight men of the 'Border Regiment'. Some of the fellows were taking Jeeps and guns. That would mean they would have to spend time on arrival taking the tail off the glider, to unload the stuff. Taking the tail off a big Horsa is bad enough when you have time to do it. Working under fire would certainly not help matters. Mick (Hall) too, had passengers, and I found he was next in the train to me. As we were taking troops of the same regiment it looked as though we could stick together after landing. That was what we wanted; we made a little pact to keep with each other throughout the operation.

When we reached the glider I found the troops all ready to emplane. The Officer in charge of them introduced himself to me and I to him. I asked him how the men were feeling. He said they were all 'keen as mustard'. I had a chat with one or two of them and told them that I would certainly get them to Holland OK and in return I was expecting them to take good care of me on the ground. They said it would be a piece of cake, once they got to Holland. It was good to see such excellent spirits.

The whole of one end of the runway was crammed with gliders and tug aircraft. There was to be another 'lift' the following morning by another flight which had joined us from another station because their place was not large enough to deal with them all. It all looked very impressive that September morning, all lined up and ready for heaven only knew what.

I walked around from one glider to the other chatting with the various pilots. I had a parting with Mick. We wished each other the best of luck on the journey. At ten minutes to ten I climbed aboard my glider; the troops were already seated inside. I quickly checked their straps and gave them one or two final instructions as to positions they should take up in case of a forced landing on the sea.

Making myself comfortable in my seat I checked over the controls with Hartford. Hartford had been my co-pilot for six months and we had got organised together perfectly. He was a splendid chap and very easy to get along with. I asked him what he thought about everything. He said he was quite confident we should make the trip OK.

Promptly at ten o' clock the Tow Master waved the first glider away. I was about twelfth down the line. In less than six minutes from the first glider taking off, I saw my tug taxiing slowly on to the runway in front of me. I gave the OK for take off to him over the intercom, and the rope stretching between us began to tighten. Then we began to move, slowly at first then with ever increasing speed. It is always a tense moment or two during take off with a full load of passengers, as everything depends on the aircraft being correctly trimmed. I watched the airspeed indicator creep round to eighty miles per hour and at that speed pulled back gently on the control column and the glider lifted off the ground. A second later the Dakota in front of me became airborne too, our first worries were over.[7]

One man who had a little more to think about than most of his fellow glider pilots that Sunday was Staff Sergeant Arthur Rigby of 'B' Squadron, who had been confined to barracks at RAF Manston with the rest of his Squadron the evening prior to take-off. Arthur however had a problem that he felt could not wait until his return from Holland:

On Saturday morning 16th September about 0830 hours I received a signal from the R.A.F. Signal office telling of the birth of my daughter Josephine! The drill was that after briefing for an operation, everyone was confined to camp, but on the receipt of this signal I decided to take a chance. I went along to see the Commanding Officer told him of the event and to my surprise he gave me ten hours leave to get home and back again, and I did it, with a half-hour to spare.

The day was a little misty at first, but cleared as the sun got up and rapidly became warm and sunny. We breakfasted at 0530 hours and collected big flasks of tea or coffee as required, and huge doorstep corned beef sandwiches as the day's rations, and by 0830 hours we loaded onto trucks, our rucksacks and weapons altogether. Staff Sergeant Ted Healey and I had a Bren gun and rifles, 4 boxes of Bren magazines, 200 rounds of .303 in bandoleers. When we arrived on the perimeter track all the squadron gliders were lined up one behind the other. Our anti-tank gun crew was already awaiting our coming. We had to do the usual checks to make sure everything was working, controls OK? Me in the cab working the column and rudder, Ted calling the instructions 'left – right – OK! up – down – OK! compression bottles etc.' and finally the hand lashings and fixtures.

We were carrying a 6-pounder anti-tank gun, all the gun-crews gear and personal weapons, plus 20 rounds of ammunition for the gun, and a jeep to tow the whole she-bang.

The gun crew consisted of three men, Sergeant Shelswell, Bombardier Lock and a driver named Hodges. We knew them quite well, having spent some time with them at Brize Norton, and we had knocked around Birchington during the time before take-off and found them quite a good bunch. When everything was checked and found to be okay we walked across and had a chat with our tug-crew who were standing in line on a parallel perimeter track in their take-off position ready to swing onto the main runway in turn. Everyone was in high spirits, jokes being bandied about, and general 'Mickey taking' on various characters' flying capabilities.

On return to the glider formation, we found two of our particular mates standing by our glider, Staff Sergeant Paddy Clenaghan and Staff Sergeant Charlie Thackeray. Poor Charles was a bit apprehensive but I hope we managed to josh him enough to take his mind off possibilities. Word came along the lines, by way of assembly marshals, to mount up and prepare for movement.

Soon everyone was in position, though by this time it was too hot to close the doors, so we left them both open and also the door in rear of the cockpit.[8]

Also sitting waiting in the heat at RAF Manston was Staff Sergeant Arthur Shackleton, in the lead Horsa with Major Ian Toler. They were at the head of 'B' Squadron column and would be the first 'B' Squadron glider to set out behind its Albemarle tug for Arnhem. They were carrying the Commanding Officer of the South Staffords and a small number of men from his Battalion Headquarters. Not only was Arthur sharing the cockpit with his own commander and carrying the South Staffords' Commanding Officer, the Albemarle tug aircraft was being flown by Wing Commander J.R. Grice, the 297 Squadron Commanding Officer. The concept of 'tactical loading' – the separation of key personnel – does not appear to have been considered when the air manifests were drawn up.

The first serial from Manston was due to lift at 1040 hours. Arthur remembers his last few minutes on English soil that clear autumn morning:

Fancy hoping you could go to war, we must have been mad or maybe someone had doctored our tea. I was just on the tow path talking to Arnold Baldwin and Joe Michie, when our load approached led by Lieutenant Colonel McCardie, he was accompanied by his batman, RSM Slater, a Jeep driver, a signaller and a few other soldiers.

Our glider was first on the runway as we were first to go, Arnold and Joe were second carrying the rest of the Battalion Headquarters staff. As Major Toler arrived I got the passengers into their seats and then strapped Major Toler into his seat. I then moved outside the aircraft to do a visual check on the controls while he moved them inside the cockpit. I had already checked the position of the Jeep and trailer in relation to our centre of gravity.

While I was outside I noticed a man setting up a tripod further up the runway, I remarked to the tow master about this and he said it was a camera man who had asked him for the best location to film us moving off.

Eventually I was in the cockpit with everything double checked, the Albemarle tug slowly moving forward, rope slack taken up followed by full revs we surged forward to eighty miles per hour on the ASI and the cameraman appeared on the port side. By this time we were airborne and level at ten feet off the ground, I remember saying 'smile to your left sir, Pathe Gazette are filming us'. At two hundred feet he handed me the controls and said 'what did you say when we took off?'[9]

The 'Pathe' news reel footage of 'B' Squadron's take-off was distributed all over the country as evidence of the launching of the airborne operation. That footage showing Arthur and Ian Toler's glider leaving the Kent airfield is now among the most familiar images of MARKET GARDEN in existence.

Following on behind their Squadron Commander's glider in the stream of 'B' Squadron Horsa's were Staff Sergeant Godfrey Freeman and his co-pilot Lieutenant Henry Cole. After take-off Godfrey became aware of the true scale of the operation and immense size and diversity of the air armada he and Henry were a part of. He absorbed the scene as he and Henry went about their business and their heavily laden Horsa climbed steadily away from the Manston runway:

Slowly we climbed following the main stream of aircraft gaining height little by little until at about two thousand five hundred feet we levelled out, took station and sailed on towards Canterbury where we had to rendezvous with other streams coming in from the north and east.

From all over southern Britain now, it seemed aircraft were converging into an endless stream, which sailed on and on over roads, railways, rivers, over built-up areas and farmland. Over all the works of man, large and small, until at last it crossed the coastline and we were out over the North Sea. Halifaxes, Stirlings, Dakotas and our own Albemarles, each with a glider in tow, swept on in relentless throng, while above, below and on the same level, fighters kept station to guard us from attack. On our way out we met Bomber Command coming back; their work was done, ours was beginning.

We flew on, terribly slowly it seemed, while the shore of Britain receded behind us, and down below we could see ships, floating like models on a sea of glass. Whatever else we were going to meet that day, at least the weather was smiling. There was a strange comfort in sitting there with Henry as though we were on an exercise and I had to remind myself that this was no exercise but the real thing. The sun shone through the Perspex windows of the cabin, we were warm, comfortable and relaxed and, except for an occasional buffet from a slipstream, the air was smooth and our passage through it unruffled.[10]

At RAF Fairford all was going well and the mood was extremely positive, George Pare was among his flock and found himself in a prime seat in distinguished company to observe the momentous events of what was his second D-Day:

Lieutenant Colonel Iain Murray was the first pilot of my glider. I had immense faith in his ability as I had also in Brian Bottomley's, his co-pilot and our Intelligence Officer, for they had delivered me safely during darkness before dawn on D-Day in Normandy. I caught sight of Peter Fletcher, our Adjutant, as he stood a little further away near his glider and waved. Our little HQ staff was a close-knit unit with a good sense of comradeship with a feigned nonchalance which we obtained from the CO. At the moment there was no feeling of bravery about me, but a genuine surprise that the operation was actually to be undertaken, mixed with genuine excitement at the thought of adventure ahead, coupled with a sublime ignorance of what we were in for.

I was fortunate to have found a place in this glider, for Major General Roy Urquhart, the Divisional Commander, was our prime passenger. I hoped that he would not share the fate of the GOC, of the Sicilian Airborne invasion who had landed in the sea, and perforce had to sit on a floating wing of his glider out at sea and watch the battle – his battle – being fought a few miles away on the island, entirely without his general-ship. At any rate our General had his Staff Officers with him in the forepart of the glider, and there was a loaded jeep with its trailer in the middle and three men in the tail.

The take-off, always an exciting business with a fully laden glider, was without incident, and we rose swaying into the air, to join the immense stream of Stirling-Horsa combinations, which were making a huge circle over England preparatory to setting course for Holland. Once we were in position the air seemed full of planes, and we could pick out Dakotas, Waco [Hadrian] gliders, Halifaxes, giant Hamilcar gliders and a great fleet of accompanying fighter planes. Over the North Sea the sight was incredibly beautiful and awe-inspiring.

The CO left his second pilot at the controls, and beckoned the General to sit in his place for a time, to watch this air fleet moving against the glittering background of sea and sky. Each of the four of us in turn was allowed to enter the cockpit to see this historic sight, and we could not help but be exhilarated.[11]

Iain Murray and George Pare would probably not been as buoyant and cheerful if they had been aware that 1 Wing had already lost a Horsa with serious loss of life. It was shortly after the first take-offs that Operation MARKET GARDEN incurred its first casualties. A catastrophic accident resulted in the loss of a 'D' Squadron Horsa flown by Staff Sergeant Leonard Gardner and Sergeant Robert Fraser. The glider was carrying twenty-one Sappers from 1 Platoon, 9th (Airborne) Field Company, Royal Engineers under command of Sergeant Arthur Oakey.

The combination had taken off without incident from RAF Keevil earlier that morning and was heading west away from Keevil to allow the rest of the serials in its block to take off and 'formate' prior to turning east to join the stream. The tug aircraft for this serial was a Stirling of 299 Squadron RAF. Sergeant 'Wally' Simpson was the rear gunner on the Stirling, and was a helpless witness to the terrible tragedy that occurred in mid-air to the south-east of Bristol.

We took off at 1025 in the morning and everything was going well. During the forming up on special routes given to us at the briefing, I was watching the glider from my rear turret. Suddenly I saw a part fall off the glider and a second later I realised it was the whole tail section. I informed our captain and watched the glider fall; the towrope broke just short of my turret and the glider crashed into a field at Paulton, near Radstock. We broke formation, circled the crash site and returned to base. We had been in the air for just one hour.

There were no survivors of the crash; all twenty three men were killed. The Operations Log for 299 Squadron RAF has a concise but grim entry recording the failure of the sortie and the fate of glider 389: 'Unsuccessful, tail of glider fell off and glider crashed at 5118N 0231W Aircraft returned to base. Glider caught fire and exploded killing the 21 troops being carried.'

There were a number of other tug-glider combinations that were forced to separate prior to leaving friendly soil, although most were less dramatic than the events over Somerset. There were a number of glider-tug separations due to mechanical failure affecting either the tug or the glider, however the most common technical cause for aborting the sortie was failure of the tow rope linking the two aircraft.

There were also more than twenty incidents of deliberate releases of the tow rope due to poor visibility – the weather encountered by the crews flying from the western airfields was not as ideal as predicted.

In order for a glider to maintain station behind its tug, the pilot must be able to see the tug aircraft; alterations to course, headings and speed were communicated by intercom cable running the length of the tow rope. The senior glider pilot had two options when in transit behind the tug: he could opt for either the high or low tow position. Flying directly behind the tail of the tug was very difficult and extremely bumpy as the glider was constantly buffeted by the turbulence generated by the tug.

The 'low tow' position, slightly lower than the tug's tail and outside the slip stream was the most stable position and it also allowed the glider pilots to see the whole length of the tow rope. The 'high tow' position was found to be more difficult to maintain and less stable than the 'low tow'. The tow rope itself was 350 feet in length; in the case of the Horsa it was split into a 'Y' shape that was attached to the leading edge of the wing either side of the cockpit, so the actual length was approximately 300 feet.

The need for both aircraft crews to be able to monitor the position of each other and the length of the tow rope itself during flight was critical if they were to maintain their respective positions. In the event of loss of visibility for any length of time, orientation became extremely difficult for both crews, particularly the tug pilot who received all of his information on the status of the glider second hand from his rear gunner. Once sight of the tug was lost, the glider pilots were dependent on an instrument in the cockpit that would indicate the position of the tow rope in relation to the glider itself; this instrument measured what the GPR referred to as the 'angle of dangle'. The angle of dangle was indicated on the 'Mk II Tow Cable Angle Indicator' (CAI), which was connected by elastic to the tow rope by the RAF ground crew prior to take-off. In flight the CAI dial in the cockpit indicated a lateral and vertical bar on its dial that the pilot could use to maintain the correct attitude to the rope and therefore keep station with his tug. That, at any rate, was the theory, however if the connection was not rigged correctly the reading in the cockpit could be wildly inaccurate or possibly fail to register at all; the instrument could only be used in the 'low tow' position.

On the morning of 17 September, more than forty glider combinations from 'E' Squadron were in formation approaching Oxford. They encountered thick cloud and were forced to fly much lower than ordered, five gliders from 'E' Squadron releasing themselves from their tugs and a single Horsa also from RAF Down Ampney being released in cloud by the tug pilot. The crew of that particular serial were Staff Sergeant A. 'Nobby' Clarke and Sergeant Gordon Pyne. Gordon recounts their experiences over Oxfordshire:

We took off on the first lift on Sunday 17th September 1944 somewhere about 1030 am. Conditions were not good, very bumpy and a lot of cloud. Sometime after take off cloud conditions worsened and Staff Sergeant Clarke decided to go into the low tow position i.e. below the tug aircraft. We had a very rough ride down through the slipstream of the Dakota and very soon after our blind flying went unserviceable. Not long after this there was a large jerk felt in the glider and the airspeed dropped off very rapidly, as we must have been in a climbing attitude.

We broke cloud and were in brilliant sunshine with not another glider or aeroplane in sight! Clarke said what did you pull us off for? I replied that I didn't. He said; 'For Lords sake, hang on to the tow-rope'. Bearing in mind that below and all around us were streams of aircraft/glider combinations and all sorts of defending fighters etcetera. Our descent back through the clouds was going to be very dangerous to say the least. With us both praying hard we dived steeply to get through the danger as quickly as possible, I called to the passengers to take up emergency landing positions as we were going to make a forced landing. Fortunately nothing collided with us on the way down, and we broke cloud at about 1700 feet.

I was told to look for a suitable field for our landing. There was a very suitable field not far from a village and nicely into wind. Clarke made a 'copy book' circuit of our chosen field but as we turned into the final approach dozens of villagers burst through the hedges onto the field. On both sides of the field were rows of tall trees. We turned to one side and managed to almost clear the trees, but the cable, which was still attached to the glider, got hooked up and stopped us very rapidly.

In the silence, which followed, I heard the click of a Sten gun being cocked. The Sergeant in charge of our passengers had fallen asleep and thought that we were on our landing zone in Holland. I managed to shout 'Don't shoot, we are still in England!' No one was injured in the landing and we started to unload the glider of its cargo, a jeep fitted with two machine guns and a trailer full of ammunition and mortar bombs.

The field we had landed in was not far from the aerodrome, 'Stanton Harcourt'. Before we had finished unloading the glider a Royal Air Force Officer appeared on the scene with a number of Royal Air Force policemen. Staff Sergeant Clarke and myself were placed under open arrest and told that we were to go to Stanton Harcourt airfield and a plane would be sent from Down Ampney to take us back to a Court of Inquiry to investigate our failure to complete our mission.

The passengers, to be escorted by some of the Royal Air Force police, were to return to Down Ampney with their equipment to get ready for a later flight. We collected the towrope and went to Stanton Harcourt. We were duly collected by an aircraft and arrived back at Down Ampney sometime in the afternoon of 17th September. Fortunately the tug pilot had informed the Court of Inquiry that he in fact had pulled us off. We were in a situation where the combination tug/glider was losing height at the rate of 2000 feet per minute and he had no other course open to him. Staff Sergeant Clarke's evidence was merely a formality. We were released from arrest and told that when our passengers and load arrived back, there was another glider ready for us to load for the second lift.[12]

Chalk Number 240 was another Horsa from 'E' Squadron that was forced to release from its tug in cloud near Oxford. As the crew attempted an emergency landing at Bessels Leigh near Abingdon, the glider crashed into high-tension cables with predictable results. The church diary for the village recorded the event: 'A Horsa glider hit a pylon at Bessels Leigh, a wide area was quickly sealed off. Staff Sergeant Thomas Joyce the first pilot was killed and his co-pilot Sergeant Hoyle seriously injured, 2 Wing GPR had also taken its first casualties of the "Op".'

The massed aerial armada that lifted from England that morning was working to a complicated joint plan produced by the combined planning staffs of 38 Group RAF and the US IX Troop Carrier Command at the Combined Troop Carrier Command Post (CTCCP) at Eastcote near Uxbridge. Each glider-tug combination was part of a stream that would take sixty–five minutes to pass each of those fixed Initial Points (IPs) on the ground.

Staff Sergeant Ron Gibson of 'F' Squadron was one of many flying in the northern stream of aircraft making progress from their base airfields to Hatfield and then on to the coast at Aldeburgh. They also encountered some cloud over Holland:

In the cabin of the Horsa we carried a 6-pounder gun and the jeep that would tow it into action. In the rear seats sat two men of the Border Regt, the driver and the gun layer. 'Sim' was my co-pilot. He was a German Jew from Berlin, a refugee who had arrived in England a few months before the declaration of war. I had only known him a few weeks ...

After passing the farm yard [at the end of the runway] we flew into some low lying mist ... We flew low, at three hundred feet in a wide circle that led us back over the airfield ... I began to sweat beneath my clothes: we were dressed in full battle order, with heavy cloth smocks over our tunics. At Cirencester I handed the controls over to 'Sim'. The Dakota began to climb ... At two thousand feet we rose into clear air. For the first time since we set off I could see the entire column of tugs and gliders receding into the distance before me. Those furthest ahead had shrunk to midget size like insects impaled on the blanket of cloud ... We saw a second train of tugs and gliders approaching from the Berkshire downs. The air was very still, and inside our cockpit we felt we were hanging motionless, whole nothing moved but the wisps of cloud that flicked past the window.

At this height the air turned colder and our legs grew numb. I asked 'Sim' to draw some hot tea from the Thermos flask. This was one of the luxuries of flying, when one could lean back in the seat, sipping at the slippery rim of the cup, and watch the other man sweat at the wheel. A few minutes later we saw one of the leading gliders cast off and turn back beneath us. It circled over a wood and headed for the aerodrome at Hatfield. In a moment it vanished behind the edge of the Perspex. We heard later that the tug pilot had ordered it to release when his plane failed in one engine.

It was midday when we reached the coast at Aldeburgh. 'Sim' was sitting at the controls. I crawled back along the fuselage over the gun and trailer to carry a mug full of tea to the BORDERS in the rear seats ... I passed the mug through a gap between the trailer and the plywood roof; it was grasped by the gun layer. The two 'Borders' looked cheerful enough. One was a corporal, short and dark, who lived in Birmingham; the other was a taller, fair north countryman from Tyneside. We had met them on the towpath only twenty minutes before we left; we had shaken hands, chatted for a few minutes and smoked each others cigarettes. From forty minutes after our landing I never saw them again.

We sighted the Dutch coast at a quarter to one ... I wondered what 'Sim' was thinking. I felt the same coldness, a vacuum of emotion, a sense of fatality that I supposed all people felt in moments of crisis. We heard the thud of exploding flak: two black smudges burst above the cloud ... When a couple of shells burst close above the tow plane, the pilot wheeled to starboard and towed us into the heart of a dense cumulus. All but a dozen feet of rope was shrouded in vapour. We tried to dive down into the blind flying position, but the rope sagged lower though 'Sim' was pushing at the stick. A second later we emerged from the cloud to see the tug a hundred feet below, half hidden beneath our nose. The rope tautened with a jerk. In twenty minutes we reached our first turning point at s'Hertogenbosch.[13]

The plan for all three lifts anticipated the likelihood of small numbers of gliders and transport aircraft not making landfall and being forced to ditch in the sea. A flotilla of RAF Marine Craft Section sea rescue launches and Royal Navy high speed launches were positioned along the route to recover crews and passengers from abandoned aircraft.

The launches were normally employed in the recovery of pilots from Allied aircraft forced to ditch on the return leg of missions over occupied Europe and Germany. These specialized boats and crews operated from the East Anglian ports of Felixstowe, Gorleston, Lowestoft and the Kentish port of Ramsgate. They would be needed to recover five Horsa gliders from the first lift that ditched in the North Sea on D-Day.

The system for the initial marking of the location of ditched gliders and the subsequent recovery of their crew and passengers was well coordinated and effective. The initial 'May Day' call would be initiated by the tug aircraft (gliders had no radio), although the call was not always required as the launches were positioned directly under the air corridor used by the glider formations and could observe any aircraft dropping out of position. Fighter aircraft were also employed as part of the safety net, flying what were known as 'team work' missions. Spitfires, Thunderbolts and other types were used to mark the location of the ditched aircraft and survivors with smoke floats. This gave rescue launches or seaplanes a reference point to head for, speeding the recovery process. The rescues completed on 17 September appear to have been completed in text book manner.

The 'D' Squadron GPR War Diary records the ditching of Horsa Chalk Number 462 piloted by Staff Sergeant Ken Beard and Sergeant Geoff Tapping, 'ditched' off Holland. The entry states that they were returned to UK the same day. The unit responsible for the rescue was Rescue Motor Launch 547 of 69th Rescue Motor Launch Flotilla, 26 A/S RMCU from Felixstowe. The Captain of this motor launch, Lieutenant J.S. Andrews, writes in his 'Report on Air Sea Rescue':

> 17/9/44 R.M.L. 547 was at waiting position 51°49'N 03°10'E. Numbers of aircraft towing gliders were passing overhead. At 1259 a glider bearing 130? true distance approximately 10 miles, height 1,000 feet, was seen to be on a different course than its tug. Course was set towards it at full speed and at 1301 it crashed. At 1310 the glider could be seen as a black dot on the water six miles away. Spitfires closed the spot, dropped smoke floats and patrolled between glider and the RML. At 1330 in position 51°40'N 03°21'E, five British glider troops were taken aboard. The glider sank at 1325 but the men were in a rubber dinghy close to it. They were the full crew of glider number 462 of 'D' Squadron, and were suffering from immersion, minor cuts and bruises. I alarmed the Warwick Call-sign 'Revive 36' of the situation and returned to my position.

Sergeant Geoff Tapping recalls the ditching and subsequent recovery:

> We took off from Keevil on Sunday 17th September for Arnhem. The towrope broke and we ditched 8 miles from the Dutch coast at approximately 1330 hours. Our load consisted of 3 paratroops, 2 jeeps, 2 motorcycles, and 100 gallons of petrol. Also Ken and I were the PIAT team for 13 Flight. We carried the PIAT and 6 PIAT missiles. Ken flew the Horsa to ditch. I went back in the fuselage to instruct the parachutists what to do. We all survived and our dinghy kept us safe until we were picked up by a naval Air Sea rescue launch, which eventually took us to Felixstowe.[14]

At around the same time, the crew of High Speed Launch 2687 from 26 A/S RMCU at Felixstowe was having a particularly busy time. Ditching gliders appeared to have assumed the proverbial frequency of unwanted London buses in their designated patrol area:

> While on our rendezvous position a glider was observed to break away from its towing aircraft, our engines were started and we kept the boat under the glider until it ditched. The boat was taken alongside the main wing and 8 survivors were taken aboard at 1220 hours.
> At 1209 hours another glider was observed to break away. Here we took off another 8 survivors. With means at disposal of a High Speed Launch it was found impossible to sink the glider after rescue was completed. 3 injured men were treated and the survivors were later transferred as follows: 7 to HSL 2557, 9 to HSL 2572. While engaged in rescue of the second glider a third glider was observed to ditch. Upon reaching it we found 2 survivors had already been picked up by HSL 2555.[15]

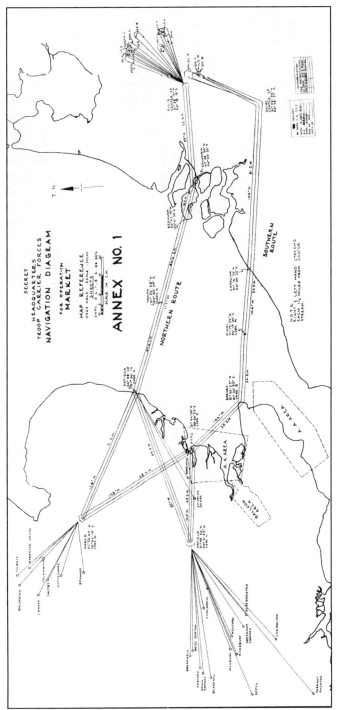

*Navigation Diagram*

Staff Sergeant Cyril Lyne and Sergeant Des Feather had been forced to ditch with Chalk Number 278; their load was an NCO and five soldiers from 3 Section, 2 Mortar Platoon of 7 KOSB Support Company. They were the second glider recovered by the RAF Marine Section Launch:

Des Feather had the controls, and I sat back and had a good look around. The sky was full of swaying black Horsas and their tugs. As I watched, one combination slowly dropped below the stream, the rope parted, and, fascinated, I watched the glider's leisurely descent towards the sea. A ring of white foam appeared on the water and I could see no more. I wondered who that poor devil was.

As I turned and looked ahead again, I saw my tug's starboard propeller slow down, and eventually stop. I barely had time to take over when the other propeller did exactly the same! I pushed the nose down as the tug began to drop, but finding myself in the embarrassing position of overtaking the tug, I had no choice but to release. 'Stand by for ditching.' Des began to call the height as the crash of rifle butts against the fuselage rang out. 'Hold on to the axe, Des, ready to chop our way out.' 500, 450, 400, still the crash of splintering plywood, glancing back I was horrified to find that there was no top left and the sides were just beginning to go. 'Stop and strap yourselves in,' I screamed. 150, 100, 50. I held off as the sea rose to the wheels. Then the sea fell away and we were stalling at 50 feet! Bump, bump, as the tail touched the swell and I remembered no more.

When I came round I was surrounded by green water. Above, below and ahead just green water. I struck out, and suddenly realised that I did not know which way was up! Kicking around I eventually broke surface in the nick of time to find Des surfacing beside me, and the glider some thirty feet or more behind. 'Swim for the glider, Des.' The clothes we wore, the equipment and ammunition were no help, but we managed to get back and climb on to the wing. We found that there was absolutely no sign whatever of the cabin. It had completely disintegrated around us. Des turned to me and. said: 'That was a bloody good joke about holding on to the axe!'

The mortar crew was climbing out, the three at the back not even damp. The last man came up, dry as a bone and promptly fell overboard. Splashing to the surface he grabbed the nearest piece of glider, the flap tab. Under his weight the flap slowly descended taking its sodden burden with it. As he struggled up again, the flap returned to its normal position, only to be grabbed again and descend again! After the third up and down journey I began to fear for the elastic and we hauled the chap aboard. I was now concerned about the length of time the heavily laden glider would float (I found later that in fact it wouldn't sink!) but a Walrus [seaplane] came up and the observer pointed in the direction from which a launch was approaching at speed.

We found the other crew already aboard, Staff Sergeant 'Bruce' Hobbs and his co-pilot Sergeant Moore of a Horsa with chalk number 266. Sitting back in borrowed clothes, drinking countless cups of tea, I speculated, as we hove to at the rendezvous, on the depth of water we had been swimming in. Two miles at least, I suggested. The Erk unrolled his fishing line, the toy sort that wouldn't even reach the water from the top of the pier. He threw it out, and had to wind half of it back to take up the slack. There was just about enough water to float the launch! But out where we ditched I know it was about two miles deep![16]

Once clear of mist or cloud, the British tug-glider combinations were flying at 2,500 feet while the American serials carrying paratroops were operating a thousand feet below them. This separation was designed to minimize the risk of any mid-air collision. A 'cast-off' height of 2,500 feet would also give the glider pilots some margin for adjustment to their approach direction and a fighting chance of orientating themselves to the ground prior to landing. They would not have much time however, as the glider serials were only separated by ten-second interval. Although the British glider combinations were intended to fly in loose 'pairs of pairs' within the column, the RAF tug commanders were not tied to a rigid time table and had, unlike the parachute serials, some freedom of manoeuvre. They could use their own judgement to adjust speed and heading if required to deliver their serial intact – this latitude to react to changes in circumstance undoubtedly increased the number of gliders that reached Arnhem safely.

The positioning of Eureka Beacons across England to mark the Initial Points assisted accurate navigation. Beacons with IX Troop Carrier Command personnel were even placed on boats at sea to mark landfall for both northern and southern streams as they approached the far coastline.

The air movement order closely resembled a previous instruction that had been drafted for LINNET 2, which had allowed for up to three streams of transport aircraft to fly parallel courses, with one and a half mile separation between them. This increased the volume of aircraft arriving over the landing and drop zones, so allowing more troops to be delivered simultaneously. In the event the American IX Troop Carrier Command elected only to use two columns to deliver the parachute element of 1st British Airborne Division.

The British parachute lift would be mounted from the American airfields at Barkston Heath and Saltby. The massed armada of 143 Dakotas would climb from the two airfields to a transit height of 1,500 feet and remain there until they were approaching their DZ; they would then descend to 500 feet to begin their run in to make the drop. Once their 'sticks' of paratroops had jumped they were clear to climb up to 3,000 feet and return on a reciprocal course to their home airfields.

The British tug aircraft, once free of the significant impediment of a fully laden glider and its tow rope, were ordered to climb to pre-designated heights and fly a reciprocal course back to their home airfield. They were directed to fly back at between 4,000 and 7,000 feet remaining within the airspace protected by the escorting fighter screen on outward and return legs of their journey. The decision to launch Operation MARKET in daylight had also allowed the further tightening of the air formations by reducing the interval between take-offs to an absolute safe minimum for such large numbers of aircraft. The interval between the tight formations of American parachute serials for example had been reduced from six minutes down to four.

The overall impact of the amendments to the MARKET plan is dramatic when measured against the Normandy night drop of the 82nd (US) Airborne Division. In the sixty-five minutes it would take to deliver 155 plane loads of paratroops and 358 gliders to Arnhem, the Normandy drop had scattered 369 sticks of paratroops over a wide area of French countryside.

A general spirit of optimism was prevalent among the majority of troops taking part in Operation MARKET – why should it not be? The intelligence reports and orders issued all describe likely German opposition to be light and the quality of enemy troops to be at best mixed. All of the GPR pilots' accounts of the build-up to 17 September and of the morning of D-Day contain a mixture of relief at finally getting back into the war, and of extreme confidence that any opposition offered by the Germans, whether in the air or on the ground, would be overwhelmed.

Irishman John McGeough was a Staff Sergeant pilot serving with 'C' Squadron GPR based at Tarant Rushton; originally an infantryman in the Essex Regiment he had completed his flying training by July 1943 and joined the GPR in North Africa the following month. He was posted to RAF Tarant Rushton in January 1944, which he was extremely happy about. Many of the men of 'C' Squadron were veteran pilots who had flown on the Sicily operation; the Squadron also had the prestige of being the only GPR squadron operating the Hamilcar heavy glider.

John was convinced that the presence of the huge 8-ton Hamilcars at the Wiltshire base was directly attributable to the calibre of pilots within his squadron. There is no evidence that this is true, however it does give a hint of the level of esprit de corps that was present across both wings of the Regiment in 1944. The Officer Commanding 'C' Squadron was Major J.A.C. 'Dickie' Dale DFC, who had flown on Operation HUSKY to Sicily as a Lieutenant in July 1943. His rapid elevation to squadron commander so soon after the disaster off the Sicilian coast is a both a tribute to his personal qualities and an indication of the scale of the reorganization required in the GPR in order to successfully prepare for and mount the Normandy lifts.

In April 1944 he had made the unusual decision to allow his first pilots (Staff Sergeants) to choose their own co-pilots. John McGeough had selected Sergeant Henry 'Wally' Woltag a first-generation Polish Jew; the two men formed the Squadron's most cosmopolitan crew. Wally was known as a happy outgoing man who was rarely seen without a smile on his face, his happy disposition balancing the sometimes serious outlook of the Celt he shared a cockpit with. John and Wally were firm friends who were frequently to be found making the most of the Sergeants' Mess bar facilities together. The ethnic origins of both pilots went some way to ensuring that they always strived to ensure they were not outdone by their Anglo-Saxon comrades in arms.

Despite John's length of service in the GPR, Operation MARKET was his first real operation; he and 'Wally' were to fly a Horsa on the first lift. John recorded a very detailed account of his experiences:

> In my Horsa there was a jeep and trailer, a bombardier of the Royal Artillery with four gunners, and an RAMC Doctor – Lieutenant Randall.
>
> Our first sight of Holland was Schouwen Island, then across the mainland to Nijmegen and then a turn to take us to Arnhem. The bridge over the Rhine there was soon visible and easily recognisable from the pictures we had been shown – then the landing zone at Wolfheze became visible (on the battle plan it was zone 'Z') and again was easily identified. Having picked out my particular landing site in a field bounded by woods on two sides and a farm track on the other I made preparations for the landing. We were at a height of 2,500 feet and I asked my tug pilot to make one or two slight alterations to course so that when I cast off I would be in the right area to enable me to land successfully. This he did and I pressed the red release knob – the tow rope fell away and the tug flew off towing it behind it.
>
> I was now in free flight and flew around for a very short while to plan my final approach and to ensure there was no risk of collision with other gliders; 350 were to land on first lift and 300 on second lift. Henry must have been concerned as he said to me 'For goodness sake get down, you never know what is going to happen.' I put down half, then full flap and as the glider was fully loaded kept my airspeed at about 85mph and touched down on Dutch soil, not a shot having been fired.
>
> Several pilots misjudged their approach and five Horsa's came in over us – did not make the field, and crashed into the wood adjoining. We did not have time to investigate or to render any assistance, as our orders were to unload and proceed from the area as soon as possible.[17]

Staff Sergeant Ken Kirkham was also involved in the first lift having successfully taken off from RAF Harwell with his co-pilot, the Squadron Second in Command, Captain Hugh Bartlett. They were part of the 'A' Squadron detachment that was carrying Lieutenant General 'Boy' Browning's headquarters to LZ 'N' outside Nijmegen. The Nijmegen serial also included 'Commander Glider Pilots' himself, George Chatterton, while members of his headquarters staff were at the controls of a number of the Horsas heading for Nijmegen.

Ken Kirkham wrote this account of his journey to Holland which includes a good description of the technical aspects of trying to land a fully laden Horsa. The manifest for his load that day is best described as eclectic, while his principle passenger was Major J. Morkowski, the liaison Officer to Browning's headquarters for the 1st Polish Independent Parachute Brigade Group. He and Hugh Bartlett were also carrying four other passengers, a Jeep, a laden trailer and four folding bicycles.

A good deal of the Dutch coastal areas had been flooded by the Germans as a defensive measure; I remember red roofs showing above the waters, a drift or two of black smoke, from downed enemy aircraft or shot-up flak positions – too far away to identify. There was an occasional glimpse of allied fighters wheeling on the flanks; the sense of air superiority was very marked. I saw nothing with a black cross on it. There may have been small-arms fire from the general direction of Germany as the Reichswald reached right to the frontier, but the mind became marvellously concentrated on the business of getting the load down safely and in one piece, if at all possible.

My position in the stream should have, in theory, afforded plenty of time to make for my allocated parcel of the landing zone, but, in practice, a general melee seemed to develop as soon as I pulled the rope-release. I was balked by other Horsas across my initial approach, and was forced to take off flap. A Horsa could descend under the effects of full flap (sort of mini barn-doors extended at more-or-less right angles beneath the main-plane, operated from compressed-air bottles) like a controlled lift, able to be pulled up in less than the length of a football pitch. With the removal of full flap, fully laden, it usually dropped like a stone, and for a few seconds, until forward speed built and the elevators were able to bite again, it was in the Hands of a Higher Power.

Most of the passengers' sick-bags had, by then, I suspect, been fully used. The motion of a glider on tow was a test for the strongest stomach among those with nothing to do but stare at each other across a narrow fuselage and consign their futures to unknown hands, but we were, in any case, only seconds away from an under-carriage-intact touch-down. 'Like a feather ...' Major Morkowski called out, clapping me on the shoulder in heartfelt relief as he bundled out of the side door.[18]

Staff Sergeant Maurice Herridge, another 'A' Squadron pilot, was also in the stream of Horsa and Hadrian gliders heading for Nijmegen. He had expected to fly with his good friend and regular second pilot Sergeant Cliff Dawson – the two trusted each other and had flown to Normandy as a crew. However, on the Saturday before the operation Cliff had been promoted to first pilot and given his own Horsa to command. Both pilots would have to get used to sharing the cockpit with a new partner. Now paired with Sergeant Alan Taylor, Maurice takes up the story of his Sunday morning. His landing would probably not have been placed in the same category as that by the grateful Major Morkowski:

As we were about to take off my new co-pilot, I guess like the rest of us a little apprehensive, said 'It's very different with a full load'... 'Haven't you trained for it?' I replied ... 'No' came his response, I could not believe what I was hearing. 'I'm sorry then I can't let you take over' ... I think he was relieved to hear me say that. How I was going to hold the weight of the fully laden Horsa for three and a half hours I did not know, but there was no alternative so I got on with it.

Approaching our landing area the 'Ack Ack' was very heavy, initially our tug was the target, then we were. We were almost at the landing area when our tow rope was severed by anti-aircraft fire. We were instantly cut off from the tug ... I had to find somewhere to land in a hurry. I saw an orchard and decided that landing in trees would be better than hitting the ground at this speed. That's what I did, in my log book I wrote 'Landed safely, no casualties, glider a complete write off.' I was not joking, it was a mangled heap but we managed to get the Jeep we were carrying out of the front of the wreckage, not the rear. The six Royal Engineers we were carrying got into it and drove off.

We started walking in the direction of our intended Landing Zone, after about half a mile we saw some woods ahead … let's get some cover in there, I thought. By now my arms and shoulders were aching and very painful to move after the flight.

A few yards into the wood we heard an American voice 'watch yourself there are Germans hiding in there, they are trying to get over the border.' There was also a railway line running through the woods which seemed strange at the time but we had our own orders so we left the Americans to it and moved on.

When we finally reached the end of the woods we found a house, a Dutch woman stood on the doorstep and called to us 'come quickly' so we went to her. In English she said 'I am so pleased you have come, come in and I will make tea.' We found it all a little bizarre, however we drank our tea and then took our leave to get to the Landing Zone.[19]

Maurice Herridge was not the only victim of bad luck with a tow rope that day. Second Lieutenant Janusz Szegda, a liaison officer from the 1st Polish Independent Parachute Brigade Group was attached to Gerald Lathbury's Brigade Headquarters. The 'D' Squadron Horsa he was travelling in contained two Jeeps, Sergeant Luitwieler a Dutch Commando of No. 2 (Dutch) Troop, No. 10 (Inter-allied) Commando and two Royal Army Service Corps drivers from Headquarters 1st Parachute Brigade. He submitted this report to the War Office after the battle explaining why he and his party of men had failed to arrive at Arnhem:

Our Horsa, with number 478, landed about 14.00 hours East of Udenhout. Our Pilots were Staff Sergeant Cram and Sergeant Whitehead. We landed near Udenhout, because the Pilot had lost sight of the tug in the clouds, and had to cast off.

The six of us moved off in two jeeps to get to Grave to join up with some American Airborne, whose objective was to take the town. On the way we passed many Germans, quite a number of which we shot from the jeep. As we proceeded, the enemy became more numerous and our ammunition would have given out if we had fought a pitched battle. So I decided to turn off in the direction of Best.

While we were going round a corner in the village of Esch at about 35 miles per hour, Sergeant Whitehead shouted to me to stop, but he had a strong Lancashire accent, I could not understand what he intended to convey. We were in the second jeep as Luitwieler being a Dutchman had been in charge of the leading jeep, so that he could ask civilians for any information. What Sergeant Whitehead had actually said was 'My mate has fallen out of the jeep.' i.e. the one we were in, but as I could not understand clearly what he said I ordered the driver to carry on. It is presumed that Staff Sergeant Cram is taken Prisoner of War. The Dutch later confirmed this.

When we first started off, we had taken a volunteer civilian with us in the leading jeep, to guide us to Grave. Knowing that there were many Germans at one of the main cross roads we decided to hide up in a wood and from here on our journey was arranged.[20]

It is not too difficult to imagine the language used by Staff Sergeant Alan Cram when he recovered from his fall from the speeding Jeep and realized that he was alone in occupied territory. Jack Whitehead and the glider passengers had better fortunes – they were hidden by the Dutch resistance until 24 October 1944 when they finally came out of hiding to assist in the liberation of the Dutch village of Boxtel.

The majority of gliders did not fall foul of the random twist of fate of a broken tow rope or the consequence of flying into dense cloud, most arriving at their intended LZ unhindered and without significant incident. This was due without doubt to the virtually impenetrable fighter escort and the suppressive activities of the UK-based Allied bomber crews. European-based ground-attack fighters of the RAF Second Tactical Air Force also attacked any German anti-aircraft gun position brave enough to engage the oncoming streams of transport aircraft.

Not all were destroyed immediately, some positions avoiding the attention of the Allied Air Forces until the air armada was actually overhead. These surviving 'flak' units did their best to inflict some damage on the formations as they flew on relentlessly towards the Rhine. The effect of a successful anti-aircraft strike on a glider was both instant and violent. Lieutenant Colonel John Place, the Commanding Officer of 2 Wing GPR, was at the controls of a Horsa with his second pilot and Wing Intelligence Officer, Lieutenant Ralph Maltby. They experienced the impact of flak on a wooden aircraft at close quarters:

> We were flying in the low-tow position and we still had half an hour to go before reaching the landing zone. Ralph had just strapped himself back into his seat when I told him to take over, as I wanted to check up on the map. I had barely got my map out in front of me and was bending over, tracing our course, when I heard a sudden very rapid and curious swish-swish sound, which was quite loud. I couldn't make out, for a fraction of a second, what was causing it, but when I looked out of my window I saw a lot of little red sparks shooting upwards from beneath the cockpit and past my port window.
>
> Next second there was a tremendous bang right in the cockpit and a thin wisp of greyish smoke. I automatically grasped the control column and as I did so I could smell high explosive; then poor Ralph rolled sideways in his seat as far as his straps would let him. I shouted for somebody to come forward and see what could be done for Ralph, and the platoon sergeant poked a startled head into the cockpit. I told him to try to get Ralph back on the floor of the cockpit, but before he could do so Ralph was dead.[21]

Lance Corporal 'Johnnie' Peters, 'B' Company, The Border Regiment, was one of the passengers in John Place's Horsa:

> Upon passing the flooded area we came under intense anti aircraft fire. The shells were bursting around the towing aeroplane and our glider, but it was a joy to see the rocket firing Typhoons swoop down on the anti-aircraft battery positions and knock them out of action. During the flight we had a near miss at the rear of the glider, a cry went up shouting that the tail was coming off, this message was relayed from the rear to the front where I was sitting. Lieutenant Colonel Place sent his 2nd pilot to investigate and he came back with the good news that all was well and he resumed his position in the cockpit, we were still under fire from the ground. I asked Sergeant Tommy Watson how long it would be before we landed and Lieutenant Maltby the 2nd Pilot said in 15 minutes time. Sergeant Watson told me that it was one o'clock when there was an almighty bang in the cockpit, a shell burst and killed Lieutenant Maltby outright.[22]

There was understandably some anxiety among the passengers about the risks of flying on with only one pilot. Sergeant Watson received a head wound as a result of the flak, but John Place flew solo on to Arnhem and successfully landed his Horsa on LZ 'S', despite the distraction of bullets passing right through the canvas fuselage as he attracted German small-arms fire on his final approach. One of the other passengers, Private Hughes, was hit in the knee by a bullet that penetrated the wooden floor of the Horsa. Ralph Maltby was later given a field burial close to the LZ near Reijerskamp Farm, just north of Wolfheze.

Having passed through the flak unscathed, John McGeough was now on the ground and out of his cockpit on LZ 'Z'. He and 'Wally' Woltag immediately busied themselves with the task of removing their tail assembly. John still had time to observe the activity around him:

> We went round to the tail unit of the glider to undo the four quick release bolts, which held it in position, remove it, and get the trailer and jeep on to terra firma. The time was 1340 hrs so we had been airborne approximately 3 hours 10 minutes.
>
> Then came the Dakotas and the sky was full of many coloured parachutes, there were over 2,000. One could not be but impressed with the sight. There is a Dutch song 'Op de grote stille heide' but on this occasion it certainly was not quiet on 'Renkumse Heath' near the glider landing area. We experienced a little trouble with one of the bolts but in a short time we were on our way. I saw that back from where we had landed there was a crashed Hamilcar, it had turned over on its back on landing and the crew were dead. It had also come from Tarrant Rushton and one of the crew was a friend of mine – Sergeant Brackstone.
>
> It was then that things began to assume a more serious note, as the realisation came that death was a possibility for all of us. Henry (or 'Wally' as he was known) and I rendezvous with other glider pilots and started to make our way to Arnhem via Wolfheze and Oosterbeek. Near Wolfheze there was a mental institution and some of the inmates were wondering aimlessly around the area terrified and bewildered. I am not quite sure how they came to be free; it may have been due to the fact that the RAF had bombed the area before our arrival.
>
> It was at this time that we nearly became casualties due to carelessness of one of the tug pilots who had been cast off from one of the gliders, which arrived after us. He dropped the towrope too soon, almost on top of us. The towropes were 'Y' shaped fitted with heavy metal couplings, three in all, one at each of the extensions of the rope. We narrowly missed being hit by the couplings, which could have caused serious injury.
>
> As we left the landing zone we saw some German Prisoners of War who had been in the area when the parachutists descended and were captured by them. Although those were the first enemy troops we had seen we were too busy to give them more than a cursory glance. I am almost certain that there was a uniformed woman amongst them.[23]

Somewhere amid the main stream of British gliders heading for Arnhem and untroubled by flak, Sergeant Brian Tomblin was at the controls of an 'E' Squadron Horsa with Lieutenant Alec Johnston. They were carrying infantrymen of the 7th King's Own Scottish Borderers. As he cast off and lined up for his approach onto LZ 'S', Brian realized that this landing was not going to be as straightforward as he first thought as there were numerous other gliders jockeying to secure a clear final approach and a safe landing. As he made his own approach he, like many others, could see over to the south of the railway embankment and LZ 'Z' where the gliders of 1 Wing and the Hamilcars of 'C' Squadron were busily 'shooting' their own approaches in equally demanding circumstances. The excitement of the final moments before landing is communicated in his commentary:

> We were not the only plane in the air; in fact it began to look a bit chaotic. There were gliders, tugs with ropes dangling, all heading to do their 'own thing'. Our landing zone was now fully clear to us, we applied half-flap and the glider responded by dipping its nose. Full flap was put on, and our angle of descent steepened to that typical Horsa attitude and we

headed towards a ground haze of smoke and fire from buildings burning in the district. The 'Red Devils' were once again landing in enemy territory.

We sank fast towards the treetops – 'Hell, we are going to hit them, can't put the flaps up again, No – it's OK' – we skimmed over the trees of the Oosterbeek woods, and the ground rushed up to us steeply. Hard back on the stick, and we shot along the ground to the accompaniment of juddering and banging that characterised a Horsa landing on a rough surface. Brakes on hard 'Mind that horse charging about scared out of its wits ...' To stop and get out quickly was our object. The brakes hissed quietly, we careered across the field, and the wheels sank into the soft sandy soil as we slowed jerkily to a halt. For a fleeting second we sat there in this smallish field tucked away in the woods – we were once again smugly satisfied that we had brought the old girl and its passengers to the right place at the right time. Our first relief was that we hadn't struck any mines placed there. The crackle of small arms brought us out of our momentary pause, we switched the flaps up out of habit, and then took part in the feverish activity to get out and we were a sitting target for any nasty Germans in the area.

The strange eeriness of that Dutch Sunday morning was then broken by the skirl of bagpipes playing 'Blue Bonnets' and our Scottish Borderers headed off in that direction for their rendezvous. Alec and I checked our operational kit, and did our quick change from pilots to soldiers. In the air above us, in chain after chain, tugs and gliders stretched back almost 20 miles, still protected by Allied fighters. Air traffic was so dense that the Pilots likened it to Piccadilly Circus. Incredibly, despite Royal Air Force predictions of intense anti-aircraft fire, this immense glider cavalcade encountered little resistance. The pre-assault bombing had been more effective in the Arnhem area then at Eindhoven and not a single tug or glider was shot down in making their approach.

Our tugs flew off, with ropes waggling behind, to be dropped at the Pilot's whim on anything that might resemble the enemy. One Horsa found the tree tops coming through the floor of the glider as they ran out of height, and the floor was ripped to pieces forcing the glider down on its nose ... remarkably no one was hurt.

Two gliders raced across our landing field and went straight into the trees, ripping their wings off as they did so. An 8-ton Hamilcar touched down on the soft soil, its nose dug into the earth and its weight and speed drove the glider into the ground to lift its tail high, and flip the Hamilcar over on its back. With the Pilots sitting in the 'hump' on the top of the Hamilcar it was useless to attempt to dig them out.[24]

It was not as simple as each individual pilot selecting their own landing site – all of the pilots had been briefed to land in pre-allocated areas within the landing zones and each of the lifts had its own area of designated ground. The idea was to leave adequate space for the gliders of the second lift the next day. Identification of respective fields was made easier by the landing aids set out by the pathfinder company, each LZ was marked with a large white letter made from marker panels to indicate its identity. The pathfinders were also firing coloured flares from Very pistols – white flares for 'S' and red for 'Z'. Both LZs had smoke generators making violet smoke to indicate wind direction to all crews. The parachute DZ was also marked with a white letter but blue smoke was used for wind indication; no flares were fired. With an average separation of nine seconds between each glider landing, selection of landing points had to be made quickly and there was little room for error once committed.

Major Peter Jackson, Officer Commanding 'E' Squadron, had successfully identified his target and was down safely on LZ 'S'. He was briefly gathering his thoughts when he was interrupted:

Immediately after landing I was surprised by one of the passengers who came forward and said: 'Please Sir, could I take off my lifebelt now?' My answer was apparently to the point and unloading was proceeded with, after which the Squadron moved towards the checkpoint. So far there had been no gunfire and everyone was suitably pleased.

There was one gentleman who did not appear to be in the least disturbed by the whole affair and that was an elderly Dutchman. He was sitting on a wall placidly smoking an ancient pipe which he removed from his mouth long enough to say 'good morning' and then resumed his smoking, just as though he had spent most of his life watching glider landings.[25]

Sergeant George Barton was in the Anti-Tank Platoon of the 7th Battalion, the King's Own Scottish Borderers. He was strapped into the rear of an 'E' Squadron Horsa with his driver Private R. McCluskey. As the glider cast off from the tug and began its descent, he remained unaware of any problem with the approach to the LZ until it was too late:

I felt the glider attempt to suddenly make a climbing movement, and then the big bang and everything came to a stop. When I came to my senses I realised we had landed in the trees, with the tail standing up in the air. I had to jump about 15 feet to the ground along with my driver. The two pilots were either dead then or unconscious. I had orders to leave them for the medical team and it was also obvious we couldn't get out the jeep and gun. I later heard the pilots, Warrant Officer [Joseph] Lee and Sergeant [Norman] Boorman, died from their injuries.[26]

The sudden climbing movement described by George Barton was presumably an attempt by the glider pilot in control of the aircraft to clear the trees that were to kill both pilots. Joseph Lee was the 27-year-old Squadron Sergeant Major of 'E' Squadron, whose loss so early in the operation would have shocked the Squadron and its commander Major Peter Jackson.

Staff Sergeant 'Syd' Neill, 14 Flight, 'F' Squadron, also had a difficult landing on LZ 'S' having lost the air pressure in the system that operated both the flaps and his brakes. He therefore had no conventional means of slowing his glider in the air or on the ground. Syd had to think quickly and find some way to reduce the landing speed of his Horsa or he would meet a similar fate to the unfortunate Lee and Boorman.

He attempted to reduce his speed by ramming the undercarriage into the ground and bouncing his Horsa across the heathland three or four times in an attempt to collapse or break off the undercarriage. If he could achieve that the glider would be landing on the central skid under the fuselage, dramatically reducing his speed.

Unfortunately his drastic actions resulted in the nose wheel breaking through the glider floor, injuring Lieutenant Commander Wolters of the Royal Dutch Navy. Trees at the end of the landing zone eventually brought Syd's wayward Horsa to a halt. Sergeant Jim Robertson, the co-pilot, suffered a badly broken leg in the crash and was carried into a nearby house where a medical officer set his leg.

Padre Pare's experience of landing in Holland was much less eventful than Syd Neill's. After a comparatively sedate landing with Lieutenant Colonel Iain Murray and his Intelligence Officer, Lieutenant Brian Bottomley, at the controls of their Horsa, George Pare watched Major General Urquhart and his small group of headquarters staff waste no time in getting away from the glider before driving away to establish the Divisional Headquarters:

As far as our own glider's landing was concerned we had known more exciting times in some of the exercises held earlier in the year. I had a glimpse of the Neder Rijn river, and espied the Landing Zone as the CO pulled his lever and our tow-rope fell away, dangled underneath our tug plane, which then veered away and dropped the rope with his blessing as he set his course for home.

Down we went and the open area, straddled with safely grounded gliders, came slowly and gently up to us. The pilot flattened out, we touched, seemed to run forward swiftly, a heap of manure flew at us which I thought might upset our equilibrium, the brakes were on, and we came to a slow, beautiful halt. I do not know the thrill a pilot gets, but I know the feelings a passenger receives at the calm ending to any touch-down. Here we were at Wolfheze, six miles east of Arnhem, just as if on an exercise. The passengers clambered out, and the General congratulated the pilots on a very good trip, which we others cordially endorsed.

The men at the rear started work and very quickly the tail was taken off the Horsa, and the jeep driven away. The General and his staff disappeared. I had with me a weighty rucksack and a heavily laden first-aid pack. The two pilots and I stood by the machine watching other gliders coming in to land. It was a magnificent spectacle, with no sign whatever of the enemy.

Again the air throbbed to the drone of many aircraft, and now the sky filled with parachutists. Some landed quite close, one at our feet. We saw a Dakota crash about half a mile away behind some trees. Our landing area was fairly open, consisting of ploughed fields dotted with clumps of trees and almost surrounded by wood. Some gliders were touching down on the other side of a line of trees about two hundred yards away, and one unlucky pilot tried to land too close to the trees, his right wing touched a tree and at once there was a rending, crashing sound as the glider broke its back. The whole machine looked as though it were a complete wreck. The CO called out, 'Come on Padre, it looks as though they're your first patients. What a fantastic thing to do – with all that space to his left!'

We dashed over and found all the occupants crawling out and grinning sheepishly, so the Colonel gave Wilkinson, our Australian pilot, a gentle admonition, as well as congratulations on a narrow escape.

I set off from here to make a tour of the gliders which looked the worse for wear and came across one in a ditch by the railway embankment. Several of the passengers were slightly hurt so I began to patch up the casualties. A news reporter joined us. In the distance there was the noise of small arms fire, but nobody knew what it was. As far as we could see the landing had been a tremendous success, a view which was later confirmed. After leaving this wreck, and seeing no more, neither being able to see any men for all had unloaded their gliders and disappeared, I rediscovered my glider after some difficulty, picked up my rucksack and staggered along in the direction I knew the others had taken. After a few minutes I heard bullets whistling near, although probably not intended for me, so I moved to the shelter of the trees and walked amongst them.[27]

As the steady influx of gliders continued on both sides of the railway line, away from George Pare another Hamilcar was approaching the increasingly crowded LZ 'Z'. Sergeant 'Geoff' Higgins was seated in the cockpit of a Hamilcar high above his load, making his own approach to LZ 'Z'. At some point over the North Sea he had lost intercom communication with his tug and to the passengers below. He and Staff Sergeant John Bonome, his first pilot, had elected to push on regardless, trusting their tug pilot to get them to within sight of their destination; he did not let them down:

As we approached the landing zone it appeared just as we had been briefed. We were flying close behind the first two Hamilcars and so, despite the lack of intercom, the pulling off procedure presented no difficulty. The thoughts and feelings of our passengers can only be guessed at as they sat or stood inside the glider unable to see what was happening.

Everything seemed to be going well until we saw the glider in front turn over as it landed over the line of trees at the edge of the landing zone. The immediate reaction of my first pilot John Bonome was to steepen the descent and so land short of the trees. This meant, of course, that we struck the ground hard and bounced and bumped towards the trees. The glider slowed to a stop clipping a wing in the process.

According to the procedure laid down, in the event of an opposed landing John and I left the cockpit and jumped down from the wings. We carried commando knives with which we were to slash the tyres on the way down. Unfortunately mine fell from its scabbard and I received a cut on my knee. It did not prove to be too bad.

The body of the glider sank to the ground and as the two of us took defensive positions to the sides we were pleased to see the truck and gun coming out through the front in good order. All around us many Horsas had arrived and were arriving, and we realised that there was no opposition. The sun was shining and it was really going to be 'the piece of cake' we had now come to believe.

John and I had been told to stay with the gun for about 48 hours when we would receive directions of where to rendezvous with the rest of the glider pilots ready to be flown back home.[28]

The puncturing of the Hamilcars tyres was intended to speed the lowering of the fuselage to the ground in order to reduce the time taken to unload the vehicle and gun carried within the cavernous glider. Thirteen Hamilcars landed on LZ 'Z' on the first lift, their fortunes were mixed. The gliders weighed close to 16 tons when fully loaded as they were for this operation, their wing span being an immense 110 feet. The combination of the weight, the almost total lack of headwind to reduce their landing speed and the very soft ground on the LZ proved disastrous in the case of three of the wooden giants.

Staff Sergeant David White and Sergeant Charles Winkworth were initially thought to have both been killed on landing. Their Hamilcar spectacularly overturned complete with the 17-pounder gun and Morris tractor they were carrying. However, Staff Sergeant White had survived, though badly injured and trapped in the wreckage by the weight the Morris tractor unit.

Colonel Graeme Warrack, the Assistant Director of Medical Services (ADMS), who had just returned to LZ 'Z' after inspecting the Medical Dressing Station (MDS) in Wolfheze, came to the crash site to see what assistance he could give:

I saw one or two Hamilcars coming in, one made a bad landing about 200 yards from the rendezvous; it appeared to have come down very fast in a potato field, collected a lot of earth under its bows which acted as a stop and turned it 'arse over tip'. One pilot was killed and the other injured and pinned down by the load inside.

Went back to the upturned Hamilcar and organised the digging out of the injured pilot. Eventually found that he was pinned by the hips and shoulders and was in considerable pain. He had already been given morphia, so we tried to move the weight from him first by manual effort, then with jacks from the vehicles, and finally by hitching a carrier to the top of the upturned 15 cwt and pulling it bodily off. The Commander Royal Engineers had to be consulted before this was done in case of a disaster. Finally it was accomplished all right and Staff Sergeant White (the pilot) was moved over to the Regimental Aid Post.[29]

David White would not survive the battle – the 22-year-old Staff Sergeant died later from his wounds in the Schoonoord dressing station in Oosterbeek. A second Hamilcar also carrying a 17-pounder and its Morris tractor also overturned, killing 23-year-old Sergeant Charles Brackstone and badly injuring Staff Sergeant Jack Shaw. Jack played no further part in the battle and was taken to a field hospital where he was later taken prisoner. Padre Pare was also witness to the efforts to recover the wounded glider pilots from the wreckage of their aircraft:

> One of our men told me a Hamilcar had overturned, and accompanied me to the spot. The machine, a giant glider carrying a seventeen-pounder gun with its three-ton towing lorry, had turned right over, burying the pilots. A crowd of soldiers was trying desperately to lever up the wreckage and after some time, as gently as they could, pulled out one survivor. The unfortunate pilot was out on a smile as the doctor ran his hands over his crushed body, and quickly he was borne away to a house the Field Ambulance had taken over as a Medical Dressing Station, about a mile away.
>
> For the rest of the afternoon I visited parties of pilots in odd places, and buried a young Sapper who had been killed in the landing. In the evening I heard that one glider had hit a tree and one or two soldiers had been killed, so I set off and found the wreck.
>
> A glider quickly smashes, for it is made only of plywood and this one looked the usual chaotic shambles. The body of a pilot was here, and I buried him. He had suffered terrible injuries and must have been killed outright. The wounded passengers had been removed to the Field Ambulance. The noise of small arms fire had increased but it did not seem very close, and as far as anybody knew everything was going well.[30]

By coincidence, both 17-pounders trapped in the wrecked Hamilcars belonged to 'D' Troop, 1st Airlanding Anti-Tank Battery, RA. The loss of these two precious guns made a significant dent in the overall anti-tank capability available to Roy Urquhart's division.

Colonel Warrack was clearly a very busy man during the initial stages of the landings and made the most of the apparent lack of German opposition to move around the landing zones and ensure his medical troops and resources were all in place. Sergeant Ollie Frazer, a 'C' Squadron pilot recounts another sighting relating to Graeme Warrack on LZ 'Z' amid the bustle of activity on 17 September:

> Major Dickie Dale, my Commanding Officer at Tarrant Rushton, told me how, shortly after landing at Wolfheze, he was approached by a very senior officer who enquired much to his surprise, 'Is Frazer down yet?' As he had just seen me making my way to the rendezvous, he replied, 'Yes, I've just seen him.' 'Good' replied the officer, 'That's fine. Carry on. Let battle commence', and hurried away.
>
> He was amazed that so much interest should be shown in one of his junior pilots, but, in fact, it was Colonel Graeme Warrack, the ADMS, enquiring anxiously about the safe arrival of my brother and the rest of 181st Field Ambulance. My brother, Major Simon Frazer, was the 2nd in command of 181st Field Ambulance. All was well, however, as they too had landed safely and Simon was already engaged on setting up the first aid post.[31]

The third Hamilcar to come to grief that day was flown by Staff Sergeant 'Reg' Garnett and Sergeant 'Paddy' Matson, who were late arriving over the LZ due to mechanical problems with their Halifax tug. Although given the option by the tug pilot to return to Tarant Rushton, Reg had elected to press on to Holland. Not only was Reg taking his chances by arriving late and flying his Hamilcar into a LZ already covered in abandoned gliders, but there was also the realistic possibility of being cast off over occupied territory by his tug if the mechanical problems deteriorated further. His load consisted of two Bren carriers belonging to John Frost's 2nd Battalion. Knowing their value to the Battalion, he pushed on and was now making his approach onto LZ 'Z'. Reg, with great understatement, summed up his landing in a 1993 issue of *The Eagle*: 'Handicapped by a faulty tug. Took the decision to press on, but as a result a late arrival over the target complicated the landing and, with brakes malfunctioning on loose ground, the flight was terminated by the railway embankment. Fortunately the rapid exit of the two Bren Carriers caused neither casualties nor damage.'

The Bren carriers broke free during the crash and burst through the wood and fabric of the nose of the Hamilcar. One of the carriers was found to be serviceable and was driven off under its own power to join the advance on the bridge; the second was thought to be unusable and remained at the embankment on the Sunday. The Halifax that had delivered Reg and Paddy Matson to their fate at the railway embankment had turned for home. At the controls Pilot Officer Herman had his own problems – he had to fly with all four engines permanently set at full throttle to maintain a safe cruising speed and height. Consequently the fuel consumption of his aircraft was increased significantly and he failed to return the 644 Squadron aircraft to RAF Tarant Rushton that day, being forced to divert into RAF Earls Colne near Colchester in Essex, where he landed safely.

With the drama of the Hamilcar landings on LZ 'Z' obscured from view by the railway embankment, Lieutenant Alec Johnston, Brian Tomblin's co-pilot, continues the story of the two 'E' Squadron pilots after their 'hairy' landing to the north of the railway embankment on LZ 'S':

> Relief at having 'pancaked' safely and avoiding mines and flak, was mixed with a burning desire to get away from the exposed glider as fast as possible, for the Germans were accomplished performers with their mortars.
>
> A period of organised chaos followed, during which the pilots of 'E' Squadron bade a hasty farewell to their live load, in this case elements of the King's Own Scottish Borderers, and hurried to their rendezvous. So far, so good! The enemy had reacted only slightly, and what firing could be heard was only desultory and not too near.
>
> Somewhere bagpipes were wailing: this was an arrangement designed to assist the King's Own Scottish Borderers in locating their rendezvous. Once 'E' Squadron had formed up with only two or three absentees, due to prangs and pull-offs, it became necessary to reach Wolfheze with the minimum of delay and take up the positions planned.
>
> Since little or nothing was known of the German dispositions, Major Jackson sent a reconnaissance patrol ahead to explore the ground. This patrol, after a stealthy approach lasting some 40 minutes, was set upon by hordes of laughing and shouting Dutch children, who presented the astonished soldiery with dozens of luscious apples, welcome gifts, too, since the afternoon was a hot one. The patrol returned more quickly and in an upright posture to render its report and, in due course, 'E' Squadron was established in Wolfheze.
>
> The reception was overwhelming. Everyone seemed to speak English; secret caches of tea and other delicacies were unearthed (often literally), news of the German dispositions given and, in turn, questions asked about the progress of the war and the whereabouts, health and activities of the Dutch Royal Family. It was all very moving, especially when the glider pilots shared out their cigarettes, chocolates and other food. The children went wild with joy.[32]

Staff Sergeant 'Reg' Grant was busy among the 'E' Squadron gliders on LZ 'S', having landed safely with his load of personnel and stores for 181 Airlanding Field Ambulance, RAMC. He describes the change in tempo and atmosphere on the ground around him as the first sticks of the 1st Parachute Brigade begin to descend to his south on DZ 'X'. The relaxed and almost peacetime mood around the gliders at the beginning of his account contrast sharply with the sound of small-arms fire coming from the direction of Oosterbeek and Arnhem. You can sense a change in mood and the first indication of concern toward the end of this passage:

Calmly and unhurriedly, we unloaded the glider. The equipment of the ambulance lads, being of fairly small bulk, all came through the main side door and down the ramp easily. The unloading was completed in under five minutes. Away to the north the air was filled with parachutes as men and supplies floated gracefully to earth. There was a feeling of unreality about the whole thing. Weather-wise, it was a very pleasant Sunday afternoon with no sign at all of enemy troops.

We left the glider and made our way across the soft ground to the cover of a line of trees, along the edge of the landing zone. Some of the lads pulling a handcart loaded with medical supplies, the Sergeant and a Corporal pushing the motorcycles. After just a few yards, the Sergeant threw his to the ground saying he could not push it over the soft ground. Why he didn't start it up and ride it I don't know. Occasionally we heard the odd shot or two from the direction of Arnhem. No doubt the men attempting to reach the bridge were clearly running into trouble, the wooded areas being ideal for ambush.

Continuing along the line of trees, on the way to our rendezvous, I was about ten yards ahead of the others when an uncanny instinct made me duck behind a low bank. Almost immediately a bullet zipped by. I stayed there for a few seconds but as no further firing took place, I rejoined the others who had moved to the other side of the trees. It was probably a stray not aimed at me at all. Gliders were still arriving and all types of airborne troops were leaving the landing zones, completely unmolested, and moving down a sandy track to their own particular rendezvous. Parting company from the ambulance unit we joined up with the other glider pilots of our own Squadron.

A long column of men, guns and Jeeps stretched up the road through the village of Wolfheze towards Arnhem. We moved slowly along with our enormously heavy rucksacks weighing us down. The paratroops were well to the fore and were running into trouble. We came across one trooper coming back up the road with a head wound and he said his entire section had been wiped out.[33]

As the lead elements of Gerald Lathbury's 1st Parachute Brigade marched away from DZ 'X' towards their objectives all appeared to be going to plan. In fact, overall the landings themselves could only be viewed as a total success, losses had been minimal and the predicted benefits of a daylight landing had been realized.

The Airlanding Brigade had every right to be satisfied with their state immediately after the first lift.

A total of 358 British gliders had taken off from their home airfields, thirty-eight headed for Nijmegen carrying Corps Headquarters. The Royal Air Force Post Operational Report stated that a total of thirty-nine gliders failed to reach Arnhem. A single combination turned around and returned to base with engine trouble, another crashed in Somerset possibly due to structural failure. A total of twenty-four gliders were released over England, the majority of releases triggered by poor visibility. Twenty-two of those glider loads and their crews would be allocated new gliders and inserted into the second lift the following day. There were five less fortunate crews forced to ditch in the North Sea and a further nine gliders adrift in occupied Holland.

The anti-aircraft positions along the route of the air corridors had been effectively neutralized or in many cases destroyed by swarms of ground-attack aircraft, preceded by a series of concerted and well-coordinated bombing raids. The reported flak concentrations around Arnhem itself and

Deelen airfield to the north had so far proved ineffective.

Deelen airfield was heavily bombed on 15 August and again on 3 September. After both Allied bombing raids, the German garrison at Deelen airfield, with the aid of forced labour, worked hard to repair damage and enable aircraft to continue using the airfield. After the raid of 3 September, the headquarters of 3 Jagddivision was withdrawn from Deelen to Duisburg in Germany.

As a result of the damage sustained to the runway, as well as the move of 3 Jagddivision, Deelen ceased to be an operational airfield after 3 September. The heavy flak guns used for the defence of the airfield were relocated to other more valuable sites. Nevertheless Deelen was still deemed to be of enough military importance to warrant protection and most of the light flak units remained in position.

Allied aircraft again targeted Deelen on 17 September. The damage sustained to the remaining 'flak' positions is not recorded. However, some operational light flak guns were subsequently moved off the airfield and attached to the 9th SS Panzer Division. They remained with the SS Division for the duration of the Arnhem battle.

The prediction of a 40 per cent casualty rate to the air transport fleet from flak had been excessively gloomy – no transport aircraft were lost to anti-aircraft fire on the first lift.

Intelligence predictions of low-calibre German troops in the area of the landings also appeared to be substantiated by the mix of German prisoners taken immediately after the landings. Some had in fact not waited for the main body to land and had surrendered to 'Boy' Wilson and his pathfinders. The first forty-seven German prisoners of war had the appearance of low-quality troops and were drawn from twenty-seven separate units. It was also noted that many were not carrying weapons or were at best only wearing side arms.

The initial surprise of the landing was total – the female prisoner referred to in John McGeough's account and by several other glider pilots was a Luftwaffe telephonist named Irene Reimann. Her Sunday stroll with a boyfriend had been disturbed by the unexpected landing of a large British Airborne force this must have shattered any romantic aspirations she or her partner had had for the rest of the day.

Arthur Shackleton also clearly recalls taking another young German soldier prisoner as he emerged from a barn struggling to put his hands up to surrender, while also holding on to his unbuttoned trousers. His amorous afternoon with a local girl had also been abruptly interrupted by the arrival of 'B' Squadron and the less than amorous South Staffs.

One component of the first day's glider lift that really did need every glider possible to reach Arnhem was Freddie Gough's Reconnaissance Squadron. The bulk of his men were carried in gliders from Tarant Rushton along with their up-gunned but unarmoured Jeeps. With their Vickers machine guns they were to spearhead the initial assault on the main Arnhem Bridge. The Recce Squadron had been allocated twenty-two 'C' Squadron Horsa gliders to deliver its Jeeps to Arnhem – twenty of them arrived safely on the landing zone.

A single Recce Squadron combination flown by Lieutenant George Stokes and Sergeant Jack Taziker had to turn back to Tarant Rushton when their tug developed engine trouble. Jack described the moment of decision over the sea in a letter to his wife written in March 1945:

> We had only been airborne about 20 minutes when one of the tug's engines conked out. So we had to return to base. When we had landed we found that a large strip of fabric was missing from the glider's wing. So it was a dam good job that we did turn back. The ground staff quickly stuck another piece of fabric on the wing and they found us another tug, so we set off about half an hour behind the others to try and catch up with them. It was hopeless; we got just out over the North Sea when the pilot of the tug saw nothing but sky and water.

He decided to turn back. We got back to Tarrant Rushton at about 3 o'clock and I was just in time to hear the BBC announcement that there had been an airborne landing in Holland.[34]

John Fairly wrote *Remember Arnhem*, an excellent account of the Reconnaissance Squadron's part in the Arnhem battle. This extract describes the events on board the same Horsa seen from the confines of the troop compartment. Bill Cook was a Driver/Operator with Recce Squadron's HQ Troop. Strapped in close to Lieutenant Graham Wadsworth and Sergeant George Kay, he was not enjoying his flight in the Horsa, despite drawing on some 'Dutch courage'. Things were about to get worse:

'I was sat', recollected Cook, 'at the rear, on the right of Sergeant Kay, and, as we swung out to sea, I well remember a feeling of apprehension which made me reach for the bottle of rum that 'Judd' (Kay) was swigging.

The next glance out of the port side turned that apprehension into fear, for I saw part of the wing fabric – a strip about a foot wide – rip off from the leading edge right to the back. At that point, it disappeared, leaving an ugly gaping hole and a wing that started to billow out. 'God,' I thought, 'this is it,' and had visions of the whole wing disintegrating. I let 'Judd' into my discovery and somehow we got Lieutenant Wadsworth, sitting at the front, to understand our predicament; he in turn passed the news to the glider pilots. 'Did we think we could make it?' was the cool, delayed response, to which our unanimous reply was, 'Get the bloody thing turned round and put her down!'

The result was that they returned to Tarrant Rushton and, after a quick patch up with glider fabric, took off again in just over a quarter of an hour, in an attempt to catch the tail end of the glider force. Failing to succeed in this, they returned to base for a second time. Later that evening, in the deserted billet, Bill Cook heard the radio announcement of the landing at Arnhem.[35]

A second Horsa flown by Staff Sergeant 'Jock' MacDonald and Sergeant J.W. Mowatt carrying two Jeeps and personnel from 'A' Troop were separated from their tug over Hampshire when they hit the turbulent slipstream of another combination in their formation. Their tow rope snapped as they fought to regain control of their glider; an emergency landing was the only option. They landed safely north-east of Andover near Doyley Manor.

One of the twenty Horsas that arrived over LZ 'Z' landed badly and overturned, killing the first pilot, Staff Sergeant George Baxter. The crash rendered an additional two Jeeps from 'A' Troop of Gough's Squadron unusable. The Recce Squadron serials had, however, been largely successful – in fact twenty-four Recce Jeeps were available for the *coup de main* mission. Four of the Jeeps that were not available to 'Freddie' Gough belonged to 'A' Troop; they were not part of the initial dash for the bridge and were intended to be held in reserve. One of the myths used to explain the failure of Operation MARKET to seize the prize of Arnhem Bridge is the loss of the Recce Squadron's Jeeps during the first lift.

There was confusion about the Recce serials that resulted in garbled messages being circulated about the non-arrival of Gough's Jeeps, but they were, in fact, spurious. Roy Urquhart, meanwhile, had been briefed that due to the lack of Jeeps, the *coup de main* could not be mounted, so was already modifying his plan. The bulk of Gough's force was intact on LZ 'Z' and preparing to seize the bridge as planned.

The *coup de main* Jeep convoy was formed and ready to move from its rendezvous point by 1530 hours. In a flurry of high-revving engines they departed at 1540 hours with 'C' Troop leading, with Lieutenant Bucknall commanding the lead Jeep. The Jeeps moved off LZ 'Z', quickly negotiating the bottleneck at the Wolfheze railway crossing, before turning right to run along a track parallel to the railway embankment on their right.

With all of the Airlanding Brigade lift and 1st Parachute Brigade on the ground, and the engine noise of the Dakotas of IX Troop Carrier Command receding into the distance, priorities rapidly changed.

As soon as their gliders were unloaded the glider pilots had other roles to perform. The two commanding officers and their squadron commanders set about regrouping their pilots and organizing them for the respective tasks as dictated by Colonel George Chatterton prior to leaving England.

**Notes**

1 Edwards, SSgt J.E., 'A' Sqn GPR, 'What did you do in the war, Grand Dad?' (unpublished).

2 Bassarab, FO, R.N., 299 Sqn, RAF, by permission of *The Eagle*.

3 Pare, Captain G., RAChD, HQ 1 Wing, GPR, by permission of *The Eagle*.

4 NA, Air 37/998 Comd Glider Pilots Report, Op Neptune, 26 July 1944.

5 Tomblin, Sgt B.A., 'E' Sqn GPR, correspondence with Luuk Buist, 1991.

6 Bassarab, FO R.N., 299 Sqn, RAF, by permission of *The Eagle*.

7 Holcroft, SSgt W., 14 Flt, 'F' Sqn GPR, 'No medals for Lt Pickwoad', September 1945, p. 8.

8 Rigby, SSgt A., 19 Flt, 'B' Sqn GPR, by permission of *The Eagle*.

9 Shackleton, SSgt A., 20 Flt, 'B' Sqn GPR, Interview with the author, 2007.

10 Freeman, SSgt, G, 19 Flt, 'B' Sqn GPR, correspondence with Luuk Buist, 1991.

11 Pare, Captain, RAChD, G.A., HQ 1 Wing, GPR, by permission of *The Eagle*.

12 Pyne, Sergeant G., 11 Flt, 'E' Sqn GPR, correspondence with Luuk Buist, 1992.

13 Gibson, SSgt R.P., 16 Flt, 'F' Sqn GPR, *Nine Days*, Ilfracombe, Arthur Stockwell Ltd, 1956.

14 RAF Marine Craft, Reports on A/S R, National Archives, AIR 29/444.

15 RAF Marine Craft, Reports on A/S R, National Archives, AIR 29/444.

16 Lynne, SSgt C., 'E' Sqn GPR, correspondence with Luuk Buist, 1991.

17 McGeough, SSgt J., 'C' Sqn GPR, correspondence with Luuk Buist, 1978 onwards.

18 Kirkham, SSgt K., 'A' Sqn GPR, correspondence with Bob Hilton, 1997.

19 Herridge, SSgt M., 'A' Sqn GPR, interview and correspondence with the author, 2008.

20 Szegda, Second Lieutenant J., HQ 1 Para Bde, National Archive, WO208/3351.

21 Peters, Corporal J., 'B' Coy, 1 Bn, Border Regt, interview with the author, May 2008.

22 McGeough, SSgt J., 'C' Sqn GPR, correspondence with Luuk Buist, 1978 onwards.

23 Tomblin, Sgt B., 'E' Sqn GPR, correspondence with Luuk Buist, 1991

24 Jackson, Major P., 'E' Sqn GPR, correspondence with Luuk Buist, 1991.

25 Barton, Sergeant G., 7th Battalion, KOSB, correspondence with Luuk Buist, 1991.

26 Pare, Captain G.A., RAChD, HQ 1 Wing, GPR, by permission of The Eagle.

27 Higgins, Sergeant G., 'C' Sqn GPR, correspondence with Luuk Buist, 1991.

28 Warrack, Colonel, RAMC, 'The Harvest of Ten Years', by permission of the Airborne Museum Hartenstein.

29 Pare, Captain G.A., RAChD, HQ 1 Wing, GPR, by permission of The Eagle.

30 Frazer, Sergeant O., 'C' Sqn GPR, by permission of The Eagle.

31 Johnston, Lieutenant A., 'E' Sqn GPR, correspondence with Luuk Buist, 1991.

32 Grant, SSgt H.C.R., 'E' Sqn GPR, correspondence with Luuk Buist, 1991.

33 Taziker, Sergeant J., 'C' Sqn GPR, letter dated March 1945.

34 Fairley, John, Remember Arnhem, Glasgow, Bel & Bain Ltd, 1990, p. 34.

# CHAPTER 7

# One Foot on the Ground

*'The pilots were dead in the branches of the tree.'*

**The Afternoon of Sunday, 17 September 1944**

The 1st Airborne Division plan was going well. Across all of the landing and drop zones, men, Jeeps, guns and Bren carriers were criss-crossing the heathland and fields. All were moving with purpose to their Rendezvous Points (RV).

The RV process was slightly more complicated for the GPR. Immediately on landing the pilots assisted in unloading their gliders, on completion of which, those glider pilots who had carried artillery units remained with their passengers to provide them with infantry protection. The anti-tank batteries of the Airlanding Brigade had however released their pilots from this duty and used their own more plentiful infantry to protect their own 6-pounders. All other pilots went with their passengers to their unit RV, where the senior glider pilot took command, formed all pilots into a body and led them on to their own Wing RV.

Once they were regrouped as formed GPR units, 1 Wing GPR came under command of Headquarters, 1st Airborne Division and 2 Wing GPR under command of Headquarters, 1st Airlanding Brigade.

The parachute drop on DZ 'X' had gone particularly well – the bulk of Gerald Lathbury's 2,283 men of the 1st Parachute Brigade and assorted other parachute-trained units, including the majority of the Reconnaissance Squadron, had made successful jumps. For various reasons, four men had refused to jump and one man, believed to have been from the 1st Parachute Battalion, was killed when his canopy failed to fully open and he 'Roman-candled' to his death.

Due to the particularly heavy loads that each paratrooper carried, even landings in ideal conditions were not without risk. Awkward landings resulted in a number of injuries and broken legs for an unlucky few, though no more than would have been anticipated on a large-scale drop such as this. As with the glider lift, men making their way off the DZ to their rendezvous had to check above their heads frequently as men and supply containers were landing all around them.

Major Peter Jackson, commanding 'E' Squadron GPR, watched the parachute landing and the successive waves of American Dakotas with the educated eye of a fellow pilot: 'By now the sky was black with parachutists, and containers and more gliders coming in to land. One thing that impressed me was the speed at which the Dakotas turned after release and made off home, and one Flight Commander of 271 Squadron was accused of turning so rapidly that his towrope cracked his windscreen.[1]

Not everybody on the landing zones had time to watch the impressive spectacle of the air armada delivering 1st Parachute Brigade. Lance Corporal Albert 'Ginger' Wilson had landed by Horsa with 11 Platoon of The Border Regiment. As he followed his platoon away from their glider, while attempting to orientate himself, he surveyed the tall trees around LZ 'S': 'Looking up into them, I saw that another Horsa had smashed into them forty feet above the ground. The pilots were dead in the branches of the tree; the anti-tank gun that the glider was carrying had smashed through the bulkhead into the cockpit.'[2] It is possible that this smashed glider was the one described by George Barton in the previous chapter.

Staff Sergeant 'Wally' Holcroft had been more fortunate and had completed a textbook landing on LZ 'S'; his platoon from 'C' Company of the Borders had left his Horsa in good order. Wally had, however, suffered a 'nasty crack to the head' in the side door as he and Sergeant Norman Hartford rushed to join their infantry passengers in cover away from their now redundant glider. Both the glider pilots and their passengers from the Borders were witness to the 1st Parachute Brigade drop as they assembled at their RV:

> Sporadic rifle fire was going on all this time and our little band of men kept a sharp look out for the enemy, but none challenged us. As soon as the glider had been unloaded of supplies we moved off to join the rest of the Border Regt, who were gathering together in a wood close by. The Glider Pilots had orders to stay with the troops they brought in until the following day when they were due to rendezvous at Wing HQ.
>
> When we arrived in the wood I found Mick [Hall] and his party, he told me his glider had been the second to land. As we stood talking and awaiting further orders, a paratrooper landed near us, rolling over and over on the ground. Getting to his feet he quickly divested himself of his 'chute' and grinned happily at us, as though this was an everyday occurrence. Now a large number of paratroops were landing, this must have been a second lot for a large number had landed before us.[3]

Things were not going so smoothly with the landing of Freddie Gough's Recce Squadron Jeeps and their 'C' Squadron Horsas. One of the twenty Recce Squadron Horsas that arrived over LZ 'Z' had landed badly and overturned, killing the first pilot, Staff Sergeant George Baxter. The crash rendered two Jeeps from 'A' Troop of Gough's Squadron unusable. There were further delays with the extraction of the armed Jeeps from six of the gliders, the pilots and Recce crews locked in a protracted and frustrating struggle to free them.

These problems were primarily due to damage caused to the Horsas on landing, distorting the tail and trapping the Jeeps, or because the Horsa had settled awkwardly nose down in soft soil after landing. There was an art or knack to removing the tail section of a Horsa even in ideal conditions – cutting the cables linking the cockpit to the rudder was only the beginning of what is consistently described as a hot and sweaty task. Two well-trained and well practised men, working in a synchronized manner, was the minimum requirement to achieve this successfully, even on a level surface in the benign environment of a training exercise.

The task of removing the tail section, and indeed a fully loaded Jeep from a nose-down Horsa during a real operation, was of an altogether different magnitude. The tail in most cases was approximately 16 feet above the ground, so climbing up inside the glider along the steep incline of the fuselage was in itself no mean feat. The removal of the bolts securing the tail to the fuselage, while struggling to avoid falling back along the troop compartment of the Horsa onto a trapped Jeep, was a frustrating and lengthy task.

Once the tail was separated from the fuselage, there was the small problem of getting the Jeep out of the fuselage and down to the ground. This was normally achieved with the aid of purpose-made metal ramps that flew with the Jeep, but these were now rendered too short by the tail-up attitude of the grounded aircraft. Some airborne ingenuity was required to get the vital Jeeps down from their lofty perch as the Recce Squadron crews and their pilots laboured through the afternoon to extract the trapped Jeeps. Eventually, by stacking supply panniers on top of each other close to the now open troop-carrying compartment, the ramps could be used. The Jeeps were driven down the very steep incline and away from the Horsa; the last Recce Jeep did not drive away from its glider until 1750 hours, just as daylight was beginning to fade.

The four Jeeps crewed by Sappers from 9th (Airborne) Field Squadron RE, who were earmarked to assist in seizing the bridge, had not been grouped in the same glider serial as the Recce Squadron which had been flown in by 'C' Squadron from RAF Tarant Rushton. The Sappers were flown in by 'D' Squadron as part of a different serial from RAF Keevil and consequently were elsewhere on the LZ at a different time. This separation of the two components of Gough's force by time and ground was an unfortunate and unintended consequence of retaining the existing Air Movement Table from the operation orders of LINNET II and COMET, but the need for a Jeep *coup de main* force and therefore its composition and collective delivery had not featured in either plan.

There was a further variable that delayed the assembly of 'Freddie' Gough's squadron – many of the Recce Squadron troopers required to crew the Jeeps did not travel with their vehicles by glider but had parachuted in among Gerald Lathbury's brigade onto DZ 'X'. The parachute element arrived after the gliders whereupon they had to orientate themselves quickly before moving across from the DZ, laden with full equipment, to the Recce Squadron assembly point 350 yards south of the railway, west along Telefoonweg on the south-east corner of a wood. Despite all of these challenges the Recce Squadron serials had been largely successful; in fact, twenty-eight of the planned thirty-one Recce Jeeps were available for the *coup de main* mission. Four of the Jeeps that were not available to 'Freddie' Gough belonged to 'A' Troop; they were not part of the initial dash for the bridge and were intended to be held back as the squadron reserve. Overall the *coup de main* force was in good shape.

By 1500 hours, 1st Parachute Brigade was formed and ready to move, lead elements pushed out from the DZ for its objectives at a steady pace. The Brigade's orders were unchanged; they were to seize the Arnhem railway and road bridges with best possible speed.

The 2nd Parachute Battalion, under John Frost, initially moved quickly east through the centre of Heelsum then dropped down onto their southern approach along the north bank of the Rhine on route LION. John Fitch took his 3rd Parachute Battalion around the eastern side of Heelsum before moving onto route TIGER, using Utrechtseweg as the axis for his advance through Oosterbeek to Arnhem, in support of John Frost and his men. At this point the 1st Parachute Battalion, under David Dobie, remained at the DZ as the brigade reserve; they were prepared to move out to the north of Arnhem using the Arnhem–Ede road which had been designated route LEOPARD.

As Lathbury's brigade began to move away from the open terrain of the Drop Zone and its columns snaked into the close wooded areas around Heelsum, the trees began to screen their radio antennae, and radio communication became more and more difficult. Roy Urquhart's tactical headquarters was still in the process of setting up in a temporary location near Wolfheze. The signallers there struggled to maintain radio communications with both brigades with increasing difficulty until eventually both links collapsed. Loss of radio communication was not uncommon at the time and the general situation still appeared favourable to Gerald Lathbury as he and his paratroops pushed on toward Oosterbeek.

The absence of radio communications with the brigades was further compounded by problems on 1st Airborne Division's Command Net. There was a very powerful but unknown station transmitting on the same frequency, its signal was effectively jamming the net. Therefore Roy Urquhart's primary means of command and control was initially denied to him. The combination of closely wooded countryside and increasing distance was also preventing his signallers from establishing a radio link to 'Pip' Hicks and 1st Airlanding Brigade. Concerned about the lack of information available to him and his headquarters about the securing of the future landing zones

Roy Urquhart set off north toward the Airlanding Brigade headquarters at Duitsekampweg with the intent of speaking to 'Pip' Hicks face to face and assessing the situation on the ground for himself.

When Roy Urquhart arrived at the Headquarters of 1st Airlanding Brigade he found that 'Pip' Hicks was also lacking a viable radio link with his leading units, and had left his headquarters to go forward to see for himself what was happening. It was while he was with the Airlanding Brigade staff that Roy Urquhart heard the spurious report that the majority of the gliders carrying the Recce Squadron Jeeps had failed to arrive on the landing zone. There was no logical reason to doubt the authenticity of the report and even if there had been doubt, verification was impossible by radio.

Believing that there would be no Jeep *coup de main* mounted on the bridge, Roy Urquhart quickly surmised that any hope of seizing the bridges now rested with the lead parachute battalions commanded by Gerald Lathbury, but unfortunately he had no radio communication with Lathbury's headquarters. The jamming of the Command frequency had resulted in the decision to change frequency on the Divisional Command Net, however this information had not yet been passed to Headquarters the 1st Parachute Brigade who were out of reach due to the jamming and the terrain. Anxious that a major component of his plan had apparently fallen by the wayside, and in an attempt to ascertain what state the Recce Squadron was in, he issued orders that 'Freddie' Gough was to report to him as soon as possible.

The false Recce Squadron report and lack of radio communication triggered a dramatic course of action from Roy Urquhart. Unable to speak to Gerald Lathbury by radio, and therefore unsure of the exact location of the 1st Parachute Brigade Headquarters, he set off from the headquarters of the 1st Airlanding Brigade in his Jeep to locate Gerald Lathbury. The best hope of success now rested with 2nd Parachute Battalion and Lieutenant Colonel John Frost, who had yet to be informed of the demise of the Recce Squadron and its implications on the overall plan. Roy Urquhart believed that the changing situation warranted his direct intervention on the ground. He was determined to ensure that John Frost was forewarned that there were no British troops waiting for him on the Arnhem bridge and to stress the even greater need for 2nd Parachute Battalion to push along route LION with all possible speed.

As the heavily laden parachute troops continued to move out towards Oosterbeek and Arnhem, by about 1530 hours the area around the landing zones appeared to be gaining some semblance of military order. The glider-borne battalions of the Airlanding Brigade were also moving themselves into defensive positions on and around the landing and drop zones allocated for the arrival of 'Shan' Hackett's 4th Parachute Brigade and the second lift the next morning.

The Airlanding Field Ambulance was established in Wolfheze and was busily treating casualties from the first lift. The Airlanding Light Regiment, RA already had the light guns of 3 Battery RA in position to the east of LZ 'Z', sited just south of Wolfheze within sight of the lunatic asylum. Glider pilots from 9 and 23 Flights GPR had been detached from 'G' Squadron, with orders to remain with 3 Battery and provide local defence. Lieutenant Mike Dauncey of 9 Flight had made a good landing and was now making the rapid transition from pilot to soldier that he and his men had been trained to do:

> We were now infantry soldiers and our job was to act as a kind of screen to the men in the Royal Artillery. It was envisaged that we would later be withdrawn and sent back to England again ready for the next operation. I felt very excited. At last I might see a little bit of action. The odd burst of gunfire could be heard in the distance. No one came close to us that evening, and so we began digging slit trenches around the gunners to give them some sort of protection.[4]

As Mike Dauncey and his comrades dug their trenches, 1 Battery, RA moved into gun positions between 3 Battery RA and the southern outskirts of Wolfheze village. Both gun batteries were on call to the 1st Parachute Brigade and 1st Airlanding Brigade should their advance on the bridge or the occupation of the LZs require artillery support. Both batteries would have to move closer to Arnhem as the advance progressed, the light guns maximum range being roughly 5½ miles, so the distance to the Arnhem bridges was well beyond their range. A future position for the guns had been selected close to Oosterbeek Church – the gunners and their attendant glider pilots would have to follow on behind the advancing Parachute Battalions.

The glider pilots of 1 Flight, 'A' Squadron were attached to 1 Battery, RA and were digging in around the light guns they had flown over from England. Sergeant Bob Shipley was among them as they hurriedly established themselves around the Battery. Bob and his fellow pilots were soon working up a sweat digging their trenches. Bob's brother Norman was also with the 1st British Airborne Division in Holland, serving as a Private with 'C' Company, 2nd Parachute Battalion. No doubt he too was building up a sweat as he moved quickly towards the river bank in full battle order along route LION.

Lieutenant Colonel Iain Murray had set the RV for the pilots of 1 Wing close to Headquarters 1st Airborne Division, his pilots arriving at the RV in a steady stream with no interference from the enemy. Headquarters 1 Wing was then set up in a defensive position in the vicinity of the lunatic asylum and patrols were despatched back out onto the LZ to rescue any glider pilots trapped in the wreckage of crashed gliders. The remainder of 1 Wing remained close to Headquarters, 1st British Airborne Division, providing defence and acting as the divisional reserve.

In fact, much of Iain Murray's Wing was not available to him as they were widely dispersed across the landing area, actively supporting other airborne units. The varieties of tasks undertaken by the GPR Squadrons at this stage of the operation justified George Chatterton's 'total soldier' concept and the strict training regime imposed on GPR volunteers during the early days of the Regiment.

The pilots of 'A' Squadron were now split between three separate locations. 18 Flight and most of 2 Flight were guarding 'Boy' Browning's Corps Headquarters in Nijmegen, 1 Flight were protecting 1 Battery RA at Wolfheze and 17 Flight were still waiting impatiently at Tarant Rushton for the second lift into Arnhem. They were now the only 'A' Squadron flight not yet deployed. Major 'Billy' Griffith, a pre-war county cricketer, commanded the Squadron having flown to Nijmegen with his squadron headquarters flight to command the main body of his squadron.

The 'G' Squadron flights were also dispersed. Captain Robin Walchli and 24 Flight were providing defence around the 1st Airborne Division Headquarters, while 9 and 23 Flights were both protecting the light guns of 3 Battery RA, with Major Bob Croot, the Officer Commanding the Squadron, personally overseeing the defence of the gun batteries and their surrounding area. The remaining 'G' Squadron sub-unit was 10 Flight GPR which had not deployed as a formed unit, but had suffered the frustration of being broken up into its component sections to reinforce other squadrons. Six crews from 10 Flight's 1 Section were attached to 'F' Squadron for the first lift and remained with them throughout the battle. The remaining three sections were spread across the second and third lifts, flying from RAF Fairford and Tarant Rushton.

Ian Toler's 'B' Squadron was in relatively good order and all of the gliders that had reached the landing zone had made successful landings without incurring casualties, although Staff Sergeant Jack Hopkins and Sergeant G. Hooker were wounded by machine-gun fire after landing. Two gliders had failed to arrive: Lieutenant 'Jimmie' Barclay and Lieutenant Roland 'Dusty' Miller had made it as far as Holland, but failed to reach Arnhem due to a broken tow rope over Tilburg, while Staff Sergeant 'Tommy' Geary and Sergeant G. Bristow had suffered similar bad luck over England. Jim Hooper's luck appeared to have changed as he and 13 Platoon of the South Staffords had landed without incident on LZ 'S'. Four of the 'X' Flight Hadrian gliders, that had been administered by 'B'

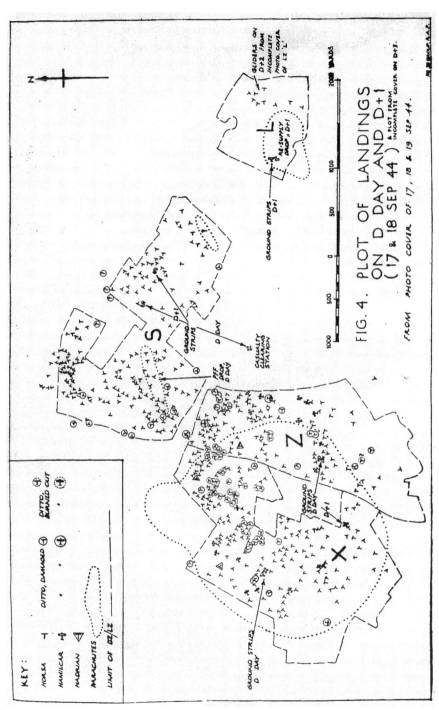

*Plot of landings, 17 & 18 September 1944*

Squadron at RAF Manston, had also landed with their special loads intact on LZ 'Z'. Ian Toler's diary entry describing the first minutes of the landing is generally upbeat:

> At Reyers Camp, the rendezvous, we met 'Boy' Wilson of the Independent Parachute Company, very cheerful. 'Did you see our marking and the coloured smoke?' he shouts. 'Yes. OK,' I reply. Apparently there were a few 'Jerry's' round the dropping zone when they landed, and shots were fired, but they gave up as soon as the Independents opened up on them. We see them now; a disconsolate lot and the first enemy prisoners we are to meet. It is altogether too quiet. We start to dig in rather too enthusiastically as I have blistered my hands in a very short time. Some more gliders are coming in. We eat our sandwiches and rest. I check up on Angus Low's Flight.

It was Captain Angus Low and 20 Flight who been nominated by their squadron commander to make the long march back to Nijmegen to reinforce the 'A' Squadron crews protecting Corps Headquarters, but he and his men were far from enthusiastic about the prospect of executing this apparently insane order. After the chaotic period of order and counter order before and after Operation COMET, Angus and his men were assembled and finally given orders for Operation MARKET on 16 September:

> We were then told that 20 Flight, my flight, were to proceed to Nijmegen after landing at Arnhem so as to assist in the defence of Corps Headquarters. We gaped in amazement at this order as apart from crossing the Rhine, it would involve going through twelve miles of enemy territory. I might add that corps headquarters were allocated thirty-eight gliders to take them to Nijmegen and there were insufficient aircraft to tow gliders to Arnhem in one lift.[5]

Ian Toler's personal view of this order is recorded in his diary entry for 16 September:

> Our military plan is in general to remain with our loads until the situation stabilizes sufficiently for the glider pilots to be drawn into a central area.
> There is one rather doubtful point. I am told to take approximately twenty crews or one flight who land on the first lift, straight to Nijmegen to assist in the defence of Corps Headquarters. This is all very well but it is through twelve miles of enemy territory. I don't think it is 'on' and say so in no uncertain terms. Major Royle [Second in Command, 1 Wing GPR] agrees and we decide to remain with the unit until Division Headquarters is established and then to see how the land lies and whether it is possible to get to Corps.

The pilots of 20 Flight never left the Arnhem area to make what would have been an extremely perilous journey. In fact, Angus Low's flight was reinforced with half of 19 Flight, attached to the South Staffords and were involved in defending the LZ. The remaining half of 19 Flight were detached from Ian Toler's command and remained with their loads, accompanying the 6-pounders of 1st Airlanding Anti-Tank Battery RA. By coincidence, Ian Toler had commanded the same battery prior to becoming a glider pilot. The second lift would include more 'B' Squadron gliders, 3 and 4 Flights, which were both waiting at RAF Manston.

The pilots of Major John Lyne's 'D' Squadron were all allocated to the defence of Roy Urquhart's headquarters. Captain James Ogilvie, the Squadron Second in Command, attracted much attention from the photographers recording the landings, having flown to Holland wearing a kilt with his battledress; the Squadron Intelligence Officer, Lieutenant K.F. Strathern also wore a kilt during the battle. The two Scots were both photographed together with Iain Murray on 18 September on the junction of Kasteelweg (Breedelaan) and Utrechtseweg near Doorwerth. Captain Stanley Cairns commanded 13 Flight and 21 Flight was under Captain F.H. 'Bull' Barclay; the two flights had lifted from RAF Keevil with a combined total of fifty Horsa gliders.

John Lyne had lost five Horsas before crossing the Channel, one of which was due to the tragic and unexplained break-up of the Horsa over Paulton that killed Staff Sergeant Leonard Gardner and Sergeant Robert Fraser. The other four gliders were spread for various reasons between RAF Keevil, St Albans, Gosfield and Chalfont St Giles. A single 'D' Squadron Horsa flown by Staff Sergeant Ken Beard and Sergeant Geoff Tapping had been forced to ditch in the sea off Walcheren, while a further two had made forced landings elsewhere in Holland. The exploits of Staff Sergeant Cram and Sergeant Whitehead, and their Polish and Dutch liaison officers, were recounted in the previous chapter. However, the fate of the majority of the missing crews remained a mystery to their squadron commander, who had managed to regroup over 130 pilots and was now focussed on their deployment.

After landing, 'D' Squadron had taken on two main tasks. 13 Flight was deployed to Wolfheze where it assisted in the defence of Divisional Headquarters. The pilots of 21 Flight were split into two sub-units, one group reinforcing Captain Stanley Cairns and 13 Flight in Wolfheze, and the other protecting the guns of 1 Battery, RA. The second lift would bring in three more flights of glider pilots, bringing the Squadron up to its full strength. The reinforcements would arrive from two separate locations: 5 Flight from RAF Blakehill Farm; 8 and 22 Flights lifting from RAF Keevil. Not everybody arriving at the 'D' Squadron RV did so without incident – Staff Sergeant Bob Cardy of 13 Flight took a less conventional route:

> We landed with no difficulty about 1.30 pm, eventually we arrived at our rendezvous. We had a little adventure between landing and reaching our rendezvous. One of the medical orderlies we carried said he knew the way to our rendezvous. So Sid Longworth and I took a lift. Unfortunately it turned out that the driver either took a wrong turn or was lost. So eventually we found ourselves on what we now know was the main road to Oosterbeek passing on the way two German Lorries, which had been shot up by other airborne troops who were now busy collecting up prisoners. Shortly after passing these vehicles we saw what appeared to be a German motorcycle and sidecar with a machine gun mounted and it was decided that we were really going in the wrong direction so we turned back from where we came.[6]

As Iain Murray gathered the pilots of 1 Wing GPR together and took stock of his situation, the *coup de main* force was finally assembled and waiting to set off on its mission, however, as the 9th (Airborne) Field Company RE Jeeps had still not arrived at the RV by 1530 hours, they were held at the RV. 'Freddie' Gough was keen to get his column out of its assembly area and onto route LEOPARD. By 1540 hours it was decided that the Recce Squadron could wait no longer for the Sappers and with Lieutenant Peter Bucknall and 8 Section in the lead, the *coup de main* Jeeps left the LZ via the Wolfheze level crossing.

The Recce crews were well drilled and keen to press on to their objective. After negotiating the crossing they turned right onto the sandy but solid track known as Johannahoeveweg. The track stretched out before them running parallel to the railway embankment and they began to move eastward along it with the high embankment on their right.

The column now had some freedom to manoeuvre and immediately began to move tactically. Each troop was broken down into sections comprising pairs of Jeeps that 'leapfrogged' each other in short tactical bounds using whatever cover was available. The troops themselves would also leapfrog each other and take a turn leading a leg of the squadron advance, the rear troops having responsibility for protecting the rear and flanks of the whole formation as it moved rapidly along.

As the column moved down Johannahoeveweg, with 'C' Troop leading the way, the sequence of 'leapfrogging' was just beginning to settle into its own rhythm, the lead pair beginning to follow the track down a gradual slope into a patch of open ground. The slope emphasized the height of the railway embankment and its tightly packed undergrowth further; across the open ground the track began to climb out of the dip and threaded between the embankment to the right and a low wooded ridge to the left.

At about 1600 hours Peter Bucknall broke cover to make another bound forward, taking his Jeep down into the dip and safely across to the other side; as he disappeared from view firing broke out beyond the trees just as the second Jeep in the pair crossed the clearing. As Sergeant Tom McGregor and his crew probed forward a series of flashes followed by a crescendo of noise erupted from the ridge to his front and the embankment to his right. German machine-gun and rifle fire swept the track, the open space framed by the steep embankment, the ridge an ideal site for an ambush. Trooper 'Dickie' Minns was immediately hit in the stomach and tumbled out of Tom McGregor's Jeep onto the ground. Lance Corporal 'Taff' Thomas and Trooper Reg Hasler reacted quickly, when ordered by Tom McGregor, to dismount from their seats and fight on foot. They found cover behind the Jeep and attempted to return fire, despite being seriously outgunned.

The fate of Peter Bucknall and his crew was unknown at the time and the crew of the second Jeep were pinned down near their vehicle. The remainder of the column was forced to halt and attempt to locate the German positions. The German positions to the left of the track were identified quickly, however, but Gough's troopers could not get forward into suitable fire positions to engage them due to enfilade fire from positions hidden high above them on the railway embankment.

The momentum of the dash for the bridge had been lost and the *coup de main* force was now stalled less than a mile from the LZ, with 'Freddie' Gough's headquarters a few hundred metres behind the head of the column. As he worked on a plan to outflank the German position the order to report to Roy Urquhart finally reached him. Assuming that the summons must be a matter of some importance, or that he was to be given new orders, he decided to leave the column and make the very short journey back to Divisional Headquarters on the other side of the level crossing. Leaving his Second in Command to deal with the ambush he departed at speed with a small escort of two Jeeps from 'D' Troop.

The German force blocking Recce Squadron's advance along route LEOPARD was 2 Company of SS Panzer Grenadier Depot and Reserve Regiment 16. This unwieldy unit title was shortened to 'SS Battalion Krafft', taking the name of its commander, Sturmbannführer Josef 'Sepp' Krafft. By coincidence, 2 Company of Krafft's battalion had already deployed for a day's field training using the woodland between Wolfheze and Oosterbeek early that morning. The training battalion numbered just over 300 officers and men, the majority of the trainees being untried in action, however 'Sepp' Krafft knew that an airborne landing was most vulnerable during its earliest stages. He entered the following in his unit war diary: 'We knew from experience that the only way to draw the teeth of an airborne landing with an inferior force is to drive into it.'

Krafft had alerted his complete battalion during the Allied preliminary air raids; they were therefore ready for action and reacted immediately when ordered to move out of Arnhem and Oosterbeek by Krafft's battalion headquarters. Led by experienced officers and battle-hardened NCOs, the young SS men quickly implemented their commander's plan to disrupt the British landings.

The Wolfheze Hotel became SS Battalion Krafft Headquarters; as the headquarters was establishing itself 'Sepp' Krafft ordered his 2 and 4 Companies to form a line of defence running from north to south just to the east of Wolfheze. He reinforced his companies with over a hundred more German troops collected en route to the defence line so that he now had over 400 men.

Although SS Battalion Krafft had no armour it was well equipped with machine guns, mortars and flame-throwers, so was a potent enough force to worry any airborne commander.

Having assessed the situation for himself, 'Sepp' Krafft had correctly concluded that an airborne landing on such a scale could have but one objective, the bridge at Arnhem. Using the intelligence available and his own knowledge of the ground, he identified four possible routes from the British LZs to the bridges in Arnhem, conluding that his battalion should block the two central routes into Arnhem. The training companies were ordered to establish a line running from a point just north of route TIGER, through Hotel Wolfheze along Wolfhezerweg, with a single platoon on the north side of the railway embankment. It was this northern platoon that was on the ridge ahead of the Recce column.

The Krafft Battalion blocking line was effectively in place by 1530 hours, at which time, 1st Parachute Battalion had only just been released from reserve and Gough's Jeeps were still static on the LZ. The swift and decisive actions of 'Sepp' Krafft had defeated the *coup de main* force before it had even left its RV; his men were also pushing patrols forward to the Landing Zones.

Luckily for Gerald Lathbury's 1st Parachute Brigade, Krafft's line did not stretch south over routes TIGER or LION, so the two lead parachute battalions advance would not be impeded by Sepp Krafft's enthusiastic men.

Although 'Freddie' Gough was also moving with haste, he and his small party arrived at Divisional Headquarters only to find that Roy Urquhart had just left hoping to catch up with Gerald Lathbury and his headquarters on route LION. He then drove from the Divisional Headquarters to the Airlanding Brigade Headquarters, in the vicinity of the Wolfheze level crossing, hoping to find his elusive Divisional Commander. It was close to the crossing that he met David Dobie, whose 1st Parachute Battalion, now released from its role in reserve, was finally on the move. As the two officers discussed the German blocking action that was preventing Gough's men from progressing along route LEOPARD, Dobie decided to bypass the ambush and go further north onto the Arnhem-Ede road and then press on toward his own blocking position north of Arnhem.

Immediately after briefing Dobie, 'Freddie' Gough set off at speed with his three Recce Jeeps along route LION to locate Roy Urquhart and find out why he had been summoned; he could then get back to his squadron who were still pinned down by their ambushers.

Roy Urquhart was mobile in his Jeep, ahead of Freddie Gough, travelling along the southern route, seeking out Gerald Lathbury's headquarters; he eventually caught up with the Brigade Headquarters column at about 1700 hours. They were following on behind John Frost's 2nd Parachute Battalion column heading east toward the bridges. Lathbury had, however, left his own headquarters to visit Lieutenant Colonel John Fitch and 3rd Parachute Battalion on route TIGER.

In the absence of Gerald Lathbury, Tony Hibbert, the Brigade Major of 1st Parachute Brigade, met Roy Urquhart when he arrived at the Brigade Headquarters. He remembered Urquhart shouting from his Jeep, urging the Brigade to move on as quickly as possible or the Germans would get to the bridge first. Urquhart then sped off in his Jeep to catch up with Lathbury and the 3rd Parachute Battalion. This frenzy of senior officer activity was directly attributable to a lack of radio communications and misinformation regarding the status of the Recce Squadron Jeeps.

Initially the decision by David Dobie to bypass the ambush on Johannahoeveweg appeared to be a good one – he knew that he must not allow himself to become bogged down in skirmishes that distracted him from his mission to the north of Arnhem. Eventually 1st Parachute Battalion began to shake out into formation and were moving north prior to swinging east and down onto the Ede-Arnhem road. Dobie had set 'R' Company off moving tactically ahead of the main column.

After progressing less than a mile up the road from the level crossing, German troops opened fire from concealed positions in the wood line ahead of 'R' Company. The paratroopers reacted decisively and immediately began to skirmish through the woods on either side of the road. They launched an assault up the left side of the road and, despite sustaining casualties, were quickly in among the German defenders. The core of this German force comprised Luftwaffe troops from Deelen airfield, but there were also some armoured cars from the Reconnaissance Battalion of 9th SS Panzer Division involved in the later phases of the action. As the battle to clear a route began to expand, 'S' Company began to be drawn in to support their comrades in the lead company. Again David Dobie attempted to bypass trouble and press on with the mission given to him by Gerald Lathbury – his battalion had to be in position to the north of Arnhem before nightfall. He ordered his companies to break clean of the battle in the woods and move eastward along the forward edge of the woods; once free of German interference they could once again attempt to drop down onto route LEOPARD.

The clean break appeared to be working and the paratroopers were beginning to make progress again. The lead elements of the Battalion had covered approximately 2,000 yards eastward when German fire again erupted from the trees ahead. The lead companies of 1st Parachute Battalion pressed forward once more, probing the German position in an attempt to break through or outflank this new obstacle in their path. Initial reports from the lead platoons informed David Dobie that the Germans were in the woods in unexpected strength. Collation of patrol reports produced an estimate of German strength to be in the region of five tanks, more than a dozen armoured cars and half tracks and at least a company of infantry. As this was not the level of resistance that had been expected, further patrols were mounted by the Battalion seeking a way around the German positions.

With Dobie's priorities changing as darkness began to draw in, his rear- link radio operator picked up a message from John Frost's 2nd Parachute Battalion. The message was an urgent plea for reinforcements and a much-needed resupply of ammunition, the content of the message confirming that all was not as it should be with Operation MARKET. The strength and ferocity of German resistance was of a much higher order than had been suggested prior to the landings – if the bridges were defended in the same manner John Frost would need significant reinforcement. Dobie decided that there was only one course of action available to him – he would abandon his original mission and now unrealistic objectives, and take his depleted battalion down to reinforce John Frost at the bridge.

Regrouping his battalion would not be straightforward in the darkness, particularly as 'R' Company had taken 50 per cent casualties and were still being pulled in from the initial battle with the Luftwaffe troops and the SS armoured cars. The casualties across the Battalion were in the region of 100 killed, wounded and missing. The remnants of 'R' Company were still not reformed by 0100 hours, so leaving guides behind to escort them along later David Dobie ordered his battalion to move off for Arnhem.

Later that night the Battalion's Australian Second in Command, Major John Bune, was ambushed and killed as he went back to guide a Jeep convoy carrying the seriously wounded. The Battalion's wounded did eventually get to British medical aid in the Oosterbeek area.

The formidable defences from which the 1st Parachute Battalion had received such a mauling were an advance element of 9th SS Panzer Division, the position they had bounced off being the northern shoulder of a German *Sperrlinie* (blocking line).

So ended a long and costly day for the men of 1st Parachute Battalion, who continued to creep east and south through the Johanna Hoeve Wood under the cover of darkness. After a series of violent encounters with German patrols they eventually emerged near the railway station in the north of Oosterbeek.

The 3rd Parachute Battalion, under Lieutenant Colonel John Fitch, had left DZ 'X' before their sister battalion at 1500 hours. As planned they had initially moved through Heelsum following route

TIGER, with 'B' Company in the lead setting a fast pace. The lack of opposition on the route was fortunate as the terrain prohibited movement in loose tactical formations. There were high garden fences along the road side interspaced with crowds of waving and cheering Dutch civilians, so the paratroopers could not see beyond the immediate vicinity of the road. In that congested landscape John Fitch's battalion was strung out in a column roughly a mile in length – shortly after the tail-end platoon finally began to get into a marching rhythm, the lead platoon was approaching the crossroads formed by Wolfhezerweg and Utrechtseweg.

The Platoon Commander, Lieutenant James Cleminson, was confronted with a totally unexpected sight: a German Citroen staff car suddenly appeared moving at speed from the direction of Wolfheze. As the staff car turned left towards Arnhem the men of 5 Platoon reacted instinctively and poured a torrent of rifle and Sten gun fire into it; the occupants had no chance to evade or return fire and were all killed. The first casualties inflicted by 3rd Parachute Battalion were notable as they included the Arnhem District Commander, Generalmajor Friedrich Kussin.

The General had just left 'Sepp' Krafft's Battalion headquarters at Hotel Wolfheze, where he had been briefed on the dispositions of the SS Training Battalion. 'Sepp' Krafft had warned the General of the likelihood of British troops using the same road and advised him to take a less direct route back to Arnhem. But General Kussin had insisted he had no time to waste and, ignoring the advice, he drove to his death. Hundreds of British airborne troops would pass by the bullet-riddled wreck of the staff car and the corpses of its occupants as they moved along route TIGER.

There was, however, little time to ponder who the high-ranking German officer in the staff car was as 'B' Company resumed its advance toward Oosterbeek. At the next crossroads, serious and unexpected German resistance was encountered in the form of a self-propelled gun, supported by infantry. The German armoured vehicle drove straight into the head of the British column, knocking out a PIAT in the process; with the anti tank weapon out of action the lead platoons had no choice other than to scatter. The men of 'B' Company threw everything they had at the advancing German vehicle. Major Peter Waddy, the Company Commander, even tried to set it alight by firing a flare at it from his Very pistol!

During the ensuing fierce firefight the German vehicle was joined by two armoured cars which managed to destroy two Jeeps and a valuable 6-pounder gun, before they and the self-propelled gun withdrew under an increasingly uncomfortable weight of fire from the paratroopers. Peter Waddy set about regrouping his company who were dispersed in fire positions all around the crossroads; once he had done this he resumed his advance east on route TIGER. The German vehicles were part of a mobile patrol from 9th SS Panzer Division who had been ordered to block the main routes into Arnhem.

While 'B' Company had been locked in their struggle with the rampaging SS vehicles, Gerald Lathbury had finally caught up with 3rd Parachute Battalion. He made contact with John Fitch in the vicinity of the crossroads and urged him to bypass German opposition so that he could maintain momentum towards his objective in Arnhem. With the intention of doing exactly what his brigade commander had ordered, John Fitch ordered 'C' Company, under Major Peter 'Pongo' Lewis, to peel off from the Battalion to the north and attempt to loop around behind any German positions that might be forming ahead of the Battalion's current position.

Peter Lewis wasted no time and had 'C' Company moving into the woods to the north by 1745 hours. Moving quickly along Breedelaan, they then turned right and moved east following the railway line toward Oosterbeek Station. This method of advance worked well, 'C' Company emerging at the railway station in Arnhem at about 2130 hours and making a dash for the bridge. As they moved through the town they ploughed through groups of Germans, leaving burning trucks, half-tracks and armoured cars in their path. After one of the most aggressive and costly attacks of the battle, Peter

Lewis and less than two platoons of his men finally linked up with John Frost and his 2nd Parachute Battalion at about 2300 hours, a truly remarkable feat.

With the remainder of 3rd Parachute Battalion still attempting to push through Oosterbeek and on into Arnhem on route TIGER, Jimmy Cleminson and 5 Platoon were at the head of 'B' Company as they probed into Oosterbeek, where he and his men entered and searched the Hotel Hartenstein at about 1800 hours. They found a well-stocked Officers' Mess in the hotel, with the table set for lunch – not knowing where or when they would next eat, 5 Platoon took advantage of their good fortune and tucked into a very late lunch.

To the west of Oosterbeek, and less than a mile from the Hartenstein, 'A' Company were now experiencing the attention of the Germans – as they moved through the crossroads they came under German mortar fire from the Bilderberg woods. As it rained down on the crossroads, Roy Urquhart finally caught up with 3rd Parachute Battalion. His timing could not have been worse as his Jeep attracted German machine gun fire as he drove up. As the crossroads were overlooked by a German observation post (OP), the intensity of the mortar fire increased causing casualties all around the position. Roy Urquhart's driver and signaller were both hit during a particularly heavy mortar 'stonk'. The German troops so effectively hindering John Fitch's advance were another of 'Sepp' Krafft's forward companies – the SS trainees were once again in the wrong place at the wrong time for the British.

Major Mervyn Dennison, the Officer Commanding 'A' Company, took decisive action, launching a counter-attack into the Bilderberg woods to clear out the mortars. He sent two platoons out to locate the mortar tubes and destroy them; during the advance into the woods the German OP was located in a water tower and destroyed. The mortar position and some supporting machine-gun posts were also found and attacked by 'A' Company. At the end of the action the Company had taken twenty casualties after inflicting a similar number on the Germans, and had also taken eighteen prisoners. The attack had delayed the Battalion's advance, and by the time the Company had regrouped and rejoined the Battalion it was growing dark.

John Fitch now had the privilege of hosting both Gerald Lathbury and Roy Urquhart at his headquarters – having finally linked up with each other neither could leave as the Germans were established to the front and rear of their host battalion. Gerald Lathbury had radio communication with the other two parachute battalions, however, there was no radio link to Headquarters 1st British Airborne Division that Roy Urquhart could make use of to influence the battle. At 2130 hours the news from 2nd Parachute Battalion was relatively good – they had made it to the bridge and although they did not hold both ends, it was intact and they were firmly ensconced around its northern end.

With the lower route to the bridge reported still clear, Tony Hibbert recommended to Gerald Lathbury that 3rd Parachute Battalion drop down from route TIGER onto route LION and move to the bridge under cover of darkness. However, Lathbury disagreed and decided that 3rd Parachute Battalion would stay in its current position and move on to the river road before first light. Both senior commanders were forced to stay with John Fitch and his battalion, remaining isolated from their headquarters and staff. Other than 'C' Company, who were proceeding with great energy along the railway line, 3rd Parachute Battalion were now static with their forward platoons in Oosterbeek.

The southern thrust by 2nd Parachute Battalion had begun to move away from the DZ at 1500 hours – from the start John Frost had elected to strike out and maintain the fastest possible speed for the bridges. Major Digby Tatham-Warter was at the head of the column with 'A' Company, setting a rapid pace from the outset, with the lead platoons making short work of German patrols that were unlucky enough to stray into their path. John Frost had been given four 6-pounders from 'B' Troop, 1st Airlanding Anti-Tank Battery, RA; there was also a single gun from 'C' Troop that had not made it to 3rd Parachute Battalion with the rest of its parent troop. The guns had been carried to Arnhem by the Horsas of 19 Flight GPR, half of the flight now employed as a defence platoon for the guns. Consequently, Sergeant Arthur Rigby and seventeen other pilots were in the midst of Frost's battalion as it moved along route LION. He describes the scenes as the column progressed toward Arnhem:

> We passed some homes on our way and there were men digging their gardens and mowing the lawns just as though it was quite usual to have an entire airborne division drop in on a Sunday afternoon and not to cause too much fuss. We arrived at our rendezvous and sorted ourselves into a column.
>
> We were the last vehicles in the line, sort of 'Tail-end Charlie's'. Hardly was there time to settle when coming down the road toward us was Staff Sergeant Clenaghan, herding about twenty-five German prisoners along with him. Apparently he had landed close to the railway line on the landing zone and had found these 'Jerry's' in a little hut drinking their mid-day bevvies, and they had surrendered to him without a murmur. First blood to us.
>
> Around 4.30 p.m. we were starting to move off toward Arnhem, some 8-10 miles away. It transpired that of the two routes into the town we were taking the road closest to the River Rhine, which led through Oosterbeek. It wasn't long before we started to travel into the populated areas. It was like a royal progress, men, women and children were standing along the pavements and in their front gardens, throwing posies of marigolds to us, giving us apples and bottles of wine, shouting 'Welcome, Welcome, four years we have waited', shaking our hands, little boys running along with us their faces shining.
>
> We stopped at a road junction and a young woman came up to me. She was carrying a little girl of about two years old in her arms. She spoke a little English and she asked me if the war was nearly over and how were things in England. I told her it wouldn't be long before peace returned and she cried. The little girl was somewhat scared by my appearance and she did not respond to my friendly approaches.
>
> The column did not stop again until we arrived in the village of Oosterbeek, quite a pretty little place with nicely situated well built houses, mostly of a bungalow type. The village stands raised above the fields, which slope down to the river and away across the fields, we could see the railway on an embankment, crossing the Rhine by way of a large iron cantilever bridge. It was still Sunday, quiet, no opposition had been met and not a shot had been fired so far. Quite a number of cattle were grazing in the fields around the village. Some Royal Engineers and infantry were sent off to the bridge and railway, but after a very short time a sharp fight developed.[7]

The infantry referred to by Arthur were the men of 'Dickie' Dover's 'C' Company, supported by Sappers from 9th (Airborne) Field Company, RE, who had peeled off from the Battalion just after Oosterbeek Church. Their mission was to secure their objective, known as CHARING CROSS, the railway bridge. Once the bridge was in their hands, 'C' Company were to cross onto the southern bank of the river and turn east towards the southern end of the road bridge. While this was in progress 'B' Company were supposed to carry on behind 'A' Company, until they came to the pontoon bridge. Having secured the pontoon they would then cross the river by pontoon and follow Dickie Dover and his men on to the southern ramp of the road bridge.

The events of the afternoon did not, however, go according to Gerald Lathbury's plan. As Lieutenant Peter Barry led 9 Platoon down towards the railway bridge, the platoon climbed to the top of the embankment, where he sensibly dropped off two of his sections to give him covering fire if required. Approaching the bridge at the head of his lead section, he moved onto the bridge itself; there was still no German fire.

Ordering a smoke grenade to be thrown to screen his advance, as the smoke poured from the grenade Barry began to run across the bridge with his men behind him. Having covered 50 yards until they were no longer screened by smoke and seeing how exposed they now were, the section went to ground. As they considered their next move, the Germans detonated the demolition charges that they had placed on the bridge to prevent its capture. The centre section of the railway bridge collapsed into the river – with CHARING CROSS gone, there would be no crossing by 'C' Company.

To make matters worse German machine-gun fire now swept the remaining span of the bridge, hitting Barry in the arm and leg. The section abandoned their position on the bridge and escaped down an access stairway. Arthur Rigby heard the demolition charges blow:

> We could hear rifle and machine-gun fire across the fields, angry fire for the first time since our arrival. Suddenly there was a tremendous roar of explosives and the railway bridge began to collapse in a wall of dust and smoke, and no doubt some of our chaps went up with it if they had made the distance to the bridge as was intended. The strange thing was the effect the explosion had on the cattle and horses which had been grazing around the area of the bridge. They appeared to collapse and were all lying on their sides as though dead. Immediately after this occurrence there was quite a dangerous delay. Quite obviously the officers in the column were taken by surprise by the sudden appearance of enemy resistance after the quiet start of the operation, and it was some little time before there was any forward movement.[8]

With the demolition of the railway bridge, the situation on route LION changed dramatically. 'A' Company were just beyond the railway bridge when they were engaged by German armoured cars firing from the road ahead. There were also a number of well-placed German positions on Den Brink, a piece of high ground to the left, which now began to pour fire down onto the road. A 6-pounder at the head of the column was swiftly brought into action and began to engage the German armoured cars, while 'A' Company continued to move forward using the surrounding houses and gardens for cover.

John Frost adapted his plan and ordered 'B' Company up off the road and onto Den Brink to clear out the German positions. This they did, led by Major Doug Crawley, their attack allowing 'A' Company and the rest of 2nd Parachute Battalion to continue their advance relatively unhindered towards the bridge. Frost's headquarters followed on in the wake of 'A' Company, passing dead Germans and burning vehicles as they edged ever closer to the prize of WATERLOO, the main road bridge. Behind Frost came Tony Hibbert and 1st Parachute Brigade Headquarters. Freddie Gough had finally located Gerald Lathbury's headquarters, and decided to remain with it and push on with 2nd Parachute Battalion to the bridge.

While the parachute troops wrestled with unexpected opposition, Lieutenant Colonel John Place had successfully moved off LZ 'S' and established Headquarters 2 Wing GPR in a house at the corner of Duitsekampweg and Lindeboomlaan. He and his men were under command of 'Pip' Hicks and were an integral part of his plan to secure the LZs for the second lift. Elements of 2 Wing GPR were already tasked to establish themselves in defence immediately after rallying at their respective RVs. John Place supervised the concentration of 2 Wing with a depleted command team – he had already lost Ralph Maltby in the air and his Regimental Sergeant Major, 'Mick' Briody, had also failed to arrive on the landing zone for reasons unknown to Place at that time. The RSM had suffered a broken tow rope over Essex and had made an emergency landing on the American airfield at Great Saling; he and Staff Sergeant Marshall, with men from 17 Platoon, C Company, of the Borders, would join the second lift.

The concentration of 2 Wing happened with little interference from the Germans. Staff Sergeant Ronald Gibson had supervised the removal of the tail from his glider. After half an hour of struggling, brute force assisted by liberal use of an axe and dogged infantry determination had triumphed over wood and steel. The men of the Borders had successfully unloaded their Jeep and trailer. Throwing their packs onto the bonnet, Ronald and his co-pilot 'Sim' had hitched a lift across the LZ to the Borders' RV, on the corner of a triangular wood in the south-west corner of LZ 'S':

A party of about sixty glider pilots were lying under the trees: others were patrolling the path by the railway. It had been planned that we should rendezvous in squadrons and march off separately towards the town park, where we would dig in for the night ... A few yards from a level crossing a sniper's bullet whizzed overhead. We jumped off the path and lay flat in the hollow between the ploughed furrows and the turf bank. Two scouts were ordered forward. At this moment the colonel walked up and ordered us to wait. I lay back, pillowed against my rucksack. 'Sim' began talking to a Dutch boy who had appeared from behind the trees ... The scouts returned with our first prisoner. He was a grey-faced little man, dressed in a shabby uniform with a peaked cap. He did not seem frightened – only a little dazed from the interruption of his Sunday afternoon.[9]

Wally Holcroft and his 14 Flight comrades were also waiting among the Borders, the flight having originally been designated as the 2 Wing reserve:

From a cottage close by, the occupants came out to greet us with apples and pears, which they distributed freely amongst us. They seemed very pleased indeed to see us and though a difficult conversation took place, laughter and smiles quickly overcame the language barrier. Some of 'F' Squadron gliders had brought in members of the 'Border Regiment' and soon the twelve pilots concerned were all present. Among them was 'Admiral' Dicky Banks, (so called because he had served in the Maritime Anti Aircraft Artillery), Staff Sergeants Dodd and Tobin and Sergeants Hogg, Davison, Graham and Parkinson.

The commanding officer of the Borders was a Scottish Major, a splendid officer whom we had already met back in England for a brief chat about the operation. Now he quickly gathered his platoon commanders about him and issued orders for the next move. We had to march about two miles to take up positions to cover the arrival next day of still more gliders and paratroops. It was quite warm now and the sun shone from a cloudless sky. Carrying a sixty-pound rucksack on my back I found the going somewhat strenuous and my clothes clung to me with sweat. A good portion of the journey lay over open country and we passed hundreds of parachutes, which had been left behind by the paratroops. The Dutch people were making hay while the sun shone, so to speak, for they were industriously engaged in gathering up the parachutes and making off with them whilst the going was good.

We met no opposition from the enemy as we moved along, it was difficult to realise this was the real thing and not some simple exercise back home, though here and there we passed the wreckage of one or two gliders. We saw several members of the Glider Pilot Regiment whom we had known in earlier days, we exchanged a little friendly banter and pressed on.

When we arrived at our destination the Officer Commanding detailed the glider pilots to defend a small area overlooking the landing field for the next day's arrivals. It was sheltered from the air by a small copse and we wasted no time in getting down to digging a few slit trenches. The time was 6 pm.

After we had prepared our positions to his satisfaction, Staff Sergeant Dodd, our Flight Sergeant, gave us permission to brew up. We took out our ration packs and made ourselves a meal, which proved a great success though I found myself regretting having left a packet of sandwiches back in the Glider. We had rations for three days, made up into little packages, each sufficient for one day. In addition we each had a small Tommy cooker for heating water, and twenty cigarettes. All the food was dehydrated and the most amazing concoctions emerged from mysterious looking little cubes.[10]

The 'F' Squadron pilots remained with the Borders at their RV until there were enough glider pilots present; they then set out for the 2 Wing RV, crossing the railway line from the western end of LZ 'S' before emerging at the northern edge of DZ 'X'. They then followed the railway line east across the top of LZ 'Z', using Parallelweg, until they crossed back over the railway at the level crossing next to Van Beeck Calkoen School. Once back on the northern side of the railway they had a short march on the road leading to Reijerscamp Farm and the Wing RV at its intersection with Duitsekampweg. Their subsequent move into defensive positions on the eastern side of Wolfheze made use of Duitsekampweg and Johannahoeveweg, passing through the heart of Wolfheze to their new position in the wood line.

The situation at the Recce Squadron ambush site had changed little during the afternoon, despite the efforts of Gough's men to dislodge or outflank the SS troops blocking their way. Sergeant Tom McGregor had been killed by machine-gun fire and the rest of his crew had all been wounded. During the skirmish, the burning wreck of Peter Bucknall's lead Jeep had also been seen surrounded by dead bodies. The wounded survivors from the second Jeep had been taken prisoner by 'Sepp' Krafft's men and all except 'Dickie' Minns, who was too badly injured to be moved, were taken back behind the German positions into captivity. After about two hours, the Recce Squadron was forced to withdraw with a number of fresh casualties under its Second in Command to its start point to seek new orders.

The forward position of the Recce Squadron on Johannahoeveweg was to become part of the Airlanding Brigade perimeter around the second lift. 'F' Squadron GPR had been given the wood line close to the ambush as part of its area of responsibility. Captain 'Robbie' Robson led the men of 16 Flight GPR east down the sandy track (Johannahoeveweg) that the Recce Jeeps had used earlier in the afternoon. During their move 16 Flight were harassed by sniper fire and strafed by German aircraft, eventually occupying the wood line from where they could see Tom McGregor's lifeless body close to his abandoned Jeep. The flight could not see Dickie Minns who, despite his wounds, had managed to crawl under the Jeep; he would not be recovered until later the next day.

The glider pilots were not only involved in a firefight with SS troops who attempted to block their advance, they were also subjected to some well-directed heavy mortar fire. Despite the German fire, the withdrawal of the Recce Squadron began at about 1830 hours. Subsequently a number of Panzergrenadiers, who had been acting as snipers, were taken prisoner. Staff Sergeants George Milburn, Joe Kitchener and 'Duffy' Edwards were given the task of moving the SS men back to the Military Police in the Brigade Admin Area in Wolfheze.

With 'Robbie' Robson's flight now firm and overlooking the ambush site, the remainder of 'F' Squadron, under the command of Major Tony Murray, occupied the rest of the wood line at Johannahoeveweg, with arcs of fire watching east and south towards Oosterbeek. Sepp Krafft was now concerned that his small unit was being surrounded by a much larger airborne force and ordered his men to withdraw to the north, which they did successfully from about 2130 hours that night.

The war diary of 2 Wing GPR records a change of headquarters location at 1800 hours. John Place and his command team moved into Wolfheze to a house at the junction of Mesdagweg and Wolfhezerweg. By 1830 hours, 2 Wing GPR had concentrated and was occupying positions around Wolfheze facing west and south-east, with a detachment at the wood north of the railway, near to the tunnel under the railway.

If the explosion in his cockpit and the death of Ralph Maltby had rattled John Place, the Dubliner was not allowing it to show. He was directing the movement of 2 Wing with his characteristic coolness and the assured air of a veteran. Situation reports were arriving in to the Wing Headquarters from the GPR squadron commanders.

Major 'Dickie' Dale and 'C' Squadron were to act as the 2 Wing reserve. About sixty strong, they moved into positions on the southern edge of Wolfheze, south of the railway line and overlooking two roads that entered the village from the south of Heelsumseweg and Wolfhezerweg. The Squadron's sixteen or so Hamilcar pilots had deployed, with the 17-pounder anti-tank guns they had carried, all over the divisional area. The second lift was scheduled to bring in reinforcements from Tarant Rushton, in the form of a further fifteen Hamilcars and their crews. 'Dickie' Dale was reinforced by 14 Flight from 'F' Squadron on the Sunday afternoon and, like all of the squadron commanders, was expecting his detached men to regroup with him after twenty-four hours.

To the north of the railway and left of 'C' Squadron, Peter Jackson had led close to a hundred 'E' Squadron pilots from their RV along Duitsekampweg to its junction with Wolfhezerweg. From here they had dispersed into defensive positions. The bulk of the 'E' Squadron force comprised 11 Flight GPR, commanded by Captain Gordon Mills. They were operating in the infantry role, with the task of guarding the south-western approach into Wolfheze and blocking any threat from the direction of Oosterbeek to the LZs. The rest of the Squadron consisted of 12 and 25 Flights, their arrival being staggered across the second and third lifts. As he directed his squadron into their new positions, Jackson remembered seeing the prisoners taken by the King's Own Scottish Borderers after a successful initial encounter with the Dutch SS.

The first prisoners were brought in shortly afterwards, large blonde men, who claimed they had been held as political prisoners, but it was not long before they were sitting amongst their guards chatting and smoking their guards' cigarettes. Such is the British Army.

Firing was then heard for the first time from a distance and a recce party was dispatched. At one house they spoke to the occupants and a bar of chocolate was given to the small boy of the family. He evidently did not know what it was and the mother explained that he had been born during the occupation and had never seen chocolate. It was about this time that we had our first sight of the Germans when an enemy armoured car appeared round the corner, stopped, fired a few rounds which fortunately missed and for some unaccountable reason pushed off.

Our people then pushed on in the direction of Arnhem and came across the railway. There they saw a magnificent spectacle, a Flak train, which had been bombed to blazes by Fortresses the day before, with the gruesome sight in addition of the German gun crews bespattered about the place. Further along were what had been the almost palatial barracks of the SS troops, before the attention paid to them by the Fortresses. Here there were numbers of dead Germans lying in the grounds most of whom had a Luger pistol placed in their hand. The Luger in each case was wired to a mine and would have been a painful surprise to any souvenir hunter.

The surviving SS troops had evacuated themselves in such a hurry that they had left the constituents of their next meal untouched. As these consisted of steaks and potatoes, the Glider Pilots made a very satisfactory meal themselves. The Squadron headquarters was established in a magnificent house, which had belonged to a Dutch collaborator and was well stocked with brandy and cigars, and being Sunday evening and so far very peaceful, those who could enjoyed a comfortable hour or so.[11]

The situation around the landing zones was certainly less fraught and confused than the testing series of events that had befallen 1st Parachute Brigade during its drive to seize the three bridges. The landing zones did not, however, escape German attention by any means. The Headquarters of the 1st British Airborne Division had initially set up in the woods to the south of Wolfheze, the divisional war diary recording its establishment at 1415 hours. At about 1630 hours the woods were shelled by German mortars, Staff Sergeant Victor 'Dusty' Miller and a small group of 24 Flight pilots had been out on a foray away from their trenches, attempting to locate the source of some German small-arms fire. Their return and the proximity of their trenches were timely:

Hardly had we reached our slit trenches when I heard sounds that froze me to the spot. They resembled the noise of a car in a high speed skid. Whoosh, whoosh, whoosh. Three times, one after the other, each followed by a faint whistle, mounting quickly to a screaming roar. By that time I was at the bottom of my slit trench.

The first rushing missile plunged into the earth about fifty yards away with a shaking explosion. The ground trembled and the sand cascaded down the sides of the trench. The second and third missiles wailed down close behind; again and again the earth shook. More sand spilled down my neck, I heard the sound of falling branches. An acrid smell floated across the clearing. I started to raise my head, but jammed it down again, as the enemy mortars sent a second trio of mortar bombs off with a spine-chilling screech. Again the faint whistles grew louder and louder. Again the angry screams and explosions. This time they fell a little further away. The noise of falling masonry indicated that they must have hit the asylum.

Almost before the sounds of the explosions had died away, a third batch of bombs shrieked down. The earth rocked once more, causing a further sandslide in my slit trench. I tried to force myself deeper into the soft earth while shrapnel rained down outside. A silence descended over the wood. The smell of burning reached my nostrils.

Peering over the trench rim, I saw flickering flames and smoke from the direction of the asylum. 'The swine, the bloody swine', I thought to myself. I sat up on the edge of the slit trench and wiped the sweat off my brow.[12]

Concern about future shelling, the danger of wood splinters and fire resulted in an order to relocate the headquarters after last light. The Royal Artillery had a more direct method of dealing with the German disruption of activity on the landing zones. The Germans had used Nebelwerfer, multi-barrelled mortars known to the British as 'Moaning Minnies', to fire into the British positions. Some of the rounds landed close enough to the light gun positions to warrant a response from the British gunners. A counter-shoot was mounted before last light, Lieutenant K. Halliday RA, a Forward Observation Officer (FOO) with 1st Airlanding Light Regiment, RA, directed the British 'shoot'. He was escorted by two pilots from 14 Flight, 'F' Squadron; Sergeant Peter Gammon was one of them:

It was not until the evening that we saw any of the enemy and that was from a distance when my first pilot Staff Sergeant Ron Jones and I acted as guards to a Forward Observation Officer and his signaller directing gun fire onto a large building set in its own grounds. The Germans were evacuating in obvious panic (this building was Wolfheze Hotel I learnt later). Except for the unfortunate inmates of a mental home which had been bombed in the morning and who were now wandering aimlessly about, all the local inhabitants had retired to their cellars. The air attack had also set fire to a house and it was uncomfortable in these initial stages to watch it burn in the night without anybody doing anything about it. We dozed that night in a garden shed.[13]

Although the artillery shoot was observed to have had some effect on the Germans, there could be no guarantee that further shelling would not take place that evening. The plan to relocate Divisional Headquarters was implemented after last light. With Sepp Krafft's mortars located only 300 metres south of the hotel building, British artillery fire was very close to its intended target.

When darkness began to fall at about 2000 hours, the men of 24 Flight GPR were tasked with defending the headquarters. Led by Robin Walchli, they moved out into the open space of LZ 'Z'. 'Dusty' Miller was among the pilots as they moved across the ploughed field; he and his co-pilot, Sergeant Tom Hollingsworth, carried the extra burden of the Flight's PIAT and its ammunition. Finally, after negotiating a path through the dark hulks of abandoned gliders, they were directed into their new position:

> Near the centre of the field we halted and the officer explained that we would be spending the night here as it would be safer out of the woods, in case the enemy started to shell the place during the night, as undoubtedly he knew we had moved in there during the afternoon. I was assigned a section of men and told to start digging in.[14]

Victor worked with Tom Hollingsworth and Sergeant Arthur Webb digging their new trenches as 24 Flight formed a laager position around the Headquarters. The Headquarters staff moved out of the woods and spent the night operating out of empty Horsas protected by the glider pilots.

Sergeant Brian Tomblin, of 12 Flight, E Squadron, was determined that after a long and eventful day his first night on Dutch soil should not be spent in the type of discomfort being endured by 'Dusty' Miller and his comrades:

> That evening our Squadron ensconced itself in positions around a large Mental Hospital. Our Headquarters had been set up in a large house previously occupied by a Dutch collaborator – he lay dead in his own Dining Room. A few others and I had been detailed to guard a road junction near a side entrance of the Hospital, and we seemed to be surrounded on all sides by relatively thick woods. We found a nice house at this road junction, and upon wandering down to its cellar I found the floor covered in blood – the house seemed to have been previously occupied by a Doctor.
>
> By now it was my normal bedtime, and by mutual agreement we split up our duties for the night. It was my turn to sleep first, thank goodness, and upon going upstairs I found a lovely bedroom. A search of the dressing table revealed a pair of largish silk pyjamas. A few minutes later I was tucked up in bed in silk pyjamas, and agreed with myself that I had chosen the right operational unit. Good things never last, and what seemed a few minutes later, a chum telling me that there was German activity in the woods aroused me. A few minutes later I was feverishly digging my first foxhole on the front lawn in my borrowed pyjamas, but I had soon to get back into more suitable clothing for the occasion. We spent the remainder of the night 'standing-to' listening to strange night noises.[15]

Some of the strange noises heard by Brian and the 'E' Squadron sentries were no doubt due to the erratic wanderings of the patients from the Wolfheze Mental Hospital. The patients were inadvertently released from the relative safety of their wards when Allied bombing breached the walls of the hospital. A number of veterans recall the staff from the hospital searching the LZ in the darkness attempting to recover their confused patients and get them back into the relative safety of the damaged hospital. Victor Miller encountered both patients and staff from the Hospital while guarding Divisional Headquarters:

> Suddenly something white flitted through the trees. Darkness had almost closed in, making

visibility very poor. Another white-clad figure moved slowly forward and I felt my scalp tingle … I eased my Sten gun forward. I heard voices coming from the trees where the white forms had been, and then one of the queer figures appeared less than ten yards away. I strained my eyes and, as the figure drew near, I could see that it was old and bent. Watching closely, I allowed it to draw nearer.

I still could not make out exactly what it was except that it was human. The figure was laughing away to itself and, when it was less than ten feet away, the glow from the burning asylum lit up the features. A shock went through me, as the wrinkled face of an old woman was revealed. I stood up.

The figure drew back. I lowered my Sten and she smiled, then threw back her head and laughed insanely. By then I realised she must have been an inmate of the asylum. I felt a wave of pity for her.

Another figure appeared out of the gloom and I could see that she was a nurse. She called out to the woman, who ran off into the darkness, holding her long, voluminous skirts up as she did.

More voices came through the trees and a column of weird white-clothed men and women filed past my trench, silhouetted against the glow of the smouldering buildings. Several nurses were herding them forward. I was standing up outside my trench now and the nurses, as well as some of the insane, smiled warmly at me. Then they were gone, fading away into the night. I could not help but shiver as I sat on the edge of my hole.[16]

Not all of the numerous Dutch civilians who strayed into the British positions were as lucky as those encountered by Victor Miller. Lieutenant Mike Dauncey recalled a tragedy that occurred close to his 9 Flight position at the 3 Battery, RA gun line:

We had clearly taken the enemy by surprise. For most of the evening the only people we saw were those from the lunatic asylum, who were extraordinarily friendly. They all came out wearing nightshirts and kept shouting, 'Hello Tommy', which I thought was very endearing.

Our rendezvous was in scrubland, just south of the lunatic asylum. We were supposed to give local protection to the 3rd Battery. Major Munford, the Battery Commander, led the Battery through the wood to the main road.

There was some sporadic firing close to our RV and in the area of the gun position. We had to dig in to form a screen round the guns; we had some more small arms fire throughout the afternoon.

Major Croot then sent me out with a small reconnaissance patrol through the wood and generally in the direction of the Arnhem main road. It was late afternoon, early evening when we were fired on by a sniper. We fired back and pushed on. It was just getting dusk when I saw a group of men in the wood ahead of us. I started shouting the password, but there was no reply. I shouted again, and then we opened up. I had a Sten and I fired two rounds and it jammed. Discretion seemed the better part of valour. We took to our heels. I rather doubt if we hit anybody.

Later that evening, when it got dark, we had our first serious casualty. A voice was heard shouting, 'Hello Tommy' and we assumed it was our friends from the asylum. In fact it was a German who must have heard these cries earlier that day. Someone shouted back a reply and a German threw a stick grenade straight into his trench. It didn't kill him but he was badly wounded, and it certainly had the effect of sharpening us up a little. In fact, it was a long first night. I couldn't sleep at all.

The next person to hail us was machine-gunned. In the morning, I walked the 30 or 40 yards away from our positions and saw the machine-gun victim. An old woman, perhaps 50 or 60 years old, dressed in a long black dress or skirt, lying in an enormous pool of blood at the bottom of a small rise.[17]

Dutch civilians and psychiatric patients feature prominently in the majority of veteran accounts of the first day. Their acceptance of the damage caused to their homes and the civilian casualties as the price of liberation clearly affected and humbled many of the troops who landed that day.

The Allied bombing raids resulted in numerous Dutch casualties with Wolfheze Mental Hospital paying a particularly heavy price – forty-five men and thirteen women patients were killed. A further thirty-five medical staff and local residents were also killed by Allied bombs, and there were also a significant number of civilian wounded, these casualties making the fervent Dutch welcome even more remarkable.

Reg Grant was with Peter Jackson's squadron, dug in just south of the railway line close to the Wolfheze Mental Hospital. His account gives a good impression of the atmosphere around Wolfheze as darkness closed in and suggests that 'E' Squadron had positions on both sides of the railway line:

By nightfall, we were still in the village and as we were part of the force, staying in the vicinity of the landing zones to hold that area for further glider landings, we were ordered to dig in for the night. RAF bombers had reduced part of this village, with its neat villas, to heaps of rubble. We met the owners of some of these buildings who seemed pleased to see us, despite the destruction. Apparently there were hardly any Germans at all in the village, and they had taken the full brunt of the attack. Some of them were wearing bright orange rosettes and ribbons, and kept asking if we were going to stay. At that time things seemed to be going reasonably well and we assured them that we were.

Syd and I dug a roomy slit trench in the sandy soil, under some trees, in line with several others made by fellow pilots, and settled down to an uneasy night of waiting. Syd went on the scrounge amid the ruins of a nearby house, and came back with a bottle of port. The night was quite chilly and we were most grateful for the occasional swig from the bottle, which helped to keep us warm. The enemy patrols became quite active, and at times, bursts of fire close by made us grip our rifles and peer into the darkness ready to fight off any attack, but until one became imminent we kept very quiet.[18]

While Reg and Syd enjoyed the spoils of war and attempted to fend off the cold of the autumn night, Lieutenant Alec Johnston and a fellow GPR officer were probably less worried about keeping warm – they had more pressing and immediate concerns:

While the Squadron watched by night, Lieutenant Bill DeAshe and I spent a nerve-wracking two hours de-booby trapping a host of abandoned enemy trucks and cars. The vast majority were smashed beyond repair, but it proved possible to get a Volkswagen going following the removal of a door booby trap. The radiator had a hole in it the size of a cricket ball and it says much for the construction of the engine that it withstood a waterless 5 mile journey the next day laden with kit and stores (and, be it whispered, at least one 'bod').[19]

Away from Wolfheze there was little respite for John Frost and his 2nd Parachute Battalion, who were still fighting to maintain their momentum and get to WATERLOO, the main road bridge. With 'A' Company still spearheading the attack along the river bank they fought on, progressing steadily on after dusk, inflicting heavy casualties on the Germans and taking over forty prisoners as they went.

When the lead sections of 'A' Company came within sight of the huge road bridge at about 2000 hours, darkness was closing in, but the main prize was apparently within their grasp. As the paratroopers moved under the shelter of the bridge they could hear German vehicles moving freely back and forth across the river. John Frost ordered his troops forward into the large houses around the northern ramp of the bridge. 'A' Company quickly occupied fire positions in the houses and began to prepare them for defence. An initial attempt to seize the southern end of the bridge, led by Lieutenant Jack Grayburn, was forced to withdraw by the combined fire of a pillbox on the bridge and a German armoured car positioned further back on the bridge.

While Jack Grayburn reformed his platoon and recovered his wounded, the remainder of the 2nd Parachute Battalion set about securing the northern ramp of the bridge against counter-attack. Sappers from the 1st Parachute Squadron, RE worked under the bridge ensuring there were no German demolition charges in place, and John Frost established his headquarters in a suitable house. Amidst all of this hurried activity, Sergeant Arthur Rigby arrived with 19 Flight and the 6-pounder guns of the 1st Airlanding Anti-Tank Battery, RA:

> We arrived at the northern end of the bridge around 8.30 p.m. When the column of troops and guns arrived by way of the riverside road leading to the bridge, we were drawn up to the side of the Rijnkade, and all glider pilots were collected together and were marched off to Brigade headquarters.
>
> My co-pilot and I, however, never reached it, for as we approached the road leading to the headquarters our jeep and gun pulled up almost opposite us. The sergeant in charge told our Flight officer that he had been ordered to take the gun up the ramp to the end of the bridge and deal with a 'pillbox' strongpoint. As the gun would have to be manhandled into position, could he have some men to assist in the operation? Captain David Simpson detailed Healey and me together with three others.
>
> With the aid of the official gun crew, Sergeant Shelswell, Bombardier Lock and Driver Hodges, we shoved and pushed the gun and ammunition up the path from road level to a position at the end of the path looking along the bridge. We had also brought along with us the Bren gun with a box of magazines. I was No.1 and Healey was No.2. However on arrival in position Sergeant Shelswell sent his driver back to his jeep and told Ted Healey to go forward with Bombardier Lock and site the Bren gun to cover the road in front in case 'Jerry' attacked.
>
> He appointed me as loader on the 6-pounder while he acted as aimer and No. 1. We proceeded to pump shells into this strongpoint on the bridge, which was pouring out quite heavy fire in our direction. After four or five rounds from the 6-pounder the opposing fire died down considerably, and then apparently the flame-thrower went in. I saw the burst of flame from the flame-thrower and a cloud of black smoke surround the structure, and I heard the screams from the occupants. The 6-pounder gun was withdrawn very soon after this, but Healey and I stayed in position on the bridge until the early hours of Monday.[20]

The gun position selected by Sergeant Shelswell was no more than 100 yards from the pillbox so Arthur Rigby was certainly in a prime position to see the outcome of the flame-thrower attack. Although there were problems with the flame-thrower's ignition system, the pillbox was doused with unignited fuel and was finally set alight when a PIAT was brought into action. The PIAT bombs ignited the flame-thrower fuel and set fire to a wooden shed behind the German position. The assault party had not realized that the shed contained ammunition for the pillbox, so the resulting explosion was spectacular. The explosion also set the recently renewed paintwork on the bridge alight, robbing the British of the advantage of darkness and preventing any further attacks that night.

John Frost had much to think about that night – the railway bridge was blown and the pontoon bridge had been denied to him as the vital centre section had been secured by the Germans on the southern side of the river; his battalion was alone in Arnhem. 'B' Company, having cleared Den Brink, were now back down on the river bank near the pontoon bridge, and 'C' Company were involved in executing their secondary task to capture a German headquarters in the town itself. The burning paintwork on the bridge was of little use to the British, illuminating the bridge and thereby denying them the cover of darkness under which they could mount another attempt on the opposite ramp. Frost could not afford the time to reflect on how well his battalion had performed – he had much to consider before first light exposed his small force to whatever response the Germans in Arnhem could muster:

> 'A' Company had fought their way from the DZ for eight miles through thick country to capture the main objective, all within six hours of landing in Holland. They had accounted for over 100 Germans and several vehicles. The company now held the northern end of the bridge. I had hoped to take the southern end also, but 'C' Company had been foiled at the railway bridge; and now despite their gallant efforts 'A' Company had been prevented from crossing here. The fires on the bridge and the intense heat made any further approach impossible for the time being.
>
> My only hope was to find some boats and get across further downstream. I planned to get 'B' Company and the Brigade Defence Platoon over the pontoon bridge and at the same time to bring 'C' Company down from their attack on the German HQ in the town; but I had no wireless communication with either company, and anyway 'C' Company seemed to be heavily engaged. I sent Major George Murray, my senior sapper with a patrol to reconnoitre, but he soon reported there were no usable boats, and that the enemy were in a position on the far side of the pontoon bridge.
>
> So I decided that I must hold a tight perimeter around the north end, the important end of the bridge, and there await the arrival of the other battalions of the brigade the next morning, I hoped.
>
> The total force at the bridge at this time numbered no more than 600 men, although some more would come through later in the night. My battalion was without two companies. There was Brigade Headquarters but no Brigadier, about two troops of sappers, and almost two troops of the Airlanding Anti-Tank Battery, the Reconnaissance Squadron Headquarters, a Royal Army Service Corps platoon with Jeeps with ammunition from our DZ, and some Glider Pilots. A mixed force but all good airborne soldiers … It was evident we were up against SS Panzer troops – tough fighting soldiers; but my biggest worry was that we were out of touch with the rest of the division. The signallers in the top room continued to call throughout the night, but there was no response.[21]

With the paintwork on the bridge continuing to burn fiercely, John Frost's mind wrestled with his tactical options as he surveyed the bridge and the ground he held. The foremost question in his mind was 'where were Gerald Lathbury and the rest of the Parachute Brigade?' Gerald Lathbury was with Roy Urquhart at the headquarters of 3rd Parachute Battalion where, despite all of the setbacks, both men remained relatively optimistic of returning to the offensive at first light. The two British commanders elected to stay with 3rd Parachute Battalion Headquarters in buildings half a mile west of the Hartenstein Hotel. With John Frost's battalion group holding the northern end of the bridge, Urquhart felt he had one hand on the prize, but chose to remain with his lead brigade, close to the battle, with the intention of influencing the battle at first light.

The veteran Roy Urquhart had been unhappy with the quality and volume of intelligence material available to his staff. Although he was also sceptical of the optimistic intelligence predictions of light

| ARMY FORM C 2136 (Large) | **MESSAGE FORM** | | Register No. |
|---|---|---|---|

| Call | Srl. No. | Priority | Transmission Instructions |
|---|---|---|---|

ABOVE THIS LINE FOR SIGNALS USE ONLY.

**FROM**
(A)  GSO 1 (Air) Eastcote

Date-Time of Origin. 171705 A

Office Date Stamp

For Action.

Tac H.Q. British Airborne Corps

**TO**

(W) For Information (INFC)

Rear H.Q. British Airborne Corps

RAF Ops          IX TCCP

Message Instructions.   G R

Originator's No.

O. 494 ⊙ TOPSEC ⊙ MARKET ⊙ XRAY hour D plus one now postponed to 1400 hrs rpt 1400 hrs ZONE A due to weather ⊙ American resupply bombers will come in at end of main stream ⊙ All aircraft flying southern route ⊙ Todays aircraft losses U.S and British negligible ⊙ All aircraft report accurate drops ⊙ Gliders cast off before leaving U.K. being flown in second lift ⊙ GENERAL BRERETON sends heartiest congratulations

*This signal, issued late in the afternoon of D-Day, paints an optimistic picture of the situation on the ground. It delays the second lift from the early morning arrival directed by Major General Urquhart to an afternoon landing. This had serious repercussions on the ground in Holland where nobody was aware of the delay.*

German resistance during the build-up to the operation, he could not, however, have expected the strength and ferocity of the counter-attacks so soon after his division's first landings that afternoon.

The aggressive and apparently well coordinated German response to the landing of his division was a cause of great concern. The presence of German armour in such large numbers, and the obvious quality of its supporting infantry, suggested that these were not the static garrison formations identified in the pre-operation intelligence summaries. Indeed, the searching of prisoners and enemy dead confirmed the presence of Waffen SS troops in and around Arnhem and Oosterbeek. There was still, however, no definite indication of the strength of the German units in the immediate area.

Unbeknown to Urquhart, the 'hornets' nest' that 1st Airborne Division had literally dropped into contained some of Germany's most battle-hardened troops, and to make matters worse, two of Hitler's most able senior commanders were on hand to direct counter-operations. By a twist of fate Field Marshal Walter Model, the newly appointed commander of Army Group B, had selected the Arnhem area as an ideal location for his personal headquarters. He and his staff were located in the Tafelberg and Hartenstein Hotels in Oosterbeek, his task being to stabilize the western front. Arnhem, with its excellent road and rail links, coupled with its proximity to the German border and the front line, was ideally suited to his needs. The Headquarters of Army Group B had only moved into Oosterbeek forty-eight hours before the start of Operation MARKET GARDEN.

The same factors that had attracted Walter Model made the Arnhem-Nijmegen area an ideal location to rest and refit battle-weary German formations that were being reconstituted and prepared to stem an anticipated Allied drive on Nijmegen and the Ruhr. One German formation under Model's command much in need of respite was II SS Panzer Corps, under the command of Lieutenant General Wilhelm 'Willi' Bittrich. The SS panzer troops had suffered significant losses during the Normandy campaign and their subsequent withdrawal across northern France. On paper, Bittrich's corps consisted of two armoured divisions: 9th SS (Hohenstaufen) Division and 10th SS (Frundsberg) Division. At full strength, each of his divisions should have been able to amass close to 18,000 effective troops and 170 main battle tanks, but the remnants of Bittrich's corps that finally arrived in the Dutch province of Gelderland were nowhere near the strength or fighting power with which they had begun the Normandy campaign.

Immediately after arriving on 10 September, II SS Panzer Corps had established its headquarters in Doetinchem, 40 kilometres from Oosterbeek. As 'Willi' Bittrich began to take stock of his fighting strength, his staff reported that the attrition wreaked on his elite divisions had been significant. The 9th SS Division, commanded by SS-Oberststurmbannführer (Lieutenant Colonel) Walther Harzer, was the stronger of the two divisions, with 3,500 troops but only twenty of its original 170 Panther tanks; Harzer could also call on a mixed fleet of armoured cars, self-propelled guns and half-tracks. The Division was scheduled to return to Germany for a full refit after handing over its serviceable vehicles to 10th SS Division. Although a shadow of its full strength, 9th SS Division retained the full spectrum of a Panzer formation capability, with elements of armour, artillery, reconnaissance, engineers and most importantly, Panzergrenadiers. The Division had begun arriving in Gelderland on 7 September and was immediately dispersed to company sized bivouac sites between Arnhem and Apeldoorn. Walther Harzer was loath to hand over any of his precious armour to his sister division, deliberately ignored Bittrich's orders and instructed his men to immobilize their vehicles by removing wheels and tracks from them. The dispersed companies were designated as *Alarmeinheiten* – small independent combat teams that could react quickly to any Allied attack. This was a role that both divisions were well practiced in – prior to the Normandy landings II SS Panzer Corps had trained and exercised regularly in the anti-airborne role. SS Brigadeführer (Brigadier) Heinz Harmel, the commander of 10th SS (Frundsberg) Division, describes the training regime leading up to the Allied invasion:

The whole II SS Corps was especially trained over the previous fifteen months via classroom and radio exercises – all directed to countering a landing supported by airborne forces in Normandy. The training benefited us enormously during the Arnhem operation. At the lower end, NCO's and officers were taught to react quickly and make their own decisions. NCO's were taught not to wait until the order came, but to decide for themselves what to do. This happened during the fighting all of the time.[22]

The 10th SS (Frundsberg) Division reported its strength as 3,000 effective men; it had been severely mauled in Normandy losing most of its armoured vehicles to Allied air strikes. The depleted division was being regrouped on the Dutch-German border to the east of Zutphen. As well as lacking tanks and other armoured vehicles, the Division was handicapped by the loss of its Signal Regiment. The few surviving units included the divisional reconnaissance battalion, an armoured infantry regiment, two artillery battalions and an engineer battalion. All of those units listed as effective were desperately short of vehicles and were classified as partially mechanized.

Although battered and lacking vehicles, spares and trained replacements the combined strength of the two SS formations amounted to 6,000 highly motivated, veteran troops. In particular, the proximity of 9th SS Division to the British LZs and objectives was a major piece of intelligence that had been picked up by Bletchley Park using ULTRA. But this mission-critical information had not been disseminated as far down the chain of command as Roy Urquhart and his staff, so the appearance of these battle-hardened troops was a total surprise to all in the 1st British Airborne Division.

The presence of Walter Model and his staff right in the centre of the British landings had an almost catalytic effect on the German forces around Arnhem. The Field Marshal had been about to sit down to lunch as the leading waves of Allied transport aircraft and gliders approached their LZs. Within minutes of receiving warning of the scale and apparent destination of the airborne formation, the Field Marshal left the Hartenstein Hotel and drove at speed in his staff car to the Garrison Headquarters in Arnhem. After issuing orders to the garrison staff, who were recovering from an Allied air raid, he returned to his staff car and again ordered his driver to make best speed, this time in the direction of 'Willi' Bittrich's Corps Headquarters in Doetinchem.

When Model arrived at the SS headquarters at about 1500 hours, he found that Bittrich had already reacted to the news of the British landings and formulated a sound plan to counter them. Having quickly assessed the situation, the astute SS veteran had issued his first warning order to his Divisional Headquarters as soon as 1340 hours, only sixty minutes after the first British boots touched Dutch soil.

Bittrich had ordered 9th SS Division to secure what he logically assumed was the British objective, the main road bridge at Arnhem. The 10th SS Division was ordered to move south via the ferry at Pannerden to secure and defend Nijmegen. Once briefed on Bittrich's plan, Model quickly approved it, his executive approval giving II SS Panzer Corps freedom to manoeuvre without constraint against the landings. While the lead battalions of the British 1st Parachute Brigade were still in the process of assembling and preparing to leave their DZ, the SS commander had already taken decisive steps to counter the British landings.

One of the key components of 9th SS Division that was to hinder the advance of 1st Parachute Brigade was Kampfgruppe Spindler. It was this hastily formed battle group, led by the commander of the divisional armoured artillery regiment, SS Lieutenant Colonel Ludwig Spindler, that was blocking Gerald Lathbury's three-pronged advance. After nightfall Kampfgruppe Spindler had also taken 'Sepp' Krafft's SS Depot Battalion under command and was establishing a practically unbroken defence line stretching from the Ede-Arnhem road (route LEOPARD) in the north down to the banks of the lower Rhine in the south.

The troops of Kampfgruppe Spindler had formed a blocking line and moved through the streets of Arnhem from east to west until they reached the western outskirts of the town. Under cover of darkness the SS troops went firm and linked their positions so that John Frost's battalion, including the glider pilots of 19 Flight, were now behind the blocking line and cut off from the rest of their division.

Both sides waited impatiently for the coming of the dawn and the opportunity to seize the initiative; for most, it was a long and restless night.

**Notes**

1      Jackson, Major P., OC, 'E' Sqn, correspondence with Luuk Buist, 1991.

2      Wilson, LCpl A., 1 Border, 'When Dragons Flew', by permission of Border Regt Museum, p. 105

3      Holcroft, SSgt W., 14 Flt, 'F' Sqn GPR, 'No medals for Lt Pickwoad', September 1945.

4      Dauncey, Lt, M, 9 Flt, 'G' Sqn GPR, interview with the author, February 2008.

5      Low, Captain A., 20 Flt, 'B' Sqn GPR, correspondence with Luuk Buist, from 1991 onwards.

6      Cardy, SSgt R., 13 Flt, 'D' Sqn GPR, correspondence with the author, 2007.

7      Rigby, Sergeant A., 19 Flt, 'B' Sqn GPR, by permission of *The Eagle*.

8      Rigby, Sergeant A., 19 Flt, 'B' Sqn GPR, by permission of *The Eagle*.

9      Gibson, SSgt R., 16 Flt, 'F' Sqn GPR, *Nine Days*, Ilfracombe, Arthur Stockwell Ltd, 1956.

10    Holcroft, SSgt W., 14 Flt, 'F' Sqn GPR. 'No medals for Lt Pickwoad', September 1945.

11    Jackson Major P., OC, 'E' Sqn GPR, by permission of *The Eagle*

12    Miller, SSgt V., 24 Flt, 'G' Sqn GPR, *Nothing Is* Impossible, Bury St Edmunds, Spellmount Ltd, 1994, p. 98.

13    Gammon, Sergeant P., 14 Flt, 'F' Sqn, correspondence with the author, 2007.

14    Miller, SSgt V., 24 Flt, 'G' Sqn GPR, *Nothing Is Impossible*, Bury St Edmunds, Spellmount Ltd, 1994,  p. 98.

15    Tomblin, Sergeant B., 12 Flt, 'E' Sqn GPR, correspondence with Luuk Buist, 1991.

16    Miller, SSgt V., 24 Flt, 'G' Sqn GPR, *Nothing Is Impossible*, Bury St Edmunds, Spellmount Ltd, 1994, p. 100.

17    Dauncey, Lieutenant M., 9 Flt, 'G' Sqn GPR, interview with the author, February 2008.

18    Grant, SSgt R., 'E' Sqn GPR, by permission of *The Eagle*.

19    Johnston, Lieutenant A., 'E' Sqn, correspondence with Luuk Buist, 1991.

20    Rigby, Sergeant A., 19 Flt, 'B' Sqn GPR, by permission of *The Eagle*.

21    Waddy, J., *A Tour of the Arnhem Battlefields*, Barnsley, Pen & Sword Ltd, 2001, p. 65.

22    Kershaw, R ., *It Never Snows in September*, Hersham, Ian Allan Ltd, 1990, p. 41.

# CHAPTER 8

# The Fog of War

*'It was now eleven o'clock and we were getting a bit anxious about the second lift.*

**The morning of Monday, 18 September 1944**

When dawn finally broke John Frost and the 2nd Parachute Battalion were still firmly ensconced around the north end of the Arnhem Bridge. Soon after first light, a small convoy of German soft-skinned vehicles and trucks had inexplicably driven through the German lines and attempted to cross the bridge. Arthur Rigby and his fellow pilots were involved in stopping the wayward German vehicles from progressing any further:

> We could see vehicles approaching at quite a rapid pace from the south side of the Bridge and the firing stopped. (I thought that XXX Corps, the troops that were to link up with us from Nijmegen had arrived) but before there was time to settle back someone shouted 'They're Jerries' and there was no doubt that they were.
>
> Every machine gun and rifle opened fire and absolutely chopped the vehicles to pieces. The leading wagon turned off the road and crashed into the parapet of the Bridge, the ones behind either collided into each other's rear or stopped any way they could. One very brave German soldier leapt out of the cab of a crashed vehicle and dashed across the road through this hail of fire and jumped up on to the parapet wall about twenty yards from where I lay. With a revolver in either hand he proceeded to pump bullets in every direction. Fortunately, he didn't last for very long before he was cut down or he might have inflicted quite a lot of damage.
>
> One of his victims was a young lad who lost his nerve and dashed across to my slit trench and promptly fell in on top of me shouting 'I've been bloody hit' over and over again. He had a rather nasty wound in the upper arm. Ted and I placed his field dressing on it and sent him off to find the Regimental Aid Post.
>
> Very soon the whole scene at our end of the Bridge was like an inferno and a firework display as the lorries which had tried to cross the Bridge caught fire and blazed away. The ammunition they had been carrying was exploding and sailing up into the night sky like so many rockets.
>
> In general, the firing between the opposing forces died down considerably and around midnight we heard a voice calling for 'Glider Pilots to reform over here'. Ted and I quickly made our way towards the direction of the voice and found Lieutenant Cole at the end of the path with two or three others of our Flight, including Charlie Watson. It seems we were detailed to stand as sentries at Battalion headquarters, which had been established in what appeared to be some sort of municipal buildings. Well, I was placed near the entrance gate

and now it all seemed unreal, dream-like, for it was quiet again, very little firing at all, an occasional burst of machine gun fire, sometimes the enemy and then our boys. You could tell which was which; the German MG 34 had a much faster firing rate than the Bren. I had only been on sentry for about an hour when I was relieved and was told to report back to the jeep. On arrival there I found Ted and Charlie and all our gun crew still intact. Nobody seemed to want our services for about an hour so I had a little 'kip'.

I was woken up to find Captain Simpson and about a dozen blokes from our Flight. His news was that we were to carry out a patrol of the area and try to find out what was going on, mainly because there was little or no radio contact with neighbouring elements. By this time it was just starting to get towards dawn and it was possible to see one's way around. We had searched the buildings and yards (it was a sort of furniture factory), and found nothing and no one, and we were just on our way out. I was tail end Charlie, and some yards behind the main party; on passing some wooden screens I suddenly heard a faint clatter. When I looked behind these screens, there was the oldest soldier I have ever seen. He must have been seventy years old and he quite obviously had no intentions of getting involved in any war-like proceedings, for as I approached him he had already laid his rifle on the ground (that probably was the clatter that I first heard). He immediately made signs that he was surrendering. Then he walked up to me with tears in his eyes and said very quietly 'Kamerad'. I took him prisoner.

There were no other incidents during the patrol, and we returned to the headquarters in broad daylight. Captain Simpson went inside to make his report and to hand my prisoner over for interrogation, and on his return, he collected about a dozen Glider Pilots who were in the headquarters, making our party up to about twenty-five. He then told us that we were to man a house on a strategic corner and off we went to find this place. It was a gorgeous house beautifully furnished and carpeted, fine glass china in cabinets, heavily upholstered chairs and settees, great soft cushions. All was smashed up to strengthen the defences; cabinets and furniture were pushed up to the windows to the sound of breaking glassware. Cushions were emptied of their soft contents and filled with earth from the garden to make sandbags and when the ground floor was completed we moved upstairs to carry out the same work.[1]

The soft-skinned vehicles were easy meat for the paratroopers around the northern ramp; a few stunned survivors were taken prisoner. Ironically the unfortunate convoy belonged to one of the V2 missile batteries that the airborne assault was intended to drive out of Holland. The prisoners, although shocked, successfully concealed their specialist role from their captors, admitting only to being conventional artillery gunners.

Later in the morning German armour and infantry began to probe the British defences from the east, they had little success apart from a solitary Panzer that penetrated as far as the underside of the northern ramp. The Panzer was knocked out by a 6-pounder anti-tank gun, the Royal Artillery gun crew probably being assisted by pilots from 19 Flight GPR.

At about 0900 hours, vehicle movement was seen at the southern end of the bridge, initial thoughts among the defenders being that XXX Corps had made good time and were about to link up with the 2nd Battalion from the south. The vehicles were in fact elements of the 9th SS Division Reconnaissance Battalion, under command of Hauptsturmführer (SS Captain) Viktor Gräbner. The mixed force of thirty armoured cars, half-tracks and trucks had been despatched south to locate any Allied airborne landings in the area of Nijmegen, and had crossed the Arnhem Bridge only an hour before Frost and his troops had secured the northern ramp.

Viktor Gräbner was confident that his force had the firepower to deal with lightly armed airborne troops quickly and effectively. He was returning to Arnhem with the intention of clearing the main road bridge; racing ahead of his main column was a troop of five armoured cars. This advance force approached the bridge at speed and weaved through the burnt-out wrecks of the dawn convoy. The sudden appearance of the fast-moving German vehicles caught the anti-tank gunners by surprise, the wrecks also providing Gräbner's men with some cover. All five vehicles forged on over the northern ramp into the town itself, only one suffering damage from a British mine.

The defenders were now 'stood to' and prepared for any further German assault as Gräbner and his main force approached the southern end of the bridge again at some speed. There was no hesitation from the British this time – as the column moved closer to the British positions a maelstrom of fire was unleashed from every British position. The full range of weapons available to 2nd Parachute Battalion was brought to bear on the SS men. Staff Sergeant George Baylis of 'B' Squadron was in the Arnhem Water Board building overlooking the north ramp: 'The big attack in armoured vehicles from the south side degenerated into shambles as they were knocked out by 6-pounders and PIATs, their crews were potted as they jumped out attempting to escape. I vividly recall thinking it was like shooting at clay pipes or moving figures at a fun-fair shooting gallery.'[2]

The guns of the 1st Airlanding Light Regiment, RA were also directed onto the German vehicles as they careered across the bridge weaving between already burning vehicles. The effect of 75mm howitzer fire on open-topped half-tracks and soft-skinned trucks was terrible, as mortars and small-arms added their weight of fire and completed the nightmare for Gräbner's men. The Reconnaissance Battalion thrust lost its momentum and the survivors fell back to the southern side of the bridge. There were now another twelve burning wrecks on the bridge, Viktor Gräbner had been killed and seventy SS men were listed as casualties.

The German pressure on the northern bridgehead continued throughout the morning as infantry continually probed the airborne perimeter and well-directed mortar fire dropped onto British positions. When John Frost made the decision to withdraw 'B' Company from their increasingly isolated position at the pontoon bridge, they took a number of casualties executing the withdrawal into the perimeter. As the day progressed the Germans increased their pressure on 2nd Parachute Battalion, using mobile flak guns to pour fire into the British-held buildings from across the river and using conventional artillery fire against any likely British positions. The threat of snipers became almost ever present and claimed many defenders lives as, apart from a few signallers and medics, every soldier within the perimeter was now involved in its defence.

While 2nd Parachute Battalion held on to its enclave around the bridge, the remainder of 1 Parachute Brigade did their best to break through and reinforce their fellow paratroopers. The 1st and 3rd Parachute Battalions were on the move before dawn, their intention being to break in and reinforce the bridgehead before the arrival of the second lift early that morning.

The remnants of 3rd Parachute Battalion moved in darkness along Utrechtseweg, through Oosterbeek following route TIGER, before heading south onto route LION. The column was initially unopposed and made good progress, covering over 2½ miles. As the lead platoon crossed the railway line and reached the Rhine Pavilion on the river bank, things were beginning to go wrong at the rear of the Battalion. As the level of daylight grew, German snipers began to harass the column from positions in treetops and machine guns became more active.

With the weight of enemy fire beginning to increase, the column separated into two halves, with the bulk of the support weapons in the rear half. Roy Urquhart and Gerald Lathbury were both at the front of the Battalion with 'B' Company. It was approximately 0700 hours and with the protection of darkness long gone, a clear conflict of interests now manifested itself between the two airborne commanders. The Divisional Commander wanted to be back at his own headquarters when the second lift landed, while Lathbury was desperate to head in the opposite direction to be with his lead battalion on his brigade's main objective, Arnhem Bridge.

As the morning progressed, the 1st British Airborne Division situation became more confused. Roy Urquhart could wait no longer and decided to attempt to get back to his headquarters. Gerald Lathbury and two officers, Captain W.A. Taylor, the Intelligence Officer of the 1st Parachute Brigade, and Lieutenant Jimmy Cleminson, commanding 5 Platoon, B Company, 3rd Parachute Battalion, escorted him part of the way, but at some point they became separated from the main body of 3rd Parachute Battalion. Cut off from any British troops the small group was forced to hide in a Dutch house from advancing German troops. Urquhart's instinct to get forward to a position where he could influence the battle had backfired on him.

After initially hiding in 135 Alexanderstraat, he and Gerald Lathbury, accompanied by the two junior officers, attempted to evade the advancing Germans. To make matters worse, Lathbury had been badly wounded and could not be moved. With more German troops closing in on the house, Urquhart had no choice other than to leave him in the care of the Dutch householders.

The General was then trapped in the attic of Anton Derksen and his family at 14 Zwarteweg, very close to St Elisabeth Hospital. He would remain frustrated and cut off from his division and the battle, with no means of communication, for the next fifteen hours.

The 1st Parachute Battalion had not stopped moving during the night. They had, however, found it impossible to break through the German positions on their original axis, having been blocked by Kampfgruppe Spindler, and were at the northern limit of the German sperrlinie. The Battalion turned south and, led by Major Ronnie Stark and 'S' Company, moved under cover of darkness through Oosterbeek. At about 0430 hours their lead platoons approached the bridge over the railway at Schelmseweg where they came under heavy machine-gun fire from Den Brink and were engaged by armoured cars. They were once again blocked by 9th SS Division in the shape of Ludwig Spindler's Kampfgruppe.

Faced with another well-established German blocking position, David Dobie continued his battalion's move south and directed his troops to turn south-east away from Den Brink. The 1st Parachute Battalion now attempted to find a gap or a weak spot where it could force its way through to John Frost's men. They were now probing along route LION on the lower road. Both 1st and 3rd Parachute Battalions would spend a fruitless day desperately throwing themselves against the line held by Kampfgruppe Spindler.

The repeated attempts to break through to the bridge were extremely costly and by last light both battalions were effectively reduced to a fighting strength of less than 100 men.

Away from the struggle to reach Arnhem Bridge, 'Pip' Hicks and the 1st Airlanding Brigade were preparing for the arrival of the second lift. The 7th Battalion King's Own Scottish Borderers were defending DZ 'Y' (Ginkel Heath), the 2nd Battalion South Staffords were defending LZ 'S', north of the railway line, and the 1st Battalion of the Border Regiment was defending LZ 'X'.

During the course of the morning, the Germans mounted several attacks against the landing zones. The Borders had an eventful morning, 'D' Company successfully repelling a series of probing attacks at the southern end of LZs 'Z' and 'X'. They called down 75mm artillery fire from the guns of the 1st Airlanding Light Regiment, RA, to break up the German attempts to overrun the vital landing zones.

The German troops facing the Borders were elements of Kampfgruppe von Tettau, another battle group named after its commander. General Hans von Tettau was a capable infantry officer who had supervised the training of German troops in Holland and had been ordered by Walther Model to form a Kampfgruppe from his command in order to put pressure on the British landing zones from the west.

Kampfgruppe von Tettau was initially quite small and comprised units of varying quality. The units committed to attack the Borders' positions on the morning of 18 September were SS Battalion Schulz and the Soesterberg Fliegerhorst Battalion. The latter battalion had been formed from redundant Luftwaffe ground personnel and was in the process of being converted to the infantry role.

Both were beaten off by the dug-in glider-borne infantry. Other units grouped under General von Tettau's command were mainly static guard battalions, coastal defence regiments and training schools. Hans von Tettau's command would continue to grow in size and capability as the battle progressed.

Approximately a mile away from the main Borders' defensive positions, 'B' Company had occupied and fortified the brickworks in Renkum. At 0700 hours, unaware of the British presence, Naval Manning Battalion 100 began to move through the small village. At the optimum moment 'B' Company, supported by mortars and Vickers machine guns, opened fire on the unsuspecting and inexperienced sailors. German casualties were high and 'B' Company were subsequently embroiled in a struggle to hold their position against increasing numbers of Germans for the rest of the morning.

The 7th Battalion King's Own Scottish Borderers had also experienced an eventful morning, their Commanding Officer, Lieutenant Colonel Robert Payton-Reid, was an officer of the old school who was determined that his battalion would hold on to the DZ 'Y' whatever the Germans threw at them. He and his men were to have their resolve tested to the full as the day progressed.

In fact, many of the 'Germans' opposing the Scots were members of SS Wach Battalion 3, a Dutch volunteer formation commanded by Hauptsturmführer (SS Captain) Paul Helle. The Borderers had already encountered Dutch troops on the Sunday afternoon, when the well-equipped glider-borne troops had made short work of the Dutch volunteers and had taken a number of prisoners. The skirmishes today would not be so one sided.

The men of 16 Platoon, 'D' Company were positioned some distance from their own company positions, having been tasked with holding a group of huts on the north-eastern corner of DZ 'Y'. The position in the huts was not ideally suited for defence and the presence of Dutch civilians inside the huts further complicated the situation. The isolated platoon was attacked and overrun by 5 Company of SS Wach Battalion 3. The unequal but fierce battle resulted in seven dead from 16 Platoon, with the survivors being taken prisoner. The Dutch SS now held a strong position from which they could overlook the majority of 4th Parachute Brigade's DZ.

Possession of the western side of the DZ was also in dispute, with 'B' Company of the Borderers, commanded by Major Michael Forman, being subjected to a series of determined attacks by SS Wach Battalion 3. The Company was already under strength as 7 Platoon's glider, flown by Staff Sergeant Hadin and Sergeant Blenkinsop of 'E' Squadron, had been forced to cast off over England. After a very bumpy emergency landing, during which the undercarriage was ripped off their Horsa, the Platoon found themselves in the grounds of Abingdon Asylum. Although the glider was badly damaged, there was only one casualty in the Platoon – the Platoon Commander's batman suffered a broken leg, but everybody else, including both pilots, walked away from the wreck. The Platoon managed to get back to their airfield and joined the second lift.

The initial encounter between the Scots and the Dutch SS had been one sided, 'B' Company having caught the Dutch mounted in their vehicles. The Scots used their anti-tank guns, commanded by the redoubtable Sergeant George Barton, to initiate their attack and then followed this up with machine-gun and rifle fire to complete their attack. There were few if any Dutch survivors. Later in the morning the Dutch mounted further determined attacks that were broken up by 'B' Company using artillery and mortar fire.

The size of DZ 'Y' had forced Robert Payton-Reid to disperse his companies over a wider area than he would have preferred, but the imminent arrival of Shan Hackett and his brigade was expected to ease the situation and allow the Borderers to regroup and move off the drop zone.

'A' Company of the Borderers were deployed on the eastern side of the drop zone well away from their sister companies. The Company Commander, Major Robert Buchanan, had had to detach 4 Platoon to overlook Amsterdamseweg on the north-eastern edge of the drop zone and the isolated platoon had been subjected to probing patrols by German units during the night. The Scots had ambushed two patrols and inflicted heavy casualties on them, but the Germans reacted quickly.

Under cover of darkness German infantry mounted a series of assaults against 4 Platoon, until finally overwhelming the hard-pressed Scots at dawn on Monday. A few survivors evaded capture and made it back to 'A' Company's position some miles to the east. The main 'A' Company position was also attacked repeatedly during the course of the morning, but the position held firm, inflicting heavy casualties on the Germans.

The Borderers were under increasing German pressure, with three platoons now missing or captured, and they spent the rest of the morning locked in a struggle to maintain their hold on DZ 'Y'. The planned arrival of the second lift was still some hours away, but Robert Payton-Reid was confident his men were up to the task.

While the airlanding battalions grappled with German attacks of increasing intensity, news of Roy Urquhart's disappearance had reached Brigade Headquarters at about 0730 hours. This development, coupled with the news that Gerald Lathbury was also listed as missing, was to have a dramatic effect on the dispositions and tasks of the airlanding battalions. 'Pip' Hicks, although the oldest but most junior brigadier in the Division, was now the senior officer in Arnhem and the staff officers at Divisional Headquarters requested he take command of the Division.

Command of 1 Airlanding Brigade was quickly handed over to the Deputy Brigade Commander, Colonel Hilaro Barlow, and 'Pip' Hicks moved to Headquarters 1st Airborne Division at 0900 hours. By this time Divisional Headquarters had moved from the shelter of the abandoned gliders into the woods west of Oosterbeek, close to Utrechtseweg and the site of the Kussin ambush. Command of 1st Airborne Division was assumed on a temporary basis by Hicks at 0915 hours.

Shortly after the change of command had taken place at Headquarters, 1st Airborne Division, fresh orders were issued to Lieutenant Colonel Derek McCardie and two companies of the South Staffords, who were to leave theirs defensive positions around LZ 'S', reorganize for an advance and break through to 2nd Parachute Battalion on the bridge.

After conferring with his new Chief of Staff, Lieutenant Colonel Charles Mackenzie, Hicks decided to reinforce McCardie with the remainder of his own battalion as soon as possible after the arrival of the second lift. This would add the weight of 'A' and 'C' Companies to the drive on the bridge, as well as the firepower of the outstanding half of Support Company. With the second lift due to arrive over the drop and landing zones from 1000 hours onwards, Hicks hoped that the weight of 4 Parachute Brigade would give him the impetus to break through to John Frost and the bridge.

The need to break through Spindler's blocking line and reinforce 2nd Parachute Battalion was viewed as critical to the outcome of the battle. As a result, a thorny decision was made. Immediately after the drop of 'Shan' Hackett's 4 Parachute Brigade, 11th Parachute Battalion would be removed from his command and ordered straight into Arnhem.

The 2nd Battalion South Staffords were now clear of their original positions, and were formed up and on the move toward Wolfheze by 0930 hours. As they moved off Padre 'Chig' Chignell, the Chaplain of 2 Wing GPR, buried four soldiers including Privates Grewcock and Higgins of the South Staffords. Their grave took the form of a recently abandoned 3-inch mortar pit at Reijers Camp.

The change of orders for the South Staffords presented Ian Toler with a choice: should 'B' Squadron remain in place or go with Derek McCardie's battalion? It did not take the tall Cheshire gunner long to choose his course of action – he elected to join the Staffords' column and follow on, with the intention of reaching Headquarters 1st Airborne Division.

The pilots of 'B' Squadron, like all of the GPR, had been issued with large rucksacks packed full of extra equipment, ammunition and rations. As they were not supported by their own integral quartermasters, each individual crew had to be entirely self sufficient. The rucksacks were not ideally suited to tactical movement and presented a problem for Ian Toler and his men, the challenge being quickly overcome with typical GPR ingenuity. The Squadron had already deployed scavenging parties around their local area and Ian Toler instructed them to search particularly for vehicles. The words in his diary were 'we mean to be mobile':

Lockwood and Chadwick turn up with a Bren carrier which they have salvaged from a Hamilcar … When the time comes the problem of the rucksacks is almost impossible. The carrier comes in very useful and a Jeep which pulls three trailers and one handcart is unbelievable unless you see it. We move off at the rear of the column, cross the railway at Wolfheze, which has been bombed heavily. The Dutch people wave to us and seem quite at home. We see two German snipers who have been captured in their camouflaged suits.[3]

The South Staffords' column moved through Wolfheze with 'D' Company leading, Support Group and Battalion Headquarters in the centre, and 'B' Company to the rear. As 'B' Company passed through the small town they were joined by 13 and 14 Platoons, bringing the South Staffords up to an all-up strength of 420 men. Staff Sergeant Jim Hooper had remained with 13 Platoon since landing and was now in the same column as the rest of his 'B' Squadron comrades:

Sergeant Johnson and I marched with the Platoon and during the trek from Wolfheze to Oosterbeek we were strafed by low flying Me 109s, luckily we suffered no casualties … When we arrived at Oosterbeek the reception we received from the recently freed Dutch townsfolk was both joyous and tremendous. Sadly we could not stop to enjoy the hospitality offered and pressed on with all speed to our objective.[4]

The pilots of 9 Flight GPR were not on the move, having spent the night at Wolfheze protecting the light guns of 3rd Battery, 1st Airlanding Light Regiment, RA. The day for them, like a number of the troops around the landing areas, had started well. The morning is remembered by most as a pleasant one, the start to Sergeant Tom Owen's day being typical of many around the landing zones:

This being the first time most of us had been in action and we were most considerate of Dutch property. Early on the second day a number of our Flight occupied a Dutch house, which as you would expect of the Dutch, was very clean and tidy. The occupier had left a bucket full of eggs in preservative so we helped ourselves and had a damn good breakfast. Being good soldiers we cleaned up all our mess including brushing the mud off the stairs. We had just finished our good deed when Jerry blew the house down on top of us. We weren't so considerate after that.[5]

The scheduled arrival of the second lift and the planned move of Divisional Headquarters triggered the move of Iain Murray's 1 Wing Headquarters. He and his small staff moved from Wolfheze to their new position astride the Arnhem-Utrecht road at Kasteelweg. With daylight came a noticeable increase in the number of casualties travelling west on the road from the direction of Arnhem. The sound of small-arms fire and support weapons was now almost constant from the same direction.

Later that morning, 9 Flight moved with 3 Battery, RA into a new position. The Battery moved into what was to be its final gun position by Oosterbeek Church and completed its first fire mission from there at 1000 hours. From this new location the light guns were in range of John Frost and 2nd Parachute Battalion, and they were used to deadly effect against the 9th SS Division's Reconnaissance Battalion shortly after establishing their positions. The Battery also engaged German mortar positions that were disrupting the advance of the 1st Parachute Battalion.

Since the arrival of the first lift, numerous Dutch civilians had come forward to offer to assist their airborne liberators, although the majority of these volunteers were rejected. The British were reluctant to use the Dutch Resistance movement, initially refusing the services of Dutch guides and Resistance fighters. The past infiltrations of the Dutch Resistance by German agents and overconfidence in their own capabilities were the primary reasons why a multitude of volunteers were politely turned away.

One offer of direct support was witnessed by Jan van Hofwegen, a Dutch teenager whose family owned the laundry in Oosterbeek. He was naturally curious about the newly arrived gun battery now established in the fields close to his home:

> Four howitzers were placed in position behind the old church. Now and then they would fire in the direction of Arnhem. We talked with the gunners and were told they had been in North Africa and Sicily and one said laconically: 'Now we are here and in six weeks we will be in Berlin.'
>
> A Dutch man was observing the action of the battery and told an officer that he had been a Dutch artillery officer and offered his service, it was declined.[6]

At this stage of the battle the area of the church was only lightly defended, with 3 Battery RA digging gun pits while Glider Pilots provided local protection. There were also two 17-pounders and three 6-pounders of the 1st Airlanding Anti-Tank Battery, RA covering the road approaches through Oosterbeek.

Lieutenant Mike Dauncey was one of the 9 Flight glider pilots deployed near the church with the gunners:

> We were sent up the road east of the church and just west of the Railway Bridge and formed a line to protect the gunners. I had about six other glider pilots with me.
>
> We took over a house, which was once used by Germans. It stank … a terrible smell. They had left quickly. There was straw on the floor and a couple of billy-cans lying about. In the dining room was a picture of Hitler tacked on the wall. I tended to move about the area, up and down the road.
>
> Near the railway bridge, which had been blown the day before, I found a wounded Para who was being cared for by the Dutch. I helped to get the man to a dressing station and went on and met another Para firing a machine gun across the meadows near the river.[7]

There were also a number of adjustments made by John Place to the 2 Wing GPR positions. Peter Jackson's 'E' Squadron moved to the wood along the Wolfhezerweg, near a home for the blind, covering arcs from the north-west to north-east. Wing Headquarters moved to a house on Wolfhezerweg, just north of the railway line. Tony Murray took 'F' Squadron east, north of the railway, to a wood between Wolfheze and Johannahoeve to link up with the Reconnaissance Squadron. They were tasked with protecting the landing zone from positions on nearby high ground. Desultory German mortar fire was encountered, but otherwise the situation appeared stable. Jackson describes the morning's activity for 'E' Squadron:

The next morning news was received of the approach of the Germans and the Squadron disposed themselves in a wood and dug in and waited for their attack. In this wood was a large mansion, which was being used as a home for blind people.

Unfortunately the previous day it had suffered from the bombing but even this calamity did not seem to affect the welcome the inmates gave to our Forces. One old man who addressed me in broad Scots surprised me. He had apparently been living in Holland for 20 years prior to the war. His main concern was to know if the German reports were true that Aberdeen had been razed to the ground by flying bombs. His joy at the contradiction of this report was overwhelming.

He then turned to more personal topics and asked me how long I was in the country. I told him 'twenty-four hours' to which the old man with an expression of disgust replied, 'Been here twenty-four hours and not got a Dutch girl yet? Bah.' All this was of course in broad dialect.[8]

One man who had gained a reputation for charming the ladies back in England was Staff Sergeant Laurie Weeden, who now had little time to meet local girls. He had been detached from 'F' Squadron to act as a runner for Headquarters, 2 Wing GPR:

Whilst there appeared to be no enemy activity in our immediate area there were already rumours of considerable opposition having been encountered between Wolfheze and the bridge at Arnhem.

Our engineers had destroyed some German field guns, which had been left behind in Wolfheze, and I was sent off on a bicycle to the 1st Airlanding Brigade headquarters with a message confirming destruction of these guns.

Brigade headquarters was believed to be in the Heelsum/Renkum area, and I rode out across the Doorwerthse Heide into the outskirts of Heelsum. No one was about in Heelsum, but about half a mile down the long straight road to Renkum I could see troops, which I thought were probably Germans. A motor vehicle approached and I hurriedly hid in a hedge until it had passed, and I then cycled back towards Wolfheze.

When about half way back across the Doorwerthse Heide some fighter planes, which I had incorrectly assumed to be the Royal Air Force escort to the second lift, started spraying the area with machine gun fire. As I was under the distinct impression that one of them was aiming at me, I fell off my bicycle into the shelter of a deep ditch by the side of the track, which must have looked rather comical but was nevertheless very effective.

On returning to the Wolfheze area I was informed that Brigade headquarters was at Kabeljauw, where I ultimately delivered the message.[9]

Wally Holcroft and his mates in 14 Flight were also waiting expectantly for the second lift, which had been due to arrive overhead at around 1000 hours:

The airlift had still not arrived at eleven o'clock so we made some tea, and discussed the possible reasons for the delay. Down in the wood a soldier of the Borders was being buried, he had been injured the day before on landing and the poor chap had died during the night.

An Officer from Brigade Headquarters arrived and told us that the battle for the bridge was going fine and the Second Army was making good progress towards us from Belgium. This was great news, but Banks said he thought three 'Ops' like this one was enough for any man. As he had already been involved in two operations he was in a position to give an opinion.

We laughed at the 'Admiral's' remarks however and I reminded him that when we were in North Africa together, he had said that he intended to avoid any operations. He looked at me for a moment and said, 'We say a lot of things we don't really mean, don't we?'

As we talked, a bunch of German prisoners came marching down the road. Perhaps these were some of the fifty we had been told to watch out for earlier. The Major came out to have a look at them, and the sight of them sent him haywire. 'Get your bloody hands up' he roared and at the same time booted one or two of them in the pants. If they didn't understand the language they certainly knew what the Major was talking about for their hands shot up like a flash. There would be about twenty of them and the poor wretches looked terror stricken as they staggered along in dishevelled array. If this was a sample of the Wehrmacht I was not very impressed and the incident made me feel good.[10]

Padre George Pare had spent the early part of the morning searching wrecked gliders for injured or dead glider pilots. On returning to the site of 1 Wing Headquarters, he was surprised to find the position empty. Having broken the unwritten rule of allowing himself to be separated from his kit, George Pare paid the price. The Headquarters had moved off, taking his rucksack and first-aid pack along with it:

It was a blow to be without my kit but since the second lift was due at 1000 hours I was determined to stay.

All the men and vehicles were moving away from the Landing Zone southwards to the main road to Arnhem, but I found half a dozen Royal Engineers under the command of a competent sergeant, who had been in a crashed glider the day before, and who were being left for a time, as their nerves were not too steady. I joined them, the sun came out, the noise of battle, which seemed to have increased, was a long way off and everything round us seemed quite pleasant.

It was now eleven o'clock and we were getting a bit anxious about the second lift. Suddenly we all heard the drone of engines and rushed excitedly into the open. There were half a dozen fighters circling overhead. 'They're here!' we called. 'What are they, sir?' asked one of the men. 'Oh, Spitfires of course,' I replied confidently. 'Of course they're Spitfires,' echoed another, amazed that anyone could think otherwise.

The Sergeant remained silent. There was a moment's pause as we gazed upwards. 'I think they're Messerschmitts!' suddenly shouted the youngest, a young engineer of about eighteen. 'Oh! Can't be!' I exclaimed dubiously. The planes were now swooping down, one after the other. 'Quick – in the trenches!' yelled the Sergeant.

We needed no encouragement. We dived in, as the first machine roared over, its guns blazing. One by one the others followed. The droning died away and we crawled out feeling very shaken and most resentful. The Landing Zone was the worse for wear, for a few gliders were now burning furiously.

At last I could wait no longer, and as a jeep went by, begged a lift. I was taken by some roundabout route, eventually landing on the main Arnhem-Wageningen road, and caught up with Colonel Murray's party, which was awaiting a movement order. Everybody was asking about our reinforcements and nobody knew.[11]

Unusually for a chaplain, George Pare later submitted a situation report to 1 Wing Headquarters. He detailed the attack by the German fighters and the damage caused by fire to a number of gliders and to a farm near the landing zone.

Not all of the German strafing runs were unsuccessful as men of 'A' Company of the Borders

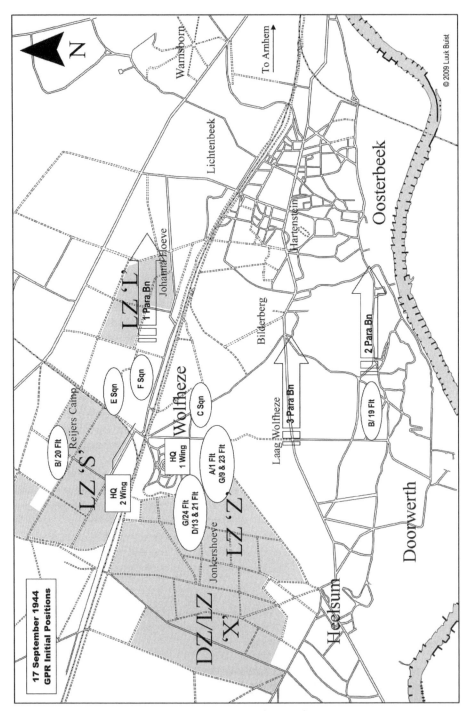

*GPR positions noon, 17 September 1944*

had also mistaken the German fighters for 'friendlies'. They had climbed out of their trenches to wave encouragement only to be met with a murderous hail of cannon and machine-gun fire. The Company reported twenty-one casualties: seven dead and fourteen wounded.

The Luftwaffe attacks on the landing zones coincided with the scheduled arrival of the second lift. Fortunately, a providential twist of fate resulted in fog and mist settling across southern England preventing the use of the Operation MARKET airfields.

The poor visibility in England resulted in a four-hour delay to the departure of the second lift, the transit across the North Sea adding a further three hours to the delay, so that it would eventually arrive over Holland much later in the day. The troops already in Holland remained unaware of the seven-hour delay to X-hour.

One can only speculate on the outcome of a determined German air attack breaking through the fighter escort to reach the lumbering columns of tugs, gliders and parachute transports. If such an attack had arrived shortly after the second lift was completed, it could still have been disastrous – an airborne landing is at its most vulnerable in its earliest stages as the troops rally and form up. Even a small number of ground-attack aircraft would have caused chaos if left to roam unhindered over the exposed troops on the landing areas. We will never know what might have happened, but it is reasonable to point out that the huge Allied fighter escort had been more than capable of protecting the first lift for the whole flight. Another fact worthy of note is that the sporadic Luftwaffe ground attacks did little to impair the progress of the 1st British Airborne Division on the ground, at this stage of the battle.

Thankfully, the English weather had played its part in ensuring the two components of this hypothetical disaster never met over Arnhem, although the Germans realized that a follow-on reinforcement lift, or at least a series of resupply drops, were almost certain to take place after the initial landings. Consequently, German anti-aircraft units were quickly repositioned along the most likely approach routes to the known Allied drop and landing zones.

The effectiveness of the Luftwaffe improved as the battle progressed, each subsequent lift and supply drop being met by more and more German fighters. Indeed, a myth has grown over the years that the Luftwaffe used documents recovered from an American glider south of Arnhem to synchronize their attacks with the Allied air plan.

It is true that a copy of the Allied air plan did find its way into German hands, but it only contained details for activity on 18 September. By the time the captured documents reached a high enough level in the German command chain to be of use, they were out of date. It is almost certain that after the first lift the Germans were aware of the Allied intent. They used their existing air-defence network and observers in the still occupied areas in the west of Holland to give advance warning of approaching Allied formations.

To the west of Oosterbeek, the second lift had not materialized as planned. Robert Payton-Reid made the following entry in the Borderers war diary. Despite the increasing weight of German pressure on the landing zones that morning, he remains optimistic:

1000 – The 4th Parachute Bde were due to make their drop at this hour and their appearance was anxiously awaited. At this time the situation was reasonably well in hand. 'B' Coy Gp were inflicting severe casualties on enemy parties on the main rd where at least six armd tracked vehs were knocked out by their atk gun and their occupants eliminated by the fire from MMGs. They were also mortaring and shooting up the Arty Barracks in EDE, and mortaring the wood at the NORTH of the DZ. 'C' Coy were covering the SW portion of the DZ and engaging any enemy seen in the open. On the EASTERN side there was the unknown factor of 'D' Coy, but they appeared to be containing the enemy, and Major

Hill's small force had the situation in hand in the SE. At the SOUTHERN end Bn HQ were holding a firm base.

Unfortunately, however, the aircraft did not appear at their appointed time.[12]

The lead elements of the South Staffords and 'B' Squadron had entered Wolfheze at about 0930 hours, the column negotiating the crowds of jubilant Dutch civilians and pushing on eastward toward Arnhem. The majority of the pilots involved in this march recall passing the grisly marker of General Kussin's bullet-ridden staff car, and then the generosity of the local population. Arthur Shackleton was with Ian Toler as they progressed toward Arnhem:

> We had salvaged a Bren Carrier from a crashed Hamilcar and we managed To cobble up its broken track with wire and rope, we took this with us. Whilst en route, we had various small fire fights. 'Busty' Baker found a motor cycle with a hole in the tank which we plugged with a piece of wood. Someone found a hand cart. These items we were going to use in our victory parade through Arnhem![13]

The South Staffords column moved steadily through Wolfheze towards Oosterbeek, meeting little resistance. A number of survivors' accounts remark on the combination of fine weather, the absence of Germans and the cheering civilians creating a peacetime exercise atmosphere. Companies marched at the regulation pace, resting for ten minutes after fifty minutes on the march; very few bodies and little wreckage littered the route.

The mood would change dramatically later in the morning when the remnants of 'R' Company, 1st Parachute Battalion, under Major John Timothy MC, were encountered. The men under his command included three young subalterns and a mixture of other ranks. Timothy could not give Derek McCardie's headquarters staff much firm intelligence on the situation to their front, other than the fact that the opposition was formidable and increasing in strength.

The paratroopers joined the rear of the South Staffords column with the intention of finding their battalion in Arnhem. The reorganized column moved off again, after replenishing the paratroops' ammunition pouches. The advance continued along Utrechtseweg into Oosterbeek, until 'D' Company was halted abruptly by machine-gun fire from north of the railway line.

German snipers were also targeting the South Staffords and more machine guns then opened fire from a wooded feature to the north, known as the Mariendaal. Major John Phillip and 'D' Company became embroiled in a firefight with the German positions and were no longer moving toward Arnhem. The South Staffords deployed platoons to outflank the machine guns with little success. Derek McCardie, aware that he only had two rifle companies, did not want to become bogged down in Oosterbeek, but he and his men would be delayed in Oosterbeek for some hours. Ian Toler and 'B' Squadron continue to move forward with the column, his diary entry describing the change in mood from the morning: 'We are now moving through the woods on the side of the road. There has been a battle here and bodies of dead Germans and our own troops are lying on the ground. My pilots are salvaging German weapons and ammunition, motorcycles and even a machine gun for future use.

**Notes**

1    Rigby, Sergeant A., 19 Flt, 'B' Sqn GPR, by permission of The Eagle.

2    Baylis, SSgt A., 19 Flt, 'B' Sqn GPR, by permission of The Eagle.

3    Toler, Major I., OC 'B' Sqn GPR, by permission of the Toler family.

4    Hooper, SSgt J., 20 Flt, 'B' Sqn GPR, interview with the author, February 2008.

5    Owen, Sergeant T., 9 Flt, 'G' Sqn GPR, correspondence with Luuk Buist, 1991.

6    Hofwegen, J.A., citizen of Oosterbeek, diary entry, 16 September 1944, by permission of The Eagle.

7    Dauncey, Lieutenant M.D.K., 9 Flt, 'G' Sqn GPR, interview with the author, February 2008.

8    Jackson, Major P., OC 'E' Sqn GPR, correspondence with Luuk Buist, 1991.

9    Weeden, SSgt L., 14 Flt, 'F' Sqn GPR, correspondence with the author.

10   Holcroft, SSgt W.,14 Flt, 'F' Sqn GPR, 'No medals for Lt Pickwoad', September 1945.

11   Pare, Captain G.A., RAChD, HQ 1 Wing, GPR, by permission of The Eagle.

12   Battalion War Diary, 7th (Galloway) Battalion, KOSB, dated 18 September 1944.

13   Shackleton, SSgt A., 20 Flt, 'B' Sqn GPR, correspondence with the author, December 2007.

14   Toler, Major I., OC 'B' Sqn GPR, by permission of the Toler family.

# CHAPTER 9

# The Second Lift

*'I did not know how we were going to land as there was hardly any land left but down we came in a steep dive until about 100 yards from the ground.'*

**Monday, 18 September 1944**

In England the ground crews of US IX Troop Carrier Command and the two RAF Transport Groups had successfully turned their aircraft around within twenty-four hours after the outstanding success of D-Day. The unexpectedly low casualty rate incurred by the transport squadrons over the Low Countries during the first lift and the near absence of battle damage had greatly assisted their progress.

The American airfields at Saltby and Spanhoe were again alive with activity as they prepared to deliver the 2,119 men of the 4th Parachute Brigade to DZ 'Y'. The two stations would launch a combined total of 126 C47 transports, Saltby producing two serials of thirty-six and Spanhoe a further two serials of twenty-seven. The American drop would also drop 51 tons of valuable combat supplies.

Preparation to mount the second glider lift of the 1st Airlanding Brigade had been equally successful, with 297 tugs and gliders being loaded and ready for their flight to LZs 'X' and 'S'. The lift carried the balance of the 1st Airlanding Brigade, including the remaining two rifle companies of the South Staffords and the guns of the 2nd (Oban) Airlanding Anti-Tank Battery, Royal Artillery.

The total number of gliders had increased overnight from 270 to 297 as crews and loads from aborted sorties and emergency landings were added to the Air Movement Table for the second lift. In this respect the bad weather and 24-hour interval between lifts appeared to have worked in the planners' favour.

One glider pilot who had managed to get himself, his co-pilot and his passengers back onto the operation was Regimental Sergeant Major (RSM) 'Mick' Briody of 2 Wing GPR. Originally an Irish Guardsman, Mick Briody was now a glider pilot. He and his co-pilot Staff Sergeant Marshall were involved in a particularly 'hairy' emergency landing after trying to cast off from their tug having lost orientation in cloud over Braintree. Their load consisted of twenty-eight men of 17 Platoon, The Borders commanded by Lieutenant Bob Crittenden.

The best account of the incident is contained in *When Dragons Flew* – the story of The Borders at Arnhem:

> The glider pilot tried to release the tow-rope from the glider, but only one side fell free, while the length on the other side swung up and tried to hammer its way through the plywood skin of the glider.
>
> However the pilot and his co-pilot managed to put the glider down; it landed heavily,

crossed two fields, tore through a hedge and eventually came to rest in a cornfield with its undercarriage, skid, fencing posts and wire in a beautiful tangle inside it.

Fortunately no one was hurt and the platoon unloaded the hand cart containing equipment, ammunition and compo rations …

It transpired that they had landed close to a US Air Force base. Here they were offered dinner by the American Colonel, but Bob Crittenden refused this insisting that they must get back to base as soon as possible.

The American Colonel arranged for them to be flown back to their start point in Marauder Bombers that were stationed on his airfield. The hand cart was underslung in a bomb bay and the platoon was split up between several bombers for the journey.[1]

In some cases pilots had little time to prepare for the operation and were only 'warned' to fly to Arnhem at the last moment. Sergeant Albert Maughan of 'F' Squadron was one such pilot:

I was a second pilot in 15 Flight, stationed at Broadwell. My co-pilot at that time was Staff Sergeant Grace, but as he was in hospital I was left at base after the take-off for the first lift. On the morning of the 18th I was 'asked' by Lieutenant Steevenson of 14 Flight, who also lost his co-pilot, if I would go as his co-pilot. Our load was a jeep and trailer with four men of the South Staffords.[2]

Albert Maughan volunteered to fly of course and took part in the second lift.

As the early morning mist began to clear at different times across England, thousands of troops and airmen waited impatiently either inside their aircraft or outside on the grass next to the runway.

The majority of personnel hanging around waiting for the second lift had flown on previous operations, or had at least endured the torturous cycle of preparing for airborne operations that were inevitably cancelled at the last moment. The second lift contained an unusual unit that had only been included in the operation at the last moment; in contrast to the soldiers around them its members had very little military training and would never have expected to take part in an airborne operation such as this.

The men of RAF Light Warning Units 6341 and 6080 were all RAF airmen trained to operate RADAR, although they were unfamiliar with the equipment they were about to accompany to Holland – Forward Director Posts (FDP), an early form of deployable RADAR. Forty airmen and five officers had been hastily assembled under the command of Wing Commander Brown, a senior Ground Control Interceptor officer. They were now loaded with their equipment into four 'A' Squadron Horsas at Harwell.

Once on the ground in Holland it was intended that the FDPs would direct Allied fighter aircraft over the landing zones by day and night. The need for this form of ground control on the operation had been reviewed just prior to D-Day and the FDP chalk had been cancelled on 16 September. It was only after Wing Commander Brown visited 'Boy' Browning personally to plead for the RAF chalk to be reinstated that they were included in the second lift.

The ground stations themselves could not be fitted into a single Horsa, so the loads had to be split into two halves. The transmitter was packed in crates in one glider and the receiver similarly packed in a second. Two stations were deployed to ensure that at least one station would be complete and serviceable after landing.

Wing Commander Brown did not accompany the FDP personnel to Arnhem but flew in another 'A' Squadron Horsa with Corps Headquarters to Nijmegen. Maurice Herridge landed at Nijmegen and remembers hearing what became of the unfortunate Wing Commander, as he busied himself cutting his trapped load free from his shattered Horsa in the orchard: 'We were attacked by a

Messerschmitt 109. I did not see what happened but it was common knowledge that on LZ (N) a senior RAF Officer with the name of Brown had been hit; he was wounded when he returned to his glider to recover his sleeping bag. He died of his wounds the next day.'[3]

Staff Sergeant 'Eddie' Edwards had been allocated a chalk number in the first lift. He had originally been due to carry a 75mm Howitzer and its Jeep but this had all changed on 15 September:

> Our curiosity was certainly aroused when the briefing officer said 'Sit down gentlemen, I have something special for you lot.' These chaps did not call you Gentlemen unless they wanted something.
>
> He informed us that it was proposed to transport a Radio Direction Unit, RADAR, to Landing Zone 'X' located south of Wolfheze Station and that we were the chosen few to see that it arrived in the correct spot where the equipment would be set up … We would be going on the second lift on the assumption that the landing zone would be in our hands. This of course met with approval from the glider crews.
>
> The RADAR equipment arrived in lorries, and so did a number of RAF personnel. The stations were crated up and some of these crates were on the large size. One crate loaded into my glider occupied most of the cargo area and for good measure, two smaller ones were fitted in.
>
> I was then informed that I was to find room for some of the RAF operators. I had to draw the line at six. I also formed the opinion that the Stirling tug captain would have to 'put his foot down' going along the runway!
>
> I did raise one question after loading my glider, what would be the procedure, if by some chance, a glider did not land in the exact spot? I got the answer I expected, that I was expected to land in the exact spot but should I decide differently, there would be plenty of transport available. I could imagine the sort of reply I would get from a Jeep driver when he saw the packing cases![4]

The 'A' Squadron gliders were allocated chalk numbers 5000–5003. The lack of military training and absence of combat experience among the RAF technicians and ground controllers concerned the glider pilots – the prospect of landing behind enemy lines with such unprepared passengers was not an attractive one:

> The four glider crews decided that a crash course in arms training would not go amiss, so we paid a visit to the armoury and pleaded with the Quartermaster to let us have enough arms and ammunition to start a private war.
>
> He must have had a few sleepless nights when he did not get most of his gear back. We did not tell him where most of it was going.

While Eddie Edwards and his fellow pilots supervised their highly precious cargo, others among the waiting lift had less glamorous but important tasks. On the runway at RAF Down Ampney, Private 'Wilf' Bell of 10 Platoon, 'C' Company, 7th Battalion King's Own Scottish Borderers could not wander far from his glider. He and the rest of his platoon had been selected to guard the five gliders containing the Battalion's ammunition resupply. A total of five Jeeps and ten trailers were strapped down inside 'E' Squadron Horsas waiting for the mist to clear. Like everybody else in England, 10 Platoon were unaware of the fierce fighting around Arnhem Bridge or of the increasing threat to their intended landing zones:

> At 1030 we were all seated in the loaded glider. Lieutenant Wayte had brought some newspapers to read and he handed them round and we were able to read about the landing

that had taken place the day before. The headlines looked good to us. Full of praise about the greatest allied air armada to take to the skies the world had ever known, we were going over a day later but we knew we were still a part of it and that people would read the same about us on the Tuesday.

There was not much in the paper about the actual fighting going on as it was too early to print any sort of report. Just as I was finishing the first page our tug started up the motors and I knew that very soon I would be on my way. I checked that I had my life jacket on the right way, as there is always a chance we would come down in the sea.

I looked out of the window, as we were to be the first glider to take off out of the hundreds behind us. As I sat there I saw the man with the flag getting ready to wave to the tug pilot to take off. A few minutes later the towrope started to tighten up and off along the runway we went and by the time you could count to ten we were off the ground and starting to climb. It was a lovely take off, hardly a flicker; we must have had a good pilot.

It was a lovely sight to see all the gliders forming up just like being on a big parade ground, and then off we went towards the channel. After a while I got tired of watching fields and a few towns passing underneath us so I carried on reading as we had a three hour trip in front of us. After a while somebody said we were just going over the coast. It was not long before all we could see was the deep blue sea below us and a few rescue launches cruising about.[5]

Staff Sergeant Arthur Mills, 22 Flight, 'D' Squadron took off from Keevil at 1140 hours with Sergeant F.H. Stapley as his co-pilot. Their load was a good example of the administrative tail that every division needed to sustain itself in battle. The equipment required could only be carried by glider, in this case a jeep with trailer, one motorcycle and three men of 6 Airlanding Light Aid Detachment, Royal Electrical and Mechanical Engineers (REME), and of course their tools:

We encountered some cloud on approaching the Suffolk coast at Aldeburgh. Our Tug had to manoeuvre to miss it, airspeed at times rising to 170 miles per hour. It was a marvellous sight, an endless stream of tugs and gliders supported by fighters crossing the North Sea. I felt very proud to be a part of it. On approaching the Dutch coast, I observed three gliders, which had parted company with their tugs and had ditched in the sea. We passed over the Schelde Islands, which had been flooded. Later I saw another two gliders force land. We encountered some anti aircraft fire, the black puffs were appearing to our height but fortunately not on target.[6]

The cloud would cause problems for many of the gliders on the second day, with reduced visibility over England and out over the North Sea. The forecast from the meteorological office had correctly predicted that rain and a low cloud base would affect the southern route. The decision was taken at HQ First Allied Airborne Army that all troop-carrying aircraft would use the northern route. American resupply aircraft were the only formations exempt from this order.

The first aircraft of 46 Group RAF began lifting from RAF Blakehill Farm at 1043 hours, with 38 Group not far behind, commencing their lift at 1100 hours. The weather forecast proved accurate with some cloud over southern England and the southern route in Holland. The glider column had been briefed to fly at 2,500 feet, however the cloud base had forced them down to below 2,000 feet over England. Generally the visibility was good on the northern route once the streams crossed the Dutch coast. The limited visibility and large number of aircraft inevitably caused incidents and forced landings. Sergeant D. Smithson and his co-pilot, Staff Sergeant 'Spinner' Newton of 'G' Squadron, were one of the unlucky crews involved in a near miss. They had been forced to reduce their altitude and came into contact with the parachute stream:

> At the beginning flying was very easy, so easy that I piloted the Horsa glider for most of the crossing of the North Sea. The Dutch coast came into view and 'Spinner' took over. Within minutes things went wrong.
>
> Over the intercom I heard the tail-gunner of the Stirling swearing at his pilot and telling that an American Dakota was out of line and swinging towards us and at the same time telling him to climb. I then looked out my left and there within yards was the wing of the Dakota that clearly had not seen us.
>
> I shouted at 'Spinner' to climb and go right, which he did. You may guess what happened next. We were flying at about 1,100 feet low and at about 160 airspeed, we went up, the tail of the Stirling went up as well, and that meant that the nose of the Stirling pointed down. The Stirling pilot not liking going down at that speed pulled back on his stick. The Stirling tail going down, the Horsa nose going up ... SNAP ... We were flying free the coast a mile or so away.
>
> We had a quick discussion, back to sea and get picked up by Air Sea Rescue after ditching. I did go back to the lads there and told them to prepare to ditch, but back with 'Spinner', land was the better bet. 'Spinner' turned for land.
>
> Very quickly land was beneath us and I was trying to help 'Spinner' in the landing. Which way was the wind? No smoke or sea gulls. Did 'Spinner' guess? We were touching down still among poles and wire but the landing was good. No time for congratulations, we had to destroy the gun and glider.

'Spinner' Newton had earned his nickname during elementary flying training after recovering an aircraft from what was thought by those who saw it to be a fatal spin. Perhaps his previous experience helped him to maintain a cool head when landing after this incident.

The majority of pilots experienced less trouble with cloud or other aircraft and the lift was generally going well. There was of course a third variable that they could not predict or control – the Germans. The amount of flak had increased on the route as the German air defence system was now expecting further lifts, or at least resupply missions, to take similar routes to the ones used by the first lift. Anti-aircraft units had been relocated along the corridors used by Sunday's air armada.

Staff Sergeant Stan Hann had started his career in the Durham Light Infantry but was now flying a 'B' Squadron Horsa as part of the second lift. He had a typically down-to-earth Geordie view on the subject of flak: 'Different people have various views on "Flak". Over the coast of Holland and near the dropping zones, I used to watch these balls like cotton wool coming up in the sky, and wondering why they never came near me, as I was never unduly worried by it and it always seemed a long way off.'[7]

Staff Sergeant Ron Watkinson and his co-pilot Sergeant Arthur Jones were also flying a 'B' Squadron Horsa from RAF Manston. Once across the North Sea they were beginning to think that they were approaching the home strait:

> Our Horsa glider with chalk number 878 was hit with 'flak' near Middelburgh, which damaged the aileron control wires and air pipes, making ailerons and most instruments, including the Air Speed Indicator, useless. No person was injured, but we had a fair number of holes in fuselage and load. I regained as much control as possible, without ailerons, but the glider continued to swing, pendulum fashion, behind the tug.
>
> I kept in contact with the tug pilot, who suggested we turn round and make our way back to the English coast, to 'ditch'. I declined and said; 'if we can go back, we can go on'. We

carried on towards Arnhem for about another 20 minutes, when the towrope broke. The glider was easier to control in free flight, but the landing gear would not jettison (found out later that the locking wires had not been removed). We had no airspeed indicator or altimeter and the flaps were not working, as well as the ailerons.

I managed to get it down close to a farm, near the village of Fijnaart. The nose wheel broke and came into the cockpit, but no one was injured. A host of Dutch men and women came out to greet us. None spoke English. After embracing us we all began to unload the glider.

We then had problems, the flak had buckled the metal troughs that the wheels should have run in and the glider was at an awkward angle. This meant that the jeep, gun and trailer of the 1st Airlanding Light Regiment, RA had to be virtually lifted out, and this was achieved, mainly due to Dutch brawn.

After getting all the gear out it was found that the flak had damaged the hitches on the jeep, gun and trailer. It was at this point, whilst we were trying to improvise some means of connecting our equipment, that we were attacked by German troops. We put up a fight and whilst doing so, we broke the dial sight, dismantled the breech and threw them into a dyke.

My co-pilot, Arthur Jones, was severely hit and one of the Gunners took a bullet through his face and we were captured whilst tending their wounds. The Germans took the wounded into the farmhouse and let us talk to them, before the remaining four of us were marched off to Dordrecht and then to prisoner of war camps.

The determination to get through to Arnhem at all costs had also figured in the fate of two other glider pilots, this time from 'D' Squadron. Staff Sergeant Tony Coombs and Sergeant Knowles were flying a Horsa; strapped in at the rear of the glider was Sergeant S.H. Cooper from the MT Platoon of 156th Parachute Battalion:

We took off from Keevil in a Horsa with chalk number 964. Our glider was loaded with a jeep and two trailers loaded with explosives and small arms ammunition. With me, in addition to the two glider pilots was my driver, Private Agnew. We had been in the air for some time when I realized we had been cast off and were going down.

We landed at an American airfield [Martlesham Heath, Suffolk] where we were quickly prepared for another take-off. The captain of the tug aircraft explained that we had been getting so much turbulence from other aircraft that he had had to cast off. Off we went again. We didn't catch up with the other aircraft and so became a lone duck for all the German anti-aircraft fire in Holland.

The tug was hit and we were going down again. Making a rough landing, we hit a tree near the edge of a field [LZ 'W' at Son] and immediately came under fire. We were just in front of 82nd US Airborne forward positions near Nijmegen.

They gave us covering fire whilst we unloaded the glider. Then with the two glider pilots hanging on the back, we made a dash for the American lines, making it without mishap. I realized that I still had a job to do to get the ammunition through to the Battalion at Arnhem. Asking for information, I was directed to the Operations Room of the 82nd.[8]

Those gliders that had better luck and arrived over the landing zones intact were not going to have the breathing space accorded to the men of the first lift. The Germans continued to press the Airlanding Brigade defenders in an effort to overrun the landing zones. The fight to hold the vital ground of the Ginkelse Heide had raged on all through the day, each German attack gaining in strength and intensity. The KOSB war diary entry for the afternoon gives an insight into the situation around DZ 'Y' just before 4th Parachute Brigade began jumping at 1406 hours:

> 1000. The 4th Parachute Bde were due to make their drop at this hour and their appearance was anxiously awaited. At this time the situation was reasonably well in hand. Unfortunately, however, the aircraft did not appear at their appointed time.
>
> 1000 to 1400. There followed now a difficult period during which the enemy pressed in all sides. Steps were taken, by using every man and weapon, to keep him in check and these were so successful that he eventually drew off the majority of his force NORTHWARD. Therefore, when the Parachute drop did eventually take place, between 1400 and 1500 hrs, the DZ was completely clean and fire on it came from only a few isolated enemy weapons situated at a distance.
>
> 1500. All parachutists down, with very few casualties.[9]

The entry was written by Robert Payton-Reid himself, who fails to mention that the Battalion Headquarters had charged German positions just before the drop. The 'charge' was with bayonets fixed and he, the Commanding Officer of the Battalion led it himself.

'Shan' Hackett's brigade had already sustained casualties before they reached DZ 'Y'. Six C47 Dakotas had been brought down by flak over Holland. The suppression of German flak by Allied ground-attack aircraft was less well coordinated on the second day, possibly due to the delay in England.

Fighter escorts were also much less evident than on the previous day, transport crews stating that they had not seen any 'little friends' within 30 miles of Arnhem. The escort did, however, prevent any of the ninety fighters put aloft by the Luftwaffe breaking up the second lift of transports and glider combinations.

Regardless of losses and flak the American formation exorcised the ghost of Sicily and pressed on to its objective, arriving just after 1400 hours. The paratroops jumped from between 800 to 1,000 feet to be met by streams of German tracer originating from the fringes of the drop zone.

There was still no hesitation on the part of the paratroops or the American Dakota crews who flew on regardless of ground fire, delivering the bulk of 4th Parachute Brigade right onto its designated drop zone as planned. Only nine paratroops failed to jump, all of these attributed to wounds or snarled equipment.

On return to England twenty-four Dakotas were reported to have battle damage, again less than the figures anticipated.

The variety in the calibre of German defenders around DZ 'Y' was apparent in the different ways they reacted to the intimidation of the mass drop of paratroopers. Many were immediately frightened by the scale and momentum of 4th Parachute Brigade's arrival and ran away from the heathlands without firing a shot. Those units that were well led and experienced opened fire on the helpless paratroopers while they were at their most vulnerable. Hanging below their parachutes in daylight, unable to return fire, the British troops were dreadfully exposed to German ground fire. The German fire killed thirty-two of Shan Hackett's men on the drop zone.

Despite losses the parachute drop was viewed as a success – the second brigade was now on Dutch soil and ready to fight. Behind the parachute drop came the glider streams. Among the hundreds of gliders and tugs was Private 'Wilf' Bell and his comrades in 10 Platoon. They had no idea of the casualties their fellow KOSBs had sustained to date or that they were fighting desperately at close quarters to retain the ground below them:

> At 1450 hours the Glider Pilot told us to take off our life jackets and fasten up the safety harness as we were nearly there. You should have seen the gliders lying in the field below.

They were as thick as flies on an empty jam tin. It was a wonderful sight.

But then the anti-aircraft fire started again and my heart came into my mouth, but that passed. Another minute and I felt our glider give a shudder and I knew we had cast off and were on our way down. I did not know how we were going to land as there was hardly any land left but down we came in a steep dive until about 100 yards from the ground. The pilot straightened her out and slid down to the ground just missing the other gliders already there by inches. It could not have been a better landing.[10]

The Airlanding Brigade phase of the second lift was now in full swing, glider after glider cast off from its tug and made its individual approach to its nominated landing zone. The Pathfinders of the 21st Independent Parachute Company were once again out on the ground marking the landing zones. The markers and beacons were all placed accurately by 'Boy' Wilson's men, although the post-operation report would show that the 'Eureka' beacon on LZ 'X' only responded to less than half the 'Rebecca'-equipped aircraft on approach. The smoke generators and coloured 'T' markers showing wind direction, however, proved more than adequate in daylight. This, combined with the accurate navigation of the transport crews of both Air Forces to the cast-off point, ensured a successful lift from an airman's point of view.

Staff Sergeant Arthur Mills and his load of REME tradesmen were now approaching the cast-off point:

I saw the Maas, the Waal and the Lower Rhine in front of me. In approaching the Rhine I could see the gliders, which had landed the day before, also I saw a field on the left-hand side of a large wood, and I decided to aim for this. I released the towrope at 3,500 feet and made a straight in full flap approach into the field. I made a good landing with no damage whatsoever to the glider.

The passengers who had never flown in a glider before were very pleased. The landing zone we were in was 'X', west of Wolfheze. We soon removed the tail section, installed the ramps and drove the jeep and trailer out with no difficulty. Unfortunately we couldn't get the jeep to start, so while the lads were working on it, I shared out an orange and a flask of tea. The fault rectified, we all piled into the jeep and drove to the rendezvous at Wolfheze railway station.[11]

It seems ironic that the only Jeep that failed to start after landing belonged to detachment of REME mechanics and tradesmen. Alternatively, maybe it was fortuitous that it was that particular Jeep on that particular glider.

Staff Sergeant Bob Rose and Sergeant Harold Hockley also encountered technical problems with their load that afternoon. They were carrying a 6-pounder gun from 2nd (Oban) Airlanding Anti-Tank Battery RA:

Our position was well over to the left of landing zone 'X'. I was surprised to find we had settled in a shallow gully, the glider settled down nicely and virtually out of sight.

The lads in the back dropped the tail and I could hear the ramps sliding into position. We set about releasing the securing chains. At that stage all seemed to be going well until I heard a lot of cussing and someone frantically wielding an axe.

The gun would not pass under the main wing-spar! Normally there was about 2-inch clearance but this bloody gun was 3 inches too high! The lads with the axes were having no effect so we let the tyres go down and with a combination of bouncing and a lot more cussing finally the jeep pulled it clear.

Before they left the Corporal said, 'Sorry Staff, we rolled it over the other day in an accident but we didn't think there was any damage.' The accident obviously had displaced the Armour plate shield.[12]

Another glider pilot struggling to unload was Sergeant Lewis Haig of 'D' Squadron. 'Lewis Haig' was actually 'Louis Hagen', an Austrian Jew who had enlisted in the British Army to fight the Nazis. Prior to the operation all Austrians had been issued with new Anglicized identity papers and names to hide their true origin and nationality if captured.

Capture was not the foremost worry in Louis Hagen's mind as he brought his Horsa in to land with his Glaswegian first pilot, Staff Sergeant 'Mac' Wheldon. What follows is an extract of Louis Hagen's book *Arnhem Lift*, which gives a comprehensive account of landing a Horsa and a very detailed and humorous description of removing a Horsa tail unit in the field under less-than-ideal conditions:

As we are now losing height, and as we cross the river we can clearly see the bridge at Arnhem which is our ultimate objective …We turn to starboard with half flaps down and our gliding angle steepens suddenly. Another fifteen degrees to starboard and we are just about over our landing area.

Full flaps down and our nose is now pointing directly to the ground, the flaps keeping our speed constant and just above stalling speed. Someone cuts in from the right and we veer off a little, and then just before we hit the ground, pull out level. We lift gently over a hedge and then touch down firmly. Brakes full on … slow skid to port … a perfect landing.

We sat there for a moment, looking pleased with ourselves, when the crackle of distant machine guns and the whistle of some nearer shots reminded us forcibly that we were not on exercise. We leapt out and got into the tail unit, which we had to remove before the Jeep and trailer could be got out.

'Mac' and I start on the heavy bolts inside the tail … meanwhile, two of the parachutists loosen the shackles on the Jeep and trailer, and the third one begins to cut the control wires. 'Mac' and I are sweating like pigs. We have to work together and reach the same stage of the operation at the same time. We have to be quick. They are still sniping at us and we are completely helpless and exposed. Safety wire cut … backwards and forwards with the release lever … one by one the bolts come out … not so hard really … pretty much like the drill on the station … I'm stuck now … the bastards are getting more and more difficult … I'm so terribly hot. I send one of the parachutists to stick the trestle under the body and he shouts that he has done … so we get to the last two bolts … must be completely together now … mine is quite loose … ready 'Mac'? … right … go! Why the hell doesn't the tail fall off? We've done everything like the practice.

We bang from the inside but it is stuck fast. I jump out to look and discover that the bloody fool of a parachutist has stuck the trestle under the tail itself … I kick it away, and with a terrific crash the whole tail fuselage breaks off and falls over on the trestle … it's in the way still … we all get our shoulders under it and heave to the left … but the trestle is jammed in the fuselage now and embedded in the ground … it's a hell of a job … eventually we manage it, sweating, cursing and using all of our strength.

The two runners slipped out and fitted beautifully, and the paratrooper driver drove straight out of the glider. As we jumped on the Jeep and drove off, we noticed just on the right a cross and grave of one of yesterday's glider pilots. We had been lucky.[13]

The pilots of both wings had been clearly briefed on how they should approach their designated landing zones. The Operation Order was clear on the matter of 'Direction on Landing':

**Plan A** – Winds from 225–045 (through N) [SW to NE]

| | |
|---|---|
| LZ 'S' | Landing direction E to W |
| LZ 'X' | Landing direction S to N |
| LZ 'Z' | Landing direction S to N |

**Plan B** – Winds from 045–225 (through S) [NE to SW]

| | |
|---|---|
| LZ 'S' | Landing direction W to E |
| LZ 'X' | Landing direction N to S |
| LZ 'Z' | Landing direction N to S |

During the first lift the wind came from the North so Plan A was used. On the second lift the wind came more or less from east to north-east to east therefore Plan B was correctly employed.

Lieutenant Peter Brazier and Sergeant Maurice Hibbert of 25 Flight, 'E' Squadron followed the operation order without incident. They were carrying an unusual load into battle. One of their passengers was Lance Sergeant Mervyn J. Potter of 3 Detachment, 261 (Airborne) Field Park Company, Royal Engineers. Being a Sapper he had developed his own method of removing the tail of his Horsa and of extracting the equipment for which he was responsible:

We had with us an Airborne Bulldozer (Clark Air Tractor Crawler), one Matchless motorcycle and one standard airborne trailer, all of which was loaded into a Horsa glider.

In order to load the bulldozer into the glider, a specially designed loading ramp was necessary. This was designed and made under my personal supervision in our Company Workshops. This was carried around from one planned and cancelled operation to another, in the same Bedford 3-tonner as the bulldozer.

From the very first planned and cancelled operation with which our detachment were concerned, I knew that we would not be able to take this 'special ramp' with us on an operation so other means had to be found, in order to unload the bulldozer.

I decided that the quickest and easiest way to achieve this was by using small charges of explosive, to blow away the landing supports struts of the glider to settle her on her belly. My idea was presented to the commanding officer of the 9th Field Company, Royal Engineers and he rapidly gave me permission. So, from this time on, I carried in my Airborne Smock, two small charges of gelignite, detonators and safety fuse for the purpose.

On landing on the 18th of September 1944, this method was used and the bulldozer with all our other gear was successfully unloaded with no damage whatsoever to anyone or anything (except the glider). The explosives were attached to the struts in such a way that the detonating wave was away from the fuselage in order that no damage would be sustained to the fuselage or its contents. Bearing in mind that our trailer, apart from other engineering equipment, contained a large quantity of explosives.

One of the aircraft that had failed to cross the North Sea at the first attempt and had been incorporated into the second lift was the 'C' Squadron Horsa flown by Staff Sergeant Jack Taziker and Lieutenant George Stokes. They were now arriving over LZ 'Z' carrying the Recce Squadron headquarters party.

They had a lucky escape on the Sunday morning, turning back to Tarant Rushton when the fabric covering the leading edge of their wing had begun to peel off. Their luck did not hold at the second attempt either. Jack Taziker wrote to his wife six months after the battle to tell her what had happened to him:

Eventually we arrived over Holland and what a sight it was. The whole of the country as far as you could see was under water. It had been flooded. But not all of it – oh no – one little dry piece contained an AA Gun, and I met my first Flak.

In fact they scored a bulls-eye right in the cockpit on my mate's side. I wondered what had hit us. It happened so suddenly. But when I saw George bleeding like a stuck pig I realized what had happened and realized that I had been hit in the left arm and both legs. Luckily I was in control of the glider at that time and the splinter didn't seem to worry me. I managed to get the kite back into position again and we carried on.

Meanwhile the Recce Officer in the back of the glider tried to stop George from bleeding. Twenty minutes later we arrived over the landing ground and it was surrounded by the enemy. They fired everything they had at us and the Sergeant passenger was hit in the arm. The glider was riddled with shots and we weren't able to make a proper landing because the AA shells had burst one of the air bottles so we couldn't use flaps or brakes. So we made a crash landing at the bottom end of the field. It wasn't as bad as I expected, there was a splintering of wood as we came to a standstill and the cockpit filled with a cloud of dust.

That was the critical moment of all the operation to me. I was still strapped in my seat when I felt an awful pain in my head and I knew that I had been hit. But I didn't know what. I sank back in my seat and said to myself 'Oh Lord, what a way to die'. Just then George shouted at me 'Come on Jack, get out'. I released my harness and made a dash for the door and threw myself under the glider. The enemy were still firing at us from a barn about 300 yards away.

When I found time to collect my wits and saw my right hand grovelling in the dust and covered with blood, I thought I must have been hit in the arm. I lifted my left arm to my head and what a shock I got. It felt as if half my head was blown away. Meanwhile the Recce Officer had got his Machine Gun out and he was engaging the enemy. George was lying behind the glider wheel whilst I tried to dig myself under the glider with my left hand.

All this time the blood was pouring down my face, dripping from my eyebrows at my nose. After about half an hour things seemed to have quietened down a bit and the Recce Officer came over to give me a shot of morphine and a drop of whisky. He put a shell dressing on my head and the Sergeant gave me a cigarette. I felt fairly comfortable. We lay there for about four hours and then the RAMC took George and me to a house that they were using as a dressing station.[14]

These differing accounts from individual gliders show that the landing zones were not totally secure on the afternoon of 18 September. Equally, German troops were not able to dominate any of the landing zones. In some areas German units were able to bring direct-fire weapons to bear close in on the second-lift gliders as they landed and as their crews and passengers subsequently unloaded – certainly not the reception envisaged for the second lift in the original plan for Operation MARKET.

Staff Sergeant Reg Grant of 'E' Squadron witnessed the landings from his position behind the home for the blind at Wolfheze:

The Germans, expecting reinforcements, and helped by this delay, had by now brought up anti-aircraft guns, and some of the gliders and Dakotas carrying paratroops got a very hot reception.

The landing zone was also covered in smoke, the enemy having set fire to the grass and gorse upwind of the area. Some of the glider pilots, unable to see the ground until they were about fifty feet above it, were landing very fast and hitting all sorts of obstacles.

One glider flying straight towards us at an impossible speed, and unable to touch down, flew slap into the trees about forty yards to our left. A grinding, splintering crash and in seconds, a graceful aircraft was just a heap of shattered wood and metal. The two pilots were miraculously thrown clear, through the nose, and escaped with bruises. The occupants in the fuselage were not so lucky however.

Another glider, flying between two trees, left its wings and tail behind and the fuselage careered like an express train through gliders, which had already landed, doing great damage and causing a number of casualties.

Yet another, perhaps the most spectacular of all, was a pilot diving the glider through the anti-aircraft barrage and dense smoke, realizing he would fly straight into a row of trees, bounced the glider on the ground high into the air again. Imagine his feelings, when clearing the obstacle by a good twenty feet, the row of trees turned out to be a whole wood, stretching several hundred yards in front of him. Sinking slowly into the wood, six-inch thick trees were snapped off like matchsticks, the glider disintegrating and spilling its load of men and equipment. Total casualties – one damaged knee. All the equipment from the wreck was recovered, including a trailer, which was perched up in the trees, inside part of the fuselage.[15]

Overall the second lift had gone well despite the delay, poor weather and German opposition. In total, 297 gliders had taken off for Arnhem, of which twenty-four had failed to arrive: one glider had crashed on take-off; seven gliders made emergency landings in England; two made involuntary landings in the North Sea; and fourteen were forced to land prematurely in Holland. This attrition was mainly due to the increased effectiveness of German flak, which was far heavier than on the previous day.

Those gliders that had reached Arnhem had a high success rate – of the seventy-three intended for LZ 'S', seventy-one made it into the landing area, sixty-seven of which landed accurately within the designated landing zone.

Originally, of a total of 224 gliders that had been allocated LZ 'X' as their destination, 202 reached the Arnhem area, of which 189 delivered their loads to the correct landing zone. Accidents on what were congested landing zones were kept to a minimum, although German ground fire was far more evident than on the previous day.

On LZ 'L', thirty RAF Stirlings completed the first resupply mission of the operation, dropping 86 tons of supplies, but unfortunately the Germans had already overrun much of this area. Only an estimated 12 tons found their way into British hands, an interesting comparison with the 14 tons landed by the three Hamilcar freight serials on the same day. Recovery parties immediately busied themselves across all of the landing zones collecting in supplies that had arrived by parachute and glider.

The arrival of the second lift had finally released 1st Airlanding Brigade from the increasingly difficult task of keeping the Germans back from the landing zones. At 1515 hours orders were issued initiating the move into Arnhem.

The activity on the landing zones did not distract Iain Murray and 1 Wing GPR from moving away from their defensive positions shortly after the last glider was down on the ground. By 1600 hours, 1 Wing GPR had moved east along the Arnhem-Utrecht road towards Arnhem, having been ordered to establish themselves in defence around the new Divisional Headquarters, the Hotel Hartenstein, about 6 kilometres from Arnhem Bridge.

The relocation into Oosterbeek created a logistical problem for Wing Headquarters – the movement of German prisoners. As the Divisional Headquarters reserve troops, Iain Murray's men had the responsibility of guarding prisoners of war (POWs).

Staff Sergeant Joe Price of 'E' Squadron and Sergeant Len Affolter of 'D' Squadron were detailed by Iain Murray to assist with the POWs. They initially escorted a number of wounded Germans to the Brigade Dressing Station in Wolfheze. After reporting back to the headquarters they left again, this time with some forty prisoners, including Luftwaffe telephonist, Irene Reimann. The prisoners were eventually secured for the night in the classrooms of the JP Heije School in Oosterbeek.

John Place and 2 Wing GPR were also due to move, although their integral role in the defence of the landing zones prevented them from leaving as quickly as their counterparts in 1 Wing earlier in the afternoon.

The orders for 2 Wing GPR were precise – Place and his pilots were to centre their position on the spot height 63.5 between the Graftombe and the Ommershof estate. Their positions were to cover up to but exclude the railway line. The Borders were on the left flank of 2 Wing holding a line from the glider pilots to Heveadorp. The GPR units would fit in with the Brigade defence plan filling the gaps created by casualties and the move of the South Staffords earlier in the day.

John Place did not realize at the time but this would be the line on which 2 Wing would fight shoulder to shoulder with their Airlanding comrades for the rest of the battle.

The Airlanding Brigade's withdrawal from the positions around the landing zones would use three separate routes. Troops would begin to move from 1900 hours, the KOSB taking the route north of the railway through Johannahoeve, 2 Wing GPR south-east through Wolfheze and the Borders east along the main Renkum-Arnhem road.

In accordance with their orders, 1st Airlanding Brigade headquarters moved off at 1900 hours with the sections of 2 Wing GPR leading the way. Brigade Headquarters followed on behind them with all the necessary paraphernalia required to sustain a headquarters in the field. The new headquarters was established at the Bilderberg Hotel.

As the move took place elements of the second lift were also on the move at the same time – the pilots flying the second lift did not have the breathing space enjoyed by their predecessors on the previous Sunday afternoon. The atmosphere and tempo of activity around the landings had changed dramatically. Things were not so well ordered and linking up with parent units was difficult. On the first lift, Sergeant Albert Midgley of 9 Flight had flown a 'G' Squadron Horsa with Lieutenant John Bewley. Their glider had been loaded with a Jeep, its trailer and about eight passengers of Headquarters 1st Airborne Royal Army Service Corps. Once on the ground they remained with their passengers under command of Lieutenant Colonel M. St John Packe RASC.

> Our instructions were to stay with them as long as they needed us. On our way, alongside troops of the South Staffords, fairly quiet at first, I faintly remember Wolfheze Station and the body of the German General Kussin hanging out of his bullet-riddled car.
>
> After many stoppages we arrived at Oosterbeek and were told we could not go any farther owing to enemy action along the road. Lieutenant Colonel Packe then commandeered a house at Hartensteinlaan on the green opposite the Hartenstein Hotel and set up his headquarters. Mr Minjauw and his family who lived there moved into the cellar.
>
> Lieutenant Bewley and I stayed with Lieutenant Colonel Packe for the next three days. With the help of a Dutch resistance man and a furniture van we collected what containers we could, which was rather hectic as we came under small arms fire frequently. Luckily the Dutchman knew his way around. With the help of Dutch civilians warning us of the whereabouts of the Germans, we survived.[16]

Staff Sergeant Mark Leaver, of 10 Flight, 'G' Squadron, landed late in the afternoon. He had a load and a destination of an altogether different nature to that on Albert Midgley's glider. Leaver was carrying Sergeant Flower and five men of No. 2 Detachment, 261 (Airborne) Field Park Company, Royal Engineers, and a Jeep and trailer packed with explosives for the bridge:

> We made our way to Wolfheze where we received orders to proceed to the bridge in Arnhem, via Oosterbeek and the lower road near the river. We made good progress until we rounded a bend in Klingelbeekseweg and ran into heavy fire from the junction with Utrechtseweg where German tanks were located.
>
> We did as speedy a turn as possible with a jeep and trailer and managed to return round the bend just as the Germans spotted us and brought their heavy guns to bear. As there was no other way available we decided to wait near the green adjacent to the Railway Station at Den Brink until reinforcements arrived.

Things did not appear to be going too badly for Sergeant Ken Bryant and Staff Sergeant George Duns. The two 24 Flight pilots from 'G' Squadron had force-landed on the first lift in England but had successfully reached Holland at the second attempt. They did not have to venture as far into Arnhem as the 10 Flight crew and their explosive laden Jeep, as their task and load were of a more conventional nature – a Jeep with radio set, and a trailer with communications and Intelligence Section equipment. One of the five passengers was Major H.P. Maguire, GSO2, Intelligence Branch, Headquarters, 1st Airborne Division:

> After unloading we crossed the railway line and met up with some other of our lift at Wolfheze. Our orders were to get the radio equipment to divisional headquarters.
>
> We drove south from Wolfheze and turned onto the road to Oosterbeek. There was some action along this road, and we came across our first sight of it when we passed the body of General Kussin and his driver lying in the German staff car. We stopped to ask directions from some Dutch civilians and they very kindly gave us some fresh water and fruit. There were no further incidents until we got to the Hartenstein Hotel.
>
> At divisional headquarters they were urgently waiting for the radio equipment, as they could not contact the units on the way to the bridge. Our Flight was ordered to defend the perimeter of the hotel grounds. By early evening we had dug our slit trenches, and had a few German prisoners to guard. We had a meal of cold canned stew and tea, and settled down in our slit trench to try and get some sleep.[17]

Not all of the lift had fared so well, Staff Sergeant George Cawthray's co-pilot, Sergeant Lawrence Thomas recalls landing with their 1st Parachute Battalion load:

> We made a good landing, after which the field became crowded with people. I was dead chuffed that we had managed to get down safely. A little girl grabbed some cigarettes from my hand. It was clear that they had not seen any cigarettes for a very long time. The onlookers thought it was brilliant that we had come down in this field. As second pilot it was my job to guard the aircraft while it was being unloaded. I lay, therefore, in front of the aircraft with my Bren, while various bystanders helped with the unloading. As this was going on two more gliders landed nearby. When we were ready to leave we went to a farmhouse about 200 metres away from our aircraft. Here we were given milk and fruit and we were also introduced to the people from the underground that would lead us to a ferry crossing.

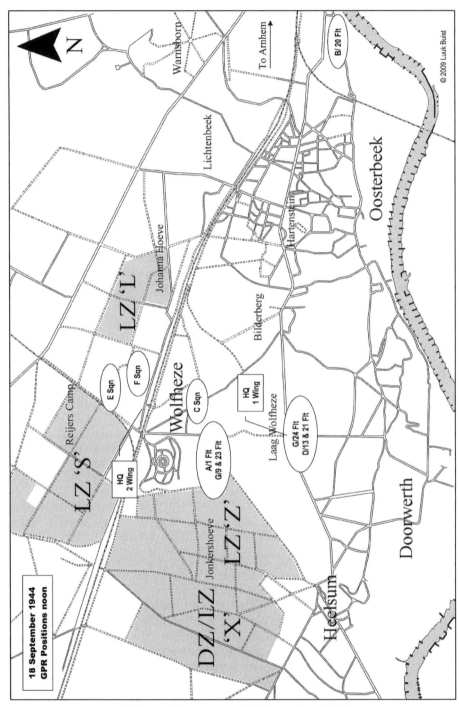

*GPR positions, noon 18 September 1944*

Miss G. Kamminga, a teacher from Zetten, recalls the arrival of two gliders and meeting passengers from Chalk 759 (South Staffords):

In the afternoon there was a stream of cyclists along the Molenweg. We crossed the Molenbrug over the river Linge and there, in front of us, stood a British glider.

A Sergeant had set himself up behind a machine gun in front of the aircraft. 'Where are the Germans?' he asked. We told him that there were none in the vicinity, which reassured him. The men from the glider dismantled the aircraft in order to unload a gun and a jeep. The amazement of those watching was further increased when, shortly afterwards, a second glider [Chalk 5000] landed close by.

The load for Chalk 5000 comprised personnel from 6080 LWU under the command of Squadron Leader Coxon RAF. There were four other RAF personnel and Lieutenant Bruce E. Davis USAF. He was a US Air Force Ground Controller from the US IX Air Force, a specialist deployed to act as liaison between the RAF ground stations and their American counterparts in the 306th Fighter Control Squadron.

The role of the RAF LWUs was to coordinate fighter activity over the ground taken by the airborne divisions. The intent was to establish runways in the newly occupied territory and operate aircraft over the Rhine. Night-capable RAF Beaufighters were to operate initially from Nijmegen and protect the bridgeheads from German bombing raids. Linked to the plan and following on in the third lift was the 878th (US) Aviation Engineer Battalion. Its task was to create the required airstrips at locations still to be identified to support Allied fighters up close to the front line. The engineers would be delivered mainly in Hamilcar gliders to repair Deelen Airfield or to establish new airstrips using wire mesh and runway repair techniques. The deployment of the RAF ground controllers in the second lift was a key advance element of what was still at this stage an open-ended plan.

Chalk 5000 was flown by Staff Sergeant 'Lofty' Cummings and Sergeant Jimmy McInnes of 'A' Squadron. The heavily loaded Horsa was roughly 8 kilometres from LZ 'X', at 3,000 feet, when German flak targeted its tug. When the Stirling was hit and caught fire, the glider cast off its tow and began to descend. The burning tug crashed near the village of Opheusden; no parachutes were seen to emerge from the stricken aircraft. The Horsa, free from damage, completed an emergency landing south of the Rhine at Hemmen.

At the same time Staff Sergeant John Harris and Sergeant Jesse Bosley were flying another RADAR serial as Chalk 5003, their load consisting of equipment and personnel from 6341 LWU. They were bracketed by the same flak batteries as Chalk 5000, their Horsa was hit by flak and fell to the ground south of Opheusden on the Dodewaard road; there were no survivors.

Finding themselves in the unfamiliar environment of an isolated location in occupied Holland, the passengers of Chalk 5000 were feeling exposed and edgy. Their pilots quickly assured them all was well and when it became evident that there were no Germans close by they began handing round cigarettes. While taking time for a smoke it became immediately clear that the bulky and secret equipment could not be moved without vehicles; it was therefore decided to destroy it.

Corporal Austin was ordered to supervise the destruction of the RADAR sets by shooting them to pieces with Sten guns, in the hope that this drastic action would render the fragile equipment useless to the Germans.

After destroying the equipment the chalk were given a lift by a group of soldiers whose glider had also force-landed. The local Dutch Resistance gathered the crews of all three wayward gliders together, the amalgamated loads producing two motorcycles, two jeeps, one with a trailer and one with a 6-pounder gun, and about seventeen men.

This composite force was then guided by the Resistance and numerous jubilant local civilians towards the ferry crossing at Driel. Lawrence Thomas was in the midst of this throng:

> We left the field followed by an enormous stream of civilians. A bit further on we made contact with the crews of the other gliders. The now complete procession took the road to the Driel ferry.
>
> Shortly afterwards we halted again. News had been received that some German soldiers were hiding in a house on the right hand side. We were ordered by Lieutenant Turrel to surround the house and take the Germans prisoner. It did not result in a battle; the soldiers were Poles who had been pressed into service by the Germans. We couldn't take them with us so they were handed over to the local police who locked them up in a police cell.

Having secured their POWs the last obstacle to confront the procession was the Driel ferry crossing. For a short time Peter Hensen, the ferryman, contemplated the dilemma of whether or not he should charge for the ferry crossing. Staff Sergeant George Cawthray:

> After we crossed the river we hastened through Oosterbeek arriving in the outskirts of Arnhem without incident. At this point we parted with our passengers, Lieutenant Turrell, second in command of the Headquarters and Support Company of 1 Parachute Battalion and the two Despatch riders Clarke and Donnerly. We turned back to try and make contact with our own Squadron, which we did, in the Church [Oosterbeek] area.

Back on DZ 'Y', 4th Parachute Brigade was regrouping – it was already clear that the situation around them was not as they had been briefed. The failure of radio communications had prevented the passage of situation reports between headquarters prior to the second lift. Shan Hackett and his staff were unaware of the absence of Roy Urquhart and Gerald Lathbury and were therefore surprised to find 'Pip' Hicks in command of the Division.

Adding to their confusion, what they had been told would be a secure and quiet drop zone could not be classed as either. The Brigade's own advance party had jumped with Lathbury on the first drop, and now set about briefing their commander and fellow staff on the current battle picture as quickly as possible.

The original mission allocated to 4th Parachute Brigade was to reinforce 1st Parachute Battalion on the high ground north of Arnhem. The orders remained unchanged despite the fact that David Dobie's battalion was not to the north but fighting desperately alongside its sister battalion, trying to reach the bridge in Arnhem.

'Shan' Hackett was unhappy with the situation he found in Arnhem. His outlook was further darkened when he was informed that 11th Parachute Battalion was to be removed from his command almost immediately. The drive to break through to the bridge needed fresh impetus – another battalion was to follow on behind the two companies of South Staffords also striking out for the bridge.

The removal of one of his battalions did not go down well with the newly arrived commander, who released them but insisted that one of the remaining airlanding battalions was given to him in exchange. The 7th Battalion King's Own Scottish Borderers were detached to 4th Parachute Brigade, although they were still very much involved in defending the landing zones. The KOSBs were holding on to LZ 'L' in preparation for arrival of the Polish Brigade and the third lift, their actions being restricted to that task until the lift was complete.

The South Staffords and 20 Flight, 'B' Squadron GPR were still advancing east away from the landing areas when the second lift, including the second half of their battalion, was finally heard approaching in the distance. Ian Toler was with his men and describes the reaction around him amongst the column:

Everyone is very anxious. The noise of aircraft and 'flak' opening up gives us hope. Later we hear a report that gliders have been seen. This cheers everyone up. There is more firing, probably our own, and I move down the street with the 'O' group. It is quite fantastic.

Our weapons at the ready looking for snipers at every turn, and the streets with civilians moving about quite normally, and shops as if it were a street in Chester. We move into a house, which has been the local Gestapo headquarters, very comfortably furnished, and well stocked with food. I take a tin of asparagus. There is continual firing and sniper hunt. A bullet comes through the window.

I meet Captain Dickinson of the Light Regiment. We now have orders to move down towards the railway. I have at last contacted Captain Angus Low and his Flight, and we move off at the rear of Major Timothy's men as usual. It must be between five and six o'clock and everyone is feeling a little tired. More fruit from the Dutch is very welcome. A Dutchman produces a Bren and ammunition, two Sten guns, a rifle, grenades, and more ammunition for which we are very thankful.

The advance is very slow and heavy rifle and machine gun fire is coming from the woods north of the railway on our left. I do a small reconnaissance to the right and see that the Railway Bridge over the river has been blown.

I rest near the Railway Station with Timothy and eat the tin of asparagus, which is not very filling. We move on to a house, which overlooks the road into Arnhem. It is getting dark and everyone is tired. The firing in the direction of Arnhem is increasing and now includes mortar, shells and lots of tracer and is altogether a very good reproduction of the Infernal Regions.

Timothy and I go down the road to recce and meet a Squadron Leader [Sqn Ldr Howard Coxon, 10 Group, RAF] in charge of a Radar section. He looks rather out of place in blue uniform in this rather unhealthy spot. His tug, a Stirling, was shot down south of the river. They force landed successfully and got across the river by the simple expedient of going to the ferry and asking to be taken across on payment of the usual fare! He is trying to join divisional headquarters so as I am trying to do the same I suggest he stays with my pilots until an opportunity arises when we can go and try to locate it. It does not look at the moment as if the opportunity will arise.

The afternoon had also been a period of heavy activity for the German units pushing against the defences of 2nd Parachute Battalion around the bridge itself. German armour and artillery continued to pour into Arnhem, the focus of attention appearing to be the defenders at the north end of the bridge. The combination of 88mm guns, assault guns and tanks began to level houses street by street and row by row. The use of high explosive and incendiary shells very soon had huge areas of the town in flames and reduced to rubble.

Arthur Rigby and the survivors of 19 Flight were still among the defenders holding on to the bridge with John Frost, with German pressure building as the day continued:

Our house seemed to bear a charmed life for despite the fact that practically all the houses around us were hit and in ruins or on fire, we were virtually unscathed. I was in dire need of a toilet so decided to try to find one downstairs. I found one and did what was necessary and was on my way back upstairs when there was a terrific crash in the upper part of the house.

Clouds of dust came pouring down the stairs. I rushed back to our room to find a great hole in the outside wall and the place full of dust and rubble. In the midst of all this stood a chap named Carter and his left arm was almost severed just above the elbow. He was repeating over and over 'look at my bloody arm'. He was taken off to the Regimental Aid

Post. I helped him down the stairs and left him in charge of a couple of other blokes with directions with which to find their way.

When I returned to my post all the dust and smoke had died down or blown away and it was surprising to find that Carter was the only casualty. All the houses in our immediate vicinity were on fire, and the roar of the flames was a bit frightening, but the worst part was the thirst.

Fortunately some bright spark had found that the water was still available from the taps when we first occupied the house and had filled the bath. So water was there, but over the period of time it had become very dusty and coloured by brick dust and smoky wood chips from the flying sparks, but it was still drinkable and we made tea, using our ration packs. That didn't include Ted and I, our rations were still on the jeep wherever that might be, but the other lads shared theirs with us, positive nectar!

We had hardly finished our drink when Charley Watson yelled up the stairs for Ted and I to rejoin the blokes below, so off we went. On arrival in the downstairs hallway we found Captain Simpson gathering all the Glider Pilots together in order to take us elsewhere where our presence was required.

We had to leave the house by the windows. Hardly had he given us our instructions and directions than Jerry mounted an attack by infantry, preceded by a tank, which came round the corner into 'our street' [Marktstraat], from the shelter of the arches under the bridge ramp. It was huge, must have been a Tiger. It seemed to fill the street. It rumbled down the middle of the road, firing its shells into each side as it advanced.

Again our house wasn't hit, but as the tank went on past us we could hear men shouting in German, and we had to beat off a very determined attack. Firing came at us from houses on the opposite side of the street and from the gardens surrounding, but we rarely saw anyone for long, just a quick glimpse as the men came forward towards our positions.

I suppose we must have put up sufficient firepower to stop them for the attack didn't develop and we were left in peace for a while. Very shortly we climbed out through the windows and dashed away through a couple of streets to arrive in a small park overhung with trees and once again we found our jeep parked under the trees.

All my cigarettes, which I carried in my smock pockets, had been smoked, but I still had another two hundred and some chocolate in my rucksack on the jeep. I went across and retrieved two packets of twenty and a bar of chocolate, together with two packs of 'K' ration, and brought them back to the place where Ted was now busy digging a slit trench.

I learned we were to stay the night in this park. Despite a large number of bombs, which did considerable damage to our equipment we were not hit and our weapons and carried ammunition were intact.

Anyway, there were slit trenches to be dug and holes to be cut through the walls to enable us to fire through to the street if need be, so we were kept busy for a while. I suddenly realised in the middle of all this that it was my birthday and called across to Ted with the news. Before he answered a lugubrious voice from a nearby 'fox-hole' said, 'Hard bleeding luck chum, save us a bit of cake!' Typical![18]

At Wolfheze, Major Peter Jackson moved 'E' Squadron back into Oosterbeek as part of the 2 Wing GPR realignment within the Airlanding Brigade defence line. The gathering darkness provided cover for all kinds of movement:

On the way along a dark road we were amazed to find ourselves preceded by a very smartly dressed high stepping young woman who trotted along quite unconcernedly hugging her handbag to her side. She eventually turned into a house but it was too dark to see the number so the troops went on.

As they proceeded there were more signs of battle to be seen, and two Opel cars, recently enemy property, whose owners had ceased to care, were requisitioned. One had a badly damaged radiator but the car was kept running by a trooper sitting on the front mudguard with a pail of water with which he kept down the temperature in the radiator. These two cars were loaded with bottles of gin and thus equipped for any emergency, the column moved on.

Wally Holcroft was also involved in the 2 Wing GPR move into Oosterbeek that evening. He was moving with 'F' Squadron and this extract from his account of the battle gives a good insight into the mindset of the average glider pilot on the second night:

Once again we marched down the road, and again the day had become very warm and sticky making the task of carrying our enormous rucksacks, very irksome and somewhat tiring.

We were held up on the road by a three-ton truck for a while. It was endeavouring to pull a 17-pounder gun up a steep track. Operations were under the direction of a very old friend of mine Sergeant Major Petrie ['C' Sqn], no less. He proudly pointed out to me that he had brought this enormous load of truck and gun in his glider. I congratulated him on his fine achievement.

Eventually we arrived at the junction of four roads, one of which led to Arnhem, and here we had to part from our friends of the Border Regiment. A large crowd of Dutch people had gathered at the crossroads to watch a large truck of German origin, which had been captured along with a party of weary looking German soldiers, about fifteen of them.

Some of the civilians were endeavouring to turn the truck in the direction of Arnhem, after which the Germans were made to load the truck with some military supplies, which lay at the side of the road. 'Doddy' [SSgt W. Dodd] decided we could commandeer the truck to take us to Division headquarters and at the same time convey the German troops to a Prisoner of War cage.

This party of Germans looked a better sample than the last lot we had seen, but they too looked very scared. 'Doddy' ordered one of them to cut off his SS insignia, which he did reluctantly and handed it to 'Doddy' who, apparently, wanted it for a souvenir.

This little episode caused an epidemic of souvenir hunting and soon all the Germans were busily engaged cutting off their badges. We arrive at divisional headquarters, which was situated in a large and beautiful hotel, set back off a road into Arnhem at Hartenstein, Oosterbeek.

German equipment lay everywhere and everything had an air of a battle going well for us. We handed over our prisoners to a guard and then went into the hotel to see if we could learn anything concerning the whereabouts of the Glider Pilots.

No one could help us at Division headquarters so as it was now getting late we decided to stay in the grounds of the hotel until the following day. It seemed to me that all was over bar the shouting and I suggested to Mick Hall that we would see the Second Army arrive next day and we should be on our way home. Mick agreed and together we dug a slit trench to accommodate us for the night.[19]

The 1st British Airborne Division war diary records the activation of the Headquarters at its new location in the Hartenstein Hotel at 1700 hours. Iain Murray and 1 Wing GPR moved in all around the hotel gardens establishing defensive positions before the Headquarters began to function. Various glider pilots remember moving into the vicinity of the new headquarters and Oosterbeek that evening,

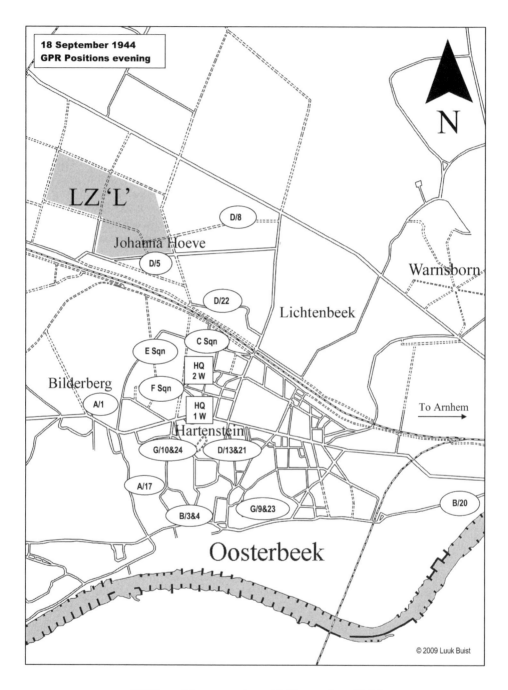

*GPR positions evening, 18 September 1944*

including Staff Sergeant John Bonome and Sergeant Geoff Higgins who were moving among the early evening shadows in the Dutch town. The two 'C' Squadron pilots had successfully landed their Hamilcar as part of the first lift and had been ordered to remain with their load, a 17-pounder gun, its tractor and crew. John Bonome:

> While awaiting the second lift, we received a visit from the Luftwaffe, who seemed to look upon us as a target as the bursts of machine gun fire came very close, but fortunately causing us no damage.
>
> They left and then the second lift arrived, but this time they were heavily opposed. There was no sign of Sergeant Higgins and myself of being relieved, so we remained with the gun crew who were now ordered to proceed towards Arnhem.
>
> We had difficulty in getting the gun over an embankment, but eventually managed to join the line of vehicles heading into Arnhem …
>
> Eventually we reached our allocated position on the corner of Hoofdlaan and Utrechtseweg and set up the gun facing west with our Bren-gun position on the other side of the road.
>
> Having dug ourselves in we waited what may befall us. It seemed that we were to defend the divisional headquarters in the Hartenstein Hotel, about 200 yards away.[20]

Other members of 'C' Squadron were migrating towards the Hartenstein, including John McGeough and Henry Woltag who had survived the day and were now deployed around the new headquarters. John gives an indication of how the glider pilots were employed and of how close the German forward elements were to the Headquarters even at this early stage of the battle:

> We reached the Hartenstein Hotel at Oosterbeek and there I was to remain for the rest of the battle. Henry, myself and a number of other glider pilots were detailed to defend Divisional Headquarters which was set up in the hotel so we set to and dug slit trenches in the grounds at the rear, ready to repulse any enemy attack.
>
> It was not long before we carried out patrol duties and on one occasion having reached the junction of Mariaweg and Utrechtseweg were pinned down by heavy machine gun fire. We could not see where the gun was, the area was heavily built up and it could have been in any of the houses in front of us.
>
> The bullets were just missing us and in retrospect it appears to me that the gunner could not get any more depression on the machine gun. On this occasion we were lucky. We endured the situation of lying flat on the roadway, expecting to be hit any time for about twenty minutes before the firing ceased. We were then able to withdraw to the Hartenstein which was only a few hundred yards away.[21]

The pilots of 1 Wing GPR were being held back as the divisional reserve and were busily establishing themselves in trenches around the Hartenstein. There were of course elements of Iain Murray's wing fighting elsewhere, including 19 Flight which remained with John Frost's battalion on the bridge. Ian Toler and the bulk of 'B' Squadron were still attempting to reach the bridge with the South Staffords. It is apparent from Ian Toler's diary entry for the evening of 18 September that the town of Arnhem was by now fully acquainted with the stark realities of war:

> All civilians are in air raid shelters, one woman is in hysterics. For want of other orders we decide to stay the night in this area. I fix positions, give the order to dig in and arrange to park the transport. We have now acquired a Jeep, which the Sergeant Major and Staff Sergeant Baker have made out of two. A house just down the road is set on fire by a shell,

flares up and lights up the whole area.

In the dark Arnhem is now looking like Dante's Inferno. We are very tired. The Dutch in the house are very helpful and we start to get some food. Alas, we have hardly started when an order comes from Lieutenant Colonel McCardie we are to advance and put in an attack with Major Timothy. Where or when is not stated. We rouse the men and start on the road again towards Arnhem from which direction the firing has not diminished.

Staff Sergeant Shackleton and I go with Major Timothy's 'O' group. The darkness helps and the firing seems to be going over our heads. The pace is very slow and we stop in a street with houses on one side and a high wall on the other. Here we lie down on the pavement and in spite of the smell of drains and the tracer bullets from the enemy position on the hill behind the houses continuously passing over our heads and mortars dropping unpleasantly close, we drop off to sleep spasmodically from sheer exhaustion. I also hear what I presume must be the enemy rocket projectors going off with a devilish hissing sound followed by an almighty 'crump'.

I lose Captain Angus Low for a while. He is looking for the transport with our rucksacks. One thing is certain; we could never have carried them ourselves. The Sergeant Major is near me.[22]

Sergeant R.K. Taylor of 5 Flight, 'D' Squadron was among one of the smaller groups of pilots attempting to locate their comrades and link up with 1 Wing Headquarters at the Hartenstein.

We glider pilots were sent along with other troops through the grounds of the asylum and past a burned out flak wagon to another collecting point.

Whilst at this point I lost touch with George Bonter, my first pilot.

Captain Morrison, our Flight commander, gathered as many of us together as he could find to form our own unit, not much more than a section. We started off in the general direction of Arnhem.

Just as darkness was falling we headed off to the left in the direction of a fire fight, hoping to give a hand. The firing died out and in full darkness we settled down on the edge of a wood. I had no idea where we were by this time.[23]

The situation amongst the units attempting to reach John Frost and his men at the bridge was equally confused. The lead elements of the South Staffords under Derek McCardie with Ian Toler's squadron were now mixed in with the remnants of 1st Parachute Battalion. David Dobie had roughly 140 paratroops including a number from 3rd Parachute Battalion who were still fit to fight; he was determined to continue his effort to break through to the bridge.

The two battalion commanders formulated a plan to mount a joint attack on the German blocking line at 2100 hours. During their planning it was agreed that David Dobie would take the lead and command the joint force as he had been on the ground longer and had better knowledge of the German defences and the local situation.

Before the two battalions could launch their attack a report reached them from Divisional Headquarters stating that 2nd Parachute Battalion had surrendered, the two battalions were ordered to disengage and return toward the Division's perimeter. Derek McCardie and David Dobie, however, did not believe the report and continued to prepare their men for the attack.

The delay to the timings was a double-edged sword, the preparation time being spent usefully disseminating orders, and preparing weapons and equipment. Also, the longer the two commanders waited, the closer the remaining companies of the 2nd Battalion South Staffords and the 11th Parachute Battalion would be to joining their force. The downside of course was that every hour that passed swiftly by was an hour less of darkness that the airborne could use for cover.

Staff Sergeant Mark Leaver was still static with his Jeep load of explosives waiting nervously for a chance to push through to the bridge:

> After dusk we had several skirmishes with German patrols but held our position. At about midnight on the 18th and after hearing a lot of heavy firing coming from the other side of the railway line, we heard quite a large group of men marching along the bottom road from the direction of Oosterbeek and approaching our position. We issued a challenge, and were very relieved when it turned out to be the South Staffords. We advised them of the position and it was decided that we would continue to the bridge at first light.[24]

## Notes

| | |
|---|---|
| 1 | 'When Dragons Flew', by permission of the Museum of The King's Own Royal Border Regiment. |
| 2 | Maughan, Sergeant A., 14 Flt, 'F' Sqn GPR, correspondence with Bob Hilton, 1997. |
| 3 | Herridge, SSgt M., 'A' Sqn GPR, correspondence with the author, December 2007. |
| 4 | Edwards, SSgt E., 2 Flt, 'A' Sqn GPR, 'What did you do in the War, Granddad?', collection Luuk Buist. |
| 5 | Bell, Private W., 10 Pln, 'C' Coy, 7 KOSB, correspondence with Luuk Buist, 1989. |
| 6 | Mills, SSgt A. , 22 Flt, 'D' Sqn GPR, correspondence with Luuk Buist, 1991. |
| 7 | Hahn, SSgt S., 3 Flt, 'B' Sqn GPR, interview with the author, February 2008. |
| 8 | Cooper, Sergeant S., MT Pl, 'HQ' Coy, 156 Para Bn, by permission of *The Eagle*. |
| 9 | Battalion War Diary, 7th (Galloway) Bn, KOSB, 18 September 1944. |
| 10 | Bell, Private W., 10 Pln, 'C' Coy, 7 KOSB, correspondence with Luuk Buist, 1989. |
| 11 | Mills, SSgt A., 22 Flt, 'D' Sqn GPR, correspondence with Luuk Buist, 1991. |
| 12 | Rose, SSgt R., 5 Flt, 'D' Sqn GPR, correspondence with Bob Hilton, 1997. |
| 13 | Hagen, Sergeant L., 8 Flt, 'D' Sqn GPR, *Arnhem Lift*, Barnsley, Pen & Sword Ltd, 2001, p. 20. |
| 14 | Taziker, Sergeant J., 'C' Sqn GPR, letter dated March 1945. |
| 15 | Grant, SSgt R., 'E' Sqn GPR, by permission of *The Eagle*. |
| 16 | Midgley, Sergeant A., 9 Flt, 'G' Sqn GPR, correspondence with Luuk Buist, 1988-9. |
| 17 | Rigby, SSgt A., 19 Flt, 'B' Sqn GPR, by permission of *The Eagle*. |
| 18 | Rigby, SSgt A., 19 Flt, 'B' Sqn GPR, by permission of *The Eagle*. |
| 19 | Holcroft, SSgt W., 14 Flt, 'F' Sqn GPR, 'No medals for Lt Pickwoad', September 1945. |
| 20 | Bonome, SSgt J., 'C' Sqn GPR, correspondence with Luuk Buist, 1991. |
| 21 | McGeough, SSgt J., 'C' Sqn GPR, correspondence with Luuk Buist, since 1978. |
| 22 | Toler, Major I., OC 'B' Sqn GPR, by permission of the Toler family. |
| 23 | Taylor, Sergeant R., 5 Flt, 'D' Sqn GPR, correspondence with Bob Hilton |

# CHAPTER 10

# High Tide

*'Glider Pilots … left flanking!'*

**Tuesday, 19 September 1944**

Amid the preparations for the combined breakthrough attack, Arthur Shackleton was approached by Derek McCardie with an idea to add weight to the South Staffords' assault:

> The Colonel said to me 'Staff, I saw you driving a Bren Carrier today. I want to use it in the attack tonight, you can drive it and I will come with you. We can use the carrier to lead the attack.' I was not too happy about the prospect for a number of reasons, not least the fact it seemed to promise certain death … I explained that the broken track on the carrier had only been bodged with fence wire and that if we attempted to do anything other than drive in a straight line it would come off. The CO seemed happy with my explanation and went off to carry on with his planning.[1]

The final orders conference for the combined attack was held at 0200 hours, in a room within a battle-scarred house. Arthur Shackleton escorted Ian Toler through the rubble strewn streets to Derek McCardie's makeshift headquarters.

Unbeknown to any of the commanders present, John Fitch was also about to attempt a breakthrough with the remnants of his 3rd Parachute Battalion. This was his last throw of the dice as a formed unit, his proud battalion launching their attack along the river bank at 0230 hours with roughly fifty men. They were beaten back under withering German fire with many casualties, including RSM John Lord. The survivors, including John Fitch, joined up with the combined attack at 0430 hours, offering to give supporting fire.

By this time the South Staffords from the second lift had been reunited with their Commanding Officer and the companies that had landed on the first day. Arthur Shackleton remembers entering the dark room just prior to the 'O' Group: 'I found a bottle and a candle and put them together … like in a romantic restaurant. The atmosphere was most eerie, the darkened room, the mortars bursting around us outside and the rattle of small arms fire. In amongst all of this we were trying to organize our own attack.'[2]

Ian Toler:

> There is a lot of wrecked transport on the road both British and German. The house is dark save for a single candle in the front parlour which might be the same in any house in any British suburb. The furniture is all there as the owners have left it and yet this house is in the middle of a battle, the only evidence for this at present being a hole in the window blind where a bullet came through a little while before.
>
> Round the candle are McCardie, looking a lot older than when I last saw him a few

162

hours ago, Lieutenant Colonel Dobie commanding 1st Parachute Battalion, Major Buchanan [OC Support Company, South Staffords] and the Adjutant [Captain J.F.K. Chapman] and Intelligence Officer [Lieutenant D.G. Longden] of the Staffords.

The atmosphere is tense and dramatic. Lieutenant Colonel Frost … reduced to about eighty men is holding the bridge at Arnhem only a mile or so away and must be relieved. To hold the bridge is the object of the whole operation. The Divisional commander has decided that it is impossible to hold the bridge without taking the high ground behind us which dominates the bridge. This he has so far failed to do.

He has not heard from Frost and assumes he has been wiped out, so he has ordered McCardie and Dobie to withdraw. McCardie knows Frost is still there as he is in wireless touch with him and knows his plight. He decides he cannot let him down.

We all go out [of the room] and McCardie and Dobie take the decision to advance on the bridge at all costs, turning like Nelson a blind eye to the Divisional Commander's orders.

The Staffords are to advance along the road into the town past the St Elisabeth Hospital … and press on to the bridge, in spite of a 20mm gun firing directly down one of the streets they have to pass. The 1st Parachute Battalion is to advance along the riverbank which is known to be strongly held by the enemy in slit trenches and covered by enemy mortar fire.

Zero hour is 0345 hours. Fortunately before this time a message comes through from Division upholding McCardie's decision having contacted Frost.

McCardie now calls me in and tells me that my pilots will not advance to the bridge with him but will return to Divisional Headquarters. As was originally intended. I must admit I am very thankful, but feel that I am deserting some very brave men on a forlorn hope. I wish the colonel 'God Speed' and retrace my steps along the road to find Angus and his flight.[3]

Ian Toler rejoined his pilots and immediately tasked Sergeant Major Billy Watt to begin to organize their withdrawal to Oosterbeek. After some time spent hunting for the Jeeps containing the Squadron's rucksacks, he realized that daylight would soon be upon them and it would surely be accompanied by accurate German machine-gun fire. At 0330 hours, still accompanied by Squadron Leader Howard Coxon from the RADAR mission, 'B' Squadron set off west toward Oosterbeek. Despite the illumination of burning buildings, flares and mortar explosions, the column did not attract any direct German fire.

As they hurried westward, they encountered Major Robert Cain leading 'B' Company of the South Staffords towards the battle. It was he who had represented the men of his own 13 Platoon when they had requested the reinstatement of Jim Hooper as their pilot at RAF Manston. Destined to be awarded the Victoria Cross for his actions later in the battle, Cain had the good fortune and further distinction of being the only one of five recipients of the medal to survive the battle.

Ian Toler gave Cain a briefing on the situation he was marching into and an outline of Derek McCardie's plan of attack for the South Staffords. The two groups then separated and moved off in opposite directions. Toler's men were by no means home and dry:

After we passed the station and crossed the railway we are going up the road we traversed earlier in the evening, when a burst of tracer comes straight down the centre of the road. Thank god we are marching on the side. Tracer is also over us from the embankment on our left. I decide this is no place for us and decide we must take a detour. Do we move quickly![4]

Arthur Shackleton:

By this time it was full light and we had to cross two streets. The Germans were firing machine guns on fixed lines down both of them. We realized that being German they were highly methodical, they were firing five second bursts with a five second interval. We timed them!

We managed to get everybody across without casualties. We were forced to leave the motorcycle behind but kept the Bren Carrier with us.[5]

At 'Zero' hour, David Dobie advanced with his battalion along the Onderlangs road closest to the river, whilst the South Staffords supported his left flank by attacking on a parallel axis along Utrechtseweg. The 11th Parachute Battalion had finally reached the forward battalions, but was to be held in reserve behind the South Staffords and played no part in the initial attack.

The opposition from the Germans has been described by all who survived as exceptionally fierce. The weight of fire was extremely intense and casualties were correspondingly heavy, with no prospect of bringing anti-tank guns forward to tackle German armour due to the confined space and the intensity of the enemy fire.

As dawn broke the South Staffords were in a particularly exposed position, between the Municipal Museum and the St Elisabeth Hospital. German tanks continually attempted to penetrate the British lines, able to roam at will once PIAT ammunition was expended.

With momentum lost and casualties mounting, Derek McCardie requested support from the 11th Parachute Battalion, asking them to work around to the left of the German positions. Lieutenant Colonel George Lea was in the process of initiating just such an attack when he received orders from Divisional Headquarters that he was not to intervene in a futile battle – orders that came from Roy Urquhart himself. Earlier the advance of the South Staffords had driven the German line back and freed the Divisional Commander from his exile close to the St Elisabeth Hospital at 0630 hours.

He had immediately secured himself a Jeep, driven by Lieutenant Edward Clapham MC, Commander of A Troop, 1st Airlanding Anti-Tank Battery, RA who was not about to refuse a Major General's request for a lift to Divisional Headquarters. It was an eventful journey as the two men drew fire from numerous German snipers as they sped toward Oosterbeek. Roy Urquhart arrived safely at the Hartenstein by 0725 hours.

Having had over thirty hours to consider his position and seen the strength and depth of the German forces in Arnhem for himself, Urquhart had decided that further attacks would be useless without reinforcements. He therefore set about finding a way to get 'Shan' Hackett and his battalions down to the bridge and into the battle.

Unaware of Urquhart's orders to 11th Parachute Battalion, Derek McCardie had already decided his men could not sustain the rate of attrition the Germans were inflicting on them and was looking for a way to extract his battalion from an increasingly desperate situation. The attack had been led by 'A' Company, who were now practically cut off from the rest of the Battalion. Nevertheless, they gave what covering fire they could to allow their sister companies to withdraw, but in the process the company was wiped out. McCardie was captured when the 'A' Company position was overrun, having gone forward to ascertain why the Company was not engaging German tanks. On reaching the forward positions he discovered that they had expended all of their PIAT ammunition. He was then blown off his feet by a blast and captured with the few survivors of 'A' Company by advancing German infantry.

The other rifle companies of the South Staffords fared little better. In their new positions, they were just as vulnerable as before as Kampfgruppe Spindler raked their exposed positions with fire from all sides. Jim Hooper had stayed with 13 Platoon after landing and had not withdrawn with the rest of 'B' Squadron. He was now in the midst of some of the most savage fighting of the battle:

We advanced beyond a badly shot up tram car until forced to halt soon after dawn's early light. We were just past the Municipal Museum and still some distance from the bridge, but only a few hundred yards from Arnhem's main station.

During the attack the Germans were able to sweep the road with 20mm, heavy machine gun and tracer fire whilst the airborne troops were advancing on a very narrow front. The enemy was also able to fire on us from the south side of the river with mortars and other heavy weapons.

The Paras' progress had been similarly disappointing and both units had taken heavy casualties. In anticipation of a German counter-attack defensive positions were established in houses on the north side of Utrechtsweg opposite the museum. These houses immediately received the attention of the German gunners on the other side of the river. Our building caught fire and 13 Platoon was forced to evacuate as it began to collapse around us.

The survivors dived into the grounds of the museum, later known as 'the Dell' where we dug in and waited for the next attack. The attack came and the weary South Staffs, short of ammunition and without heavy weapons, were over-run by Panzers, self propelled guns and SS Infantry.

I lost contact with my second pilot Sergeant Peter Johnson, who was killed in action – 'no known grave'. I was taken prisoner.[6]

The South Staffords fought tenaciously, but by midday Derek McCardie's veteran battalion had been practically annihilated. Only 'C' Company had escaped from the killing zone around the St Elisabeth Hospital as a formed unit. The survivors of 1st Parachute Battalion now numbered no more than forty effective paratroopers.

A few survivors from the other companies of the South Staffords doggedly fought their way out of the carnage, but most were either dead or taken prisoner like their CO and Jim Hooper.

Hooper remembers contemplating his fate as he was being stripped of his weapons and searched by members of 9th SS Panzer Division. Ironically at around the same time, his RAF tug pilot, Flight Sergeant Edwin Flavell, was writing a reassuring letter to Jim's parents from RAF Brize Norton:

Dear Mr & Mrs Hooper,

As you no doubt expected Jimmy took part in a large airborne landing in Holland. Before we took off Jimmy asked me to drop you a line as the mail position with the airborne forces would be obscure.

There is no need to worry it really was a 'large piece of cake' everything went like clockwork.

The take off was from an advance base; myself as Jimmy's tug pilot. It was a completely uneventful trip, the only thing that shook us both was the number of aircraft in the sky.

The trip over Holland was very interesting, I think it was the first time both of us had been on a daylight operation.

The target turned up OK and after positioning ourselves we said cheerio and Jimmy went on his way, my gunner watched the glider make for the landing zone. I also visited the landing zone the following day with another glider it all looked very peaceful indeed, I heard a remark passed to the effect that the smoke coming from the woods was probably afternoon tea being brewed up.

Well I must close now and if I get any news of Jimmy I won't hesitate in writing to you.

I remain yours

Sincerely

Edwin Flavell

A world away from Brize Norton the battle for possession of the bridge was increasing in ferocity as the Germans mounted a series of concerted attacks in an effort to reopen the highway south. In the absence of Gerald Lathbury, John Frost had moved into the 1st Parachute Brigade Headquarters and assumed command of the Brigade.

Frost's force was running desperately low on ammunition. There were also a steadily increasing number of casualties streaming into the cellars, below the now shattered houses around the northern ramp. Despite the ever-increasing German pressure, a demand for a British surrender was rejected out of hand by John Frost. The struggle would go on.

Arthur Rigby and 19 Flight were still playing their part in the defence of the bridgehead. Despite all that was happening around him, Arthur had the same basic priorities as every soldier through history, 'Where is my next meal coming from?':

Tuesday morning dawned a bit misty but not sufficient to obscure the view around our flat, all quiet, and the sun began to shine weakly. I now noticed that my boots had suffered rather badly from the burning debris I had walked through and they were in very poor shape, but there was nothing I could do so I forgot about them.

We were hungry again and we had only our 'K' rations. Ten 'K' rations between eleven of us. Ted and I had eaten one of ours the night before, so Ted had a scout round the cupboards in the flat and came up with potatoes, carrots, onions and a tin of 'something' (no label). We got a fire going (the smoke from the chimney would not show against the fires and smoke which still hung over the town) and after finding a large saucepan and mug I managed to bale enough water from the lavatory cistern to provide cooking liquid.

Ted got cracking on the vegetables and the dehydrated meat cubes form the 'K' rations. The rest of us returned to our posts, taking turns to wash and shave with water from an outside water butt. The stew that Ted prepared was good. Hot and tasty, but the tin without a label which he found had been punctured and the meat inside was off but the dehydrated cubes made a very meaty flavour. Well enough to be able to call it 'Beef Stew', and for dessert we found some apples in a dish on the sideboard.

We discovered later that had we been on the ground floor we would have had quite a choice of fruits, for in a sort of coach house in the yard there was a cart loaded with all kinds of local fruit. All was laid out as if on a market stall ready for sale but we didn't find this until we were leaving the home later.

Across the rooftops, visible from the window from which we observed, was a tall Cathedral belfry, quite clearly to be seen through the smoke, and it seemed as though the bells were chiming, softly at times, and quite loudly at others. Some of the boys reckoned that Jerry had some spotters up in the tower and they were signalling our whereabouts to their mortar teams, so that they could pinpoint us fairly accurately. But in time we realised that the soft tinkles and the loud clangs coincided with the intensity of their mortar attacks and concluded that bomb fragments causing the illusion of 'signals' were striking the bells.

Later in the morning the Luftwaffe had a 'go' at us. A gaggle of Messerschmitts came in low over the houses with their cannon and machine guns blazing away. Going like the 'clappers'. Unfortunately for one of the pilots the smoke was a little denser at that moment and he didn't notice the cathedral spire until it was too late to avoid it. He banked steeply to try to get past but his starboard main plane hit the tower and the impact broke it off. The aircraft flipped over on to its back and dived into the homes about a mile from us. They didn't try any more strafes after that.

The situation with 1st Airlanding Brigade in its positions around Oosterbeek and the landing zones was relatively stable – the weight of German attacks was not yet as heavy as those falling on the 1st Parachute Brigade. Brigade Headquarters moved to the houses in the Pietersberg area, just to the south of the Hartenstein.

Major 'Dickie' Dale DFC and the pilots of 'C' Squadron GPR were being held as the Brigade reserve. They moved with the headquarters and were deployed in defensive positions to the east of Brigade Headquarters, to act as local protection.

The task of defending the western flank of the Brigade was the responsibility of the 1st Battalion, The Border Regiment, who had established their headquarters in a house at Breedelaan. The Battalion had performed well against the Dutch SS and Kampfgruppe Von Tettau, despite the absence of their veteran Commanding Officer, Lieutenant Colonel Tommy Haddon. He had as yet failed to reach Arnhem despite two attempts.

Major John Blatch, the Second in Command of 2 Wing GPR, and his co-pilot Sergeant John Lester had taken off from RAF Broadwell with the first lift carrying the Borders CO. They flew into cloud soon after take-off, and had been forced to pull off and land on the Berkshire Downs. The load consisted of Tommy Haddon, the CO, his Intelligence Officer Lieutenant Ronald Hope-Jones, a few headquarters personnel, a Jeep and trailer.

Having extracted the Colonel's Jeep from the Horsa, they had all raced back to the airfield to join the second lift. The group succeeded in securing a new glider and took off without incident on 18 September. All went well this time until a point on the Albert Canal just West of Herentals in Belgium. Both pilots had noticed that they seemed on their own, the rest of the stream had disappeared and there was no sign of the promised fighter cover. John Blatch recalls:

> Then the flak started. Tug and glider were hit. The tug pilot shouted down the intercom to pull off as he and his co-pilot were wounded; we did just that and saw the tug go down in a steep dive we thought could only be fatal.
>
> Our own aircraft had several holes in it but no-one hurt; however a large part of the port aileron was missing. Control could only be kept by flying fast and doing shallow left hand turns.
>
> Luckily we had height enough to pick a couple of fields with a hedge between for a crash landing, and went in – fast. The flaps worked and improved stability. Speed was lost by rubbing the skid hard into the first field and bursting through the hedge.
>
> We came to rest just short of a second hedge where the whole complement unloaded without much difficulty. Relieved to have made landfall just on the Allied side of the canal line, we found our way to the nearby Headquarters of a Unit of 7th Armoured Brigade which was about to advance.
>
> We made our way with them to the corridor up which the sea-tail of 1st Airborne Division was proceeding. We joined them and reached Airborne Corps Headquarters at Nijmegen but could get no further, having to content ourselves with odd jobs there until evacuated after the battle.
>
> The saving grace was to find on returning to Broadwell that the crippled tug and injured crew had somehow made it home.

While a very frustrated Tommy Haddon was battling his way east to catch up with his battalion,

Major Henry Cousens, his Second in Command, had stepped up into his appointment and was handling the Borders extremely well in his absence. This incident is another example of the absence of 'tactical loading' – a battalion commander and the Second in Command of 2 Wing GPR were both travelling in the same glider. Dispersal and separation of key personnel does not appear to have been considered a priority when loading the aircraft.

The Borders were holding their own and were deployed as follows: 'A' Company were dug in around the Graftombe, with 'B' Company in the vicinity of the high ground of the Westerbouwing. Control and defence of the key crossroads of Utrechtseweg and Wolfhezerweg was allocated to 'C' Company, whilst 'D' Company was dug in at the Zilverberg.

The 7th Battalion King's Own Scottish Borderers were still tied to their original mission – to maintain control of LZ 'L'. The Scots had moved east and north of the railway, to secure the landing zone in preparation for the arrival of the third lift of gliders. These gliders would carry the heavy weapons and equipment of Major General Stanislaw Sosabowski's 1st Polish Independent Parachute Brigade Group.

Despite incurring 10 per cent casualties en route to Arnhem and during the drop itself, the 4th Parachute Brigade was in good shape at the start of the day. 'Shan' Hackett had visited Divisional Headquarters during the night, where he had spoken with 'Pip' Hicks. The two brigadiers had agreed that 4th Parachute Brigade was to advance westward, using the Ede to Arnhem road north of the railway line as its axis. They were to secure the high ground at Koepel, keeping a firm left flank on the road.

The vacuum created by the detachment of 11th Parachute Battalion to the battle for the bridge had to be filled. With a third of his infantry missing, the Brigade's engineer squadron was instructed to deploy in the infantry role and act as 'Shan' Hackett's reserve. The Sappers were held back in a backstop role behind the two battalions.

There were also glider pilots among 'Shan' Hackett's brigade who were required to play a part in the attack. Captain Barry Murdoch was the Officer Commanding 8 Flight, 'D' Squadron. He and his flight remained with the 10th Parachute Battalion where they had already found gainful employment, north of the railway line:

> Most glider pilots have to be prepared to drive jeeps. At that time I was driving Lieutenant Colonel Smyth's jeep, officer commanding the 10th Parachute Battalion. We set off at 3 o'clock in the morning for north side of the railway line. Task was to protect the landing zone from enemy infiltration, and hold the ground for next day's gliders.
>
> At dawn we were just north of the railway line with the 10th Parachute Battalion – about 600 men. We were driving along a road, to get into our positions when an 88mm gun at the end of the road suddenly opened up on us. Shells were bursting very close, so we quickly took cover on the side of the road.
>
> A few minutes after leaving the jeep a shell hit it and blew it up. This annoyed both Lieutenant Colonel Smyth and myself, because all our kit went west, including cigarettes. Then we reported to nearest company and asked for some help; we were provided with a walkie-talkie wireless set. After that we went into action against the 88mm gun. It died down eventually, and we took one house.[7]

Two other 'D' Squadron flights were also operating north of the railway in support of infantry battalions. Captain John Morrison had taken 5 Flight to support the King's Own Scottish Borderers in their task defending the Polish landing zone. Captain Ian Muir was in command of 22 Flight, who were attached to 156th Parachute Battalion.

The KOSB had been returned to the command of the Airlanding Brigade. The 4th Parachute

Brigade would attack with its two remaining battalions. The advance would be led by Lieutenant Colonel Sir Richard des Voeux's 156th Parachute Battalion, with Lieutenant Colonel Ken Smyth's 10th Parachute Battalion in support on their left flank.

The aim was for 156th Parachute Battalion to take three areas of high ground consecutively. The first overlooked Johannahoeve Farm near LZ 'L'; the second key feature was in the woods near Lichtenbeek House. Once the first two objectives were secured the Battalion was to attack the Koepel feature. If successful in 'rolling up' these key pieces of high ground, they would be within striking distance of Arnhem Bridge.

Ken Smyth's attack on the left flank would use Amsterdamseweg as its axis and ensure there was no enemy interference with the main attack. Once the third objective at Koepel had been secured, 4th Parachute Brigade was to quickly regroup and then attack in the direction of Arnhem. The new attack would bring 'Shan' Hackett's brigade into the battle, where the left flank of the 1st Parachute Brigade was thought to be.

South of the railway line in Oosterbeek, daylight had brought the opportunity for consolidation around the Hartenstein Hotel. Early in the morning it was decided to concentrate all prisoners in the tennis courts behind the Hartenstein Hotel. The glider pilots, guarding the prisoners in the J.P. Heije School, were involved in escorting the POWs out of their classrooms and up to the new divisional prisoner cage.

During the morning, both GPR Wing headquarters located each other and established communications. John Place left 2 Wing Headquarters and visited Iain Murray at the Hartenstein Hotel at 0930 hours. Whilst the two commanding officers met, Headquarters 2 Wing had completed its move to a house at Nassaulaan.

During the move the Wing had attracted the unwanted attention of several ME109s which loitered over the position for thirty minutes strafing the exposed glider pilots, the men of 2 Wing obviously responding with whatever weapons they had to hand. While good for morale, returning fire in such a position was rarely successful and the amount of ammunition expended was clearly a cause for concern to Wing Headquarters.

Shortly after the attack, an order was circulated to all squadrons and flights to the effect that returning fire was a waste of valuable ammunition and also signposted the firers' positions to the attacking aircraft.

Staff Sergeant Cliff Wedgbury had been detached from 'F' Squadron to act as a runner for 2 Wing Headquarters; his account appears to vindicate the thinking behind the order:

When we moved to Nassaulaan, Padre Chignell found that he had left his haversack containing a chalice and a bible at our previous house. I was ordered with another glider pilot to accompany him so he could retrieve it.

As it had been rumoured that the Germans had overrun this house I didn't feel too happy about it. However we set off through some allotments and woods.

As we went along I could hear and feel the thumps of mortars being fired. My reaction was to fling myself flat on the ground, but the Padre, a brave man, stood there, resplendent in his 'Red Beret', walking-stick in hand, looking as though he was going to pick blackberries and completely oblivious of any danger. I felt most humble! The haversack and contents were safely retrieved and we started to make our way back to Wing headquarters.

On the way back through a drive in the woods, we heard the sounds of fighter aircraft, which we assumed to be ours. I was wrong; the aircraft were FW190's and ME109's. After they had been fired at by airborne troops, they circled and came back, firing their cannons in our direction. The noise was horrific both from the planes and the crashing of trees as

169

they were chopped down. My immediate response was to seek cover.

I spotted a chap in a trench and dived in on top of him. By the time the air attack had finished I found I was underneath him. I was glad I was still alive.[8]

At 1100 hours an urgent message came direct from Headquarters 1st Airborne Division: 'F' Squadron were to move to the east edge of a wood in the grounds of Dennenkamp house. They were also to maintain a standing patrol in the Lebretweg/ Zaaijerplein area.

Wally Holcroft had moved with 'F' Squadron into their new position, just before the German air attack began:

Lieutenant Clarke ordered trenches to be dug. We had hardly begun to take up positions when over came a flight of Messerschmitts … we were busy digging trenches as the enemy attacked at low level.

We had no experience of this kind of warfare; in fact most of us had no experience of any kind of warfare. Not surprising perhaps we all dashed for shelter beneath the trees. Lieutenant Clarke in command of the situation insisted we kept on digging. We did but not too enthusiastically.

Soon after the last aircraft had passed over one of the boys made the discovery that the wood was honey-combed with deeply dug holes. These had apparently been machine dug by the Germans. I found myself a good one and Mick [Hall] and I entrenched ourselves.

We were busy making ourselves comfortable when 'Ginger' Rice came breathlessly up to us. 'Banks [SSgt] and McLaren [SSgt] have had it" he said, 'and several of the boys are wounded.'

This news stunned me for a few moments. 'Admiral' dead, it couldn't be; for only minutes before he had passed me as he went down the wood with a cheerful smile on his face. Burly McLaren too, this was indeed depressing news and I recalled 'Admiral's' words of only the day before, 'Three of these Operations are enough for anybody'. 'Admiral' had not survived his third.

These being our first battle casualties, and among friends who had lived in a tightly knit community for the past six months, caused some despondency to fall over 'F' Squadron for a while, but it served no purpose to fret and we had to forget. Mac and Admiral were gone, and nothing we could do would bring them back. We learned later that though they died when one of the bombs exploded near them neither of them had a wound but had been killed by shock waves from the blast.

There was a large house [Dennenkamp] in the wood and this had been taken over as our Squadron headquarters. Towards dinner time someone found a large greenhouse full of grapes and tomatoes. It didn't take long for the boys to empty it and I was able to get a share, which I divided with Hartford who was very pleased for after a couple of days on reconstituted food, fresh fruit certainly tasted delicious.[9]

About a mile to the south of 'F' Squadron, on the west of the Oosterbeek perimeter, was 'A' Squadron's position. Staff Sergeant Clarence 'Curly' Harman, 17 Flight, 'A' Squadron, was on the south-western edge of the Oosterbeek perimeter, in the area of a house called Oorsprong on van Borsselenweg:

I heard an ME109 coming straight for us. I pushed Staff Sergeant [Dennis] Daniels and his co-pilot to the side of the track and Sergeant Christian and I climbed over a gate to the cover of the trees. The Messerschmitt turned and flew up and down the ride looking for us. I kept the biggest oak tree between the plane and me. Eventually I heard it throttle right back as it came looking for us. When the plane was gone Sergeant Christian and I went looking for the others, only to find out they were killed.[10]

Sergeant Norman Ramsden was a target of the same Messerschmitt:

We lay up under cover around a large house [Oorsprong Estate]. Here we were strafed by an ME109. Staff Sergeant Daniels and his co-pilot Sergeant [Lewis] Pattinson, both of 17 Flight, were killed outright. Our Padre supervised the burial in a lawn in front of the house. I joined up with the rest of 17 Flight and dug positions alongside a roadway for the night.[11]

Staff Sergeant Reg Grant of 'E' Squadron was less disturbed by the activities of the Luftwaffe – he was using the sound of the fighting in Arnhem to monitor its tempo and build his own picture of the battle to the east of his position. Peter Jackson's squadron were centred on Oranjeweg, running north off Utrechtseweg, in the west part of Oosterbeek. Reg Grant could clearly hear the sound of battle and yet he was just a few hundred yards north-west of Divisional Headquarters at the Hartenstein:

We moved back to a position nearer the road on top of a slope. At about nine o'clock the first enemy fighters we had seen began strafing us. So long as we kept in our slit trenches they did little damage. Our only casualty was one of the Flight commanders who received a wound in the shoulder.

We had no idea whatever just what was happening at the bridge although occasionally we heard sounds of intense bursts of fire, now mostly from the enemy. You could tell by the very high rate of fire from their automatic weapons.

By midday the enemy seemed to be moving in from all directions and was obviously bringing up armoured vehicles from the sound of the tracks. On the move all the time – as soon as we had prepared defences in one area, so we moved to another.

On one occasion I was told to dig a trench in what was probably one of the best lawns I had ever seen, but when the officer moved on, I dug it in a flowerbed instead, just a few feet away.[12]

Later that morning Major Peter Jackson was in the process of laying out 'E' Squadron's new position, when he was rudely disturbed:

I went ahead to survey the ground accompanied by one of the Sergeants. Whilst looking round deciding where to dispose the troops the Sergeant was heard to say, 'Look Sir, aren't those Typhoons.' I looked skywards and to my horror saw that black crosses decorated the 'Typhoons' that were already diving down on us.

The Sergeant got to the only available hole and I was forced to take cover beneath an army handcart, which was the thinnest thing one could ever find to put between oneself and a bullet. The enemy aircraft sprayed them with bullets but fortunately without causing injury, but the action completely wrote off the two cars with their precious cargo of liquid refreshment.[13]

Staff Sergeant William Gordon of 'C' Squadron had landed a Hamilcar glider, with two Bren carriers of the South Staffords, during the second lift. As the glider touched down and ran along the ground, the undercarriage hit soft ground. The wheels sunk in immediately, bringing the huge glider to a sudden stop. The tail of the aircraft reared up suddenly and the pilots were thrown out. William Gordon was slightly dazed and Sergeant Charles Symmonds sustained a broken arm. A corporal in one of the carriers was also injured.

They managed to free the carriers, which both remained serviceable. William Gordon:

I took the place of the injured Corporal. I accompanied the Canadian Lieutenant [Lieutenant Art Godfrey] in the inspection of perimeter posts, probed the road leading to Arnhem and collected dropped supplies. A large part of the supplies dropped into enemy hands and we seemed not to have any means of correcting the errors. The enemy firepower increased as they moved in to surround us. Multiple barrelled mortars were quite startling and a flight of FW190's strafed the area.

The nearest I got to the Road Bridge was when in company of the Canadian Lieutenant and another Lieutenant, we went by carrier to try and recover a half-shaft from a damaged and abandoned jeep, within sight of the destroyed railway bridge. During examination of the jeep, the enemy opened up with a mortar but we managed to withdraw one of the shafts, the officers provided cover, and we didn't remain long in the area.[14]

Although Roy Urquhart now had an understanding of the level of German resistance in Arnhem itself and John Frost was still clinging on to the north end of 1st Airborne Division's primary objective, the overall situation remained confused.

Rather than offering the promise of much-needed reinforcements, the imminent arrival of the third lift later in the day and the protection of its landing zones had become another difficult task. The hard-pressed airborne troops were already struggling to hold the landing zone north of the railway. The third lift had been due to take off from England at 0745 hours and had been due to land in Holland at 1045 hours, this timing being designated as Z-hour.

Sergeant Peter Gammon was part of an 'F' Squadron patrol that morning; he, like his divisional commander, was beginning to realize the gravity of the situation. He saw some of the survivors withdrawing from the direction of the bridge:

We had 'stood to' at dawn … It was quiet and my water bottle virtually empty. Somebody had located a pump in the courtyard of a nearby stable block so we all took turns to go and fill them and have a wash.

Half way through my ablutions, I was called outside to find the rest of the flight marching off southwards. Passing the Hartenstein and the Oosterbeek church down by the river, we turned eastwards towards the demolished railway bridge.

We met marching towards the church dejected groups of soldiers, most were silent but some shouted warnings ahead of us and a few cursed the authority that had put them in impossible positions. Some had arms and equipment but many were in various states of undress revealing field dressings.

A few hundred yards short of the railway embankment we took up positions in a row of bungalows. Our action was obviously a morale booster for none of us had anything more potent than rifles and grenades with which to resist any German follow up to our retreating forces.

Toward lunch time the numbers moving east dwindled to nothing and we joined the last small group spurred on by the distant rattle of tank tracks on the hard road.[15]

Not all glider pilots succeeded in reaching their designated RV points and rejoining their fellow squadron members. Due to the circumstances, a lot of them found themselves fighting in a totally unexpected role in a corner of the battlefield they had not chosen for themselves.

The training they had received under the direction of George Chatterton was to save many of their lives – the 'total soldier' concept was to be vindicated at Arnhem. One glider pilot who fought much of his battle away from his comrades was Staff Sergeant Edward Browne of 9 Flight, 'G' Squadron.

His Horsa was loaded with a jeep and trailer, with six members of a medium machine gun section of Support Company of 3 Parachute Battalion:

> After we landed one of the gunners was killed. I volunteered to act as gunner, as I had been trained on Vickers. The Para Sergeant, Ted Bradshaw, set up one gun, and I operated the other, so we were stuck right out on the perimeter. As I was isolated from my Squadron, I hardly knew what happened to any of them. One first rate Flight officer, Lieutenant Bewley, used to come out and check on me but he was unfortunately badly wounded.[16]

North of the railway line the 4th Parachute Brigade attack began at 0700 hours, with 10th and 156th Parachute Battalions attacking as planned. Both battalions made repeated and determined attacks through the morning. They were repeatedly blocked by 9th SS Panzer Division who were firmly established and holding a blocking line running from Oosterbeek station along Dreijenseweg to the Ede-Arnhem road.

Losses were heavy – 156th Parachute Battalion, for example, encountered self-propelled guns, armoured cars and determined infantry. 'A' Company lost all of its officers and the Battalion was also strafed by Messerschmitts, causing more casualties.

The Company Commander of 'A' Company was Major John Pott. Like every soldier in 4th Parachute Brigade, he was determined to break through to the bridge and relieve John Frost's beleaguered force. One of his platoons had been left at the drop zone to protect the casualties from the brigade drop. Just prior to the attack, his company had been reinforced with the pilots of 22 Flight from 'D' Squadron, under the command of Captain Iain Muir.

Staff Sergeant Arthur Mills was with 22 Flight that morning:

> We went into action with 'A' Company, 156 Parachute Battalion. We fought in the woods all day, but it seemed that the German fire was coming at us from all directions. The 'moaning minnies', multi-barrelled mortars, were very frightening. The shrapnel was stripping the leaves from the trees and falling amongst us.
>
> I saw a jeep about 30 yards away get a direct hit leaping into the air and landing on its back .We had another brew and a bit of chocolate. We were being strafed by ME109's and FW190's but fortunately the trees hid our positions.

John Pott takes up the story later in the morning, just after his company had secured their initial objective overlooking Johannahoeve Farm and were pushing on to take Lichtenbeek:

> The woodland was thick to the west of the road, so when we bumped into the enemy on the line of this road, there was just time for the briefest order: '5 Platoon … fire platoon, 4 platoon and Glider Pilots … left flanking!' In we went … the assault overran well hidden infantry with two half tracks firing down the road from our right.
>
> It was a cheer to see them pull back, as our chaps charged towards them, but they inflicted heavy casualties … We had little time dig in before the first counter-attack came in, but we held our fire till they were close, and we cheered as they ran back … We were out of ammunition when the second attack came in, so we laid low until they were very close and then tried to charge into the flank of their assault line, but a bullet through my femur felled me and that was 'A' Company's last effort.
>
> I was overrun by a platoon of youngsters led by a fine looking Unteroffizier, who said in perfect English, 'Sorry we can't see to you now, but your chaps will be back soon anyway.'[17]

Roy Urquhart was out actively seeking information again and visited Headquarters 4th Parachute Brigade at 1400 hours. During his visit 'Shan' Hackett reluctantly sought permission to withdraw his hard-pressed brigade south over the railway line. He intended to pull his troops back through Wolfheze, to the comparative safety of the Oosterbeek perimeter. It was hoped that the surviving units would gain enough respite to reorganize themselves and attack from Oosterbeek on the southern side of the railway embankment.

Permission to withdraw was given by Urquhart, although there was a significant complication. LZ 'L' was also north of the railway line and the third lift had been due to begin landing that morning at 1045 hours. Without effective communications with England, there was no way of knowing if the lift was even still coming that day.

The scenario of the second lift on the previous day was repeated for the third. Headquarters 1st Airborne Division knew nothing of any delay or postponement to the take-off, and so could only wait expectantly and hopefully until the gliders and parachutes appeared overhead.

The lack of information on the arrival of the lift presented 'Shan' Hackett with a stark dilemma. Not only were the 10th and 156th Parachute Battalions under growing pressure from German infantry, supported by artillery and armoured vehicles, but he had no reserve other than 4 Parachute Squadron RE and his own headquarters staff. The King's Own Scottish Borderers were already spread thinly around the landing zone and could not be expected to hold on to the ground indefinitely in the face of the oncoming German tide. With both parachute battalions already sustaining such heavy losses, the prospect of withdrawing in contact with the enemy was not an attractive one.

There was a real prospect of being driven back across the open space of LZ 'L' while exposed to German fire. If this nightmare scenario came to be, not only would losses be high, there was the awful prospect of the landing zone being overrun and occupied before the gliders arrived. The third lift gliders would cast off unaware of the withdrawal and would be landing amongst the Germans. There could only be one outcome: a horrific turkey shoot.

By 1500 hours, communication between 10th Parachute Battalion and Brigade Headquarters was becoming difficult. In fact, Ken Smyth's men had found more than one of their nominated withdrawal RVs already occupied by the Germans. The resulting mêlées were no holds barred affairs, creating yet more confusion.

Unaware of the 10th Parachute Battalion's situation, 'Shan' Hackett's thoughts were focussed on not allowing his brigade to be trapped between the advancing Germans and the significant obstacle of the railway embankment.

There were only two obvious crossing points for vehicles, and more importantly guns. These were the level crossings at Oosterbeek (Hoog) and Wolfheze railway stations. It was assumed that both of these were in German hands, or very soon would be. An attack on the Wolfheze crossing by 10th Parachute Battalion was being planned, when information on the imminent arrival of a large German force from Kampfgruppe von Tettau from the west was reported by the Dutch Resistance.

Not wanting to be trapped between the two German forces, the decision was taken to break out to the south over the Wolfheze crossing as quickly as possible. The situation north of the railway line, at about 1530 hours, can only be described as perilous.

'Shan' Hackett's situation could accurately be described as being between a rock and a hard place. The KOSB remained pinned to the landing zone, waiting for what might possibly be a non-existent third lift. His two parachute battalions were withdrawing towards the landing zone, with enemy infantry and self-propelled guns snapping at their heels from three directions.

What Hackett really did not need at that moment was the untimely arrival of the third lift in the midst of his withdrawal. The added complication of the gliders carrying the Polish Brigade's guns and vehicles could only result in chaos.

**Notes**

1    Shackleton, SSgt A., 20 Flt, 'B' Sqn GPR, interview with the author, June 2008.
2    Shackleton, SSgt A., 20 Flt, 'B' Sqn GPR, interview with the author, June 2008.
3    Toler, Major I., OC 'B' Sqn GPR, by permission of the Toler family.
4    Toler, Major I., OC 'B' Sqn GPR, by permission of the Toler family.
5    Shackleton, SSgt A., 20 Flt, 'B' Sqn GPR, interview with the author, June 2008.
6    Hooper, SSgt J., 20 Flt, 'B' Sqn GPR, interview with the author, February 2008.
7    Murdoch, Captain G., 8 Flt, 'D' Sqn GPR, by permission of the Airborne Museum Oosterbeek.
8    Wedgbury, SSgt E., 14 Flt, 'F' Sqn GPR, correspondence with Luuk Buist, 1991.
9    Holcroft, SSgt W.,14 Flt,'F' Sqn GPR, 'No medals for Lt Pickwoad', September 1945.
10   Harman, SSgt C., 17 Flt, 'A' Sqn GPR, correspondence with Bob Hilton.
11   Ramsden, Sergeant N., 17 Flt, 'A' Sqn GPR, correspondence with Bob Hilton, April 1998.
12   Grant, SSgt R., 'E' Sqn GPR, correspondence with Luuk Buist, 1991.
13   Jackson, Major P., OC 'E' Sqn GPR, correspondence with Luuk Buist, 1991.
14   Gordon, SSgt W., 'C' Sqn GPR, correspondence with Bob Hilton, 1997.
15   Gammon, SSgt P., 14 Flt, 'F' Sqn GPR, correspondence with the author.
16   Browne, SSgt E., 9 Flt, 'G' Sqn GPR correspondence with Luuk Buist, 1991.
17   Waddy, J., *A Tour of the Arnhem Battlefields,* Barnsley, Pen & Sword Ltd, 2001, p. 112.

# CHAPTER 11

# The Third Lift

*'The landing was a bit eventful.'*

### Tuesday, 19 September 1944

The third lift was to be very different in scale and character to the two much larger and well-coordinated lifts that had been completed before it. The core of the Air Movement Table for the day was formed by the thirty-five gliders allocated to lifting the vehicles and anti-tank guns of Major General Stanislaw Sosabowski's Polish Brigade. The glider element of the Polish lift had been grouped at RAF Keevil and Tarant Rushton. The bulk of the Brigade would jump by parachute, from US IX Troop Carrier Command C47s, flying from Lincolnshire.

There were nine other gliders added on to the original Air Movement Table for the day. These were all serials that had, for various reasons, been unsuccessful in their first attempt to make the crossing. As such, they were a disparate mix scattered across all of the glider airfields as there was not enough time to concentrate the smaller serials at Tarant Rushton or Keevil. The glider and tug crews were, therefore, briefed that they were to rendezvous with the main formation over the English Channel.

The English Channel was to be the location of the rendezvous, and not the North Sea, as the much larger second lift had used the northern route the previous day. The third lift was switched to the southern route in the hope that the German defences would still be focussed on the previous day's route.

There was one combination flying from Down Ampney. This 'E' Squadron Horsa, with chalk number 272, was flown by Staff Sergeant Melrose and Sergeant McDonald. They were unsuccessful on the first lift, landing their Horsa loaded with seventeen troops and six handcarts of 1 (HC) Mortar Platoon, 7 KOSB at RAF Martlesham Heath, near Ipswich.

There were three 'G' Squadron Horsas scheduled to join the lift from RAF Fairford, all attempting the crossing for the second time, the three tugs being provided by two separate RAF Squadrons. A single 'A' Squadron Horsa, piloted by Staff Sergeant John 'Timo' Jenkins and Sergeant 'Timber' Wood, was to lift from RAF Harwell, with the intention of joining the glider stream over the Channel.

A single 'B' Squadron Horsa, crewed by Staff Sergeant Arthur Proctor and Sergeant J. McCulloch, would be towed by a 296 Squadron Albemarle from RAF Manston. Another lone 'D' Squadron Horsa, carrying medics and equipment from 133 Parachute Field Ambulance, had also been added on to the Keevil lift. This Horsa, flown by Staff Sergeant Stocker and Sergeant Allen, bumped the Keevil total up to sixteen.

There were other crews in amongst the Keevil chalks, many joining the lift at short notice. Soon after the departure of the second lift from RAF Harwell, Staff Sergeant Bert Gibb and Sergeant Ron Driver of 'A' Squadron were detailed, with little warning, to fly an empty Horsa to Keevil. It was a routine flight, a relatively short hop of about 30 or 40 miles. They were, however, ordered to go in full fighting order and on arrival reported to the Duty Officer, who allocated them a bell tent that was set up by the perimeter road:

> We had a very early briefing, followed by breakfast, then two more briefings. The first briefing outlined what the operation was – the third lift to Arnhem.
>
> Thirty Horsas mainly taking in the Polish headquarters, and Hamilcars taking in Engineers with bulldozers and equipment to put down a metal airstrip with if I recall correctly, about the same number.
>
> At the next two briefings the Hamilcars were not mentioned again. At one of them, we had aerial photographs of our destination; landing zone 'L' situated northwest of Oosterbeek near Johannahoeve Farm. The landing zone was quite a distinctive shape and proved very easy to see from the air.
>
> We all were told that it would be a 'piece of cake' and that the fighting would very likely be over by the time we got there.[1]

Ron Driver's comments on the withdrawal of Hamilcars from the Air Movement Table are interesting. Ten of the heavy gliders had been earmarked to deliver the engineering equipment and bulldozers of the 878th US (Airborne) Aviation Engineer Battalion to Arnhem. The British gliders would be supplemented with American Waco gliders from the American airfields at Chipping Ongar and Boreham in Essex. The smaller Wacos would be carrying the remainder of the specialist American unit.

It was intended that the American engineers would be used to repair the runway at Deelen and establish an airhead to receive 52 (Lowland) Division, and much-needed combat supplies. There was also the plan to establish a forward airstrip for the night-capable Beaufighters, which would of course require engineer support. The uncertain situation on the ground and increasing losses incurred by resupply aircraft to flak led to the abandonment of this plan.

There was, however, another practical factor that might have affected this decision: a shortage of British glider pilots. The 'Parade State' for the Regiment at the time shows barely enough pilots to cover the three main lifts, let alone an additional lift including Hamilcars. A later lift would, of course, have been possible if crews had been recovered from Holland and regrouped for a fourth lift.

The shortage of pilots is illustrated further by a study of the composition of the crews of the sixteen gliders that took off from RAF Keevil to join the lift. The crews were drawn from 'A', 'B', 'D' and 'E' Squadrons, with some of the cockpits manned by pilots from different squadrons. One 'B' Squadron pilot who found himself operating away from his home airfield was Staff Sergeant Roy Howard. He had flown one of the six Horsas that took part in Operation DEADSTICK, the dramatic coup de main assault on the Orne bridges in Normandy. Roy Howard had successfully landed his glider next to the bridge over the Orne River – 'Horsa Bridge'.

Whereas the Normandy mission had been preceded by three months of intensive training and rehearsals, this operation and the third lift in particular could not have contrasted more. Roy was nominated to fly one of the Polish Brigade gliders:

> I was in 'B' Squadron for the whole of my time but was temporarily posted to 'D' Squadron at Keevil for Operation Market only. No idea why!
>
> I met Sergeant Davy, my second pilot, on the 19th September for the first time and never saw him again after that fateful day ... I never met the crew of our Stirling tug aircraft.[2]

Although RAF Keevil had a respectable number of gliders to launch, RAF Tarant Rushton had responsibility for the main body of the lift. Twenty Horsa and a single Hamilcar, from the second lift, were scheduled to take off from the Somerset airfield. The single Hamilcar was chalk number 903, crewed by Captain Bernard Halsall and Sergeant Lodge. The composition of the crews was a similar disparate mix to those that were formed at Keevil, the gliders being manned from a cross-section of GPR squadrons. In this case 'A', 'C' and 'G' squadrons had all provided pilots to deliver Jeeps, trailers and most importantly ten 6-pounder guns of the Polish Brigade.

The 'met' on the morning of 19 September was not good: large swathes of England were covered by banks of fog that showed no sign of clearing that day. The fog was particularly dense over Lincolnshire and the American airfields used by US IX Troop Carrier Command, which meant that the Parachute element of the third lift could not take off at all. However, later in the morning the fog did begin to clear from RAF stations Down Ampney, Fairford, Keevil, Harwell Tarrant Rushton and Manston. Eventually, the decision was taken that the glider component of the lift was to take off independently, leaving the parachute component behind on its fog-covered airfields.

After a very busy day at Keevil, Ron Driver finally thought that he had some idea what was going on:

After the briefing, I think it was the last, when we were allocated the glider that we, Bert Gibb and I, were going to fly, we walked over to it and found that it was already loaded with two fully loaded Jeeps with the two Polish drivers standing by. We soon found out that they did not speak English and as neither of us spoke Polish communication between us was difficult and mainly by gestures. We checked the controls, the lashings on the Jeeps and tested the correct loading by the unofficial way by one of us hanging on to the tail to see if we could take the weight off the nose-wheel. It all seemed satisfactory.

Eventually we were given the order to emplane. It was my job to make sure that the two Poles were correctly strapped in for take-off, the tug had of course, been warming up its four engines, it was a Stirling.

We had met the crew at one of the briefings. Soon take-off commenced and eventually it was our turn, the Stirling moved onto the runway from where it had been parked, straightened up and slowly took up the slack of the cable and we began to move.

The glider eventually became airborne and the glider pilot has to keep the Horsa to flying just a few feet above the runway to help the tug to get airborne. All seemed well, a good take-off and we steadily climbed to our designated height, and after some positional manoeuvring, set course for our destination.

Flying conditions were not all that good, it was quite cloudy and very hazy, and for most of the time we could only see two or three glider-tug combinations.

We concentrated on keeping in the correct position in relation to the tug, at times this needed all our concentration and due to the deteriorating flying conditions we took it in turns of about twenty minutes to pilot the glider.[3]

The 'Headquarters Commander Glider Pilots' war diary records the cloud base over the English Channel at between 1,000 and 1,500 feet. Some turbulence was encountered and flying conditions were recorded as 'uncomfortable' under tow.

The final tally of gliders forming the lift included the nine gliders making their second attempt and the thirty-five carrying the guns and vehicles of the Polish Brigade to LZ 'L'. The last combination was clear of its airfield by 1250 hours.

Poor communications created further problems for the third lift so that the delay to Z-hour was not communicated to the fighter squadrons that had been tasked to escort the gliders and that day's re-supply mission. Consequently, 127 RAF Spitfires and a US Eighth Air Force Mustang squadron loitered aimlessly at the RV, before abandoning their mission. The third lift and the resupply mission would fly to Arnhem unescorted.

Only a day before the first lift, Lieutenant Peter Wood had arrived in Somerset to join 'C' Squadron. He had just completed his flying training and had to curtail his own plans for the coming week:

> I had been given a leave pass after completing my course, and someone said, 'just before you go on leave, you are wanted at Tarrant Rushton', where I went immediately. Here I was paired with Sergeant Jackson, my second pilot for the third lift.
>
> Our load was a jeep, a trailer with ammunition and explosives, two motorbikes and four men, none of whom spoke English.
>
> The weather was foul over southeast England and we flew through heavy cloud until over the sea. Flying on the 'angle of dangle' with a full load behind a Halifax was not exactly easy.
>
> Over Holland we encountered lots of light flak and the Halifax took strong evasive action, diving, climbing and turning. It was very difficult to keep a tight rope in those circumstances. This went on for what must have been about 45 minutes. Most of the flak was well aimed but they had our speed wrong and most of it passed between the tug and the glider.[4]

Ahead of the glider stream, and also heading for Arnhem, were 163 RAF transport aircraft carrying supplies. Without a fighter escort to suppress the German flak batteries, the slow and unarmed aircraft were subjected to sustained and accurate fire from German flak batteries, now concentrated around Arnhem.

Forced to run in on the supply drop point at 900 feet, they were a perfect target for the German gunners. Damage and losses to the formations were heavy, nine Stirlings and four Dakotas being shot down with a loss of fifty-two aircrew.

The bravery of the RAF aircrew and their RASC dispatchers was admired and remembered by all who witnessed the drop that afternoon. Ninety-seven of the aircraft that returned to England had sustained damage from flak. One of the aircraft lost on this mission was flown by Flight Lieutenant David Lord who, like many others, flew into the maelstrom of German fire with little regard for his own safety. As a result of his own personal bravery and sacrifice, he was posthumously awarded the Victoria Cross.

Staff Sergeant Arthur Mills was north of the railway line with 22 Flight. Although he had problems of his own, he witnessed the bravery of the RAF crews over the Supply Drop Zone: 'I saw a supply Stirling shot down, the crew baling out, another on fire, and two Dakotas diving towards the ground. It was very depressing. Our Flight's second in command, Lieutenant Smith, was killed. I could see him lying in the trees, but none of us could get to him.'[5]

It was here again that the breakdown in radio communications had played a fateful part in the conduct of the battle. The RAF crews were unaware that the Germans had overrun the supply drop point and that they were in fact running the gauntlet of fire to drop their precious supplies into German hands. The desperately needed supplies were denied to 1st Airborne Division, who had no way of informing the RAF of the need to relocate the drop zone.

The German troops around Arnhem viewed the British supply canisters as 'manna from heaven', having been deprived of such high-quality rations for many years. The contents of the canisters were much sought after, particularly chocolate and cigarettes, which were always in short supply in occupied Europe.

Coming in at a higher altitude, and behind the supply drop, were the glider-tug combinations of the third lift. There had been the expected attrition to the formation. One combination was forced to return to base as the glider load had shifted and the aircraft had rapidly become uncontrollable.

Mechanical reliability also played its part, as some of the tug aircraft began to show the strain of the past few days; two combinations turned back because of engine failure. A third glider was forced to land in England, just short of the coast at RAF Manston, also due to engine failure on the tug.

Those gliders that crossed the English coast and pushed on out over the channel found the weather and visibility began to improve. One tow rope had broken and another had been severed by flak off the coast, so ditching two gliders. Perhaps because of the weather, or the comparative size of this lift, the flak encountered over the coast was not serious, but during the flight up to the rendezvous several glider crews reported light and medium flak in quantity.

One combination appears to have been selected as a special target for flak positions north of the Escaut Canal, and another glider was shot down, crashing out of control. Five others force-landed in Belgium and Holland, due to broken ropes, and in one case, to the late arrival of the combination and the consequent lack of fighter cover.

Staff Sergeant John 'Timo' Jenkins of 'A' Squadron could claim to have completed one of the shortest flights of the first lift. Forced to abort on take-off, he completed an emergency landing just inside the perimeter of Harwell airfield. He was now flying one of the lone glider combinations attempting to join the third lift:

> We took off again on the 19th September, this time as a lone glider combination, with orders to link up with the Polish Airborne over the channel. Owing to patchy cloud we failed to locate them and on approaching the enemy coast we encountered troublesome flak.
>
> I called up the tug pilot on the intercom, and asked him what he thought of the situation. He replied that he heard over the radio that all landing zones at Arnhem were in enemy hands, but he left the final decision to me.
>
> The flak started again as we turned north towards the Dutch border and so I decided to pull off, in order to give the Stirling better evasive action, and to continue our journey by road, with the jeep and trailer. We eventually arrived at Nijmegen and reported to the headquarters where Major Griffith and Squadron Sergeant Major Mew were stationed.[6]

The gliders were approaching Arnhem at the much higher altitude of 2,500 to 3,000 feet, but the supply aircraft had run in for their drop at 900 feet, making them far more vulnerable to anti-aircraft fire.

The gliders had to cast off once over the landing zone and then begin their slow descent – with no engines it was a one way ticket. They had no choice but to glide down through an intimidating barrage of flak and small-arms fire.

Ron Driver and Bert Gibb, of 'A' Squadron, flying from Keevil, were across the Channel and looking out of their Horsa cockpit for landmarks to confirm their position over Holland. About to make their descent through the barrage thrown up by the German defenders, and whilst scanning ahead of their tug's flight path, they observed the first indication that they were nearing the objective:

> We became aware of some black puffballs of flak straight ahead. As we got nearer this increased in density until when we were only about, I suppose, a mile away ... I remember saying to Bert 'The tug's heading straight for it, surely he's not going to go into that?' but he ploughed remorselessly on.
>
> We concluded that we had arrived; I took over the controls from Bert while he concentrated on looking for our landing site. In next to no time we had entered the box barrage. After a while, probably only seconds, there was a tremendous bang near us, it seemed the glider was pushed sideways, for a split second the controls went 'sloppy', no feel at all.

Lieutenant Colonel John Rock RE, the first Commanding Officer of the Glider Pilot Regiment.

Successor to John Rock after his death in a flying accident, Lieutenant Colonel George Chatterton.

A group in front of a Tiger Moth at 16 EFTS, RAF Burnaston near Derby in 1942. Back row: R.J. Scott – Redfearn. Middle row: Wedge – Phillips – R. Scott – Spellman – Ramsey – Mee – Whittle – Mould. Front row: Richardson – King – McGeough – Ansey – Withnall – Martin – Reardon.

Soldiers volunteered from all over the British Army to join the newly formed regiment. Here a group of students plan a training sortie at one of the GTS under the direction of their RAF instructor.

Corporal Cliff 'Wedge' Wedgbury at the Glider Training School in a staged propaganda photograph entering the cockpit of a Hotspur glider. Cliff served with 14 Flight, 'F' Squadron during the battle.

Summer 1944 – A group of 'F' Sqn Pilots off duty at Broadwell. Back (L to R) Bennett, Mather, Richards, Wilson, Howard, Firth. Front (L to R) Redway, Boyce.

Tarrant Rushton, summer 1944 - a Section of 'C' Squadron Glider Pilots pose with their RAF Ground crew in front of a Hamilcar.

The heady days of the Normandy campaign – within days of landing jubilant pilots of 10 Flight, 'G' Squadron head for home complete with souvenirs.

Down Ampney, Sunday Morning, 17 September 1944. Pilots of 'E' Squadron form up for muster parade in fighting order outside their Nissen huts. Note the rucksacks worn by pilots nearest the camera.

Waiting for takeoff at Broadwell, the command team of 2 Wing found time to gather for a photograph with their CO Lieutenant Colonel John Place. L to R : ?, Lt Maclaine of Lochbuie ('F' Sqn), , Maj Tony Murray ('F' Sqn), Maj John Blatch (2 i/c 2 Wing), Lt Col John Place (CO 2 Wing), Capt J. Hooper (Ops Officer 2 Wing), Padre Chignell, Lt Joe Maltby (IO 2 Wing), Capt Donald Shuttleworth (Adj. 2 Wing).

The Hamilcars of 'C' Squadron would deliver Bren Carriers and a nasty surprise for the Germans in the form of the newly developed airlanding variant of the 17-pounder anti-tank gun.

RAF Keevil, Wiltshire – Sunday morning, Stirling tugs of 196 and 299 Squadrons RAF and Horsa gliders of 'D' Squadron marshalled into order by serial on the runway.

Horsa glider en route in the low-tow position below its tug. Note the 'Y' shape of the tow rope and absence of invasion stripes on the upper surfaces.

Nijmegen bound, an 'A' Squadron Horsa (Chalk 414) forced landed in a field 3 miles north of Melksham. One of the passengers was Major Russell ACSO. The load consisted of 1 jeep, 1 trailer, 1 motorcycle and 9 passengers from Browning's Corps HQ.

Pilots struggled to find space to land at Landing Zone 'Z'. Note the gliders at the top of the picture that have run off the LZ into rougher terrain.

The gliders of 'E' Squadron delivered 7th Battalion KOSB en masse to the NW corner of Landing Zone 'S'.

Shortly after the last glider touched down the Paratroops of 1st Parachute Brigade leave their aircraft and jump onto Drop Zone 'X', west of Landing Zone 'Z'.

Safely down on LZ 'S', chalk number 280 flown by Staff Sergeant Rumble and Sergeant Booth. The 'E' Squadron Horsa is being unloaded by passengers from Headquarters, D Company, 7th Battalion KOSB. The tail remains in place and the side door is in use.

One of the four Waco/Hadrian gliders flown by pilots of Lieutenant 'Peggy' Clark's 'X' Flight on DZ 'X'. These gliders, designated to fly on the second lift to Landing Zone 'X' were at the last minute brought forward from the second lift to the first lift.

Unexpected guests in Wolfheze, 17 September – Staff Sergeants Joe Kitchener, 'Duffy' Edwards and George Milburn of 16 Flight, 'F' Squadron escort POWs of Krafft's SS-Panzergrenadier-Ausbildungs- und Ersatz-Bataillon 16 to Oosterbeek.

Staff Sergeant Joe Price of 'E' Squadron lights a cigarette for Irene Reimann, the Luftwaffe telephone operator captured on Sunday afternoon.

Staff Sergeant Godfrey Freeman was among the men of 19 Flight, 'B' Squadron that were attached to Lieutenant Colonel John Frost's 2nd Parachute Battalion.

Sergeant Geoffry Lawson of 19 Flight, 'B' Squadron who was killed in the vicinity of Arnhem Bridge. He is wearing second pilot wings.

Arnhem Bridge, 18 September – a photo-recce picture of the bridge gives some indication of the intensity of the fighting. Abandoned and destroyed German vehicles litter the northern ramp after Viktor Grabners failed attempt to rush the bridge.

Monday, 18 September – On the corner of Utrechtseweg & Kasteelweg – kilted Captain James Ogilvie (R) and Lieutenant 'Jock' Strathern (L, behind in kilt) of 'D' Squadron with Lieutenant Colonel Iain Murray (in trousers), CO of 1 Wing GPR.

Wolfheze, 18 September – Staff Sergeant John McGeough (kneeling, with wings) of 'C' Squadron assists in the recovery of a resupply pannier.

The scale of Operation MARKET is apparent from this picture of the LZs taken after the second lift. Note second-lift gliders have landed in opposite direction.

POW Sergeant Jack Bruce, of 17 Flight, 'A' Squadron, still wearing lifebelt after forced landing.

Major Peter Jackson, OC of 'E' Squadron.

Staff Sergeant Arthur Shackleton of 'B' Squadron.

Oosterbeek, 21 September – Lieutenant Des Turner of 'E' Squadron on his 21st birthday with his co-pilot Staff Sergeant Walford in front a house at Hartensteinlaan.

Staff Sergeant Peter Clarke and a picture of the house he used as an improved dressing station on Oranjeweg.

Oosterbeek, 22 September, GPR patrol in the garden of 8 Stationsweg, (L to R) Sergeant Candrick, Captain Cairns, Sergeant Williams and Sergeant Shipp of 'D' Squadron.

Glider Pilots and Pathfinders outside 8 Stationsweg, L-R  Sgt Stan Graham (5 Flight), Sgt Louis Hagen (8 Flight), Sgt 'Sonny' Binick, Pte James Cameron, Pte Frank McCausland, L/Cpl 'Tug' Wilson and Cpl Max Rodley. Kneeling: Sgt Ben Swallow and Pte John Jeffery.

Germans tour LZ 'Z' after the battle, note the Polish graffiti on the fuselage of the Horsa.

Oosterbeek, 20 September – wounded soldiers from MDS Vreewijk are evacuated by the Germans. Among them are Captain Robbie Robson (lying left of guard) and Staff Sergeant 'Duffy' Edwards (behind Robson) from 16 Flight, 'F' Squadron.

The ruins of Weverstraat in Oosterbeek, the scene of some of Lieutenant Mike Dauncey's actions and his brave, final stand. (9 Flight, 'G' Squadron)

228 Glider Pilots were killed in action and would never be coming home, the Glider Pilot Regiment would never fully recover from its losses at Arnhem.

Staff Sergeant John Bonome of 'C' Squadron pictured shortly after his return to England on Urquhart's aircraft.

Then Bert yelled above the din 'OK Ron I've got it', seconds later he yelled, 'release!' I pulled the cable release and Bert immediately banked to port and put the glider into a steep dive.

The landing zone was straight ahead and we were doing a fair lick of speed. Bert called for flap and we started to reduce speed, he took it down and I thought we are going to make a perfect landing. The ground ahead was fairly smooth, looked as though it had had some crop on it that had been recently lifted and we touched down.

Immediately the cockpit canopy was showered with soil, grass, stones etcetera and we were thrown violently about. We eventually came to rest and the dust outside started to settle. We undid our safety belts and got out of the door that the Poles had opened. We looked up at the barrage and the combinations still coming in.

I remember saying to Bert 'Christ have we come through that lot'. We just stood there then moved away from the glider still looking at the sky and the planes still arriving and those that were hit diving down with smoke trailing.

I remember one Horsa that came down towards the west of us. It ended up in a kind of flat spin, hit the ground with a hell of a whack and seemed to fall to pieces. I had been conscious of things buzzing by my ears and I shouted to Bert 'there's a lot of June bugs about', he replied, 'What the hell are they?' I replied 'they are flying beetles, if they hit you in the face they will give you a nasty smack'. No sooner had I said it, about fifty yards or so away a fountain of earth appeared and the horrible truth dawned. I screamed at Bert 'they are not beetles but bullets'!

We looked at each other, and then both crawled back to the glider. The reason why we had slewed round on landing was that we had lost a landing wheel, I expect, by the explosion near to us in the air, it had also taken off a couple of feet of the wing tip. The undercarriage was still intact and it was this that had dug in the soft ground.[8]

Staff Sergeant William Blanthorn was in a similar situation to Ron Driver, as he too made the dramatic transition from the orderly environment of the cockpit to the immediate chaos of the battlefield:

There were many planes dropping containers and gliders coming to land. I applied full flap but realised that they were unserviceable probably due to flak. Realising that landing zone 'L' wasn't on, I selected a hay field across the railway line, crashed through trees to reduce speed and applying brakes crashed the glider on the ground.

The front wheel snapped and all the underside of the fuselage damaged with dirt and soil all over us. Luckily none of us were hurt and we jumped out and lay on the ground underneath the glider for about 10 minutes.

All was quiet so we assessed the damage deciding that we would need help to unload and made our way to the rendezvous, passing a farm with a notice up 'Wipe your feet please' which gave us a little heart.

Eventually we reached Wolfheze but there was heavy machine-gun fire in the vicinity and we had met Jerry for the first time.[9]

The thirty gliders that had pulled off within sight of LZ 'L' were exposed to everything that the German troops surrounding the landing zone could throw at them. Many of the gliders were hit as they made their final approach and the tugs were also sustaining damage from the heavier anti-aircraft guns, now grouped around the area.

Staff Sergeant James Bonham and Sergeant John West had cast off from their Halifax tug, as it was damaged by flak and turned for home. The 'C' Squadron crew had lifted from Tarant Rushton, carrying a Jeep and Polish gunners from 1 Troop, Polish Anti-Tank Battery. Sergeant Tom Pearce of 'D' Squadron, who had flown in with the second lift, was on the edge of the landing zone watching their approach:

> We heard gunfire to the north and west but nothing came our way until the third lift arrived. One Horsa had just cast off at about 1,500 feet when there was a black burst very near the glider that immediately went into a vertical dive.
>
> It looked to be doing 200 mph. At about 500 feet it levelled off ... the 'G' force was so strong that it broke the back of the Horsa and the inverted shallow 'V' it [the glider] now formed went along in the air until it ploughed into the ground a few hundred yards from us.
>
> The cockpit broke away from the fuselage and went along the ground like a huge 'spinning top'.
>
> Shortly afterwards another Horsa came to a halt very near us. We went to help the troops get the vehicle out. Immediately after this we were ordered to retreat through the tunnel under the railway.[10]

The dramatic crash landing had distracted Bert Gibbs and Ron Driver from the urgent task of unloading their own Horsa:

> The pilot made a perfect touchdown, but suddenly its nose dug in, throwing up a wave of earth that obscured the fuselage, so that only the tail could be seen sticking up at a crazy angle.
>
> This galvanized us into action; we dashed over to the Horsa. As we did so, we could see that the cockpit had disappeared. We started frantically to dig away the soil, clods of earth, pieces of plywood and Perspex etc. Until we came across a piece of uniform and pulled out one of the pilots.
>
> He was of course dead. We re-doubled our efforts to find the other but were unsuccessful. We left the two Poles who had survived the crash, though dazed, to their own devices.
>
> They could do nothing about their own load, I think it was a six-pounder gun. We ran back to our own glider and began to get the two Jeeps out.[11]

Ron and Bert's efforts were in vain – both pilots had been killed outright in the crash. There were actually four of the Poles on board, all of whom survived the crash, but took no further part in the battle as they were hospitalized. The senior Pole on the glider was Second Lieutenant Wroblewski, who was destined to have his leg amputated as a result of his injuries. As the two 'A' Squadron pilots counted their blessings, they set about unloading their own glider. The remaining serials of the lift continued to land around them.

The amount of German flak had increased since the second lift and would continue to grow in effectiveness as the battle progressed. Every day more German anti-aircraft units moved into the Arnhem area, from other parts of Holland and Germany itself.

The King's Own Scottish Borderers were desperately holding on to the perimeter of the landing zone. Their actions prevented the Germans from firing at the gliders once they dropped below tree height level. However, while on their final approach, and above the tops of trees surrounding the landing zone, the gliders were still visible to the German units closing in on the landing zone.

At this height and speed, the gliders were extremely vulnerable to small-arms fire, every German soldier who could bring a weapon to bear pouring fire into the fuselage of the nearest glider. They were huge black targets that were difficult for even the rawest German recruit to miss.

The lift had not gone well and as the surviving gliders finally landed, there were a higher than normal number of heavy landings. The subsequent damage to the gliders, and in many cases to the load itself, had a detrimental effect on the overall success of the third lift.

Casualties among the Poles were close to 10 per cent of the ninety-three personnel who had left England. In all, nine of the ninety three glider-borne Polish personnel involved had been killed or would die as a result of their injuries. The toll on equipment was much worse, with only three of the Polish Brigade's ten anti-tank guns that had left England on the ground and battle ready.

Not all of the surviving gliders had made it to the correct landing zone, two Horsas having landed intact on LZ 'S', which the Germans had retaken on Tuesday morning.

The unfortunate crews were unaware that their landing zone was in enemy hands as they had not received an updated briefing after the second lift. Oblivious of the orders for the third lift, they had stuck to their original orders and found themselves cut off in the middle of an occupied landing zone. It is believed that a few lucky individuals were able to slip through the Germans and rejoin friendly troops, however the other part of the 7th King's Own Scottish Borderers mortar group were quickly surrounded and taken prisoner.

Lieutenant Peter Wood was enjoying better fortune on his first operation. He had cleared the English Channel, flown through German flak and was about to make his first combat landing:

> The landing was a bit eventful, with the Germans on the north side of of the landing zone and our troops on the south, with a bit of a battle going on between them. I landed exactly on target to within 10 yards, close to a corner of dense woods.
>
> We unloaded with some difficulty with lots of things going on around us. My co-pilot was wounded. Cylinders containing goodness knows what were plonking down around us, missing us by a yard or two. We moved quickly into the woods with the Germans, fortunately too thick to see them and difficult to distinguish between the shouts, whether German or Polish.
>
> We decided there was no future in staying where we were. From memory we were down to four (including the wounded co-pilot). We made a dash, south across the landing zone to join our own forces, three in the jeep and myself on one of the bikes. We must have crossed at fifty miles per hour, a ploughed field, across the ruts, through barbed wire with the Germans potting at us.[12]

Sergeant Sid Dadd, of 'C' Squadron, was by now in the thick of the fighting on the north side of the railway, having remained with the gunners he had brought in on his Hamilcar:

> We stayed with the seventeen-pounder gun crew and were supporting the paratroopers on a left flanking move on the third day, when the third lift came in. It looked like they were shot out of the sky.
>
> The paratroopers were driven out of the woods in front of us by flame throwing tanks and we retreated back over the level crossing at Wolfheze. Staff Sergeant White was shot in the lung.
>
> Later we had the gun positioned in a drive through woods next to the crossroads and knocked out a tank. Finally we could not move the gun as the tyres were shot to pieces.

The battle north of the railway line had not abated to allow the third lift to land, with ever-increasing German pressure beginning to tell. The 10th Parachute Battalion had been embroiled in a bloody struggle to take the water pumping station at the junction of Amsterdamseweg and Harderwijkerweg. With mounting casualties, and little prospect of breaking through the

Kampfgruppe Spindler blocking line, they had been ordered to withdraw.

Under cover of smoke, the Battalion executed a textbook withdrawal 'in contact' and was leapfrogging back, company by company, towards the railway embankment. German armour was close behind them and they were continually harassed by accurate German mortar fire.

As the lead companies cleared the wood line and began to emerge onto LZ 'L' to continue the rhythm of their tactical bounds, they were confronted with the chaos of the third lift.

Gliders were on the ground unloading directly in their path and there were more making final approaches, under a steady stream of German fire. There was little time to consider the scene to their front, as pursuing German armour and infantry began to fire at them from the woods to their rear.

The lead elements of 10th Parachute Battalion ran into some very confused Polish survivors who, because of the chaos around them, believed they had landed in the middle of the Germans. The situation was not helped by the language barrier and the proximity of the Germans. As a result there were exchanges of fire between British and Polish troops.

At roughly 1600 hours, Staff Sergeant Les Frater was with Sergeant Tom Pearce, his co-pilot, having stayed with the gunners they had brought in on the second lift. Les and Tom were soon involved in the chaos:

> We were on the road toward Wolfheze, with Tom and I riding perched on the back of the Jeep, ready for any attack from our rear. The attack, when it did come, was, however, from above. German fighters streaked low overhead as we leapt for the safety of a ditch. We fired back with little hope of success as we were armed only with rifles.
>
> As soon as the attack was over, we carried on to the crossroads at Wolfheze, where we stopped to search some buildings in the vicinity of the track. As we did not find any sign of the enemy, we pressed on towards Arnhem.
>
> We made good progress until we reached the area where the third lift was due to arrive, and took up positions at the edge of the landing zone. As the gliders carrying the Polish troops arrived, Tom and I dashed out to help remove the tail of one glider, which was obviously refusing to budge.
>
> As we finally enabled the passengers to unload, we came under very heavy fire from tanks and troops emerging from the surrounding woods. On returning to the road, one soldier of our group told me that a direct hit had blown up our Jeep and killed Battery Sergeant Major Baxter.
>
> As our packs were also on the vehicle, we lost all our spare ammunition, food, spare clothing and many other items. Fortunately, we had strewn ourselves with bandoleers of .303 ammunition, and assumed that this would suffice.
>
> Subsequently, we received the order to move back toward Oosterbeek, and we joined many others moving in the same direction. It then became apparent to us that things were not going according to plan, and optimism started to wane.[13]

One of the German units causing 'Shan' Hackett's men concern was a greatly reinforced SS Battalion Krafft. Having withdrawn from his original blocking position on the first night, Sepp Krafft had been absorbed into Kampfgruppe Spindler. He and his battalion were now attacking LZ 'L' from the north-east and were pressing 'D' Company of the KOSB as they withdrew back towards the landing zone.

But Krafft's men had become overconfident and 9 Company were overeager in their effort to prevent the British airborne troops from escaping. Close behind the Scots as they emerged from the wood line into the open, their chase came to an abrupt halt when they were met by a hail of well-directed fire from 'HQ' and 'D' Companies of the KOSB. The SS men took heavy casualties and were thrown back off the landing zone.

On the north side of the landing zone, 'A' Company of the KOSB were in an exposed position having attempted to time their withdrawal so that it would fall 'in step' with the rearward bounds of 10th Parachute Battalion. However, the synchronization of the bounds had not worked well for the Scots and 'A' Company became isolated. They were penned in on three sides by German troops and were eventually left with no option but to surrender, only thirty men succeeding in slipping away to rejoin the Battalion.

The withdrawal had also isolated smaller groups of British troops, particularly those whose gliders had landed in amongst the infantry companies as they made their rearward bounds to the railway line. Lieutenant Conchie and Sergeant Kilbryde, both from 'C' Squadron, were cut off in a 'no-man's-land' on the edge of the landing zone. Sergeant Kilbryde: 'The Polish soldiers had disappeared. We decided to wait till dark before rejoining other units. After exchanging fire for some hours we were eventually surrounded and captured from the rear. We were taken to a casualty centre and marched out of Arnhem the following morning.'[14]

The unremitting German pressure on LZ 'L' and its outnumbered defenders continued to build. The problem faced by 4th Parachute Brigade was to get its heavy weapons, vehicles and equipment to the other side of the railway embankment. Once south of the railway, it was hoped that there would be some respite under the cover of the woodlands beyond. If they could then regroup, the Brigade would be able to move through Oosterbeek and join the rest of 1st Airborne Division.

The embankment was not really a great hindrance to individual soldiers on foot, although there was the very real danger of snipers. The brigade staff themselves withdrew via this exposed route, as did the bulk of the KOSB and 156th Parachute Battalion. Sir Richard des Voeux had managed to get 156th Parachute Battalion back over the railway line in relatively good order. However, as they crossed the obstacle things started to go wrong for his battalion and there was some confusion as to where the Battalion was heading, once over the embankment. The majority of 'B' and Support Companies headed into Wolfheze, taking a single platoon of 'C' Company with them, while the rest of the Battalion marched toward Oosterbeek; the two halves of the Battalion were never reunited.

The Wolfheze-bound half of 156th Parachute Battalion linked up with elements of Ken Smyth's 10th Parachute Battalion. This composite force set about preparing Wolfheze for defence.

The extraction of 4th Parachute Brigade's vehicles was more problematical, as control of the two level crossings at Wolfheze and Oosterbeek could not be guaranteed. The Royal Engineers had, however, found a solution to the problem. They had located a tunnel through the railway embankment half a mile east of the Wolfheze crossing. Although it had a very low ceiling, a Jeep could pass through it.

Ron Driver used the tunnel to escape to the southern side of the embankment. He witnessed the inevitable congestion and confusion, as the single small tunnel was used to evacuate all of the remaining brigade vehicles:

It was chaotic in this area by the railway line. It soon became evident why … Everyone and everything was trying to get through a small tunnel through the railway embankment.

There was no organisation; no one appeared to be in charge and as more and more troops arrived, the pressure increased at the front. Some attempted to go over the embankment only to be met with heavy small arms fire; they were like ducks in a shooting alley. Bert and I eventually managed to get through the tunnel between two jeeps.

To my surprise the situation there was just as bad. We went down a couple of short dirt roads, and then came out onto a metal road, lined on both sides with woods. The road became more and more crowded with troops, so much so that, when the men in front of you stopped, you had to stop.[15]

Ron and the men around him needed breathing space, to get themselves and their equipment through to Oosterbeek. This valuable time was created by a rearguard that remained on the northern side of the railway embankment, keeping the oncoming Germans at bay.

Two defensive positions were established, a quarter of a mile out from the tunnel entrance to the left and right. They were to act as buffers against the German advance and protect the withdrawing troops who would be extremely vulnerable, if attacked, as they waited to use the tunnel, or while climbing the embankment.

The left-hand (north-west) position was held by 'A' Company of 10th Parachute Battalion, under the command of Captain Lionel Queripel. They were using the cover of some woods to inflict as much damage as possible on any German troops threatening the withdrawal.

To the right (north-east), 'B' Company, 7th King's Own Scottish Borderers had an identical task. The Scots halted one German advance with some very accurate bursts of Bren gun fire from Corporal Berry. He targeted a German cart loaded with ammunition or explosives, the resulting explosion killing numerous Germans and breaking the momentum of their attack.

Despite the ferocious defence by the rearguard positions, the Germans remained determined to press home their attack on 4th Parachute Brigade. They realized that 'Shan' Hackett's brigade was at its most vulnerable. Both rearguard positions were subjected to heavy fire and sustained attacks from Kampfgruppe Spindler. Fighting went on at close quarters around these positions after darkness fell and through to the next morning.

Whilst the rearguard fought fiercely to hold on to their positions, the rest of 4th Parachute Brigade and the survivors of the third lift continued to withdraw. Les Frater was now safely on the south side of the railway line: 'We kept moving back until we reached an area west of Oosterbeek, and found ourselves on a track running through the woods beyond the Bilderberg hotel. Tom and I took up a position behind a low shelter of piled logs just before it became dark. We stayed the night in the environs of the 'Bilderberg'.[16]

Ron Driver had negotiated the tunnel and was also on the south side:

Bert and I during this period discussed the events of the day and how things had all gone wrong to what we had expected, and been briefed to expect, but being optimistic, thought that the situation would improve. We had a further period of 'stop-go' when a voice shouted, 'The two glider pilots come here!'

I must admit my heart sank when I heard it. It was the voice of Lieutenant Kenneth Chittleburgh of the Glider Pilot Regiment. He was a tough stocky man, broad shouldered, and because of his hard discipline during training, was, to put it mildly, not very well liked. In fact many a man returning to barracks after a hard time under his command during a training exercise gave vent to his feelings by proclaiming to one and all what he was going to do to him if we ever go into action.

Lieutenant Chittleburgh instructed us to stay with him and the handful of glider pilots that were with him and also to collect any other glider pilots that we came across. Up till then, when the troops in front of you stopped, you did the same and just waited till the column moved again.

Lieutenant Chittleburgh, however, has already organised us into sections, and sent us into the woods as 'flank protection'. We went into the wood just out of sight of the column, dropped down on the ground and waited for the recall whistle and generally moaning about fate that had put us under his command. When we heard the whistle we rejoined the column and moved on until the next stoppage when we repeated the process.

We did a number of trips into the woods and back, then on one occasion we were ordered in and came to a small clearing, in it was a shallow depression that we made for and made ourselves comfortable in.

I happened to be at the far end of this depression and during a lull in the conversation thought I heard voices coming from the south. I warned the section and we listened for a while, we could hear nothing and I received some whispered jibes about my hearing and imagination, then we heard voices that I would imagine were about forty or fifty yards away. Someone whispered 'Jerries'; I remarked that it could be Poles that were parachuting in south of the river.

The voices seemed to be arguing; as the sounds got nearer soon we could see shadowy shapes coming towards us. There was a line of silver birch saplings at the edge of the clearing; their trunks were only an inch to an inch and a half thick, the figures stopped behind them, still arguing.

Then two stepped through the trees and we could see that they were Germans. We opened fire; we had all got rifles. I remember thinking I must fire just above the ground and when I had exhausted my pannier, turned slightly to get some more clips, when to my horror, I saw the back of the last man of the section about twenty yards away, running towards the road. My first reaction was 'the rotten sods, they have left me to fight the German army on my own'.

Then I thought, don't panic, I remembered that I was carrying some grenades in my left pannier pouch; I took one out, collected my kit, pulled the pin and then threw the grenade. When it had exploded I grabbed my kit up and ran like hell. I am positive I broke the world record for the distance!

When I rejoined my section I berated them for leaving me on my own, their reply was slurs on my hearing and I should have heard the whistle. I asked what the Lieutenant had said when it was reported, the reply was evidently 'Don't worry about them, they will be miles away by now'. We carried on in much the same manner until it started to get dark.

Lieutenant Chittleburgh came to us and told us to stay where we were until he returned. He returned an hour or two later and told us to follow him. We trekked behind him in single file, now and again conscious of various activities going on around us, troops digging in, and moving in various directions like ourselves. We stopped again for a short time, then moved on again, posted to individual spots, and told to dig in, with stand-to half an hour before dawn.

I must admit that my digging in was half hearted; just a shallow trench as near as I could get to a tree, made my self as comfortable as possible and fell asleep. I don't recall having to do any sentry duty or anything like that.[17]

Ron's experience was not unique – it was apparent that the divisional perimeter that was slow in forming around Oosterbeek was far from solid. Even the area close to Roy Urquhart's own headquarters was not secure.

Staff Sergeant Reg Dance of 'E' Squadron was with Lieutenant John 'Tommy' Tomson in the area of the Hartenstein, enduring what he described as heavy shelling. He was informed that there was a German breakthrough occurring 1,000 yards to the south of their position. Reg and his hastily formed patrol moved down into the area to the rear of 1st Airlanding Brigade Headquarters:

I gathered eight other Glider Pilots among them were Staff Sergeant Taylor, Sergeants Ranger, Whawell and Turl. We moved off until we came to a house called 'Vreeberg' where I put our small party into four defensive positions, covering the main tracks through the woods and fields leading from the South West [the corner of Pietersbergseweg and Kneppelhoutweg].

Within a few hours we came under concentrated shell and mortar fire. Later, whilst I was going around the positions I saw a patrol of seven enemy troops with a machine gun advancing towards me.

I called out to Sergeant Ranger to fire on the left track and I ran forward firing my sub-machine gun. The patrol was wiped out, but during the night we could hear one of them moaning and calling out; 'Tommy, Tommy, Kamerad'.

Staff Sergeant Taylor and I got a chair from the ruins of 'Vreeberg' and brought the poor devil in. Our last drink of tea had been made and I gave my share to the German. He thanked me, mainly with his eyes, and then he died.[18]

After their march back from the bridge, Ian Toler and 'B' Squadron were now established in a position around a house, at the south-east edge of the Oosterbeek perimeter. The Squadron Headquarters was located inside one of the houses.

Ian Toler:

Captain Angus Low is with me. Captain John Neale, my second in command, who was in charge of my Squadron's second lift, appears, and reports all well with the second lift and no casualties. Says he is off to join Major Linton [OC 2 Airlanding Light Battery RA] with the Light Regiment, to whom he is attached, and to 'keep away from Wing Headquarters.'

That is the last time I ever see him. I get a little sleep. There is rifle fire, mortaring or shelling going on in the distance. Aircraft overhead. It is the first re-supply. Stirlings and Dakotas. The flak is fairly heavy. A Dakota is hit and bursts into flames. We do not know then that the dropping zone is in enemy hands. An enemy aircraft tries to machine-gun us.

The owners of the house return and start collecting this and that. A canary has disappeared. We search for it and eventually find it. It is agreed that we keep half the food in the cellar. Language is the great difficulty but Angus Low makes a hit with the daughter who is young and attractive. We might almost think the battle was over!

Major Royle and the Colonel who say we have to take up defensive positions round the [Hartenstein] Hotel at once rudely shake our comparative peace. I go off on a recce with Staff Sergeant Shackleton and meet Brigadier Hicks and Lieutenant Colonel Murray and am told to hold the area of a small house south east of divisional headquarters.

Unfortunately it is rather close to a Hospital. The occupants of the house are still in residence. I advise them to move, and order the Flight to proceed to dig-in in their garden. We are rather isolated but fairly well sighted for fire except to our immediate front.

I share a slit trench in very sandy soil with Shackleton. It is just about big enough for one and we entwine our legs together in a most intimate fashion. Cramp is inevitable and every time we move brings a cascade of sand on top of us. Sleep is practically impossible but comes spasmodically all the same. Rather as an animal I should imagine, as one wakes automatically at every noise or movement and then drops off again.[19]

Throughout the day, the battle around the bridge had continued to rage. While 4th Parachute Brigade made their dramatic fighting withdrawal, over and under the railway embankment, Lieutenant Mike Dauncey had remained with 'G' Squadron protecting the gun positions in the vicinity of the Oosterbeek church:

In the afternoon a trail of men started coming along the road from Arnhem into our area, not well organised. Major Croot [OC 'G' Sqn GPR] organised them into a proper line stretching from the river to the road and any fresh straggler was pushed into their 'Croots

Cut'. After a bit they got their form back.

We, Frank Derbyshire and I, with Staff Sergeant Mack and Sergeant Wild and a few paratroopers, had the job of seizing the telephone exchange in Oosterbeek, as the Germans were still using the phone lines.

We travelled to the telephone exchange in a jeep, probably one belonging to the Light Regiment. Very friendly and helpful Dutch people directed us to the telephone exchange. We eventually found it, unfortunately locked, so we had to shoot out the locks.

The exchange was completely empty, with ticking and clicking noises going on in locked rooms. We wondered at first about the possibility of time bombs and booby traps, but soon realised that it was an automatic exchange.

We then found the main fuses, which stopped the exchange from working. We then took up positions in the building, not very good from our point of view, because we were about a mile from any of our own troops and the field of fire in the building was poor. We also had no Anti-Tank weapons of any kind.

Later in the afternoon the caretaker of the exchange appeared. He was very good about the damaged lock, but said he would have gladly opened the door, had we asked him! Later more Airborne troops arrived with a carrier and jeep.

We were told that we were to destroy the telephone exchange, so that it could not be used. When done we were to report to a Brigadier ['Pip' Hicks], with a view to helping the western flank of the perimeter, which was forming.

An automatic telephone exchange is not easy to destroy. We cut wires and undid connections in different rooms, but it was only a temporary way of putting the exchange out of action. In one room, we let off a grenade, but it had little real effect.

About this time the Royal Air Force re-supply came in, despite the heavy Anti-Aircraft fire, which greeted them. The Brigadier [Hicks] then had a change of plan and we were told to return to the Light Regiment once more, to act as local protection.[20]

Later that afternoon, further small groups of stragglers and walking wounded began to appear in the Light Regiment area, from the direction of Arnhem. They represented a disparate cross-section of the four battalions that had been decimated while attempting to break through to John Frost and his force on the bridge.

At 1900 hours, Major 'Dickie' Dale was ordered to deploy a standing patrol to dominate the ground between the railway bridge and Oosterbeek railway station. The GPR patrol's mission was to prevent any German advance, through this area toward Oosterbeek and the guns of the Light Regiment RA. The glider pilots were to remain in position until after last light, when it was intended that they would be withdrawn.

Wally Holcroft was with 14 Flight, 'F' Squadron, in the grounds of Dennenkamp, when Lieutenant Clark called his section together and informed them they were to undertake a fighting patrol towards the town of Arnhem:

We had to leave everything except our fighting kit and join Lieutenant Pickwoad with our section at the bottom of the wood in ten minutes time. After joining Pickwoad's men we received more information, both sections to proceed along the southerly main road towards the town of Arnhem and engage the enemy when we found him.

Where this would be no one seemed to know, but off down the road we went, I for one feeling quite apprehensive and though I tried to put on an air of unconcern I could feel a trickle of sweat running down my neck. However I had some consolation here, for I noticed that Lieutenant Clark, who was immediately in front of me, was suffering the same discomfort.

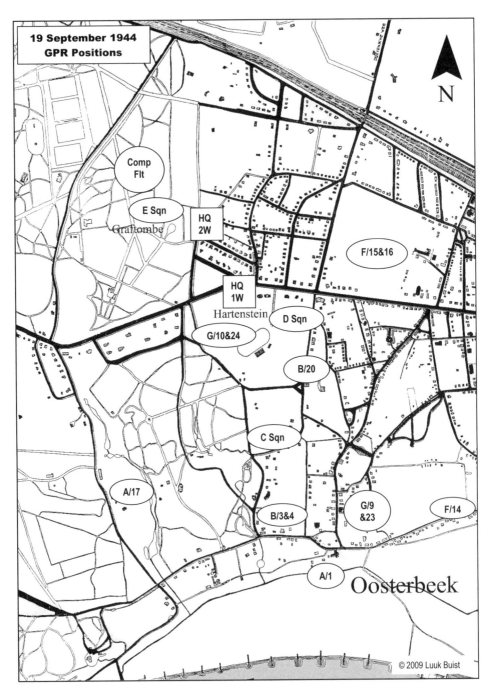

*GPR positions, 19 September 1944*

We approached the church at Oosterbeek and here a roadblock had been set up with some six-pounder guns and a couple of Jeeps. A number of paratroops were here who, we were told, had run out of ammunition. We halted here for a few moments on the orders of Major Alec 'Dickie' Dale DFC of the Glider Pilot Regiment, whilst he conferred with a Brigadier ['Pip' Hicks] who had suddenly appeared.

There was not much activity at this time apart from some sporadic rifle fire and as soon as the Major had finished his conference he ordered us to proceed.

Soon we came to a Railway viaduct that spanned the road and here we met some enemy opposition. Lieutenant Pickwoad rushed his men towards the railway to bring their weapons to bear on the Germans whilst Lieutenant Clark took another man and me to a house on the roadside.

The owner had locked the door, but Clark without hesitation put his revolver butt through the window in the door, pulled back the catch and in we went. Hurrying up to the attic we found a large portion of the roof had been removed by mortar fire and from here we had a bird's eye view of the railway.

The railway line was situated on a high bank directly in front of us whilst about fifty yards to our left was the railway station for Oosterbeek. On the right Pickwoad's men were being kept busy by a party of Germans coming towards them down the railway bank.

The Lieutenant was urging his men to 'Let them have it.' Which they promptly preceded with and from the room at the top of the house I was occupying, I could plainly see the rifles and Bren guns firing up the bank.

Clark ordered me to fire into the station buildings and I did so but as I could see no sign of any enemy there, I pointed out to him that it was little use wasting ammunition on invisible targets, to which he agreed and I ceased my little fusillade.

The Lieutenant decided he would have a look round outside again and after telling me to keep a wary eye on the railway station off he went. There was no activity near our house; it all seemed to be across the road where Pickwoad appeared to be quite at home with his private war.

I think he was quite enjoying it. After a few minutes Clark called me down from the attic where I had just discovered a quantity of very tasty looking apples. Stuffing a few in my pockets I withdrew.

The battle on the embankment subsided and Clark told us we were to occupy a few of the houses on the roadside and deny the road to any enemy that might approach. As we were discussing this, a motorcyclist rode by and called to us the information that a number of enemy tanks were approaching from the direction of Arnhem.

We were ordered into the houses at once, a party of six men to each house. We took up defensive positions in the upper rooms and began to barricade the doors and windows with furniture.

Our house was beautifully furnished but the occupants had already fled and obviously in a great hurry, for on the bed in my room was a half-packed suitcase. The bedclothes were untidy and among them lay a lovely silk nightgown, and a pair of pyjamas. I tried to picture the owners in my mind. Man and wife no doubt and quite young too by the lingerie.

Where could they have gone? They had certainly not taken much with them; I reflected on the fact that only three nights ago they would be in this bed together, completely ignorant of the toils of war about to engulf them. By the time we had secured the house it was five o'clock in the afternoon.

I had not bothered to barricade my window, as I did not expect to see any tanks approaching from the west side of Oosterbeek, which it overlooked. I noticed Major Dale walking down towards our house wearing no cap or helmet of any kind. He was sauntering along as though he was on some kind of Bank Holiday tour.

He called for Lieutenant Clark and soon I could hear them talking quite plainly. Lieutenant Clark expressed the opinion that it was of little use trying to defend the road with rifles and Bren guns against heavy vehicles and suggested withdrawing to the rear of our guns and armour back along the road. The Major replied saying we would have to do our best where we were, until further orders were forthcoming. Major Dale then withdrew and proceeded back up the road as calmly as ever.

I resigned myself to impending doom. Some of our boys were on the other side of the road lying on a bank that sloped away from the houses, and the road down to the riverside. A German self-propelled gun lobbed a few shells towards them whilst a battery of machine guns peppered them with lead, chipping up the ground in front of them. They seemed to be in a very tough spot.

Then shells and mortar bombs began to come over wholesale and two houses close by disappeared in a great explosion and a mushroom of smoke. When the pall of smoke disappeared, what remained of one of the houses was burning furiously.

As dusk fell the rattle of gunfire became more intense and fires sprang up in all directions as high explosive shells and mortar bombs fell like rain. In the half-light it seemed as though the whole world was on fire, and I expected a bomb to crunch into our house at any moment.

I thought there couldn't be much future for us in this, especially when the German tanks arrive. So, to console my depressed state of mind I munched on one of the apples I had stolen, it tasted as good as it looked.

Now a new sound impinged upon my ears, sounding like distant thunder and I guessed that I knew who was making the noise and from whence it came. I felt certain it was the British Second Army fighting on the south side of the river.

Strange how hope does spring eternal in the human breast. The sound of our own guns from the south completely revitalised me and a little later we received orders to withdraw from the houses and fall back on our positions in the wood, which we had held earlier on that day.

We lost no time in evacuating the houses and as we formed up outside we could see a big red glow in the night sky. The guns sounded louder now and I thought they'd be here tomorrow to save the situation. We marched back up the road; it was very dark by now and fairly quiet.

Back through the village and back into the wood, where it was so pitch black I could not find my trench. Wandering about like a lost sheep I tripped over a tree stump and fell into someone else's pitch. However I found my own place eventually and it seemed like the Grand Hotel.[21]

Late in the afternoon, Staff Sergeant Andy Andrews of 'E' Squadron found himself to the south of the railway line, in the north-west corner of the divisional perimeter.

He and the rest of the pilots around him were ordered back to 'E' Squadron's headquarters located to the rear in an empty house:

We moved rapidly back through the woods east towards Oosterbeek. After digging in we had a meal from food dropped by air supply in another house nearby, serving as a Squadron dump for our large kit bags and cookhouse.

Shortly before dark we moved to the south of this house along a thin strip of woods shielding us from the Germans thought to be about 200 yards away across an open field.[22]

As darkness closed in, and information trickled in to the Roy Urquhart's staff at the Hartenstein, it was becoming increasingly obvious that the initiative no longer rested with 1st Airborne Division. The Germans had blocked all attempts to break through to Arnhem Bridge. The decision was therefore taken to hold on to the existing bridgehead and to establish a strong perimeter around Oosterbeek. The battle was now one to hold on, until relieved by the armour of XXX Corps.

Orders were issued at 2030 hours, directing units to consolidate their positions and link up to form a small perimeter centred on the Hartenstein. With every unit needed to bolster the perimeter, the GPR squadrons were to play a prominent role in establishing and defending the Oosterbeek perimeter.

The north-west sector of the perimeter was divided between the GPR, the Royal Engineers and the Pathfinders of the 21st Independent Parachute Company. Peter Jackson and 'E' Squadron were ordered to dig in and hold positions between Graaf van Rechterenweg and Nico Bovenweg, facing north, linking up with the 21st Independent Parachute Company on the right, in the grounds of a house called 'Ommershof', with the KOSBs to the east of the 21st.

Other groups of glider pilots were also being integrated into the defensive plan. 'Pip' Hicks released thirty pilots from duties in reserve with 'C' Squadron and these pilots, most likely the survivors of 14 Flight, formed a composite GPR force with another thirty pilots from 1 Wing GPR. The latter had not managed to join their parent squadrons after the second lift.

Lieutenant Kenneth Chittleburgh was placed in command of this new sixty-man flight, and was ordered to hold the ground from the junction of Valkenburglaan, Graaf van Rechterenweg and down the track following Beelaertslaan. This placed Kenneth Chittleburgh's command in the perimeter, with the familiar faces of 'E' Squadron on their right and 'A' Company the Borders on their left flank.

Ian Toler and 'B' Squadron were now close to the Hartenstein, acting as part of the Divisional Headquarters defences. Ian's diary entry eloquently captures the mood of the night:

> Lieutenant Colonel Murray and Major Royle come round after dark to see that all is well and sentries posted. A mad woman walks down the road past our position and away into the distance singing an unintelligible song in a high pitched monotonous voice without any intermission until she is out of earshot.
>
> It is as if she is afraid to stop singing at the peril of her life. Most eerie particularly as the sounds of battle have stopped at this moment and there is a background of silence.
>
> After she has gone a gun keeps firing close to our position. I hope it is ours but hardly care, as it keeps sleep even further away.

At the Arnhem Bridge there was to be little respite for Arthur Rigby – 19 Flight were on the move:

> Captain Simpson arrived and took Ted Healy and myself with our Bren and ammunition into the garden of the house, over the wall at the bottom. Up on to the roof of an outhouse and in through the back window of a house whose front window overlooked the orchard at the back of what appeared to be a nursing home or hospital.
>
> I noticed that smoke was curling up through the tiles on the roof of this building and shortly afterwards it erupted into flames. Clenaghan, Higginbotham and Miller presently joined us and as the fire grew in intensity it became increasingly hot in our house.

**Notes**

1    Driver, Sergeant R., 1 Flt, 'A' Sqn GPR, by permission of The Eagle.

2    Howard, SSgt R., 'B' Sqn GPR, correspondence with Bob Hilton dated August 1997.

3    Driver, Sergeant R., 1 Flt, 'A' Sqn GPR, by permission of The Eagle.

4    Wood, Lieutenant P., 'C' Sqn GPR, correspondence with Luuk Buist, 1991.

5    Mills, SSgt A., 22 Flt, 'D' Sqn GPR, correspondence with Luuk Buist, 1991.

6    Jenkins, SSgt J., 2 Flt, 'A' Sqn GPR, correspondence with Bob Hilton, 1997.

7    Driver, Sergeant R., 1 Flt, 'A' Sqn GPR, by permission of The Eagle.

8    Driver, Sergeant R., 1 Flt, 'A' Sqn GPR, by permission of The Eagle.

9    Blanthorn, SSgt W., 1 Flt, 'A' Sqn GPR, correspondence with Robert Sigmond, date unknown.

10   Pearce, SSgt T., 5 Flt, 'D' Sqn GPR, correspondence with Luuk Buist, October 1991.

11   Middlebrook, M., *Arnhem 1944: The Airborne Battle*, London, Penguin Books, 1994, p. 271.

12   Wood, Lieutenant P., 'C' Sqn GPR, correspondence with Luuk Buist, 1991.

13   Frater, SSgt L., 5 Flt, 'D' Sqn GPR, correspondence with Luuk Buist, 1991.

14   Kilbryde, Sergeant G., 'C' Sqn GPR, correspondence with Luuk Buist, 1991.

15   Driver, Sergeant R., 1 Flt, 'A' Sqn GPR, by permission of The Eagle.

16   Frater, SSgt L., 5 Flt, 'D' Sqn GPR, correspondence with Luuk Buist, 1991.

17   Driver, Sergeant R., 1 Flt, 'A' Sqn GPR, by permission of The Eagle.

18   Dance, SSgt R., 'E' Sqn GPR, by permission of The Eagle.

19   Toler, Major I., OC 'B' Sqn GPR, by permission of the Toler family.

20   Dauncey, Lieutenant M., 9 Flt, 'G' Sqn GPR, by permission of The Eagle.

21   Holcroft, SSgt W., 14 Flt, 'F' Sqn GPR, 'No medals for Lt Pickwoad', September 1945.

22   Andrews, SSgt A., 11 Flt, 'E' Sqn GPR, 'So you wanted to Fly, eh?' Institute for Studies in Teacher Education, Burnaby, BC, 1997.

# CHAPTER 12

# A Steel Grip

*'There was no doubt that the others looked to the glider pilots to lead,
which we did.'*

**Wednesday, 20 September 1944**

As another day dawned on Arnhem it was clear that the men still holding the northern end of the road bridge were running out of time. Their combat supplies were continuing to dwindle at a rapid rate and there was no immediate prospect of any resupply.

The German forces around the fiercely held but ever-diminishing British perimeter continued to grow in strength and confidence. Movement between British-held positions was a high-risk undertaking as German machine-gunners poured fire into buildings or open spaces at the slightest hint of British movement. There was also the ever-present menace of snipers.

The Germans were beginning to dominate John Frost's enclave around the north ramp, having effectively split the British force into two separate halves on either side of the ramp. The Geneva Conventions were generally respected by both sides, with stretcher bearers being allowed freedom of movement. However, mortars rounds and artillery fire do not recognize the Red Cross so that medics and stretcher bearers were frequently cut down by both sides when caught out in the open.

The defenders faced a desperate dilemma when the Germans mounted a direct assault on the building they were holding. The choice was stark: fight to the death, surrender, or attempt to cross bullet-swept killing zones to reach the nearest British-held building. In many cases they were driven out of the building by flames but returned to reoccupy the rubble.

Arthur Rigby and his fellow pilots were still hanging on to their position in the bridgehead. As the sun rose, they could see the burnt-out tower of the cathedral that had been set on fire during the night. The building immediately in front of their position had also been ablaze for most of the night, obscuring their view. The flames and smoke had hidden the cathedral tower, but now that the fires had died down, it was possible to survey their arcs of fire and beyond.

In daylight the town was now revealed to be a scene of complete devastation, with few buildings around the ramp being unscathed. The incessant German mortar and artillery fire continued to add to the ruined landscape. The Germans were also making use of phosphorous shells to set buildings alight, the intention being to use the resulting flames to drive the airborne troops out of their positions.

Despite the Germans best efforts and the shortage of food, water and ammunition the British remained defiant. Arthur Rigby:

> Captain Simpson arrived and together we went outside into an alleyway to the left of the house. From here it was possible to look across the top of the Market Square to what seemed to be troops milling about and through his binoculars Captain Simpson identified them as Germans.
>
> I fired a couple of bursts from my Bren and he reckoned that I had brought three or four

soldiers down. I couldn't tell really, anyway they scattered and after about a half an hour I was sent off to get some food, leaving my gun with Captain Simpson and a paratrooper.

After a quick meal I returned to the alleyway and the word was passed around that the British forces were only 2¼ miles away, south of the river, and if we could hold on for another 3 hours we would be relieved. I got the impression that things were not going well.

We had lost a lot of our troops and we were quite obviously hemmed in on all sides and our ammunition was getting very short and no re-supply had come our way as had been expected.

A little later we were told that Thirty Corps would attack the bridge at 6 o'clock in the evening. This was considerably longer than 3 hours away and almost immediately after this information we were ordered to evacuate the houses and gather in the gun-park (the place we had started from). Well, all except Ted and I, we were left behind to engage some machine gunners who were firing from the windows of the local jail into the gun park, found our target and pumped two or three magazines into the windows and the opposition died down.

We withdrew into the gun-park and joined [Paddy] Clenaghan, [George] Miller, [J] Higginbotham and [Geoffrey] Lawson who were busy digging in. We joined in with gusto, for by this time Jerry was really getting cracking with everything he had. Self-propelled guns and tanks were shelling the area and mortar bombs were raining down, together with a considerable volume of small arms fire.

I saw Captain Simpson talking to an artillery officer on the corner of the street opposite the gate to the park and after a few moments the artillery bloke came into the park and spoke to another artillery officer. Then he returned to Captain Simpson and dashed off down the road to our left. The houses and buildings around us were all on fire again, and the heat was intense and still we were getting fired on from all sides.

Our casualties were mounting, dead and wounded men were everywhere. The artillery officer who had gone off with Captain Simpson suddenly came into the street out of a little alleyway and started to walk down to the park gate. When he was only about twenty yards from us he was hit by a sniper and flung right across the road into the opposite gutter, shot clean through the head, and he was dead before we got to him.

Yet so far, neither Ted nor I had a scratch, but my boots were so badly charred they were falling rapidly to pieces. A Paratrooper noticed my forlorn state and told me that at the far end of the park, standing in the road outside the entrance, there was a German lorry loaded with all kinds of loot, including army boots. So I handed my Bren to Ted and Charlie Watson, borrowed Charlie's rifle and set off to try to find this treasure trove.

Sure enough, there it was, just as the man had said. I had a quick look round and it was somewhat quieter in this area, so I ran smartly over and climbed into the back of the lorry and there were literally dozens of pairs of boots besides other army gear. I reckon it was a Quartermaster wagon abandoned for some reason, or perhaps had been parked there on Sunday afternoon before we arrived?

Anyway I got myself a new pair of boots to replace my burnt ones. Very nice ones they were too, soft brown leather uppers and hobnailed soles. The only snag was that they were a wee bit tight but in view of the fact that we would probably be relieved during the next day or so, I thought they would serve their purpose.[1]

The 2nd Parachute Battalion and the other airborne units holding the bridge remained disciplined and aggressive, although they were limited by the absence of heavy weapons. The Germans had a seemingly endless supply of ammunition and were now maintaining an almost constant barrage on the British positions. With limited stocks of all ammunition natures, for the British it was now a case of hanging on and weathering the storm.

German infantry supported by self-propelled guns and panzers continued to threaten the battered perimeter from all directions as the day wore on. The airborne defenders remained more than capable of dealing with unsupported infantry and consistently beat them back. Panzers were, however, becoming a real problem as stocks of PIAT bombs were exhausted. Without PIAT ammunition John Frost's men could not engage the German armour.

The positioning of the few 6-pounders meant that little could be done to stop them from simply driving at will into the perimeter from the east. These marauding German vehicles added to the devastation as they methodically engaged buildings at point-blank range. The 6-pounder positions covering the bridge and the western side of the perimeter remained active and continued to take a toll of any advancing self-propelled guns, armoured cars and Panzers.

During the course of the morning radio communications were established between the bridge and Roy Urquhart at the Hartenstein. John Frost explained his situation and asked the Divisional Commander for desperately needed reinforcements and ammunition. Urquhart explained that he was unable to offer the men at the bridge any support and that he was in an equally desperate position.

Both halves of 1st Airborne Division had no alternative but to hang on for the arrival of XXX Corps from Nijmegen. John Frost and his men could hear the sound of the battle around Oosterbeek but there was no indication of any fighting across the bridge to the south. The lead elements of XXX Corps were in fact still 11 miles away locked in a desperate struggle of their own.

Stanislaw Sosabowski and the main body of his Polish parachute brigade were the only troops uncommitted to the battle. They were, however, still 'fogged in' on their Lincolnshire airfields and they would remain trapped in England for the rest of the day.

The 4th Parachute Brigade rearguard north of the railway line had held on through the night, but were now being driven out of their positions by overwhelming German pressure. It was at some point that morning that Captain Lionel Queripel, Second in Command of 'A' Company, 10th Parachute Battalion was to sacrifice himself in the action that would ultimately result in the award of a Victoria Cross. Here is an extract from the full citation:

> Captain Queripel found himself cut off with a small party of men and took up position in a ditch. By this time he had received further wounds in both arms. Regardless of his wounds and of the very heavy mortar and Spandau fire, he continued to inspire his men to resist with hand grenades, pistols and the few remaining rifles.
>
> As, however, the enemy pressure increased, Captain Queripel decided that it was impossible to hold the position any longer and ordered his men to withdraw. Despite their protests, he insisted on remaining behind to cover their withdrawal with his automatic pistol and a few remaining hand grenades.
>
> This was the last occasion on which he was seen.
>
> During the whole period of nine hours of confused and bitter fighting Captain Queripel displayed the highest standard of gallantry under the most difficult and trying circumstances. His courage, leadership and devotion to duty were magnificent and an inspiration to all.

Mortally wounded, Lionel Queripel was captured and died in hospital; his award was posthumous. His efforts and those of the rearguard had bought 'Shan' Hackett's now depleted brigade valuable time and breathing space. Much of the Brigade's heavy equipment and Jeeps had used the tunnel to escape the German trap north of the railway embankment. The King's Own Scottish Borderers had reached their new location at about midnight and started digging in.

Under cover of darkness the previous night 4th Parachute Brigade had moved south of the railway where they had run into further opposition. Blocked at the Breedelaan behind the Bilderberg Hotel they moved to the east and spent an uncomfortable and uneasy night in the woods surrounded by German troops.

In the morning, attacks on a small scale developed along the Utrechtseweg against the Border Regiment and intense activity in the woods north of the railway was reported by the KOSB.

The initiative was now definitely in German hands as more and more reinforcements poured into the Arnhem area from all over Germany and Holland. There were numerous formations closing in on the survivors of 4th Parachute Brigade as they withdrew towards the positions held by 1st Airlanding Brigade.

General Hans von Tettau's command had now grown to divisional strength and was attacking the Borders' position south of Utrechtseweg. North of the same road Hans von Tettau had deployed Kampfgruppe Lippert which was also pushing toward Oosterbeek. Both formations were advancing from west to east using Utrechtseweg as an inter-formation boundary. Kampfgruppe Spindler and Kampfgruppe Bruhns attacked from north to south over the railway embankment with the intention of driving into Oosterbeek. Lieutenant Ron Johnson of 'E' Squadron was commanding a section in the north-west part of Oosterbeek when, during the night, his unit became mixed with troops of the KOSB:

I decided to stay with the King's Own Scottish Borderers, and placed my section under the orders of their Commanding Officer. We were positioned on the edge of their defensive area, a large white house [Hotel Dreyeroord].

We dug trenches again, this time along a fence, with no field of fire. This was dangerous as we could easily be subjected to a grenade attack. We had some minor skirmishes during daylight hours.[2]

Sergeant Russell 'Fred' Tilley of 11 Flight, 'E' Squadron was already with the Scots. He had flown one of their mortar platoon detachments in on the first lift, remaining with them after landing. He was described by Robert Payton-Reid as one of the most active members of his battalion, high praise indeed from a man who was renowned for the highest standards. During the course of the day, the Battalion's Medical Officer and some of his staff had been captured.

Fred Tilley took it upon himself to do something about this and attached himself to the undermanned RAP. He attended to the needs and comfort of the wounded, some of whom he had carried into the RAP under fire. Later when the RAP itself was hit and caught fire he coolly organized the evacuation of wounded, rejoining the battle in a more conventional role when the RAP was reinforced with new medical staff.

Another ad hoc RAP had been established on Oranjeweg on the north-west side of the perimeter behind 'F' Squadron's positions. Luckily for Tony Murray's squadron, among the reinforcements they had received prior to leaving RAF Broadwell was Staff Sergeant Peter Clarke.

Peter had plenty of flying hours under his belt as had been one of the earliest recruits into the GPR. It was Peter who with Sergeant Arnold Phillips had carried Corporal Jim McDowell and his mortar section from 1st Battalion The Border Regiment on the first lift. Jim McDowell and the rest of his section became possibly the most famous mortar crew of the war as a result of the photographs taken of them by Sergeant Dennis Smith of the Army Film & Photographic Unit.

Before the outbreak of war Peter had served as a Territorial in the Royal Army Medical Corps; he then became a Regular Army medic until he joined the GPR in 1942. His skills saved many lives during the fierce fighting that took place around his RAP.

Flying Officer Reginald Lawton was navigator in Stirling LJ939 from 190 Squadron Royal Air Force stationed at RAF Fairford. When hs aircraft had been hit by flak during a resupply drop on the afternoon of the 19th he had bailed out and descended by parachute into the middle of the battle below. The stricken Stirling crashed into the woods to the north of the Bilderberg Hotel.

This was not familiar territory for an RAF navigator and he had spent some nerve-racking hours evading capture by hiding in the Bilderberg woods. Eventually he chanced upon a Royal Artillery foot patrol which took him back to the 1 Battery Command Post. At the RA headquarters he was reunited with Squadron Leader F.N. Royle-Bantof, a staff officer from Headquarters 38 Group who had come along as a passenger on the ill-fated Stirling.

During the night the two airmen moved with the gunners to the area of the Old Church in Oosterbeek. After digging a slit trench they spent the night in the shelter of a large barn at Benedendorpsweg:

> At dawn we went out to make a few improvements to our trench. Then someone said to me 'Didn't you mention a Captain Corrie last night?' I said 'Yes' and was told he was in an adjacent house. We had been living with the airborne Troops in our mess back at base for months so I knew many of the officers who had been dropped here.
>
> The Squadron Leader and I were shown the way to the house. Captain Corrie was in the kitchen when the two of us walked in. He was surprised to see me of course, and I sat in the drawing room while he made me a cup of tea and prepared some breakfast.
>
> The kitchen had a good stove going and there seemed to be a good supply of food. The drawing room was large and lofty and very much over furnished in a Victorian style. The walls were covered with family photographs and there were several small tables loaded with photographs and oddments.
>
> There was some knitting lying unfinished. Captain Corrie told me he had advised the family to go and they left only the previous night. Later we hurried up the road past large attractive houses some of which we still occupied, a few hundred yards to the Old Church where I met Major Croot and one or two others whom I knew. From the Field Dressing Station a jeep took us to divisional headquarters.

The night had not been as comfortable for 'F' Squadron as things took a turn for the worst early in the morning when they were attacked by SS infantry supported by self-propelled guns. Outnumbered and outgunned 'F' Squadron were forced out of their positions in the woods on the Dennenkamp Estate. They withdrew with considerable losses toward the Hartenstein. Sergeant Peter Bond: 'I was taken prisoner by, I believe 9th SS troops, on the 20th with Captain Robson, Staff Sergeants Appleton, Edwards, Hope, Cobbold, Sayles, and Sergeants Mahoney, Price, Wetherall, Bowden, Maughan, Seaman and Walsh while on patrol. My first pilot, Staff Sergeant Castle, was killed in action.[3]

Sergeant Johnny Wetherall:

Sergeant Gordon Wright had been detailed off somewhere as a runner I was teamed up with Staff Sergeant Sayles who was No. 1 on the PIAT. I was his No. 2. We dug in short of the railway line, more or less north of a house called Dennenkamp.

When we were attacked the next morning, I stuck my head up when I should have kept it down and got an explosive bullet in the right side of the face, its casing stuck in my cheekbone but punctured the eye.

We were duly rounded up, drubbed several hundred metres eastwards and handed over to guards of a different calibre, one of whom tried to remove our helmets with rifle blows. I recall Sayles shouting 'he wants our helmets off' but I didn't come to until about four days later.

Ron Gibson was in one of the 16 Flight trenches during the SS assault. In November 1944, he wrote a letter describing the attack to the parents of his co-pilot Ernest 'Sim' Simion:

In the evening [19th] we moved out to Oosterbeek park … Beech Wood … and dug ourselves in, but it was very thinly held. I was separated from Simion again, he was in a fox-hole about fifty yards from mine … all through the night we were mortared.

Early on the Wednesday morning a party of Jerries … suddenly burst through the corner of the woods where Simion was and threw some grenades into the backs of the trenches. At the same time another party of SS troops dashed across the road under cover of Spandau fire and attacked with grenades and sub-machine guns.

I looked down into Simion's corner and saw it occupied by the SS who were hauling our wounded out of their trenches. I saw one man standing up and being searched by an officer but couldn't recognize him as Simion. I made a dash and was able to join the rest of the squadron who had drawn back. This is all the information I can give up to the moment Simion is missing.[4]

Sergeant Ernest Simion is buried in the Commonwealth War Graves Cemetery at Oosterbeek and is recorded as 'Killed in Action' on 20 September 1944. This is probably fortuitous – one can only speculate as to the fate he may have met once identified as a German Jew by his SS captors.

The SS attack on 'F' Squadron was well executed, using a combination of self-propelled artillery, mortar fire and smoke to support their attacking infantry. The mortar barrage wounded Sergeant Pat Mahoney together with Staff Sergeants 'Bob' Hope and 'Appy' Appleton, who were evacuated before the SS overran the position:

We were evacuated to a dressing station in Oosterbeek where our wounds were dressed. During the morning of the 20th the hospital was heavily shelled, and all patients who were able were sent into the cellar.

Later an orderly came into the cellar with a German of the SS and said, 'Sorry boys, but the hospital has been captured and you are prisoners.' We were made to go to a field 200 yards away, those who could not walk being helped by the more lightly wounded.

The Germans took away our smocks and helmets, and began to search us. They were taking watches, both civilian and military, and rings. The SS man found my escape purse and put it in his right hand jacket pocket, after tearing off the waterproof cover.

I had hidden my ring in my mouth, and hung my watch on the 'dog-tags' round my neck. After searching me the German put his left hand round my waist, and my right arm round his waist to help me over to the other prisoners. While he was doing this, I managed to extract my escape purse from his pocket and conceal it in my sleeve.[5]

Staff Sergeant Holcroft of 14 Flight:

Lieutenant Clark ordered me to go back up the wood to locate some members of our Flight who had gone astray, including Hall, Rice, Tobin, Davison, and Davidson. I found Hall, but Clark still not happy with the size of his Section sent Mick Hall and I back up the wood for a further search but we were only able to locate one more member.

By the time we reached the point of departure again, Clark and the rest had departed. The three of us did not know what to do now so when an Officer we met in the wood told us to lie up until morning we readily took his advice for we had no idea where the Flight had gone.

At first light we set off to find our Flight, an officer directing us to Wing headquarters which was situated in a large house [Nassaulaan] not far from divisional headquarters where we found Captain Mills [OC 11 Flight 'E' Squadron] patrolling outside with a German rifle. He looked extremely tired and worn out but he took a keen interest in our inquiry and informed us that 'F' Squadron was in the wood almost directly opposite Wing headquarters so off we hurried to join them.

After walking for about five minutes along a path that ran through the wood we came upon a series of trenches. There were no soldiers about and all was very quiet. The area looked as though it had been hurriedly evacuated for there were all kinds of equipment lying on the ground. We discussed the situation for a while but arriving at no satisfactory conclusion we proceeded a little further into the wood.

There were still no signs of any activity, not a single soul to be seen, so we returned on the path we had taken to Wing headquarters. I went into the house and saw the Wing Adjutant, Captain Donald Shuttleworth, a splendid officer whom I had known since my earliest days with the Regiment.

He listened sympathetically to my story and then suggested we assisted in defending Wing headquarters for a while. He asked when we had eaten last and when we said not since the day before, he said he would do what he could for us but couldn't promise much. The Germans, he told me, had cut off the water supply, and that commodity was becoming very scarce. I went back into the garden and told Mick what I had learned and as I was talking, Laurie Weeden came out the house and gave us a cheery greeting.

Laurie's favourite topic was girls and he could tell a risky tale better than anyone I knew could. When I asked him if he had one or two to tell us now, he laughed heartily and said no, but he had got his eye on a choice piece of Dutch-ware.

The Adjutant came out with some chocolate and a drink of tea. He apologised for not being able to offer us anything better, but we were most grateful to him for his kindness towards us.

We were discussing the general situation when a shower of mortar bombs descended in the area. We all fell flat on the ground and I held my breath waiting for the explosions which came one after another for a few seconds; then there was silence broken only by the sound of a few tiles falling to the ground from nearby houses. After the initial shock we recovered and laughed at our own discomfiture.

The Adjutant went off with Weeden on some patrol whilst Mick and I sat down on some supply baskets to wait developments. As we sat talking an old friend turned up in the form of Staff Sergeant Wedgbury. Old 'Wedge' looked as though he had been having it rough but he cheered up considerably when he saw us.

Laurie Weeden went on what was to be an eventful patrol with the 2 Wing GPR Adjutant, Donald Shuttleworth:

During the morning I accompanied the Adjutant, Captain Shuttleworth to 1st Airlanding Brigade Headquarters in Pietersberg area. The entrance to the headquarters building was a grisly spectacle, as a cluster of mortars had recently found their target, killing a number of the occupants [Captain E.A. Moy Thomas, Staff Captain, Captain R. Burns, Brigade Intelligence Officer, Captain S. Blatch, Brigade Signals Officer, brother of Major John Blatch, Second in Command No. 2 Wing and Lieutenant A.E. Thomas, Defence Platoon Commander were killed].

On our way back along Hoofdlaan it seemed that the western defence line of the perimeter was disintegrating, with a substantial number of our troops retreating in rather a disorderly manner towards the Hartenstein Hotel.

An officer restored order with a revolver threatening to shoot anyone retreating further. In the event no German troops appeared, but this rather alarming episode occurred just about the time that elements of 4 Parachute Brigade were arriving in the perimeter, and I have often wondered whether they were mistaken for the enemy by some of our own troops.

During this incident I met up with Staff Sergeant Sydney Wilkinson, an Australian who joined the regiment at the same time as me, in May 1942. He died of wounds on 25th September.[6]

Captain Harry Brown, Officer Commanding 3 Troop, 4 Para Squadron, Royal Engineers was in the line close to 'E' Squadron and the composite flight:

The next morning our position [Ommershof] was attacked by 2 half tracks but after a few near misses from a PIAT they sheared off and did not disturb us again. Almost immediately afterwards our position was very heavily mortared and Captain Nigel Beaumont-Thomas and two other ranks were killed. After intermittent mortaring a further four other ranks were wounded and evacuated.

A hundred yards to the south-west of the Captain Brown's trenches was Ken Chittleburgh's composite flight. Sergeant Ron Driver had been woken well before dawn.

Just before dawn I heard a tank engine start up, then the creaking as it began to move. It was to the right of my position and a few of our troops came running back. The tank was firing its gun every minute or so, there were a number of machine guns firing; we only had one Bren gun in our section, as far as I know there were no PIAT's or Mortars only rifles.

The first sight of the tank proved that we were wrong, it was a self-propelled gun, there was no cover and we had to run through the edge of the wood bordering a kind of cart track.

Two hundred yards away was an open field, when we reached it the track turned left, running alongside the end of the wood. We ran down this track, it was, I suppose, about a hundred and fifty yards long, then came to a road. On the other side of was a gravel drive, leading to the front of a fairly large white house [Sonnenberg].

The drive continued to the front of the house where there was a circular raised flowerbed, surrounded by ornamental stonework about a foot high. Dug-in in the centre of this was a Sergeant of the Border Regiment with a Vickers machine gun, together with a Lance Corporal to feed the belt.

When we ran up to them he asked me 'What's up Sarge?' I replied 'there is a German self propelled gun coming round that corner any minute now'. He said 'OK, get behind me, we'll deal with the bastard'.

I don't remember where the others went, but I got down on the gravel path, behind the ornamental stonework. As the gun appeared, the Vickers opened up. The gun stopped and fired, I remember the shells screaming overhead but was not conscious of hearing them explode. The firing stopped, the gun reversed back round the corner of the wood, a few minutes later came back and the duel started all over again.

At the Hartenstein Hotel the officers of 1 Wing GPR were working hard to maintain links with their squadrons and keep an eye on the perimeter defences. Captain Peter Fletcher, Adjutant 1 Wing, and Lieutenant Brian Bottomley, Intelligence Officer 1 Wing, went out together as a pair, with Captain A. Taitt and Sergeant Tony Streeter as another.

Iain Murray was also out and about on his own 'recce' patrol; on his return later in the morning, after his patrol, he attended a divisional conference. He briefed the staff that the general situation was good, but despite this optimism the Hartenstein area continued to come under heavy shellfire and casualties continued to mount.

During the morning, the fighting around the crossroads in Oosterbeek had intensified. The Main Dressing Station (MDS) was located on the crossroads in the Schoonoord Hotel, and news that SS troops had overrun it was an immediate cause for concern for Roy Urquhart and his staff a few hundred yards away in the Hartenstein.

While the Geneva Conventions ensured both sides would treat each other's wounded, the loss of the MDS and its medical staff would prevent some of the lightly wounded retuning to the battle after treatment. Urquhart needed to confirm whether the report was true so he ordered Major John Royle, the Second in Command of 1 Wing, GPR to go to the Schoonoord Hotel and investigate.

At 1130 hours John Royle departed from the 1 Wing positions with Captains Taitt, Ogilvie and Murdoch, and their sections, on patrol. Half an hour later the patrol met with machine-gun fire in the area of the MDS crossroads, Royle was killed and James Ogilvie was wounded. Captain Barry Murdoch:

> Not much sleep had been had at all, and we were pretty continually mortared, and shelled. This morning we were trying to re-take the crossroads 100 yards from divisional headquarters.
>
> The medical station there had been captured and we were in urgent need of it. We, Major Royle, Captain Ogilvie and myself with our sections, went down and after a bit of a battle chased Jerry away.
>
> 'Bit of a battle' was described thus: we crept through some woods and on the edge of the woods, some 50 yards away we saw a machine gun post. Major Royle was about to fire his Bren gun at it, and discovered that it wouldn't work. Just behind us somebody yelled, 'They're moving, Jerry's running back,' so we chased after them. The next thing we knew was that a machine gun was firing from a tank at us.
>
> I jumped behind a car and ran back 30 yards. Later orders were received to move into the house on the corner of Stationsweg, Utrechtseweg ['Quatre Bras', held by 1 Platoon, 21st Parachute Company]. Captain Ogilvie and Lieutenant Colonel Murray were with me then.
>
> Major Royle was killed, whilst we were standing by the car previously mentioned.

Private Hardy was a medic in 16 Parachute Field Ambulance:

> I went as a Medic with a party of Glider Pilots led by Major Royle and Captain Ogilvie, to clear out a nest of snipers who had been worrying divisional headquarters.
>
> In this sortie Major Royle and three of the pilots were killed and Captain Ogilvie was wounded. They successfully knocked out a machine gun nest killing four Germans and taking two prisoners, but another position was covering the machine gun nest.

Roy Urquhart was saddened by the loss of John Royle and had this to say about his fellow Scot in his own book *Arnhem*:

> When I heard that the dressing station had been overrun, I sent out Major John Royle, second in command of a wing of the Glider Pilot Regiment, to find out what was happening. He was killed in the middle of the road at the dressing station.
>
> At one time before the war, Royle had been a regular subaltern in the Highland Light Infantry. On the outbreak of war he joined up in the ranks and became a Warrant Officer in the Scots Guards. Later he was commissioned in the Glider Pilot Regiment.

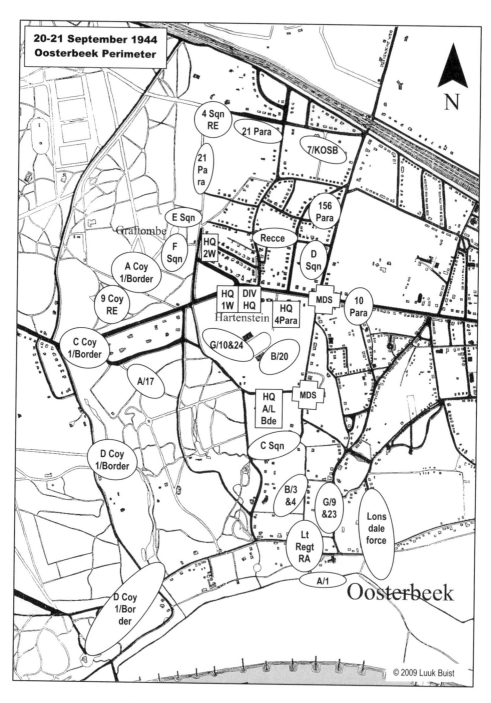

*GPR positions, 20 & 21 September 1944*

However fatalistic it is possible to get in the matter of casualties, one cannot but be sad when these are caused as a direct result of a personal order.[7]

While the situation all around the Oosterbeek perimeter remained fluid, the Hartenstein itself had not yet been subjected to a direct attack. John McGeough:

All of the time I was there it was not possible to delineate our and the enemies territory – we did hold the Hartenstein and its grounds but away from there no one knew whether friend was in the next garden, house or street.

Constant vigilance was required and we fully expected that at any time the Germans would attempt to overrun our positions at the Hartenstein, but our morale was high and we were determined that they would have to fight for every inch of ground.

The tactics they adopted however was to try and knock out Divisional Headquarters not by frontal assault but by subjecting the comparatively small area we occupied to an intense barrage of mortar fire and tank fire which rained down on us by day and night increasing in ferocity as time went on.

Being an ex-mortar man myself I appreciated more than most the skill with which they laid their barrages, and this combined with the sound of tanks moving up to shell us caused great anxiety, especially as the casualties from shrapnel began to mount up.

Nothing is worse than seeing comrades killed and even more distressing than the outcries of pain from the wounded was our inability to do much for them other than dress their wounds with our field dressings … at one time the collection point for our dead was by a rear wall of the Hartenstein.[8]

Sergeant Tom Pearce was also close by, digging a trench in the garden of a cottage near the Hartenstein:

It was fairly easy because the ground was soft and sandy. Trenches of other people were so close that the earth formed a pyramid between us. Suddenly we heard 'Moaning Minnies' coming; they were going to be very close.

I sat in the trench looking at Les Frater and my stomach muscles were twanging like a banjo being played fast, I knew real terror. The mortar bombs landed in the pyramid showering us with earth but we were below the blast-level so we were unhurt, several men in adjoining trenches were killed.

We were then collected together, all glider pilots, about 20 of us to go on a 'fighting patrol' we were told by Squadron Sergeant Major Oliver. We crossed the road in front of the Hartenstein and moved across allotments towards Stationsweg as I now know it to be.

I was in the Infantry before joining the Glider Pilot Regiment and as we were across those allotments there seemed to be no order to our movements; again I thought if the Germans are in the houses we shall be mown down.

No enemy fire came. We took over the houses, two of us in every other house, we were two or three houses from the crossroads [Utrechtseweg/ Stationsweg] on the right. Looking through the upstairs window of the house we were in we saw a park, a lone cottage (like an estate lodge) and a plantation. To the left was a rather open area and another street junction.

We spent the night in a bedroom getting a little uncomfortable sleep on the spring frame of the bed; there were no mattresses or bedclothes. I don't remember getting any food or even a drink.[9]

Sergeant John Haller, 24 Flight, 'G' Squadron was defending Divisional Headquarters at the

Hartenstein Hotel when he was detailed to be a Bren gunner in an ad hoc group of glider pilots:

> The group comprised Lieutenant Bob Palmer, Staff Sergeants 'Butch' Wilmot and 'Vic' Vickers and Sergeants 'Yanto' Evans, 'Jock' Faulkner and myself.
>
> We ended up guarding a crossroad on the right wing of the remnants of 10 Parachute Battalion and held it. SS infantry fighting patrols and a succession of snipers until the afternoon of Saturday the 23rd when a Tiger tank rolled up just about the limits of a PIAT range.
>
> A great little Para PIAT gunner joined us and hit it smack on the nose. Our rejoicing was short lived. After spitting out their loosened back-tooth fillings the gun swung round and down onto our positions. Inevitably we were literally blown out and crawled away under heavy machine gun fire. I was wounded in my arm and taken to a hospital.

At the 'B' Squadron command post, south-east of the Hartenstein, Ian Toler was working hard to keep track of his men and their dispersed locations. Other officers were attempting to do the same. Captain Terry Miller, the OC of 3 Flight, visited the CP and stated that his position was with the Light Regiment by the church at Oosterbeek. Captain Bill Barrie (Second in Command of 'G' Squadron) and Major Tony Murray (OC 'F' Squadron GPR) visited 'B' Squadron seeking to update their own maps and information.

The 1 Wing Intelligence Officer, Lieutenant Brian Bottomley, delivered the latest intelligence report and orders for the Squadron to retire into the Divisional Headquarters perimeter 100 yards behind them. This relocation was intended to tighten up the defence line around the Hartenstein and separate the Squadron from the MDS located in the Tafelberg Hotel.

Ian Toler's squadron, consisting mainly of 20 Flight, were to slot into the new line with 10 Flight, 'G' Squadron, under Captain Maurice Priest, on their left, and 24 Flight, also 'G' Squadron and led by Captain Robin Walchli, in position on their right flank. The orders were passed on quickly and 20 Flight retired to new positions along a line of trees to the rear of their original trenches.

To the south of the Hartenstein, in the vicinity of Oosterbeek Church, Staff Sergeant Mark Leaver and Staff Sergeant Eric Holloway of 'G' Squadron had occupied the rear bedroom of the second house in a row at the back of the laundry (van Hofwegen); they are in a good position looking out over open land towards Arnhem.

This area had been relatively quiet apart from the firing of the British gun batteries in the fields around the church, but this was about to change. Mark Leaver:

> During the morning we spotted a German squad of about 8 men setting up a mortar position about 400 metres to our left. We opened fire and cleared the site. There was no time for congratulations for where the mortar site had been there now appeared a Tiger tank, which wasted no time in demolishing our position, causing us to evacuate with great speed.
>
> We then crossed the road at the back of the laundry under cover of a phosphorous grenade. We were very lucky to get across this road without casualties as a few minutes later a self-propelled gun with infantry support came down the road towards the laundry.
>
> With the assistance of Major Cain and his men, plus gunners from the 75mm Howitzer site, this menace was suitably dealt with. We then occupied a house at the side of the laundry and adjacent to the Gun Battery.[10]

Lieutenant Mike Dauncey, was also still in the old church area close to the laundry:

There was a certain amount of shelling in the area. The remnants of the South Staffords and some paratroopers were about quarter of a mile up the road, in very good order protecting the ground to the west of the railway bridge.

In due course the Jerries put in an attack over the railway embankment but it was very easily smashed by good machine gun fire.

A certain diversion was caused by the fact that we all stopped firing because the word got round that they were Poles. However this was eventually remedied and the machine gunners amused themselves by warming up the area with sharp bursts while the Jerries were trying to get back.[11]

By midday the first small groups of survivors of the 4th Parachute Brigade withdrawal began to arrive at the Hartenstein. The fighting of the day before and the withdrawal back to the railway line had taken a severe toll, with the subsequent confusion and fighting that night south of the railway line causing yet more casualties.

The state of 'Shan' Hackett's brigade can be gauged by the fighting strength of 10th Parachute Battalion when it finally reached Oosterbeek and the Hartenstein at midday. The Battalion could offer Roy Urquhart a total of sixty paratroopers who were able to fight on.

Hackett himself was having difficulties getting back into the perimeter – he and his brigade staff were now facing the familiar dangers of being surrounded. Despite being able to talk to Divisional Headquarters by radio he was unsure of its location or of the perimeter boundaries.

The Germans had kept the pressure on the 4th Parachute Brigade positions right through the night by use of mortars and patrols that continually probed their defences. Early in the morning the Brigade had begun to move toward Oosterbeek only to run into German patrols after only a few hundred yards. The rest of the morning was spent fighting a running battle with ever-increasing numbers of German troops and armour.

The Germans meanwhile were tightening their grip. Kampfgruppe Krafft were moving through the woods to the north, while SS Battalion Eberwein were advancing from the west and SS-Unterführerschule 'Arnheim', under command of SS Standartenführer Michael Lippert, were also driving in through Heelsum and Wolfheze. The battle in the woodland was increasing in intensity, with ferocious hand-to-hand fighting creating a mounting number of casualties.

Sir Richard des Voeux, the Commanding Officer of 156th Parachute Battalion and his Second in Command were both killed during the morning. Ken Smyth the Commanding Officer of 10th Parachute Battalion was also wounded during the fight to reach the perimeter, although despite his wounds he remained with his battalion.

Eventually after eight hours pinned down by German fire at roughly 1700 hours, a desperate bayonet charge was launched, and 'Shan' Hackett and 150 officers and men from his shattered brigade broke through into the divisional perimeter.

Inside the perimeter things were far from comfortable. The tightening of the German grip around Oosterbeek and the damage to the town's infrastructure was beginning to take effect. At Divisional Headquarters the water mains had ceased to function and water was in increasingly short supply. There was a brief glimmer of hope at 1405 hours when formations of Mustangs and Thunderbolt fighters flashed over, heralding the arrival of another valiant attempt to drop supplies by the RAF.

The battle on the perimeter continued through the day, despite tenacious resistance. John Place and the pilots of 2 Wing GPR were forced to relinquish their hold on the high ground at Hill 63.5 and 'E' Squadron withdrew into the woodland near the Ommershof house. Here they quickly regrouped and moved into position with the 21st Independent Parachute Company on their right, with 'A' Company, 1st Battalion Borders on their left.

All around the perimeter fragmented units were joining together in order to survive and to fight on. Staff Sergeant William Blanthorn of 'A' Squadron attached himself to some of the 10th Parachute Battalion who were digging in and after some heavy fighting they were forced to withdraw into the woods:

Before first light we tried to contact the remainder of the 4th Parachute Brigade, but were forced back. There was heavy fighting, machine gun and mortar fire and there were many casualties. We fought all day in the woods with Jerry closing in.

Met up with Jack Robson and Dickie Grant, and with Fred Parker, my co-pilot, the four of us kept together. There were some medical officers with the wounded, a few being carried on a jeep, and at about 3.30 pm one of the officers hoisted a white flag.

All the Jerries were shouting and screaming, when a British patrol came back and seeing the Germans started shooting on us, more casualties. Eventually things quietened down and we were searched then marched away in column of threes to the main road, which was lined with tanks and soldiers. We passed a hotel on our right where a dead civilian was laying outside.

Suddenly a machine gun opened up on us and we all dived for cover, but one of the German guards and a Glider Pilot officer were killed, I was shot in the left leg and another chap in the neck. Fred Parker put a field dressing on and gave me a shot of morphia, which we carried with us.

Eventually the casualties were taken away in a truck to a Regimental Aid Post but we received no medical attention.[12]

Staff Sergeant A.E. Mills, 22 Flight, 'D' Squadron was also a witness to the incident:

Many wounded lay round us, many of them dying. I was next to the officer commanding our Flight, Captain Muir, when we were completely surrounded by SS Panzers. This would be about 3 p.m. Before they got to us, we quickly buried our fighting knives and threw the bolts from our rifles away. As we stood up, a Polish soldier at my rear fired past my shoulder at the Germans and we had to dive flat on the ground, but luckily they did not shoot at us. We were now prisoners of war and formed up in lines by our captors. I was at the front of the column when a shot rang out and Captain Muir fell dead. Apparently a 'trigger happy' German had mistaken us for active troops and had opened fire. Then we were put in trucks and taken to a Hospital.

The bulk of 'A' Squadron were now in the south-east of Oosterbeek in the old church area where they were engaged by German self-propelled guns supported by infantry. Despite the best efforts of the Germans the gun batteries in the church fields remained in action.

The battle to dominate the area and prevent a direct attack on the vital gun line was not without cost. Captain Norman Hardie was killed at 1200 hours, and Staff Sergeants Bob Barratt, Maurice Clayton, and Luther Kirkman were also wounded while on patrol, as was Staff Sergeant Dennis Houghton. Maurice Clayton lived to tell the tale:

Wednesday in the afternoon, a tank was reported coming down the road from Arnhem [Benendendorpsweg] towards the guns. A small patrol of us went hunting for it. Captain Norman Hardie, our commanding officer, led the patrol. On locating the tank, a shell was fired at us.

This killed Captain Hardie outright and wounded Staff Sergeant Barratt in the thigh, and shattered my right leg below the knee. Barratt and I were eventually reached by a patrol of Paratroopers and then taken to the Regimental Aid Post of the Royal Artillery.[13]

Staff Sergeant Freddie Chapman was in the same patrol:

Our patrol went off and the panzer tank opened fire, killed Captain Hardie and mortally wounded Staff Sergeant Clayton and Staff Sergeant Bob Barratt. I returned to our position by the laundry and I was bowled over by a mortar shell. I yelled across the road at the house we occupied without response. I eventually crossed the road to find the house had been shelled. I then returned to our unit. During the heavy mortaring and shelling from 88 mm, I received shrapnel wounds in the neck.[14]

Mark Leaver was joining a composite force formed in the main from the survivors of the four battalions that had attempted to break through to the bridge. In all, the remnants of 1st, 3rd, 11th Parachute Battalions and 2nd Battalion South Staffords never amounted to more than a very understrength battalion. It was clear, however, that every man counted now more than ever.

As Kampfgruppe Spindler pushed west out of its blocking position between the bridge and the Oosterbeek perimeter, the survivors were being regrouped, rearmed and integrated into the defensive positions on the east side of Oosterbeek.

Lieutenant Colonel 'Sheriff' Thompson, the Commanding Officer of 1st Airlanding Light Regiment, RA had managed to halt what was a leaderless and confused stream of survivors on the edge of Oosterbeek. He and Major Robert Cain had set about organizing them into a cohesive military unit again.

Once in their new positions the men were issued with rations, ammunition and most importantly leadership. Major 'Dickie' Lonsdale DSO, Second in Command of 11th Parachute Battalion was appointed to command what became known as 'Lonsdale Force'. Dickie Lonsdale was a veteran of Sicily with a reputation for unconventional thinking, and he set about the task of defending the most vulnerable area of the perimeter with great energy.

Lonsdale Force was destined to fight a series of desperate actions against the men of Kampfgruppe Spindler as they tried to break into Oosterbeek and threaten the gun batteries around Oosterbeek old church. The fighting was intense, vicious and often hand to hand. Despite this the rejuvenated men of 'Lonsdale' force held their ground inflicting heavy casualties on their opponents.

During the fighting on the 20th, Lance Sergeant John Baskeyfield of the South Staffords anti-tank group was killed while engaging German tanks. Maintaining his nerve when his position on the junction of two Oosterbeek streets (Benedendorpsweg and Acacialaan) was attacked by two German Panzers and a self-propelled gun, John Baskeyfield allowed each target to come up to 100 yards from his gun in order to ensure a kill. He was awarded the Victoria Cross for his actions, the following extract giving some idea of the courage witnessed by those around him:

Manning his gun quite alone, Lance Sergeant Baskeyfield continued to fire round after round at the enemy until his gun was put out of action. By this time his activity was the main factor in keeping the enemy tanks at bay. The fact that the surviving men in his vicinity were held together and kept in action was undoubtedly due to his magnificent example and outstanding courage.

Time after time the enemy attacks were launched and driven off. Finally when his gun was knocked out Lance Sergeant Baskeyfield crawled under intense enemy fire to another six-pounder gun nearby, the crew of which had been killed and proceeded to man this single handed.

With this gun he engaged an enemy self-propelled gun which was approaching to attack. Another soldier crawled over open ground to assist him but was killed almost at once. Lance Sergeant Baskeyfield succeeded in firing two rounds at the SP gun, scoring direct hits, which rendered it ineffective.

Whilst preparing to fire a third, however, he was killed by a shell from a supporting enemy tank.

If John Baskeyfield and the men of Lonsdale Force had not stood firm there was a real danger that German armour would have penetrated the Oosterbeek perimeter from the east. Such a thrust into the area of the old church would have immediately threatened the guns of the 1st Airlanding Light Regiment, RA and potentially gone on to cut 1st Airborne Division off from the river to their south.

Lieutenant Mike Dauncey and other men from 'G' Squadron moved into a new position on Weverstraat, roughly a thousand metres from the scene of John Baskeyfield's action:

> That afternoon the Para chaps were withdrawn to our houses for a rest. We took over the area to the north of our area with a mixed bag of glider pilots, parachutists and airborne infantry under Lieutenant Max Downing on the left, Captain Mike Corrie with Lieutenant Frank Derbyshire in the centre and myself on the right. It took a bit of sorting out, but once that had been done the situation looked far better.
>
> That evening we spent digging in and getting to know the men a little. I had Staff Sergeant Halliday and Sergeant Wyatt, both of whom were invaluable. There was no doubt that the others looked to the glider pilots to lead, which we did. Incidentally the parachutists all called Bob Croot the 'Mad Major'.

To the north of Mike Dauncey, Ian Toler and 20 Flight were settling in to their new positions on the tree line close to the Hartenstein:

> During the afternoon the Flight dug in. Major 'Tiny' Madden [GSO2 Air Branch, Div HQ] came over and said there were some snipers in a house opposite our position. We organised fire from everything we had including the PIAT. It was most impressive and satisfied the urge to hit out at something but I doubt whether the sniper was really there.
>
> I heard that Major Royle had been killed and later Bill Barrie. We are lucky not to have had casualties so far. There is another supply drop in the evening. The flak is heavier but we are powerless to do anything. Those chaps are marvellous but again much of the drop goes astray. I clean my Sten gun yet again and sleep in a slit trench by myself this time.

In the grounds of the Hartenstein Hotel Reg Lawton had miraculously met up with another member of his crew, Flying Officer Cullen, their Bomb Aimer. Together they went around and found a line of trenches over to the left of Hartenstein Hotel commanded by two officers they knew, Captain Priest and Captain Barry.

> We learned that the enemy had captured the Field Hospital, the roof of which we could see beyond some trees. This meant that our Engineer, Flight Sergeant Byrne, was now a prisoner.
>
> We were in these trenches only a few hours, before we decided to move again. We returned to the house and set off down the grounds. I chose a spot on the edge of the wooded part and almost on a corner of the running track. This commanded the open ground of the running track and tennis courts, beyond which was Captain Priest's line of trenches, about 12 feet long and seven feet deep. Cullen was a couple of trenches away with Captain Walchli and Bob Smith, his runner.[25]

In the north-west corner two flights of 'E' Squadron were heavily attacked and, after a stiff fight against overwhelming odds during which they were cut off from the main Allied position, they decided to break out. Major Peter Jackson, officer commanding 'E' Squadron:

This they did in a gallant dash through the enemy lines giving Jerry everything they had as they came through, and succeeded in regaining the main position which was strongly held.

The Germans made another attack after heavily shelling our men with mortars but this was beaten off. The enemy then brought up a broadcasting van and called to the British troops saying 'British Tommies, why do you fight for the English Lords? Churchill and Montgomery have left you to die. We are going to attack you with the SS Panzer Division.'

One British Officer, a titled member of the English aristocracy, is reported to have turned to his comrades and said; 'What, fight for me? Good God!'[26]

Sergeant Ron Driver was in the composite body, which was moving south-west into the positions of the Border Regiment:

A group of us were taken to the edge of a wood, facing an open field we were told to dig in at the corner with the field fan shape in front of us. We started digging with gusto, two to a slit trench, one chap got out for a breather and then said, 'Hey there's some other guys digging the other side of the road.'

We all stopped and looked to where he was pointing. There was a road skirting the field in front of us, three to four hundred yards away, the other side of the road, the ground was a tree plantation with a track-fire break, at the bend in the road. It was at this point that the men, Germans we concluded, were digging away.

We all got our rifles and fired away. They didn't take the slightest notice of us. We stopped firing and looked amazed at each other. One chap, with a look of incredulity on his face, said, 'Bloody-Hell, they have issued us with blanks!' Someone said, try the Bren, it was amazing, one burst had the diggers diving into the trench.

We continued with the digging in, all the time keeping a watchful eye on the Germans opposite. I don't even remember seeing any of them again. We did get subjected to bouts of mortar-fire, but nothing that troubled us. You had to take advantage of the quiet periods for essential personal things.

I had quite a stock of tea cubes. These looked like dirty sugar lumps. The tea, sugar and the powdered milk were all compressed together. If you wanted to mash, you put the water in your mess-tin, lit a solid fuel tablet in its holder, placed the mess-tin on it and when the water boiled, popped in the cube and hey-presto-a cup of tea. If you wanted something to eat, in the two twenty-four hour ration packs that we were issued with, were the tea cubes, some hard blocks of various shades of colour, the oatmeal coloured one turned out to be just that. You put the water on, and then scraped away at this block until the porridge was the thickness you wanted. The milk and sugar was also included. The brown block, given the same treatment was supposed to be mincemeat, certainly not like Mother made! I think there were some hard-tack biscuits, and Barley sugars but I couldn't be certain. I don't think we had any ration issue while we were at Arnhem. I know I had an inside pocket of my smock with a plentiful supply of tea cubes but, later on, getting up water was a big problem.

14 Flight, 'F' Squadron returned to their previous positions in the north-east part of the perimeter. Wally Holcroft:

We were not long in the garden when an Officer commandeered us to assist with the defence of a road junction close by. He had three men with him with rifles, but he felt that the addition of Mick's Bren [Staff Sergeant Hall] to his armoury would be a distinct advantage. We were glad to help and we returned with him to his slit trench where we set up the Bren.

The Officer informed us that they belonged to the Royal Army Service Corps but as they had little to do they were acting as infantrymen and he was determined to hold this position to the last man with knives and grenades if necessary. Mick enquired if he had any news, but he had heard only contradictory rumours and he felt that none of these were reliable. He thought the Second Army was pushing on fast, and no doubt if we could hold our positions for another day or two all would be well.

Our position was attacked several times during the day with mortar bombs, whilst the battle in the wood warmed up from time to time and the crackle of rifle fire was incessant. In the afternoon the Dakotas arrived with more supplies and they ran into a hostile reception worse than the previous day. It was heartbreaking to watch the planes seemed to be flying into hell. Parachutes carrying supplies came floating down in hundreds, but the wind carried most of them away northwards into what I estimated must be the enemy's lines.

A couple of supply panniers fell across the road, one hitting the roof of a house where it dislodged a few tiles before slithering off the roof and into the garden below. The other, falling without its parachute opening fairly smashed into the ground and most of the contents were ruined.The Royal Army Service Corps boys left us now to collect what supplies they could of those that had fallen in our lines. Later in the afternoon they returned saying they had found a number of their own men in a house down the road and they wished to take one of us with them for a meal. Mick went with them.

When he returned about an hour later he said that he'd had a lovely meal in a house where the owners were still living. They had cooked him some chicken. I consoled myself with a bar of chocolate. We took turns to watch during the night, it never became really dark for houses burning here and there kept the area well illuminated.[17]

In Arnhem, despite the tenacious resistance of the airborne troops around the northern ramp, the situation around the bridge continued to worsen. John Frost had been wounded in the morning and had been forced to hand command of the remnants of his force over to 'Freddie' Gough.

German attacks grew bolder and the defenders' numbers continued to dwindle as the day went on. By midday the battle for possession of the bridge had reached a critical point. The perimeter was receding rapidly as the Germans continued to blast and burn the defenders out of their positions on both sides of the ramp.

After some last desperate counter-attacks, all surviving British troops were withdrawn into the 'HQ' Company position just to the north of the bridge. The majority of John Frost's officers had by now been killed or wounded and it was clear that relief was not about to appear from the rest of 1st Airborne Division in Oosterbeek.

The remaining troops fought on in the hope that the rumours of relief by XXX Corps at 1700 hours were true. By nightfall there was no sign of any relief force and the last British-held houses were well and truly ablaze. The defenders had no firm positions left to hold as the Germans continued to push into the streets and buildings, no longer deterred by airborne troops.

Eventually a short truce was arranged and the British wounded were surrendered to the German medical services. By the light of burning buildings many of the wounded and dead were recovered from the ruined streets around the bridge. All of the time more German troops and armour were arriving to reinforce the final German effort to retake Arnhem bridge. During the truce Arthur Rigby was moved out of his fire position:

From somewhere in the rear of our positions I heard a voice shouting, 'Glider Pilots, this way' repeatedly, and on looking around I saw that I was practically alone. So gathering my Bren and the remaining bit of ammo I started to make my way through the debris toward the voice, falling over a pile of bicycles onto a dead soldier in the process. Eventually I located the voice of Lieutenant Cole and found about a dozen glider pilots gathered round him, including Ted Healey and George Miller. The rest I didn't know.

As soon as I arrived Lieutenant Cole set off down an alleyway. We passed Lieutenant Meakin standing at a junction of two alleys pointing the direction to follow saying quite calmly, 'Pass right down the car please, don't hang about' and we finally arrived outside what appeared to be a school or Technical College and found the doors locked.

Lieutenant Cole stepped forward to do his 'cowboy act' by shooting the lock open. It didn't work. Five rounds from his 45 automatic and the door stayed firm. However, a chap came along and said he had found a basement door open and we followed his direction and guidance into the building.

Quite a large number of troops were gathered in the basement rooms. We were sent upstairs and told to get rid of our fighting knives, and then lie low and keep quiet in the upper rooms (which appeared to be classrooms) and wait for Thirty Corps to arrive in the night.

So we settled down, whilst outside we could hear the clatter of AFV's and Jerry troops shouting about in the streets, and finally fell asleep for a short while.[18]

Sergeant Godfrey Freeman, also of 19 Flight, had been wounded during the battle to hold the bridge. He remembers lying on the stone floor of a cellar that was being used to shelter the wounded:

Boots were passing me by, and not caring much whether they trod on me or not. I think I must have roused myself then and am now bewildered and confused, but growingly aware that the situation is dire.

Upstairs, small-arms ammunition was exploding in the fire like jumping squibs on Guy Fawkes Night. Next to the Dutch civilians, standing upright like outsize altar candles, were a few rounds of six-pounder anti tank ammunition, abandoned for want of a gun to fire them from.

From time to time I caught a glimpse of Lieutenant Colonel Frost as he lay, white as wax from loss of blood, on a kind of stretcher rigged out for him by the medics, from which he issued orders and instructions.

A visit from a German interpreter to enquire whether he was prepared to surrender proved fruitless. He was sent back with a message to the effect that Lieutenant Colonel Frost would accept unconditional surrender from the other side. From then on it was only a matter of time.[19]

After the truce those still fit enough to fight attempted to re-establish defensive positions in the burning houses, but it was to be a forlorn hope. Those remaining were in fragmented groups with little ammunition. They fought on but after incurring yet more casualties while attempting to stem an irresistible tide of German armour and Panzergrenadiers, John Frost's battalion and its supporting elements ceased to be a fighting force.

The next morning the battle of Arnhem Bridge was over, the main objective of Operation MARKET was, after three days and four nights, back in German hands. Private James Sims was one of the survivors from 2nd Parachute Battalion, in his own account of the battle entitled *Arnhem Spearhead* he recalls being marched away from the bridge as a POW:

The road we turned into had trees down each side and under these parked nose-to-tail, were never ending lines of German mark IV tanks. In the dusk it was a truly impressive sight. Seeing my wonder a young enemy soldier remarked 'Yes Tommy, those were for you if you had not surrendered'. Several of the tank men called out to us 'well fought Tommy,' 'Good fight, eh Tommy?' They seemed to regard war in much the same way as the British regarded a football match.[20]

During the day some radio communication had been possible. At 1505 hours Headquarters 1st Airborne Division had transmitted the following message to 'Boy' Browning's Corps Headquarters in Nijmegen:

Enemy attacking main br in strength. Situation critical for 1 Para Bde. Enemy also attacking Div posn EAST from HEELSUM and WEST from ARNHEM. Situation serious but am forming close perimeter defence round HARTENSTEIN 6978 with remainder of Div. Relief essential both areas earliest possible. Still retain control of ferry crossing HEVEADORP.

The message was the first contact between the headquarters, therefore the first indication of the gravity of the situation to Browning and his staff. At midnight Roy Urquhart's headquarters was informed that the Guards Armoured Division had secured the Nijmegen Bridge. They had in fact rushed the bridge at 1830 hours but had remained bogged down in heavy fighting in Nijmegen itself and further to the south.

**Notes**

1     Rigby, Sergeant A., 19 Flt, 'B' Sqn GPR, by permission of *The Eagle.*.

2     Johnson, Lieutenant R., 'E' Sqn GPR, correspondence with Luuk Buist, 1991 onwards.

3     Bond, Sergeant P., 16 Flt, 'E' Sqn GPR, correspondence with Luuk Buist, 1991.

4     Gibson, SSgt R., 16 Flt, 'F' Sqn GPR, letter to Simion family, November 1944, courtesy of Alan Sugerman, AJEX Archive.

5     Mahoney, Sergeant P., 16 Flt, 'F' Sqn GPR, Evasion Report, National Archives file WO 208/3324.

6     Weeden, Sergeant L., 14 Flt, 'F' Sqn GPR, correspondence with the author, March 2008.

7     Urquhart, Major General R., *Arnhem*, London, Cassell & Co Ltd, 1958, p. 113.

8     McGeough, SSgt J., 'C' Sqn, GPR, correspondence with Luuk Buist, 1978 onwards.

9     Pearce, Sergeant T., 5 Flt, 'D' Sqn GPR, correspondence with Luuk Buist, 1991.

10     Leaver, SSgt M., 'G' Sqn GPR, correspondence with Bob Hilton, 1997.

11     Dauncey, Lieutenant M., 9 Flt, 'G' Sqn GPR, interview with the author, February 2008.

12     Blanthorn, SSgt W., 1 Flt, 'A' Sqn GPR, correspondence with Robert Sigmond, date unknown.

13     Clayton, SSgt A., 1 Flt, 'A' Sqn GPR, correspondence with Bob Hilton, 1998.

14     Chapman, SSgt A., 'A' Sqn GPR, correspondence with Luuk Buist, 1991.

15     Lawton, Flight Lieutenant R., RAF, 'Harvest of Ten Years', by permission of Airborne Museum Hartenstein.

16     Jackson, Major P., OC 'E' Sqn GPR, correspondence with Luuk Buist, 1991.

17     Holcroft, SSgt W., 14 Flt, 'F' Sqn GPR, 'No medals for Lt Pickwoad', September 1945.

18     Rigby, Sergeant A., 19 Flt, 'B' Sqn GPR, by permission of *The Eagle*.

19     Freeman, Sergeant G., 19 Flt, 'B' Sqn GPR, correspondence with Luuk Buist, 1991.

20     Sims, Private J., 2nd Para Bn, *Arnhem Spearhead*, Imperial War Museum, 1978, p. 88.

# CHAPTER 13

# The Cauldron

*'We only had personal weapons and nothing to stop a tank with and were ordered to retire in the direction of Oosterbeek.'*

**Thursday, 21 September 1944**

During the course of Wednesday evening, Divisional Headquarters at the Hartenstein received a radio message from the Guards Armoured Division, stating that the Guards would spearhead an all-out drive on Arnhem Bridge at first light on Thursday morning.

There had also been a desperate attempt to rush a flying column through the German lines from Oosterbeek to the bridge, with ammunition and medical supplies. This forlorn hope comprised two Jeeps commanded by Lieutenant Leo Heaps, a Canadian officer from 1st Parachute Battalion. He and his men had made a successful high-speed dash of this nature as far as St Elisabeth's Hospital on the second day of the battle. His platoon was now much depleted and the German grip on the routes to the bridge was by now almost air-tight. After a short meeting with Roy Urquhart in his headquarters, the brave Canadian agreed to attempt another vehicle-borne run through the German defences to John Frost and his men at the bridge.

Leo Heaps was not a man to shy away from a challenge as his presence at Arnhem already proved. Although not a fully trained paratrooper, he had made his first jump with David Dobie's battalion on D-Day, and had shown himself to be quite fearless during 1st Parachute Battalions battle to reach Arnhem. Despite his obvious bravery, he could not accomplish his resupply mission alone as he would need men to crew his Jeeps. He looked around the area of the Hartenstein for volunteers. Eventually, enough men were found to crew the two Jeeps and the plan was explained. The group would drive the vehicles down to the Heveadorp ferry; once at the ferry the intention was to cross the river to the less densely defended south bank. The Jeeps would then speed along the south bank, through the startled Germans and across the main road bridge into the beleaguered positions around the north ramp.

At midnight on Wednesday, the Jeep crews had climbed aboard their heavily laden vehicles; they were a mixed bunch. Two more officers had joined the mission: Lieutenant Maarten Knottenbelt, a Dutch commando of No. 2 (Dutch) Troop, No. 10 (Inter-allied) Commando, who had put his role of liaison with the Dutch Resistance on hold until the fighting subsided. Lieutenant Johnny Johnson, a United States Air Force Support Signal Team officer, also came forward as he currently had no useful role to fulfil in the headquarters. In his own account of that night, *The Grey Goose of Arnhem*, Leo Heaps also mentions two sleepy Glider Pilots (unknown) armed with Thompson sub-machine guns, who climbed on board the Jeeps to act as gunners.

The undoubted bravery of Leo Heaps and his band of men was, in the end, to prove futile as they could not get across the river. The Heveadorp ferry was out of action and fog obscured the bank that night; the members of his very small force became separated from each other and had to find their own way back from the river bank to the Hartenstein. The identity of the two glider pilots remains unknown to this day.

Any effective resistance in the area of Arnhem itself ceased later in the morning. At 0500 hours, the last defiant airborne troops were forced to surrender. Many of the bone-tired defenders attempted to evade capture and reach Oosterbeek, but most were in German hands by the end of the morning. Arthur Rigby was among those who did their best to avoid capture and break through the German lines to the west:

> In the early hours of the morning (around 2.00 am) we were again called into the corridor and shepherded back down into the cellars, and there we found upwards of a hundred troops, various regiments altogether. We stayed together, parties of five or six and were told to set off and hide up in the town, to try to better our chances of not being discovered. Our party consisted of Ted [Healey], George Miller, an artillery officer, a paratrooper and myself.
>
> It all seemed dreamlike. We were all dog-tired and the setting was eerie. The area was still burning fiercely and among the roar of the flames we could hear voices shouting in German and there we were, a little group of blokes tired out, thirsty and red eyed from the smoke, which swirled around us, looking for shelter.
>
> I suggested we make for the river and as we were still wearing our air jackets (deflated) we could possibly slip into the water and inflate the jackets and drift downstream and join the main body around Oosterbeek. Hoping the artillery officer knew in which direction the river lay, turned to consult him, but he had disappeared off on his own I guess. The other three thought the idea was sound, but as we didn't know which way to go why not lay up for the rest of the night, possibly get some sleep, gather strength the next day and try the river stunt on Thursday night.
>
> So this was settled and we found a garden in the rear of a house, which included a shrubbery. I got myself well under the bushes, spread my camouflage net scarf over myself, lay down and went sound asleep. Whilst I was doing this Ted and George found a pile of garden refuse, grass cuttings and leaves and dug themselves into this and buried themselves and slept. The paratrooper bedded down in the outside toilet. I awoke in broad daylight to the sound of crackling burning timber and saw with horror that the house that Ted and George had bedded down against was ablaze and burning debris showering down onto them.
>
> They were sound asleep. I got them aroused and away from the danger and fortunately no harm or injury had been sustained, but there was no sign of the paratrooper. He must have scampered during the night. The problem was where to go? Daylight, danger of being seen and probably shot at.
>
> So we decided to each take a look at possibilities and rendezvous back in the garden in 30 minutes. George set off to look out of the front of the house. I was going over the wall into the alleyway and Ted was going opposite ways to me. It all went disastrously awry. George had hardly got into the front part of the house when there was a terrific burst of firing, automatic pistols and rifles. We heard George shout 'not this way' and then silence, except for German voices shouting to each other.
>
> Ted went to the rear of the house and shouted to George but the only reply he got was Schmeisser pistol fire down the passageway. Ted didn't stand on ceremony, he dashed across to my side of the garden and together we cleared the wall. The German voices seemed far away and at least we were not being pursued. As we were travelling along this alley, we noticed a small cottage standing alone, behind the other houses, and decided to make for it, over the fence and into the back door.

We were astonished to find about twenty other blokes inside, and one young officer. Most of them had weapons but no ammunition. I spoke to the officer and asked him what he planned to do and he said he thought we could lie up till nightfall and then get down to the river, and possibly escape. As we had the same in mind, we decided to stay with them at least until they moved off and then go our own way.

We decided to get some more sleep in readiness for the night adventures and laid ourselves out on the bed. I hardly seemed to have closed my eyes (though in fact it was over two hours later) when I was awakened by raucous German voices shouting outside 'We know you are in there Tommy, are you coming out or do we have to fetch you!' Dead silence – a sudden burst of machine gun fire and the same question asked. This time, I heard the young officer say that he was coming out and they were not to shoot.

Ted and I decided to stay put and hope that we would be forgotten, but there was no such luck. Having got the main body outside the Germans decided to search the home and we had no time to hide. We were marched downstairs and out through a window to join the others in the courtyard. German soldiers, all young lads, surrounded us, Panzer Grenadiers 18 to 20 years of age. They were laughing and joking, slapping us on the back, congratulating us on the fine battle we had put up.

We were lined up and marched off toward the centre of the town. On the way we saw Staff Sergeants Higginbotham and Clenaghan carrying a wounded officer into a German Regimental Aid Post and when we arrived in the square by the Cathedral George Baylis joined us, also Frank Dennis. We were all searched again, and after this 'going-over' we were told to sit on the pavement. After about an hour we were moved into the Cathedral and by this time our numbers had swelled enormously. Various airborne units all mixed up. Thus began captivity.[1]

Godfrey Freeman had also remained in the cellar underneath the house used as 1st Parachute Brigade Headquarters, but was eventually taken prisoner and led out of the cellar and up onto the street. The house above was by now burning quite fiercely:

A small group were gathered together, some standing, others sitting or lying on the grass, with an SS officer who, for the time being, was absorbed in the spectacle of the fire. I made my way towards this group and soon recognised my Flight commander, Captain Simpson, but there was nobody else there that I knew.

I made myself known to him and asked whether anyone had seen anything of Henry Cole, my skipper. 'I was going to ask you the same thing' he replied, 'No, I haven't seen anything of him at all.' 'Perhaps he'll turn up' I muttered, and turned to regard the SS officer who was still watching the fire, staring over the top of the embankment. 'Have you seen anything of the anti-tank?' I asked, 'The anti-tank commander we brought over?' For answer Simpson jerked his head in the direction of one of the figures that were lying on the grass. 'Over there' he said. Rocking slowly from side to side rather like a contented infant, and humming what sounded like snatches of song, was the barely recognisable person of the Battery Commander.

'What...?' I began. 'Bomb happy' replied Simpson tersely. 'Hallo Major' I said. To my astonishment he recognised me instantly. 'Hallo Freeman' he replied, 'Where's old Yellow Scarf?' It was the nickname he had given to Henry Cole, who liked to wear a yellow silk scarf, decorated with foxes' heads. 'I'm afraid I don't know' I answered, "I haven't seen him for two days. We got separated.'

Just then some louder explosions boomed out from somewhere nearby, and the Major began to chortle and chuckle with bizarre inner content. 'There's a good one!' he almost cheered, as a much louder explosion sounded closer at hand. His body shuddered with each explosion but he bore no sign of a wound. I took comfort from that, and the fact that whatever had happened to him had left him remarkably cheerful.

Meanwhile, Captain Simpson appeared to have developed a severe limp, and I looked down and saw a fairly bulky dressing bound round his ankle. 'I am terribly sorry' I said sympathetically, 'I didn't realise you'd been hit.' Captain Simpson looked about him quickly, and I thought rather furtively. 'Don't be a bloody fool' he whispered as loudly as he dared, 'I haven't been hit. This is a fake!' 'A fake?' I echoed the word stupidly. 'To get into hospital, of course!' The spectacle of my Flight commander brazenly swinging the lead was too much for my enfeebled mind to grasp. 'What on earth for?' I asked. Simpson lowered his voice and looked about him again. 'Because, my dear Freeman,' he explained, in the sort of tones commonly reserved for backward children or the very naive, 'it is easier to get out of a hospital than it is to get out of a prison camp.'

My mind suddenly seemed to find a kind of second wind: escape! My heart took another leap. Escape? Why not? The more I thought of it the more the idea attracted me. 'That's a bloody good idea,' I said admiringly. While having different fantasies about a way to escape I found myself looking down at the Gunner Major, and slowly an idea began to form in my mind. I made a snap decision. 'All right,' I said, 'from now on I am bomb happy, so please take no notice of anything I say or do from this moment on.' Simpson eyed me thoughtfully. 'OK,' he agreed, 'I'll back you up all I can.' So began nearly four weeks of the most demanding role I have ever played![2]

Whilst the last throes of the bridge battle were in progress, the remainder of the Division had spent the night regrouping and preparing for what would undoubtedly be another day of intense fighting around the Oosterbeek perimeter.

Later in the morning, at 0730 hours, Roy Urquhart held an Orders Group with his surviving staff and senior commanders at the Hartenstein. With his thoughts on holding on to Oosterbeek, in order to maintain a bridgehead for XXX Corps, he formally divided responsibility for the perimeter between his two brigade commanders.

'Pip' Hicks was given the western side of the boundary, from the junction of Stationsweg and Graaf van Rechterenweg down Valkenburglaan, and Van Borsselenweg to Heveadorp, which included the Driel ferry crossing site. The Airlanding Brigade commander positioned his troops from right to left as follows: Reconnaissance Squadron; 7th Battalion King's Own Scottish Borderers; 21st Independent Parachute Company; 4th Para Squadron, Royal Engineers; 2 Wing, Glider Pilot Regiment; and 1st Battalion, Border Regiment.

The eastern side of the perimeter was allocated to 'Shan' Hackett; he positioned his force right to left: 11th Parachute Battalion west, south and east of Oosterbeek Church; 2nd Battalion, South Staffords east of Church, from south of the Hofwegen laundry to the crossing of Benedendorpsweg and Polderweg to the river bank.

The remnants of 1st Parachute Brigade troops were spread from the junction of Rozensteeg and Weverstraat to the flank of 10th Parachute Battalion, who were positioned east of the Schoonoord Hotel, in four houses astride Utrechtseweg. To the north of the crossroads, glider pilots from 'D' Squadron held a thin line from the crossroads to a rather indeterminate boundary, with 156th Parachute Battalion in the area of Stationsweg and Joubertweg. At this point, both east and west met, to the left of the paratroopers were the Reconnaissance Squadron and 7th Battalion, King's Own Scottish Borderers.

It has to be remembered that the formations listed were all well below their fighting strength by now and many junior commanders were either wounded or dead. They were essentially battalions, companies and squadrons in name only. However, they remained determined to fight on, until relieved by the tanks of XXX Corps.

At the start of the day there were glider pilots deployed in nearly every section of the Oosterbeek perimeter. The core of 1st Airborne Division's only real reserve was made up of 20 Flight from 'B' Squadron, and 10 and 24 Flights from 'G' Squadron. Major 'Dickie' Dale and 'C' Squadron were still operating as 1st Airlanding Brigade's only reserve. The GPR force defending the vulnerable south-east corner of the horseshoe was made up of 1 Flight from 'A' Squadron, 3 and 4 Flights from 'B' Squadron, and 9 and 23 Flights from 'G' Squadron.

The GPR grouping, fighting in the woods to the north-west, was made up of the remnants of 'E' and 'F' squadrons. Scattered all over the divisional area there were numerous glider pilots fighting as individuals, or in sections still fighting alongside the troops they had carried in their respective gliders. Many never regrouped with their own comrades, but spent the whole of their time in Oosterbeek within the ranks of an adopted unit. Their unique training and SNCO status made them a real asset to a depleted unit within the perimeter.

Sergeant Fred Tilley was a prime example of the positive impact they were to have on those units and the battle itself. Robert Payton-Reid, the Commanding Officer of the 7th Battalion, KOSB had this to say of Fred:

> [Tilley] had, from no known reason, decided to remain with us instead of rejoining his own unit and had appointed himself my 'bodyguard'. On one occasion I was going round the front with him and when we arrived near where I expected to find a platoon he shot ahead round some houses to locate it. He shot back even faster, however, seizing me by the arm, dragged me along with him, whispering: 'there's a trench round there cram full of Bosche'.
>
> As he thought they could not have failed to see him we deemed it wise to get out of sight, so leapt through a window of a damaged house nearby. Our leap took us further than anticipated, because the floor had been demolished with the result that we dropped right down into the cellar. And there we were, caught in a trap, expecting at any moment to see Hun faces peering down at us. Only Tilley's strength and agility saved the situation. By standing on my hands he could just reach ground level. With what help I could give him he managed to pull himself out, and then, by a stupendous effort, he hauled me up after him. A few minutes later we reached the proper platoon position [12 Platoon, 'C' Company] where, now it was safely over, our adventure took the appearance of a huge joke.[3]

Fred Tilley was awarded the Distinguished Conduct Medal in recognition for his behaviour during the battle. His contribution as a substitute medic in the KOSB Regimental Aid Post was briefly described in the previous chapter. As the battle progressed and casualties among the Scots battalion mounted, Fred took on more roles. This extract from his full citation gives some detail of the tasks he undertook, and as well as being a worthy tribute to him, it encapsulates the versatility and qualities George Chatterton sought to imbue in its recruits when he assumed command of GPR training in 1942:

> During the operations near Arnhem this NCO was attached to the KOSBs and distinguished himself throughout by his personal gallantry, initiative and unflagging cheerfulness under the most trying conditions. On 20th September, when the MO [Medical Officer[ and part of his staff were captured, Sgt Tilley attached himself to the RAP [Regimental Aid Post] and did sterling work in attending to the comfort and moral well being of the wounded, many of

whom he himself brought in under fire. When the RAP was hit and set on fire he saved several lives by his coolness in organising the evacuation of the wounded. Later when the medical staff were reinforced and when casualties had decimated battalion HQ, he voluntarily assumed the duties of RSM. In this capacity he maintained the supply of ammunition making numerous hazardous journeys to forward positions to do so. When rations ran out he organised a central kitchen from which he produced out of the products of the country, a hot meal for every man daily. In addition to these activities, he volunteered whenever there was dangerous work to be done and was constantly on anti- sniper patrols in and about the battalion area.

On one of these on 23rd September, he discovered an enemy post on which he immediately organised and led an attack as a result of which six enemy were captured and many killed. This NCO's enthusiasm, complete disregard for his personal safety and confident bearing had a most marked effect on all ranks of the battalion and his conduct throughout the battle was in accordance with the highest traditions of the British Army.[4]

Fred Tilley was not alone. Many other glider pilots were decorated for bravery during the battle (their citations are shown at Appendix 12). The intensity of the fighting within the area bounded by the Oosterbeek perimeter had by now caused the German troops to christen the area with the ominous nickname of 'Der Kessel' – The Cauldron. Conditions inside the cauldron were becoming more and more difficult as German pressure continued to mount, but the British would not give way and were described by one German as 'fighting like cornered tigers'. The tenacity of their defence and their aggression even in defence only added to the heat of the cauldron.

Much of the German mortar and artillery fire was centred on the Hartenstein and its surrounding gardens. The Germans were not aware of the hotel's role as the British headquarters but had selected it as a suitably prominent landmark to act as an objective for their attacking troops. Consequently there was a regular flow of German ordnance directed into the grounds around the hotel. This made even the most mundane tasks that soldiers had to complete to administer themselves potentially hazardous for all concerned.

Iain Murray, who had attended Roy Urquhart's 'O' Group, returned to his own headquarters in one of the rooms of the Hartenstein shortly afterwards. The routine of disseminating information from the briefing was shattered just after 0900 hours, when German mortar fire, coupled with heavier 'Moaning Minnies', began to rain down on the divisional area.

Sergeants Dennis Andrews and Denis Raggett of 'B' Squadron were both killed; also wounded in the same attack was Captain Angus Low, the 20 Flight's commander. Ian Toler's squadron was further weakened when Staff Sergeant Watt, and Sergeants Albert McCarthy and Ken Consterdine were brought in wounded, after being hit during the same attack. Sergeant Major 'Billy' Watt took the wounded to the MDS for treatment and then supervised the construction of overhead cover on all squadron trenches. As well as casualties amongst its pilots, 'B' Squadron also lost one of the prized vehicles it had acquired just after the first lift. The pride of Ian Toler's fleet, a captured German staff car, had not survived the mortar attack.

Once the mortar fire had ceased, Sergeant Dennis Andrews, who had flown in with Angus Low, was buried alongside his comrade Sergeant Denis Raggett, and others, within the grounds of the Hartenstein. The lull in the fighting also allowed the wounded to be attended to. Private James Hardy of 16 Para Field Ambulance, Royal Army Medical Corps was attached to Divisional Headquarters:

A glider pilot from a defence post nearby came in and asked if we could spare a medical orderly and I volunteered for the job, as it was work I was accustomed to. Upon arriving at the defence post which was a house about 100 yards from divisional headquarters I found four wounded glider pilots and these I immediately evacuated to a Main Dressing Station.[5]

Angus Low was among the wounded. He was naturally far from happy at being wounded and less so with the prospect of leaving the men of 20 Flight, although he was to find that life as a casualty at the Tafelberg MDS did have its compensations:

I was wounded in the right hand. I also sustained an injury to my ears through the blast and the dirt and sand, which was blown up in my face, temporarily blinded me. I was taken down to a nearby cellar and about 20 minutes later after the shelling died down I was removed to 181 Field Ambulance which was located in a house nearby.

I lay on the first floor and was duly seen by the Medical Officer while lying on a table. I was still very shocked and rather annoyed that I could not see very well because of the sandblasting of my eyes. I heard the Medical Officer giving instructions to the orderly to wash my wounded hands and 'to be very gentle'. The medical staff were tremendous, the orderly washing my hands was so gentle that I hardly believed a man could be so soft to the touch.

I decided I really must open my eyes in spite of the sand. I found the 'orderly' was a lovely blonde with shoulder length hair and wearing a white dress, which seemed so out of place amid all the filth around. Plaster and dust crashed down from the ceiling as another mortar bomb hit the building. It was an effort to open my eyes even slightly, but I felt I must as she was smiling at me.

Although not in my best smiley mood, I felt I owed it to her and gave a sickly smile back. She knew I was watching her because she kept smiling while she gently bathed my hands.[6]

While Angus enjoyed the briefest of respites in the MDS, the battle continued all around him. Shortly after the artillery strike on the 1 Wing positions, Iain Murray and his adjutant, Captain Peter Fletcher, set out with a section of glider pilots to retake the crossroads by the Schoonoord Main Dressing Station. This they did but the cross-roads continued to change hands regularly throughout the battle as the advantage shifted from one side to the other.

The morning had also got off to a lively start on the western side of the perimeter too, the Germans having mounted a concentrated assault on the key high ground overlooking the Driel-Heveadorp ferry crossing. The high ground, known as the Westerbouwing, was the lynch pin of the south-west corner of the new perimeter. A small restaurant sat in its own gardens, overlooking much of the perimeter and, critically, both sides of the ferry crossing. Whoever held the Westerbouwing dominated the ferry and much of the surrounding area.

The feature was held by 'B' Company of the Borders who were attacked at 0800 hours that morning by artillery, Char B tanks and infantry from the Hermann Goering Schule Regiment. Despite a determined defence that inflicted heavy casualties on the Germans, the speed and ferocity of their attack overwhelmed 'B' Company. The Germans pushed forward, taking many of the defenders prisoner, but were eventually halted by the Borders after they had captured the restaurant itself.

The loss of the Westerbouwing was a blow to British plans – after the loss of the main Arnhem Bridge it was intended to use the Driel ferry to reinforce the perimeter from the south bank. The long-awaited drop of the Polish Brigade was due to take place later in the day near Driel and the ferry was to be used to reinforce the Division with Poles after the drop. This would be impossible with German troops sat on top of the Westerbouwing dominating the river.

The German assault on the Westerbouwing had driven into the heart of the defences on the western side of the perimeter. The width of the perimeter base had been dramatically reduced to less than a thousand yards, so that, in military terms, 1st Airborne Division was hanging on to the river bank by a thread. If the Germans could continue to force an armoured wedge between the river and the airborne troops, the battle would be over almost instantly. The Borders counter-attacked on three occasions, attempting to regain the vital high ground, but each time were driven back.

Amid the confusion of the Westerbouwing battle, Major Charles Breese, the acting Second in Command of the Borders, rallied the survivors of 'B' Company and reorganized them. He also added two depleted platoons from 'A' Company to what became known as 'Breese Force', later to be reinforced with soldiers from the South Staffords and some paratroopers. These men operated in a similar role to Lonsdale Force on the eastern flank, showing great tenacity and preventing any further German advance along the river. The defences established by Charles Breese were so well organized that the Germans abandoned infantry attacks and resorted to artillery as their primary weapon to dislodge Breese Force.

The loss of the high ground had a direct bearing on the fighting in the area for the rest of the day. With the other companies of the Borders heavily engaged with accurate German mortar fire, all the battalion's positions were overlooked by enemy observation posts which could direct machine guns, artillery and mortars onto the Borders at will. Consequently, movement between positions, or relocation of equipment, was exposed to well-directed fire from heavy weapons, coupled with the ever-present threat of snipers.

The fighting in the south-west corner of the perimeter continued through the day, with all of the Border Regiment's companies embroiled in the struggle to hold their ground and block any German advance into the Division's rear area. The support of the Airlanding Regiments' light guns and use of their own bayonets and grenades held off a series of well-organised German attacks.

The composite flight was also dealt a blow during the morning at about 0945 hours when its commander, Lieutenant Ken Chittleburgh of 'D' Squadron, was killed by mortar fire. To the north-east of Oosterbeek, Lieutenant Ron Johnson of 'E' Squadron had stayed with his section within the KOSB's area:

> Last night the Germans set some houses near our position on fire. It was a real blaze and the sky was lit up. A young lady called out to us to be allowed to come from the blazing houses into our position. Having shouted to everyone locally to hold his fire, I called to the lady to come across to us. Unfortunately someone opened fire, shot her down and she lay in the road crying. Again I called to everyone to hold their fire and went out to carry her back into our lines. She had a part of her foot shot away. I handed her over to one of the Sergeants who took her to the First Aid Post.[7]

On the eastern side of the perimeter defences, the Germans also attacked close to the Rhine, with similar intent to the attack mounted from the west on the Westerbouwing feature. German infantry attacked along the river bank in the morning, but they were vigorously engaged by small-arms fire from Lonsdale Force and the guns of the Light Regiment.

Undeterred, the Germans quickly adapted their tactics and heavily shelled the area, causing a number of casualties among the gun crews of the Light Regiment. The gunners' Commanding Officer, Lieutenant Colonel 'Sherriff' Thompson, was also wounded. Later in the day German tactics were changed again, when armour was brought into play along the river bank. This in turn was held and then driven off by a combination of anti-tank guns, PIAT and sheer guts. Major Robert Cain, by now commanding the South Staffords, featured prominently in this action. His bravery and personal example under fire resulted in the break-up of the attack and in him being awarded the Victoria Cross. An extract from his citation:

On 20th September a Tiger tank approached the area held by his company and Major Cain went out alone to deal with it armed with a PIAT. Taking up a position he held his fire until the tank was only 20 yards away when he opened up. The tank immediately halted and turned its guns on him, shooting away a corner of the house near where this officer was lying. Although wounded by machine gun bullets and falling masonry, Major Cain continued firing until he had scored several direct hits, immobilised the tank and supervised the bringing up of a 75 mm. howitzer which completely destroyed it. Only then would he consent to have his wounds dressed.

The next morning this officer drove off three more tanks by the fearless use of his PIAT, on each occasion leaving cover and taking up position in open ground with complete disregard for his personal safety. During the following days, Major Cain was everywhere where danger threatened, moving amongst his men and encouraging them by his fearless example to hold out. He refused rest and medical attention in spite of the fact that his hearing had been seriously impaired because of a perforated eardrum and he was suffering from multiple wounds.

On the 25th September the enemy made a concerted attack on Major Cain's position, using self-propelled guns, flame throwers and infantry. By this time the last PIAT had been put out of action and Major Cain was armed with only a light 2-inch mortar. However, by a skilful use of this weapon and his daring leadership of the few men still under his command, he completely demoralized the enemy who, after an engagement lasting more than three hours, withdrew in disorder.

Staff Sergeant Wally Ashworth of 'B' Squadron witnessed the action:

Staff Sergeant Dickie Long was No. 1 on the Bren and I was No. 2. About 200 yards away, near some fences, was a great bloody Tiger. Major Cain was firing a PIAT from behind the corner of a building we called the laundry. His method was to hold the PIAT in the firing position and after firing at the enemy tanks he rolled sideways behind the laundry, reloaded, rolled sideways and fired again. This happened several times. The next thing I saw was a flash that sent the major staggering backwards. He had his hands to his eyes and I thought he was blinded. I didn't know what happened, but it never occurred to me that the PIAT had exploded. A couple of bods went and got him.[8]

Major Cain was treated by medics for his injuries and then, despite a burst eardrum, he insisted on returning to command his sector. To the north of the river, in the centre of Oosterbeek itself, the 10th Parachute Battalion faced attacks in similar strength from Arnhem to the west along Utrechtseweg. Initially, the much-depleted battalion was able to hold its ground and prevent a German breakthrough. After their initial success, a self-propelled gun was brought into action against the paratroopers, which, without support weapons, was extremely difficult to deal with. The gun proceeded to move systematically along the street, firing high-explosive shells into any buildings believed to be held by the British. The use of high-explosive shells, and the increasing numbers of German infantry, caused significant casualties amongst the defenders. German infantry infiltrated what was now a porous position. Once in amongst the defenders, they steadily began to outflank and eject 10th Parachute Battalion from their positions, the fighting being at close quarters and well within earshot of the Hartenstein. The Battalion was by now close to being totally overrun, with all of its officers killed or wounded. Lieutenant Colonel Ken Smyth, the Commanding Officer, had been fatally wounded and was among the dead. Despite their dire situation, and with no prospect of reinforcement, isolated pockets of resistance fought on under the command of Captain Peter Barron of the 2nd Airlanding Anti-Tank Battery. These isolated groups held on right through the day, until 'Shan' Hackett was able to send in the 21st Independent Parachute Company to relieve them the following day.

In the north-west part of the perimeter, Lieutenant Alec Johnston, recalls a lighter incident, which boosted the morale of 'E' Squadron:

Early in the morning of the fifth day, Lieutenant Desmond Turner, looking like a cross between a coal heaver and a scarecrow, marched up to the Wing Adjutant, Captain Shuttleworth, halted, saluted smartly and delivered himself of these memorable words: 'Please Sir, it's my 21st birthday today, can I have the day off?' Another incident that did much for the morale of the Squadron at about this time was the escape of Lieutenant 'Tommy' Tomson.

Tommy was exploring some houses in the vicinity of his positions when suddenly, on entering the sitting room of one such dwelling, he found himself face to face with a German patrol that was seated round a fireplace. For perhaps three seconds the Germans stared in amazement at the Englishman who, feeling like a rabbit confronted by a snake stared back. Then the spell was broken. Tommy turned and fled.

The Germans grabbed their guns and by the time they had got out of the front door Tommy was 80 yards away, going like the wind. Even as they fired at his swiftly departing figure, it leapt clean over a high fence and disappeared into the nearby shrubbery. If not one of the classic escapes of the war, it was nevertheless 100 per cent effective.[9]

Close by to 'E' Squadron, Wally Holcroft was reunited with some survivors from 14 Flight, after their battle on the Dennenkamp estate with the Dutch SS Panzer-grenadiers':

The morning dawned damp and misty, and we kept alert for a surprise attack, but nothing developed and later the sun broke through the haze and it became a glorious day. I suggested we made an excursion back to the wood for our kit, as it contained all our food supplies and we hadn't seen it since Tuesday.

As we made our way down we met 'Doddy', he looked really done in and when he saw us he railed at us for some time. 'Half the Flight is dead or wounded,' he said, 'There's not many left besides myself.' Then he went on to tell us how, after losing us, they had gone on the Tuesday to fight a really fierce battle with the enemy and had been bombed, shelled, and blasted right left and centre.

One mortar bomb had dropped into a trench occupied by four of the boys killing three of them outright and mortally wounding the fourth. Graham [Sergeant John] was among the dead, he was only about twenty years old and one of my closest friends. 'Doddy' seemed to think that we had been dodging the column a bit, but when I reminded him of what had actually happened he calmed down somewhat. We left him eventually looking very dejected, and proceeded on our way.

The wood was much as we had left it two days before but was now occupied by another Flight. We continued the search for our kit, which we found quite intact, and after gathering it up we made our way back to Wing headquarters. We passed Captain Shuttleworth on our way and he gave us a friendly word or two; we were never to see him alive again. Reaching our trench without mishap we prepared a scanty meal from our ration packs which we consumed and then enjoyed a cigarette.

If my memory serves me right it was on this day that we saw Major General Urquhart standing close by us talking to another Officer and he looked so confident and self assured I thought everything must have been going well.[10]

Staff Sergeant Laurie Weeden had moved into the same area, with a number of other glider pilots from 'F' Squadron. The evening before, he had met his flight commander, Lieutenant Aubrey Pickwoad DFC, who told him to return to 14 Flight, as their numbers were dwindling due to casualties. They were now reinforcing their comrades on the perimeter to the north-west of the Hartenstein Hotel.

I spent the night in the first floor room of a house in Nassaulaan and during the night I challenged some movement at the bottom of the garden. At daylight I realised that I had been challenging a tame rabbit in its hutch. We were on the edge of a wood looking out over a large field towards Manege and Sonnenberg. I was sharing a trench with Staff Sergeant Eric Stubley, from whom I acquired a Bren gun, with Staff Sergeants Tim Mathews and Rice in the next trench on our south side. A few metres away to the north were the bodyies of Sergeant Laurie Howes and also, I believe, the body of my co pilot Sergeant John Graham. Both had been killed the previous day – it was suggested that they might have given their position away when lighting a cigarette.

During the morning, a number of Germans, some of whom were shouting in English 'cease fire', advanced across the field in front of us, presenting rather an easy target and sustaining a number of casualties, including two dead immediately in front of us near a re-supply pannier.

I spent much of the day cleaning the Bren gun, which seemed unsuited to the sandy soil at the top of the trench. So far as I recollect we had no food and little or no water. We could hear the German NCO shouting commands from across the field as they fired their mortar.[11]

Sergeant Tom Pearce of 5 Flight, 'D' Squadron, found himself with another group in a house in Oosterbeek itself, just two or three doors away from the junction of Stationsweg and Utrechtseweg:

Someone cooked potatoes and apples from the gardens and we had a typical army meal. Some odd Soup 'SOS' as we used to call it in the Infantry. Someone else found Port Wine in the cellar. I didn't have any, as I don't like it. At this time we had an officer with us, Captain Ogilvie. He was wounded, a bullet in his shoulder I was told, and lay in a bed in the downstairs room at the right when entering the house from the rear.

Somewhere during our occupation of these houses the following things come to mind. I spent some time lying at the side of the house I called headquarters aiming my rifle at the garden of the lone house across the street, holding it between the pump and the wall.

The house across the street had been destroyed by fire before we got there and I was told that a Dutch lady came out and crossing the street and asked to be allowed to stay with the glider pilots on this side.

In perfect English she said, 'Do please tell me if this one goes up in flames won't you?' I also spent some time aiming my rifle through a small hole (one brick) in the wall of the outhouse at the rear of the house, looking across the allotments, which we had crossed on taking over the houses. I could see soldiers moving along the houses and gardens but the distance was such that I didn't know whether they were Germans or ours.

While lying by the water pump three soldiers climbed out of the ruins across the road and dashed to the right. The distance to cover was very short and they moved very fast, again I could not decide whether they were friend or foe, so I didn't fire.[12]

On the other side of Utrechtseweg, in the Hartenstein area, Ian Toler was with 20 Flight, holding the ground on the east side of the tennis courts, which were being used as a divisional prisoner cage for German POWs, taken after the landings and during subsequent fighting. Such a facility requires routine administration, even during the heat of battle, as Ian Toler was about to find out:

I had made my headquarters in the Pavilion and in particular in the cellar below. I well remember a soldier bringing a German woman in uniform across and asking if she could use my cellar as a toilet, a somewhat unusual request in the middle of a battle! Rather grudgingly I left the comparative safety of the cellar with my co-pilot Staff Sergeant Shackleton for the lady's convenience.

She was an unconsciously long time and must have been in extremis. When we returned to the cellar it appeared to be completely flooded with urine, and uninhabitable. As a result we hurriedly dug a slit trench in another part of the garden from which we were blown out by a shell.[13]

South of the Hartenstein, in the south-east corner of the perimeter, although exhausted, Lieutenant Mike Dauncey and his men continued to protect the RA gun batteries by holding their ground on Weverstraat:

Somehow we were kept awake all night and in the morning started a bit of a link-up. Our post covered the crossroads and also got some chaps out to cover round the top of the battery. Company Sergeant Major Smith, of 'B' Company, 11 Parachute Battalion and I were in the top two houses on either side of the road, so we formed a link-up.

Then occurred my first piece of luck. I never wore my helmet, relying instead on my beret as a morale booster for the others. I was standing outside near a slit trench when a sniper put a bullet through the front of my beret and out the back. The bullet grazed my scalp, sending a flood of blood down into my face. I fell to the ground and lay perfectly still for several seconds, then I warned Sergeant Major Smith I was going to scramble into his trench. I rolled into the trench just as the sniper's second shot hit the ground where I had been.[14]

Communication between the splintered groups of glider pilots was increasingly difficult. The 1 Wing GPR war diary has the following entry at 1330 hours: 'Casualties, as far as can be ascertained, are 9 killed, 15 wounded, but owing to Squadrons and Flights being split information is very hard to obtain.'

During the afternoon two eight-man tank-hunting patrols were mounted by 1 Wing GPR. Lieutenant Brian Bottomley, the Wing Intelligence Officer, with seven other glider pilots formed one patrol; Lieutenant Herman Futter the Adjutant of 'B' Squadron, with a further seven pilots, made up the second patrol.

On returning from his patrol later in the afternoon, Brian Bottomley reported a German propaganda unit was broadcasting an appeal for the British to surrender. The broadcast was clearly heard in the 'B' Squadron positions – a German voice emanating from a loudspeaker located out to their front. The accented voice mentioned Lieutenant Colonel McCardie (now a POW) of the South Staffords by name. The Squadron replied to the request with some well-aimed bursts of Bren gun fire that silenced the irritating voice.

The increased intensity of German artillery fire was causing even more casualties around the Hartenstein. At 1600 hours the dispositions around Divisional Headquarters were reviewed, and troops and stores were dispersed over a wider area in an attempt to reduce the effect of the artillery fire. The perimeter defence positions, however, could not fall back or be dispersed any further. The glider pilots and the Defence Platoon therefore had no option but to sit tight in their original positions. Iain Murray and his Adjutant, Captain Peter Fletcher, waited for the dust to settle and at 1730 hours set out to visit their men and the 1 Wing forward positions. Murray had also distributed the following upbeat Situation Report to all of his squadron and flight commanders:

> Situation well in hand. Nine fire tasks given to XXX Corps Artillery to neutralise enemy fire. Guards Armoured Division trying to get up tonight but may not get through until morning. Supply drop successful. Local enemy opposition consists few self-propelled guns and quickly gathered units from 50 different divisions. We are superior in numbers; several self-propelled guns have been knocked out in last twelve hours. Several Germans are surrendering along the River. The Poles have dropped. You are doing a splendid job, keep it up and most important, keep cheerful.[15]

As the early evening began to close in, glider pilots were taking over more positions around the perimeter in their usual willing manner. Sergeant Ron Driver of 'A' Squadron:

> It was late afternoon when we were moved away from the orchard, we were told to wait where we had stopped, for some reason. We waited some time then the officer came back; he put his arm through the centre of the group and said, 'Those to the right, follow me, those to the left go with the Sergeant Major.'
>
> Bert and I were in opposite groups; there was nothing we could do. We mouthed a 'cheerio' at each other as we walked off, that was the last I saw of Bert during the operation. He was lucky; he got back over the river and back to England unharmed. We went back down the road, along another road some way, then through the garden of a house and into the garden of a house in the next road.
>
> The back door of the house was open, the Captain went in and I followed close behind. He knew exactly were he was going, evidently had done a recce. There was a door facing the back door, but slightly to the left and another door on the wall to the right at the far end, the Captain made straight for this door, passing on the left in the corner a table, still laid for a meal. I saw that there was a bowl of biscuits on the table and a tall slender bottle.
>
> The Captain opened the door in the corner, and turned sharp right up the stairs that went towards the back of the house. The second he disappeared from my sight, I grabbed a handful of the biscuits, stuffed them into a smock pocket, then the bottle, and followed the Captain up the stairs, stuffing the bottle in an inside pocket as I did so. We went back along a landing towards the front of the house and turned into the front bedroom on the right. He went to the window, turned to me and said 'We are expecting an attack along that road opposite, get all the glass out of the windows and put the mattress in front of you for added protection' and went out of the room.
>
> It was just beginning to get dark. I smashed all the glass out of the windows with my rifle butt, put the mattress below the window and peered along the road. In front of me, the road went off at a slight angle so that I couldn't see the end. Time went on and no attack arrived.
>
> It was very difficult in the darkness, first you thought you saw movement in the road and after tensely waiting some time, realised that it was probably only tricks of the imagination. After an hour or two I got a bit bored, if that is the right word, with the situation. I started to make myself a bit more comfortable.
>
> I collected bedclothes etcetera to make things easier sitting or kneeling by the window, and then started to eat some of the biscuits. They were some sort of toasted biscuit, about

an inch and a half-long, half-inch square and all the edges were rounded. They were very nice and most welcome. After sampling a nice few, I pulled out the bottle, tried to make out the contents by the label and took a tentative swig. It was a bottle of wine, very nice. I spent the most pleasant time I had had in Holland eating the biscuits and having an occasional swallow, periodically looking out of the window for any signs of the enemy.[16]

Sergeant Ken Bryant, 24 Flight, 'G' Squadron was trying to get some sleep in the bottom of his slit trench in the respite after a mortar barrage. Both he and Sergeant Otto witnessed the strangest of sights:

A part of the Hotel grounds had been fenced to make a compound; there was a herd of tame deer in it. There was a woman's voice coming from the broken trees, she seemed to be calling to somebody. I looked over the top of the trench and saw her in some sort of white dress, standing against the fence of the deer compound. For a moment I thought it may be imagination, but she turned and ran off into the broken trees.[17]

To the east, the Germans started to probe the defences and to put pressure on the perimeter. During the afternoon, 156th Parachute Battalion were attacked in their houses by small numbers of infantry from the north, but saw them off. German movement in the wood to the east of Stationsweg was observed and reported by 'D' Squadron GPR and patrols from 10th Parachute Battalion were also attacked at about the same time.

In the south-east, Lieutenant Mike Dauncey was still doggedly defending some houses in the area near the river held by Lonsdale Force. His luck continued to hold:

In the afternoon we were attacked by armour for the first time. We gave it to them with the PIAT, which shook them. Two chaps in my area were hit; one of them was Staff Sergeant Halliday. I was lucky, a bullet hit the fleshy part of my nose, and it tended to exhilarate me more than anything does.

Today a self-propelled gun started being unpleasant from the East, but was knocked out by a PIAT. The anti tank gunners retired down the street and our PIAT was withdrawn for division, I was told.[18]

In the north-west corner of the perimeter, a self-propelled gun moved up to support German attacks into the woods, in the vicinity of Sonnenberglaan, making life unpleasant for 'F' Squadron for a while. The remnants of the Squadron moved into a wood opposite the junction of Oranjeweg and Verlengde Paul Krugerstraat to fill the gap between 'E' Squadron and the Borders. Later a 6-pounder anti-tank gun and a Vickers machine gun helped to stiffen the 'F' Squadron front. Eventually, later in the afternoon, 'F' Squadron launched a counter-attack, cleared the infiltrating Germans out of the wood and drove them back. At roughly 1800 hours, John Place relocated the 2 Wing headquarters to the next house – 2 Wing were back in control of their area.

Staff Sergeant Andy Andrews was with 'E' Squadron in the same area. Also on the move, he had been ordered to shift his location during the fighting:

We were alongside the road … mortaring continued very heavily south of our position. It did in fact kill many of our people and Lieutenant Turner then moved myself, leaving Paddy Senier and Len King, Larry Goldthorpe and himself with four others to the positions receiving heavy fire.

The others, including Gordon Midgley and Hank Holdren, must then have closed up to the road, maybe even putting one in each trench. I know Paddy was by himself. When we got to the new position we were then heavily shelled until nightfall. On my left, as I was on the extreme left of 'E' Squadron's position, I contacted the Royal Artillery Lieutenant. There was a narrow road between our positions.[19]

The fighting for the woods at the north-west corner of the perimeter was continued throughout daylight hours. Staff Sergeant Reg Grant, who was involved in 'E' Squadron's battle to hold the woods, describes the intensity of the fighting and the tactics employed by the German troops:

The section of which I was a member, and under the command of Lieutenant Briscoe, occupied four slit trenches in a line of about fifty yards, divided into two units by a six-foot wire mesh fence running through the middle. There were large piles of logs scattered about, which gave us some cover, in what was a rather open situation.

We appeared to be almost a hundred yards in front of the main line of defence. Salvoes of mortar bombs were beginning to come over and the curious wailing noise that their passage through the air made gave you the impression they were trying to seek you out personally.

The Germans were by now moving up considerable numbers of infantry and self-propelled artillery, the nearest self-propelled gun being approx. eighty yards to our immediate front. The German infantry lads kept up this drill, shouting to each other the whole time.

Our weapons consisted of rifles and bayonets, and some had knives strapped to their legs. We had no automatic weapons or grenades. There appeared to be utter chaos with no information at all regarding the true position, and Lieutenant Briscoe told us he was going back to headquarters for orders.

Then almost as if they had been given a direct order, the occupants of the two trenches on the other side of the wire suddenly moved out and made for the main forces behind us. I saw two of them hit and fall as they crossed the open ground. That left just four of us in two trenches close to the wire fence. The Germans were now commencing to attack, and I saw a grenade coming through the air straight for us. I shouted a warning to Syd Price as I leapt out of the trench and dived under a log pile. Fortunately, the grenade was deflected by the wire and exploded a few feet from where Syd was crouching.

I was just about to return to the trench, when the 88mm gun to our front opened up on our lads to the rear, and the shells were passing just over the top of my woodpile making an unearthly noise. It was a cross between a shriek and the tearing of calico playing havoc with the eardrums. Some of the infantry had obviously spotted me, as small arms fire was splintering the bark off the logs above me, so I decided it was time to get back in the trench.

It was a bit crowded; the two lads in the other trench had joined Syd as their dugout had become untenable. One of them was wounded in the leg and was obviously in some discomfort. Syd was looking very dazed – I think he must have taken quite a bit of blast from the grenade. Although we had seen the other trenches evacuated, we still had not been given any direct order to do so, and we decided to hold on where we were.

There was now no sign at all of our own chaps behind us although they must have been there, as the Germans were keeping up heavy small arms fire and occasional rounds from the self-propelled gun. Our return fire seemed to be puny compared with the weight of fire coming into our positions. It was about this time that I saw big Jock Smith lying in a small depression, twenty yards in front of us, and much closer to the enemy. There was no movement from him, so we could not tell if he had been hit or was playing possum, but he was in full view of the Germans.

There was still a great deal of shouting between the enemy troops, and suddenly they put in a classic infantry attack very similar to exercises we had taken part in at battle school. Very heavy automatic fire from the right flank, directed on us, and the positions further back forced us to keep our heads down, as their lads came storming through the trees.

What happened next is almost dreamlike. I had visions of figures in field grey coming straight over our positions and I felt a blow, which knocked me against the back of the trench. A young German who could not have been more than sixteen or seventeen, screamed at me in his own tongue and held a machine pistol at my chest. There was little we could do and we scrambled out of the trench, the wounded lad with some difficulty, and in a few seconds we were standing behind the self-propelled gun, where an officer in a black uniform began to go through our pockets.

Unlike the troops who were still shouting to each other, he was very polite. When he found my fighting knife still strapped to my leg he said 'Tut tut' and carefully removed it and stuck it into the soft ground – at the same time keeping me covered with his automatic.[20]

Staff Sergeant George Davis was with 'F' Squadron in a defensive position alongside 'E' Squadron:

We were dug-in in gardens behind a street of houses. Michel Long took every other man from this line to go on a patrol. Jim Wells on my left and my second pilot Alec Williams on my right were included. Shortly after this my position came under heavy bombardment. I felt extremely lucky not to be injured and when the firing ceased I hoped to be able to get back in the cover of the nearby trees and try to rejoin my Flight. Unfortunately the enemy troops had decided to use the house, in whose garden I had my slit trench, as their temporary headquarters. I was discovered and made prisoner of war before I could make my escape.[21]

Sergeant Alec Williams:

We hadn't gone far when we heard incoming mortars. We got behind a tree and saw George and the slit trenches at either side disappear in the smoke and flames of mortar bursts. Meanwhile we heard another salvo of mortars arriving and the patrol and I retired at a rapid pace to the squadron headquarters.

We told them what happened and we all moved out towards George Davis and the others but didn't get far when we ran into a tank with infantry support. We only had personal weapons and nothing to stop a tank with and were ordered to retire in the direction of Oosterbeek where we regrouped under the command of Major Murray.

We cleared a wood of the enemy inflicting casualties and taking prisoners, once more we dug in at the far edge of the wood. During this action Major Murray was wounded in the neck.[22]

Tony Murray was treated by Colonel Graeme Warrack who described the squadron commander's wound as 'a through and through bullet wound of the throat, a very lucky young man'. The popular squadron commander would play no further part in the battle. Command of 'F' Squadron passed to the Squadron's Second in Command, Captain Thomas Plowman.

Whilst the battle raged around Oosterbeek, the weather finally began to offer a window of opportunity for the last lift of troops into the Arnhem area. Major General Stanislaw Sosabowski and the 1st Polish Independent Parachute Brigade Group were finally going to leave their fog-bound airfields and jump into battle. The poor weather and the resulting two days of delays had naturally created a mood of frustration among the Poles.

As well as the weather, the changing tactical situation on the ground in Holland had also come into play. Roy Urquhart had managed to communicate the fact that the landing zones had been overrun and that the Poles would have to drop on a new drop zone on the southern side of the Rhine. The Poles therefore now had to contend with planning for a drop on a different drop zone. They would jump close to the small village of Driel and hopefully be brought across the Rhine on the Heveadorp ferry under the cover of darkness. The 1,500 Poles were desperately needed to bolster the embattled Oosterbeek perimeter. In a flurry of activity lasting three hours the drop was replanned and the aircrews and their passengers were rebriefed, repacked where necessary and formed for the lift.

Despite less than ideal weather conditions and poor visibility the 114 American C47s of IX Troop Carrier Command were loaded and began to take off into overcast English skies. Almost immediately the bad luck that appeared to continually plague the third lift intervened again. Even as the lead American pilots struggled to coax their aircraft through the low cloud and fog to a safe altitude, the order to abort the lift was given. The weather forecast and local conditions suggested that the formations might well get to Arnhem, but the visibility over their home airfields was set to deteriorate so dramatically that they would not be able to find their way back. The situation was further complicated as the encoded abort instruction could not be authenticated correctly by the aircrews because the codes issued for the mission were incorrect. Confusion resulted in every cockpit as each aircraft commander had to make his own individual decision on the authenticity of the abort signal.

Forty-one commanders accepted the signal for what it was and turned their aircraft back towards home. The weather conditions were, however, already so bad that they could not retrace their course to land at Spanhoe or Saltby – aircraft and paratroops were consequently spread across eastern England. One unfortunate C47 even put down in Ireland! Close to 500 Polish paratroopers were now out of the battle and it would take a further forty-eight hours to recover them and regroup their chalks together. They were eventually dropped in to reinforce the 82nd US Airborne Division near Grave, having played no direct part in the Arnhem battle.

The remainder of the Polish brigade flew on in seventy-three C47s, just over 1,000 Poles reaching the drop zone. The first combat drop made by 1st Polish Independent Parachute Brigade Group finally began at 1700 hours. The German anti-aircraft crews were as effective as usual, managing to down five of the American transports. The Poles managed to jump from their stricken aircraft but a total of ten American aircrew gave their lives. The evasive manoeuvring of the C47s did spread the formations and slow the exit of the paratroopers, but despite this the drop was generally successful, if not widely dispersed. German ground fire did kill five Poles and wound a further twenty-five as they descended, but they were unable to interfere with the Poles once they were on the ground.

Stanislaw Sosabowski's brigade shook out into its positions quickly. The Polish forward companies occupied the southern bank of the river opposite the Oosterbeek church and the Heveadorp ferry. While the discovery that the ferry was inoperable was a body blow to Roy Urquhart's plans for a Polish river crossing, Sosabowski was furious. A reconnaissance of the ferry itself by Polish engineers also revealed that the positions on the opposite side of the crossing were held by German troops. The ferry itself had been put out of action by its Dutch owner immediately after the Germans had overrun the Westerbouwing feature.

Communication between the two generals was hampered by the lack of a radio link across the Rhine. Urquhart had watched the Polish drop as it happened, but was unable to communicate with Sosabowski directly. All messages between the two men were carried by Captain Zwolanski, the Polish liaison officer working in Urquhart's headquarters. The brave Pole swam the Rhine with orders from the British General that the Poles were to retake the Westerbouwing and secure both sides of the ferry crossing. As the light began to fade in the early evening, engineers on both sides of the river were busy constructing makeshift rafts to carry the Poles across the river.

The attempt to capture Westerbouwing failed and the construction of the boats proved to be a painfully slow process; by dawn they were still nowhere near ready. Similar efforts to build rafts and locate boats were made on the Polish side of the river, but this also ended in failure. With no hope of transferring any of his men across the Rhine, Sosabowski ordered his brigade to take up defensive positions around Driel.

The resupply of those already in Oosterbeek was also beginning to test the mettle of the Allied aircrews. The day's resupply mission had been extremely costly to the Allied air forces, with 117 Stirlings and Dakotas involved in the drop. However, the longer the battle went on the less likely it was that MARKET GARDEN could monopolize the Allied fighter squadrons. The escort for the resupply was much less numerous than on previous drops as US fighters were tasked to escort a large bombing raid on Germany that day. The poor weather in England had also prevented some RAF squadrons from getting airborne to join the mission.

The Luftwaffe made best use of what was for them a rare opportunity to outnumber an Allied formation. The Me 109s and FW 190s managed to penetrate the limited fighter escort and inflict serious damage on the slow-moving transport formations. The anti-aircraft batteries were as effective as they had been against previous missions. The combined efforts of fighters and gunners downed twenty-nine RAF aircraft, a 25 per cent hit rate against the British formation. 190 Squadron RAF alone lost seven out of ten of its Stirling on the mission. Again the greatest tragedy was that the bulk of the supplies delivered at so great a cost were dropped into German hands.

The cost of the day's fighting had been heavy for both sides, although with the exception of gaining the Westerbouwing the Germans had little to show for an intense day's fighting. The ferocity of the British resistance in Arnhem and in the Oosterbeek cauldron had taught the Germans to show some caution. The Germans were now also very aware of the proximity of XXX Corps as during the day British heavy guns had begun to strike German positions around Arnhem with some effect. The guns of 64th Medium Regiment, RA were being directed with success from within Oosterbeek by Headquarters RA using it's more powerful 19HP radio sets to call in fire. This was an extremely timely development as the stock of ammunition held by the Light Regiment in Oosterbeek was now running very low. The XXX Corps guns were brought to bear on various German attacks as they developed around the perimeter or even within the cauldron. The heavy weight and accuracy of this fire was to be decisive throughout the rest of the battle.

The day had been an exceptionally tough one across the whole perimeter, with about 150 British troops being killed hanging on to the perimeter since first light. Meanwhile, the arrival of the Poles on the southern bank and the dramatic intervention of the XXX Corps guns seemed to give some hope of victory. Nobody talked of defeat and every man prepared himself for another day of struggle the next day.

That night at 2200 hours, the divisional perimeter was reduced in the north by withdrawing further south. 7th Battalion, King's Own Scottish Borderers were moved to the area of the edge of the wood at area Hartenweg and Bothaweg. They maintained contact on their left with the glider pilots of 'E' and 'F' Squadrons. The Reconnaissance Squadron remained on their right with 9 Field Company, Royal Engineers in reserve just behind them. With the Poles now on the ground, 1st Airborne Division had no more cards to play and it was clear that the gilder pilots would not be leaving early as planned.

## Notes

1      Rigby, Sergeant A., 19 Flt, 'B' Sqn GPR, by permission of *The Eagle*.
2      Freeman, Sergeant G., 19 Flt, 'B' Sqn GPR, by permission of *The Eagle*.

3   Payton-Reid, R., Lieutenant Colonel, CO 7 KOSB, by permission of KOSB Regimental Museum, Berwick-upon-Tweed.

4   Tilley, Sgt F., 'E' Sqn GPR, DCM citation.

5   Hardy, Private J., 16 Para Fd Amb, RAMC, IS9 Escape Report NA WO208/3351.

6   Low, Captain A., 20 Flt, 'B' Sqn GPR, correspondence with Luuk Buist, 1991 onwards.

7   Johnson, Lieutenant R., 'E' Sqn GPR, correspondence with Luuk Buist, 1991 onwards.

8   Ashworth, SSgt W., 20 Flt, 'B' Sqn GPR, interview with Robert Shawn, September 1967.

9   Johnston, Lieutenant A., 'E' Sqn GPR, correspondence with Luuk Buist, 1991.

10  Holcroft, SSgt W., 14 Flt, 'F Sqn GPR, 'No medals for Lt Pickwoad', September 1945.

11  Weeden, Sergeant L., 14 Flt, 'F' Sqn GPR, correspondence with the author, March 2008.

12  Pearce, Sergeant T., 5 Flt, 'D' Sqn GPR, correspondence with Luuk Buist, 1991.

13  Toler, Major I., OC 'B' Sqn GPR, by permission of the Toler family.

14  Dauncey, Lieutenant M., 9 Flt, 'G' Sqn GPR, by permission of *The Eagle*.

15  War Diary, 1 Wing, GPR, dated 21 September 1944.

16  Driver, Sergeant R., 1 Flt, 'A' Sqn GPR, by permission of *The Eagle*.

17  Bryant, Sgt K., 24 Flt, 'G' Sqn GPR, correspondence with Luuk Buist, 1991.

18  Dauncey, Lieutenant M., 9 Flt, 'G' Sqn GPR, interview with the author, February 2008.

19  Andrews, SSgt A., 11 Flt, 'E' Sqn GPR, *So you wanted to Fly, eh?* Institute for Studies in Teacher Education, Burnaby, B.C., 1997.

20  Grant, SSgt R., 'E' Sqn GPR, by permission of *The Eagle*.

21  Davis, SSgt G., 14 Flt, 'F' Sqn GPR, correspondence with Luuk Buist, 1991.

22  Williams, Sergeant A., 14 Flt, 'F' Sqn GPR, correspondence with Luuk Buist, 1991

# CHAPTER 14

# 'Up Agin It'

**Friday, 22 September 1944**

The character and tempo of the battle changed significantly as a result of the Polish landing at Driel. The Germans were almost immediately forced into a rethink of their troop dispositions in Arnhem and Oosterbeek, and their tactics. The presence of the Poles to the south of Arnhem was viewed by the Germans as an obvious threat to their supply route to Nijmegen. There was potential for 10th SS Panzer Division to be cut off from its sister formation on the north bank, or even the threat of a Polish attempt to take Arnhem Bridge from the south. The threat of the Poles, and the advance of XXX Corps further south, triggered the establishment of *Sperrverband Harzer* to the south of the Rhine. This new blocking line tied up close to 2,400 German troops who could have been thrown into the fighting in Oosterbeek.

Stanislaw Sosabowski and his men had no intention of embarking on either of the courses of action anticipated by the Germans, however the latter were not to know that. The Poles remained inexplicably static in their positions as, away from German view, they prepared whatever boats they could for a river crossing and waited anxiously for nightfall. In an attempt to prevent a Polish breakout, the Germans threw everything they could at this new threat on the south bank. Throughout the day the Poles endured heavy mortar bombardment and repeated infantry attacks, supported by Panzers. The German assaults were well coordinated and determined, and they managed to force the equally determined Poles out of some of their outer defensive positions around Driel. The battle around Driel raged for much of the day, with neither side gaining any advantage, but the village still remained in Polish hands at nightfall.

The attrition of vehicles and men suffered by the Germans in and around Oosterbeek on Thursday, for little gain, also forced a change in tactics. The fighting on the northern bank of the river also changed in character, as German tactics had been adapted overnight. There was no appetite to engage in close-in fighting with the tenacious and extremely aggressive British airborne troops. From the German point of view, the recapture of Arnhem Bridge had isolated the remnants of the British division in Oosterbeek with little hope of relief. They elected not to be drawn into a fight in an urban environment, where the British could use all of their training and fighting spirit to maintain parity and inflict casualties, preferring to use their superior firepower to blast the British out of their positions, whilst also keeping them at arm's length.

With every passing hour and day, more and more artillery units were arriving in the Oosterbeek area to join the battle. Eventually over one hundred pieces of field artillery would be employed in the bombardment of the British defences. The proximity of the town to the German border and supply dumps ensured a plentiful and constant supply of ammunition to feed the mortars and guns, so that the bombardment was relentless, placing mental strain on the defenders inside the perimeter. Steady streams of casualties caused by shrapnel and shell splinters were received in the medical posts inside the perimeter. The only practical means of defence was to seek shelter for the wounded in the cellars of the village. Those still able to fight remained outside and could only dig deeper trenches and add overhead cover if time and defence stores were available. Many of those defending Oosterbeek endured terrible mental strain as a result of the continual shelling, coupled with extreme levels of fatigue.

Friday was a critical point in the battle – if the perimeter and most importantly the positions on the north side of the river could be held for another twenty-four hours relief looked possible. Under cover of the early morning mist, two troops of armoured cars of the Household Cavalry had managed to work their way forward and link up with the Poles outside Driel. The presence of the lead element of the Guards Armoured Division on the southern bank seemed to indicate that XXX Corps were close to coming within reach of the 1st British Airborne Division. If the Poles could maintain their hold on Driel and the ferry crossing then there was a chance of reinforcement. The key to any such crossing would be control of the north bank of the river. Although sections of the north bank were in British hands the Westerbouwing and other areas had been lost to the Germans. It was doubtful that the surviving British units had enough strength to oust the Germans from the Westerbouwing hill or the river bank itself.

The rhythm of the battle had now become routine at the Hartenstein, the 1 Wing GPR war diary recording a busy morning around the headquarters. After waiting for a lull in the shelling, Iain Murray personally led a burial party for his Second in Command, Major John Royle. Accompanied by Captain Taitt and Lieutenant Brian Bottomley, he selected a burial site about a hundred yards to the west of the Hartenstein where they completed a field service and burial for the brave Scotsman.

With shell and mortar fire continuing to inflict casualties all around the perimeter positions, casualties were recorded as being heavy throughout the morning. Despite the hazards of moving about in the open, officers from 1 Wing GPR units visited Iain Murray's headquarters to update their commander on their situation and to glean information from the Wing staff. When Ian Toler came across from 'B' Squadron, he was followed by the two kilted Scots of 'D' Squadron, Captain James Ogilvie and his Intelligence Officer, Lieutenant 'Jock' Strathern. The information they received was positive: 43rd (Wessex) Division had crossed the Waal River at dawn and were now pushing north towards Arnhem. This news and the arrival of the Household Cavalry in Driel seemed to bode well; the mood was therefore positive. British artillery was firing overhead and all seemed possible. At 1150 hours the following message was issued from Headquarters 1 Wing GPR: '43 Division attacking main bridge, Arnhem on a two Brigade front, 1000 hours. 2nd Household Cavalry contacted Polish Parachute Brigade.'

The casualty situation at 2 Wing GPR was now becoming serious, the fighting having taken a particularly heavy toll among the officers. Captain Peter Fletcher, the Adjutant of 1 Wing, was sent with a sergeant from 2 Wing to a house where there were a number of men without an officer to lead them. The detachment of a member of the 1 Wing headquarters staff from his staff duties gives an indication of the gravity of the situation.

Ron Driver was blissfully unaware of the deteriorating situation – he had succumbed to fatigue and lack of sleep, and had committed the cardinal sin of snatching some sleep. He was rudely awoken by the shock of someone kicking him in the ribs, although luckily for him it was a British ammunition boot inflicting the pain and not a German jackboot:

> It was a furious Sergeant Major, cursing me something awful. He threatened to have me court-martialled and said that if the Captain had found me, I would have been shot. He gave me another verbal going over, ordered me to stand-to and threatened me with all sorts of dire punishment if anything happened like that again and went out of the room. It gradually began to get light, still no signs of any activity at all up the road, and some time in the morning, we were on the move again. After stops and starts, dropping to the ground or into

slit trenches if there were any handy, when there was a mortar attack, we eventually ended up in the wood by the open field, that we had left the day before.

This time I think we were under the command of Lieutenant Haeffner of 'A' Squadron. The mortaring became more and more intense. In fact it had been intensifying in its ferocity for the last few days. We were continually under heavy fire, in the shrinking perimeter, by mortar, artillery, small arms and snipers. The times that we heard the supply planes of the Royal Air Force coming, only to see the parachutes and canisters float away out of our reach. Food and especially water was extremely scarce. Ammunition was getting very low. Things on the whole didn't look too good. Because of the increasing bombardment, mainly by mortars, a fair bit of time was spent in digging our slit trench deeper and deeper, in fact, the one that I was in with another glider pilot was so deep that we couldn't see out, if we stood up on the bottom. To see out, we each had an ammunition box that we stood on.[1]

The battle continued to rage close to the river bank, as Kampfgruppe Spindler again tried to drive into the heart of the British defences. The threat posed by these armoured thrusts along the river bank was significant. There was desperate fighting as the 9th SS Division troops pushed towards the gun batteries and Oosterbeek Church from the east, threatening to get behind the British positions and isolate them from the river crossing. To the west the von Tettau division still controlled the Westerbouwing and were still actively probing the western defences. Many of the units being thrown into the battle had been hastily formed from training units, troops on leave or even from naval and Luftwaffe personnel with limited infantry training.

The ad hoc nature of some of the German units prevented them from conducting effective and well coordinated urban operations. The less well trained units were no match for the battle-hardened British airborne troops and were not inclined to venture too deeply into the cauldron. The veterans of 9th SS Panzer Division, however, were well versed in the intricacies of fighting in built-up areas, continually threatening the eastern flank and base of the perimeter with their Panzers and infantry.

The German method of attack remained artillery heavy throughout Friday and the remaining days of the battle. Infantry assaults continued, but they were more deliberate and methodical in their application. Individual buildings or areas of wood line were isolated by artillery and mortar fire prior to attack by infantry with Panzer support. The intention was to drive the British out of key buildings and wrest control of bite-sized chunks of specific areas from them. Despite these concentrated attacks, and their superiority in numbers and firepower, they made little progress. The British remained in place and continued to inflict casualties on every German attack.

The German Panzer crews were not enjoying the same advantages in the Oosterbeek fighting as they had over 1st Parachute Brigade during the battle for Arnhem Bridge. The Airlanding Brigade had more time to consider the sighting of its integral anti-tank guns which were deployed in defence at key points in Oosterbeek, where the urban terrain was ideal for tank ambush. The German armour could not operate in the same aggressive manner as it had in Arnhem without paying a very heavy penalty. The nature of the fighting now also favoured the tank-hunter. Panzer crews forced to close down inside their vehicles were stalked and killed at close range by brave individuals, or pairs of infantrymen using the PIAT.

In the early hours of Friday morning, roughly 160 pathfinders of 21st Independent Parachute Company, under command of Major 'Boy' Wilson, had moved into a new defensive position in the perimeter. They occupied positions in houses and gardens from the junction of Pietersbergseweg and Sandersweg down to the MDS crossroads. In the process they relieved the exhausted survivors of 10th Parachute Battalion at Utrechtseweg. Another unit that would not normally expect to be employed as front-line infantry was 250 (Airborne) Light Composite Company, Royal Army Service

Corps. The RASC troops, under Captain John Cranmer-Byng, were also deployed into new positions early in the morning. The supply troops occupied a line from the track junction of Bildersweg and van Deldenpad, to the road junction of Pietersbergseweg and Sandersweg. Both of the reinforcement units were ordered to move forward if possible.

Brigadier 'Shan' Hackett was busy visiting the units under his command. When he visited the glider pilots occupying houses along Stationsweg he was briefed on the German infiltration that had been taking place in the area and the now ever-present sniper threat – snipers were becoming an increasing nuisance and were hindering movement. This sniper activity was not restricted to the areas recognized by both sides as the 'front line' – there was a sniper threat well inside the perimeter, behind the British forward positions. The cover of darkness was exploited by some very brave Germans to infiltrate what was by now a porous perimeter and from first light these behind-the-lines snipers caused numerous British casualties. The park land in the southern half of the perimeter was ideal terrain for this type of infiltration and sniping was a constant hazard in that area. One particular sniper was making use of the rear door of the Hartenstein a dangerous undertaking.

Countering the potent threat posed by German snipers was another task given to the GPR. Glider pilots were already spending the night hours patrolling the numerous gaps in the perimeter and were now employed stalking German snipers in daylight. The glider pilots generally deployed as an eight-man patrol which split down into four pairs to hunt for snipers. They became very effective in this role. Staff Sergeant George Milburn of 'F' Squadron was involved in many of the anti-sniper patrols:

> One of our pilots – I can't remember his name, but he was a Londoner. He had a Bren Gun and thought he saw a sniper high in a tree. He replaced his magazine with a full one, took careful aim and fired off the whole magazine of at least twenty-eight rounds. The sniper fell straight down and hit the ground like a sack of coal. Then we heard the chap with the Bren Gun say 'Watch him; he might not be dead.' Typical soldiers humour, the German had been hit several times and had fallen at least fifty feet out of the tree![2]

The pressure on the glider pilots holding Stationsweg increased as the day went on, the mortar and artillery bombardments also becoming more frequent and intense. At least one self-propelled gun had remained in the neighbourhood and improved its position from dusk on Thursday night. Sergeant Louis Hagen of 'D' Squadron wrote in his book *Arnhem Lift*:

> During the morning, the first German self-propelled gun started moving around the top cross-road. We heard the engine revving and the Jerries shouting before the attack started. The immediate job was to put our PIAT in a position where it could dominate the road and prevent the self-propelled gun from moving down. The noise of the tank got louder, we could hear the tracks squeaking and grinding along the road. Then the first shots were fired and tore away some bricks from the front of the houses.

German armour made its presence felt in 'D' Squadron's area throughout Friday using a mix of self-propelled guns and tanks. The German method of operation appeared to be for the armour to move up and down Stationsweg blowing holes in the walls of the houses. Supporting infantry would then attempt to use these breaches to enter the defended houses, but the infantry assaults were not pressed home with great determination and the houses remained in British hands. Fighting of this nature is difficult and high in casualties on both sides.

Staff Sergeant Arnold Baldwin was a 'B' Squadron pilot who had spent most of the battle so far with Captain Angus Low and 20 Flight. He had spent Wednesday and Thursday dug in to the east of the tennis courts at the Hartenstein Hotel:

During the morning Squadron Sergeant Major Watt collected a group; me and Sergeant Michie, Staff Sergeants Bert Stroud, Bill Thomson, Ginger Eardley and Sergeant Harry Crone and, I think Cliff de Rungary, though Joe Michie cannot remember him there. He said we were being seconded to the Parachute Regiment [21st Independent Parachute Company] and led us round the northern end [Utrechtseweg] of the allotments which lay between the Hartenstein and the road running south from the Main Dressing Station crossroads to the Tafelberg Hotel [Pietersbergseweg].

Some way down this road he turned into an alley between houses on the eastern side of the road [Paasberg] where we came under fire. Bill Thomson suffered a badly shattered shin; Watt and I dragged him into shelter and got him away to a dressing station. Bill Watt then left us in the house and returned to the Hartenstein.

Not long after Bill had departed, a Paratrooper arrived who said we were to follow him to another house, a large detached building on the same side of the road. This proved to be the nearest house to the Schoonoord Hotel on the Main Dressing Station crossroads, then being used as a hospital. He also said whoever was in charge must accompany him to the Para headquarters. There being three of us of equal rank, a hasty decision had to be made and I was elected.

The Para headquarters was a house a little further back down the road, on the opposite side. The commanding officer was wounded, half reclining on a settee, covered with a blanket and I cannot recall ever knowing his rank or name. He said that we were to remain in the house until further orders and to keep a sharp lookout for a possible German attack. There was water in the bath upstairs in this house, of which we could draw some for drinking purposes only.

The house we were to hold had no windows or only very high lights on the north side so no view of the Schoonoord Hotel or the crossroads was possible. A pair of heavy front doors led into a large room or hall, a door and passage on the right hand led to a smaller room, a door on the left hand of this room led to a small kitchen or scullery. A window in the rear wall of this scullery revealed a paved yard outside with a tall warehouse about five or six yards away.

This warehouse had the double doors on first, second and possibly third floors usual in such buildings. A wall ran off from the left hand side of the house, forming a passageway between it and the warehouse; on the other side of this wall were more allotments which ran up to the rear of the houses lining the road from the Main Dressing Station crossroads to Arnhem. The allotments and the houses were only visible from the first and second floor rear windows.

It was assumed that Germans occupied these houses, though at first none were visible. A door in the right hand wall of the scullery led down a few steps to a garage with double doors at each end, the rear doors opening to the small yard in front of the warehouse, the front doors leading out to the street. The bedroom windows at the rear of the first and second floors were the only available lookout points and these were manned – most of the time. Most of the furniture had been removed from the house and the only food to be found was row after row of bottled plums in the cellar.[3]

During Thursday evening the divisional perimeter was contracted in the north-west. This reduction in the Division's frontage led to some changes in the 2 Wing GPR dispositions. The 'F' Squadron lines remained unchanged, but 'E' Squadron moved from their wood back onto the left flank of 'F' Squadron, at the corner of Hartensteinlaan and Oranjeweg. Once settled into their new position, 'E' Squadron linked up with 'A' Company of the Border Regiment on their left flank. On the right flank of 'F' Squadron were the King's Own Scottish Borderers, holding positions in houses at Paul Krugerstraat. The two GPR squadrons now had the psychological comfort of once again fighting side by side.

Command of 2 Wing remained with Lieutenant Colonel John Place, the Wing itself remaining under command of 'Pip' Hicks and 1st Airlanding Brigade. The Brigadier was no doubt aware of the serious situation facing his men when he included the following phrase in one of his messages to Headquarters, 2 Wing GPR: 'We're up agin it'. The 2 Wing headquarters moved to a house at Hartensteinlaan during the reorganization of the line. The 'E' Squadron sector was further strengthened during the morning when a second 6-pounder was sited within the Squadron's boundaries.

The continual shelling and mortaring of the area led to the decision to resite the Airlanding Brigade headquarters to a less obvious location that could not be identified by German mortar fire controllers, the new location being in a wood on the Hemelsche Berg estate. The brigade reserve of 'C' Squadron GPR was now holding a line from the Kneppelhout monument to a house called Hemelsche Berg. Two 6-pounder guns of the South Staffords were integrated into the defence plan, one to cover the approach to the east, and the other facing west at the road junction at the corner of Hoofdlaan and the entrance to the Hemelsche Berg estate.

Wally Holcroft's account gives some indication of the proximity of the 2 Wing positions to each other on the Friday morning, after the reorganization:

Early in the morning I walked across to Wing headquarters to get some water. The place was a complete ruin now, everything being covered in plaster and dust. In one chair sat the Padre [Chignell] staring straight in front of him and apparently seeing nothing. I had never seen the Padre without a kindly smile on his face but now he looked a picture of despair. I didn't disturb him but successfully begged a mug of water and hurried back to Mick Hall.

We made a little breakfast and discussed the prospects of the day. Mick pointed out that we thought it was the end, two days ago, and we were still in the fight. Perhaps the Second Army would make it today; it was now Friday the 22nd of September. About nine o'clock that morning we heard the steady tramp of marching feet coming up the road. It was 14 Flight with Lieutenant Pickwoad leading them, or at least what was left of them.

They marched over to us and we learned that Pickwoad had formed a composite section of what was left of 3 sections, Lieutenants Clark and Steevenson were both casualties along with many others. Pickwoad decided that his men would take up defensive positions near us; they had brought some rations and cigarettes, which they cheerfully shared with us. It was good to have them around again. During the morning we had the usual heavy spate of bombing, two of them falling just outside our trench, showering us with earth. The fighting flared up again, not in the wood this time but in the opposite direction down the street.

A number of troops came hurrying up the road led by a Lieutenant Colonel carrying a large box of ammunition on his shoulder. He turned into the street and as he ran towards the sound of strife he half turned and called to his men 'Hurry up you lads or we'll miss the battle. The war is going to be over before we arrive.' Having delivered this lengthy discourse to his men he turned and fairly flew down the street whilst his men galloped faithfully after him. I had to laugh at this little cameo, but I not only admired that man, I envied him for he was a real soldier if ever I saw one. How he and his men fared in the battle I never found out for I did not see them again, though shortly afterwards the sound of conflict diminished. Perhaps the very gallant Lieutenant Colonel and his men had put the enemy to flight, I would not have been at all surprised.

The fine houses on the street which we were on the corner were looking very battered now. Every salvo seemed to knock a little more off. One had hardly any roof left on and all the windows were long gone. The street was strewn in rubble and broken glass.[4]

As the day wore on the tempo of battle showed little sign of abating and there was still no sign of relief from XXX Corps from the south. During the afternoon, Headquarters, 1 Wing GPR came under heavy fire again, one shell bursting in an adjoining room to the command post causing substantial damage. Iain Murray went out again to tour his Wing positions and monitor the morale of his men. The whole of the area remained under heavy shell and mortar fire for much of the day. Sergeant Ron Driver of 'A' Squadron clearly remembers Murray on his rounds:

It was during the afternoon, I think, that we were in the bottom of our trench during one mortar session in progress, when a voice up above said, 'Are you all right down there?' We looked up, and then jumped up when we saw that it was Lieutenant Colonel Ian Murray. He had his beret on, not his steel helmet. He said 'Hang on chaps you're doing a grand job, the Second Army will soon be here' then strolled towards the next trench. We stood on our ammunition boxes and watched him out of sight. He must have had a charmed life.

He actually made us feel a bit ashamed of ourselves. We didn't spend so much time crouched in the bottom of the trench, until a particular heavy barrage forced us to. This one seemed particularly heavy and close, in fact, one felt that it would drive you mad, or deaf, or both. You huddled in the bottom of the trench trying to make yourself as small as possible and eventually there was an almighty bang, the nearest one had ever been. I received a bang on the right side of my head and was struck in my right chest and left shoulder. I shouted to my companion that I had been hit and asked him if he was all right, he replied that he had been hit in the back of his head and shoulders. I could feel the blood starting to trickle down my face and body. There was nothing we could do but sit and wait for the barrage to finish. With the bombs dropping all round, mainly from multi-barrelled mortars, your thoughts were on whether you were going to be hit again. It was a great relief when the bombing stopped; we stood on our boxes and looked out.

We hardly recognised the place, it was littered with branches from the trees, and the ground was churned up with the bombing. Somehow we managed to get out of the slit trench then scrambled our way towards the Hartenstein, I suppose three or four hundred yards away. We ran up to the back, down the cellar steps to the dressing station there. A medical orderly greeted me with 'where are you hit mate?' I told him head and both shoulders, he gave me a jab of morphine, put a shell dressing on my head wound. Then he took a big pair of scissors, and, starting at the wrists, cut through all my clothes, up the arms, to my neck. He peeled the clothing back and put shell dressings on my wounds, sticking them on with adhesive plaster about six inches wide. This had taken place with me lying on a stretcher. Two orderlies then lifted me up, still on the stretcher, and put me in the corner of the cellar. Shortly after this the barrage started again and soon more casualties came in and the place began to get pretty crowded.

A Captain came in and called for our attention. He said, 'It's getting very crowded here, so we are going to move some of you. We will be taking you on a jeep to other accommodation and on one part of the route we will be going along a road on which the Jerries are one side and our lads on the other, but don't worry, they have not fired on us yet.' They then started taking stretchers out and eventually it became my turn. I was lifted out by two orderlies who placed the stretcher on the bonnet of a jeep outside.

We started off, through the grounds of the Hartenstein, I had no idea where we went, and all I could see was a large Red Cross flag waving over me. We traversed the 'danger road' without incident, any firing stopped as we went through. We arrived at the new place a few minutes later. It looked like a fairly large empty house. I was taken off the jeep, taken into the house down a long hall and into a room on the right. I was the first one in this room and was put in the far corner on the right. A steady stream of stretchers arrived until the room became full. A medical orderly, a corporal, came in and told us that he had been assigned to look after us.[5]

Near to the Concert Hall, in the south of Oosterbeek, Staff Sergeant Stan Hann of 3 Flight, 'B' Squadron had been involved in defending the guns of the Light Regiment. The day had not gone well:

Sergeant Moon, my second pilot was killed … He was shot through the head by a sniper whilst trying to rescue Captain John Smellie who had been shot by I would think the same sniper. Sergeant Moon dashed across the open ground and had managed to lift Captain Smellie on his shoulders when he was killed. Staff Sergeant Bowen, Sergeant Collett and myself later brought in Captain Smellie. I think he was still alive, but was later killed when the enemy mortared the First Aid Post.[6]

Some hundred yards to the east, Lieutenant Mike Dauncey was still involved in holding Weverstraat:

We had another fight with the Germans but they were driven off easily. The self-propelled gun was back again; unfortunately he got us this time. Sergeant Wyatt was killed and eight men were wounded. Major Croot was with me and we were both cut slightly at the hand. No glider pilots were with me now.

We had seen the Poles with Captain Miller's chaps behind us in the direct ring round the gunners. The remainder of my chaps about 3 or 4 were sent to give local protection to the gunners for the night to give them a rest while Major Croot and I went towards the gunner's headquarters to try to dig out some more folks. Suddenly we realised how hungry we were and Bob Croot and I both put down a large tin of beans each, almost cold, in great spoonfuls. In the whole time we only had three properly prepared meals and twice they were blown up, once by the self-propelled gun and the other time by a mortar. By now it was so dark and late that we had our first proper sleep, which was marvellous.[7]

In the north-west corner of the perimeter 'F' Squadron were still holding firm. Staff Sergeant Laurie Weeden was maintaining a constant watch of his area of responsibility using field glasses. He received an unpleasant surprise when he located an expertly camouflaged self-propelled gun, or tank, in front of a house adjacent to a stable, only 250 metres from the 'F' Squadron position:

As we had no weapons to deal with this threat, I went to divisional headquarters at the Hartenstein Hotel, where I saw the Commander Royal Artillery. He said that he was not prepared to bring the anti-tank guns to the tanks as he had already lost some guns that way. He arranged for a forward observation officer to come with me to our position with a view to bringing XXX Corps artillery fire on to the German position. He also arranged for me to have a PIAT gun and six rounds of PIAT ammunition, and whilst still at the Hartenstein I managed to get a bucketful of water from a trailer outside the hotel.

The shoot by XXX Corps commenced with a shell, which exploded very close to our trenches and a second one, which exploded behind the German occupied house at the present Manege. The forward observation officer then received a message to the effect that the XXX Corps battery had to move forward and that it could no longer give us supporting fire. He told us that he would arrange a further shoot and that night, after dark, XXX Corps shelled the area, catching houses alight and illuminating the German troops on to whom we were able to bring our own small arms fire to bear.

The self-propelled gun or tank at the Manege had not, to our knowledge, fired at us, until we left that position on the Saturday afternoon.[8]

The response from the senior gunner officer may seem unreasonable at first, however, a number of anti-tank guns had been overrun by the Germans when taken forward into exposed positions at the request of infantry units. As the guns were not easy to manoeuvre in an urban environment, it was far more practical and less hazardous if the tanks were allowed to come to the guns. Wally Holcroft was in the same area as Laurie Weeden:

In the afternoon, Lieutenant Pickwoad returned from Wing headquarters. He said the situation was very serious and we should have to do our best to hold on. He promised us some work for that night to keep us busy and prevent us from getting morbid. True to his word he collected us at 5.30 in the afternoon and took us into Wing headquarters where he issued his orders.

Ten of us had to take up positions in the wood taking with us as much ammunition as we could carry. It was dark and everything was quiet by the time we moved off for the wood [West of junction Oranjeweg/Nassaulaan]. We were taken to the northern perimeter where a series of slit trenches had been dug that looked out across a large field, the other side of which was German.

The enemy had a tremendous bonfire burning which, aided by one burning near us, illuminated the whole area with a soft light setting off the trees and shrubs in strange silhouettes. Mick Hall and I, having a Bren gun were sent down to a corner of the wood, which formed a hinge to our position. Staff Sergeant Boucher was allocated to us and we were given special instructions by Lieutenant Pickwoad to watch the front carefully for intruders, meanwhile the party defending the area previously departed for a well earned rest. The Germans incessantly fired tracers at us but owing to their low position their shots sailed harmlessly overhead.

We had a heavy machine gun positioned a few yards away, which never stopped firing; where they got all their ammunition from heaven only knows. Taking turns to watch during the night we would occasionally fire off a round or two to let the enemy know we were not asleep. I did not see anything unusual and Boucher didn't seem to care whether he saw anything unusual or not. He was a regular cool half back that one.[9]

Sergeant Norman Ramsden of 17 Flight, 'A' Squadron was west of Divisional Headquarters when he and members of his flight were called to the Headquarters to make up a patrol to clear the area around :

Before we could set out we were heavily mortared. Lieutenant Eric Markwick was mortally wounded and Staff Sergeant Carlton was wounded in the arm. Both were taken to the Regimental Aid Post. The patrol was abandoned and we returned to our position. At this time Captain Norman Smillie and Staff Sergeant Crook [F Sqn] joined us. That night a few of us went down to the river to meet the Poles and guide them back through our position.[10]

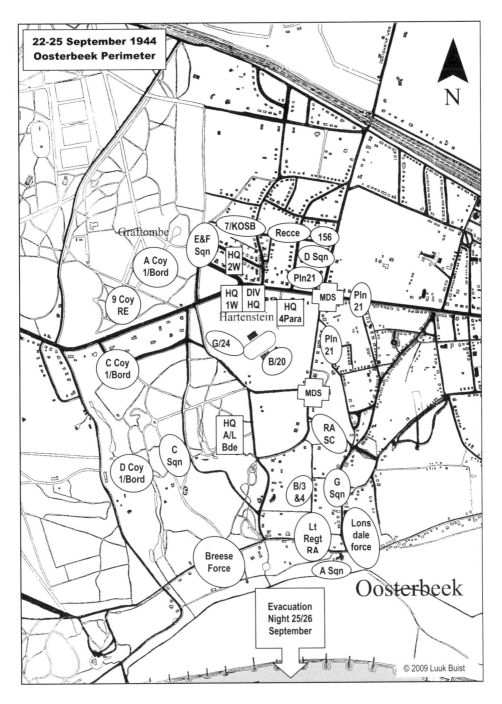

*GPR positions, 22-25 September 1944*

At about 1725 hours arrangements were made to receive reinforcements from the Polish Brigade, who were to cross the river after dark. A number of glider pilots were selected to act as guides to meet them and lead them to their new positions. Captain Harry Brown, commander of 3 Troop, 4 Para Squadron, RE was given command of the task of ferrying the Polish Parachute Brigade reinforcements across the Rhine. It was hoped that 200 Poles could be brought across that night. The group set off at dusk with a total of fifteen men, six recce boats, a single RAF survival dinghy, tracing tape to mark the route and some signal wire. They were accompanied by a Royal Artillery Forward Observation Officer whose radio would provide communications with Divisional Headquarters. The marking of the river bank and the route into the perimeter was critical, as the base line of the perimeter that ran along the river bank was estimated to be 500 metres in length at best. Locating the British-held section of the north bank, while crossing the fast-flowing Rhine in an inflatable boat at night, would be no mean feat. The Polish troops had no watermanship training so would need all the help they could get. Staff Sergeant Fred Ponsford of 'A' Squadron was one of the glider pilot guides:

> Five glider pilots, myself included, were selected to make our way through the German lines to the Rhine. We were to meet the Poles, who would be crossing the Rhine in small boats and lead them back to reinforce the perimeter defence at Oosterbeek with the possibility of mounting a counter attack.
>
> At 2230 hours the five of us made our way to Oosterbeek church where at the base of a wall an officer briefed us as to what was required. We were each given a compass bearing, which he hoped would take us through gaps in the enemy lines but could not be certain of the accuracy. Also the enemy was firing on fixed lines and where gaps existed in the hedges these were regularly subjected to automatic fire. I was a little apprehensive to learn that we would proceed as individuals, not as a patrol. I think we left at five-minute intervals and I was number three.
>
> Believe me there is no lonelier place than being alone in no-man's land between two opposing forces that give no quarter. It was about ten minutes after I set off that I heard voices and recognised them at once as the enemy. I made a slight detour, went forward again and after about twenty minutes heard the sound of water, the Rhine. I had made it, and then promptly fell over the glider pilot who had been number two.
>
> The briefing officer joined us, informed us that the German position was about forty yards away, and absolute silence was paramount. Again the German habit was confirmed when between exchanges of artillery fire we could hear their voices. We were now to suffer the most exasperating part of the operation.
>
> We became aware that small boats were on the Rhine passing to and fro in front of our position and these quite obviously were our Polish comrades. Had we attempted to call out the Germans would have immediately become aware of our intentions and I doubt if any of us would have survived. Lying there in a quandary of what to do next I suddenly have an idea. Of all people surely the Poles would recognise the 'V' signal if it were given by means of a whistle! I mentioned it to my fellow glider pilot and we decided to give it a try by whistling together. I never discovered if the signal was the means of success that followed but almost at once boats started to come ashore with 4 or 5 Polish Paratroops in each.[11]

Mr R. Wegrzyn is a descendant of one of the Polish paratroopers who attempted the crossing that Friday night. He wrote a letter to the Glider Pilot Regimental Association Magazine, *The Eagle*, in August 2000:

My late grandfather was a member of the Independent Polish Parachute Brigade, which was dropped at Driel during the Arnhem Operation. His favourite story concerns the night of Friday September 22nd when he and his company were instructed to make way to the Rhine, some six miles away. Here they would be met by manned small boats that would ferry them across to join up with the main defensive perimeter around Oosterbeek. This part of the operation was quite successful but when the boats were approaching the far bank, German voices could be heard and it was obvious that it would be quite impossible to land at that point without arousing the enemy.

The boats were allowed to drift downstream where it was hoped to get ashore without raising an alarm. Suddenly from out of the darkness came the distinct whistle of Beethoven's Fifth Symphony, i.e. the 'V' for Victory sound. The boats were immediately directed to the signal, which came from a section of Glider Pilots who, conscious of the German proximity, used the 'V' signal to attract the boats to their location.[12]

Fred Ponsford takes up the story:

We thought about fifteen would be sufficient to take back at this stage, me and my colleague set off on a reciprocal course. However after about ten minutes there was a terrific outbreak of small arms fire and it was obvious he had stumbled into a German strong point.

I now had picked up about a dozen Poles and before starting back I had a short briefing with them where I outlined my intentions should we be challenged or come under direct fire. Briefly this involved throwing my last grenade and then running like mad, during which they must follow my voice, as I would be maintaining communications by this means. I took a fairly wide detour so as to avoid the previous part's misfortune and was, as I thought, making excellent progress when suddenly the Teutonic challenge came ringing out. I immediately threw the grenade in the direction of the challenge I think the next seven seconds was the longest I shall ever experience.

I was about to rise and charge forward convinced the grenade was a dud when it exploded. I was away like the wind, shouting my head off screaming out anything that came in my head. The Poles, bless them, didn't hesitate and followed my voice to the letter. The astonishing thing is that we got away with it Scot-free. I like to think it was my acting like a screaming maniac may have kept them in their slit trenches. As I said earlier I made quite a detour in order to return to British lines and that section had not been informed of the possibility of friendly faces coming in.

For days this section had engaged several hundred enemies and as far as they were concerned any movement to their front was the enemy and was to be treated accordingly. In fact the officer in command was about to give the command 'open fire' believing he was being subjected to a mass infantry attack when he recognised the strong west country accent which as he told me later was unmistakable.[13]

Despite the bravery of the Poles themselves, and the efforts of Captain Brown and his battle-weary men, only fifty-five Poles successfully crossed the Rhine to reinforce the perimeter. If there was to be any hope of a link-up with XXX Corps and a subsequent bridgehead on the Rhine, many more Poles would have to make the hazardous crossing. The resources available to support further crossings were sparse and combat supplies inside the perimeter were dwindling rapidly. Food was becoming as scarce as ammunition and hunger was becoming a problem for many of the defenders. There had been no resupply drop by the RAF. The predicted arrival of XXX Corps on the south bank, as well as the bad flying conditions over the UK, had resulted in the cancellation of any resupply drop for Friday. The RAF had spent the day regrouping, repairing battle-damaged aircraft and resting fatigued aircrew.

There had, however, been a positive development on the south bank of the river as the Poles prepared to begin their crossing to the north bank. An armoured column had approached the Polish lines south of Driel at speed. After one of the lead tanks had been knocked out by a Polish anti-tank mine, there then followed an exchange of fire between the Poles and the rest of the tanks in the column. After a brief skirmish, the identity of the column became clear: the tanks were British. The column was a mix of infantry from the 5th Battalion of the Duke of Cornwall's Light Infantry and a squadron of tanks from the 4/7th Dragoon Guards, both units of 214 Infantry Brigade. The infantry, under command of the dynamic Lieutenant Colonel George Taylor, had travelled on the rear decks of the tanks to complete a dramatic 10-mile drive to Driel. The 35-minute drive along narrow roads in the fading light of early evening later became known as the 'Driel dash'. Unfortunately the new arrivals could do little to affect the battle – as they had no boats they could do nothing but wait for the remainder of their brigade and 43rd (Wessex) Division to join them at Driel.

The situation to the south of Driel was far from stable, and the narrow corridor along which XXX Corps had to travel was under constant attack from east and west. The German formations between Nijmegen and Arnhem also recognized the vulnerability of the British and American corridor and were making every effort to cut the Allied route. The road link had been designated 'Route Club' but had been christened 'Hell's Highway' by the Allied troops who were attempting to run the gauntlet of German fire to get to Arnhem. With fighting still going on to the south and German strength around Oosterbeek increasing all of the time, the prospect of a successful crossing looked extremely slim.

## Notes

1     Driver, SSgt R., 1 Flt, 'A' Sqn GPR, by permission of *The Eagle*.

2     Milburn, SSgt G., 'F' Sqn GPR, conversation with the author, 1994.

3     Baldwin, SSgt A., 20 Flt, 'B' Sqn GPR, by permission of *The Eagle*.

4     Holcroft, SSgt W., 14 Flt, 'F' Sqn GPR, 'No medals for Lt Pickwoad', September 1945.

5     Driver, SSgt R., 1 Flt, 'A' Sqn GPR, by permission of *The Eagle*.

6     Hann, SSgt S., 3 Flt, 'B' Sqn GPR, interview with the author, February 2008.

7     Dauncey, Lieutenant M., 9 Flt, 'G' Sqn GPR, interview with the author, February 2008.

8     Weeden, SSgt L., 14 Flt, 'F' Sqn GPR, correspondence with the author, March 2008.

9     Holcroft, SSgt W., 'No medals for Lt Pickwoad', Sep 1945.

10    Ramsden, Sergeant N., 17 Flt, 'A' Sqn GPR, correspondence with Bob Hilton, 1998.

11    Ponsford, SSgt F., 17 Flt, 'A' Sqn GPR, correspondence with Luuk Buist, 1991.

12    Wegrzyn, R., letter to *The Eagle*, vol. 9, No. 6, August 2000.

13    Ponsford, SSgt F., 17 Flt, 'A' Sqn GPR, correspondence with Luuk Buist, 1991.

# CHAPTER 15

# Forlorn Hope

*'You don't mind if I join you, do you?'*

## Saturday, 23 September 1944

Saturday started badly, with a heavy downpour of rain that looked set to remain over the town for some time. Those troops occupying trenches out in the open had to endure the discomfort of being wet, as well as the ever-present danger of artillery and sniper fire. Lieutenant Aubrey Pickwoad DFC was in command of 14 Flight, who were fighting in the 'F' Squadron sector of the line. The Squadron was deployed in the north-west corner of the perimeter alongside 'E' Squadron. Wally Holcroft's account of the battle, 'No medals for Lt Pickwoad', contains an excellent narrative that describes the routine administration required to keep 14 Flight in the field. The account begins on Friday afternoon:

> The afternoon wore on and it commenced to rain heavily causing weapons to seize up as water seeped into the barrels. At this time we were having a brisk exchange of fire with the enemy. It was fortunate therefore that Lieutenant Pickwoad had organised a weapon cleaning room in a house on the eastern perimeter of the wood. We took weapons up to the house and exchanged them for clean ones. As darkness fell on yet another day the small arms fire became more sporadic. Bonfires were stoked up again and blazed brightly in both camps, spreading an eerie light across the field that separated friend and foe.
>
> About nine o'clock we were ordered to withdraw from our trenches whilst a fresh batch of Glider Pilots took over for the night. We were taken to some reserve trenches that lay in the rear of the ones we were vacating. But as by now it was quite dark we couldn't tell exactly where except that we knew we were deeper in the wood. When we were told that we were being withdrawn for a rest I was naive enough to think it was just for that purpose, for after Lieutenant Pickwoad had arranged for sentries to be posted in pairs my turn was not until five o'clock in the morning. I thought I was well set for a good night's sleep.
>
> That Saturday night we experienced the worst bombardment from enemy mortars than we had as yet experienced. There seemed to be no end to the number of missiles heading our way and the miracle was that though the bombs exploded with great sheets of flame and ear splitting detonations, casualties were very light. It would not have been unreasonable to think that after what seemed like hours of non-stop explosions no one could have remained unscathed. It came, as a relief therefore when I began my tour of sentry duty, though apart from the bombing there had been no other enemy activity. At dawn I went round the trenches to tell the lads to man their positions in case of an enemy attack They were all in good spirits, and as I went round I found one where 'Ginger Palfreeman' was lying hidden under a big piece of carpet. When I shook him and told him to get out, he simply lifted up the carpet, pushed out his red head and said, 'Come inside for heavens sake and shut the bloody door.'
>
> Ginger Palfreeman was someone quite noteworthy and deserves a special mention. He was not a Glider Pilot and though he had come with the Glider Pilots had no business to be in Arnhem at all. 'Ginger' was a tow-master, that is to say he was responsible for signalling

247

the tugs and the Gliders on to the runway and into the air. After that was accomplished the tow-master's task was done until the next operation, but this was not sufficient for 'Ginger' who insisted on accompanying his friends to Arnhem. We had tried to make him see sense but his heart was set on going so he went to see the Wing Commander who told him flatly, nothing doing. Not to be outdone he carried out his duties as tow master at take off on September 17th. But as the last two or three gliders were due to be signalled away, he handed over his signalling equipment to a friend, climbed aboard a Glider and took off with the rest for the Battle. Well, here he was now in a trench; I had not seen him since Tuesday when McLaren and Banks were killed. When I realised who it was I asked him if he was sorry he had come when he could so easily have been still safe at home. His large freckled face split into a wide sheepish grin as he replied 'I'm not complaining, I can stick it if you lot can.' He was certainly 'Sticking it', what a man![1]

Laurie Weeden was also with 14 Flight. This extract from his account gives us further insight into the rhythm of the battle. Despite nearly a week of concerted German attacks and the strain of almost continual artillery bombardment, most units remained effective and ready to fight:

Some time after midday we were informed that we were to be taken out of the line for a rest. Our relief arrived, possibly observed by the Germans, as further mortars greeted their arrival and we left in some haste and made our way to a house, which was probably in Nassaulaan. Here we attempted to sleep, disconcertingly there was not only the noise of the artillery and mortars but also the clatter of German armour on the move.[2]

Divisional Headquarters had been under heavy shell and mortar fire since 0800 hours. Iain Murray's small Command Post had suffered some blast damage, and shards of shrapnel were embedded in the walls of the room that he was using to orchestrate 1 Wing GPR's defence of the Hartenstein grounds. The rain and artillery fire were to set the tone for the rest of the day around the Hartenstein.

Away from the headquarters, Sergeant Geoff Higgins of 'C' Squadron was still with the gunners he had carried into Arnhem in his Hamilcar on the first lift. He and Staff Sergeant John Bonome had accompanied them since landing, assisting in the operation and defence of their 17-pounder gun. The two glider pilots, the gunners and the powerful gun were now located in a defensive position, on the corner of Hoofdlaan and Utrechtseweg. As the rain and mortar bombs continued to fall, he reflected on the events of the past few hours:

Last night, a rather frightening experience was to hear coming up the lane the sound of troops moving. The language was foreign. I was convinced they must be Germans and so was ready to engage them. It was good to recognise them quickly enough as Polish. Then came our most terrible and frightening experience. The mortar fire came closer and this time it was mixed with the rather terrifying squeal of 88mm shells some of which seemed to hit the trees above. There was nothing for it but to stay down in one's trench and hope for the best for there was no enemy to engage. For how long this devastation went on I do not know, but as I remember it, it seemed like hours. The truck containing the ammunition and all the other equipment belonging to the gun received a direct hit and was soon ablaze. Ammunition was exploding, and it seemed that this must be the end. However there came a sense that the sound of the explosions was receding and that the 88mm shells had become less frequent and more distant. So I shook the sand, which had fallen from the sides of my trench, off my head and crawled out to see what had happened.

The towing truck was completely burnt out. The first person I looked for was John

Bonome, my first pilot, but he was not about. Fearing the worst I visited his trench. The other Staff Sergeant had gone and John was face down and quite obviously very distressed. I lifted him and found that he was very confused and obviously had no idea what was happening. As I had previously taken the Sergeant to the first aid post I also took John there and handed him over to one of the orderlies. I returned to the gun-site to see one of the gunners helmetless wandering about in the direction of the Hartenstein, somewhere in the area where the deer were kept. He was incoherent and when I went towards him to take his helmet I could see that he had been wounded. He had been hit on the side of his head and I applied two field dressings and held them there as we set out for the Hotel. He quickly became less steady and as there was still evidence of mortar fire our progress became more and more haphazard. I remember as one burst of firing that seemed quite near, I jumped in to a slit trench. There was radio equipment and later on I became aware that we had made a brief call on a broadcasting unit. The gunner was almost out when we reached the door and was assisted by another soldier. After the gunner had been taken away I sat down in the hallway.

During the short time I was there I saw several wounded and also was aware that not far away a Padre was conducting a burial service for several casualties. I asked a passing orderly about the lad I had brought in. He said, 'He died, he was one of those being carried out.' I cannot be sure that this was so, but I then returned to the gun site where I was told by the bombardier that another soldier who was occupying a larger trench with two others had been killed as a result of the blast. The gun had been hit on the shield probably by a 88mm shell. It was fractured and bent.[3]

Sergeant 'Wall' Mullett of 24 Flight was in the grounds of the Hartenstein, close to the tennis courts, where his flight remained dedicated to the defence of Divisional Headquarters. The torrent of German artillery and mortar fire continued to whittle down the numbers of 24 Flight, and 'Wall' was about to become a casualty himself:

I was joined in my trench by Staff Sergeant [Thomas] Stewart also of 'G' Squadron, who, after a short while, suggested that we move to a quieter spot. I agreed and as he led the way out of the trench a mortar bomb exploded against the tennis court fence and killed him outright. He took most of the whole force of the explosion and I was knocked back into the trench. I discovered that there was little I could do for him and found a trickle of blood running down my face which had come from a scalp wound caused when the mortar bomb had opened up a hole in my tin hat, the size of a golf ball. Although I was concussed and suffering a degree of shell shock I considered myself very fortunate and made my way very unsteadily to the dressing station in the basement of the Hotel. Although I had seen many wounded taken to dressing station I was surprised when they told me that supplies of dressings etcetera had run out and nothing could be done for me but, that treatment would be available at the Schoonoord Hotel, although it was in German hands. My shell dressing was placed on my head covering the wound and together with a German Prisoner of War we staggered through a so-called 'No man's land' to the Schoonoord Hotel.[4]

The men of 'B' Squadron were subjected to very heavy and continual mortar and artillery fire throughout Saturday morning, the shelling going on for over four hours. During the 'stonk', one of the Squadron's Jeeps was set on fire and several dugouts were blown in, although miraculously nobody was wounded or killed. Ian Toler was making his morning rounds of his positions when the shelling began:

I hear one of the shells coming – we are learning to judge them pretty well now. Just as I reckoned it was about to land I make a dive for the nearest slit trench. I must have timed it a fraction late as I have a vivid memory of seeing the burst that which hit our Jeep as I was upside down completing my dive below ground.

Later Shackleton and I were in our pit when the shells really got our range. The concussion in the pit was appalling. I was not any happier when 'Shack' said 'This is it, Sir, I think we've had it.' I didn't like to let him know I entirely shared his view. I know I was as frightened at that time as ever I have been and felt certain death was only a second or two away. The top of the pit was blown in, my Sten gun blown in the air, and we were covered in earth. The pit was no longer any protection and as there was a couple of seconds lull, both 'Shack' and I without saying a word, jumped out of our pit and ran the three yards to Sergeant Geary's trench which was still intact. I remember, again as I dropped in head first, saying politely to the occupants 'You don't mind if I join you, do you?' I was certainly surprised to still be alive.[5]

The Squadron was now involved in the defence of houses outside their own positions, each section rotating in turn between the Hartenstein trenches and the task of defending the houses. On the Friday afternoon, Staff Sergeant Bill Thomson's section had been ordered to occupy a house close to the pathfinder company headquarters at 16 Pietersbergseweg. With Bill Thomson wounded by mortar fire as he led his section into the new position, Arnold Baldwin assumed command of the section. There was still no definite news of troops crossing the river, other than a few Poles. Water was becoming particularly scarce, but some was still obtainable from a nearby well. Arnold Baldwin took stock of his own on Saturday morning, as he and his section kept watch from their fire positions in the house:

Saturday started with a heavy burst of firing fairly early in the morning. The most pitiful cries and groans from outside a window followed this on the south side of the hall. A cautious glance revealed a civilian lying on the ground, dressed in a light blue-grey boiler suit. He was obviously mortally wounded and it was impossible to go to his aid. This revealed a curious situation – to travel up or down the street was comparatively safe; to enter the passages at right angles to the street was definitely not. But who was firing and from which direction remained a mystery. Otherwise nothing much happened that day. The watch on the houses across the allotments showed shadowy movements behind some of the windows and it is possible that our lads took occasional pot shots, if only to relieve the boredom. Rations had run out, or so it was thought, and they were now on a diet of bottled plums.[6]

Brigadier 'Shan' Hackett kept a close eye on the units holding the eastern flank of the perimeter. He was regularly seen visiting his forward positions – during the morning it was 'Boy' Wilson's 21st Independent Parachute Company and 'D' Squadron on Stationsweg. That night German movement was detected in the wood north-east of the Main Dressing Station and in the built-up area to the west of it. Further movement, indicated after first light, was thought to suggest attacks by mid-morning on 156th Parachute Battalion and 'D' Squadron GPR. The Germans worked hard through the night to infiltrate Hackett's lines from the north, this aspiration being described in the 4th Parachute Brigade war diary as 'established fact by midday'. The strongpoints in the houses hung on through the morning, but conditions were described as 'grim'. At 0742 hours a strong attack was mounted on 'D' Squadron's positions. Headquarters 4th Parachute Brigade called down artillery onto the corner of Stationsweg and Joubertweg, in front of the glider pilots. The Light Regiment responded with an artillery shoot into the area at 0750 hours which broke up a determined German attack.

The shortage of PIAT bombs among the defenders allowed German armour to close in on the British-held houses and blast the defenders out room by room. As a direct result of this, the defenders moved out of the houses and dug trenches in the surrounding gardens. Staff Sergeant Harry Gibbons of 'D' Squadron was a Bren gunner occupying one of the houses in Stationsweg; he experienced the consequences of attempting to hold houses without adequate anti-tank weapons:

> We had made an observation point in the loft of a house overlooking a forward German sand bagged position from which much activity was in evidence and we were able, with Bren-gun fire, to eliminate the activity. Some hours later a German armoured vehicle approached firing a shell which scored a direct hit, killing my second pilot Dave Newman and wounding Staff Sergeant Alfie Coates. I was unharmed.[7]

Staff Sergeant Les Frater and his mates in 5 Flight were having a very busy time defending another house on Stationsweg; they were also part of the 'D' Squadron effort to keep the houses on the normally pleasant, leafy road in British hands. They continued to hold out and were doing well:

> We were attacked by tanks, which we could see from an upstairs window, refuelling before making their noisy way toward us again. We were spared mortaring, as the Germans were in the house opposite and eventually, across the way in Stationsweg. Food was no longer available, and our stock of ammunition was very low. Three of us ran the gauntlet of the snipers in a dash to the Hartenstein, which, by this time was a very sad sight, with dead and dying lying around the hotel, both inside and outside. We managed to scrounge a box of .303 and a 2inch mortar and two bombs. That afternoon we beat off a frontal attack by our neighbours in Paul Krugerstraat without loss to ourselves. Sometime during a lull in the fighting, we were able to bury one of our dead, Sergeant David Newman, and to evacuate a casualty to a house nearer to the crossroads. Although the enemy was only just across the road, most of us had survived even the tank attacks, which were rapidly reducing our house to a ruin.[8]

Lower down in Oosterbeek, in the south-east part of the town near the old church on the river bank, the indomitable Mike Dauncey, was fighting with Lonsdale Force. He was looking for a way to take the battle to the Germans who had killed and wounded so many of his comrades during the fighting around Weverstraat:

> We dug out some chaps who were resting at the church and the music hall and went over the road to Captain Mike Corrie, as Lieutenant Max Downing was killed [the previous day] and Lieutenant Frank Derbyshire was missing from patrol. We still had no PIAT. German infantry was however still rather wary of rushing about wildly. We had our positions in upper floors of houses so as to get a more commanding view which was ok except for the mortars, and self-propelled gun which had things much its own way except that it was too cautious to come really near. If the anti tank chap had only been there or even a PIAT would have done.
>
> The Germans who had been darting about all day were finally pretty well pinpointed by the evening. We thought we'd have our own back on them in return for their self-propelled guns. Two paratroops and I went out on a patrol, and supported by a little Bren-gun fire we caught them with their trousers down. After chucking a No. 36 [Grenade] in through a hole in the wall and shouting that we would shoot them if they didn't come out, eight sheepish Germans filed out, three of them wounded. We were so pleased with ourselves that the

whole party marched straight across the open to our own lines. This was too much to ask and the mortars came down on us. Major Croot was waiting for us. He was delighted and no one took any notice of the mortar, except the Germans who were terrified, until one landed five yards away and wounded three of them and two of us. We were standing under a large leafy tree and we were all buried in the branches, which had been severed by the mortar. We got a machine gun and plenty of Lugers, which were becoming very fashionable. This was the last time I saw Major Croot.[9]

On the opposite side of the cauldron, Saturday had also been a long day for the men of the Borders holding their sector of the perimeter, the worsening situation having resulted in the detachment of two platoons to bolster their hard-pressed neighbours in Breese Force. Despite the subsequent arrival of welcome reinforcements in the shape of sappers and some paratroopers, they were still very much struggling under pressure. The increasing intensity of the attacks mounted from the west by Hans von Tettau's Division were particularly felt by 'A' Company, who were heavily attacked by German infantry supported by self-propelled guns and flame-throwing Panzers. Stubbornly both they and 'C' Company, who also bore the brunt of these attacks, held on to their positions inflicting heavy casualties on attacking German infantry. The gravity of the situation on this side of the perimeter can be gauged by the fact that 'A' Company had been forced to strip the German dead of their weapons and ammunition. With over half their number so equipped, the Borders managed beat back a further three assaults during the course of Saturday. As the day progressed and the fighting became more confused, 'D' Company of the Borders was isolated from the rest of the Battalion and the Division as a tide of German units washed around their positions. Undeterred, 'D' Company fought on and continued to hold their ground.

Staff Sergeant Ron Gibson had been awake since before dawn and had 'stood to' in the rain with the rest of 16 Flight. After the flight had stood down, he had made himself a hot drink and eaten a soggy bar of chocolate, a suitable treat as it was his birthday that morning. The squadron position had been attacked in the morning, but Ron's section had played no part in that action as they were inside a wood line. This could, of course, not last and this would inevitably be a memorable birthday:

Our line at this point was well armed; we had two 6-pounders at either end of the hedge and a Vickers Gun between them. They had a wide field of fire over a ploughed field. The first warning came when the assault guns began blasting a row of trees above the heads of the gun crews and riflemen along the hedge. The ground soon became littered with broken boughs and the trunks were seared with white scars. Three or four casualties were taken away to the roadside. Then I hear a series of whistles from across the field. The Vickers opened up with a long burst and one of the 6-pounders fired. There was little difference between the deafening crack from the charge of our guns and the close-range fire of the self propelled gun. The attack fell back.

They made five assaults in the rain and mist of the morning, but all were repulsed. One time an assault gun crawled half-way across the open field before it was smashed by two successive shells from the 6-pounders; it stood scorched and derelict poised on the edge of an old gun pit, with its dead crew sprawled behind the shield.

At twelve o'clock the rain stopped. My clothes and rifle were smeared with wet sand. When the last attack had fallen back, I sat in the bottom of my trench and cleaned as much of my rifle as I could with a strip of parachute silk. I lit the Tommy cooker and brewed the last of my tea ration.[10]

Saturday's 'morning hate' continued to add to the now significant list of dead and wounded all around the perimeter, including an increasing number of glider pilots appearing on that list. Colonel Graeme Warrack, the Division's senior medical officer in Arnhem, wrote the following comment in his report for Saturday:

> At about 0900 hours five casualties were brought in, including Captain [Thomas] Plowman of the Glider Pilot Regiment. He was in a very shocked state and had his left arm and right ankle wounded. He had been on a 6-pounder gun and had been laying up for a tank or Self Propelled gun, which he had eventually got, a damn stout show! The next day he was killed when the Tafelberg received a direct hit.[11]

News of the dire situation had reached beyond the bounds of the perimeter and what was to be the final resupply mission attempted by the Royal Air Force was mounted on Saturday afternoon. The formation included seventy-two Stirling and fifty C47 Dakotas, protected by a strong fighter escort. The fighters were sufficient in number to deter any German interceptors and the resupply mission reached the Arnhem drop zone unmolested by the Luftwaffe. A fighter escort can do little to prevent attrition by flak, however. The German defences damaged over half of the formation and brought down six of the Stirling and two C47s. The bulk of the supplies dropped were gleefully accepted by the waiting German ground troops encircling Oosterbeek. Many British unit war diaries commented that it was only during the resupply drops that Allied fighters were seen overhead.

The shelling of the perimeter continued through the day, using conventional guns and mortars, as well as the dreaded 'Moaning Minnie' multi-barrelled mortars. The Hartenstein again appeared to be at the centre of this maelstrom of high-explosive ordnance, the hotel and its surrounding gardens being subjected to an unrelenting stream of incoming fire. Adding to the hazards of working around Divisional Headquarters, the entrance to the battered hotel was also under sniper fire from first light until dusk.

The unit war diaries give no indication of the physical and mental strain that those inside the perimeter were being subjected to on Saturday. Captain Frank 'Bull' Barclay, OC 21 Flight, 'D' Squadron reported that his section had been under heavy fire all morning and had had a number of casualties. Lieutenant 'Jock' Strathern reported that his section had been under continuous shell and mortar fire since seven o'clock in the morning. Certainly the bombardment was causing casualties and placing stress on those who were already tired through lack of sleep, but morale remained good.

Staff Sergeant George Voller and his co-pilot Staff Sergeant Alan Richards had remained with the 6-pounder anti-tank gun they had flown in on the first lift. They were deployed away from the Hartenstein and so were not forced to endure shelling of the same ferocity. During a lull in the shelling, they had both been released from the gun position and allowed to take a short break. The two 'B' Squadron pilots had taken the opportunity to 'brew up', were enjoying a hot mug of tea near their trench and were no doubt discussing the latest rumours of relief, the arrival of the Poles and news of casualties among their own squadron. Their respite from battle was to be short lived, as George Voller recalls:

> We were standing outside the trench having a cup of tea when a shell landed nearby. I was hit in the right elbow by some shrapnel. We decided it ought to be dressed properly so Staff Sergeant Richards and I set out to walk to divisional headquarters. We did not realise it when we set off but the surrounding area was completely flattened and under constant shelling. I was hit twice more. Staff Sergeant Richards left me at divisional headquarters, and returned to the gun. The medical officer [Lieutenant D.M. Randall] apologised that he had no facilities at all. He said that if we could walk he would provide a Red Cross escort for us to go to another casualty station nearby. The Red Cross flag was made up of bloodstained bandages on a white cloth. Some five or six followed the medic. The casualty station was a

requisitioned private house. All the Airborne signs were still in place. The medic went to the front door of the house, pushed it open and said 'Go in'. I went into the hall of the house and a German soldier closed the door. I was a prisoner.[12]

That evening Brigadier 'Shan' Hackett held an Orders Group to discuss the situation on the east side of the perimeter. He gathered in the commanders of the sectors for which he had responsibility. In attendance were Major Geoffrey Powell of 156th Parachute Battalion, Major 'Boy' Wilson of 21st Independent Parachute Company and Iain Murray of 1 Wing, Glider Pilot Regiment. The group discussed the current situation and reached the conclusion that a shortening of the line was required if they were to continue to hold their side of the perimeter. Under cover of darkness they would withdraw from the north-east corner into houses between Paul Krugerstraat and Utrechtseweg west of Stationsweg. This would not be straight forward as some of the houses they were moving into were currently held by the Germans. A liaison officer from the glider pilots' detachment at Stationsweg came into 1 Wing headquarters at about 2000 hours and was issued a walkie-talkie radio by Captain Ogilvie, one of two produced by Iain Murray after the briefing in order to co-ordinate the withdrawal onto the new line. The shortening of the line was helped by two artillery shoots from XXX Corps 25-pounders, south of the river. They were directed onto the area north-east of the MDS crossroads, where German movement had been reported.

That night the Poles were also preparing to attempt a second river crossing to reinforce Oosterbeek. During the day XXX Corps had managed to locate and deliver purpose-built assault boats to the Polish brigade's forward positions on the south bank. There was some confusion over the carrying capacity of the boats, which resulted in a delay as the Poles were forced to reduce their troops from loads of sixteen men down to twelve per boat. The boats also arrived without boat handlers, the Poles having expected Royal Engineers to crew the boats for them. The absence of handlers caused more delays as the untrained Poles got to grips with the boats in the dark.

The crossing operation did not get underway until 0300 hours on Sunday. The Germans on the north bank were alert to the possibility of a second crossing and brought heavy fire down onto the crossing area as the untrained Poles struggled to cross the fast-flowing river. The intention when planning the operation had been to get close to a Polish battalion over the river but this was unachievable using untrained troops after so many delays. In the event 153 Poles were inside the perimeter by day-break. They were too few in number to have any great affect on the battle, but nobody could question their bravery that night.

**Notes**

1    Holcroft, SSgt W.,14 Flt, 'F' Sqn, GPR, 'No medals for Lt Pickwoad', September 1945.
2    Weeden, SSgt L., 14 Flt, 'F' Sqn GPR, correspondence with the author Mar 08.
3    Higgins, Sergeant G., 'C' Sqn GPR, correspondence with Luuk Buist 1991 onwards.
4    Mullet, Sergeant W., 24 Flt, 'G' Sqn GPR, by permission of *The Eagle*.
5    Toler, Major I., OC 'B' Sqn GPR, by permission of the Toler family.
6    Baldwin, SSgt A., 20 Flt, 'B' Sqn GPR, by permission of *The Eagle*.
7    Gibbons, SSgt H., 8 Flt, 'D' Sqn GPR, correspondence with Luuk Buist, 1991.
8    Frater, SSgt L., 5 Flt, 'D' Sqn GPR, by permission of *The Eagle*.
9    Dauncey, Lieutenant M., 9 Flt, 'G' Sqn GPR, interview with the author, February 2008.
10   Gibson, SSgt R., 16 Flt, 'F' Sqn GPR, *Nine Days*, Ilfracombe, Arthur Stockwell Ltd,

1956.

11    Warrack, Colonel Graeme, RAMC, *The Harvest of Ten Years*, Airborne Museum, Oosterbeek, 1988.

12    Voller, SSgt G., 19 Flt, 'B' Sqn GPR, correspondence with Luuk Buist, 1991.

# CHAPTER 16

# Morning Hate

*'Never was darkness more eagerly awaited.'*

**Sunday, 24 September 1944**

Saturday night had been eventful, with little opportunity for rest or sleep. The strain of six days and nights of fighting was beginning to tell on all of the men holding the perimeter. Up in the north of the cauldron, 2 Wing GPR were braced for whatever the grey light of dawn would bring. Staff Sergeant Peter Gammon was with the survivors of 14 Flight, defending the houses in Nassaulaan:

> Dawn on Sunday broke strangely quiet so we decided to take stock of our situation. Whilst we had been in the woods, the house, though not hit, had got into a discreditable state with the windows and doors blown off and plaster and grass fragments covering the carpeted floors. Nevertheless the Dutch family were still sheltering in the basement, and said they were alright. Finding a broom, I swept the living room clean only to have my efforts negated by mortars falling behind the house. More to the point a piece of shrapnel took the skin off my knuckle just as I was putting in my mouth a small cake that which the family had given me. In spite of this our morale improved when the artillery barrage from south of the river started up.[1]

Staff Sergeant Ron Gibson was also in the 2 Wing GPR area, preparing himself for the uncertainty that accompanied yet another day of fighting. He was with some of the survivors of 16 Flight, close to Peter Gammon in the 'F' Squadron trenches. His account outlines the state of the troops still fighting to hold the north-west of the perimeter – though tired their morale was still good and they remained disciplined and full of fight:

> I had a two hour sleep, returning to my post an hour before dawn. For the first few hours of the day we were left in peace. The Mortar fire was directed over our heads in the direction of divisional headquarters, the hotspot of the whole bridgehead. Our ammunition was re-sorted, the rations checked, and the trenches deepened … An attack through the thick cover of beech and oak saplings was anticipated. As a fighting unit the squadron was a conglomerate force. It was formed from the remnants of 'E' and 'F' squadrons. There were two 6 pounders and their crews from the Border Regiment, in the hedge was a Vickers gun manned by two parachutists and in the slit trenches … were several men from the other squadrons.[2]

The mortar fire, referred to by Ron Gibson started early in the morning and continued through the day. The Hartenstein remained at the epicentre of the storm of German artillery fire. Arthur Shackleton clearly remembers how helpless he and his comrades felt when subjected to the ferocious early morning barrage that regularly descended on the Hartenstein and its devastated environs:

> Every morning just after the sun rose, we had what became known as the 'morning hate'. For a solid hour the Germans plastered our positions with shells and mortar bombs. One mortar known to us as the 'Moaning Minnie' fired off nine rockets in one salvo.
>
> One morning I watched a creeping barrage coming steadily toward our positions. I was certain that the next barrage would land on top of us but for some unknown reason, the Germans ceased firing – relief all-round!
>
> Later on in the day [Saturday] a shell landed on the lip of our trench and we were buried up to our waists in sandy soil and rendered as deaf as posts. On clambering out, we dived into the next trench and finished up with Arnold Baldwin on the bottom and Joe Michie on top of him. Me on top of Joe and Major Toler on the very top, with his legs sticking out. Eventually the barrage moved away and we sorted ourselves out. While starting to re-dig the trench [on Sunday] I found an unexploded 88mm shell by the side of the trench ... It was about this time I decided I didn't go much for this dying for King and Country lark![3]

Ian Toler's diary entry for Sunday compliments Arthur Shackleton's memories of the shelling and the subsequent discovery of the German shell. It also illustrates just how intense the bombardment was:

> Looking at the remains of our weapon pit we see an unexploded shell lying just on the lip of it. If it had gone off I should certainly not have been writing this. We get the sappers to blow it up which they do with great glee. My shaving kit, which I had left above ground as I was starting to shave when yesterday's bombardment started, has gone for a Burton. I am so tired by now that I don't care.
>
> During one shelling ... I am sharing a slit trench with the Sergeant Major. I am lying on top of him, being pretty tall, I can't get all of my legs in. The toe of one boot is protruding. After the bombardment I notice a piece of shrapnel has taken a neat piece out of the toe cap of my boot, but missing the foot.[4]

Artillery shells are not noted as great respecters of rank, the shells and bombs landing among the British positions on Sunday morning being no different. Brigadier 'Shan' Hackett was away from his own headquarters, preparing for the reception of the Polish paratroops who had crossed the river the previous night. The Poles were due to reinforce his brigade on the north-eastern corner of the perimeter. It was while he was busying himself with this task that he was wounded in the stomach and thigh with shell splinters. His wounds required surgery that could not be provided inside the perimeter. The seriously wounded Brigadier was evacuated from the area at about 1400 hours and taken to the St Elisabeth hospital behind the German lines in Arnhem for treatment.

The loss of such a senior commander triggered a reorganization of the chain of command in 4th Parachute Brigade. The terrible casualty rate accrued by the Brigade during its fighting withdrawal and battle to get into Oosterbeek had been particularly high among 'Shan' Hackett's senior officers. There were no battalion commanders or staff officers able to step up into the position of Brigade Commander. The only commanding officer surviving and capable of taking on the role was Lieutenant Colonel Iain Murray GPR. The handover of command between the two men took place in the Divisional Headquarters RAP, as the wounded Brigadier was treated and the battle continued around them.

The elevation of Iain Murray to command of 4th Parachute Brigade in turn resulted in him handing over the command of 1 Wing GPR to Ian Toler:

During the afternoon I am told to go to Wing HQ which is in the Hartenstein Hotel, only one-hundred yards from our position. Here I am told that as Brigadier Hackett has been wounded and taken prisoner, Colonel Murray is to take over his brigade and I am to assume command of the Glider Pilot Wing.

Around the hotel there was still a great deal of sniping and I was warned not to go across the entrance as the sniper was shooting at anything that moved. It seemed so quiet I could hardly believe that, so I put my steel helmet on the end of a stick and moved it about by the entrance. To my great astonishment immediately there was a loud crack as the sniper fired at it and the bullet embedded itself in the doorway.[5]

Divisional Headquarters are traditionally viewed by front-line soldiers as a 'cushy billet' behind the lines and out of harm's way. Flying Officer Reg Lawton visited the Hartenstein on the second Sunday of the battle. His description of conditions inside the hotel leaves the reader in no doubt as to the dangers faced by the remaining staff officers, clerks and signallers of Roy Urquhart's staff:

I went into one of the rooms of the Hartenstein Hotel and found Flying Officer Cullen there. He said that Lieutenant Colonel Murray of the Glider Pilot Regiment, whose room it was, had said we could stay there, so we settled down. Besides Lieutenant Colonel Murray there was Major Toler, a lieutenant, two corporal runners and one or two officers were always coming and going for instructions. The room, although on the ground floor, was a bedroom. It was large and lofty, a huge gilt-framed mirror ran up one wall, smashed by bullets, and there was a large modern yellow bed. A wardrobe had been pushed against one of the windows but snipers in the trees outside made it impossible to stay anywhere in the room except in two of the corners. Accordingly we all lay down in these corners and if we had to move, did so at the run.[6]

The news of Ian Toler's appointment and the move out of the trenches and into the Hartenstein was initially well received by his co-pilot and battle partner, Arthur Shackleton:

I immediately thought 'good' we shall have the shelter of stone walls. How wrong I was. Our duties consisted of visiting the various Glider Pilot positions noting casualties and re-distributing the surviving pilots to keep the perimeter manned. This entailed us wandering around the positions above ground with lethal objects flying around while others were snug in their trenches.[7]

As the changes in command took place, the reinforcements that had made it into the perimeter were being introduced to the battle. The 153 Poles who had made the river crossing the previous night were allocated as reinforcements to 4th Parachute Brigade. It was decided that the bulk of the paratroops should be used to bolster 'D' Squadron, who were under command of Captain James Ogilvie. One hundred of the Poles, from the 3rd Polish Parachute Battalion, were guided to their new positions on the north-east corner of the perimeter at Stationsweg. The Squadron sent Lieutenant Brian Bottomley and Sergeant Streeter to lead the Poles into the 'D' Squadron lines. On their way into the front line the whole party was pinned down in one of the houses by heavy machine-gun fire, which killed two Poles, one of whom was their commander, Captain Ignancy Gazurek. The group remained pinned down throughout the day, their move eventually being completed under cover of darkness later in the night. The remaining fifty-three reinforcements were detached from the main group and sent to reinforce Major 'Dickie' Dale's 'C' Squadron in the area between the Kneppelhout monument and the Borders' positions at van Lennepweg.

The fighting on the eastern side of the perimeter remained intense for most of Sunday. Just south of the medical crossroads, on Pietersbergseweg, Staff Sergeant Arnold Baldwin and his section from 20 Flight were taking their turn away from the Hartenstein trenches holding the 'B' Squadron house:

> Sunday, commenced with another outburst of small arms fire, heavier and more prolonged than the previous day, followed by a furious hammering on the front door. I approached the door with extreme caution and while stood pondering what to do a voice cried 'Come on, open up for f...'s sake, its f...ing naughty out here.' This was shouted in an unmistakably cockney accent that the cleverest German mimic could never have achieved. Through the door stepped an obviously very hard-nut sergeant major of the parachutists, the scarf or camouflage netting he wore on his head instead of a helmet giving him a decidedly piratical look. He seemed genuinely surprised by the commotion he had caused and when asked what he was up to, replied angrily that 'nobody told anybody anything, nobody knew what was going on, nobody knew just where the Germans were' so he had walked up to the crossroads on a one-man reconnaissance. After getting his breath back he returned to his unit.
>
> Some while after this there was further knocking on the door and I, wondering if this was visitor's day, decided to fall back on the old 'Who goes there?' 'Captain – Royal Army Medical Corps, I have an urgent message from the Germans.' Inside the door he stated that he was tending the wounded in the Schoonoord Hotel. The local German commander had sent him to say that he was bringing up tanks to blast them out of the house if they did not leave voluntarily, regardless of what might happen to the wounded in the Hotel. I said they couldn't leave without orders and took him down the road to the Para headquarters where he repeated his story to the wounded officer, who said 'Go back and tell him we'll knock his tanks out with our anti-tank guns.' This clearly enraged the Captain who said 'Don't talk bloody rot, they know you haven't got any ammo.' After pondering this for a few seconds the Para officer said 'OK, tell them we'll withdraw', at the same time motioning to me not to leave with the Captain. He then told me to move out of the house into the next house, stay the night there and go back again in the morning. This we did.[8]

The situation for those dug in close to the hotel building continued to worsen, as the German grip on Oosterbeek continued to tighten. The supply of water had been cut off since Thursday reducing the men of 'B' Squadron to desperate measures, such as extracting dirty water from toilet cisterns and animal troughs. A liberal use of issued water purification tablets rendered this water technically fit for human consumption. Arthur Shackleton:

> Major Toler and I moved into the Hartenstein. From there, we visited the various Sections of Glider Pilots at intervals to check on casualties. I remember while I was in the Hartenstein another Glider Pilot coming in with the news that he had found a well, but it was under sniper fire. I was 'volunteered' to go with him to investigate. We found the well with four or five bodies lying close by. This was the moment that the coward in both of us took over. We decided that we did not want a VC or even a mention [in despatches], so we would return at dusk with some water bottles, which we duly did. By tying string around them we managed to half-fill five of them with very discoloured liquid. We gave the bottles to a very grateful Medical Officer in charge of the wounded in the cellar of the Hartenstein. We decided that we would pay another visit to the well just before dawn. However, there was a very heavy bombardment during the night and when we reached the well again it had taken a direct hit and was just a heap of rubble and muck … no more water.[9]

In the south-east corner of the perimeter, Lieutenant Mike Dauncey, was in command of a mixed section of Lonsdale Force troops holding Weverstraat:

There was a certain noisy activity during last night with shots flying about and bags of shouting, but it didn't materialise. Got some little bits of mortar in the shoulder and on the forehead, not bad. The usual form of sniping, mortar and self-propelled gunfire. Several amusing things occurred today. The game was 'spot the sniper'. To get a better angle I went down the road to the school with a very reliable private of the South Staffords. We took up our position upstairs, but after about half an hour smoke started filling the room and eventually became so dense that we couldn't see. I went downstairs to investigate and found some gunners round a huge fire in the school hall on which was a huge tin bath full of chickens! They were cooking for the Battery.[10]

Staff Sergeant Laurie Weeden of 'F' Squadron stayed in one of the houses at Nassaulaan during Saturday night and in the morning his section moved from the house into the trenches. As they completed the move they were informed that they were now the second line of defence behind the KOSBs, any feeling of relative safety being short lived:

A Bren gun was required urgently and as I ran forward round the corner of Paul Krugerstraat into Hartenweg I was somewhat surprised to be confronted by a German soldier, only about fifteen metres away, and advancing towards me. I dropped to the ground, cocked the Bren gun, and squeezed the trigger. The Bren gun jammed ... Fortunately the German turned and ran back to his own lines, being hit in the process by British rifle fire. During the morning I observed, through my field glasses, a German soldier at the top floor window of a house in Bothaweg and I emptied a magazine of my Bren gun in his direction. We were to have trouble from that quarter at dusk that day.[11]

On the eastern side of the perimeter, a platoon of about thirty enemy infantry had managed to establish a foothold in the wood close to the crossroads of Kneppelhoutweg and Vijverlaan (a track leading to the Brigade HQ). They were now trying to cross the road and infiltrate the woods adjacent to the Airlanding Brigade headquarters. The brigade staff had reacted aggressively to the threat. A Bren gun manned by brigade signallers caught the Germans in the open as they attempted to dash across the road from one wood to the other. Withering bursts of fire from the Bren team felled at least a section of the Germans crossing the road, the remainder making it into the wood. A firefight quickly broke out in the woods, during which a number of the surviving Germans were killed by small-arms fire. Despite the rapid response from the brigade staff, a small German enclave had been established in the British wood. An enemy position in such close proximity to the headquarters was deemed unacceptable and a clearing patrol was deployed, under the command of Lieutenant G.N. Austin, a liaison officer from the South Staffords, and Sergeant Major Morgan of the Army Physical Training Corps. The composite patrol proved unsuccessful and both men were reported killed. Later, a party of about twenty glider pilots from 'C' Squadron, led by Lieutenant Robert 'Blubber' Boyd, also tried, without success, to oust the interlopers from the wood. In spite of their numbers the larger GPR patrol was not strong enough to drive the Germans out of their position. The Germans had by now been reinforced by two Panzers that were ensconced on the junction of Pietersbergseweg and Kneppelhoutweg, from where position they were threatening the road and supporting the infantry enclave in the wood.

Similar actions were taking place all around Oosterbeek as the Germans used their superiority in numbers and weight of armour to grind their way into the perimeter. Sergeant Hugh Carling had flown into Arnhem as co-pilot to Lieutenant 'Blubber' Boyd. In his book *Not Many of us Left* he describes the severity of the fighting that Sunday afternoon:

We made our way to the house where a Dutch lady had given me some food a few days before, now derelict and occupied by some of the South Staffords, whose officer had gone off to look for a tank and had not come back. The place was in chaos, with dead lying where they had fallen and wounded men groaning in the gardens, unable to make it to the doubtful shelter of the ruined house. I gathered from those who could talk that a tank had come around the end of the road and the civilians had been taken off under a white flag, and then they had simply been plastered and were waiting to go into the bag any minute. The young Captain had taken the PIAT to see if he could retaliate but had not been seen again. I found Staff Sergeant Reg Dance, one of 'E' Squadron pilots, lying in the garden, his face obliterated in a great froth of blood and presumably dead, if not from his wounds, from a long period of exposure, for he was blue and stiff and had no perceptible pulse. I crawled on into the wood and found my chaps huddled in a hole. They had seen enemy troops following a tank. I had a quick look in the direction indicated and, sure enough, there was a bunch of Jerries, about 700–800 yards away, moving across our front with a vehicle of some kind ahead of them.[12]

Back with Lonsdale Force Lieutenant Mike Dauncey had survived yet another close shave, as he and his small band of men contested the vital roads and buildings between the Hartenstein and the river bank with 9th SS Panzer Division:

The game was still spotting the sniper that afternoon. To get a better view of where I thought he was, I went up to the top of the house to get a view from a dormer window. Unfortunately he spotted me first and the bullet hit a stovepipe just by my head. A piece of pipe or the bullet striking me in the left eye was blinding me at once. One paratrooper tried to get the metal out of my eye with a couple of matches, but this was not possible so it had to be left. It was later this day that a paratrooper paid the glider pilots a real compliment when he said how glad he was to be fighting with us. It was so simple yet so sincere.

Things were fairly sticky that evening. The Germans were making a real effort. Still no anti tank equipment for us. We had to send away for it each time and it did not seem to appear. Two Self Propelled Guns were level with us in the same street belting away at everything. We let them do it and waited for the infantry. I must say the chaps with me were excellent. It was a question of taking tanks and self-propelled guns, mortars and shells and I am glad to say no flame-throwers, and then giving their infantry stick if and when they came.

One chap got a German officer with a No36 [Grenade] He was creeping into our cellar while we were upstairs, so we did not notice him. His binoculars were quite good. Captain Mike Corrie who threw a couple of 36 grenades at them eventually frightened off the tanks. He was in excellent form that night. I expect they thought they were mines. Oh for a PIAT or an anti tank gun!

Later that night when things had quietened down a paratrooper helped me down to our Regimental Aid Post but the Doc could not be found and the Corporal hadn't any means of getting the metal out so we returned to our houses where they tried the match trick again. As I was not feeling up to form I did not stay awake but had a good sleep to try to get myself fit for the following day.[13]

The battle was equally savage in the 2 Wing sector, Glider Pilots of 'E' and 'F' Squadron were badly mauled when the Germans introduced flame-throwing tanks to their sector of the perimeter. Despite the menace of the flame-throwers, Lieutenant Colonel John Place's 2 Wing GPR showed great tenacity and held on. During the struggle two of the Panzers were destroyed by 17-pounders. The German attack had come very close to overwhelming the 2 Wing defences, as a result of which John Place needed to reinforce his lines or withdraw. He approached the headquarters of 7th King's Own Scottish Borderers and asked them to 'dispose themselves in greater depth so as to cover the rear of the Glider Pilot positions'. Lieutenant Colonel Payton-Reid agreed to this suggestion and realigned his own front to give 2 Wing more support. The Germans then reformed and mounted another concentrated attack on the GPR trenches, using a combination of artillery, mortars, self-propelled guns and a flame-throwing tank. In the face of this vigorous assault 2 Wing, even with the support of the Borderers, had no option but to give up the wood opposite the junction of Oranjeweg and Paul Krugerstraat. Staff Sergeant Ron Gibson witnessed the cost of defending the wood:

> From my position I could not realize what had happened, but on the following day I learnt that the southern section … had been attacked by a flame-thrower tank. The section had been pushed back, leaving two of my friends sprawling in their holes, burned to death. For some inexplicable reason the tank had turned back at the end of the line, and then trundled off into the wood.
>
> Several of these flame-throwing tanks had been prowling around the outside of the division's perimeter during the preceding days but this was the only occasion on which our sector was attacked. These and the assault guns were the most formidable threat to our defences, for the infantry attacks by the SS were ill timed and undetermined and always announced beforehand by the usual whistles and guttural shouting.[14]

Major Peter Jackson and 'E' Squadron were alongside 'F' Squadron in the battle with the flame-throwing panzers. He witnessed the long overdue and very welcome intervention of Allied fighter ground-attack aircraft at a critical moment in the fighting:

> Typhoons came over and blasted the German positions with rockets and most effectively silenced the Hun, but, unfortunately, only for a while and he next produced against our ground troops the flame-thrower. One Flight of men was burnt out, and a 17-pounder anti-tank gun used against the flame- throwing tank was blown up and its crew killed. Then another gun was brought into play and one tank was blown to blazes. One officer of the Glider Pilot Regiment grabbed a PIAT, walked up to another tank and blew a hole in it, and out of the wreckage tumbled panic stricken Germans. A self-propelled German gun appeared on the scene at this juncture and the crews were dispersed into the undergrowth by automatic fire. To deal the knockout blow to the gun a British 6-pounder was pushed into position and then it was realised that no one in the particular party knew how to lay the gun. Someone had a bright idea and suggested opening the breach and peering through the barrel until it was level with the self-propelled gun and then loading and firing.
>
> This was done and the Germans now had one self-propelled gun less to play with. They were also down one gun crew. The Squadron, now sadly depleted, was withdrawn to some houses covering the wood and shortly after this another attack by some 150 Germans was launched. Out of these approximately eighty-five were killed in the first twenty minutes. The remainder withdrew and almost immediately there came a re-occurrence of heavy mortaring, which continued the whole afternoon.[15]

Staff Sergeant Brian Vincent was in one of the 'E' Squadron trenches as the flame-throwing Panzers commenced their attack. He describes the desperate methods employed by the glider pilots and other airborne troops, who had no anti-tank weapons to hand to deal with armoured vehicles.

Brian Vincent waited as one of the Panzers advanced across open terrain to get within range of the 'E' Squadron positions:

> The tank halted and threw a flame at us through the trees. The two of us in our slit trench threw ourselves flat in it. The flame slightly scorched the back of my jacket, since I was on top of my trench colleague. After a little while we sat up, ready to dive again if necessary. No more came from the tank. Someone near us fired a Tommy gun at the drivers' slot. Another glider pilot threw something at it that burst into flames as it hit the tank, but it missed and landed low near the tracks. No one came from the tank, but after some time it moved away.[16]

Lieutenant Alec Johnston, also with 'E' Squadron, was in command of some of the 2 Wing positions in the woods on Sunday afternoon. There was little prospect of tanks entering woodland, where they would be vulnerable to infantry weapons. The threat to Alec and his men, in their trenches in the woods, was infantry. During the afternoon, the mortar barrage intensified and then suddenly began to peter out:

> As the enemy mortar barrage stopped, I could see the grey-clad figures flitting about in the trees, vague and shadowy, creeping nearer. We held our fire, for we had very little ammunition left after a week's fighting. Our casualties were very heavy: there were only a few men left in the Flight I had taken over that morning after the commander had been badly wounded.
>
> The Germans had opened up first. Their fire was heavy; evidently they meant business this time. Then we started, and the whole wood seemed to be alive with the whistle and crack of small arms fire. All the time, shells from the Second Army's guns from the other side of the river whined over our heads into the enemy positions, their dull crump-crump forming a percussion accompaniment to this Devil's symphony. Suddenly my Sten gun clicked it was empty. Desperately, I hunted around for another magazine although I knew only too well that there was not one to be had. 'Hande hoch, raus, raus!' a voice screeched. I whipped round and there, standing over me, sub-machine gun in hand, was a wild looking youth not more than 17 years old. 'Raus, raus!' he shrilled once again, gesticulating violently with the barrel of his gun. I remembered wondering why he didn't shoot and then, as I clambered out of the trench, thought how dangerous it was to be out in the open with all those bullets whistling around. Next I stumbled through the trees, prodded from behind by my captor's gun.[17]

Staff Sergeant Frank Sullivan of 15 Flight was among the 'F' Squadron trenches, acting as part of a Bren gun crew, when the flame-thrower tank attack began. He survived the attack and remembers the effect of the flame-throwers as a weapon and the hasty withdrawal from the forward trenches:

> As Number 3 on the Bren my job was to make sure there were enough properly filled magazines. I was standing in the slit trench with three filled magazines in each hand, trying to make sense of the little areas of fire, which kept springing up. We could hear a tracked vehicle in the offing, and suddenly I was getting my first and last experience of a flame-thrower. I turned to warn the Bren gunner and his mate, and found I was quite alone! I don't remember getting out of the trench, but next was running in a zigzag to avoid the Schmeisser bullets that seemed to be following me. My Flight was now occupying a declivity in the ground, and I was just in time to see Lieutenant Bill Happer drop as he was shot, that reminded me that cover was desirable.

Catching up with the Bren gunner, Sergeant G. Moss, I was standing astride him behind a tree, and trying to tell him we were being outflanked on the left, when a bullet clipped his neck and passed on between my legs to hit him in the ankle. I helped him back and returned for the Bren. Going back, I found Moss again, who was obviously in trouble. I helped him on a jeep that was just about to leave with some wounded for the Regimental Aid Post. As it went off over the uneven ground there was a cry from Moss who was slipping off, so I held him on, running behind the jeep until it got to the road. I never saw my Flight again, as I couldn't find them.[18]

Laurie Weeden had managed to remain with 'F' Squadron and was now occupying one of the new trenches at the west end of Paul Krugerstraat:

At the eastern end of that long street the enemy was obviously attacking the perimeter, as we could see their mortar shells rising almost vertically and then falling on the British positions. Groups of German troops were also running across Paul Krugerstraat but, at that range, we had some difficulty in hitting them with any accuracy with our small arms fire. At one stage … a German self-propelled gun was visible just to the north of us, but I believe it was either disabled or otherwise persuaded to leave by one of our 6-pounder anti tank guns.

Approximately fifteen glider pilots were holding this position at the end of Paul Krugerstraat on the northern extremity of the perimeter. At dusk we were ordered to withdraw about fifty metres into houses in Nassaulaan, which involved running across a patch of ground, believed to be covered by enemy machine gun fire. Sergeant Fred Greenhill ['E' Squadron] offered to help me with my Bren gun ammunition and we ran across this patch of ground together. When I reached the cover of a house I looked back and saw that Sergeant Greenhill had been hit, probably in the head, and that his steel helmet had been knocked off. We could not get out to him in daylight as an enemy machine gun in a house in Bothaweg was now firing tracer bullets directly across the green. Staff Sergeant Dennis Briggs of 'E' Squadron, who was with us, told us that Fred Greenhill was his co-pilot. About ten minutes later I went to see Padre Chignell, who was supervising stretcher bearing, and informed him of the incident.

About three months later I happened to see Staff Sergeant [Andrew] Anderson of 'E' Squadron. He told me that he went out after dark that night to fetch Fred Greenhill in, but by that time the enemy was only about twenty metres from where he lay, so nothing could be done.[19]

Staff Sergeant Andrew Smith Anderson survived the battle but was tragically killed in an air crash in the Pyrenees in December of the same year. All of the accounts regarding the fighting over the second weekend of the battle give prominence to a marked increase in the casualty rate. The increased intensity of the fighting, since the formation of the Oosterbeek perimeter, had in fact generated a relatively large number of wounded for the medical services, inside the perimeter, to cope with. In fact, by Sunday morning the British dressing stations were bulging well beyond their capacity. Including German wounded, the RAMC were treating over 1,200 casualties and could not accommodate many more.

The fluid nature of the battle had resulted in the capture of many of the British medical personnel. Less than half of the fourteen Regimental Aid Posts landed were now operational – the front-line facilities closest to the battle. Two of the three Main Dressing Stations were functioning and able to provide more complex medical support. The real problem for Colonel Graeme Warrack and his medics was that many of his surgical teams had been captured during the confusion of Wednesday when the perimeter was still being formed.

The dire medical situation was further worsened by a shortage of medical supplies. The resupply drops were as critical to the medics as they were to the fighting troops, particularly as stocks of basic items such as bandages were exhausted. Many wounded received nothing more than an improvised bandage, as stocks of medicines and drugs had long been used up.

By Sunday morning, every available area that could shelter the wounded had been filled beyond its capacity. Casualties were now being treated out in the open, with all of the hazards that accompany living in the open, in the midst of a battle. The scene around Oosterbeek Church was particularly grim. The Regimental Aid Post of 1st Airlanding Light Regiment, RA was located in that area and was also servicing the remnants of the battalions that were now fighting with Lonsdale Force. The RAP occupied the house and garden of the Ter Horst family, very close to the church. Mrs Kate Ter Horst had filled her home to capacity with wounded and did all she could to comfort the wounded and the dying.

With the British medical chain about to be overwhelmed by numbers of wounded and medical supplies exhausted, Colonel Graeme Warrack, the 1st Airborne Division's senior medical officer, obtained permission to arrange a truce with the Germans, which was generously granted by Obergruppenführer 'Willi' Bittrich, commander of the II SS Panzer Corps. As many wounded as possible were moved out of the perimeter by the Germans: 250 stretcher cases by vehicle, while a further 200 walking wounded marched out on foot. Many were operated on by British surgical teams who had been allowed to carry on operating in St Elisabeth Hospital theatres after the Germans had retaken it. One can only speculate about the SS commander's motivation for allowing the truce to take place – the cynical view is that he had one eye on the end of the war and his reputation after it. It is also true that both sides were practical, and respected the Red Cross, each others' casualties and medical personnel – a state of affairs the SS troops had not encountered in Russia.

Whilst the truce was being organized, a flurry of planning was under way to the south of the river. At last XXX Corps had pushed through to Driel in strength, and a properly organised, large-scale crossing was being planned for Sunday night. The crossing would not, however, be on the scale hoped for by the majority of 1st Airborne Division, nor was it to be an attempt to expand the perimeter. At 0700 hours on Sunday morning, Major General Ivor Thomas, the commander of 43rd (Wessex) Division, and Lieutenant General Brian Horrocks, the commander of XXX Corps, had climbed the stairs of the church tower at Driel. The appearance of two such senior officers atop the church tower was a complete surprise to the Forward Observation Officer of 220 Battery, 112 Field Regiment, RA. The gunners were busy at the time, making good use of the tower to direct their own 'morning hate' onto the German positions in and around Oosterbeek. General Thomas's recollections of the thirty-minute meeting are recorded in the divisional history of 43rd (Wessex) Division:

> Lieutenant General Horrocks faced the facts. The position held by the Airborne Division had no military value. It was merely a nebulous area in wooded hills with very little control over the riverbank, which ran dead straight for over half a mile. The enemy held the high ground overlooking the river and the approaches to it. It would therefore be impossible to bring bridging Lorries down in daylight. Even if a bridge were built it would be under direct fire from the opposite bank above and below the bridge site. He therefore instructed 43rd Division to carry out the evacuation.

Later in the morning a longer and more formal meeting took place at 43rd (Wessex) Division headquarters, in the village of Valburg. The two British generals were joined by Major General Stanislaw Sosabowski and Lieutenant Colonel Eddie Myers, the Commander Royal Engineers, who represented Roy Urquhart. The meeting started at about 1000 hours; it did not go well. As soon as the decision to withdraw the airborne troops across the river was announced, the discussions became heated. Sosabowski, unaware of the extent of the difficulties faced by XXX Corps and the two American airborne divisions, refused to accept the decision. The Polish general was, no doubt, influenced by the fact that the glider element of his brigade and some of his 3rd Parachute Battalion were committed to the battle on the north side of the river. He also felt marginalized, as the plan involved the removal of some of his remaining Poles from his command. The notoriously stubborn Pole became angry and initiated a bitter exchange with Horrocks. The difficult moment was witnessed by Brigadier Hubert Essame, the commander of 214 Brigade:

'I am General Sosabowski, I command the Polish Brigade. I do what I Like.' Lieutenant General Horrocks and Major General Thomas exchanged glances. Then Lieutenant General Horrocks said: 'You are under my command. You will do as I bloody well tell you.' To this forthright statement, General Sosabowski replied: 'All right, I command the Polish brigade and I do as you bloody well say.' The conference then continued on more formal lines.[20]

Despite the imminent withdrawal, the XXX Corps commander also ordered a reinforcement of the perimeter that night, with the objective of expanding, or at least stabilizing, the perimeter boundary in preparation for the evacuation. The crossing was to be made by the 4th Battalion The Dorsetshire Regiment, followed by 1st Polish Parachute Battalion. The concern voiced about the lack of engineers and equipment was borne out later in the day, when the Polish crossing had to be cancelled due to a lack of enough assault boats to mount two simultaneous crossings.

Sunday was a grim day for the troops south of Driel, where much of XXX Corps had been bogged down in intense fighting and were unable to move north up the corridor. The German forces continued to gain strength and were launching regular and concerted counter-attacks with the intention of severing the corridor. Even if 'Hells Highway' was not physically blocked by German troops, long sections of it were rendered impassable by fire from German artillery, mortars and anti-tank guns. Movement was only practical at high speed and in small numbers, so a lengthy transit north of slow-moving engineer equipment was certainly not a practical proposition. In the unlikely event that such a convoy survived the journey and attempted to get to Driel, the roads that were in British hands were far too narrow for heavy vehicles. The roads leading up to Driel were, in fact, nothing more than muddy water-logged tracks in many places, and therefore unsuitable for heavy vehicles or bridging equipment.

The river crossing was bravely attempted by the Dorsets at 0100 hours. In the interests of operational security, the men taking part were not told of the impending withdrawal or their part in the overall plan. The Battalion had taken heavy casualties during the battle for Hill 112 in Normandy, the survivors of which therefore recognized the scale of the task facing them. The Dorsets' held their pre-mission briefing in the church tower at Driel. Major Phillip Roper commanded 'C' Company:

We could see everything up to the trees which came down to the edge of the river on the north bank, but nothing in the trees on the ground which sloped steeply upwards from the river. Colonel Tilly said 'Gentlemen we've bought it this time.' I think he realized it was a pretty hairy operation. As for myself, I thought it unlikely we would get back. When I had my company 'O' Group I tried to water it down as much as possible and told them we were going to do an important job to help the airborne people.[21]

Despite their best efforts, the crossing was a dismal failure: 375 of the Dorsets succeeded in crossing the fast-flowing river downstream from the Westerbouwing, but once on the far bank they had little chance to regroup and many were captured or killed in the darkness. Only seventy-five of the West Country men evaded capture and fought their way into the perimeter; the majority were split into ten-man sections and used to reinforce companies of the Border Regiment. A notable exception who did not join a rifle company was Captain Rose RA, who was leading one of the two FOO parties attached to the Dorsets. He and his team were quickly in action the next morning. Using his powerful radio, he directed a heavy weight of fire from the guns of the Second Army into the German lines – one of the few positive outcomes of the Dorsets' ill-fated crossing. The Dorsets were to be saddled with the unenviable distinction of being the British battalion with the most soldiers missing in action on the western front. Indeed, their actions that night are frequently overlooked, for over the period 24-26 September they were to lose a total of 275 men. It is especially grim to note that only fifteen of their number have a marked grave on the northern bank; around 200 were taken prisoner. Critically, none of the desperately needed medical supplies, ammunition or rations reached 1st Airborne Division that night. The Dorsets did, however, succeed in delivering the orders for the evacuation to Headquarters, 1st Airborne Division.

Late on Sunday evening, the Germans mounted a fresh attack and were astride the corridor at Koevering between Sint Oedenrode and Veghel, blocking the XXX Corps main supply route. Lieutenant General Horrocks had finally met with his superior, General Sir Miles Dempsey, of Second Army. The two men had concluded that the Oosterbeek bridgehead was untenable and a withdrawal should be made. The news of the German blocking attack and the failure of the Dorsets' crossing reinforced the decision – 1st Airborne Division must be extracted from Oosterbeek. There would be no further attempts to expand the bridgehead.

On the other side of the perimeter, Padre George Pare was looking after the pastoral needs of those sheltering inside the Schoonoord MDS. The battered hotel remained an oasis in the centre of the fighting on the eastern boundary of the perimeter. As darkness fell on Sunday evening, he held a field service for the wounded and their attendant medical staff:

> That evening was particularly noisy and as I took my evening service, I could hardly hear my own voice at times above the fury of the battle outside. I was constrained to consign the din to the devil, and managed to sing the whole of 'Abide with me' in the large ward. Men who could either sang or hummed, or just lay listening. The sombre words 'When other helpers fail and comforts flee, God of the helpless, O abide with me' were never sung in a more appropriate setting … At this particular service, with men stretched out all over the floor, and a couple of lamps flickering, I really felt the presence of the Almighty.[22]

### Notes

1     Gammon, SSgt P., 14 Flt, 'F' Sqn GPR, correspondence with the author, March 2008.

2     Gibson, SSgt R, 16 Flt, 'F' Sqn GPR, *Nine Days*, Ilfracombe, Arthur Stockwell Ltd, 1956, p. 76.

3     Shackleton, SSgt A., 20 Flt, 'B' Sqn GPR, interview with the author, February 2008.

4     Toler, Major I., OC 'B' Sqn GPR, by permission of the Toler family.

5     Ibid.

6 Lawton, FO R., 190 Sqn RAF, by permission of Airborne Museum Hartenstein.

7 Shackleton, SSgt A., 20 Flt, 'B' Sqn GPR, interview with the author, February 2008.

8 Baldwin, SSgt A., 20 Flt, 'B' Sqn GPR, by permission of *The Eagle*.

9 Shackleton, SSgt A., 20 Flt, 'B' Sqn GPR, interview with the author, February 2008.

10 Dauncey, Lieutenant M., 3 Flt, 'G' Sqn GPR, interview with the author, February 2008.

11 Weeden, SSgt L., 14 Flt, 'F' Sqn GPR, correspondence with the author.

12 Carling, Sergeant H., 'C' Sqn GPR, *Not Many of us Left*, Hailsham, J &KH Publishing, 1997.

13 Dauncey, Lieutenant M., 3 Flt, 'G' Sqn GPR, interview with the author, February 2008.

14 Gibson, SSgt R., 16 Flt, 'F' Sqn GPR, *Nine Days*, Ilfracombe, Arthur Stockwell Ltd, 1956, p. 77.

15 Jackson, Major P., OC 'E' Sqn GPR, correspondence with Luuk Buist, 1991.

16 Vincent, SSgt B., 'E' Sqn GPR, correspondence with Bob Hilton, February 1997.

17 Johnston, Lieutenant A., 'E' Sqn GPR, correspondence with Luuk Buist, 1991.

18 Sullivan, SSgt F., 15 Flt, 'F' Sqn GPR, correspondence with Luuk Buist, 1991.

19 Weeden, SSgt L., 14 Flt, 'F' Sqn GPR, correspondence with the author, March 2008.

20 Essame, Major General H., *The 43rd Wessex Division at War 1944-4*, London, W. Clowes & Sons Ltd, 1952.

21 Watkins, G.J.B., *From Normandy to the Weser*, Dorchester, The Keep Military Museum, 2006.

22 Pare, Captain G.A., RAChD, HQ 1 Wing GPR, by permission of The Eagle.

# CHAPTER 17

# Operation BERLIN

*'Glider pilots would act as guides through the enemy lines.'*

**Monday, 25 September 1944**

The medics and the wounded in the Schoonoord survived the shelling and, after a fitful night with little sleep, the sun rose. Padre George Pare was again moving from room to room, making his rounds of the shattered hotel:

> The night passed as usual, and Monday dawn brought new hope of relief once again. I had to answer a thousand times a day the question 'When will we be relieved Padre?', 'How is it going, Padre?' Are the boys sticking to it well?' and although I wanted to be truthful, I always gave optimistic but inaccurate replies … about nine o'clock I was standing in the wrecked reception room talking to our ever cheerful old sergeant, when to our amazement a little German car came quickly from the Arnhem direction, drew up smartly in front of our little sub hospital across the road, and a German officer jumped out. We watched incredulously, for our men were dug in almost facing the car. Rapidly two cracks from rifles rang out, he fell and the driver lurched forwards. I rushed across the road with the stretcher party the driver had a bullet hole in the centre of his forehead and the officer was wounded in the right upper lung. We brought them in but despite the care of our surgeons the officer died before noon. Our soldiers might be few and in desperate straits, but they allowed no liberties, as the Germans should have known full well. Obviously he had been given a wrong briefing.[1]

Only a few hundred yards uphill from the reception room, the 43rd (Wessex) Division plan had been delivered by the Dorsets to the Hartenstein at 0600 hours. After scrutinizing the document, Roy Urquhart was now left in no doubt that there would be no further attempt by XXX Corps to reinforce his exhausted division. He was instructed to plan to withdraw south across the Rhine, as soon as was practical. With the perimeter holding on by a thread in places, his options were extremely limited. After two hours considering the situation, he had made his decision. Contact was made with Major General Ivor Thomas – 1st Airborne Division would withdraw that night.

Although the previously unthinkable decision to withdraw had been taken, nightfall was still many hours away. The cover of darkness was essential if any crossing was to stand even a slender chance of success. The men still fighting in Oosterbeek would have to hold on until well after dusk; meanwhile, it would be a long and eventful day for all of them. The withdrawal plan required the glider pilots to play a vital role in the final chapter of the battle.

Unaware of the new British intent, the Germans were preparing for another momentous day of fighting. The 9th SS Panzer Division were readying two veteran Kampfgruppen to land what was intended to be the killer punch on the British division. Kampfgruppen von Allwörden and Harder were ordered to strike at the south-east corner of the British defences. Once again the German intention was to overrun the gun lines of the Light Regiment and cut the British off from the river bank. Once more it would be the disparate survivors that made up Lonsdale Force, along with the South Staffords and the glider pilots of 'G' Squadron who would endure the brunt of a complete day of concerted SS attacks. The Germans would not have it all their own way, especially the radio operators of the Light Regiment RA had picked up the German radio net and listened in to its traffic during the night. The German orders and preparations for the attack were overheard, and the troops in the likely path of the attack were warned accordingly.

The morning started with heavy rainfall and the customary 'morning hate', the first attack penetrated the British line and a number of the Light Regiments gun pits were overrun. The German attack, supported by two Mark V Panther tanks and self-propelled guns, came perilously close to reaching Oosterbeek Church. The gunners of the Light Regiment fought to stem the flow of German troops and armour. As the tanks closed on the gun lines, they depressed their howitzers and bravely engaged the formidable Panthers over open sights, their stubbornness slowing the German attack long enough for help to arrive. Relief came from their fellow gunners across the river on the south bank – the 64th Medium Regiment broke the attack up with a heavy fire mission that dropped shells amongst the British positions. This large-scale artillery fire mission was made possible by the radios carried over the river by the 4th Dorsets and their attached FOO parties. With direct communications to the Commander Royal Artillery of 43rd (Wessex) Division, coordination of artillery support was far more effective. The initial German attack was eventually beaten off with dogged determination, grenades and the bayonet. Close by, the South Staffords were locked in an equally savage struggle with the SS, the mêlée later being described as 'a snowball fight' with grenades. The Light Regiment guns were again firing over open sights, this time to blast the Germans out of one of the houses they had just wrested from the South Staffords. Lieutenant Mike Dauncey spent most of the day close to the guns fighting to hold back the SS attacks:

As the morning wore on the ominous squeak of enemy tanks began to get louder and louder. One of the parachutists gave me a gammon bomb and armed with this I went up the road accompanied by another airborne soldier to await the tanks' arrival. Eventually a tank came into sight and I ran forward and threw the bomb. Nothing happened for a long time and I began to wonder if it was ever going to explode. Then suddenly there was an enormous blast. Dust was everywhere. The tank didn't move. I just hoped and prayed it had done enough damage. Certainly it stayed stationary. When I looked around, though, my comrade had gone. As I didn't feel I could do very much more with only a German Luger pistol in my hand, I made my way back to a group of soldiers a little behind me and we formed a place to stop the enemy infantry.

More tanks soon began to roll into the vicinity. We threw a few grenades in their direction and they threw one or two at us. Slowly but surely the enemy crept towards us and I was hit in the thigh by a bullet that fortunately just went straight in and out. It certainly made me fall but it didn't break my leg. The time had now come to seek refuge in a slit trench. Wandering around the battlefield had become a very bad idea. On taking shelter, I suddenly heard a noise to my left and looked down to see a German stick grenade beside me. It went off and broke my jaw in two places. Amazingly I could still think all right, but I couldn't very easily speak and my face was a mess.

The two paratroopers put a shell dressing over my mouth. I could think clearly but felt very weak. The two chaps then helped me to the Regimental Aid Post [Ter Horst house], which unfortunately was so full that I couldn't get inside. I was left outside by the side of a dead man where I stayed for some time until awakened by the rain when I managed to put the dead man's blanket partly over myself. I couldn't get into that house though and stayed there until someone came outside and I managed to attract his attention. The medical officer had been hit and it was impossible for the orderly and Padre to do anything, as there must have been at least three-hundred chaps there.

The drill was to get a blanket, find a spot to lie down and a cup of char. Unfortunately this came out again through the hole in my chin, which I have since heard from other people was a most amazing sight. After the sleep I had recovered a little but could not talk properly. I learnt later that there were two fractures and the centre loose piece had been shoved out of position.[2]

The Germans launched similar assaults throughout the morning against British positions all around Oosterbeek, but the men of Roy Urquhart's stoical division clung on against overwhelming German pressure. The fighting close to the Airlanding Brigade headquarters was increasing in intensity. Under the cover of incessant heavy rain, a section of German infantry seized houses to the north of the Kneppelhoutweg and Sandersweg junction, thereby threatening to cut off Brigadier 'Pip' Hicks and his headquarters from the Hartenstein. As the German position was ideally situated to interrupt movement between the two British headquarters, it had to go. The task of ejecting the troublesome Germans was given to Major Dickie Dale and the glider pilots of 'C' Squadron. This they did with vigour, eliminating the threat to communications between the Airlanding Brigade and 1st Airborne Division.

The decision to withdraw over the river triggered a fresh bout of planning inside the Hartenstein. Roy Urquhart based his plan on the template of the British withdrawal from the Gallipoli peninsula in 1915. He had studied the extremely successful evacuation in great detail at Staff College, and so his own plan for the evacuation of Oosterbeek drew on lessons learnt from military history.

Outside the Hartenstein, rain and mortar bombs continued to fall, although a reduction in the frequency of the incoming mortar fire was noticed by those dug in around it. This was welcome relief for the men of 'B' Squadron, although there were still casualties. The number of pilots in 20 Flight continued to dwindle: Staff Sergeant Ernest Baker was picked off by a sniper and shortly after that Staff Sergeant Johnny Gowens was wounded when a shell splinter penetrated the overhead cover of his dugout. Staff Sergeant John McGeough of 'C' Squadron was in the vicinity of Divisional Headquarters when he too was hit:

> During a particularly heavy mortar barrage shrapnel in the left hand wounded me and Henry Woltag's back was peppered by minute bits of the same shell. Neither of us was seriously wounded but at the same time was not able to man our positions. I made my way to the regimental aid post near the Hartenstein, for some reason Henry did not come with me and I did not see him again until after the War. To my surprise I found that the doctor who dressed my wounded hand was Lieutenant Randall who had been a passenger in my glider. I did not have time to leave the aid post after treatment as it was taken over by German infantry and all of us in there were made Prisoner of War.[3]

Staff Sergeant Robert Ashby of 3 Flight, 'B' Squadron was to the south of the hotel, where he and his comrades experienced the full spectrum of weapons available to the Germans: 'My group was in a re-entrant, near Bildersweg and Benedendorpsweg where we experienced mortaring, shelling, sniper-fire, and air attack. Eventually, on the last morning, a tank drove us out. We then attached ourselves to another Glider Pilot unit in the direction of Heveadorp.'[4]

Over the course of the week, the battle had developed a routine of its own, which allowed for little respite. At their house on Pietersbergseweg, Staff Sergeant Arnold Baldwin and Staff Sergeant Bert Stroud were occupying the first-floor rear bedroom. Like everybody inside the perimeter, the two 'B' Squadron pilots were feeling the effects of battle. The cumulative stress and strain of a week's fighting were beginning to wear them down and both men must have been close to exhaustion. Arnold Baldwin recalled an incident where fatigue affected their behaviour:

Standing well back from the window, against the opposite wall, we were amazed to see a German face, wearing a German helmet, pressed up against the glass of a first floor window of a house across the allotments on the Arnhem Road. Just like a child looking into a sweet shop. The sheer stupidity of the German provoked an equal stupidity in Stroud and me. Without any thought for the consequences, we agreed he simply had to go and after a brief argument as to who had the right, which I settled by pulling rank, a round was fired with satisfactory results, the range being about 150 to 200 yards.

Shortly after this someone, I think it was Sergeant de Rungary, found a dehydrated meat cube in their kit. Bert Stroud was despatched to the cellar with a Dixie, the cube, a little water and a Tommy cooker and everyone was exhilarated at the thought of one, or possibly two, spoonfuls of stew. From here on everything began to fall apart. The smell of the stew, percolating up through the house, proved too much for some of us to resist and presently Joe Michie, Harry Crone and I were in the small room behind the scullery, which was also close to the steps to the cellar. For some unknown reason Harry Crone walked over to the door to the scullery, immediately turned about and tiptoeing back whispered, 'There's a Jerry looking through the window, what shall I do?' I could think of nothing brighter to say than 'Shoot the bastard'. We then made the uncomfortable discovery that none of us was carrying a weapon. Harry Crone rushed to a corner of the room and took a grenade from his pack and before I could stop him – I feared the partition between might be of flimsy construction – Harry had pulled the pin and lobbed it into the scullery. It made quite a noise in that small space. After a brief interlude it was possible to see, by squinting at a very acute angle through the scullery window, the potato masher grenade that the German had dropped in his panic. Bert called up from the cellar, after he heard our voices, 'What's going on up there?' I assured him that everything was OK and asked him how the stew was coming along. 'There isn't any,' said Bert. Hearing the grenade, and alarmed that the glow from the Tommy cooker might be seen, he tipped the stew over it to douse it. Quick thinking but it didn't send him up in the popularity chart.

Speculation as to what could happen next was answered early in the afternoon. I was summoned to the Para headquarters where the officer told me that a tank attack was expected shortly and our party was to move into the allotments on the other side of the road, occupy empty slit trenches and be ready to repel the attack. When I told this to the others they were as dumbfounded as I was. The only weapons we had were rifles, with very little ammunition; Joe Michie had a Sten gun and maybe Harry Crone had one or two grenades. Morale was already pretty low and this order raised all sorts of questions. Why us? Where were the Paras? Apart from the wandering sergeant major, the wounded commanding officer and his orderly, we had not seen a paratrooper anywhere. And if we were to hold the house at all costs, why abandon it in such a casual manner? The suspicion grew in my mind that the officer might be delirious from his wounds. So it was a very disgruntled party that moved into the slit trenches. All the growth in the allotments had been flattened by now, so a general view of the area was possible.

For the first time we saw the Schoonoord Hotel, standing well back from the crossroads. Occasionally German motorcycle combinations would bring wounded into the open space in front of the hotel and then leave for more. After an hour or so of waiting, and no sound, let alone sight of a tank, everyone became restless and a return to the house was suggested and in general approved. However, it was decided to hang on a bit longer. About this time I decided to walk about in a last effort to find any sign of an attack. At the same time a German motorcyclist walked out of the hotel across to his machine, we both stood looking at each other, barely a hundred yards apart, and with what could have been a look of disgust, the German started his bike and rode away. Pressure to return increased, leaving me in a very divided state of mind. On the one hand I wanted to return as much as anyone else. On the other hand I was aware that to leave without an order could mean a court martial and as I was nominally in charge, I would be the one for the high jump. But after what must have been an hour-and-a-half we trickled back to the house. We must have been under observation from the rear of the Para headquarters because soon after our return I was again summoned to the headquarters. 'Why did you leave without an order?' I was asked. Although I had spent a lot of thought on this the question was of course, unanswerable. As I stood shuffling my feet the officer said 'Never mind about that. The order has come through for our withdrawal'. He followed this up with general instructions, boots to be muffled etc.[5]

Whilst the glider pilots and the other men of his division contested every inch of ground with the much stronger Germans, Roy Urquhart and his staff rapidly formulated the orders for the withdrawal. The Division had parachuted or glided about 11,850 men into Arnhem, but the attrition of a week's fierce fighting had reduced the fighting strength of the Division to just over 2,500 men capable of making the crossing. Ironically, the operation was christened 'Operation BERLIN'. The plan, like the Gallipoli operation it had been derived from, was complicated and hinged on deception. The Germans must not realize the British were withdrawing, or they would launch a final overwhelming assault when the withdrawing airborne troops were at their most vulnerable. They had to remain convinced that the British were still fighting. The perimeter would collapse like a slowly deflating balloon; those who could not be moved would maintain the impression that the British positions were manned. The orders for Operation BERLIN were issued at 1030 hours, although by now not every unit was in contact, with the German attacks biting off chunks of the perimeter. A number of units were cut off completely, or isolated from their neighbours. Those who could not be reached by radio, or by runner, knew nothing of the withdrawal and fought on oblivious of the impending operation. One glider pilot who heard the orders directly from their author was Staff Sergeant Arthur Shackleton:

General Urquhart came into our room and called a meeting telling us that he had been ordered to evacuate the division across the river that night. Glider Pilots would act as guides through the enemy lines. We were told to keep it quiet from the division until he had notified all officers in charge. My brief was to go around Glider Pilot positions [1 Wing] informing them of what was happening and their role in the withdrawal.[6]

While the redoubtable Arthur Shackleton was completing his task carrying the order to withdraw around the 1 Wing positions, Major Ian Toler had a rare few moments of respite:

Very tired, finding it difficult to concentrate and thinking is an effort. At 1200 hours, we hear from Colonel Murray that orders for withdrawal across the river have been given ... Up till then Colonel Murray has had the Pegasus divisional flag ready for when the Second Army arrived. It never did so now we put it away. I am unshaven and in my present state probably would not have cared less. Colonel Murray is wonderful. He very tactfully suggests that if we are getting out tonight we don't want the rest of the Army to think we are tramps and offers to lend me his razor and a minute bit of lather which he has conserved over many shaves. It is amazing how much better I felt, both mentally and physically. Colonel Murray was probably suffering more than I of fatigue and mental and physical exhaustion but his example and leadership were better than mine. He was a Grenadier Guardsman, it counts for something I cannot explain.[7]

The 'B' Squadron war diary states that the Squadron received their orders for that night at 1300 hours. The men of 20 Flight would withdraw with the Squadron headquarters section, under command of Major 'Boy' Wilson. Those pilots involved in the defence of the Light Regiment RA, close to the old church, were ordered to remain with the gunners and withdraw in company with them. Operation BERLIN was set to begin at 2045 hours. The glider pilots were also tasked to mark the two withdrawal routes, Sergeant Major Billy Watt, Squadron Sergeant Major of 'B' Squadron, Captain Maurice Priest, OC 10 Flight, 'G' Squadron, and Lieutenant Herman Futter, Adjutant of 'B' Squadron were ordered to select glider pilots to act as piquets along the route.

The deception measures built into Urquhart's plan would not survive close scrutiny, or a determined attack by the Germans who he needed to keep at arms length for as long as possible. The guns on both sides of the river were to play a crucial part in suppressing any urge that the enemy might have to venture forth from their own positions that night. At 2050 hours, the Light Regiment would act in concert with the massed artillery of XXX Corps, launching an intense artillery barrage. Throughout the night, the gunners would follow a complicated and well-thought-out artillery plan designed to shield the withdrawing troops while they were at their most vulnerable. The barrage would also have the additional benefit of masking the sound of withdrawing troops. The artillery fire plan had been formulated by the gunners on the north bank of the river. Major Philip Tower and Lieutenant Paddy de Burgh worked under difficult conditions to compile the intricate details. Once complete, an element of the fire plan was laboriously encoded into 'Slidex' and transmitted to the gunner headquarters at XXX Corps. The remainder of the document, which could not be transmitted, was delivered by Major Reggie Wight-Boycott RA, who swam the river to ensure that it arrived intact. Ammunition stocks were low on both sides of the river, but there would be no holding back that night – without the guns the withdrawal would be an even more high-risk operation.

Most of the medical staff would remain behind to tend the wounded, and several radio operators would stay with their sets for a time to transmit a series of fictitious orders and associated signals traffic, to give the Germans something to listen to. There were several of the Division's units, however, which were in such isolated positions that they could not be contacted and so never received word that an evacuation was taking place. 'D' Company of the Borders, which had been effectively surrounded in the south-west of the perimeter and reduced to just nineteen men on the previous day, was one such unit, and only five of their men got away.

Those units that were able to communicate with Divisional Headquarters were ordered to fall back from their positions one by one. It was hoped that this phased withdrawal, under cover of the artillery bombardment, would maintain the deception until the last safe moment. It was in some of these positions that some of the wounded personnel who could not make the journey were employed to man weapons and radios. Noise had to be avoided, so all loose equipment had to be left behind and strips of cloth were to be wrapped around boots to deaden the distinctive sound of ammunition boots on cobbles. The heavy rain was now viewed as an ally for the withdrawing troops – it was hoped that it would further muffle the sound of movement and restrict German visibility.

The routes down to the river bank would be marked by a combination of guides and white mine tape, laid by the Royal Engineers. Glider pilots, predominantly from 1 Wing GPR, were detailed to act as guides at critical junctions, ensuring that withdrawing troops stayed on the correct track in the darkness. The first troops would begin to abandon their positions and heavy equipment at 2030 hours, before heading for the river bank. The men of 2 Wing GPR were included in the withdrawal plan for 1st Airlanding Brigade. With the surviving Poles of 3rd Polish Parachute Battalion under command, John Place was ordered to begin the extraction of his men at 2240 hours.

Whilst the plan was being circulated to headquarters and then disseminated to forward positions, fighting continued all around Oosterbeek. Like most men outside the Hartenstein, Sergeant Len Affolter was unaware of the developing plan. He and the rest of 5 Flight, 'D' Squadron, had moved with the battle back and forth from house to house on Stationsweg. By Monday morning, his flight had become widely scattered and he was now one of just two pilots holding a single house:

> After my colleague went out to see what the situation was like and did not return I was alone in a house. A little old lady came up from the cellar with a cup of tea. I didn't feel so lonely after that. An officer from another unit came in and gave me details of the proposed evacuation. When we pulled out at night the first guide I met in the woods was my missing colleague and together we made it back to base.[8]

In the south part of the perimeter, Staff Sergeant Wilf Harrison of 3 Flight, 'B' Squadron, was assisting a Polish 6-pounder gun crew, who were defending the Light Regiment's gun lines near the Old Church:

> We stayed with this gun and ended up in a defensive position of the Artillery adjacent to the old church in Oosterbeek. We were mortared incessantly during the daylight hours. We engaged a tank, which appeared through a row of cottages. Then amid all the smoke and dust my second pilot and friend, John Hunter, was killed, he was assisting on the anti tank gun. After dealing with John and covering him with a ground sheet, I made contact with two more glider pilots, Staff Sergeant Teddy Norris and Staff Sergeant Norman Jenkins of 4 Flight, 'B' Squadron, in an adjacent trench and from there at about 2200 hours we joined a column of troops wending their way to the river.[9]

Close by a group of 3 Flight pilots were among Lonsdale Force and were also fighting to hold off the German thrust toward the old church. Staff Sergeant George Nye was among them:

> At about 1700 hours, the remaining five glider pilots in our group were mustered and taken away from the Lonsdale Force by Lieutenant Rex Norton. We were to hold and defend a crossroads to the west, the position to be held until 2300 hours, later amended to 0100 hours, or until the return of Lieutenant Norton. Whilst holding the crossroads at about 1830 hours a re-supply drop was made with a pannier landing on our position and on opening it we discovered a seven-day pack of rations and most welcome cigarettes. We all took turns to sit at the bottom of the trench eating tins of food and smoking at the same time. The Lieutenant returned shortly before 0100 hours and we withdrew moving southeast towards the river.[10]

To the north of the perimeter, 2 Wing GPR were still holding their section of the Airlanding Brigade's line. Staff Sergeant Peter Gammon and 14 Flight were playing their part by resolutely holding onto the houses on Nassaulaan:

Daylight came on Monday, with it came an intense Mortar barrage hitting houses all around us. But the expected attack did not come when the barrage lifted. Instead our flight commander, Lieutenant Aubrey Pickwoad came running down the road. A most welcome sight in spite of the sad instructions about we were to retreat across the river that night. As we stood in the hall listening to what news he had, my knees started to shake and no matter what conscious effort I made, they would not stop. Accepting our assurance that there were no others in the vicinity he left with our best wishes as desultory bombs were still falling all around us. We considered now whether to booby trap the house with the two grenades we had left but decided against it as the Dutch family were still in the basement and from whom the decision to retreat had to be kept a secret.[11]

Staff Sergeant Laurie Weeden was also still with 'F' Squadron holding the house in Nassaulaan. He too remembers the receipt of the orders for BERLIN and 2 Wing's subsequent preparations that night. He was to play his own role in the extraction plan formulated by his flight commander Lieutenant Pickwoad:

Despite the ever-closer proximity of the enemy it is my recollection that it seemed remarkably quiet in our sector. I had acquired a new No 2 on my Bren gun – Nobby Smith who, so far as I can remember was from the King's Own Scottish Borderers. There was an unexploded 88mm shell just outside the front door of the house. During the afternoon one person from each house was summoned to 2 Wing headquarters and we were informed that we would be withdrawing across the Rhine that night. In the wood near the junction of Paul Krugerstraat and Hartenweg a German machine gun had been positioned, and as we were about to assemble for the withdrawal Lieutenant Pickwoad instructed me to occupy a trench nearby and to keep the machine gun covered with my Bren gun. I wonder whether Nobby Clarke and I, in our trench covering the Spandau, were now the northernmost operational troops of the Allied armies in North West Europe.[12]

West of Divisional Headquarters, just south of Utrechtseweg, 17 Flight of 'A' Squadron had been defending a position in amongst the Border Regiment. Sergeant Norman Ramsden and his mates were about to join a silent column of troops that was moving slowly south towards the river:

Staff Sergeant Flowers, Sergeant L. Jackaman and Sergeant King came crashing into our position having being cleared out by flame-throwers. In the scattered foxholes of our position we now had Staff Sergeants Lawson, Meiklejohn, Catt, Harman, Jenkins, Flowers, Ponsford and the Sergeants Harrison, Christian, Haines, King, Saunders and myself with Captain Smillie and Staff Sergeant Crook. Late in the afternoon of the 25th Major Dale came up and told us the evacuation plan. Later it started to rain steadily which certainly covered much of the movement noise. As we made our way to the river all the positions we came to were already unmanned.[13]

In the fading autumn light, Major Ian Toler watched his men prepare for their role in the river crossing and their chances of success. His diary entry sums up his mixed emotions and the mood of the men around him:

As the evening draws near a feeling of relief overcomes everyone. We feel we have not acquitted ourselves too badly and it is time to get out. Whether we shall live to see the withdrawal is another matter. The Glider Pilots are to act as guides down to the river where the Canadians are to be waiting to ferry us over in boats. Second Army will put on a hell of a bombardment to cover us and tracer across the river to mark the crossing places. We are to muffle our boots and fade away very quietly.[14]

On the south side of the river, 43rd (Wessex) Division were preparing to play their part in the evacuation: 130 Brigade would control operations, while 129 Brigade mounted a deception operation to the west near Heteren. On the river bank itself, four field companies of Sappers would work, under command of the Commander Royal Engineers, 43rd (Wessex) Division, Lieutenant Colonel M.C.A. Henniker. They were tasked with overseeing the ferry operations and manning the boats that had been gathered from the Division's column. There would be two crossing sites, the eastern crossing being roughly in line with the centre line of the perimeter. The Sappers of 43rd (Wessex) Division's 260 Field Company, RE would operate sixteen collapsible, canvas assault boats on this route. They would be supported by Canadian Sappers, from 23 Canadian Field Company, RCE, which was equipped with fourteen very robust wooden storm boats complete with outboard motors. The western crossing site was just half a mile downstream on the Heavadorp-Driel ferry route, having been established on the assumption that the Dorsets' operation had been successful. The opposite bank was, in fact, still in German hands, as was the Westerbouwing feature that dominated the ferry. A similar number of boats were allocated to the western crossing operation, manned by British Sappers from 533 Field Company, RE and Canadians from 20 Field Company, RCE. Gathering this mixed force of Sappers and their equipment was no mean feat, and not without difficulty – not all of the boats made it up to the crossing sites. The Canadians were part of the Second Army's Engineer Group, and they had to haul their boats through XXX Corps and along Hell's Highway before they could contemplate undertaking the crossing operation. The Sappers' problems were not over once they reached the assembly area. Major Michael Tucker commanded 23 Field Company:

Two floodwalls blocked the path from the off loading area to the launching sites. The first of these was about twenty feet high with banks sloping to about forty-five degrees, the second was about half the height and the slope much less severe. These obstacles became most difficult to negotiate. The heavy rain softened the ground and the churning of the men's feet, as they struggled over with the storm boats, soon created a slippery mess, which lent no footing whatsoever. Hand ropes were fixed but even with these the going was extremely difficult.[15]

On the north bank, the Commander Royal Engineers, 1st Airborne Division, Lieutenant Colonel Eddie Myers, had selected the two evacuation routes and was to coordinate the activity at both crossing sites. His remaining Sappers were laying white mine tape along sections of the route; they would also be responsible for the marshalling of troops in the reception area on the Oosterbeek side of the river.

Staff Sergeant Victor Miller and the men of 24 Flight, 'G' Squadron were detailed to mark the second route down to the river bank. As night fell, the guides were given their orders and allocated their posts:

We gathered around Captain Walchli, our Flight Commander. He called out one man, and assigned him to the spot we were standing on. 'Right Sergeant', he whispered to the man, 'you are the first one. When the men begin to file back here, direct them down this direction.' He pointed out into the darkness. 'I'll post the next man about fifty yards further on, and this will be repeated for the next half mile to a mile down towards the river.'[16]

**Notes**

1     Pare, Captain G.A., RAChD, HQ 1 Wing GPR, by permission of *The Eagle*.

2     Dauncey, Lieutenant M., 9 Flt, 'G' Sqn GPR, interview with author, February 2008.

3     McGeough, SSgt J., 'C' Sqn GPR, correspondence with Luuk Buist, 1978 onwards.

4     Ashby, SSgt R., 3 Flt, 'B' Sqn GPR, correspondence with Luuk Buist, 1991.

5     Baldwin, SSgt A., 20 Flt, 'B' Sqn GPR, by permission of *The Eagle*.

6     Shackleton, SSgt, A, 20 Flt, 'B' Sqn GPR, correspondence with the author, February 2007.

7     Toler, Major I., OC 'B' Sqn GPR, by permission of the Toler family.

8     Affolter, Sergeant L., 5 Flt, 'D' Sqn GPR, correspondence with Luuk Buist, 1991 onwards.

9     Harrison, SSgt W., 3 Flt, 'B' Sqn GPR, correspondence with Luuk Buist, 1991.

10    Nye, SSgt G., 3 Flt, 'B' Sqn GPR, by permission of *The Eagle*.

11    Gammon, SSgt P, 14 Flt, 'F' Sqn GPR, correspondence with the author, March 2008.

12    Weeden, SSgt L., 14 Flt, 'F' Sqn, GPR, correspondence with the author, March 2008.

13    Ramsden, Sgt N., 17 Flt, 'A' Sqn GPR, correspondence with Bob Hilton, April 1998.

14    Toler, Major I., OC, 'B' Sqn GPR, by permission of the Toler family.

15    Tucker, Major M., OC 23 Fd Sqn, RCE, War Diary.

16    Miller, SSgt V., 24 Flt, 'G' Sqn, GPR, *Nothing is Impossible*, Bury St Edmunds, Spellmount Ltd, 1994.

# CHAPTER 18

# The Final Hurdle

*'Then to my great relief I found the tapes, and the glider pilot in a gap in a hedge who asked, "What unit?" Then he told us which way to go.'*

**The night of 25/26 September 1944**

As dusk approached, Staff Sergeant Arnold Baldwin, like men all over the perimeter, prepared to leave his position and make his way through the darkness to the waiting Sappers and their boats at the river bank. His instructions were clear: he and the rest of the 'B' Squadron glider pilots had to wait for the troops to their front to fall back through their position, and then they could join on behind the column:

> The men withdrawing would be coming up from the direction of the church in single file, when the end of the line appeared we were to cross the road and join them. Although there was immense relief, everyone was aware that before we left, approximately 9.30 pm, there was ample time for the Germans to attack the house, as everyone was sure they would. So a plan was made to secure us as well as possible. It was decided to leave the house and stay in the garage. The handles of the double doors at the rear, facing the warehouse, were tied together with cable and when ready to move we crouched down, close to the walls on either side of the garage, keeping a sharp lookout to the street.[1]

Before the forward troops could begin their move south, they had to have confidence that the Germans would not be able to follow on close behind them. They waited for the darkness, anxiously glancing at their watches, waiting for the promised artillery support from their own guns and the heavier guns south of the river. Brigadier Hubert Essame, commanding 217 Infantry Brigade, was on the south bank, also waiting for the gunners to open fire. He described the moment the barrage began in the 43rd (Wessex) Division official history:

> At nine o'clock the whole divisional artillery opened up with overwhelming effect, tracer from the Light Anti Aircraft Regiment marking the flanks of the crossings. 'A' and 'C' Companies of the 8th Battalion the Middlesex Regiment thickened up the fire [with mortars and medium machine guns]. The noise was deafening and awesome as the first parties of Sappers carried the assault boats over the dyke walls down to the waters edge. The crews dipped their oars and disappeared into the darkness. More boats followed. Punctually, at 2140 hours, the first reached the far side and waited for the Airborne troops who were due at 2200 hours.[2]

During the day, the Main Dressing Station at the Schoonoord Hotel had been elevated to the status of Casualty Clearing Station. This was not due to any increase in capability or capacity, but to the destruction of all the other Dressing Stations by shellfire. Padre George Pare remained inside with the wounded:

> Rumours spread amongst us that the almost legendary relieving force was almost upon us, and we thought tonight we might see our liberators over the river. In the evening, the rumour that they were on the other side (which was actually true) was very strong. The fighting seemed particularly fierce, judging by the crescendo of noise, and we thought the tanks I had seen were attacking in strength. Because of the extra ferocity of fire everybody was cautioned to lie flat on the floor, and as far as possible patients were moved away from the empty window frames. Over the window spaces each evening we had contrived to rig up some sort of black-out, because the orderlies had to have a little light for their works of mercy. There were no combatant German soldiers left in the hospital as we prepared for the night. This Monday evening the former spick and span hotel was reduced to a terrible mess but somehow as a hospital it continued to function. The Operating theatre had continued to work (somehow) at full pressure, however severe the battle outside.[3]

For the men working on the south bank, the barrage was an awesome spectacle; they could not help but pause from their preparations and watch as the guns pounded the opposite bank. On the north bank, however, the Germans were feeling the full weight of an overwhelming whirlwind of high explosive and shrapnel. SS Hauptsturmführer Hans Moeller endured the withering barrage:

> The artillery bombardment intensified; explosions followed almost without let up. The earth was trembling and a curtain of fire and dirt of hitherto unknown dimensions rose over and between our positions. We ducked down and sought shelter but we still remained exposed to the blind raging of the shells. Houses burned brightly and collapsed; tree tops splintered; and the new impacts dealt death and destruction.

The withdrawal got underway as the barrage reached a crescendo, pinning many Germans down and destroying their vehicles and positions. The volume of fire made any movement in the open a dangerous and foolhardy activity. The northernmost British positions were abandoned first, as the 7th King's Own Scottish Borderers extracted themselves stealthily from their positions, carefully leaving their heavy weapons and radios unusable for Division von Tettau to find in the morning. The balloon was beginning to deflate – Operation BERLIN was in progress. There could be no turning back now – 1st Airborne Division was at its most vulnerable. With blackened faces and all loose equipment discarded or secured, the first troops were moving as silently as possible through the darkness. The two columns began to form and continued to grow in size as they passed through their waiting comrades, slowly moving towards the river. Sergeant Ernest 'Bunny' Baker was ready to leave the 2 Wing area:

> On the last day everyone was in low spirits. My pal Joe [Sergeant John W. Brown] had the lobe of his ear shot off and my right arm was painful from all the firing. We were hungry, wet and tired out. It was only a matter of a short time before we would run out of ammunition and food and would have to surrender. When informed that we would have to pull out, Joe and I had a good look at a map to make sure we knew where we were heading for. We decided to disregard the order to wrap our boots with cloth to muffle our movements because we thought it possible we would have to run, and these might trip us. We needed no urging to depart. It was agreed that, rather than creep along the sides of houses for cover, we would make a dash right across the space where the Airborne memorial now stands. Despite all that we had been through, we sped like Olympic sprinters. A mortar went off but we never heard a cry.

Gasping for breath, we arrived at the Hartenstein. This was a scene of unbelievable misery – the stench of bodies awaiting burial, the stink as the wounded were sick, the smell of medications, the groans of dying men, the words of Padres as they gave the last rites … no words of mine can convey the utter devastation that existed. However there was no sign of Joe. Around seven of us had begun the dash together and we had kept close. Nobody saw him fall or heard him cry out. In the hope that he had got through somehow I allowed myself to be rushed out and down to the river. Should I have tried to go back and find Joe? This question I can never answer to satisfy myself.[4]

Bunny's friend Joe had made it as far as the river and attempted a crossing. It is thought that he drowned as his body was later found on the south bank of the river. Sergeant Alec Williams of 'F' Squadron was among the King's Own Scottish Borderers. They were now sharing the hazards of the evacuation with them:

I was ordered to take the men in my house, after dark, to the road on the west side of the green in front of the Hartenstein. We had to wait for others to come down the road and follow them to the river. Just in case things went wrong, I was given a full briefing to take us to the river. We wrapped our boots in bits of curtain and moved out as ordered and lay alongside the road with others ahead of us in the same road. We waited and after a while a machine gun opened up firing across the green and some men ahead of us were hit. I decided not to wait any longer and told my group to follow me, holding on to the bayonet scabbard of the man in front. I followed the route given to me at the briefing and went south towards a crossroads. The King's Own Scottish Borderers behind me would persist in asking me: 'Are you sure Sarge?' at each change of direction. We walked to the road junction at the bottom of the green and turned right. Looking back I could see a long file of men following us a short way down the road. Then we turned left. The road went through trees. Our guns were firing across the river onto German targets with tracer at each side of the route to the river. It had started to rain, which was helping in hiding any noise we might make. Then an extraordinary thing happened. There was a bright light scattered on the road ahead on the right hand side, which looked like phosphorus, so I crossed to the left-hand side and walked round it. On the far side was a German soldier in a slit trench guarding a tank. He must have been asleep or thought we were Germans. We pointed our weapons at him and he raised his arms. No one said a word and the King's Own Scottish Borderer behind me wanted to put a grenade in the turret of the tank. I said no, it would rouse the Germans in the area, which would be disastrous for those following behind. We carried on past the sleeping tank towards the river. I must admit I was worried about finding the white tapes laid by other glider pilots and could imagine what I would have been called if I had led those following into an ambush or captivity. Then to my great relief I found the tapes, and the glider pilot in a gap in a hedge who asked, 'What unit?' Then he told us which way to go.[5]

The distance back to the river bank was relatively short, but it was by no means straightforward. The rain was falling heavily and it was a dark night. There was also the added complication of straying into a German patrol, or stumbling into one of their positions. The perimeter was far from secure – by the final day of the battle the British positions were not all physically linked to each other. They resembled a group of islands surrounded by hostile water, rather than a solid breakwater. German troops were able to penetrate the perimeter quite easily under cover of darkness. With all of these factors in mind, the weary columns moved slowly along their designated routes, following the white mine tape and the directions given by the glider pilots positioned at track junctions and prominent landmarks.

Despite the careful planning, several groups became disorientated in the darkness and were inevitably captured by the Germans. Staff Sergeant Bert Harget's experiences illustrate just how easy it was to become lost and confused in the rain and darkness that night:

> We had a fit man at the front and myself bringing up the rear. We all held onto the smock of the man in front. At one point we passed within a few metres of a German position – we could hear them talking – but the heavy rain deadened any noise we made and we were not seen. After about fifteen minutes I slipped on a muddy bank, lost my grip on the man in front and by the time I had regained my feet the column had disappeared. I was completely alone, so I walked in the general direction of the river and finally made contact with others near the riverbank.[6]

More than once during the night the two columns became mixed and confusion reigned for a short time. Eventually, the leading groups reached the assembly area close to the river bank, where they were received by the Sappers and marshalled into the waiting boats. Priority was given to the wounded, those who were fit waiting in line regardless of their rank. The first lift of troops from the central point was underway promptly at 2200 hours, but the boats at the Driel crossing to the west were experiencing problems.

There were few troops at the crossing point on the old ferry site and only a total of forty-eight soldiers (mainly 4th Dorsets) managed to get to the waiting Sappers, for whom it was a fruitless night, working in the shadow of the Westerbouwing feature. By the time it was realized that there were no troops able to get down to the Heavadorp ferry site, it was too late to adjust the plan and shift the vital boats the half mile west to bring them into play. The central crossing point therefore remained the main focus of the ferrying operation for the whole of the night. Despite the handicap of only using a single crossing point, the ferrying went well and for the first few hours there was little interference from the Germans.

With the withdrawal well ordered and going to plan, Staff Sergeant Bert Stroud waited his turn to join the exodus. He was to find that the Germans, although suppressed by the artillery bombardment, were not totally dormant:

> Presently the first shadowy figures passed by on the far side of the road. Then, just as they were thinking that they were safely out of it, there was a tremendous outburst of automatic fire. At first I thought that the withdrawal had been detected and was being attacked but nobody fell. The file moved steadily on and then we realised that the Germans had occupied all floors of the warehouse and were pouring fire into all floors of the house, at a range of fifteen yards.[7]

Sergeant Alec Williams of 'F' Squadron and his group had successfully extracted themselves from the 2 Wing area to the north of the perimeter. He and his fellow pilots joined a queue in the open area leading to the river:

> We came under fire and lay down in the open. The order was passed to send down the walking wounded which we did. The queue was very slow moving. An officer came down the line asking for any glider pilots. I stood up and said 'Here Sir!' He then numbered off a group of men. 'Take these to the next long groyne along the riverbank'. I led the group alongside the river until I found a groyne protruding into the water. We waited anxiously hoping we had got the right groyne. Then above the noise of gunfire we heard an outboard motor and a boat appeared. We waved at it and it came alongside, we jumped aboard urged on by the Canadian Engineer in the stern. We weaved across the river to the other side. I was

about to urge our group out of the boat and up a steep bank when mortars dropped in the river behind us and they went up the bank like racehorses.[8]

In spite of the German mortar fire, and recurring engine problems on the Canadian assault boats, the evacuation continued at a steady pace relatively unhindered. Later in the night, the situation changed as the Germans became aware of the activity on the river. Believing that XXX Corps were attempting another reinforcement operation, they began to shell the south bank. By 0130 hours the glider pilots, assigned to guarding the prisoners held in the Hartenstein tennis courts, were withdrawn and told to make their way to the boats. Staff Sergeant Joe Michie, who was ready to move off from the house he and his mates were holding, was to have an unexpected encounter with a German before he crossed the river:

Finally and not unexpectedly … we were told we were withdrawing. We moved out into the front garden. Soon, while waiting in the dark to move off, we heard the sound of grenades and Schmeisser fire in our house. Jerry had already moved in. Shells burst near us, which we were told were our own artillery from across the river. We moved back across the allotments and through the woods, behind lines of ghostly figures, with muffled boots, holding onto each others 'smock tails'. We lay face down, a hundred yards from the river. The pouring rain began to soak us from the ground up … The call came to line up for the boats, it was very orderly, like a bus queue. In the middle of our group was a chap wearing a ground sheet and a German helmet, which seemed a good idea, if he'd lost his own. A fellow queuer spoke to him. He answered in what I thought was good German. A bit of a humorist? But he continued to speak what became obvious was the real thing. This was because he really was a German – middle-aged, the war was ending! He was not a prisoner. Everybody was sympathetic, so he just came back with us. We were soon called to embark.[9]

The German guns and mortars were also directed onto the river itself, slowly whittling away the numbers of boats available to ferry troops, and causing further casualties among the boat crews and their Sappers. Undeterred by German fire, the Canadian Sappers of 23 Field Company estimated that they made close to 150 crossings in the darkness. As a consequence, they suffered seven men killed and four wounded. The slower and smaller British assault boats made less trips, so were not exposed to as much artillery fire and therefore suffered no casualties. Regardless of the nationality of the Sappers, or the size of their boats, they were a welcome sight for the men waiting on the north bank. Sergeant Frank McCaig of 2 Flight waited together with some other pilots from 'A' Squadron for a boat to cross the river:

At about 2.30 a.m. whilst crouched in a waterlogged ditch on the banks of the Neder-Rhine with all hell going on, shells and burning buildings, and this little figure trudging along on his own, a quick shout of 'Peter' and he was in the ditch with us with a gasp of sheer relief. We got one of the last boats which survived and I have his signature on the front of an 'Een Gulden' note together with those with whom I came out, K. Hiller, R. Milne (a towmaster), J.E. Edwards, Cyril Rose, Sammy Johnstone and me. These lads were mostly from A Squadron from Harwell.[10]

Staff Sergeant Arthur Shackleton, detailed off to act as a guide, made his way to the riverside:

Major Toler and I set off at about 2200 hours to take up our allotted positions in the woods. People started to come through, it started to rain. We spent the next two or three hours directing people along the safe route. Eventually the flow of people began to slow down until there were no more new arrivals. We decided to make our own way down to the river. We came across a small group of stragglers, who they were I never discovered, however Major Toler told them to keep quiet and that me being a Senior NCO would take charge of them, he would find a way to the river and return. I got them all to lay down by a bank of earth, but just then there was a burst of machine gun fire, I found myself on the ground with my right shoulder and arm numb, I called to them, but there was no answer so I looked at the first one and I realized that he was dead, as indeed were all of the others. Realising that it was useless to remain, I set off in the direction of the river meeting Major Toler on the way. We both set off for the river, I slipped down a bank into a stinking dyke, he pulled me out and off we went again. My shoulder was very painful. On reaching the river there was a boat being loaded with the wounded so Major Toler helped me into it. While crossing the river there was an explosion and I found myself in the river with a sharp pain in my left leg. It was very noisy with bursting shells and mortars, but as my ears filled with water it all went rather quiet. Not being able to swim I resigned myself to the inevitable, I felt very detached and calm, the cold water deadened the pain. I tried to think … if my body would be washed out to sea near Rotterdam or Amsterdam. Alternatively, I might get caught up in the reeds and never be found. Although I was a married man with a baby son, my only thought was for my mother who might never know what had happened to me. What strange things go through one's mind in times of battle. I felt my right leg touch the bottom of the river and thought 'it's not so deep after all' then my head hit something solid and at the same time I heard a voice say 'I have a body here, would you help me out with it?' I replied 'I am not a body, I am alive.' I think my rescuers were Canadian engineers. They dragged me out and carried me into some sort of building which was being used as a Dressing Station. There I was placed on a stretcher to await treatment. While I was waiting, a small medical orderly asked if he could have my fighting knife. I agreed on condition that he got me a packet of cigarettes, he cut the knife off my trousers, promising to return with cigarettes, I never saw him again – I will never trust the medical services again.[11]

Unaware of his co-pilot's fate, Major Ian Toler remained on the north bank, watching the boats moving back and forth by the combined light of flares, tracer and burning buildings:

The next thing I remember was seeing a boat loaded with men hit by something and start to sink. It seemed the men could not swim and were drowning. I think this simply made me go into the water although I could not get to any of them. However, once in the water I was immediately out of my depth. I have since gone back to the spot and the water is very deep and fast flowing. Although I am a fairly strong swimmer I should probably have not been able to swim the river under those conditions had it not been for another lucky break. We had been issued with an inflatable rubber ring which was for use if we had to ditch when flying our gliders. Discussing this with my second in command John Neale when we were issued with them some weeks before, I remember him saying 'I'm going to keep mine with me during the operation; it is not much weight and would be a fine thing to help one across a river in full equipment.' Remembering this I had kept mine under my smock and just before reaching the river I had blown it up. It now saved my life because I was easily able to keep afloat and swim where I liked.

My troubles were not over. I was swimming slowly, wondering whether I should strike out across the swift flowing river, which was like a picture out of Dante's Inferno – tracers ripping across where our troops were marking the crossing, flashes of guns and shells bursting all around, and mortar bombs dropping in the water. I wondered for a minute whether I would be safer totally submerged but remembered a vivid picture of fishes coming to the surface, stunned by an exploding grenade. However I decided to risk it and went right under for as long as I could hold my breath while the mortars dropped in the water all around. It seemed to work. I felt no great concussion. When I came to the surface I was just by a loaded boat with an outboard motor so hanging on to the side I let it pull me to the other side. Before going into the water I had time to take off my boots, in the approved fashion I hung around my neck. Unfortunately the books had not catered for someone being towed. When I arrived at the other side and climbed up the bank I found my boots had disappeared![12]

Ian Toler was not the only squadron commander waiting on the river bank. Major Peter Jackson, OC 'E' Squadron, arrived at the embarkation point only to find that there were no boats waiting for his men. He immediately volunteered to swim across the river to fetch one:

I divested myself of trousers, blouse and boots and entered the water, but eventually I had to give up in the face of a strong current and struggled back to the shore. Here I found all my clothes bar my trousers so I had to compromise by pulling on a long sleeved pullover using the arms as legs. This was quite comfortable except for an awkward draught where the neck of the pullover was. At last we found a boat, which was manned by four or five men who apparently knew nothing about propelling their vessel. They were all paddling on the same side with the result that they were going round in circles. We were soon brought to the shore and the party went across. On the road from the other bank we met a very old soldier tramping along in the opposite direction and asked him what he was doing. 'I am going to lay smoke, Sir' he said. 'Why?' I asked him. 'I dunno' said the soldier 'but my Officer says "Lay Smoke" and I'm bloody well going to lay smoke.'[13]

Staff Sergeant Wally Holcroft of 'F' Squadron had waited in line patiently, until finally obtaining a seat in one of the boats. He had a much less eventful crossing than Peter Jackson and reached the south bank without incident:

I was thankful when we reached the other side where willing hands helped us ashore and guides directed us along a road to the south. These guides, I believe, were men of the Dorset Regiment. It was a great relief to be among them as they went about their work silently and efficiently, though they looked strange in their 1915 style tin hats, which were so markedly different from these worn by the Airborne forces. We had to walk two or three miles to a rest centre that had been set up for us. Wet through and weary, each step I took was painful as, without socks my boots felt like sandpaper. I trudged slowly on away from the holocaust of Arnhem, I was quite content in my mind now and if I had been ordered to march to Brussels I would cheerfully have done so. The number of men already at the rest centre surprised me somewhat when I arrived. As we waited in a long queue outside a large wooden hut for a meal I began to shiver and feel the effects of my immersion in the river. I longed for a cigarette and though, during the whole of my sojourn in Holland I had missed many a meal I had never before been without a smoke. Not for long however, for soon we were admitted to the hut and served with two tins of piping hot stew, tea, cigarettes, a blanket and a tot of rum. Ron Jones waiting next in the queue to me must have thought I looked to be at death's door for he insisted that I drank his tot of rum as well. I shall never forget Ron Jones for that noble gesture.[14]

Not all were lucky enough to reach the river bank, or to cross the river. In some cases it was not possible to inform these men because they were in isolated positions, or were thought to have already been overrun by the enemy. Others lost their way en route down to the river, missed a checkpoint, or ran into an enemy position. Finally some tried to swim and drowned because they underestimated the current, or their boat was hit and they just couldn't swim. Sergeant David Hartley of 'C' Squadron stood in one of the queues waiting for assault boats to arrive:

It was here that I met up with Peter Hill, also 'C' Squadron. He also happened to come from the same home town, Darlington. Peter told me that he could not swim and was very frightened of the water. I told him I would look after him. The first thing we did was taking off our boots, and next was sitting together right on the edge of the boat. We had just started when we received a mortar bomb right in the middle of the assault boat. We were in the water before we knew it. Peter was a very good pupil, I soon got him into the long tow position and he was using his legs quite well, and most important we were getting away from the boat crossing area. The current was very strong and our plan was to let it help us all it could. Peter was starting to lag, the other side, what we could see of it, did not seem to be any nearer and I could really feel my shoulder stiffening up. I had a job to hold Peter, and after a brief struggle I lost him. I can not remember getting out of the water, changing my clothes, or being taken to a field hospital were a doctor took the rest of the shrapnel out of my shoulder.[15]

Trevor Francis was a 9 Flight Staff Sergeant attached to one of the gun batteries close to the riverbank; he and the Gunners were among the last to abandon their posts, as they were located at the base of the collapsing perimeter. He moved past the old Oosterbeek church and the home of Kate Ter Horst at about 0400 hours. Before setting off for the river, he had assisted the Gunners in making their gun unusable to the Germans by removing the gun's breech block and hiding it in a deep ditch full of water. Now, as dawn's light drew nearer, time was running out for Trevor and the men around him:

Feeling very much alone I ran through a field to the Rhine in the dark, falling over a dead cow and finally reaching a queue about one-hundred yards long, waiting for their chance to board a boat and reach the other side. They stood motionless and quiet looking like a hedge when flares came over, also the odd mortar. It was an impressive display of the discipline of the British soldier. Eventually reached the water with about one-hundred plus men in front and with daylight and two boats only left, plus the fact that a machine gunner was opening up from the broken railway bridge about five-hundred yards upstream. I decided to swim, so did about thirty others. Never having been a good swimmer, I threw my clothes in the river plus the rifle I had acquired. I saw about eight men hit by the gunner which I think gave me extra strength. After arriving at the other side, I crossed a field eventually coming across a typical country lane, so I continued along it. Now starting to worry what I would do if in my naked state I came across some Dutch women.

Fortunately this was soon solved because I came across an armoured car that had been slewed across the lane falling backwards into a ditch, lying on the front seat was a gas cape which I immediately donned. Continuing, I heard what I thought was a tank approaching, so I rolled down the bank to the hedge at the bottom and laid there motionless. The vehicle stopped and turned out to be an armoured car and to his relief, a voice called out 'Come on up mate, we saw you.' Eventually, after being given a blanket and a hot mug of tea laced with rum, I arrived in Nijmegen where I was given a bunk in a captured German barracks.[16]

At about the same time, Staff Sergeant Richard Long, of 'B' Squadron's 20 Flight, was close to the river. After making his way through the incessant rain and mortar fire with six fellow glider pilots, and after three hours of patient queuing, he had finally reached the embarkation point on the river bank. He was concerned about the ever-increasing light levels:

We saw literally hundreds of survivors awaiting their turn to board the boats that were coming into the shore only a couple at a time. They were small boats carrying only about twenty survivors. At around 5am, it was now almost daylight, we were told that a few more boats were to make the journey, otherwise the targets. As one of the boats started to pull away, another glider pilot, Jack Appleyard from Pudsey, Leeds, and I, who had been together all the time, ran by other bystanders getting onto another boat and scrambled aboard, amid shouts of 'There's too many of us as it is'. Reaching the other side of the Rhine seemed ages, yet it took only about ten minutes. We were all ushered into a large hut and given a tot of rum, almost black in colour, by someone in naval uniform. Looking back across the other side of the river we could see those left behind, several hundred I would imagine waiting to be taken as POWs, spending the rest of the war in prison camps.[17]

Sergeant Geoff Higgins of 'C' Squadron was a member of a 17-pounder gun crew situated west of the Hartenstein on the corner of Utrechtseweg and Hoofdlaan. Unaware of the plan to fall back over the river, he was awake, listening out in the darkness for German patrols:

In this situation of comparative isolation it is not surprising that we were not informed of the withdrawal. In the early hours of the morning I heard the considerable noise of heavy gunfire, and some shuffling sounds of people moving on the road. When I had summoned sufficient courage, I got out of my trench and recognising those passing as our men, I asked one what was happening. 'We are going out,' he said, 'hurry up and catch hold of my coat tails and follow on.' I informed those of the crew still left and took my place in that long line that moved slowly down towards the river. Flares lit up the sky and the line in front looked like a hedgerow. It was raining heavily, and it was cold and windy, but apart from the sound of gunfire and of the storm there was an eerie silence. I recall that although it was obvious that time was short, there was no panic. We crossed the rubble of the Old Church and came to a stop. The dawn was making its inevitable appearance, the sound of boats ceased and suddenly excited Germans firing rifles and throwing stick grenades surrounded us.[18]

As dawn drew near, most of those at the embarkation area had been evacuated but, with no more serviceable boats in operation, those that remained behind either had to surrender or brave the strong river and swim across. Stripping their battle dress off, most of those who chose to swim successfully made their way across, but the strong currents swept many of the exhausted men downstream, often washing them up into the hands of German patrols on the northern bank and a large number of men also drowned. It has been estimated that ninety-five airborne soldiers died during the evacuation and 500 men, possibly far fewer, were left on the river bank to become prisoners of war. The Germans began their usual attacks on the British positions at dawn and were greatly surprised by the ease of their progress. The wounded who had stayed behind to simulate the Division's presence, finally laid down their arms and surrendered. There was no further opposition from 1st Airborne Division – Operation MARKET GARDEN was over. Sergeant Brian Tomblin of 'E' Squadron knew nothing of the evacuation that had taken place overnight as, in the half light of dawn, he prepared for another day of fighting. However, soon after first light, the unmistakeable sound of the creaking and grinding of tank tracks indicated that something unpleasant was about to happen:

A heavy barrage of mortar shells fell on us, and, to my horror, I saw a flame-throwing tank charging through the woods at us. I retreated into my hole to avoid the belching flames of oil, and I heard the tank go straight over the top of my trench – luckily the sides didn't collapse. Looking out I saw Mike Brown run across the front of a tank, only to be shot down through his legs. The tanks trundled on past us, and those of us left alive simultaneously decided to run across an open field to the next copse of trees. Halfway across the fields machine-gun bullets ripped into us and we fell onto the Dutch soil, some wounded, some dying, but to my amazement I didn't feel anything that seemed to hurt. Nobody around me moved, so I lay there motionless for about two hours, not daring to twitch a muscle. It began to pour with rain, and as things had gone unusually quiet I reckoned that if I could get back into the last wood I might be able to work my way in another direction. Glancing around slowly I could not see anyone that appeared to be hostile; most of my comrades were dead. I jumped up and ran back to the wood; someone nasty fired at me. The bullet whined past my head, I leapt through the shrubbery and jumped straight into a slit trench containing two German soldiers, who had been sitting there resting. They seemed to be as surprised and alarmed as I was. 'Hande hoch' they shouted at me, and I had no alternative but to surrender gracefully. For me 'der var' was over.[19]

**Notes**

1       Baldwin, SSgt A., 20 Flt, 'B' Sqn GPR, by permission of *The Eagle*.

2       Essame, Major General H., *The 43rd Wessex Division at War*, London, William Clowes & Sons Ltd, 1952.

3       Pare, Captain G.A., RAChD, HQ 1 Wing, GPR, by permission of *The Eagle*.

4       Baker, Sergeant E., 16 Flt, 'F' Sqn GPR, by permission of *The Eagle*.

5       Williams, Sergeant A., 16 Flt, 'F' Sqn GPR, correspondence with Luuk Buist, 1993.

6       Harget, SSgt H., 'E' Sqn GPR, correspondence with Luuk Buist, 1991.

7       Stroud, Staff Sergeant B., 20 Flt, 'B' Sqn GPR, by permission of *The Eagle*.

8       Williams, Sergeant A., 16 Flt, 'F' Sqn GPR, correspondence with Luuk Buist, 1993.

9       Michie, SSgt J., 20 Flt, 'B' Sqn GPR, correspondence with the author.

10      McCaig, Sergeant F., 2 Flt, 'A' Sqn GPR, correspondence with Ken Greenough, 1988.

11      Shackleton, SSgt A., 20 Flt, 'B' Sqn GPR, correspondence with the author, February 2008

12      Toler, Major I., OC 'B' Sqn GPR, by permission of the Toler family.

13      Jackson, Major Peter, OC 'E' Sqn GPR, correspondence with Luuk Buist.

14      Holcroft, SSgt W., 14 Flt, 'F' Sqn GPR, 'No medals for Lt Pickwoad', September 1945.

15      Hartley, Sgt D., 'C' Sqn GPR, correspondence with Bob Hilton, 1997.

16      Francis, SSgt T., 9 Flt, 'B' Sqn GPR, by permission of *The Eagle*.

17      Long, SSgt R., 20 Flt, 'B' Sqn GPR, by permission of *The Eagle*.

18      Higgins, Sgt G., 'C' Sqn GPR, correspondence with Luuk Buist, 1991.

19      Tomblin, Sgt B., 'E' Sqn GPR, correspondence with Luuk Buist, 1991.

# CHAPTER 19

# Aftermath

*'The Glider Pilot Regiment had nearly ceased to exist.'*

The evacuation of 1st Airborne Division had gone relatively well, considering that it had ultimately hinged on a single crossing route, and that it had been executed under artillery and machine-gun fire. There were few complaints from the airborne troops about the conduct of the British and Canadian engineers, who had risked so much making repeated crossings to rescue them. The reception centres, manned by troops from 130 Brigade, had been established at short notice to administer the withdrawing airborne troops. Hot tea laced with rum had been gratefully received by most, as well as a very welcome dry blanket per man.

There was, at the time, some antipathy between the veterans of XXX Corps and those of 1st Airborne Division, each thinking the other could have done more to win the battle. There are even anecdotal accounts of barracking between the two groups as the airborne troops were driven away from the front line. The airborne troops were naturally frustrated that, despite the fact that they had fought so tenaciously to hold their perimeter long after the two days they had been expected to hold, the operation had failed. This failure was blamed on XXX Corps' inability to reach them in time. But the men of XXX Corps had been in the front line since Normandy and resented the fact that their airborne brethren were being taken out of the line so quickly. They were at the time, of course, unaware of the intensity of the fighting endured in Arnhem and Oosterbeek.

This was of little importance to those who were still on what was now the German side of the river – these issues mattered little. The arrival of dawn was greeted with some uncertainty and natural anxiety. During the night fatigue had finally overcome George Pare, and he had fallen into a deep and exhausted sleep. In the early morning light, he awoke with a sense that something was not quite right in the Schoonoord Clearing Station. The atmosphere had changed:

There was something different. What was it? I could not understand for a moment, and then I realised. Everywhere was unnaturally quiet. I struggled up and joined the RSM standing by a window space. 'Hullo Padre. Heard the news?' I had heard nothing and looked with stupefaction at the group of German soldiers standing carelessly about the road. 'No I've heard nothing, what news?' 'They've gone!' 'Who've gone?' 'The Division! Or what's left of them.' 'The Division! What? Why that was the Second Army crossing last night in all of that hell of a noise!' He looked at me with sorrow. 'Afraid not sir. Look for yourself, we really are prisoners now. I don't know why but the Army hasn't crossed over to us. Our chaps have had to retreat to them.'

My sleep sodden wits had not yet taken in the news. I shook my head. My faith in the Second Army's arrival was too strong to be shattered in a moment. 'I can't believe it.' 'Nor could I. I never thought this could happen. I …' He shrugged his shoulders in bitterness. 'Do the patients know yet?' 'A few of them in the yard. They'll have to be told – I haven't got the nerve to tell them. I think you'll have to break the news, it's the worst they'll ever have.'

My wits were beginning to function and the ugly reality began to grip me. A fit of deep depression shook me, and judging by other gloomy faces everyone suddenly felt forlorn. With a heavy heart I began my round and broke the unhappy news to the patients upstairs. Everyone tried to take the news of the calamity in good heart, but the news was too bitter, and the pretence too much. I was relieved to finish the miserable business.[1]

Shortly after, the guns of XXX Corps fell silent and the Germans began to emerge from the positions they had sheltered in overnight. SS Hauptsturmführer Moeller described his reaction as the barrage came to an unexpected and abrupt end: 'But then it stopped – all of a sudden – the silence appeared treacherous to all and almost "hurt". Was it all over? Would it start again? The Red Devils had withdrawn and disappeared during the night behind the curtain of dirt and destruction.[2]

A few miles away, safe on the other side of the river, Staff Sergeant Wally Holcroft of 'F' Squadron was directed to one of 130 Brigade's collection centres, where he received a warm meal, rum and a cigarette. No time was wasted; he remembers being ushered out to waiting transport and conveyed to Nijmegen, some 7 miles away. Any illusion of relative safety was rudely shattered:

Nijmegen as I remember it was like a town in peacetime for all the streetlights were burning. We passed over the celebrated bridge and arrived eventually at a Barrack like building which might have been a school and here another reception party awaited us. Here of course back in civilization as it were, they had facilities to deal with us. Hot water, another hot meal, and best of all beds. I slept all night like someone dead, and awoke next morning with the sound of an explosion. I thought I was back in Arnhem until I noticed the bed I was lying in. The Germans were shelling the town and one stray had dropped beneath our bedroom window shattering all the glass but blackout boards saved us from the blast. A few moments later we were ordered to get out of the building as an ammunition truck had caught fire nearby. Gathering up my clothes, which were still wet through, I dressed and went out into a large garden that surrounded the building. It was a bright and fine September morning, there seemed to be hundreds of soldiers about together with a small army of reporters and photographers who were busily engaged interviewing the survivors. I met Stanley Graham from 'E' Squadron looking most cheerful and we sat down and talked for a while discussing the past week. A few minutes later Mick Hall appeared; I was very pleased to see him. He told me he had had no difficulty getting across the river.[3]

Flying Officer Reg Lawton was also safe on the other side of the river; he too had been conveyed to Nijmegen:

The next morning I found I still had the remnants of the rags wrapped round my shoes, but it was difficult to distinguish between my socks and rags and what was left of my shoes. We found that our building was a large, four-storey block, standing on the outskirts of the town. It had a stumpy tower with a Chinese-style roof, and had been a training school for Dutch missionaries to China. My companion was a lieutenant of the Glider Pilot Regiment wearing a kilt [Jock Strathern], which excited a lot of interest as we walked through the suburb. I learned gradually the fate of several of my friends. Captain Ogilvie was seen to set off swimming, dressed only in his kilt, with a Sten gun round his neck. He was never seen again. Bill Barry had been killed while out on patrol in the woods. Shy, little Mike Dauncey was last seen by his men on top of a German tank, stuffing something through the slots.[4]

In fact, Mike Dauncey was still on the wrong side of the river, inside the home of Kate Ter Horst.

He, like many others, had been so badly wounded that he could not be evacuated. He and everybody else still in the house and its garden were taken prisoner when the Germans reached the river bank early on Tuesday morning. Although the German treatment of wounded had been exemplary, there were still those among them who believed that the victor was entitled to claim the spoils of war:

The first thing they did was take my watch, much to my annoyance, I couldn't do much about it. Things from now on were going to be different. After a few hours I was taken to a nearby house manned by nuns. Nothing happened in the way of treatment, and the following day we were taken further afield to a little known town of Apeldoorn, about ten miles away. I was with about thirty other British officers in a room when a German intelligence officer came in and told us he was very worried about the fact that there were wounded British soldiers who had yet to be found, and he wanted to know where they were. It was hard to forget the silence that greeted him. Not a word was said by anyone.

By this stage I still hadn't had any treatment for my wounds, and my condition was fast deteriorating. There was a hole in the lower part of my face, and every time I drank anything the liquid just came out. Fortunately, our regimental padre [Pare] happened to come in and saw me. To my delight I was sent to a local Dutch hospital, which gave me marvellous treatment.

Staff Sergeant Peter Clarke was fit and could have taken his chances crossing the river, but had decided not to follow his comrades out of the perimeter. Staff Sergeant Joe Kichener had come to the house on Oranjeweg, where Peter was still caring for a number of wounded. Joe Kichener had informed Peter of the withdrawal and offered him a place among the 'F' Squadron glider pilots withdrawing that night. Despite knowing this would result in his capture, he had declined the offer and remained with four casualties he had been caring for in his makeshift aid post:

Quite simply, in no way was I going to leave them on their own. It didn't occur to me to do otherwise though in retrospect I suppose it could have been argued that I was worth more as a trained Glider Pilot than as a medical orderly. Anyway when it became light on the Tuesday morning, a German officer appeared at the front door, was sympathetic and perfectly courteous and my four temporary guests were taken away to receive attention. Before long I was a prisoner and on my way to King Willem III Barracks in Apeldoorn.[5]

Joe Michie had by now reached Nijmegen, and was beginning to think about enjoying some rest:

Tommy Geary and I were sunning ourselves on a large lawn. It was wonderful to relax in the sun, everything was so calm. I pointed out a high flying Me 262 jet, there was a very sharp crack nearby! Something stuck in my scalp, blood poured down my face. Utter panic! I ran to the nearest building where I was instantly surrounded by nuns in large white hats – Angels? Tommy appeared, I said 'Am I dead Tom?' After nearly sixty years I still could not swear I was joking. I soon realised that I was in a hospital and the nuns were nurses, who picked a tiny piece of shrapnel out of my scalp – not as big as a dried pea. It was Hitler's idea to use that wonderful jet fighter to drop anti-personnel bombs instead of shooting down bombers – the purpose for which it was designed – making me one of the first people to be a casualty to a jet![6]

Staff Sergeant George Cooper was in Nijmegen where he had time to reflect on his rain-sodden experiences during the withdrawal. He had been making good progress through the darkness, when his journey was violently interrupted by an incident with a confused Polish soldier. The Pole had mistaken George for a German and opened fire on him. Luckily for the 'D' Squadron man, he was only wounded and still able to walk; in spite of his wound, he made it into a boat and managed to get across the river. He, too, was to find that Nijmegen was no safe haven:

> Having got across the river, which was running at about 5 knots thanks to the conditions, I was eventually taken to a church at Nijmegen where I was sprayed and given some medicine. Later I was taken to a wooden hut beside the main bridge in Nijmegen. A German aircraft dive bombed the bridge but it missed but succeeded in blowing my wooden hut to smithereens. By now I was not feeling too good.[7]

Staff Sergeant Trevor Francis was recovering from both the battle and his efforts to swim the river in the early hours of Tuesday morning. Like so many of the survivors of the battle, he was mentally and physically exhausted:

> In Nijmegen I was given a bunk in a former German barracks, immediately falling asleep for thirty-six hours. Realising on waking I had not eaten for eight days, I entered a barrack square where I was immediately approached by an English newspaper reporter. To my surprise I could not speak, being full of concern about the disaster of the previous ten days. The reporter just walked off in a huff. I was then taken to the cookhouse, fed and was then issued with a new battle dress. Finally I walked outside where at that precise moment a truck pulled up and Major Croot stuck his head out saying 'Are you on the Advance Party?' I instantly reacted by saying 'yes'. Twelve hours later I found myself landing back at Fairford. I felt rather lucky until a few days later I learnt that I was the only survivor to return to the hut I had shared with nine other pilots. A very nasty feeling which I found turned me away from making any further personal friendships.[8]

Major Ian Toler recorded his own experiences of the journey to Nijmegen on Tuesday, 26 September. It is obvious from his account, and comments from other veterans, that even at this stage the corridor was far from secure:

> We eventually were taken to Nijmegen, to a hospital. At some time we were in an ambulance and the driver had obviously lost his way. We felt it would be pretty ironic if he drove us back into enemy territory which we knew was not far away. However after a council of war we decided on a direction which fortunately was the right one.[9]

The administration of the survivors of 1st Airborne Division after the battle was well organized and swift. The air bridge that had been supporting MARKET GARDEN was utilized to repatriate the troops back to England as quickly as possible. Those who were wounded but fit to fly were given priority, followed by the uninjured. At ground level, things did not appear to be quite so well oiled and slick, but there were few complaints. Staff Sergeant Wally Holcroft:

> Wednesday the 27th of September found Mick and I about early. There was still no food to be had but we did scrounge a cup of tea from somewhere. Later we met Lieutenant Pickwoad who requested me to prepare a roll of all those who had got across the river, and another one of the casualties. He said it was likely that an advance party might be leaving for England that day and we might be needed. Staff Sergeant Dalzell, who was wounded at the crossing of the river, joined us later. Hartford, my Co-Pilot was wounded at the river but managed to get across and was flown direct to an English Hospital. Lieutenant Clarke also turned up later. Mick took the lists to the Lieutenant whilst I had a few words with Sergeant Major Petrie. A YMCA van arrived and I joined an enormous queue that soon formed. I

must have been waiting there for half an hour when Ginger Rice arrived to inform me to report to Lieutenant Pickwoad with all my kit and ready to move. As I had no kit, only what I stood up in, I didn't have to waste any time and when I met the Lieutenant he already had with him Mick Hall and Stanley Graham of 'E' Squadron and about twenty others from the various Squadrons. We were to be taken by road to Grave about twenty miles nearer Brussels to board a plane for England. We eventually reached a large airstrip near Grave, which had not long been in our possession and was now occupied by some Royal Army Service Corps personnel and a detachment of the Pioneer Corps. After half a day of waiting a Dakota of Transport Command was seen to be circling the field and preparing to land, so we all rushed over to the arrival point. It seemed that on the way up from Brussels the Dakota had run in to some heavy anti aircraft fire for the main planes and fuselage showed signs of a large number of hits. If the pilot was concerned about it he showed very little evidence of it. He said he had no orders to take us back to England but agreed to take us as far as Brussels. Without further ado we all climbed aboard the plane. The pilot decided the load was too great for take off and Major Croot ordered one from each, 'E' and 'F' Squadron, off the plane. I tossed a coin with Mick Hall and lost. Stan Graham was the other unlucky one. We reluctantly jumped off, feeling very disappointed, whilst the Dakota wasting no time at all flew off into the blue. Graham didn't want to return to Nijmegen nor did I for that matter, so we got in touch with the Pioneers who kindly provided a meal and suggested we might get accommodation at a nearby farmhouse for the night. The next morning we went back to the airstrip. Hours passed with not a sign of any aircraft but a party of about twenty Paratroops arrived by road, whose Officer was a supercilious looking young Captain. At half past three in the afternoon we had about given up hope and were on the point of trying to hitch hike by road to Brussels when four Dakotas came zooming over the field and after doing a circuit came in to land. The markings on the aircraft were familiar to me for they were from Blakehill Farm my own station. The Pilot whom I knew quite well invited us to his cabin and told us it would be touch and go for the machine to get off the ground for it was virtually packed with kit and men. We were last to take off so we were able to watch how the others fared. They thundered across the grass and rose with grace and majesty into the air. Away we went after them across the field at an ever-increasing speed. The perimeter of the strip seemed to race towards us and just when it appeared we must hit the fence the Pilot eased back on the control column and we rose effortlessly into the sky.[10]

Whilst Wally Holcroft and the hundreds of other survivors were being looked after and flown back across the Channel, there were still glider pilots who had evaded capture, but were marooned on the wrong side of the Rhine. Lieutenant Oliver 'Blubber' Boyd of 'C' Squadron had made an abortive attempt to cross the river during the evacuation. Now cold, wet and even more tired, he had been hiding close to the river bank for two days, in company with Captain Gordon Mills, the Flight Commander of 11 Flight, 'E' Squadron. The two officers, who were desperately looking for an opportunity to make another attempt at crossing the river, moved away from the river under cover of darkness, looking for an alternative crossing point, or a better place to lay up, when suddenly their luck ran out: 'At about 2100 hours on the 27th, as we were making our way north from the river, the enemy surprised us. Captain Mills was shot, dying instantly, and I had no option but to surrender.'[11]

Most of the survivors were moved by road through Holland and into Belgium where they were delivered to the town of Louvain. Louis Hagen described the journey back through XXX Corps lines of communication in his book *Arnhem Lift*:

On Thursday morning, the whole division left in one huge convoy along the main

Nijmegen–Brussels road. All the way to Louvain, we passed one continuous stream of transport, tanks, artillery, petrol lorries, jeeps, DUKWs and RAF vehicles. In parts of the road, where the corridor was especially narrow, we were still shelled by German artillery, and British tanks were covering the crossroads. Right down to Brussels, the road was lined with burnt-out Allied and German transport, armoured cars and tanks. Here and there were groups of crosses with German or British steel helmets on them. Everything was prepared for us in Louvain, and we lined up for our supper, tea and dinner combined, as soon as we arrived in the late afternoon. We spent the evening pub-crawling and making friends with the Belgians. The next morning we were taken to an aerodrome and embarked for England.[12]

Staff Sergeant Joe Michie made the same journey:

We were trucked along the corridor, which was not yet totally secure, passing many knocked out tanks, with Typhoon 'cab ranks' overhead. Finally excited mobs were cheering us as we entered a devastated Louvain. The next morning we took off from Brussels, flying just under heavy dark clouds, over a very rough English Channel. As usual with the 'Dak' the wings were flexing, would they fall off? Nobody seemed to have heard of post traumatic stress in those days. We landed at Lympne, then on to a USAAF station. Finally trucks to Brize Norton. I dropped off at the gate, Brenda had heard we were back and ran along the dark road repeating 'Is it really you?' I had an impressive white bandage around my head, courtesy of the Dutch nuns.[13]

Not all of the returning glider pilots experienced such seamless, stress-free flights home. Lieutenant Derek Steedman of 'D' Squadron may have felt that, having survived Arnhem, he and his fellow passengers had made the proverbial jump from the frying pan into the fire:

There were three Dakotas flying from Brussels and the lead ship got lost over the North Sea en route to Keevil. After two hours we were still over the sea when I pointed at some land far to the west. It turned out to be Bradwell. The next morning the Yank pilot offered to fly us on to Keevil. 'Not b….. likely,' the Glider Pilots replied. We opted for road transport.[14]

Major General Roy Urquhart had a less eventful and more direct trip home, in a Dakota flown by a very capable and experienced pilot. The General was flown back to England on 29 September, in Major General Paul L. Williams' personal aircraft, flown by Major Heinz of the IX Troop Carrier Command USAAF. It is ironic that, having been carried into Arnhem by Horsa, his fellow passengers on the American aircraft were a group of Glider Pilot Regiment SNCOs. The lucky men were: Staff Sergeants John Bonome, Harry Caunter and Albert Bowman, and Sergeants David Hartley and John Woodward. The return of the General was recorded by a US Signal Corps photographer at Northolt, the pictures of Roy Urquhart emerging from the Dakota, with his entourage of glider pilots, being among the most well-known images of MARKET GARDEN.

All over England, the other survivors of the battle were returning to their home airfields anxious to find out what had happened to their mates. The geography of the Arnhem area, and the confusion of battle, had dispersed the GPR squadrons over a wide area. Most were unaware of the true cost of the fighting in terms of casualties to their regiment. During the run-up to the launching of MARKET GARDEN, the GPR had been at the zenith of its strength and capabilities. The success of the glider landings in Normandy had blotted out the painful memories of Sicily, and morale and confidence had been high, as the gliders had released from their tugs over Holland.

The GPR had managed to crew a total of 667 gliders of all types, with 1,334 pilots at their controls. This total does not include the two wing padres, who flew in with their respective commanding officers. There were also a total of twelve stowaways, some of whom were RAF riggers and tug masters. A full breakdown of GPR casualties is included in the appendices of this book. Both wings had suffered heavily. 1 Wing GPR had begun the battle as the divisional reserve, a role that had resulted in their deployment close to the headquarters in the Hartenstein. This central position, and their role in the defence of the Light Regiments gun positions, had placed many of its pilots in harm's way. Lieutenant Colonel Iain Murray would eventually report that his squadrons had suffered a combined total 131 pilots killed in action and a further 253 taken prisoner. Ian Toler's 'B' Squadron and Captain Ogilvie's 'D' Squadron (Major John Lyne did not go to Arnhem as he was recovering from a broken foot suffered retrieving gliders from Normandy) had fared particularly badly, taking well over half of the dead and wounded between them.

Lieutenant Colonel John Place carried out the same grim task of collating the casualty figures for 2 Wing GPR. The grouping of his wing, under the command of 1st Airlanding Brigade, had resulted in their employment in the front line for the majority of the battle around the landing zones and the subsequent withdrawal into Oosterbeek. This prominent role in the fore of the Brigade's order of battle had come at a bloody price for the veterans of 2 Wing GPR. We can only speculate at the mood of the Wing staff as they pieced together the figures from the post-battle returns from their squadrons. The total number of 2 Wing pilots killed was eventually finalized at 228, added to which were the 466 of their comrades captured by the Germans. The largest proportion of killed, wounded and captured from 2 Wing were from 'E' and 'F' Squadrons, who had fought as an ad hoc infantry unit alongside the two remaining airlanding battalions, after the detachment of the 2nd Battalion of the South Staffords. There were forty-six glider pilots whose bodies could not be accounted for – to this day they still have no known grave. Twenty-nine of these were from 1 Wing GPR, a higher proportion compared to 2 Wing GPR, perhaps due to the weight and frequency of German artillery fire that fell in their area.

The confusion of battle meant that individual pilots were unaware of these totals, but they would soon be able to gauge the awful cost of MARKET GARDEN with their own eyes as they made their own way back to their squadron airfields. Staff Sergeant Richard Long's experiences, on his return to his 'B' Squadron billet at RAF Brize Norton, are fairly typical of those initial days:

> Going into our hut we could see the empty spaces of those who were now prisoners or who had been killed in action. After a long soak in the bath, removing about ten day's growth of beard, and with a change of clothing I felt on top of the world. Several of us from the hut made our way over to the RAF Sergeants Mess bar for a survival drink, and met an avalanche of well-wishers, back slappers, hand shakers and 'nice to see you back' echoes, although this appeared to be too much for one or two of us.
>
> At a parade next morning for a roll call to determine losses, it was found that our squadron had lost nearly sixty per cent of its pilots and as all seven squadrons were sent on the operation, it was obvious that the Glider Pilot Regiment had nearly ceased to exist.[15]

Sergeant 'Bunny' Baker had made it safely back to 'F' Squadron's home airfield in Gloucestershire. He too was anxious to find out which of his friends had made it over the river and out of Holland:

> We quickly got back to Broadwell, our base, and the following morning we were paraded. It was the saddest sight ever … the miserable few that assembled. While many who had set out were POWs, far too many were known to be dead. Perhaps the worst part of it for me was losing Joe. Despite much effort in the time which followed by his wealthy father, not a trace of Joe emerged.

The journey back home was a nightmare. It just seemed impossible that I was really on my way in one piece to see my loved ones. It was very early morning when the train pulled into Rochdale. My legs seemed like jelly as I walked the ten minutes or so to see my wife of only a few months. I had the feeling that I was in a dream and would awake back there [Arnhem].[16]

It would be weeks, or even months, before the true cost of Operation MARKET GARDEN could be calculated. Roughly 2,500 men had reached the south bank and the protection of XXX Corps. Amongst that number were 160 survivors from the 1st Polish Independent Parachute Brigade Group, and seventy-five of the ill-fated 4th Dorsets. It was estimated that ninety-five men were killed by enemy fire, as they withdrew to the river bank, or as they crossed the river. An unknown proportion of that number were drowned when their boats were hit by mortar bombs, or whilst attempting to swim the fast-flowing river. The 1st Airborne Division had taken over 11,500 men over into Holland, of which 1,440 men were killed in action or subsequently died of wounds. Five hundred had not made it into boats and were still evading capture in and around Arnhem. Eventually 200 of that number made it back to Allied lines with the aid of the Dutch Resistance. Over half of the Division were now POWs, 5,960 being in German hands. The ferocity of the fighting is reflected by the fact that nearly 3,000 of the POWs were wounded when they went into captivity. The bulk of the Division's medical staff and chaplains had remained with the wounded, 300 of whom were also taken prisoner. The Polish paratroopers who had made the hazardous crossings to reinforce the Oosterbeek perimeter had suffered fifty casualties during the initial landings and river crossings. The Poles had lost another forty-nine men killed in action, taking and holding the village of Driel. The 4th Battalion of The Dorset Regiment had lost 275 of its men after their disastrous attempt to capture the Westerbouwing feature.

Those who did make it back to England and safety were able to contact their loved ones by telephone, or by telegram, and put their minds at rest. Many had waited at home on edge since the news of the first landings had broken in the British newspapers. Not all would experience the great relief of knowing that their husband, son or brother had survived the battle in Holland. A story was written by a journalist named Grace O'Brien which explored the experiences of one family as they waited to hear what had become of their husband and father. Coincidentally, the soldier concerned was Staff Sergeant Stanley Lewis, a glider pilot in 19 Flight, 'B' Squadron. The article was published in the *News Chronicle* shortly after the battle.

Mrs Eileen Lewis had been evacuated with her two children from Watford to Whitchurch Road in Cardiff and it was here that she received a letter from Stanley's commanding officer. The letter informed the 33-year-old Eileen that her husband had been left behind in Arnhem. She was also given a letter that her husband had written prior to the operation, to be opened in the event that he did not return:

Kiddie darling,

You may never read this letter. I broke my ring yesterday. As you know I am not superstitious normally but I can't get rid of a premonition. Kiddie dearest I want to come back to you and the children more than anything in the world. I'm quite certain that I know myself better than anybody else and that includes you Kiddie. I realise my own limitations and shortcomings. I haven't exactly been the ideal husband. But I do love you, always remember that. Shortly, tomorrow maybe the show will be on and I'll be in it. I volunteered in 39 and again for this mob in 42, just because I realised this job had to be done and that it's bigger than you, me and the kiddies. I love this England, to me it is you, the kiddies, our home, and our life together. England IS home so therefore when I go tomorrow on this 'do' I'm going for you, I can't love you anymore than that. Look after the children Kiddie, I know you will. You're still young and attractive, and the best wife a man could hope for. So when the opportunity arises, as it will, don't be bound by any stupid sense of faithfulness to me, but remember I'll be far happier to know that you and the children are cared for. Can't write anymore now Kiddie, I feel a bit choked. Tell the kiddies Daddy loved them.

Your Stan

The days after receiving her letter dragged by for Eileen Lewis as she worried about Stanley and what would become of her and their children: two-year-old Pamela and nine-month-old son, Kenvyn. Some time later another letter arrived – the handwriting was unfamiliar and Eileen feared the worst. The opening words could have done little to allay her fears, but she read on: 'I'm afraid this is a rather difficult letter for me to write, but don't imagine from these few words that anything is seriously wrong. Far from it, your husband was quite cheerful and comfortable when I last saw him and believe me.'

As Eileen felt a wave of relief flow over her, she realized the letter had come from Staff Sergeant George Cawthray, Stanley's closest friend in the Glider Pilot Regiment. George filled in the gaps in the knowledge that Eileen had of the battle. He told her that he and Stan had been together when they received the order to fall back and withdraw over the river. Stan had some serious shrapnel wounds and was not able to make it across the river. The two friends shook hands, before separating and Stan insisted that George took his wallet saying 'Get this wallet back to Kiddie for me.'

George had made Stan as comfortable as possible, before leaving to make his way down to the river bank, with the precious wallet stuffed in the pocket of his smock. George had ended up in the river, swimming for his life, as mortar rounds landed in the water all around him. He had been wounded in the head but, blinded by blood from head wounds, he had continued to swim desperately for the opposite shore. It was from hospital that he had fulfilled his promise, and posted the letter and his friend's wallet to Stan's precious 'Kiddie'. The letter continued: 'I am very lucky to be alive myself, having had my nose and both lips shot away as well as bullet wounds in the head. Once again please don't worry bout Stanley, he's being well cared for.'

Grace O'Brien's article concluded with the information that Eileen Lewis had also received official notification that her husband was safe and well as a prisoner of war in Germany. Stanley was imprisoned with many fellow glider pilots in the north of Germany, in Stalag 11B, outside the town of Fallingbostel.

The wives and sweethearts of the 1st Airborne Division were, of course, not alone in their grief and anxiety. The battle to protect the aerial armada, and the subsequent resupply operations, had also come at a cost. The attrition of Allied aircraft and crews had been almost constant – the sometimes suicidal bravery of the transport crews has been singled out by almost every surviving veteran. The price of that bravery was also painfully high, with seventy-nine aircraft being lost around Arnhem itself. The RAF lost sixty-eight aircraft from 38 and 46 Groups, 160 British and Commonwealth aircrew were killed and a further eighty taken prisoner. The Royal Army Service Corps also suffered significant casualties: among its air despatchers, seventy-nine of their number were killed and forty-four taken prisoner. American transport crews also paid a penalty for their participation in the operation, with twenty-seven USAAF aircrew being killed and three captured. The absence of fighter cover and ground-attack aircraft is, understandably, a contentious subject for many veterans. However, the activity of many of the Allied fighter squadrons took place at high altitude and out of view of the troops on the ground. A total of 110 Allied fighters failed to return from missions mounted in support of MARKET GARDEN.

Many seriously wounded glider pilots were unaware of the true cost of the operation for weeks, being in limbo as they were moved slowly back to England through the medical evacuation chain. One of these unfortunate casualties was Staff Sergeant Arthur Shackleton. Although he had made it across the river, Arthur had been too badly wounded to be evacuated immediately by air. He, like many others, would have a longer, more complicated and less glamorous journey back to England:

On the operating table the surgeon had told me that I had a bullet in my shoulder, it was embedded in the bone which he was reluctant to play about with. The shrapnel in my leg may work itself free in later years he then told me, the shrapnel and the bullet are still there! I was placed in an ambulance and taken to the civilian hospital in Nijmegen where I was given morphine and placed in a corridor, still on my stretcher. While there, they brought me a bowl of soup, it tasted like nectar, but fifteen minutes later it all came back up. It was at about this time that the Germans dropped a bomb on the hospital shattering the window above me. I remember thinking 'The buggers are determined to have me.' Later, I was given some sort of liquid food, this I managed to keep down, and I remained on this diet for the next three days.

During one night I was placed in an ambulance which was part of a convoy taking the wounded to the rear area. We were under the command of a Major who told us that we might be stopped by the Germans further down the corridor, so if we had any arms or ammunition to get rid of them now. Sure enough we were stopped, the door opened and a German soldier came aboard, looked around and went out again. Soon we were moving again. By this time dawn was breaking and I saw through my window we were on some kind of airstrip. I later found out that this was Eindhoven. We were loaded onto an aeroplane, I was still on my stretcher. The next stop was Brussels where we were taken to another civilian hospital. More probing, same result, bullet far too embedded in the bone to remove. I remember that the nurses were all nuns and very dedicated. They introduced me to solid food again and kept my morphine going and most importantly they brought me fifty cigarettes!

The next morning an elderly nun arrived to tell me that they were going to give me a bath, they took me into a bathroom and began to undress me. I was embarrassed at first, but soon lost my inhibitions. They helped me into a lovely warm bath full of soap suds, and left me to soak off twelve days of sand and grime, it was heavenly. I lay there soaking and smoking … what bliss. They then returned to finish me off, I felt like a normal man again.

That night, someone came to take me to an ambulance (along with more wounded) to an airfield where they loaded us all onto a Dakota (still on my stretcher). While there the pilot came on board, he noticed my red beret and my cap badge which I had hung on to. I remember him saying he was stationed at RAF Broadwell and that we would be landing at Down Ampney where there were facilities to deal with the wounded. On landing, we were taken to a building (still on my stretcher). While there they took all of our particulars, redressed our wounds and fed us all. I had just got to sleep, when I was woken up and told that we were going to a railway siding to be put on an ambulance train. 'Why did they always move us by night?'

Arriving at the station, a long Red Cross train awaited us, floodlights all over the place, lots of nurses bringing cups of tea, cakes and cigarettes. All of this about 3 am in the morning. We were loaded onto the train, me on the top rack (still on my stretcher). I remember some reporter coming into the carriage saying that he had heard there was a soldier from Arnhem on board. I did not feel like talking about the battle so I kept quiet.

Eventually we moved off and ended up at New Street Station in Birmingham. From there we moved by ambulance to The Queen Elizabeth Hospital where I was put into a proper bed. I finally said a tearful goodbye to my stretcher! I had wonderful care while at this hospital. I was discharged in November and found my way back to 'B' Squadron which by this time had moved to RAF Earls Colne in Essex.[17]

Arthur's return to Earls Colne, rather than to Brize Norton in Oxfordshire, was linked to the preparations for another airborne assault on the Rhine. The terrible losses incurred by the Regiment at Arnhem were proportionally higher than any other unit that had fought in the battle, but there could be no let-up in the effort to gain a foothold in Germany. The reasons for the failure of MARKET GARDEN were under investigation almost immediately. Major General James Gavin, the commander of the 82nd US Airborne Division, was sure he had identified one of the weaknesses in the American element of the plan. The issue featured so prominently in his mind that even as the 1st Airborne Division was preparing itself for Operation BERLIN, he had taken the time to write a lengthy and detailed letter on the subject. He wrote to General Paul L. Williams, the commander of IX US Troop Carrier Command. The letter was dated 25 September 1944, and the subject was the training and employment of American Glider Pilots:

In looking back over the past weeks' operations, one of the outstanding things, in my opinion, and one thing in most urgent need of correction, is the method of handling our glider pilots. I do not believe there is anyone in the combat area more eager and anxious to do the correct thing and yet so completely, individually and collectively, incapable of doing it, than glider pilots.

Despite their individual willingness to help, I feel that they were definitely a liability to me. Many of them arrived without blankets, some without rations and water, and a few improperly armed and equipped. They lacked organization of their own because, they stated, frequent transfer from one Troop Carrier Command unit to another. Despite the instructions that were issued to them to move via command channels to Division Headquarters, they frequently became involved in small unit actions to the extent that satisfied their passing curiosity, or simply left to visit nearby towns. In an airborne operation where, if properly planned, the first few hours are the quietest, this can be very harmful, since all units tend to lose control because of the many people wandering about aimlessly, improperly equipped, out of uniform, without individual or unit responsibilities. When the enemy reaction builds up and his attack builds up and his attack increases in violence and intensity, the necessity for every man to be on the job at the right place, doing his assigned task, is imperative. At this time glider pilots without unit assignment and improperly trained, aimlessly wandering about, cause confusion and generally get in the way and have to be taken care of.

In this division, glider pilots were used to control traffic, to recover supplies from LZs, guard prisoners, and finally were assigned a defensive role with one of the regiments at a time when they were badly needed.

I feel very keenly that the glider pilot problem at the moment is one of our greatest unsolved problems. I believe now that they should be assigned to airborne units, take training with the units and have a certain number of flight hours allocated periodically for flight training. I am also convinced that airborne unit co-pilots should have flight training so as to be capable of flying the glider if the pilot is hit.[18]

One can only speculate what would have happened in Arnhem and Oosterbeek, if British glider pilots had been trained and deployed in similar fashion to their American counterparts. Conversely, it is also difficult not to wonder how the availability of two battalions of American glider pilots, modelled on the Glider Pilot Regiment, could have influenced the outcome of the battle for Nijmegen Bridge. Certainly the presence of such a credible force might have released more American airborne infantry from the defence of their landing zones, to complete their division's primary task of seizing the vital bridge. The role played by the officers and men of the GPR, from the heady moments of the first landing until the low point of the evacuation back across the river, vindicated the 'total soldier' doctrine imbued into the training of the regiment by Colonel George Chatterton. It was, however, that ability to fulfil so many roles, combined with their status as reserve troops, that led to their frequent employment in harm's way. The cost to the Regiment in terms of casualties was to be irreparable.

A major effort was underway to reconstitute the GPR in time for the next operation; this also involved the relocation of glider squadrons and their supporting tug aircraft to English airfields, closer to Germany. The decimation of the Glider Pilot Regiment at Arnhem accelerated a decision, taken by the Air Ministry shortly after the Normandy landings, to augment the Regiment with surplus RAF pilots. The original decision had been taken due to the cost of training glider pilots, using the 'total soldier' template, and the abundance of surplus plots trained overseas for the RAF. These pilots volunteered for duties with the GPR and arrived in their squadrons after Arnhem. They were integrated as quickly as possible and bravely flew into Germany, alongside their GPR colleagues. In spite of their minimal training in fieldcraft and basic infantry tactics, they acquitted themselves well. There were, of course, some new GPR pilots who had been undergoing training during the Arnhem operation and joined the Regiment for what was to be the last British airborne operation of the war.

The failure to secure a crossing point over the Rhine had been a setback for Montgomery, but there could be no turning away from the barrier of the river. There was no alternative route, no flank to be turned. The Rhine had to be crossed, and airborne troops would be needed to play a part in it. The men of 6th Airborne Division were destined to land on the far bank of the river, and they would need gliders to carry their own Airlanding Brigade, its troops, guns and equipment.

The plan, for what was to be the final battle of the Glider Pilot Regiment, incorporated all of the still bitter lessons from MARKET GARDEN. The plan for Operation VARSITY was kept as simple as possible. This time the airborne troops would be delivered in one single overwhelming lift. The attack would be supported by powerful artillery bombardments, in conjunction with huge bombing raids. Most importantly, the ground forces would cross the river before the first paratrooper, or glider, touched German soil. The initial landings, which began at 1000 hours on 24 March 1945, were a great success. This time resupply flights were overhead six hours after the initial landings. The final operation to cross the Rhine was declared a success at about 1500 hours on the same day. Although it was deemed to be a great success, it was no walkover. The Glider Pilot Regiment and its RAF reinforcements suffered a significant number of casualties as they made their landings under fire from German defences. A total of 101 pilots were killed, the majority in the first hour of the landing.

In spite of the success of Operation VARSITY and the landings in Normandy, it is MARKET GARDEN that dominates the brief history of this unique regiment of soldier pilots. The operation that Field Marshal Montgomery declared 90 per cent successful had torn the heart out of the GPR just at the moment when it was at the peak of its strength and capability. Even if Arnhem Bridge had been held, and XXX Corps had managed to fight through and relieve the shattered remnants of 1st Airborne Division, the outcome could only have been classed as a pyrrhic victory.

The conduct of the men of the Glider Pilot Regiment in Arnhem and Oosterbeek, as individuals and as a regiment of soldiers, was truly exemplary. However, many have never heard of what was one of the most capable, but short-lived, regiments in British Army history. We hope that this book will go some way to rectifying this, and that it will ensure that their courage and sacrifice will be remembered by future generations. It is difficult to summarize the contribution made by the GPR to the battle, looking back from a distance of sixty or more years. We have, therefore, looked to a man who commanded some of them and witnessed their actions during the battle. It is Brigadier 'Shan' Hackett, the commander of the 4th Parachute Brigade at Arnhem, a man renowned for setting the highest of standards for troops under his command, who will have the last word. It was he, who wrote this enduring epitaph to the Regiment:

> Our Glider Pilots were not only very high grade airmen – I believe that the Glider Pilot Regiment was the finest body of soldiers that the British Army produced in World War Two.

## Notes

1      Pare, Captain G.A., RAChD, HQ 1 Wing, GPR, by permission of *The Eagle*.

2      Moeller, Hsf and Kershaw, R., *It Never Snows in September*, Hersham, Ian Allan Ltd, 1990, p. 301.

3      Holcroft, SSgt W., 14 Flt, 'F' Sqn GPR, 'No medals for Lt Pickwoad', September 1945.

4      Lawton, FO R., 190 Sqn RAF, 'Harvest of Ten Years', by permission of Airborne Museum Hartenstein.

5      Clarke, SSgt P., 10 Flt, 'G' Sqn GPR, correspondence with the author, November 2007.

6      Michie, SSgt J., 20 Flt, 'B' Sqn GPR, correspondence with the author, 2007.

7      Cooper, SSgt G., 13 Flt, 'D' Sqn GPR, correspondence with Major Steve Elsey AAC, March 2005.

8      Francis, SSgt T., 9 Flt, 'B' Sqn GPR, by permission of *The Eagle*.

9      Toler, Major I., OC 'B' Sqn GPR, by permission of the Toler family.

10     Holcroft, SSgt W., 14 Flt, 'F' Sqn GPR, 'No medals for Lt Pickwoad', September 1945.

11     Boyd, Lieutenant O., 'C' Sqn GPR, Account of Escape, National Archives WO208/3352.

12     Hagen, Sergeant L., 8 Flt, 'D' Sqn, GPR, *Arnhem Lift*, Barnsley, Pen & Sword Ltd, 2001, p. 82.

13     Michie, SSgt, J, 20 Flt, 'B' Sqn GPR, by permission of *The Eagle*.

14     Steedman, Lt, D, 13 Flt, 'D' Sqn GPR, correspondence with Luuk Buist

15     Long, SSgt, R, 20 Flt, 'B' Sqn GPR, by permission of *The Eagle*.

16     Baker, Sgt, E, 16 Flt, 'F' Sqn GPR, by permission of *The Eagle*.

17     Shackleton, SSgt, 20 Flt, B' Sqn GPR, correspondence with the author Feb 2007.

18     Devlin, Gerard M., *Silent Wings*, Mackays of Chatham Ltd, Kent, 1985.

# Appendix 1

*GPR Wing - Establishment Table*

**I/120/1** (3 pages)
Notified in A.C.Is. 9th February, 1944
Effective date 29th December, 1943

Copy No.............

| Amdt. No. | -- |
|---|---|
| Date    ... | 29 Dec., '43 |
| Officers ... | 8 |
| O.Rs.    ... | 36 |
| Total    ... | 44 |
| M.Cs.   ... | 7 |
| Vehicles ... | 7 |
| Trailers  ... | |

## HEADQUARTERS, A GLIDER PILOT WING
(Designed to command from 2 to 6 glider pilot squadrons)
(Not to be implemented until receipt of instructions from the War Office)
### WAR ESTABLISHMENT
#### (i) PERSONNEL

79/W.E./8315 (S.D.3)

**Headquarters section-**

| | |
|---|---|
| Wing commander (lieutenant-colonel) | 1 |
| Second-in-command (major) | 1 |
| Adjutant (captain)    ...    ...    ...    ...    ... | 1 |
| Administrative officer (subaltern)    ...    ...    ... | 1 |
| **Total, officers**    ...    ...    ...    ... | **4** |
| Regimental serjeant-major (pilot)    ...    ...    ... | 1 |
| Clerk    ...    ...    ...    ...    ...    ... | 1 |
| **Total, warrant officers and serjeants**    ...    ... | **2** |
| Clerks (includes 1 corporal)    ...    ...    ... | 2 |
| Batman    ...    ...    ...    ...    ...    ... | 1 |
| Batman-driver    ...    ...    ...    ...    ... | 1 |
| **Total, rank and file** ...    ...    ...    ... | **4** |
| **Total, other ranks**    ...    ...    ...    ... | **6** |
| **Total, headquarters** ...    ...    ...    ... | **10** |

[B 161-I]

# HEADQUARTERS, A GLIDER PILOT WING
## WAR ESTABLISHMENT  - Continued
### (i) PERSONNEL  -  Continued

**Operations and intelligence section section -**

Captain (operations)

Intelligence officer (subaltern)

| | | | | | |
|---|---|---|---|---|---|
| **Total, officers** | ... | ... | ... | ... | **2** |

| | | | | | |
|---|---|---|---|---|---|
| Intelligence serjeant | ... | ... | ... | ... | 1 |
| Clerks (includes 1 lance-corporal) | | ... | ... | ... | 2 |
| Batman-driver | ... | ... | ... | ... | 1 |
| **Total, other ranks** | ... | ... | ... | ... | **4** |
| **Total, operations and intelligence section** | ... | | ... | | **6** |

**Administrative section -**

| | | | | | |
|---|---|---|---|---|---|
| Quarter-master | ... | ... | ... | ... | 1 |
| **Total, officers** | ... | ... | ... | ... | **1** |

| | | | | | |
|---|---|---|---|---|---|
| Regimental quarter-master-serjeant | | ... | ... | ... | 1 |
| Batman | ... | ... | ... | ... | ... | 1 |
| Batman-driver | ... | ... | ... | ... | 1 |
| Clerk | ... | ... | ... | ... | ... | 1 |
| Driver-mechanic (lance-corporal) ... | | ... | ... | ... | 1 |
| Drivers, I.C | ... | ... | ... | ... | 3 |
| Equipment repairer | ... | ... | ... | ... | 1 |
| Motor-cycle orderlies | ... | ... | ... | ... | 3 |
| Orderlies | ... | ... | ... | ... | 2 |
| Postman (lance-corporal) | ... | ... | ... | ... | 1 |
| Sanitary dutyman | ... | ... | ... | ... | 1 |
| Storeman | ... | ... | ... | ... | 1 |
| Water dutyman (trained as driver, I.C.) | | ... | ... | ... | 1 |
| **Total, other ranks** | ... | ... | ... | ... | **18** |
| **Total, administrative section** | ... | ... | ... | **19** |

Attached-

| | | | | | |
|---|---|---|---|---|---|
| R.A.Ch.D.-Chaplain | ... | ... | ... | ... | 1 |
| R.A.M.C.- Nursing orderly (corporal) | | ... | ... | ... | 1 |
| R.A.O.C.-Shoemaker (corporal) | ... | ... | ... | ... | 1 |

# HEADQUARTERS, A GLIDER PILOT WING
## WAR ESTABLISHMENT - Continued
### (i) PERSONNEL - Continued

**R.E.M.E. -**

| | | | | | |
|---|---|---|---|---|---|
| Armourer (serjeant) ... | ... | ... | ... | ... | 1 |
| Vehicle mechanic (corporal) | ... | ... | ... | ... | 1 |
| **Total, officers** | ... | ... | ... | ... | **2** |
| A.C.C. - Cooks (includes 1 for officers) | | ... | ... | ... | 3 |
| A.P.T.C. - Instructor ... | ... | ... | ... | ... | 1 |
| **Total, attached** | ... | ... | ... | ... | **9** |
| **Total, headquarters, a glider pilot wing** | | ... | ... | **44** |

### (ii) TRANSPORT

| DETAIL | HEADQUARTERS SECTION | OPERATIONS AND INTELLIGENCE SECTION | ADMINISTRATIVE SECTION |
|---|---|---|---|
| Bicycles ... ... ... | ... | ... | 2 |
| Motor-cycles, solo ... ... | 1 | 2 | 4 |
| Cars- | | | |
|     2-seater, 4x2 (1 in headquarters section for chaplain) | 1 | 1 | ... |
|     4-seater, 4x2 ... ... | 1 | ... | ... |
| Trucks, 15-CWT., 4x2- | | | |
|     G.S. ... ... ... | ... | ... | 2 |
|     Water ... ... ... | ... | ... | 1 |
| Lorry, 3-ton, 4x2, G.S. ... ... | ... | ... | 1 |

### NOTE ON FIRST REINFORCEMENTS

| | | | | | |
|---|---|---|---|---|---|
| First reinforcements - | | | | | |
|     Subaltern (pilot) | ... | ... | ... | ... | 1 |
|     Rank and file | ... | ... | ... | ... | 2 |

3000 2/44 W.O.P. 655 (6_)

# Appendix 2

*GPR Squadron - Establishment Table*

**I/121/1** (2 pages)
Notified in A.C.Is. 9th February, 1944
Effective date 29th December, 1943

<table>
<tr><td colspan="2">

**CONFIDENTIAL**

THIS DOCUMENT IS THE PROPERTY OF H.B.M. GOVERNMENT, and is issued for the information of officers and responsible officials.

The officer or official in possession of the document will be responsible for its safe custody and that its contents are not disclosed to any unauthorised person The document will be kept under lock and key when not in actual use.

Officers commanding units and establishments. &c., are responsible that appropriate circulation is given to this document.

</td></tr>
</table>

Copy No............

| | |
|---|---|
| Amdt. No. | -- |
| Date ... | 29 Dec., '43 |
| Officers ... | 4 |
| O.Rs. ... | 17 |
| Total ... | 21 |
| M.Cs. ... | 3 |
| Vehicles ... | 4 |
| Trailers ... | ... |

## HEADQUARTERS, A GLIDER PILOT SQUADRON
(Designed to command from 2 to 6 glider pilot flights)
(Not to be implemented until receipt of instructions from the War Office)
### WAR ESTABLISHMENT
(i) PERSONNEL

79/W.E./8317 (S.D.3)

| | |
|---|---:|
| Squadron commander (major) | 1 |
| Second-in-command (captain) | 1 |
| Subaltern (for intelligence duties) | 1 |
| Adjutant (subaltern) ... ... ... ... ... | 1 |
| **Total, officers** ... ... ... ... | **4** |
| Squadron serjeant-major (pilot) ... ... ... ... | 1 |
| Squadron quarter-master-serjeant ... ... ... | 1 |
| Duty serjeant ... ... ... ... ... | 1 |
| **Total, warrant officers staff-serjeants and Serjeants** ... | **3** |
| Batman ... ... ... ... ... ... | 1 |
| Batman-driver ... ... ... ... ... | 1 |
| Clerks (includes 1 corporal) ... ... ... ... | 2 |
| Drivers, I.C. ... ... ... ... ... | 2 |

[B 161-I]

305

# HEADQUARTERS, A GLIDER PILOT SQUADRON
## WAR ESTABLISHMENT  - Continued
### (i) PERSONNEL  - Continued

| | | | | | | |
|---|---|---|---|---|---|---|
| Orderlie   ... | ... | ... | ... | ... | ... | 1 |
| Sanitary dutyman | ... | ... | ... | ... | ... | 1 |
| Storeman  ... | ... | ... | ... | ... | ... | 1 |
| Vehicle-mechanic | ... | ... | ... | ... | ... | 1 |
| Water dutyman (trained as driver, I.C.) | | ... | ... | ... | ... | <u>1</u> |
| Total, rank and file   ... | | ... | ... | ... | ... | <u>11</u> |
| Total, other ranks   ... | | ... | ... | ... | ... | <u>14</u> |
| Total, all ranks | | ... | ... | ... | ... | <u>18</u> |
| Attached- | | | | | | |
| R.A.M.C.- Nursing orderly | | ... | ... | ... | ... | 1 |
| A.C.C.-Cooks   ... | ... | ... | ... | ... | ... | 2 |
| Total, attached   ... | | ... | ... | ... | ... | <u>3</u> |
| Total, headquarters, a glider pilot squadron | | | | | ... | <u>21</u> |

### (ii) TRANSPORT

| | | | | | | |
|---|---|---|---|---|---|---|
| Bicycles   ... | ... | ... | ... | ... | ... | 2 |
| Motor-cycles, solo | ... | ... | ... | ... | ... | 3 |
| Car, 2-seater, 4x2 | ... | ... | ... | ... | ... | 1 |
| Trucks, 15-CWT., 4x2 - | | | | | | |
| G.S.   ... | ... | ... | ... | ... | ... | 1 |
| Water   ... | ... | ... | ... | ... | ... | 1 |
| Lorry, 3-ton, 4x2, G.S.   ... | ... | ... | ... | ... | ... | 1 |

### NOTE ON FIRST REINFORCEMENTS

| | | | | | |
|---|---|---|---|---|---|
| First reinforcements - | | | | | |
| Subaltern (pilot) | ... | ... | ... | ... | 1 |
| Rank and file | ... | ... | ... | ... | 2 |

3000  2/44  W.O.P.  655  (6_)

# Appendix 3

*GPR Flight - Establishment Table*

**I/121/1** (2 pages)
Notified in A.C.Is. 9th February, 1944
Effective date 29th December, 1943

<table>
<tr><td rowspan="8">

**CONFIDENTIAL**

THIS DOCUMENT IS THE PROPERTY OF H.B.M. GOVERNMENT, and is issued for the information of officers and responsible officials.
The officer or official in possession of the document will be responsible for its safe custody and that its contents are not disclosed to any unauthorised person
The document will be kept under lock and key when not in actual use.
Officers commanding units and establishments. &c., are responsible that appropriate circulation is given to this document.

</td><td colspan="2">Copy No.............</td></tr>
<tr><td>Amdt. No.</td><td>--</td></tr>
<tr><td>Date ...</td><td>29 Dec., '43</td></tr>
<tr><td>Officers ...</td><td>4</td></tr>
<tr><td>O.Rs. ...</td><td>47</td></tr>
<tr><td>Total ...</td><td>51</td></tr>
<tr><td>M.Cs. ...</td><td>4</td></tr>
<tr><td>Vehicles ...</td><td>1</td></tr>
<tr><td>Trailers ...</td><td>...</td></tr>
</table>

## A GLIDER PILOT FLIGHT
(Not to be implemented until receipt of instructions from the War Office)
### WAR ESTABLISHMENT
(i) PERSONNEL

79/W.E./8317 (S.D.3)

| DETAIL | HEADQUARTERS | THREE SECTIONS (EACH) | TOTAL, A GLIDER PILOT FLIGHT |
|---|---|---|---|
| Flight commander (captain) | 1 | ... | 1 |
| Section commanders (subalterns) (pilots) ... | 1 | 3 | |
| **Total officers** ... ... | 1 | 1 | 4 |
| Staff-serjeants and serjeants (pilots) (a) ... | 1 | 13 | 40 |
| Towmaster ... ... ... | 1 | ... | 1 |
| **Total staff-serjeants and serjeants** ... | 2 | 13 | 41 |
| Clerk (lance-corporal) ... ... | 1 | ... | 1 |
| Badmen ... ... ... | 2 | ... | 2 |
| Driver, I.C. ... ... ... | 1 | ... | 1 |
| **Total, rank and file** ... ... | 4 | ... | 4 |
| **Total, other ranks** ... ... | 6 | 13 | 45 |
| **Total, all ranks** ... ... | 7 | 14 | 49 |

[B 161-I]

307

# A GLIDER PILOT FLIGHT
## WAR ESTABLISHMENT  - Continued
### (i) PERSONNEL  -  Continued

| DETAIL | HEADQUARTERS | THREE SECTIONS (EACH) | TOTAL, A GLIDER PILOT FLIGHT |
|---|---|---|---|
| Attached- | | | |
| A.C.C.-Cooks          ...          ... | 2 | ... | 2 |
| **Total, a glider pilot flight**   ... | 9 | 14 | 51 |

### (i) TRANSPORT

| | | | |
|---|---|---|---|
| Motor-cycles, solo          ...          ... | 1 | 1 | 4 |
| Trucks, 15-CWT., 4x2 G.S.  ...          ... | 1 | ... | 1 |

### (i) WEAPONS

L.M.Gs., .303-inch          ...          ...          ...          2

(a) 50 per cent may be staff-serjeants

### NOTE ON FIRST REINFORCEMENTS

First reinforcements -

Subaltern          ...          ...          ...          ...          1

Staff-serjeants or serjeants          ...          ...          ...          2

3000  2/44  W.O.P.  6553

308

# Appendix 4

*Airlanding Battalion Loading Plan*

## APPX A TO III FD SERVICE MANUAL PART IV.

### SUMMARY OF ALLOTMENT OF PERSONNEL, VEHS AND 6 PDRS TO GLIDERS

| No. of gliders | Sub-unit | Tpt | | | | | | | | HQ Coy | | | | | | SP Coy | | | | Rifle Coys | (a) Att | Total | Remarks |
|---|---|---|---|---|---|---|---|---|---|---|---|---|---|---|---|---|---|---|---|---|---|---|---|
| | | FC's | MkV Cycles | MC's Lt | MC's Hy | HC's | Jeeps | Trailers | 6 Prs | Bn HQ | HQ | Sig Pl | Pnr Pl | Tpt Pl | Adm Pl | HQ | A Tk Gp | Mortar Gp | MMG Gp | | | | |
| 1 | Commanding Officer | 2 | | | | | 1 | 1 | | 6 | | 2 | | 1 | | | | | | | | 9 | |
| 1 | Second in Command | 2 | | | | | 1 | 1 | | 4 | | 2 | | 1 | | | | | | | 2 | 9 | |
| 1 | Medical Officer | | | | | | 1 | 1 | | 4 | | 2 | | 1 | | | | | | | 2 | 9 | |
| 1 | Brigade Signals | | | | | | 1 | 1 | | 3 | | 3 | | | | | | | | | 3 | 9 | |
| 1 | HQ & Sp Coy pers No.1 | 6 | | 2 | 2 | | | | | 8 | | 3 | 2 | | | | | | 6 | | 3 | 22 | |
| 1 | HQ & Sp Coy pers No.2 | 6 | | 1 | 3 | | | | | 4 | 1 | 3 | 1 | | | | 6 | 2 | 4 | | | 21 | |
| 1 | Pioneer Platoon | | | | | | 1 | 2 | | | | | 1 | 1 | | | | | | | | 2 | |
| 2 | Transport Platoon | | | | | | 2 | 4 | | | | | | 2 | 2 | | | | | | | 4 | |
| 1 | Sp Coy personnel No.1 | 3 | | 8 | | | | | | 1 | | 3 | | | | 3 | 7 | | 7 | | | 21 | (b) |
| 1 | Sp Coy personnel No.2 | 3 | | 8 | | | | | | 1 | | 2 | | | | 1 | 10 | | 7 | | | 21 | (b) |
| 1 | Support Company | | | | | | 1 | 2 | | | | | | | | 1 | | | 1 | | | 2 | |
| 1 | Anti Tank Group | | | | | | 1 | 1 | | | | | | | | | 6 | | | | | 6 | |
| 4 | 1 Anti Tank Platoon | | | | | | 4 | | 4 | | | | | | | | 8 | | | | | 8 | |
| 4 | 2 Anti Tank Platoon | | | | | | 4 | | 4 | | | | | | | | 8 | | | | | 8 | |
| 3 | 1 (HC) Mortar Platoon | | | | | 18 | | | | 3 | | | 1 | | | | | 47 | | | | 51 | |
| 6 | 2 (BB) Mortar Platoon | | | 6 | | | 6 | 6 | | 1 | | | | | | | | 35 | | | | 36 | |
| 3 | 1 MMG Platoon | 4 | | | | | 3 | 3 | | | | | | | | | | | 18 | | | 18 | |
| 3 | 2 MMG Platoon | 4 | | | | | 3 | 3 | | | | | | | | | | | 18 | | | 18 | |
| 6 | A Company | 5 | 2 | 2 | | 6 | 1 | 2 | | | | 3 | 2 | 1 | | | 4 | | | 121 | 2 | 133 | (c) |
| 6 | B Company | 5 | 2 | 2 | | 6 | 1 | 2 | | | | 3 | 2 | 2 | | | 4 | | | 121 | 1 | 133 | (c) |
| 6 | C Company | 5 | 2 | 2 | | 6 | 1 | 2 | | | | 3 | 1 | 1 | | | | 4 | 1 | 121 | 2 | 133 | (c) |
| 6 | D Company | 5 | 2 | 2 | | 6 | 1 | 2 | | 1 | | 3 | 1 | 2 | | | 4 | | | 121 | 1 | 133 | (c) |
| 60 | Total | 50 | 8 | 33 | 5 | 42 | 33 | 33 | 8 | 35 | 1 | 32 | 14 | 12 | 0 | 5 | 57 | 88 | 62 | 484 | 16 | 806 | |

(a) Under att are shown all personnel NOT on WE.

(b) If Pig-tail harness is NOT available, only 19 men can be carried in each glider.

(c) If Pig-tail harness is NOT available, only 20 men can be carried in each Coy HQ glider instead of 23.

309

## DETAIL OF ALLOTMENT OF PERSONNEL, VEHS AND 6 PDRS TO GLIDERS

| No. of gliders | Glider Designation | Personnel | Tpt | | | | | | | | Bn HQ | HQ Coy | | | | | SP Coy | | | | | (a) Att | Total | Remarks |
|---|---|---|---|---|---|---|---|---|---|---|---|---|---|---|---|---|---|---|---|---|---|---|---|---|
| | | | FC's | MkV Cycles | MC's Lt | MC's Hy | HC's | Jeeps | Trailers | 6 Prs | | HQ | Sig Pl | Pnr Pl | Tpt Pl | Adm Pl | HQ | A Tk Gp | Mortar Gp | MMG Gp | Rifle Coys | | | |
| 1 | Commanding Officer | CO | | | | | | | | | 1 | | | | | | | | | | | | | |
| | | Batman | | | | | | | | | 1 | | | | | | | | | | | | | |
| | | IO | 1 | | | | | | | | 1 | | | | | | | | | | | | | |
| | | Batman | | | | | | | | | 1 | | | | | | | | | | | | | |
| | | Int. Pte | 1 | | | | | | | | 1 | | | | | | | | | | | | | |
| | | LMG No | | | | | | | | | 1 | | | | | | | | | | | | | |
| | | Sigs | | | | | | | | | | | 2 | | | | | | | | | | | |
| | | Dvr | | | | | | 1 | 1 | | | | | | 1 | | | | | | | | 9 | |
| 1 | Second in Command | 2IC | | | | | | | | | 1 | | | | | | | | | | | | | |
| | | Batman | | | | | | | | | 1 | | | | | | | | | | | | | |
| | | Loading Offr | 1 | | | | | | | | 1 | | | | | | | | | | | | | |
| | | Batman | 1 | | | | | | | | 1 | | | | | | | | | | | | | |
| | | Sigs | | | | | | | | | | | 2 | | | | | | | | | | | |
| | | Dvr | | | | | | 1 | 1 | | | | | | 1 | | | | | | | | | |
| | | Bde Sigs | | | | | | | | | | | | | | | | | | | | | 2 | 9 | |
| 1 | Medical Officer | Regt Police | | | | | | | | | 1 | | | | | | | | | | | | | |
| | | MO | | | | | | | | | 1 | | | | | | | | | | | | | |
| | | Batman | | | | | | | | | 1 | | | | | | | | | | | | | |
| | | Pte RAMC | | | | | | | | | 1 | | | | | | | | | | | | | |
| | | Pnr Sjt | | | | | | | | | | | | 1 | | | | | | | | | | |
| | | Pnr | | | | | | | | | | | | 1 | | | | | | | | | | |
| | | Dvr | | | | | | 1 | 1 | | | | | | 1 | | | | | | | | | |
| | | Chaplain | | | | | | | | | | | | | | | | | | | | 1 | | | |
| | | Batman | | | | | | | | | | | | | | | | | | | | 1 | 9 | |
| 1 | Brigade Signals | Bde Sigs | | | | | | 1 | 1 | | | | | | | | | | | | | 3 | | |
| | | Bn Sigs | | | | | | | | | | | 3 | | | | | | | | | | | |
| | | LMG Nos | | | | | | | | | 2 | | | | | | | | | | | | | |
| | | Clerk | | | | | | | | | 1 | | | | | | | | | | | | 9 | |

## DETAIL OF ALLOTMENT OF PERSONNEL, VEHS AND 6 PDRS TO GLIDERS (CONT.)

| No. of gliders | Glider Designation | Personnel | FC's | MkV Cycles | MC's Lt | MC's Hy | HC's | Jeeps | Trailers | 6 Prs | Bn HQ | HQ | Sig Pl | Pnr Pl | Tpt Pl | Adm Pl | HQ | A Tk Gp | Mortar Gp | MMG Gp | Rifle Coys | (a) Att | Total | Remarks |
|---|---|---|---|---|---|---|---|---|---|---|---|---|---|---|---|---|---|---|---|---|---|---|---|---|
| | | | | | | | | | | | Bn HQ | HQ | Sig Pl | Pnr Pl | Tpt Pl | Adm Pl | HQ | A Tk Gp | Mortar Gp | MMG Gp | | | | |
| 1 | HQ & Sp Coy personnel No. 1 | Adj | | | | | | | | | 1 | | | | | | | | | | | | | |
| | | Batman | | | | | | | | | 1 | | | | | | | | | | | | | |
| | | Int Sjt | 1 | | | | | | | | 1 | | | | | | | | | | | | | |
| | | Int Pte | 1 | | | | | | | | 1 | | | | | | | | | | | | | |
| | | RSM | | | 1 | | | | | | 1 | | | | | | | | | | | | | |
| | | Clerk | 1 | | | | | | | | 1 | | | | | | | | | | | | | |
| | | Pro Cpl | | | 1 | | | | | | 1 | | | | | | | | | | | | | |
| | | Pte RAMC | 1 | | | | | | | | 1 | | | | | | | | | | | | | |
| | | FOO, 2 OR Sigs (incl DR) | | | | 1 | | | | | | | 3 | | | | | | | | | 3 | | |
| | | Pnr Offr | 1 | | | | | | | | | | | 1 | | | | | | | | | | |
| | | Batman | 1 | | | | | | | | | | | 1 | | | | | | | | | | |
| | | OC MMG Gp | | | | 1 | | | | | | | | | | | | | | 1 | | | | |
| | | Batman | | | | | | | | | | | | | | | | | | 1 | | | | |
| | | OR 1 MMG Pl | | | | | | | | | | | | | | | | | | 4 | | | 22 | |
| 1 | HQ & Sp Coy personnel No. 2 | Int Cpl | 1 | | | | | | | | 1 | | | | | | | | | | | | | |
| | | Int Pte | 1 | | | | | | | | 1 | | | | | | | | | | | | | |
| | | Pro Sgt | | | 1 | | | | | | 1 | | | | | | | | | | | | | |
| | | Sjt RAMC | | | | | | | | | 1 | | | | | | | | | | | | | |
| | | CSM HQ Coy | 1 | | | | | | | | | 1 | | | | | | | | | | | | |
| | | Sig Offr | 1 | | | | | | | | | | 1 | | | | | | | | | | | |
| | | Batman | 1 | | | | | | | | | | 1 | | | | | | | | | | | |
| | | Sig DR | | | | 1 | | | | | | | 1 | | | | | | | | | | | |
| | | Pnr | 1 | | | | | | | | | | | 1 | | | | | | | | | | |
| | | OC A tk Gp | | | | 1 | | | | | | | | | | | | 1 | | | | | | |
| | | Batman | | | | | | | | | | | | | | | | 1 | | | | | | |
| | | Det 2 A tk Pl | | | | | | | | | | | | | | | | 4 | | | | | | |
| | | OR's 2 MMG Pl | | | | | | | | | | | | | | | | | | 4 | | | | |
| | | OC Mortar Gp | | | | 1 | | | | | | | | | | | | | 1 | | | | | |
| | | Batman | | | | | | | | | | | | | | | | | 1 | | | | 21 | |
| 6 | | *Carried fwd* | *16* | | *3* | *5* | | *4* | *4* | | *29* | *1* | *13* | *5* | *3* | | | *6* | *2* | *10* | | *10* | *79* | |

## DETAIL OF ALLOTMENT OF PERSONNEL, VEHS AND 6 PDRS TO GLIDERS (CONT.)

| No. of gliders | Glider Designation | Personnel | Tpt | | | | | | | | HQ Coy | | | | | | SP Coy | | | | Rifle Coys | (a) Att | Total | Remarks |
|---|---|---|---|---|---|---|---|---|---|---|---|---|---|---|---|---|---|---|---|---|---|---|---|---|
| | | | FC's | MkV Cycles | MC's Lt | MC's Hy | HC's | Jeeps | Trailers | 6 Prs | Bn HQ | HQ | Sig Pl | Pnr Pl | Tpt Pl | Adm Pl | HQ | A Tk Gp | Mortar Gp | MMG Gp | | | | |
| 6 | | *Brought Fwd* | 16 | | 3 | 5 | | 4 | 4 | | 29 | 1 | 13 | 5 | 3 | | | 6 | 2 | 10 | | 10 | 79 | |
| 1 | Pnr Pl | Pnr & Dvr | | | | | | 1 | 2 | | | | | 1 | 1 | | | | | | | | 2 | |
| 2 | Tpt Pl | Pnr & Dvr | | | | | | 2 | 4 | | | | | 2 | 2 | | | | | | | | 4 | |
| 1 | Support Coy personnel I | OC Sp Coy | | | 1 | | | | | | | | | | | | 1 | | | | | | | |
| | | Batman | | | 1 | | | | | | | | | | | | 1 | | | | | | | |
| | | Tpt Sjt | | | 1 | | | | | | | | | | | | 1 | | | | | | | |
| | | Cpl Med Orderly | | | | | | | | | 1 | | | | | | | | | | | | | |
| | | Sig | | | | | | | | | | | 1 | | | | | | | | | | | |
| | | OC 1 A tk Pl | | | 1 | | | | | | | | | | | | | 1 | | | | | | |
| | | Batman | | | 1 | | | | | | | | | | | | | 1 | | | | | | |
| | | Sig att 1 A tk Pl | | | | | | | | | | | 1 | | | | | | | | | | | |
| | | Det 1 A tk Pl* | | | 1 | | | | | | | | | | | | | 4 | | | | | | |
| | | Pl Sjt 2 A tk Pl | | | 1 | | | | | | | | | | | | | 1 | | | | | | |
| | | OC 1 MMG Pl | | | 1 | | | | | | | | | | | | | | | 1 | | | | |
| | | Orderly 1 MMG Pl | | | | | | | | | | | | | | | | | | 1 | | | | |
| | | Sig att 1 MMG Pl | | | | | | | | | | | 1 | | | | | | | | | | | |
| | | OR's 1 MMG Pl | 3 | | | | | | | | | | | | | | | | | 5 | | | 21 | |
| 1 | Support Coy personnel II | CSM Sp Coy | | | 1 | | | | | | | | | | | | 1 | | | | | | | |
| | | Med Orderly | | | | | | | | | 1 | | | | | | | | | | | | | |
| | | OC 2 A tk Pl | | | 1 | | | | | | | | | | | | | 1 | | | | | | |
| | | Batman | | | 1 | | | | | | | | | | | | | 1 | | | | | | |
| | | Sig att 2 A tk Pl | | | | | | | | | | | 1 | | | | | | | | | | | |
| | | Two Dets* 2 A tk Pl | | | 2 | | | | | | | | | | | | | 8 | | | | | | |
| | | OC 2 MMG Pl | | | 1 | | | | | | | | | | | | | | | 1 | | | | |
| | | Sig att 2 MMG Pl | | | | | | | | | | | 1 | | | | | | | | | | | |
| | | OR's 2 MMG Pl | 3 | | 2 | | | | | | | | | | | | | | | 6 | | | 21 | |

## DETAIL OF ALLOTMENT OF PERSONNEL, VEHS AND 6 PDRS TO GLIDERS (CONT.)

| No. of gliders | Glider Designation | Personnel | Tpt | | | | | | | | HQ Coy | | | | | | SP Coy | | | | Rifle Coys | (a) Att | Total | Remarks |
|---|---|---|---|---|---|---|---|---|---|---|---|---|---|---|---|---|---|---|---|---|---|---|---|---|
| | | | FC's | MkV Cyc.es | MC's Lt | MC's Hv | HC's | Jeeps | Trailers | 6 Prs | Bn HQ | HQ | Sig Pl | Pnr Pl | Tpt Pl | Adm Pl | HQ | A Tk Gp | Mortar Gp | MMG Gp | | | | |
| 6 | | *Brought Fwd* | | | | | | | | | | | | | | | | | | | | | | |
| 1 | Sp Coy | Dvr | | | | | | 1 | 2 | | | | | | | | 1 | | | | | | | |
| | | OR 2 MMG Pl | | | | | | | | | | | | | | | | | | 1 | | | 2 | |
| 1 | A/Tk/Gp | Pl Sjt 1 A tk Pl | | | | | | | | | | | | | | | | 1 | | | | | | |
| | | Det 1 A tk Pl* | | | | | | | | | | | | | | | | 4 | | | | | | |
| | | Dvr of 1 A tk Pl | | | | | | 1 | 1 | | | | | | | | | 1 | | | | | 6 | |
| 4 | 1 A Tk Pl | Gun Nos. & Dvr's | | | | | | 4 | | 4 | | | | | | | | 8 | | | | | 8 | |
| 4 | 2 A Tk Pl | Gun Nos. & Dvr's | | | | | | 4 | | 4 | | | | | | | | 8 | | | | | 8 | |
| 1 | 1 (HC) Mortar Pl | Offr | | | | | | | | | | | | | | | | | 1 | | | | | |
| | | Sig | | | | | | | | | | | 1 | | | | | | | | | | | |
| | | Med Orderly | | | | | | | | | 1 | | | | | | | | | | | | | |
| | | OR's | | | | 6 | | | | | | | | | | | | | 14 | | | | 17 | |
| 2 | | Med Orderlies | | | | | | | | | 2 | | | | | | | | | | | | | |
| | | OR's | | | | 12 | | | | | | | | | | | | | 32 | | | | 34 | |
| 1 | 2 (BB) Mortar Pl | Offr | | | | | | | | | | | | | | | | | 1 | | | | | |
| | | Batman | | | | | | | | | | | | | | | | | 1 | | | | | |
| | | Sig | | | | | | | | | | | 1 | | | | | | | | | | | |
| | | OR's | | | 1 | | | 1 | 1 | | | | | | | | | | 3 | | | | 6 | |
| 5 | | OR's | | | 5 | | | 5 | 5 | | | | | | | | | | 30 | | | | 30 | (a) |
| 1 | 1 MMG Pl | OR's 1 MMG Pl | | | | | | 1 | 1 | | | | | | | | | | | 6 | | | 6 | |
| 1 | | OR's 1 MMG Pl | 4 | | | | | 2 | 2 | | | | | | | | | | | 12 | | | 12 | |
| 3 | 2 MMG Pl | As for 1 MMG Pl | 4 | | | | | 3 | 3 | | | | | | | | | | | 18 | | | 18 | |
| 36 | | *Carried fwd* | 30 | 25 | 5 | 18 | 29 | 25 | | 8 | 34 | 1 | 20 | 8 | 6 | | 5 | 45 | 84 | 61 | | 10 | 274 | 1 |

## DETAIL OF ALLOTMENT OF PERSONNEL, VEHS AND 6 PDRS TO GLIDERS (CONT.)

| No. of gliders | Glider Designation | Personnel | Tpt | | | | | | | | HQ Coy | | | | | | SP Coy | | | | Rifle Coys | (a) Att | Total | Remarks |
|---|---|---|---|---|---|---|---|---|---|---|---|---|---|---|---|---|---|---|---|---|---|---|---|---|
| | | | FC's | MkV Cycles | MC's Lt | MC's Hy | HC's | Jeeps | Trailers | 6 Prs | Bn HQ | HQ | Sig Pl | Pnr Pl | Tpt Pl | Adm Pl | HQ | A Tk Gp | Mortar Gp | MMG Gp | | | | |
| 36 | | *Brought Fwd* | 30 | | 25 | 5 | 18 | 29 | 25 | 8 | 34 | 1 | 20 | 8 | 6 | | 5 | 45 | 84 | 61 | | 10 | 274 | |
| 1 | Officer Commanding A Company | OC Coy | | | 1 | | | | | | | | | | | | | | | | 1 | | | |
| | | Batman | | | 1 | | | | | | | | | | | | | | | | 1 | | | |
| | | CSM | | 1 | | | | | | | | | | | | | | | | | 1 | | | |
| | | Clerk | | | | | | | | | | | | | | | | | | | 1 | | | |
| | | Coy Sp Sec | | | | | 2 | | | | | | | | | | | | | | 5 | | | |
| | | Pte IC HC | | | | | | | | | | | | | | | | | | | 1 | | | |
| | | Ptes RAMC | | 1 | | | | | | | | | | | | | | | | | 2 | | | |
| | | OR's from res Pl | | | | | | | | | | | | | | | | | | | 4 | | | |
| | | Sig | | | | | | | | | | | 1 | | | | | | | | | | | |
| | | Det* 1 A tk Pl | | | | | | | | | | | | | | | | 4 | | | | | | |
| | | CMP | 1 | | | | | | | | | | | | | | | | | | | 1 | | |
| | | Cameraman | | | | | | | | | | | | | | | | | | | | 1 | 23 | |
| 1 | Sec in Command A Company | Coy 2IC | | | | | | | | | | | | | | | | | | | 1 | | | |
| | | Batman | | | | | | | | | | | | | | | | | | | 1 | | | |
| | | OC Pl | | | | | | | | | | | | | | | | | | | 1 | | | |
| | | Batman | 1 | | | | | | | | | | | | | | | | | | 1 | | | |
| | | Med Ord | | | | | | | | | | | | | | | | | | | 1 | | | |
| | | OR's | | | | | 1 | | | | | | | | | | | | | | 20 | | | |
| | | Sigs | | | | | | | | | | | 2 | | | | | | | | | | 27 | |
| 3 | Pln A Coy | Offrs & OR's | 3 | | | | 3 | | | | | | | | | | | | | | 80 | | | |
| | | Pnr | | | | | | | | | | | | 1 | | | | | | | | | 81 | |
| 1 | Tpt A Coy | Pnr & Dvr. | | | | | | 1 | 2 | | | | | 1 | 1 | | | | | | | | 2 | |
| 6 | B Coy | As for A Coy | 5 | 2 | 2 | | 6 | 1 | 2 | | | | 3 | 2 | 2 | | | 4 | | | 121 | 1 | 133 | (b) |
| 6 | C Coy | As for A Coy | 5 | 2 | 2 | | 6 | 1 | 2 | | | | 3 | 1 | 1 | | | | 4 | 1 | 121 | 2 | 133 | (c) |
| 6 | D Coy | As for A Coy | 5 | 2 | 2 | | 6 | 1 | 2 | | 1 | | 3 | 1 | 2 | | | 4 | | | 121 | 1 | 133 | (d) |
| 60 | | *Total* | 50 | 8 | 33 | 5 | 42 | 33 | 33 | 8 | 35 | 1 | 32 | 14 | 12 | 0 | 5 | 57 | 88 | 62 | 484 | 16 | 806 | |

(a) Incl 1 from 1 (HC) Mortar Pl.
(b) L Cpl fitter REME is carried in place of cameraman.
(c) 1 OR 1 MMG Pl, 4 OR's 1 (HC) Mortar Pl and 1 cameraman and CMP are carried.
(d) Regt. Policeman carried in place of cameraman and 2 OR's from 1 MMG Pl & Tpt Sgt carried.
  *Less 2 men

# Appendix 5

*Field Return of Officers for the Week Ending 16 September 1944*

### HEADQUARTERS GLIDER PILOT REGIMENT:

| | | | |
|---|---|---|---|
| Colonel | G.J.S. | Chatterton | Officer Commanding |
| Major | P.G. | Harding | Deputy Assistant Adjutant & Quarter Master General |
| Major | K.J.S. | Andrews | GSO 2 Operations |
| Captain | G. | Rostworowski | GSO 3 Intelligence |
| Captain | I.A. | MacArthur | Staff Captain 'A' |

### HEADQUARTERS NO. 1 WING:

| | | | |
|---|---|---|---|
| Lieutenant Colonel | I.A. | Murray DSO MC | Officer Commanding |
| Major | J.P. | Royle | Second in Command |
| Captain | P.N. | Fletcher | Adjutant |
| Captain | A.R. | Taitt | Operations Officer |
| Captain | G.A.F. | Pare | Chaplain |
| Lieutenant | J.B. | Bottomley | Intelligence Officer |
| Lieutenant | E.E. | Nicholls | Quartermaster |
| Lieutenant | S.A.M. | Johnson | Administrative Officer |
| Warrant Officer I | G.W. | Bayford | Regimental Sergeant Major |

### 'A' SQUADRON:

| | | | |
|---|---|---|---|
| Major | S.C. | Griffith | Officer Commanding |
| Captain | H.T. | Bartlett | Second in Command |
| Lieutenant | W.G. | Dyson | Adjutant |
| Lieutenant | C.H.D. | Michell | Intelligence Officer |
| Warrant Officer II | K. | Mew | Squadron Sergeant Major |
| Captain | N.G. | Hardie | Officer Commanding 1 Flight |
| Captain | R.K. | Cross | Officer Commanding 2 Flight |
| Captain | N.A.C. | Smillie | Officer Commanding 17 Flight (att. T. Rushton) |
| Captain | W.L. | Tallentire | Officer Commanding 18 Flight |
| Lieutenant | H.B. | Haeffner | Section Commander |
| Lieutenant | C.C. | Tayler | Section Commander (att. Keevil) |

| Lieutenant | E.J. | Markwick | Section Commander (att. T. Rushton) |
|---|---|---|---|
| Lieutenant | H.K. | Chapman | Section Commander |
| Lieutenant | A.G.C. | Turner | Section Commander |
| 2nd Lieutenant | J.W. | Urquhart | Section Commander |

**'B' SQUADRON:**

| Major | T.I.J. | Toler | Officer Commanding |
|---|---|---|---|
| Captain | F.J.T. | Neale | Second in Command |
| Lieutenant | H.J. | Futter | Adjutant |
| Lieutenant | G.E. | Stilton | Intelligence Officer |
| Warrant Officer II | W. | Watt | Squadron Sergeant Major |
| Captain | T.G. | Miller | Officer Commanding 3 Flight |
| Captain | J.F. | Smellie | Officer Commanding 4 Flight |
| Captain | D.A. | Simpson | Officer Commanding 19 Flight |
| Captain | A.F.W. | Low | Officer Commanding 20 Flight |
| Lieutenant | D.G. | Anderson | Section Commander |
| Lieutenant | H.M.R. | Norton | Section Commander |
| Lieutenant | K.W. | Powell | Section Commander |
| Lieutenant | H.C.L. | Cole | Section Commander |
| Lieutenant | G.R. | Millar | Section Commander |
| Lieutenant | R. | Irvine | Section Commander |
| Lieutenant | J.H. | Barclay | Section Commander |
| 2nd Lieutenant | R. | Meakin | Section Commander |

**'D' SQUADRON:**

| Major | J.F. | Lyne | Officer Commanding |
|---|---|---|---|
| Captain | J.G. | Ogilvie | Second in Command |
| Lieutenant | N. | Baxter | Adjutant |
| Lieutenant | K.F. | Strathern | Intelligence Officer |
| Warrant Officer II | W.E. | Oliver | Squadron Sergeant Major |
| Captain | J.A. | Morrison | Officer Commanding 5 Flight |
| Captain | B. | Murdoch | Officer Commanding 8 Flight |
| Captain | S.G. | Cairns | Officer Commanding 13 Flight |
| Captain | F.H. | Barclay MC | Officer Commanding 21 Flight |
| Captain | I.C. | Muir | Officer Commanding 22 Flight |
| Captain | H.J.K. | O'Malley | Attached from Depot |
| Lieutenant | H.R. | Sykes | Section Commander |
| Lieutenant | K.T. | Chittleburgh | Section Commander |
| Lieutenant | P.T. | Scott | Section Commander |
| Lieutenant | S.J.D. | Moorwood | Section Commander |

| Lieutenant | N.V.M. | Adams | Section Commander |
|---|---|---|---|
| Lieutenant | E.J.A. | Smith | Section Commander |
| Lieutenant | D.N.C. | Steedman | Section Commander |
| Lieutenant | S.R. | Smith | Section Commander |
| Lieutenant | K.S. | Mills | Section Commander |
| Lieutenant | J.H. | Kershaw | Section Commander |

## 'G' Squadron:

| Major | R.S. | Croot | Officer Commanding |
|---|---|---|---|
| Captain | W.N. | Barrie DFC | Second in Command |
| Lieutenant | M.W. | Downing | Adjutant |
| Lieutenant | J.M. | Langley | Intelligence Officer |
| Warrant Officer II | F.H. | White | Squadron Sergeant Major |
| Captain | M.T. | Corrie | Officer Commanding 9 Flight |
| Captain | M.W.D. | Priest | Officer Commanding 10 Flight |
| Captain | E.H. | Leschalles | Officer Commanding 23 Flight |
| Captain | R.O. | Walchli | Officer Commanding 24 Flight |
| Lieutenant | J.M. | Bewley | Section Commander |
| Lieutenant | M.D.K. | Dauncey | Section Commander |
| Lieutenant | R.D. | Telfer | Section Commander |
| Lieutenant | R.V.D. | Palmer | Section Commander |
| Lieutenant | F.A. | Derbyshire | Section Commander |

## HEADQUARTERS NO. 2 WING:

| Lieutenant Colonel | J.W. | Place | Officer Commanding |
|---|---|---|---|
| Major | J.F.B. | Blatch | Second in Command |
| Captain | D.H. | Shuttleworth | Adjutant |
| Captain | J.H. | Hooper | Operations Officer |
| Captain | W.R. | Chignell | Chaplain |
| Lieutenant | R.A. | Maltby | Intelligence Officer |
| Lieutenant | A.B. | Maker | Quartermaster |
| Lieutenant | T.P. | Breach | Administrative Officer |
| Warrant Officer I | M.J. | Briody | Regimental Sergeant Major |

## 'C' SQUADRON:

| Major | J.A.C. | Dale DFC | Officer Commanding |
|---|---|---|---|
| Captain | W. | McNeill | Second in Command |
| Lieutenant | E.H. | Cookson | Adjutant |
| Warrant Officer II | M.G. | Petrie | Squadron Sergeant Major |

| | | | |
|---|---|---|---|
| Captain | F.C. | Aston | Officer Commanding 6 Flight |
| Captain | B.H. | Halsall MC | Officer Commanding 7 Flight |
| Lieutenant | P.B. | Clark | Officer Commanding 'X' Flight |
| Lieutenant | T.W. | Taylorson DFC | Section Commander |
| Lieutenant | J. | Baldwin | Section Commander |
| Lieutenant | R.O.F. | Boyd | Section Commander |
| Lieutenant | R.B. | Stevens | Section Commander |
| Lieutenant | G.R.I.M | Stokes | Section Commander |
| Lieutenant | F. | Davies | Section Commander |
| Lieutenant | J.R. | Prout | Section Commander |
| Lieutenant | P.W. | Wood | Section Commander |
| Lieutenant | R.H. | Conchie | Section Commander |
| Lieutenant | T.A.D. | Godman | (of R.A.) |

## 'E' SQUADRON:

| | | | |
|---|---|---|---|
| Major | B.H.P. | Jackson | Officer Commanding |
| Captain | P.F. | Robson | Second in Command |
| Lieutenant | R.F. | Glynn Jones | Adjutant |
| Warrant Officer II | J.B. | Lee | Squadron Sergeant Major |
| Captain | G.T. | Mills | Officer Commanding 11 Flight |
| Captain | C.B. | Dodwell | Officer Commanding 12 Flight |
| Captain | A.A.R. | Oxenford | Officer Commanding 25 Flight |
| Lieutenant | P.J. | Brazier | Section Commander |
| Lieutenant | R.W. | Briscoe | Section Commander |
| Lieutenant | R.O. | Johnson | Section Commander |
| Lieutenant | J.H. | Tomson | Section Commander |
| Lieutenant | R.H. | Garnett | Section Commander |
| Lieutenant | N.C. | de Courcy Ashe | Section Commander |
| Lieutenant | D.N.S. | Turner | Section Commander |
| Lieutenant | A.G. | Catford | Section Commander |
| Lieutenant | A.F. | Johnston | Section Commander |

## 'F' SQUADRON:

| | | | |
|---|---|---|---|
| Major | F.A.S. | Murray | Officer Commanding |
| Captain | T.A. | Plowman | Second in Command |
| Lieutenant | I.M. | Roberts | Adjutant |
| Lieutenant | S.M. | Culverwell | Intelligence Officer |
| Warrant Officer II | I.J. | Blackwood | Squadron Sergeant Major |

| | | | |
|---|---|---|---|
| Lieutenant | A.E. | Pickwoad DFC | Officer Commanding 14 Flight |
| Captain | E.J. | Thomas AFC | Officer Commanding 15 Flight |
| Captain | F. | Robson MC | Officer Commanding 16 Flight |
| Lieutenant | R.E. | Spence | Section Commander |
| Lieutenant | S.R. | Maclaine of Lochbuie | Section Commander |
| Lieutenant | M.W. | Long | Section Commander |
| Lieutenant | P.R. | Clark | Section Commander |
| Lieutenant | D.A.A. | Treherne | Section Commander |
| Lieutenant | R.V.C. | Steevenson | Section Commander |
| Lieutenant | W.R.A. | Happer | Section Commander |
| Lieutenant | J.H. | Stephens | Section Commander |
| Lieutenant | R.B. | Stevens | Section Commander |

# Appendix 6

*Appreciation of the Situation*
*by Colonel G.J.S. Chatterton DSO*

## 1. OBJECT.

After landing, to withdraw into defensive positions, less units detailed for special duties, until evacuation.

## 2. FACTORS.

(a) Landings should commence at about 1340 hrs.
<u>Therefore</u> – Troops will reach R.Vs in daylight.

(b) The R.Vs are 1- 2 miles from the L.Z.
<u>Therefore</u> – Troops should reach R.V. within 2 hours (Note: 30 mins unloading).

(c) Topography of L.Z. outstanding.
<u>Therefore</u> – Good concentration - troops form up quickly.

(d) Troops move with loads in direction of R.Vs.
<u>Therefore</u> – Adequate protection moving across country.

(e) Air Umbrella over L.Zs during daylight.
<u>Therefore</u> – Movement should be safe from enemy recce or fighter aircraft.

## 3. COURSES.

A. Individual escape by pilots.

<u>Advantage.</u>

(a) immediate effort before enemy reaction.
(b) comparative ease of individual infiltration into enemy posns.

<u>Disadvantage.</u>

(a) terrain – two rivers and 10 miles of difficult country.
(b) numbers – some 1200 pilots.
(c) uncertainly of NIJMEGEN being held.

B. Immediate evacuation as formed body.

<u>Advantage.</u>

(a) immediate effort.
(b) country believed held lightly.

<u>Disadvantage.</u>

(a) terrain – as before.
(b) the Regiment is only equipped for defensive actions.
(c) uncertainty of NIJMEGEN – as before.

C. To remain individually with loads.

<u>Advantage.</u>

(a) protection.
(b) simplified administration.

Disadvantage.

(a) no regimental control
(b) possibility of pilots being involved in costly offensive fighting.
(c) difficulty of evacuation in later stages.
(d) no immediate effort to withdraw.

D. Remain a formed units within Division.

Advantage.

(a) protection of Div weapons.
(b) regimental control.
(c) troops employed in defensive role, less those detailed for special duties with R.A. and R.E. units.
(d) evacuation, when possible, simplified.

Disadvantage.

(a) supply and medical.
(b) no immediate effort to withdraw.

4. CONCLUSION.

Of these courses I prefer (D). It will involve less casualties than (C), and the possibility of successful infiltration in (A) and (B) is retarded by nature of the country.

5. PLAN.

Pilots will reform Squadrons on landing, and some under command of their respective Wing H.Qs. No 1 Wing will be under command H.Q. 1st Airborne Div., and No 2 Wing under command 1st A/L Bde., whom they are carrying. They will carry out such tasks as are allotted by the Div Commander, and withdraw as soon as the situation allows.

A.P.O. England

Colonel.
H.Q. Commander Glider Pilots.

Appreciation of the Situation
Operation "MARKET" (ARNHEM)
By Colonel G.J.S. Chatterton, DSO.

OBJECT.

1. To land 38 Hamilcar, 588 Horsa and 4 CG4.A. gliders carrying elements of 1 British Airborne Div., the Polish Para Bde., 878 U.S. Engineering Aviation Bn., and Airfield control Units in four landing zones in area ARNHEM.

FACTORS.

2. Ground.

(a) The ground is arable, parcelled into two large holdings. There are a few ditches, and the hedges are thin. Transverse tracks may offer some obstructions.
Therefore – the surface should be suitable for glider landings.

(b) The area is of a distinctive shape, subdivided by clearly defined tracks.
Therefore – recognition of individual areas should not be difficult.

(c) The area, although surrounded by trees, is comparatively large from the number of aircraft employed.
Therefore – there should be sufficient space to absorb most of the overshoots, eliminating a high percentage of potential crashes into the surrounding woods.

## 3. Time.

It is impracticable to carry out mass landings on this scale in darkness.
Therefore – all gliders must release between first and last light.

## 4. Weather.

(a) Sustained cloud flying is impracticable for large formations of glider trains.
Therefore – there should be a "safe" cloud base at the accepted heights.

(b) The surface wind may not be as forecast at final briefing.
Therefore – provision must be made for slight wind variations, although downwind landings with wind strength of up to 15 m.p.h. may have to be, in some cases, accepted.

## 5. Ground Aids.

Three types of aids are being prepared, i.e. smoke, panels and lights.
Therefore – pilots should be able to rely on a minimum of one recognition aid, should map reading prove difficult.

## 6. Release Height.

This is governed by considerations of flak and Air Cover, and generally by the entire Air Plan.
Therefore – the release height must be accepted as that defined by the Air Plan.

## 7. Direction of Approach.

This is governed by R.A.F. routing, and cannot be adjusted.
Therefore – the approach must be made from SW to NE.

COURSES.

8.

(a) A mass landing within the general area without definition of individual areas for groups or units.

(b) Landing of Army units or Station groups in defend areas.

(c) A varying approach for two conditions of wind, i.e. approach either West of the L.Z. or East of the L.Z.

(d) A fixed approach over the centre of the L.Z.

PLAN.

9. The approach to the landing zones will be made from S.W. to N.E., the final run up being the centre of the areas over a fixed point. On L.Z. "S" aircraft carrying individual units of the Airlanding Bde., will be allotted separate areas. On L.Zs X, Z, and L, gliders from each R.A.F. Station will be allotted areas, Hamilcar aircraft taking preference of the longest run.

Pilots will release on track at their discretion, landing according to the briefed plan for the surface wind given by the tug navigator, and confirmed by ground signals.

The sub division of the area will remain unchanged for any condition of wind, to assist the construction of the military plan.

A.P.O. England

Colonel.
H.Q. Commander Glider Pilots.

# Appendix 7

*Airlanding Plan*

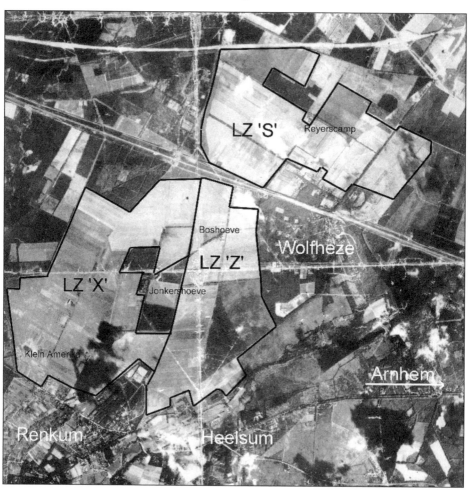

Landing Plan;

Plan 'A'. Winds from 225° - 045°

| Landing Zone | Direction of landing |
|---|---|
| S | East to west |
| X | South to north |
| Z | South to north |
| L | East to west |

Plan 'B'. Winds from 046° - 224°

| Landing Zone | Direction of landing |
|---|---|
| S | West to east |
| X | North to south |
| Z | North to south |
| L | West to east |

Ground Aids are set out as follows;

|  | Landing Zone | Panels | Very Signals | Smoke |
|---|---|---|---|---|
| 1st lift | LZ S | White S | White | Violet |
|  | LZ Z | White Z | Red | Violet |
|  | DZ X | White T |  | Blue |
|  |  | White X |  | Blue |
| 2nd lift | LZ S | White S | White | Violet |
|  | LZ X | White X | Red | Violet |
|  | DZ Y | Red T |  | Green |
|  |  | White Y |  | Green |
| 3rd lift | LZ L | White L | White | Violet |

# Appendix 8

*Air Load Manifest Operation MARKET - First Lift*

| RAF Stn | Tug/Glider combinations | RAF Sqn | GPR unit | DZ/ LZ | Chalk No | Airborne Unit | Abortive gliders |
|---|---|---|---|---|---|---|---|
| Broadwell | 24x Dakota/Horsa | 575 | HQ 2 Wing, 'F' Sqn - 16 Flt, 'G' Sqn - det 10 Flt | S | 161-184 | Bn HQ; HQ Coy; A,B & D Coy (less 19 Pl); | 162, 165, 166, 174, 183 |
| | 20x Dakota/Horsa | 512 | | | 243-262 | A/Tk and MMG Plns; 23 Mortar Pl, 1 Border | |
| | 1x Dakota/Horsa | 512 | | | 263 | Section, 181 A/L Field Ambulance | |
| | 2x Dakota | 512/437 | | | 264-265 | Elms 250 Coy, RASC | 265 |
| Blakehill Farm | 12x Dakota/Horsa | 233/437 | 14 Flt, 'F' Sqn | S | 185-196 | Bn HQ; elms HQ Coy and A Coy; 1 x 6-pdr; 1½ mortar Sect and one MMG sect, 7 KOSB | 185 |
| | 12x Dakota/Horsa | | | | 197-208 | C Coy and 24 Mortar Pl, 1 Border | |
| | 10x Dakota/Horsa | | | | 209-218 | 1 A/L Bde HQ and HQ Defence Pl; L Sect, Div Signals & 3 Sect, Provost Coy | |
| Down Ampney | 24x Dakota/Horsa | 271 | 11 Flt & elms of 'E' Sqn | S | 219-242 | elms HQ Coy; B Coy; 6 x 6-pdrs; 2 x MMG and 1½ Mortar Sect, 7 KOSB | 222, 229, 237 239, 240 |
| | 20x Dakota/Horsa | 48/437 | | | 266-285 | C Coy (minus 10 Pl); D Coy; 1 x 6-pdr; 1 x MMG and 3 x Mortar Sections, 7 KOSB | 266, 272, 277 278, 283 |
| | 5x Dakota/Horsa | 48 | | | 286-290 | Nos. 1 and 2 Surgical Teams and 3 sections, 181 A/L Field Ambulance RAMC | |
| Manston | 22x Albemarle/Horsa | 296/297 | 20 Flt & HQ 'B' Sqn | S | 291-312 | Bn HQ; HQ Coy; B and D Coy; No. 1 Mortar and No. 1 MMG Pl, 2 Bn South Staffs | 296, 298 |
| | 6x Albemarle/Horsa | 297 | | Z | 348-353 | elms 1 Bty, 1 A/L Lt Regt, RA | |
| | 1x Albemarle/Horsa | 296 | | S | 313 | Section, 181 A/L Fd Amb RAMC | |
| | 17x Albemarle/Horsa | 296 | 19 Flt, 'B' Sqn | Z | 327-347 | HQ, A, B, C and Z Tp, 1 A/L A/Tk Bty, RA (16x 6-pdr) * minus - 329, 331, 333, 335 | 336 |
| | 4x Albemarle/ Waco | 296 | X (Independent) Flt | Z | 329, 331, 333, 335 | USAAF Air Support Signal Teams | |
| | 6x Albemarle/ Waco | 296/297 | | N | 488-493 | AB Corps HQ; USAAF Air Support Signal Teams | |

| RAF Stn | Tug/Glider combinations | RAF Sqn | GPR unit | DZ/LZ | Chalk No | Airborne Unit | Abortive gliders |
|---|---|---|---|---|---|---|---|
| Tarrant Rushton | 8x Halifax/Hamilcar | 298/ 644 | 6, 7 & X Flt, 'C' Sqn | Z | 314-321 | D and P Tp, 1 A/L A/Tk Bty, RA (8x 17-pdrs) | 355, 364 |
| | 3x Halifax/Hamilcar | | | | 322-324 | 1, 2 and 3 Para Bn carriers (6 x carriers) | |
| | 2x Halifax/Hamilcar | | | | 325-326 | 7 KOSB and 1 Border carriers (4 x carriers) | |
| | 22x Halifax/Horsa | | | | 354-375 | Recce Sqn (39 x Jeeps, 2 x Polsten guns) | |
| | 3x Halifax/Horsa | | | | 376-378 | D & P Tp, 1 A/L A/Tk Bty, RA | |
| | 2x Halifax/Horsa | | | | 379-380 | 3 Para Pln, 250 Coy, RASC | |
| Keevil | 16x Stirling/Horsa | 299 | 21 Flt, 'D' Sqn | Z | 381-396 | 9 Fd Coy; det 261 Fd Pk Coy; HQ Gp, RE | 385, 389 |
| | 9x Stirling/Horsa | | | | 397-405 | A Tp, 1 Bty, 1 A/L Lt Regt, RA | 399 |
| | 3x Stirling/Horsa | | | | 456-458 | 1 FOU, 1 A/L Lt Regt, RA | 457 |
| | 20x Stirling/Horsa | 196 | 13 Flt, 'D' Sqn | | 459-478 | 1, 2 and 3 Para Bn Jeeps; 1 Para Sqn RE equipm Bde Signals; Bde HQ, 1 Para Bde (total 38 Jeeps) | 462, 468 474, 478 |
| | 2x Stirling/Horsa | 196 | | | 479-480 | 3 Para Pl, 250 Coy, RASC | |
| Harwell | 25x Stirling/Horsa | 295 | HQ GPR, 18 Flt & Elms of 2 Flt, 'A' Sqn | N | 406-430 | HQ, I AB Corps | 413, 414, 421 |
| | 7x Stirling/Horsa | 570 | 1 Flt, 'A' Sqn | N | 481-487 | HQ, I AB Corps | |
| | 12x Stirling/Horsa | 570 | | Z | 494-505 | Tac HQ; elms 1 Bty, 1 A/L Lt Regt, RA | |
| Fairford | 10x Stirling/Horsa | 190 | HQ 1 Wing & 24 Flt 'G' Sqn | Z | 431-440 | Div HQ; Div Defence Pl; No. 4 Section, Provost Coy; CRE; AA&QMG; ADMS; A, B, C & G Section Div Signals; PR team. | 435 |
| | 14x Stirling/Horsa | 190/ 620 | 23 Flt, 'G' Sqn | | 441-454 | E Tp, 3 Bty, 1 A/L Lt Regt, RA | |
| | 13x Stirling/Horsa | 620 | 9 Flt, 'G' Sqn | | 506-518 | F Tp, 3 Bty, 1 A/L Lt Regt, RA | 509, 516, 518 |
| | 1x Stirling/Horsa | | | | 519 | 3 Para Pl, 250 Coy, RASC | 519 |

# Appendix 9

*Air Load Manifest Operation MARKET - Second Lift*

| RAF Stn | Tug/Glider combinations | RAF Sqn | GPR unit | DZ/ LZ | Chalk No | Airborne Unit | Abortive gliders |
|---|---|---|---|---|---|---|---|
| Broadwell | 22x Dakota/Horsa | 512 | | S | 750-771 | A & C Coy; No. 2 Mortar, No. 2 MMG and Nos. 1 & 2 A/Tk Pls 2 Bn South Staffords | |
| | 18x Dakota/Horsa | | | S | 816-833 | | |
| | 1x Dakota/Horsa | 575 | 'F' Sqn | X | 834 | elms 1 Para Bde HQ | 759 |
| | 1x Dakota/Horsa | | | X | 835 | elms 250 Coy, RASC | |
| | 2x Dakota/Horsa | | | X | 836 | elms 250 Coy, RASC | |

| Blakehill Farm | 21x Dakota/Horsa | 233/437 | 5 Flt, 'D' Sqn | X | 772-792 | 2 A/L A/Tk Bty, RA (12 x 6-pdrs) | 773 |
| | 1 Dakota/Horsa | 437 | | | 793 | elms 250 Coy RASC | |

| Down Ampney | 6x Dakota/Horsa | | | | 794-799 | 10 Pl and Transport Pl, 7 KOSB | |
| | 6x Dakota/Horsa | | | | 800-805 | 19 Pl and Transport Pl, 1 Border | |
| | 5x Dakota/Horsa | 48 | | S | 806-810 | Reserve section, 181 A/L Fd Amb RAMC | |
| | 5x Dakota/Horsa | | 'E' Sqn | | 811-815 | elms RAOC, elms 250 Coy, RASC | 813 |
| | 6x Dakota/Horsa | | | | 837-842 | elms 2 Bty, 1 A/L Lt Regt, RA | |
| | 6x Dakota/Horsa | 271 | | X | 843-848 | elms 9 Fd Coy; det 261 Fd Pk Coy, RE | |
| | 10x Dakota/Horsa | | | | 849-858 | elms REME, 261 Fd Pk Coy, RE and elms 250 Coy, RASC | |

| RAF Stn | Tug/Glider combinations | RAF Sqn | GPR unit | DZ/LZ | Chalk No | Airborne Unit | Abortive gliders |
|---|---|---|---|---|---|---|---|
| Manston | 4x Albemarle/Horsa | 296 | 19 Flt, 'B' Sqn | X | 886-889 | elms HQ 1 A/L A/Tk Bty, RA | 865, 878 |
| | 27x Albemarle/Horsa | 296/297 | 3 and 4 Flt, 'B' Sqn | | 859-885 | elms 2 Bty, 1 A/L Lt Regt, RA (8 x guns) | |
| | 10x Albemarle/Horsa | | | | 890-899 | Adv HQ; 3 Tp, A/Tk Bty (5 x 6-pdrs) Engineer Coy, Polish Para Bde | |
| | 1x Albemarle/Horsa | 297 | | | 900 | 21 Indep Para Coy (transport) | |
| Tarrant Rushton | 8x Halifax/Hamilcar | | 6 and 7 Flt, 'C' Sqn | X | 901-908 | F and X Tp, 2 A/L A/Tk Bty, RA (8 x 17-pdrs) | 901, 903 |
| | 3x Halifax/Hamilcar | | | | 909-911 | 10, 11 and 156th Para Bn carriers (6 x carriers) | |
| | 1x Halifax/Hamilcar | 298/644 | | | 912 | 2 South Staffords carriers (2 x carriers) | |
| | 3x Halifax/Hamilcar | | | | 913-915 | Admin (bulk stores) | |
| | 3x Halifax/Horsa | | 17 Flt, 'A' Sqn | | 916-918 | elms 2 A/L A/Tk Bty, RA | 927 |
| | 11x Halifax/Horsa | | | | 919-929 | 1 Para Pl, 250 Coy, RASC | |
| Keevil | 20x Stirling/Horsa | 299 | 8 & 22 Flt, 'D' Sqn | X | 950-969 | 4th Para Bde HQ; 156th Para Bn Jeeps; 4th Para Sqn RE - Equipment; det 261 Fd Pk Coy, RE; 6 LAD, REME | 956, 964 |
| | 20x Stirling/Horsa | 196 | | | 1010-1029 | 10th and 11th Para Bn Jeeps; 133 Para Fd Amb, RAMC transport | 1011, 1026 |
| Harwell | 5x Stirling/Horsa | 570 | 'A' Sqn | X | 970-974 | 2 Para Pl, 250 Coy, RASC | 974 |
| | 4x Stirling/Horsa | 295/570 | | | 974a-974d | elms 250 Coy, RASC | 974c-974d |
| | 4x Stirling/Horsa | | | | 5000-5003 | Nos. 6341 and 6080 Light Warning Units, RAF | 5000, 5003 |
| Fairford | 15x Stirling/Horsa | 620 | 'G' Sqn | X | 930-944 | elms Div HQ; DAAG; DAQMG; CRASC; ADOS; CREME | 934 |
| | 5x Stirling/Horsa | | | | 945-949 | 16 Para, Fd Amb, RAMC transport | |
| | 14x Stirling/Horsa | 190 | | | 990-1003 | 1, 2 and 3 Para Bn and 1 Para Sqn RE Jeeps | 994, 996 |
| | 6x Stirling/Horsa | | | | 1004-1009 | 2 A/L A/Tk Bty, RA (4 x 6-pdrs) | 1005, 1007 |

| RAF Stn | Tug/Glider combinations | RAF Sqn | GPR unit | DZ/ LZ | Chalk No | Airborne Unit | Abortive gliders |
|---|---|---|---|---|---|---|---|
| Broadwell | 5 Dakota/Horsa | 512 | HQ 2 Wing and 'F' Sqn | S | 162 | Bn CO, 1 Border | 162 |
| | | | | | 165 | HQ/Signals Pl, 1 Border | |
| | | | | | 166 | 13 Pl, 1 Border | |
| | | 575 | | | 174 | B Coy 2ic, 1 Border | |
| | | | | | 183 | elms 1 Border | |
| Blakehill Farm | 1x Dakota/Horsa | 233 or 437 | 14 Flt, 'F' Sqn | S | 185 | 17 Pl, 1 Border | |
| Down Ampney | 1x Dakota/Horsa | 48 | 'E' Sqn | S | 222 | 7 Pl, 7 KOSB | |
| | 1x Dakota/Horsa | | | | 229 | No. 3 Section, No. 2 MMG Pl, 7 KOSB | |
| | 1x Dakota/Horsa | | | | 237 | section, No. 1 MMG Pl, 7 KOSB | |
| | 1x Dakota/Horsa | 271 | | | 239 | section, A/Tk Pl, 7 KOSB (1x 6-pdr) | |
| | 1x Dakota/Horsa | | | | 240 | section, A/Tk Pl, 7 KOSB (1x 6-pdr) | |
| | 1x Dakota/Horsa | 48 | | | 277 | No. 5 Det. No. 3 Section, No. 2 Mortar Pl, 7 KOSB | |
| Manston | 1x Albemarle/Horsa | 296 or 297 | 20 Flt, 'B' Sqn | S | 296 | OC B Coy, 2 South Staffords | |
| Tarrant Rushton | 2x Halifax/Horsa | 1 x 298 | 'C' Sqn | Z | 355 | 2ic HQ Tp, Recce Sqn (1 jeep) | |
| | | 1 x 644 | | | 364 | No. 2 Section, A Tp, Recce Sqn (2 jeeps) | |

330

| RAF Stn | Tug/Glider combinations | RAF Sqn | GPR unit | DZ/ LZ | Chalk No | Airborne Unit | Abortive gliders |
|---|---|---|---|---|---|---|---|
| Keevil | 1x Stirling/Horsa | 196 or 299 | 21 Flt, 'D' Sqn | Z | 385 | det No. 3 Pl, 9 Fd Coy, RE | |
| | 1x Stirling/Horsa | | | | 399 | Tp Ldr, A Tp, 1 Bty, 1 A/L Lt Regt, RA | |
| | 1x Stirling/Horsa | | 13 Flt, 'D' Sqn | | 457 | elms 1FOU, 1 A/L Lt Regt, RA | 457 |
| | 1x Stirling/Horsa | | | | 474 | elms 1 Para Bde HQ | |

| RAF Stn | Tug/Glider combinations | RAF Sqn | GPR unit | DZ/ LZ | Chalk No | Airborne Unit | Abortive gliders |
|---|---|---|---|---|---|---|---|
| Harwell | 1x Stirling/Horsa | 295 or 570 | 18 Flt, 'A' Sqn | N | 414 | elms Signal Section I A/B Corps HQ | |

| RAF Stn | Tug/Glider combinations | RAF Sqn | GPR unit | DZ/ LZ | Chalk No | Airborne Unit | Abortive gliders |
|---|---|---|---|---|---|---|---|
| Fairford | 1x Stirling/Horsa | 190 or 620 | 24 Flt, 'G' Sqn | Z | 435 | elms Div HQ | |
| | 1x Stirling/Horsa | | 9 Flt, 'G' Sqn | | 516 | F7 gun, F Tp, 3 Bty, 1 A/L Lt Regt, RA | |
| | 1x Stirling/Horsa | | | | 519 | 3 Para Pl, 250 Coy, RASC | |

# Appendix 10

*Air Load Manifest Operation MARKET - Third Lift*

| RAF Stn | Tug/Glider combinations | RAF Sqn | GPR unit | DZ/LZ | Chalk No | Airborne Unit | Abortive gliders |
|---|---|---|---|---|---|---|---|
| Tarrant Rushton | 4x Halifax/Horsa | 298 & 644 | Composite Flight | L | 120-123 | HQ A/Tk Bty, Polish Para Bde | 126, 130, 133 |
| | 7x Halifax/Horsa | | | | 124-130 | No. 1 Tp, A/Tk Bty, Polish Para Bde | |
| | 7x Halifax/Horsa | | | | 131-137 | No. 2 Tp, A/Tk Bty, Polish Para Bde | |
| | 2x Halifax/Horsa | | | | 138-139 | 1st Para Bn, Polish Para Bde | |
| Keevil | 15x Stirling/Horsa | 196 & 299 | Composite Flight | L | 140-154 | Bde HQ; 2nd & 3rd Para Bn; Signals; and Supplies Polish Para Bde | 144, 149, 152, 154 |
| Aborted sorties from First and Second lift regrouped on the Third lift | | | | | | | |
| Down Ampney | 1x Dakota/Horsa | 48 | 'E' Sqn | S | 272 | 1 Mortar Pl, 7 KOSB | |
| Blakehill Farm | 1x Dakota/Horsa | 233 | 5 Flt, 'D' Sqn | X | 773 | 2 A/L A/Tk Bty, RA | |
| Manston | 1x Albemarle/Horsa | 296 | 3 Flt, 'B' Sqn | X | 865 | 2 Bty, 1 A/L Lt Regt, RA | 865 |
| Tarrant Rushton | 1x Halifax/Hamilcar | 644 | 7 Flt, 'C' Sqn | X | 903 | F Tp, 2 A/L A/Tk Bty, RA | 903 |
| Fairford | 3x Stirling/Horsa | 620 190 | 'G' Sqn | X | 934 994 996 | Elms 1 (Br) AB Div HQ 1st Para Bde | 994 |
| Keevil | 1x Stirling/Horsa | 196 | 8 or 22 Flt, 'D' Sqn | X | 1026 | 133 Para Fd Amb RAMC | 1026 |
| Harwell | 1x Stirling/Horsa | 570 | 'A' Sqn | X | 974 | 2 Pl, 250 Coy, RASC | 974 |

# Appendix 11

*Alphabetical Nominal Roll of Members of the Glider Pilot Regiment*
*Deployed in Operation MARKET GARDEN*

**ABBREVIATIONS**

| | |
|---|---|
| A/1 or * | = 'A' Squadron No. 1 Flight or Flight unknown |
| D | = Died Prisoner of War |
| E | = Escaped |
| KIA | = Killed in Action/Died of Wounds |
| POW | = Prisoner of War |
| RAR | = Returned to Nijmegen 25/26 September 1944 |
| F/L | = Forced Landed |
| CN | = Chalk Number |
| Nijm | = Landed at Nijmegen |

**ABBREVIATIONS POW CAMPS**

The prefix 'O' indicates that the camp is an Oflag.

| | |
|---|---|
| O79 | = Braunschweig |
| O9A/H | = Spangenburg bei Kassel |

The absence of a prefix indicates that the camp is a Stalag; the prefix 'L' stands for Stalag Luft.

| | |
|---|---|
| 4B | = Mühlberg (Elbe) |
| 4F | = Hartmansdorf Chemnitz |
| 7A | = Moosburg (Isar) |
| 8C | = Kunaukz Sprottau/Sagan |
| 9B | = Wegscheide Weilberg bei Bad Orb. |
| 9C | = Muhlhausen |
| 11A | = Altengrabow |
| 11B | = Fallingbostel |
| 12A | = Limburg s.d. Lahn |
| 13C | = Hammelburg am Main |
| 344 | = Lamsdorf |
| DL | = Dulaf Luft at Wetzlar |
| L1 | = Barth Vogelsang |
| L3 | = Sagan and Belaria |
| L7 | = Bankau |
| * | = Name mentioned in POW Book but no camp number given. |
| Apel | = Apeldoorn, Dutch town, hospital |
| Ensch | = Enschede, Dutch town, hospital |
| Frei | = Freising, German town, hospital |

## PRISONERS OF WAR BRITISH ARMY 1939–1945

Alphabetical Nominal Registers (including Number, Rank, POW Number, Regiment or Corps and Camp Location Details) Listing over 107,000 British Army Prisoners of War of All Ranks held in Germany and German Occupied Territories. First published 1945 by HMSO; the 1990 edition published by War Museum Department of Printed Books. All lists corrected generally up to 30 March 1945. In some cases information not listed but added as the result of own research.

# GPR Nominal Roll & Casualty List

## A

Abel, L. Sgt. 2149270, C/6, POW 11B, CN-325
Adams, R.A. Sgt. 14426135, E/*, KIA , CN-837
Adams, N.V.M. Lieut. 129156, D/13, F/L-KIA , CN-457
Adams, D.M. S/Sgt. 136331, G/9, POW 12A, CN-*
Affolter, L.M. Sgt. 165251, D/13, RAR, CN-396
Agar, G.S. S/Sgt. 2151406, G/9, POW 11B, CN-*
Aitken, P. S/Sgt. 2879361, F/16, POW *, CN-265
Aldridge, T. S/Sgt. , D/*, F/L , CN-152
Allan, P.J. S/Sgt. , F/*, RAR , CN-*
Allen, C.H. S/Sgt. B/*, RAR , CN-*
Allen, D.M. S/Sgt. G/10, RAR , CN-*
Allen, G.R.E. Sgt. 2579984, C/6, POW 12A, CN-908
Allen, S. Sgt. 134105, D/8, F/L , CN-1026
Allison, G.S. Sgt. 2061978, E/*, KIA , CN-*
Anderson, A.S. S/Sgt. 2984513, E/11, RAR , CN-*
Anderson, D.G. Lieut. 123863, B/4, KIA , CN-*
Anderton, K. Sgt. D/21, RAR , CN-390
Andrews, K.J.S. Maj. GSO2 (Ops) 12136, HQ GPR/*, Nijm , CN-*
Andrews, D. Sgt. 14311885, B/20, KIA, CN-293
Andrews, DFM, H.N. S/Sgt. 2078059, E/11, RAR, CN-*
Annand, J. S/Sgt. 2760190, B/3, POW 11B, CN-876
Appleton, F. S/Sgt. 5121712, F/16, POW DL, CN-754
Appleyard, J. S/Sgt. 1802300, B/20, RAR, CN-352
Ashby, R.F. S/Sgt. 170154, B/3, RAR, CN-869
Ashleigh, F. Sgt. 14417002, A/2, POW L7, CN-*
Ashworth, W. S/Sgt. 6291865, B/20, POW 4B, CN-353
Askew, D.G. Sgt. 5393164, B/3, POW 11A, CN-881
Aston, F.C. Capt. 90059, C/6, RAR, CN-904
Atkins, W. S/Sgt. 6465564, C/X, RAR, CN-335
Attwood, W. S/Sgt. 723790, E/*, RAR, CN-270
Attwood, P.A. S/Sgt. 6293864, C/*, RAR, CN-324
Atwell, D.O.E. S/Sgt. 5672772, C/*, RAR, CN-370
Augty, S. Sgt. 4617488, D/5, F/L-POW DL, CN-773
Ayton, B. S/Sgt. F/14, RAR , CN-*

## B

Baacke, F.W. S/Sgt. 2120521, B/4, F/L , CN-149
Bailey, W.R. Sgt. 7357123, F/16, RAR, CN-*
Baker, D.E. S/Sgt. 4979177, C/*, POW 11B, CN-371
Baker, A.W. S/Sgt. 1431080, F/16, RAR, CN-*
Baker, E.D. Sgt. 3972044, F/16, RAR, CN-*
Baker, R.R. Sgt. 833884, B/19, POW 11B, CN-345

Baker, E.J. S/Sgt. 6468601, B/20, KIA, CN-306
Baldwin, A. S/Sgt. 1916518, B/20, RAR, CN-292
Baldwin, J. Lieut. 269414, C/7, POW *, CN-314
Banks, R. S/Sgt. 6015841, F/14, KIA, CN-*
Banpier, Sgt. C/HQ, F/L , CN-901
Barclay, J.H. Lieut. 182663, B/20, F/L, CN-298
Barclay, F.H. Capt. 99951, D/21, RAR, CN-*
Barnes, R. Sgt. 7602157, F/*, POW 11B, CN-*
Barratt, R.E.A. S/Sgt. 90573, A/1, POW 11B, CN-*
Barrie, W.N. Capt. 138718, G/HQ, KIA, CN-*
Bartlett, H.T. Capt. 1807080, A/HQ, Nijm, CN-*
Bartley, R.R., Sgt, 1880346, A/2, Nijm
Bashforth, A.L. S/Sgt. 4750116, D/8, KIA, CN-*
Basnett, E.F. Sgt. 1655127, G/10, RAR, CN-1004
Bates, J.B. S/Sgt. 912044, G/10, POW *, CN-*
Baxter, G.S. S/Sgt. 2597407, C/*, KIA, CN-365
Baxter, I.N. S/Sgt. 2765213, B/19, POW 8C, CN-886
Baxter, N. Lieut. 172276, D/HQ, RAR, CN-*
Bayford, G.W. W.O.I R.S.M. 6843827, 1 Wing/HQ, POW *, CN-*
Bayley, W.J. S/Sgt. 129586, C/X, POW 12A, CN-329
Baylis, G.S. S/Sgt. 6206242, B/19, POW DL, CN-332
Beard, K. S/Sgt. 6291974, D/13, F/L, CN-462
Begum, C. Sgt. 7904031, C/X, POW *, CN-329
Bell, A. S/Sgt. 812185, E/*, KIA, CN-*
Bennett, J.C. Sgt. 3185886, F/*, RAR, CN-*
Bermingham, C. S/Sgt. 151747, B/3, RAR, CN-867
Berry, D. Sgt. A/2, F/L-RAR , CN-414
Bestall, S.S. S/Sgt. 7022602, D/*, POW L3, CN-*
Betts, G. Sgt. 14233066, D/8, POW 12A, CN-*
Bevan, E. S/Sgt. 2891593, D/*, RAR, CN-*
Bewley, J.M. Lieut. 180516, G/9, KIA Apel, CN-*
Binnington, G.L. S/Sgt. 1427764, F/*, KIA , CN-*
Binns, A. Sgt. 3390495, F/*, POW 12A, CN-*
Birch, N. S/Sgt. B/20, RAR , CN-351
Bird, W. Sgt. 2082863, E/11, POW *, CN-282
Bird, R. S/Sgt. 2929814, D/13, RAR, CN-*
Birkett, W. Sgt. G/*, RAR , CN-*
Bishop, C.W., S/Sgt, 7044162, A/*, Nijm
Bishop, R.G. S/Sgt. 1872087, G/10, POW 11B, CN-43
Black, B. S/Sgt. 884545, D/22, F/L-POW *, CN-956
Blackledge, J. Sgt. 940321, B/19, POW 12A, CN-337
Blackwood, I.J. W.O.II S.S.M. 2881235, F/HQ, POW 11B, CN-166
Blake, H.S. S/Sgt. 3190596, A/1, F/L, CN-144
Blake, B. Sgt. 14200012, D/21, RAR , CN-400

Bland, S.A. S/Sgt. 6020324, E/25, POW 11B, CN-850
Blanthorn, W. S/Sgt. 8228874, A/1, POW 11B, CN-141
Blatch, J.F.B. Maj. 94149, 2 Wing/HQ, F/L, CN-162
Blenkinsop, Sgt. E/11, RAR , CN-222
Blinkhorn, R. Sgt. 5188375 A/*, RAR , CN-*
Dlock, J. S/Sgt. 6157987, B/4, RAR, CN-13?
Blundell, K. S/Sgt. 4460360, B/3, POW 12A, CN-866
Bode, Sgt. 72337, B/20, RAR , CN-305
Boland, O.F. S/Sgt. 1449953, C/*, RAR, CN-359
Bond, P.J. Sgt. 14417457, F/15, POW *, CN-*
Bone, S.G. S/Sgt. 2162088, B/*, RAR, CN-*
Bonham, J.F. Sgt. 2720768, C/*, KIA, CN-124
Bonner, I.K. Sgt. 14423232, D/*, POW L7, CN-151
Bonney, J.J.P. Sgt. 7601227, E/11, POW Apel, CN-227
Bonome, J.W.R. S/Sgt. 6853401, C/*, RAR, CN-317
Bonsey, R.A. Sgt. 5387698, D/*, KIA , CN-*
Bonter, S.G. S/Sgt. 1918620, D/5, POW 11B, CN-791
Boorman, N. J. Sgt. 1580835, E/HQ, KIA , CN-221
Booth, T. Sgt. 3608135, E/*, RAR, CN-280
Bosley, J. Sgt. 7356434, A/1, F/L-KIA, CN-5003
Boswell, C. Sgt. 10539450, D/*, POW DL, CN-*
Bosworth, A.J. S/Sgt. 5729053, A/*, POW 11B, CN-125
Bottomley, K.L. S/Sgt. 5510945, F/*, POW 12A, CN-*
Bottomley, J.B. Lieut. 74469, 1 Wing/HQ, RAR, CN-*
Boucher, A. S/Sgt. F/14, RAR , CN-*
Bowden, S.K. Sgt. 71237, F/16, POW *, CN-*
Bowen, J. S/Sgt. 1930900, B/4, POW 12A, CN-*
Bowerman, J.W. S/Sgt. 6461238, D/13, RAR, CN-*
Bowles, R. Sgt. 215930, B/*, RAR, CN-3
Bowman, A. S/Sgt. 6350228, C/*, RAR, CN-321
Boyce, R.R.W. S/Sgt. 5727510, F/16, POW 11B, CN-*
Boyd, R.O.F. Lieut. 71012, C/*, POW E, CN-354
Boyd, J. F. S/Sgt. / SQMS 7013328, B/HQ, KIA , CN-N.F.
Boyle, P.B. S/Sgt. 4983193, B/3, POW 12A, CN-880
Brackstone, C.T. Sgt. 2083005, C/*, KIA, CN-319
Bradbeer, A.L. Sgt. 14230534, F/16, POW 4B, CN-*
Bradburn, W Sgt. 2577105, D/*, RAR , CN-*
Bradbury, J.A. Sgt. 14547304, D/22, POW DL, CN-*
Bradshaw, W. S/Sgt. 85698, A/2, Nijm, CN-*
Bralee, S. Sgt. 5127615, F/14, KIA , CN-*
Bramah, M.A. S/Sgt. 2765856, A/2, RAR, CN-*
Bratt, F. Sgt. 4128898, A/17, RAR , CN-924
Brayley, A.H. S/Sgt. 107607, F/14, POW 9C, CN-*
Brazier, P.J. Lieut. 214774, E/25, KIA , CN-848
Breach, T.P. Lieut. 2 Wing/HQ, RAR, CN-*
Bridgewater, W.G. S/Sgt. 6088816, D/*, RAR, CN-*
Briggs, G.A. Sgt. 4984260, E/*, KIA, CN-*
Briggs, G.R. S/Sgt. 6294891, B/4, KIA, CN-*
Briggs, D. S/Sgt. 909929, E/11, POW *, CN-226
Bright, G. S/Sgt. 5388254, A/17, RAR, CN-929
Brighton, J. S/Sgt? , E/*, RAR , CN-*
Briody, M.J. W.O.I R.S.M. 2717183, 2 Wing/HQ, RAR, CN-185
Briscoe, R.W. Lieut. 299603, E/*, KIA O9A/H, CN-269
Bristow, G. Sgt. 1888394, B/20, F/L-RAR, CN-296
Broadley, D.S. S/Sgt. 1468299, G/10, POW *, CN-1009
Brookfield, J. S/Sgt. 85942, C/6, POW 12A, CN-908
Brooks, G. Sgt. 7590893, D/*, POW DL, CN-*

Brooksmith, E. S/Sgt. 7686373, F/16, RAR, CN-*
Brown, G.W. S/Sgt. 6405962, F/*, KIA 11B, CN-*
Brown, H.V. S/Sgt. 2929604, F/16, KIA, CN-165
Brown, J.W. Sgt. 1779063, F/*, KIA , CN-*
Brown, N.E. S/Sgt. 714883, C/*, RAR, CN-379
Brown, K. Sgt. A/1, RAR , CN-*
Brown, M. C. Sgt. 7948850, E/11, POW 11B, CN-225
Brown, A.S. Sgt. 14569245, F/16, RAR, CN-259
Brown, A. Sgt. B/19, RAR , CN-889
Brown, N.F. S/Sgt. G/24, RAR , CN-516
Browne, G. S/Sgt. 2034827, D/5, F/L-RAR, CN-773
Browne, E.W. S/Sgt. 5730039, G/9, POW 12A, CN-*
Bruce, R.C. Sgt. 6203726, F/*, KIA, CN-*
Bruce, J. Sgt. 6211584, A/17, POW 4B, CN-927
Bryant, P. Sgt. 6475118, C/*, RAR, CN-366
Bryant, K.L. Sgt. T/78480, G/24, RAR, CN-435
Bryce, C. S/Sgt. 3254730, E/*, POW L7, CN-128
Buckley, Tpr. D/*, RAR , CN-N.F.
Bullivant, L. Sgt. 4804561, B/20, RAR , CN-350
Bullock, R.V. Sgt. 5252386, G/9, RAR, CN-*
Bunkall, C.N. Sgt. 911333, C/X, POW 12A, CN-331
Burge, J.G. Sgt. 7955094, C/*, KIA , CN-379
Burgess, D. S/Sgt. E/11, RAR , CN-229
Burgoyne, W.A. Sgt. 4749099, B/HQ, POW 12A, CN-859
Burridge, G.H. Sgt. 2009014, E/*, KIA, CN-*
Burrow, J.G. Sgt. 14348730, F/16, RAR, CN-256
Buttler, H. Sgt. , E/11, RAR , CN-230
Buxey, W.T. Sgt. 1876657, G/10, POW DL, CN-*

## C

Cairns, S.G. Capt. 164161, D/13, RAR, CN-*
Calder, R.R. S/Sgt. 3859441, E/*, POW DL, CN-*
Cameron, Sgt. D/8, RAR , CN-*
Campbell, G. S/Sgt. 3601755, F/*, RAR, CN-*
Campbell, A. S/Sgt. 2694009, A/*, POW 12A, CN-413
Candrick, Sgt. D/*, RAR, CN-*
Cardy, R.W. S/Sgt. 6091457, D/13, RAR, CN-*
Carling, H. Sgt. T/175486, C/*, RAR, CN-354
Carlton, A. S/Sgt. F/*, POW *, CN-*
Carlton, E.N. Sgt. E/*, POW 11B, CN-*
Carlton, E. S/Sgt. 1902688, A/17, RAR, CN-924
Carr, J. Sgt. 1440700, C/X, Nijm , CN-491
Carter, C. S/Sgt. 1905999, C/*, RAR, CN-374
Carter, A. Sgt. 3607994, B/19, POW *, CN-347
Cartlidge, J.A. Sgt. A/2, Nijm , CN-*
Cartlidge, D. S/Sgt. 1504859, G/9, KIA, CN-*
Carver, J. Sgt. 1079146, E/*, RAR , CN-*
Cason, D. S/Sgt. 5192242, C/X, Nijm, CN-491
Casswell, T.R. Sgt. 14291794, C/*, POW 8C, CN-360
Castle, V.E. S/Sgt. 912746, F/16, KIA, CN-*
Catford, A.G. Lieut. E/*, RAR , CN-*
Catt, L.J.T. S/Sgt. 6400643, A/17, RAR, CN-922
Caunter, H. S/Sgt. B/20, RAR , CN-304
Caves, J.J. Sgt. 7020145, B/3, KIA *, CN-867
Cawthray, G. S/Sgt. 4695914, G/9, F/L-RAR, CN-1001
Cean, Sgt. F/14, RAR , CN-*
Chadwick, R. Sgt. B/20, RAR, CN-301
Chamberlin, B. S/Sgt. 2759851, A/1, RAR, CN-*
Chambers, W. Sgt. F/*, RAR , CN-*

Chandler, F.J. Sgt. 14650728, B/20, KIA, CN-348
Chapman, H.K. Lieut. 128777, A/2, Nijm, CN-*
Chapman, H.A.F. S/Sgt. 4267802, C/*, POW 12A, CN-366
Chapman, A.G. S/Sgt. 3966517, A/1, RAR, CN-*
Chappell, K. S/Sgt. 938773, D/5, POW 11B, CN-*
Chatterton, G.J.S. Col. 91149, HQ GPR/*, Nijm, CN-*
Chignell, W.R. Capt. / Rev. 291948, 2 Wing/HQ, RAR, CN-N.F.
Chittleburgh, K.T. Lieut. 186045, D/5, KIA, CN-*
Christian, T.G. Sgt. 3774210, A/17, RAR, CN-916
Christieson, J.J.R. S/Sgt. 2695065, C/*, POW 12A, CN-906
Clark, A.A. S/Sgt. 2094037, A/*, KIA, CN-*
Clark, P.R. Lieut. 149279, F/14, RAR, CN-*
Clark, P.B. Lieut. 109544, C/X, Nijm, CN-490
Clarke, C.S. Sgt. 2118896, E/*, RAR, CN-*
Clarke, L.R. Sgt. E/*, RAR , CN-*
Clarke, R.E. Sgt. 7949735, E/*, POW 12A, CN-*
Clarke, P. S/Sgt. 7356321, G/10, POW 11B, CN-184
Clarke, A.E.B. S/Sgt. E/11, RAR, CN-237
Clarke, B. Sgt. 5886642, B/20, RAR, CN-300
Clarke, J.R. S/Sgt. 5726667, B/3, POW 7A, CN-881
Clarke, E.E. S/Sgt. 951404, G/9, KIA, CN-*
Clarke, L. Sgt, A/*, Nijm
Clayton, M.J. S/Sgt. 1941921, A/1, POW *, CN-*
Clenaghan, H.C. S/Sgt. 133139, B/19, POW *, CN-328
Clowe, S.G.A. S/Sgt. 2081291, E/*, POW 11B, CN-*
Coates, P. S/Sgt. 2340879, B/20, RAR, CN-308
Coates, A.E. S/Sgt. 2093098, D/8, POW 11B, CN-*
Cobbold, G.A. S/Sgt. 2575349, F/16, POW *, CN-*
Cole, H.C.L. Lieut. 193639, B/19, KIA, CN-327
Cole, H.W. Sgt. 14203578, B/20, RAR, CN-308
Collett, G.E.H. Sgt. 6291721, B/3, POW 12A, CN-866
Collins, G.H. Sgt. 2879664, E/11, RAR, CN-223
Collins, C.T. S/Sgt. 2931611, B/3, POW 12A, CN-860
Conchie, R.H. Lieut. 304609, C/*, POW L1, CN-121
Consterdine, K. Sgt. 910222, B/20, POW 8C, CN-295
Cook, L.A.L. Sgt. 7943128, G/10, F/L-KIA, CN-518
Coomber, H. Sgt. 7264009, F/15, RAR, CN-*
Coombs, A. S/Sgt. 1155255, D/*, F/L, CN-964
Cooper, G.A.H. S/Sgt. 1436462, D/13, RAR, CN-*
Cooper, D.L.G. Sgt. 7346124, B/20, RAR, CN-302
Coppack, P.M. S/Sgt. 937504, F/16, POW *, CN-*
Corfield, R. Sgt. 14344873, E/*, POW *, CN-*
Cornish, R.F. Sgt. 2118009, E/*, RAR, CN-798
Cornish, D. Sgt. 903724, F/15, POW DL, CN-*
Corrie, M.T. Capt. 177502, G/9, RAR, CN-*
Cotterill, J. S/Sgt. 5109253, B/3?, RAR, CN-*
Coulthrop, S/Sgt. G/24, RAR, CN934
Cowan, E.A. Sgt. 14418015, F/*, KIA Apel, CN-*
Cowper, G. Sgt. 14528420, C/*, RAR, CN-372
Craddock, A. S/Sgt. 4980721, G/9, POW 11B, CN-*
Cram, A. S/Sgt. 3643512, D/13, F/L-POW L7, CN-478
Crawley, R. Sgt. 7662022, D/8, RAR, CN-*
Creevy, D.W. S/Sgt. 204205, F/14, RAR, CN-*
Crockett, G. Sgt. 5625607, C/X, POW 12A, CN-333
Crockford, P.R. S/Sgt. 2063433, G/*, POW 12A, CN-*
Croft, N. S/Sgt. A/*, Nijm , CN-*
Croft, R.M. Sgt. 4929130, B/20, KIA, CN-351
Crone, H. Sgt. 2051585, B/20, RAR, CN-309

Crook, J.M. S/Sgt. 177208, F/*, POW *, CN-122
Croot, R.S. Maj. 40686, G/HQ, RAR, CN-*
Crossland, B. Sgt. 3387229, G/23, RAR, CN-*
Culpan, E.H. Sgt. 2081536, D/*, POW DL, CN-*
Culverwell, S.M. Lieut. 216816, F/*, KIA, CN-*
Cummings, G. Sgt. B/*, RAR, CN-*
Cummings, S/Sgt. A/2, Nijm , CN-*
Cummins, B.A. S/Sgt. 14287144, A/2, F/L-KIA, CN-5000
Curley, J. S/Sgt. 7377256, G/9, KIA, CN-*
Cutler, J. Sgt. 912610, D/13, RAR, CN-*

# D

Dadd, S.L. Sgt. 2362599, C/7, RAR, CN-905
Dale, R.R. S/Sgt. 5112070, B/19, POW L3, CN-342
Dale, DFC, J.A.C. Maj. 149290, C/HQ, RAR, CN-314
Dallimore, A.J. Sgt. 1918346, B/*, KIA, CN-*
Dalzell, Sgt. F/14, RAR, CN-188
Dance, A.V. S/Sgt. 6018787, E/11, POW 11B, CN-282
Dance, F.V. Sgt. 1878141, F/15, RAR, CN-*
Daniels, D.D. S/Sgt. 5340429, A/17, KIA, CN-917
Dauncey, M.D.K. Lieut. 184739, G/9, POW E, CN-*
Davey, T.E. Sgt. 2189607, B/3, KIA , CN-876
Davidson, W. S/Sgt. 7942480, A/*, POW *, CN-*
Davidson, D.N. Sgt. 14413964, F/14, RAR, CN-*
Davidson, T.M.W. S/Sgt. 915972, F/16, RAR, CN-*
Davies, D.G. S/Sgt. 7400698, B/*, KIA, CN-*
Davies, J. Sgt. 1103621, A/*, POW *, CN-*
Davies, V. S/Sgt. 3254551, D/*, RAR, CN-*
Davies, W.H. Sgt. 2622598, C/*, POW 7A, CN-357
Davies, F. Lieut. 117932, C/*, POW L1, CN-909
Davies, J. Sgt. 91615, G/10, RAR, CN-*
Davies, S/Sgt. F/14, RAR , CN-*
Davis, J.R.V. S/Sgt. 5568956, E/*, POW 7A, CN-*
Davis, G.E. S/Sgt. 2045543, F/16, POW DL, CN-*
Davison, V. Sgt. F/14, RAR , CN-*
Davy, Sgt. D/*, F/L , CN-154
Dawson, C.D. S/Sgt. 997529, Nijm A/*, CN-*
Day, S.P. S/Sgt? B/*, RAR , CN-*
de Courcy Ashe, N.C. Lieut. 219857, E/11, POW *, CN-224
De Rungary, C. Sgt. B/20, RAR, CN-297
Deakin, S/Sgt. E/11, RAR , CN-230
Dean, C. Sgt. 14433795, B/19, POW 11B, CN-888
Dean, W.V., Sgt, F/16, RAR, CN-253
Deasy, W.R. S/Sgt. 985314, D/8, POW 11B, CN-*
Deeley, G. Sgt. 5127622, D/*, POW DL, CN-*
Delahunty, B.J. Sgt. 1402270, F/*, RAR, CN-*
DeLiss, D.C. Sgt. 13046281, F/16, RAR, CN-174
Denby, C. S/Sgt. G/9, RAR , CN-*
Denholme, W.B. S/Sgt. 2759257, F/14, RAR, CN-*
Dennis, F. Sgt. 5887705, B/19, POW DL, CN-341
Dennison, G.J. Sgt. B/*, RAR , CN-*
Dent, H. Sgt. 3088938, C/*, RAR, CN-315
Derbyshire, F.A. Lieut. 304446, G/9, KIA, CN-*
Devey, J. S/Sgt. 3601654, E/*, POW L3, CN-*
Didsbury, N. Sgt. 14574025, E/*, POW *, CN-130
Ditch, R.R. S/Sgt. 6149774, A/1, KIA, CN-501
Dobbings, W.D. Sgt. 907776, A/2, KIA, CN-*
Dodd, S.T. S/Sgt. 850843, F/14, POW 11B, CN-*

Dodd, W. S/Sgt. 5123264, D/22, KIA, CN-*
Dodwell, C.B. Capt. 166383, E/12, POW O9A/H, CN-*
Dolling, B. Sgt. 6296397, D/13, RAR, CN-*
Donaldson, J.C. Sgt. 1919565, B/3, POW 12A, CN-869
Donaldson, D. S/Sgt. D/5, POW *, CN-*
Doorn, H. S/Sgt. 849351, A/17, RAR , CN-921
Douglas, R.G. S/Sgt. 2336371, E/*, RAR, CN-*
Dowling, W.L. S/Sgt. 927650, E/*, POW 11B, CN-271
Downing, R.C. S/Sgt. 5252854, D/*, POW 11B, CN-*
Downing, M.W. Lieut. 156901, G/HQ, KIA, CN-*
Dowse, P. S/Sgt. F/14, RAR , CN-*
Dray, R.F. Sgt. 5735906, D/8, RAR, CN-*
Driver, R.J. Sgt. 6206076, A/1, POW 11B, CN-*
Drurey, B. S/Sgt. 889599, F/14, KIA, CN-*
Duffy,  D.S. Sgt. E/11, RAR , CN-239
Dunbar, W.S. Sgt. 2572042, E/*, POW L3, CN-*
Dunham, C.W. S/Sgt. 7382702, F/*, POW 11B, CN-*
Dunn, H. S/Sgt. 2929572, D/*, KIA, CN-*
Duns, G. S/Sgt. 4453864, G/24, RAR, CN-435
Dyall, W.A. Sgt. 853162, E/*, POW 12A, CN-794
Dyson, W.F. Lieut. 259921, A/HQ, RAR, CN-*

## E

Eardley, T.J. S/Sgt. 1455441, B/20, RAR, CN-295
Eardley, R.E. S/Sgt. 5349629, B/20, RAR, CN-309
Eason, F.C. Sgt. 2068480, D/*, POW 11B, CN-*
East, S.J. S/Sgt. 2933454, D/13, RAR, CN-*
Eastwood, J.W. Sgt. 2657864, F/*, POW, 11B, CN-*
Eburn,  Sgt. A/*, Nijm , CN-*
Edge, C.A. Sgt. 14661799, F/*, POW 11B, CN-*
Edney, F.H.G. Tpr. 5670763, B/HQ, POW, CN-N.F.
Edwards, K. S/Sgt. 3654436, D/13, F/L-POW, CN-468
Edwards, A. S/Sgt. 4126093, F/16, POW 11B, CN-*
Edwards, J.E. S/Sgt. 5387319, A/2, RAR, CN-5002
Egan, R.G. Sgt. 7885602, G/*, POW 11B, CN-*
Ellin, J.B.C. S/Sgt. 886069, G/9, F/L-KIA, CN-994
Elliott, D.G. Sgt. 7536323, D/*, POW 11B, CN-*
Ellis, J.A. S/Sgt. 1901936, E/*, POW *, CN-276
Elton, E.N. S/Sgt. 1871244, E/11, RAR, CN-284
England, E. S/Sgt. 3387172, D/8, RAR, CN-*
Ennis, B.B. S/Sgt. E/*, RAR , CN-837
Evans, J. Sgt. 4127426, D/*, KIA , CN-*
Evans, R.G. S/Sgt. 129643, E/*, F/L, CN-813
Evans, A.E. S/Sgt. E/11, RAR , CN-227
Evans, E.J. Sgt. 5393051, B/19, POW 11B, CN-886
Evans, W.E. S/Sgt. 3976318, B/20, KIA, CN-349
Evans, A. S/Sgt. G/23, CN-*
Evans, T.I. Sgt. 13040742, G/24, POW K, CN-*

## F

Fairgrieve, J.M. S/Sgt. 915952, F/15, RAR , CN-*
Fairweather, J.S. S/Sgt. 3056208, G/*, KIA *, CN-*
Farnes, W.J. S/Sgt. 5115491, E/11, POW 11B, CN-241
Faulkner, P.M. Sgt. , G/24, RAR , CN-*
Feather, D. Sgt. , E/*, RAR , CN-278
Feehily, B.P.S. S/Sgt. , F/16, RAR , CN-*
Fendick, H. S/Sgt. 1432800, G/10, KIA , CN-1002
Fenge, W.J. Sgt. 6207685, A/17, POW 11B, CN-918
Ferguson, T. Sgt. 7758018, F/14, RAR , CN-188
Ferguson, W.S. Sgt. 3061632, A/2, KIA *, CN-5002

Ferrar, R. S/Sgt. 1432374, D/13, RAR , CN-*
Firth, E.H. S/Sgt. 1880649, F/16, KIA , CN-*
Fisher, C. S/Sgt. 3458590, D/5, KIA , CN-*
Fisher, W.K. S/Sgt. 4278476, E/11, RAR , CN-286
Fisher, F.W. Sgt. 93245, B/20, RAR , CN-303
Fitchett, S. S/Sgt. , C/*, RAR , CN-*
Fletcher, P.N. Capt. 299274, 1 Wing/HQ, RAR , CN-434
Flowers, S. S/Sgt. 188726, A/17, RAR , CN-818
Follington, D.C. Sgt. 1875955, E/*, KIA , CN-277
Ford, H. S/Sgt. 6269287, F/*, RAR , CN-*
Forrester, R. Sgt. 14000080, D/*, KIA , CN-*
Foster, E. S/Sgt. 6401145, A/*, POW 12A, CN-*
Foster, L. S/Sgt. , D/*, RAR , CN-*
Foster, A.J. S/Sgt. , F/16, RAR , CN-183
Foster, L. Sgt. , B/19, F/L , CN-336
Foster, F. Sgt. 6139233, G/24, RAR , CN-*
Fowkes, T. Sgt. 4983080, E/*, KIA , CN-*
Fowler, C. S/Sgt. 6031567, E/11, RAR , CN-231
Fox, G.E. Sgt. 6145573, B/19, POW 11B, CN-344
Francis, T. S/Sgt. 327651, G/9, RAR , CN-*
Franks, R. Sgt. 1561122, D/13, KIA , CN-*
Fraser, H.N. S/Sgt. 2135945, D/*, POW 7A, CN-*
Fraser, R.A. Sgt. 953786, D/21, F/L-KIA , CN-389
Frater, L.J. S/Sgt. 5188314, D/5, RAR , CN-*
Frazer, O. Sgt. 180492, C/*, RAR , CN-324
Freem, J.S. Sgt. 2077123, G/*, POW 12A, CN-*
Freeman, G. Sgt. 5392493, B/19, POW E, CN-327
French, J. Sgt. 4626702, A/17, RAR, CN-921
Frew, E. S/Sgt. 1083001, G/10, KIA, CN-*
Futter, H.L. Lieut. 261666, B/HQ, RAR, CN-N.F.

## G

Gabbott, G.H.G. S/Sgt. 83787, C/*, RAR, CN-907
Gammon, P.J.F. Sgt. 10555020, F/14, RAR, CN-194
Garbutt, W.M. Sgt. 816515, F/14, POW 4B, CN-*
Gardner, L.J. S/Sgt. 878764, D/21, F/L-KIA, CN-389
Garnett, R.H. Lieut. 172350, E/*, POW O9A/H, CN-*
Garnett, R. S/Sgt. 1518965, C/*, RAR, CN-323
Garnham, R.A.D. Sgt. 3966566, A/1, POW 12A, CN-501
Garrard, S.W. Sgt. 10577268, F/*, POW *, CN-*
Garrett, B. Sgt. E/*, F/L , CN-149
Gault, B.T. Sgt. 26213833, B/19, KIA, CN-340
Gear, R.H. S/Sgt. 806683, E/11, POW 11B, CN-225
Geary, T. S/Sgt. 4983001, B/20, F/L-RAR, CN-296
Gell, C. Sgt. 410229, D/*, KIA , CN-*
Gibb, B. S/Sgt. A/1, RAR , CN-146
Gibbons, L.N. S/Sgt. 860893, D/5, RAR, CN-*
Gibbons, H.A.J. S/Sgt. 6481491, D/8, RAR, CN-*
Gibson, R.G. S/Sgt. 892357, F/16, RAR, CN-*
Gillow, C. S/Sgt. 894370, D/*, POW L7, CN-1014
Girvin, R. S/Sgt. 7022767, B/19, POW L7, CN-340
Gittings, J.H. Sgt. 4917002, 2 Wing/HQ, KIA, CN-*
Glover, J. S/Sgt. 6970561, C/X, POW 12A, CN-333
Godman, T.A.D. Lieut. 109394, C/6, POW L1, CN-914
Goldsack, R.L. S/Sgt. B/19, F/L, CN-336
Goldthorpe, L. Sgt. 4546883, E/12, RAR, CN-*
Goodwin, W. S/Sgt. 1508988, B/3, KIA, CN-880
Goold, D.S. S/Sgt. 5679922, A/2, KIA, CN-*

337

Gordon, C.J. Sgt. 5673163, F/*, POW 11B, CN-822
Gordon, W.D. S/Sgt. 934693, C/*, POW 11B, CN-912
Gordon, W.J. S/Sgt. 5391601, B/3, POW 12A, CN-873
Gordon, T. Sgt. 3192114, C/6, RAR, CN-904
Gosney, R. Sgt. 7900545, C/X, Nijm, CN-492
Gough, R. Sgt. B/3, RAR , CN-879
Gould, R.P. S/Sgt. 2087378, E/*, KIA, CN-*
Gow, N.G. Sgt?, A/*, RAR? , CN-*
Gowens, J.R. S/Sgt. 6211777, B/20, POW 11B, CN-303
Graham, J.W.M. Sgt. F/*, RAR, CN-*
Graham, S. Sgt. E/*, RAR , CN-*
Graham, J.F. Sgt. 1946447, F/14, KIA, CN-190
Graham, S.G. Sgt. 2003648, D/5, RAR, CN-*
Grant, H.R.C. S/Sgt. 2342594, E/*, POW L3, CN-288
Grant, R.S. S/Sgt. 6474934, A/1, POW L7, CN-147
Gray, T. S/Sgt. 1914661, C/*, RAR, CN-357
Gray, W.D. Sgt. G/10, RAR , CN-*
Green, K.W. Sgt. 14251832, C/*, KIA, CN-*
Green, K.P. Sgt. F/14, RAR, CN-129
Green, J. Sgt. D/5, RAR , CN-*
Greene, J.C. Sgt. 819826, B/3, KIA, CN-871
Greenhill, F.W. Sgt. 5947872, E/11, KIA, CN-226
Greening, B.H. S/Sgt. 5952783, G/*, POW 12A, CN-*
Greenslade, G.C. S/Sgt. 6086559, G/10, POW *, CN-*
Grieve, D.G. Capt. GSO3 (Ops) , 1 A/B Div HQ/*,
    RAR, CN-N.F.
Griffith, S.C. Maj. 73789, A/HQ, Nijm, CN-407
Griffiths, R.O. Sgt. 14625110, E/*, POW *, CN-274
Griffiths, D.J. Sgt. 4189898, E/*, F/L , CN-813
Griffiths, W.G. Sgt. 4192348, G/10, POW 12A, CN-
    1008
Griffiths, J.D. Sgt. 2574023, A/17, POW 12A, CN-925
Griffiths, R.L. Sgt. 3976492, B/20, POW *, CN-352
Grimshaw, W.S. S/Sgt. 3449926, F/16, POW 11B, CN-
    259
Grisman, K.J. S/Sgt. 4105192, B/HQ, POW 9B, CN-
    862
Guild, D.G. S/Sgt. 1919122, D/21, RAR, CN-390
Gustard, H.O. S/Sgt. 1890541, F/16, RAR, CN-*
Guthrie, D.D. Sgt. 917912, F/*, POW *, CN-*
Guthrie, L. S/Sgt. 4749793, C/15, RAR, CN-359
Gwinn, M.A. Sgt. 2598378, G/*, KIA Apel, CN-*

# H

Hadfield, G.F. Sgt. 3531592, G/24, POW 7A, CN-934
Hadin, S/Sgt. E/11, RAR, CN-222
Haeffner, H.B. Lieut. 117210, A/1, RAR, CN-*
Hagen, L.E. Sgt. 14623984, D/22, RAR, CN-*
Haines, L.F. S/Sgt. 5623039, A/17, RAR, CN-919
Hall, D.A. S/Sgt. 1779297, E/*, POW 11B, CN-*
Hall, M. S/Sgt. F/14, RAR , CN-*
Hall, R.E. Sgt. 5127631, G/9, RAR, CN-*
Haller, B.J.F. Sgt. 14291815, G/24, POW *, CN-516
Halliday, A.E. S/Sgt. 177067, G/9, POW 11B, CN-*
Halsall, B.H. Capt. 134176, C/7, F/L, CN-903
Halse, E. S/Sgt. 6029666, A/17, RAR, CN-928
Hamilton, D.A. Sgt. A/1, RAR, CN-*
Hands, W.E. Sgt. 14537821, B/19, POW 12A, CN-887
Handsom, G.D.L. S/Sgt. 1890895, B/19, POW 8C, CN-
    330

Hann, S. S/Sgt. 4469214, B/3, POW 4B, CN-*
Hannam, I.C. Sgt. 4617015, D/8, KIA, CN-*
Hannon, K.W. S/Sgt. 5511619, A/*, POW 11B, CN-*
Hanson, R.E. Sgt. 14323788, F/*, POW *, CN-*
Happer, W.R.A. Lieut. 210484, F/*, POW O9A/H, CN-*
Hardie, N.G. Capt. 149735, A/1, KIA, CN-*
Hardwick, J.G. Sgt. 3054186, D/*, POW 12A, CN-*
Hardy, D.G. Sgt. 4749826, E/11, RAR, CN-241
Hardy, E. Sgt, 4755630, F/*, RAR
Harget, H.G. S/Sgt. 7367500, E/25, RAR, CN-849
Hargreaves, A.W. Sgt. 1922641, F/*, POW 4B, CN-*
Harman, C.A. S/Sgt. 1518658, A/17, RAR, CN-916
Harne, A. Sgt. 908304, B/3, POW *, CN-873
Harper, C.G.R. S/Sgt./SQMS 886629, G/24, RAR,
    CN-*
Harris, A.A. S/Sgt. 883334, E/*, KIA Apel, CN-*
Harris, J.W.R. S/Sgt. 4201321, A/1, F/L-KIA, CN-5003
Harris, H.S. S/Sgt. 5113745, B/4, KIA, CN-*
Harrison, D. S/Sgt. 326753, C/*, POW 11B, CN-368
Harrison, P. Sgt. A/17, RAR , CN-922
Harrison, D. S/Sgt. 5112206, B/19, RAR, CN-346
Harrison, W.F. S/Sgt. 7537196, B/3, RAR, CN-892
Hartford, N. Sgt. 1444913, F/14, RAR, CN-*
Hartley, D.P. Sgt. 880337, C/*, RAR, CN-373
Harvey, L. Sgt. 6026018, D/13, F/L-RAR, CN-474
Hatch, Sgt. 2589688, D/13, RAR, CN-*
Hatch, R.E. Sgt. G/9, RAR , CN-*
Hatton, D.G. S/Sgt. 325605, C/*, RAR, CN-911
Healey, E. S/Sgt. 3775315, B/19, POW *, CN-343
Heap, J. Sgt. F/14, POW *, CN-189
Hebblethwaite, B. Sgt. 6350200, F/14, KIA, CN-*
Hebden, J.R. S/Sgt. 5393601, B/19, RAR, CN-313
Hedderman, P. Sgt. G/24, RAR , CN-*
Hedgecock, L. S/Sgt. 2584748, B/3, POW 12A, CN-
    863
Hempstead, J. S/Sgt. 1454458, G/10, RAR, CN-*
Herbert, W.C. S/Sgt. 5507459, E/*, RAR, CN-*
Heritage, G. Sgt. 4752278, B/4, RAR, CN-*
Herridge, M. S/Sgt. 5511321 A/*, Nijm , CN-*
Herron, J.F. S/Sgt. 2991950, F/14, POW 12A, CN-212
Hibbert, M. Sgt. 14598314, E/25, RAR, CN-848
Higginbotham, J. S/Sgt. 905927, B/19, POW *, CN-347
Higgins, G. Sgt. 7911243, C/*, POW 12A, CN-317
Higgs, W.W. S/Sgt. 5347593, D/5, POW 11B, CN-*
Higham, R.B. Sgt. 3714069, B/3, KIA , CN-872
Hilburn, F.J. Sgt. 4031474, E/11, POW 11B, CN-290
Hill, E.W. S/Sgt. 129350, F/*, POW 11B, CN-*
Hill, P.B. S/Sgt. 5511117, C/*, KIA, CN-326
Hill, J.J. Sgt. 1874750, C/*, POW 11B, CN-910
Hill, R.G. Sgt. 207763, A/1, POW 11B, CN-*
Hiller, K. S/Sgt. A/2, RAR, CN-*
Hobbs, P.H. S/Sgt. 6897785, B/*, RAR, CN-*
Hobbs, B. S/Sgt. E/*, F/L , CN-266
Hockley, E. H. Sgt. 2323238, D/5, POW 12A, CN-*
Hodges, K.S. S/Sgt. 5189555, B/20, KIA *, CN-294
Hogben, A.A.R. S/Sgt. 6850065, G/*, POW 11B, CN-*
Hogg, G.H. Sgt. 3385251, F/14, KIA, CN-*
Holcroft, W. S/Sgt. F/14, RAR, CN-*
Holden, L. Sgt 14405769, C/6, RAR
Holdren, C.R. S/Sgt. 2698914, E/11, KIA, CN-238

338

Hole, C. Sgt. 14222864, F/*, RAR , CN-*
Hollingsworth, T. Sgt. 14276776, G/24, KIA 11B, CN-440
Holloway, E.J. S/Sgt. 3968405, G/10, KIA, CN-1003
Holman, E. Sgt. 5507089, F/16, POW *, CN-*
Holmes, A.B. S/Sgt. 934165, C/*, RAR, CN-367
Holt, B.R. S/Sgt. 7598921, E/*, RAR, CN-794
Honey, A.E. Sgt. 5342557, C/*, POW 11B, CN-*
Honey, P.J. S/Sgt. F/*, RAR, CN-*
Hooker, G.S.H. Sgt. 2600495, B/20, POW 11B, CN-307
Hooper, J.M. S/Sgt. 2584037, B/20, POW L7, CN-299
Hooper, J. Capt. 130100, 2 Wing/HQ, RAR, CN-167
Hope, R. S/Sgt. 325601, F/16, POW DL, CN-*
Hopkins, J.A. S/Sgt. 136231, B/20, POW 11B, CN-307
Hore, J.G. S/Sgt. 5192692, D/*, POW 11B, CN-*
Horrobin, S. Sgt. 5334373, B/19, POW 7A, CN-330
Horton, J.R. Sgt. 14413159, G/10, POW 12A, CN-1009
Hoskins, R.J. L/Cpl. 6411830, B/HQ, POW, CN-N.F.
Houghton, D.G. S/Sgt. 6404069, A/1, POW 11B, CN-*
Housley, J.E. Sgt?, D/*, RAR , CN-*
Howard, H. S/Sgt. T/82013, F/16, POW 11B, CN-*
Howard, L.E. S/Sgt. 6207012, E/*, POW 4F, CN-281
Howard, R.A. S/Sgt. 14200103, B/*, F/L, CN-154
Howe, J. S/Sgt, 1077879, D/5, RAR
Howe, J.A. S/Sgt. 3387214, D/13, POW 11B, CN-*
Howell, H.G. S/Sgt. 4917288, F/*, KIA, CN-*
Howes, L.H. Sgt. 5771829, F/14, KIA, CN-*
Hoyle,  Sgt. E/11, F/L , CN-240
Huard, J.F. Sgt. 10568347, C/*, KIA Ensch, CN-915
Hudson, F.P. Sgt. 14218054, D/22, F/L-POW *, CN-956
Hudson, F. S/Sgt. G/10, RAR, CN-138
Hughes, F. Sgt. 14409950, E/12, RAR, CN-*
Humphreys, C.H. S/Sgt. 5730489, E/*, KIA, CN-*
Hunter, J.S. Sgt. 14281802, B/3, KIA, CN-892
Hursk, W.C. Sgt. 14428616, E/*, POW 12A, CN-*
Hutley, J.C. S/Sgt. 5385668, C/X, Nijm, CN-488
Hutton, F.C. Sgt. 1139014, F/*, POW 12A, CN-*
Huxley, B. Sgt. 5620711, B/*, KIA, CN-134

## I

Install, A.C. Sgt. 5734412, E/*, POW 12A, CN-*
Irons, H. S/Sgt. A/*, Nijm, CN-*
Irvine, R. Lieut. 140040, B/4, KIA, CN-*
Isaacs, S.G. S/Sgt. 6149848, E/11, RAR, CN-289
Isch, R. S/Sgt. D/*, RAR , CN-*
Ison, R. S/Sgt. 5347997, D/*, POW 11B, CN-*
Ivey, A.W. S/Sgt. 1480721, B/3, POW 12A, CN-870

## J

Jackaman, L.R. Sgt. 6208421, A/17, RAR, CN-818
Jackson, B.F. Sgt. 14668607, C/*, POW 11B, CN-131
Jackson, C.J. Sgt. 2583498, B/3, POW 4B, CN-863
Jackson, B.H.P. Maj. 95473, E/HQ, RAR, CN-219
James, D.W.M. S/Sgt. 944489, E/11, POW DL, CN-279
James, A.A. Sgt. 5891665, G/24, POW 7A, CN-*
James, J. Sgt. C/X, Nijm , CN-490
Jeavons, W.T. Sgt. 5113593, C/*, KIA, CN-913
Jenkin, L. S/Sgt. 2021927, B/4, RAR, CN-*
Jenkins, J.H. S/Sgt. 1945032, A/17, POW 11B, CN-923

Jenkins, J.H. S/Sgt. 5627278, A/2, F/L, CN-974
Jenkins, N. S/Sgt. 10556149, B/4, RAR, CN-*
Jenks, G.T. S/Sgt. 3311634, C/*, POW 12A, CN-316
Jenner, A.S.L. Sgt. 872865, F/14, POW *, CN-200
Johnson, R.O. Lieut. 293326, E/25, POW O9A/H, CN-852
Johnson, S.E. Sgt. 14259380, Γ/*, POW 11B, CN *
Johnson, A.W. Sgt. 182901, C/*, POW *, CN-365
Johnson, D.A. Sgt. 2344943, A/1, KIA *, CN-*
Johnson, M. Sgt. F/14, RAR, CN-*
Johnson, E.E. Sgt. F/14, RAR, CN-205
Johnson, A.W. S/Sgt. 6018062, A/2, Nijm, CN-*
Johnson, P.D. Sgt. 1878043, B/20, KIA, CN-299
Johnston, A.F. Lieut. 112939, E/11, POW L1, CN-220
Johnston, R.B. S/Sgt. 4269644, B/20, RAR, CN-300
Johnstone, J. Sgt. 4619254, G/10, KIA , CN-*
Johnstone, S.Y. S/Sgt. 3131087, A/2, RAR, CN-*
Jolliffe, R.T.N. S/Sgt. 958807, D/8, POW 7A, CN-*
Jones, I. Sgt. F/*, RAR, CN-*
Jones, L.V. Sgt. 2080721, D/*, KIA, CN-*
Jones, W.S. S/Sgt. 1910052, B/*, RAR, CN-*
Jones, J.G. S/Sgt. 5185381, B/*, POW 4B, CN-134
Jones, D. Sgt. 14395807, C/*, POW 12A, CN-906
Jones, R.W. S/Sgt. F/14, RAR, CN-194
Jones, P.R. S/Sgt. 2580296, B/3, KIA, CN-872
Jones, A.L. Sgt. 2052660, B/3, F/L-KIA, CN-878
Joyce, T.A. S/Sgt. 2653210, E/11, F/L-KIA, CN-240

## K

Keegan, N.H. Sgt. 14307378, D/*, POW 11B, CN-*
Keeley, M.J. Sgt. 6013234, D/*, POW 8C, CN-*
Kelly, T. Sgt. 7666986, E/11, POW *, CN-232 / 233?
Kendrick, J. Sgt. 5183855, D/13, RAR, CN-*
Kennedy, J.W. S/Sgt. 1433719, A/2, POW 11B, CN-5001
Kerr, D.F. S/Sgt. 3387884, B/4, KIA, CN-*
Kershaw, J.H. Lieut. 71848, D/*, POW O9A/H, CN-*
Kettley, A.E. Sgt. 3967285, G/*, POW E, CN-*
Key, J.W. S/Sgt. , G/23, RAR, CN-120
Kiff, L.T. Sgt. 10589771, F/15, KIA, CN-*
Kilbryde, G.H. Sgt. 4922900, C/*, POW L7, CN-121
King, L. S/Sgt. 2044286, E/12, RAR, CN-*
King, A. Sgt. 203662, C/*, RAR, CN-363
King, C. Sgt. 277060, A/17, RAR, CN-929
King, C.E. S/Sgt. 5340471, G/9, RAR, CN-*
Kingdon, J.H. S/Sgt. , A/2, Nijm, CN-*
Kirkham, K. S/Sgt. 5734557, A/2, Nijm, CN-*
Kirkman, L. S/Sgt. 3779960, A/1, POW 8C, CN-*
Kitchener, J.H. S/Sgt. 6461042, F/16, RAR, CN-256
Kitts, E. Sgt. 2571666, A/1, RAR, CN-*
Klee, G. Sgt. , B/3, F/L , CN-133
Knapman, P.S. S/Sgt. 4865458, E/11?, POW 11B, CN-267
Knapman, R. Sgt. 109748, D/5, RAR, CN-*
Knowles, L. Sgt. 3909933, D/*, F/L , CN-964
Knox, S. Sgt. 820096, C/*, RAR, CN-371
Knox, W.H. Sgt. 11000594, A/1, POW L3, CN-147

## L

Lambell, L.H. S/Sgt. 6028441, D/*, POW 11B, CN-*
Langham, W. S/Sgt. , E/11, RAR, CN-236

Langley, J.M. Lieut. 113485, G/HQ, RAR, CN-*
Langton, V. S/Sgt. , E/*, RAR, CN-268
Law, J. S/Sgt. 973467, B/19, RAR, CN-887
Lawler, W. Sgt. 5249925, E/11, RAR, CN-287
Lawrence, A.C. S/Sgt. 7584739, B/4, KIA, CN-*
Lawson, E. Sgt. 133755, E/11, KIA, CN-271
Lawson, G.E. Sgt. 2580482, G/10, POW 8C, CN-138
Lawson, G. S/Sgt. 3248605, A/17, RAR, CN-918
Lawson, G. Sgt. 5348091, B/19, KIA, CN-342
Laycock, C. Sgt. 4540391, A/1, RAR , CN-*
Le Grand, J. S/Sgt. 1014589, D/13, RAR, CN-*
Leaver, M. S/Sgt. G/10, RAR , CN-1003
Ledger, J. S/Sgt. 5111304, G/9, POW 7A, CN-*
Lee, A. Sgt. 325615, C/*, RAR, CN-911
Lee, A. Sgt. 1895351, A/1, F/L , CN-144
Lee, J.B. W.O.II, S.S.M. 822574, E/HQ, KIA, CN-221
Leeder, R.C. Sgt. 6293746, B/3, POW 12A, CN-870
Leeper, B.F. Sgt. 6022527, B/4, POW 11B, CN-*
Lees, F. Sgt. 109636, B/3, POW 12A, CN-864
Legg, T. Sgt. D/21, RAR, CN-*
Legge, E. S/Sgt. D/*, F/L , CN-399
Leggett, R.J. Sgt. C/*, RAR, CN-380
Leschalles, E.H. Maj. 55754, G/23, RAR, CN-120
Lester, J. Sgt. 2 Wing/HQ, F/L , CN-162
Lesty, P.A. Sgt. 14369876, E/*, POW 12A, CN-130
Letto, G. Sgt. 1458101, E/11, POW 11B, CN-224
Levison, J.O. S/Sgt. 1478958, E/*, KIA, CN-*
Levy, L. Sgt. G/*, RAR, CN-*
Lewis, J.E. Sgt. 14218794, F/14, RAR, CN-205
Lewis, S.G. S/Sgt. 2182524, B/19, POW 11B, CN-889
Leyshon, L. Sgt. 5730411, E/11, KIA , CN-273
Liles, R.W. Sgt. 5837805, E/11, POW 11B, CN-277
Lindsay, A.B. S/Sgt. 918329, E/*, POW 4B, CN-*
Lister, M. Sgt. F/14, RAR, CN-*
Liversidge, K. Sgt. A/18, F/L, CN-421
Livingston, D.M. Sgt. 6211353, D/*, KIA, CN-*
Locke, R.B. Sgt. 5577124, F/*, POW 11B, CN-*
Locke, P. Sgt. 2588319, A/2, RAR, CN-*
Lockwood, S/Sgt. B/20, RAR, CN-301
Lodge, L. Sgt. C/7, F/L, CN-903
Logie, P. S/Sgt. 2697840, A/*, Nijm, CN-*
Long, R.A. S/Sgt. 10538193, D/5, POW *, CN-*
Long, M.W. Lieut. 245325, F/16, POW O9A/H, CN-*
Long, R.C. Sgt. 6469368, B/20, RAR, CN-353
Longworth, A. Sgt. 14405134, D/13, RAR, CN-*
Lovett, J. S/Sgt. 128577, E/11, F/L-POW *, CN-283
Low, A.F.W. Capt. 187708, B/20, POW E, CN-293
Lowe, D.B. S/Sgt. 2084363, F/14, POW 4B, CN-*
Lund, R. S/Sgt. 2005243, D/5, POW *, CN-*
Lyne, C. S/Sgt. 1441411, E/*, RAR, CN-278
Lyon, A.B.D. Sgt. 14216954, F/16, POW SL111, CN-*
Lyon, M. Sgt. 61691, G/9, KIA, CN-*
Lyons, C.H.C. Sgt. 4267924, F/*, POW 11B, CN-*

# M

MacDonald, D.J. S/Sgt. 985899, C/*, POW E, CN-364
MacIntosh, R.D.G. Sgt. B/*, RAR, CN-*
Mack, C. S/Sgt. 2578155, G/9, POW 12A, CN-*
Mackenzie, B.W. Sgt. 6461073, E/*, KIA, CN-*
Maclaine of Lochbuie, S.R. Lieut. F/14, RAR, CN-*
Maddison, H.T. S/Sgt. 5438033, F/14, POW 11B, CN-*

Mahoney, P.J.D. Sgt. 858565, F/16, POW E, CN-762
Mail, J. S/Sgt. 66814, F/16, POW 11B, CN-*
Main, R.C. Sgt. 3909746, D/13, RAR, CN-*
Maker, A.B. Lieut. 2 Wing/HQ, RAR, CN-*
Mallison, G.N. S/Sgt. 4348337, F/*, POW *, CN-*
Maltby, R. A. Lieut. 73034, 2 Wing/HQ, KIA, CN-161
Manby, H.M. S/Sgt. 2885595, A/*, KIA, CN-*
Mann, J.R. Sgt. 6291394, G/*, KIA, CN-*
Mann, T. Sgt. 6345976, F/*, POW 11B, CN-*
Mansfield, J.J. S/Sgt. 20565026, D/*, POW 12A, CN-*
Markwick, E.J. Lieut. 293609, A/17, KIA, CN-920
Marlow, A.J. Sgt. 14509116, F/16, POW 11B, CN-165
Marriott, C. Sgt. 2657028, F/14, KIA, CN-*
Marshall, P. S/Sgt. 3054274, B/*, RAR, CN-*
Marshall, E. S/Sgt. 1994845, E/11, RAR, CN-232
Marshall, B. S/Sgt. 2 Wing/HQ, RAR, CN-185
Martin, I. S/Sgt. 75923, A/2, RAR
Martin, P.L. S/Sgt. 420786, A/*, POW 11B, CN-*
Martin, R.J.W. Sgt. D/8, RAR, CN-*
Martin, G.W.F. S/Sgt. 822571, G/9, POW 11B, CN-*
Mason, V.E.C. Sgt. 6343054, E/11, RAR, CN-284
Mather, W. S/Sgt. 62606, F/15, POW 11B, CN-822
Mathews, S.F. S/Sgt. 6093032, F/14, KIA, CN-*
Mathison, Sgt. C/*, RAR, CN-361
Matson, E.G.W. Sgt. 6985100, C/*, RAR, CN-323
Maughan, A.S. Sgt. 4270235, F/15, POW L7, CN-*
Maxwell, M. Sgt. 13106631, B/3?, POW 11B, CN-*
May, E.W. S/Sgt. 904193, E/*, POW 11B, CN-*
May, W. S/Sgt. 854844, C/X, POW 12A, CN-331
Mayes, T.W. S/Sgt. 7673174, G/9, KIA, CN-*
McBenn, S/Sgt. C/*, RAR , CN-370
McCaig, F. Sgt. 3775140, A/2, RAR , CN-*
McCarter, L. Sgt. F/16, RAR, CN-*
McCarthy, A.F. Sgt. 14416034, B/20, KIA, CN-306
McCracken, R. S/Sgt. 2929859, A/1, POW DL, CN-*
McCuish, D.C. S/Sgt. 2931669, F/*, POW 7A, CN-*
McCulloch, J. Sgt. 1646991, B/3, F/L, CN-865
McDonald, J.F. Sgt. 2881342, E/11, POW DL, CN-272
McEwan, N. S/Sgt. 983111, E/*, RAR, CN-*
McGeough, J.O. S/Sgt. 6030074, C/6, POW 11B, CN-376
McGowan, D. Sgt. 1453907, C/*, KIA , CN-377
McGregor, A.J. Sgt. 14615855, A/*, POW *, CN-*
McInnes, J. Sgt. 5961161, A/2, F/L-POW 11B, CN-5000
McIntyre, J.G. Sgt. D/21, RAR
McKay, J.M. S/Sgt. 2823181, D/*, POW 12A, CN-*
McKimm, A.S. Sgt. 6979236, F/14, RAR, CN-*
McLaren, W.C. S/Sgt. 1604219, F/14, KIA, CN-*
McLean, H.W. S/Sgt. 6103971, F/16, POW *, CN-*
McLeavy, D. Sgt. 5350002, D/*, POW 11B, CN-*
McManus, V.D. S/Sgt. 1876510, A/2, KIA, CN-*
McMillan, A.C. S/Sgt. 6296502, E/11, KIA, CN-234
McNeill, D.W. S/Sgt. 13100760, B/19, POW 11B, CN-338
McNeill, W. Capt. C/HQ, F/L, CN-901
Mead, K.A. Sgt. 1878306, F/15, POW 12A, CN-*
Meakin, R. 2nd Lieut. 314146, B/19, POW *, CN-341
Meekin, H. S/Sgt. 4345899, C/*, POW 11B, CN-377
Meiklejohn, A. S/Sgt. 3251388, A/17, RAR, CN-925
Melrose, W.G. S/Sgt. 1464667, E/11, POW 12A, CN-272

Melvin, G. Sgt. 2571165, E/11, RAR , CN-281
Merryfield, J. Sgt. D/5, RAR
Mew, K. W.O.II, S.S.M. 4122908, A/HQ, Nijm, CN-407
Michell, C.H.D. Lieut. 72247, A/*, RAR, CN-*
Michie, J.H.R. S/Sgt. 5255333, B/20, RAR, CN-292
Midgley, G. Sgt. 2701336, E/11, KIA, CN-238
Midgley, A.H. Sgt. 3531974, G/9, RAR, CN-941
Milburn, G.W. S/Sgt. 905003, F/16, RAR, CN-*
Miles, L. S/Sgt. 819078, A/18, Nigm
Millar, G.R. Lieut. P/178150, B/20, F/L, CN-298
Miller, C.A. S/Sgt. 937499, D/*, POW 11B, CN-*
Miller, G.F. Sgt. 1562235, B/19, POW *, CN-328
Miller, V.D. S/Sgt. G/24, RAR, CN-440
Miller, T.G. Capt. 134055, B/3, POW DL, CN-860
Mills, K.S. Lieut. 255204, D/*, KIA Ensch, CN-*
Mills, K.H.G. S/Sgt. 5511404, A/1, POW 12A, CN-143
Mills, G.T. Capt. 220201, E/11, KIA, CN-223
Mills, A.H. S/Sgt. 4918127, D/22, POW 11B, CN-969
Milne, R. Sgt./Towmaster , A/2, RAR, CN-N.F.
Minall, L.J. S/Sgt. 5341633, C/*, RAR, CN-373
Minards, A.H. Sgt. 2067655, C/*, POW Apel, CN-374
Mitchell, E. Sgt. 10555051, E/*, POW 4B, CN-285
Mitchell, A. Sgt. 10538003, A/1, POW L3, CN-*
Mitchell, J. Sgt. E/11, RAR , CN-231
Monk, D.E. Sgt. 1134580, A/*, POW *, CN-413
Moon, E.B. Sgt. 2589784, B/3, KIA , CN-*
Mooney, T.J. S/Sgt. 10564104, F/15, RAR , CN-*
Moorcock, D.E. S/Sgt. 1779342, F/14, KIA , CN-*
Moorcroft, G.E. S/Sgt. 10545541, E/12, RAR
Moore, H.G. S/Sgt. A/*, Nijm
Moore, S.W. Sgt. 132845, E/11, F/L , CN-266
Moore, T.R. S/Sgt. 4541252, F/14, RAR , CN-205
Moorwood, S.J.D. Lieut. 89110, D/*, F/L , CN-1011
Morgan, E.J. Sgt. 2007942, D/21, F/L-POW 11B, CN-385
Morgan, B. S/Sgt. B/20, RAR , CN-349
Morgan, W.D. S/Sgt. 4754804, D/5, RAR , CN-*
Morgan, C. Sgt. G/9, RAR , CN-*
Morrish, T. S/Sgt. D/21, RAR , CN-400
Morrison, J.A. Capt. 88880, D/5, POW L1, CN-772
Morrow, G.A. S/Sgt. D/*, RAR , CN-*
Moss, G. Sgt. 2588320, F/15, POW *, CN-*
Moss, H. S/Sgt. 2047777, G/9, RAR , CN-*
Mowatt, J.W. Sgt. 2818874, C/*, POW 12A, CN-364
Muir, I.C. Capt. 172724, D/22, KIA , CN-*
Mulholland, A. Sgt. 1876583, C/X, Nijm , CN-493
Mullett, W. Sgt. 2578702, G/24, POW 11B, CN-*
Murdoch, B. Capt. 73111, D/8, RAR , CN-*
Murdoch, A.N. S/Sgt. 6666261, G/9, POW 12A, CN-*
Murphy, T. Sgt. 2030823, B/4, KIA , CN-*
Murphy, J.R. Sgt. 6292625, 2 Wing/HQ, POW 7A, CN-167
Murray, T. Sgt. 894524, D/13, RAR , CN-*
Murray, F.A.S. Maj. 85686, F/HQ, RAR , CN-*
Murray, I.A. Lieut. Col. 99246, 1 Wing/HQ, RAR , CN-*
Musson, I. Sgt. 14291633, D/*, POW 12A, CN-*

# N
Naden, J.E.P. S/Sgt. 3453001, F/16, KIA , CN-174

Naismith, W. S/Sgt. F/14, RAR , CN-*
Naylor, C. Sgt. 1429025, E/*, KIA , CN-*
Neale, F. J.T. Capt. 73653, B/HQ, KIA , CN-859
Neil, S.H. Sgt. 2761994, F/14, POW 11B, CN-*
Neill, S. S/Sgt. 4343970, F/14, RAR , CN-210
Neilson, J. S/Sgt. 2754514, D/*, RAR , CN-*
Neilson, R.C. Sgt. 14424139, E/*, KIA , CN-*
Nettell, R.F. Sgt. 913987, D/*, POW 12A, CN-*
Newark, M.C. Pte. /RAMC 7365820, G/*, KIA , CN-N.F.
Newman, R.F. Sgt. 14418028, B/4, KIA , CN-*
Newman, D.H. Sgt. 5256366, D/8, KIA , CN-*
Newton, A. S/Sgt. 913044, G/10, F/L-POW 12A, CN-1007
Nicholson, J.L. Sgt. C/X, Nijm , CN-489
Nicklin, G.L. Sgt. 7955175, A/*, POW 11B, CN-122
Nixon, B.H. S/Sgt. 1509305, B/*, RAR , CN-*
Norbury, R. S/Sgt. 3656036, F/*, RAR , CN-*
Norris, D.E. S/Sgt. 1470905, G/*, POW 11B, CN-*
Norris, T. S/Sgt. 6853858, B/19, RAR , CN-312
North, A.J.W. Sgt. 14269986, G/10, POW 11B, CN-*
Norton, H.M.R. Lieut. 233268, B/3, RAR , CN-861
Nunn, J.M. Sgt. 1871217, C/*, RAR , CN-322
Nutter, R. S/Sgt. 4537370, D/*, POW DL, CN-*
Nye, G.H.E. S/Sgt. 7344366, B/3, RAR , CN-879

# O
Oakes, W.A. Sgt. 14573970, E/11, POW 12A, CN-275
O'Brien, D. Sgt. 14612011, B/3, POW *, CN-877
O'Brien, T. Sgt. 2938276, G/9, RAR , CN-*
O'Donnell, E. Sgt. 7013133, A/1, POW DL, CN-140
Ogden, P. Sgt. 14642484, B/20, RAR , CN-294
Ogg, Sgt. B/*, RAR , CN-137
Ogilvie, J.G. Capt. 140041, D/*, KIA , CN-*
Oliver, W.E. W.O.II, S.S.M. 3056895, D/HQ, RAR , CN-*
O'Mally, H.J.K. Capt. 44556, D/*, POW *, CN-*
Oppenshaw, T.L. Sgt. 4198648, C/*, RAR , CN-326
Oram, A.W. Sgt. 14426890, D/13, F/L-RAR , CN-468
Orford, L.W. S/Sgt. B/4, RAR , CN-*
Osborn, R.E. S/Sgt. 6398942, A/*, F/L-KIA, CN-126
Osborn, B.A. S/Sgt. 1432386, B/19, RAR, CN-312
Osborne, R.F. S/Sgt. 922174, A/*, F/L-POW *, CN-414
Otto, F.E. Sgt. 6898136, G/24, POW 11B, CN-*
Ousey, Cpl. 5627197, 1 Wing/HQ, RAR, CN-n/f
Owen, T.H. Sgt. 7517384, G/9, RAR, CN-*
Oxenford, A.A.R. Capt. 138945, E/25, KIA Apel, CN-*
Oxford, C.J. Sgt. 4859963, E/*, POW *, CN-276

# P
Page, D. S/Sgt. E/*, RAR , CN-*
Page, P. S/Sgt. 934521, B/19, POW 11B, CN-888
Page, T.G. Sgt. 1595241, D/8, RAR, CN-*
Paget, C.B. S/Sgt. 4977181, F/*, POW 11B, CN-*
Painter, G. Sgt. 1441244, B/*, KIA, CN-*
Painter, F. Sgt. 1881749, A/17, RAR, CN-928
Palett, B. Sgt. G/*, RAR , CN-*
Palfreeman, C. Sgt. 2162344, F/14, RAR, CN-*
Palmer, A.E Sgt. 4803786, D/*, POW *, CN-*
Palmer, J. S/Sgt. 1550711, D/*, KIA, CN-*

341

Palmer, R.V.D. Lieut. , G/24, RAR, CN-*
Palmer, Sgt. B/4, RAR , CN-*
Pare, G.A.F. Capt. /Rev. 175561, 1 Wing/HQ, POW E, CN-N.F.
Parker, D.S. Sgt. 5586465, D/5, POW 12A, CN-772
Parker, F.C. Sgt. 6469399, A/1, POW L7, CN-141
Parker, W. S/Sgt. 3390201, D/*, POW 9C, CN-*
Parkinson, H. Sgt. 3451219, F/14, KIA , CN-*
Parsons, B. S/Sgt. B/*, RAR, CN-*
Parsons, H.A.V. S/Sgt. 1768669, E/12, POW 11B, CN-*
Paton, N. S/Sgt. 1479373, E/*, POW *, CN-*
Pattenden, E. Sgt. 5506112, A/*, RAR, CN-*
Pattinson, L.R. Sgt. 277062, A/17, KIA, CN-917
Pavitt, W.C. S/Sgt. 6019251, D/13, RAR, CN-*
Pearce, T.W. Sgt. 4914090, D/5, RAR, CN-*
Pearson, C. S/Sgt. 1884747, A/1, RAR , CN-*
Pearson, S. S/Sgt. 7895376, C/*, RAR, CN-358
Pember, L. S/Sgt. D/13, RAR , CN-396
Pennicott, F. S/Sgt. 1990833, C/X, Nijm, CN-492
Pepper, M.R. Sgt. 7595239, B/3, POW *, CN-136
Percey, V.D. S/Sgt. 5951478, G/24, POW 11B, CN-*
Percival, R. S/Sgt. 2137984, G/10, RAR, CN-*
Perfect, E.J. S/Sgt. C/*, RAR , CN-380
Perkin, R.G. S/Sgt. 4126532, G/*, RAR, CN-*
Perry, W. Sgt. 860875, E/11, POW 11B, CN-289
Petrie, M.G. W.O.II, S.S.M. , C/HQ, RAR, CN-902
Phillip, R.H. Sgt. 885295, F/*, POW *, CN-*
Phillips, E. S/Sgt. 893156, F/*, KIA, CN-*
Phillips, A. Sgt. 14523956, G/10, KIA, CN-184
Phillips, H. Sgt. 8452655, D/13, RAR, CN-*
Phillips, P.G. Sgt. 989770, F/16, RAR, CN-*
Pickford, E. S/Sgt. 4129928, G/9, KIA , CN-*
Pickles, J. S/Sgt. 2111451, B/19, RAR , CN-310
Pickwoad, A.E. Lieut. 180092, F/14, RAR, CN-209
Picton, R.K. S/Sgt. 894207, B/3, KIA, CN-873
Pidduck, D.F. Sgt. 14409988, E/*, KIA, CN-267
Pinnock, J.D. Sgt. D/21, F/L , CN-399
Place, J.W. Lieut. Col. 51885, 2 Wing/HQ, RAR , CN-161
Plant, J.E. Sgt. 5952261, D/8, RAR, CN-*
Plowman, T.A. Capt. 138799, F/HQ, KIA , CN-*
Ponsford, F.C. S/Sgt. 5393177, A/17, RAR, CN-920
Poole, A.M.S. Sgt. F/*, RAR , CN-*
Potts, W.W. S/Sgt. 365546, G/*, F/L, CN-509
Powell, H.E. S/Sgt. 994148, D/13, KIA, CN-*
Powell, F.G. Sgt. 190364, D/5, POW L3, CN-*
Pragnell, D.R. S/Sgt. 6025696, D/*, POW 11B, CN-*
Prentice, A. Sgt. 5510144, D/8, RAR, CN-*
Preston, J.F. S/Sgt. 9103680, C/*, POW DL, CN-362
Preston, A. Sgt. 65678, C/*, RAR, CN-909
Price, J.W. S/Sgt. 6015515, E/*, RAR, CN-*
Price, S.R. Sgt. 2388139, E/11, POW *, CN-288
Price, A.E. Sgt. F/14, RAR, CN-*
Price, S.H. Sgt. 5891328, F/16, POW 11B, CN-*
Priest, M.W.D. Capt. 135830, G/10, RAR, CN-998
Prince, A.E. Sgt. 14219063, F/*, POW 11B, CN-*
Pritchard, P. Sgt. , E/11, RAR, CN-236
Privett, K. S/Sgt. 1441656, A/*, POW 11B, CN-125
Proctor, A. S/Sgt. 7377924, B/3, F/L, CN-865
Proudfoot, W. S/Sgt. 922985, E/*, POW 4B, CN-*

Puddle, G.E. S/Sgt. 2005449, D/*, POW 11B, CN-*
Pyne, G.F. Sgt. 6090857, E/11, RAR, CN-237

# R

Raggett, D.B.F. Sgt. 5630314, B/20, KIA, CN-311
Ralph, E.E.S. S/Sgt. 1434775, A/17, POW 11B, CN-926
Ramsbottom, W.J. S/Sgt. 920299, D/13, F/L-POW DL, CN-474
Ramsden, N.T. Sgt. 2073596, A/17, RAR, CN-926
Ramsey, D. S/Sgt. 6030688, C/*, POW *, CN-*
Ranfield, H. S/Sgt. 3448888, A/17, POW L7, CN-927
Ranger, N.J. Sgt. 110820, E/*, KIA, CN-*
Raspison, E. S/Sgt. 3131992, B/4, RAR, CN-*
Rathband, H.H. Sgt. 1544344, C/*, POW L3, CN-316
Read, N.J. Sgt. 3314330, C/X, RAR, CN-335
Reading, P. S/Sgt. B/*, RAR, CN-137
Readshaw, D. Sgt. 6146491, F/*, POW *, CN-*
Reardon, M.P.P. S/Sgt. 934721, G/10, POW 12A, CN-1008
Redding, F.G. Sgt. 6897587, F/*, KIA, CN-*
Redfearn, V. Sgt. 10568027, G/9, RAR
Redknap, P. S/Sgt. 5501839, C/X, Nijm, CN-493
Redway, G.E. S/Sgt. 6457896, F/16, POW 11B, CN-*
Reed, R. Sgt. 5337811, E/*, POW 11B, CN-*
Reith, A.M. Sgt. 2067142, A/8, Nijm
Renard, B. Sgt. 14436953, B/3, RAR, CN-874
Rennison, C. S/Sgt. 7023047, A/2, Nijm
Rice, D. S/Sgt. F/14, RAR , CN-205
Richards, A.E. S/Sgt. 7599895, F/15, KIA, CN-*
Richards, F.A. S/Sgt. 2589301, B/19, RAR, CN-339
Richardson, C.D. S/Sgt. 2045308, D/*, KIA, CN-*
Richardson, W.K. Sgt. 1492872, E/*, KIA, CN-*
Rickwood, G.A. S/Sgt. 2044667, D/8, KIA , CN-*
Rigby, S.R.A. Sgt. 3390554, G/*, RAR, CN-*
Rigby, A.A. Sgt. 5833342, B/19, POW *, CN-343
Riley, G. Sgt. 1419099, E/*, RAR, CN-*
Roberts, D.K. S/Sgt. 86030, C/*, RAR, CN-322
Roberts, S. Sgt. 4808556, G/9, POW 8C, CN-*
Roberts, I.M. Lieut. F/HQ, RAR, CN-*
Robertson, J.K. Sgt. 14407312, F/14, POW 11B, CN-210
Robertson, S/Sgt. D/5, RAR, CN-*
Robinson, C.F. Sgt. 5830482, D/13, POW *, CN-*
Robson, J.E. S/Sgt. 3963615, A/*, POW L7, CN-123
Robson, F. Capt. 182390, F/16, POW O9A/H, CN-*
Robson, P.E. Capt. 112954, E/HQ, POW 7A, CN-*
Rodgers, P. Sgt. 784676, C/*, RAR, CN-315
Roe, F. Sgt. 6400990, A/*, POW *, CN-*
Rogers, S. S/Sgt. D/5, POW, CN-*
Roscoe, A.L. Sgt. 6923978, G/9, RAR, CN-*
Rose, C.P. Sgt. A/2, RAR, CN-*
Rose, R.D. S/Sgt. 2070307, D/5, POW 11B, CN-*
Rosenberg, S/Sgt. E/*, RAR, CN-273
Rostworowski, G. Capt. GSO3 (Int) , HQ GPR/*, Nijm, CN-*
Rowland, W.F. Sgt. 1538780, E/*, RAR , CN-*
Rowland, R.R. Sgt. 2045148, G/10, F/L-KIA, CN-518
Royle, J.P. Maj. 66172, 1 Wing/HQ, KIA, CN-*
Rubenstein, T.A. Sgt. 14219614, E/*, KIA, CN-*

Ruff, K. Sgt. 14401873, D/*, RAR, CN-*
Rumble, W. S/Sgt. 2051082, E/11, RAR, CN-280
Rushton, D. S/Sgt. 10666246, A/*, POW *, CN-*
Ryan, R.W. Sgt. 2589852, G/*, POW 12A, CN-*
Ryans, D. S/Sgt. 4696494, D/13, RAR, CN-*

# S

Saertoris, F. Sgt. F/16, RAR, CN-*
Sampson, F.E.J. S/Sgt. 6408294, D/5, RAR, CN-*
Sanders, E. S/Sgt. 937965, A/*, Nijm
Sanderson, E. Sgt. 937039, D/*, POW DL, CN-*
Sandilands, R. Sgt. 14595939, G/10, RAR, CN-*
Sant, L. S/Sgt. 4130319, G/9, RAR, CN-*
Sargent, R. Sgt. 4617321, G/9, F/L-POW L7, CN-994
Sarjantson, J.W. S/Sgt. 2764064, B/19, POW Apel, CN-334
Saunders, A.G. S/Sgt. 5253875, C/*, POW 11B, CN-*
Saunders, R.H. S/Sgt. 6148206, C/*, KIA, CN-*
Saunders, L.J. Sgt. 5437322, A/17, RAR, CN-923
Saunders, L.P. Sgt. 4804127, B/3, POW 12A, CN-868
Sayles, B. S/Sgt. 850767, F/16, POW *, CN-*
Scott, L. Sgt. D/*, RAR, CN-*
Scott, P.T. Lieut. 149360, D/*, POW O9A/H, CN-*
Scott-Malden, C.P. Capt. GSO3 (Int) 1 A/B Div HQ/*, RAR, CN-*
Seaman, F.G. Sgt. 876231, F/16, POW DL, CN-754
Senier, P. Sgt. 1870855, E/11, RAR, CN-*
Shackleton, A. S/Sgt. 942449, B/HQ, RAR, CN-291
Sharp, H. Sgt. 5891189, E/11, KIA, CN-229
Sharrock, J.J. Sgt. 3606728, C/6, KIA, CN-320
Shaw, J. S/Sgt. 1507455, C/*, POW 11B, CN-319
Sheath, A. S/Sgt. D/*, RAR, CN-*
Shell, L. Sgt. 319389, E/*, POW 12A, CN-*
Shepherd, F. S/Sgt. 932328, F/*, POW 12A, CN-*
Shepherd, A.M. S/Sgt. 5507617, B/20, POW 11B, CN-350
Sherlock, D. Sgt. F/*, RAR, CN-*
Sherry, W.T. Sgt. 2078110, F/14, POW 11B, CN-*
Shields, G. Sgt. 7343117, A/2, Nijm, CN-*
Shingleton, D.R. Sgt. 14527704, G/10, RAR, CN-*
Shipley, R.F. Sgt. 4859506, A/1, RAR, CN-*
Shipp, D.H. Sgt. 1808711, D/*, KIA, CN-*
Short, G.F. S/Sgt. 920186, G/*, POW *, CN-*
Shorter, H.M.J. S/Sgt. 1876535, B/4, POW 12A, CN-*
Shovel, R. Sgt. 14564670, F/*, RAR, CN-*
Shuttleworth, D.H. Capt. 174177, 2 Wing/HQ, KIA, CN-163
Simion, E. Sgt. 13803084, F/16, KIA, CN-*
Simons, D.H. S/Sgt. 119641, F/*, POW DL, CN-*
Simpson, A. S/Sgt. 856791, D/*, POW Apel, CN-*
Simpson, D.A. Capt. 193137, B/19, POW L3, CN-332
Simpson, R.J. Sgt. 2933255, C/6, RAR, CN-914
Slaven, T. Sgt. A/*, Nijm , CN-*
Slee, J.D. S/Sgt. 7590943, B/3, RAR, CN-136
Smallwood, W.A. S/Sgt. 5504408, A/*, KIA, CN-*
Smart, A. Sgt. 14588092, D/*, POW DL, CN-*
Smellie, J.F. Capt. 158421, B/4, KIA, CN-884
Smillie, N.A.C. Capt. 144234, A/17, RAR, CN-919
Smith, G.W. S/Sgt. 5891307, A/*, RAR, CN-*
Smith, H.W. Sgt. 4460217, F/*, KIA, CN-*

Smith, W.E. Sgt. 5113184, B/*, POW *, CN-*
Smith, J.H. Sgt. 2596863, E/*, POW *, CN-127
Smith, T.M. Sgt. 2145760, E/11, KIA, CN-269
Smith, C.A. Sgt. 6400991, C/*, POW 12A, CN-362
Smith, A.W. S/Sgt. 1445045, D/21, F/L-POW 11B, CN-385
Smith, T Sgt. 898588, G/10, RAR , CN-1002
Smith, E.J.A. Lieut. 292210, D/13, RAR, CN-*
Smith, J.F. S/Sgt. 6468819, B/20, RAR, CN-348
Smith, S.R. Lieut. 229896, D/22, KIA, CN-*
Smith, A.J.A. S/Sgt. 14206556, B/3, POW 12A, CN-874
Smith, J.C. Sgt. 3962547, B/3, KIA, CN-875
Smithson, D.G. Sgt. 1886189, G/10, F/L-POW 12A, CN-1007
Snowden, E. Sgt. 7662064, A/*, Nijm
Snushall, J.A.W. Sgt. 2889275, D/*, KIA, CN-*
Southall, J. Sgt. A/1, RAR , CN-143
Southey, M. S/Sgt. 5958543, C/*, POW 11B, CN-360
Sparks, D.W. Sgt. E/11, RAR, CN-234
Spelman, D.G. S/Sgt. 2036287, G/10, RAR, CN-*
Spence, R.E. Lieut. 132734, F/*, RAR, CN-*
Spencer, B. Sgt. G/*, RAR, CN-*
Spencer, H.H. Sgt. T/167842, E/*, KIA, CN-*
Spencer, Sgt. B/*, RAR, CN-129
Sprott, H. Sgt. 909159, F/*, RAR, CN-*
Standerwick, R.L. Sgt. 5385190, E/*, POW 11B, CN-*
Stapley, F.H. Sgt. 1539742, D/22, POW *, CN-969
Startup, F. S/Sgt. 2019102, B/3, F/L, CN-133
Statham, W.J.G. S/Sgt. 77644, D/*, KIA *, CN-*
Stead, J.E. S/Sgt. 794717, A/*, POW L7, CN-*
Steedman, D.N.C. Lieut. 307632, D/13, RAR, CN-*
Steel, T.P.O. S/Sgt. 2046512, B/3, RAR, CN-871
Steevenson, R.V.C. Lieut. 284568, F/14, POW O9A/H, CN-*
Stephens, J.H. Lieut. 166162, F/*, POW L1, CN-*
Stephenson, E.J. S/Sgt. 6343264, D/*, POW 11B, CN-*
Stephenson, J.A. Sgt. 4616329, D/*, POW *, CN-*
Stephenson, G. Sgt. 850562, G/*, F/L, CN-509
Stephenson, E. Sgt. 1156141, B/3, RAR, CN-890
Stevens, R.B. Lieut. 165811, F/*, POW O79, CN-*
Stevens, T.B. Sgt. 3713627, G/*, POW *, CN-*
Stevens, R.A. S/Sgt. D/*, RAR , CN-384
Stevens, S.J. S/Sgt. 3658861, D/22, RAR, CN-*
Stevenson, F.J.R. S/Sgt. 351667, D/*, F/L, CN-1011
Stevenson, Sgt. G/9, RAR , CN-*
Stewart, T.W. S/Sgt. 85421, G/24, KIA, CN-*
Stilton, G.E. Lieut. 156218, B/HQ, POW L1, CN-862
Stockden, R. Sgt. E/12, RAR, CN-*
Stocker, E. S/Sgt. 1128278, D/8, F/L, CN-1026
Stokes, G.R.I.M. Lieut. 243119, C/*, POW O9A/H, CN-355
Stones, H.R. Sgt. 4537089, D/22, POW *, CN-*
Strathern, K.F. Lieut. 99754, D/HQ, RAR, CN-*
Street, J. S/Sgt. D/21, RAR
Streeter, T. Sgt. 1 Wing/HQ, RAR, CN-434
Stremes, G.F. S/Sgt. 6297726, F/*, POW 11B, CN-769
Stringer, F. S/Sgt. 2888362, D/*, POW *, CN-*
Stroud, B. S/Sgt. B/20, RAR, CN-305
Stubley, E. S/Sgt. 14422511, F/14, RAR, CN-*

Sullivan, J.A. Sgt. 6915850, D/*, POW 11B, CN-*
Sullivan, F. S/Sgt. 2013498, F/15, RAR, CN-*
Sutton, G.E. S/Sgt. E/11, RAR, CN-285
Swanson, W. Sgt. 2824942, E/11, RAR, CN-279
Swift, W.H. Sgt. 7948876, E/*, POW 11B, CN-*
Sykes, H.R. Lieut. 197752, D/5, POW L1, CN-*
Symmonds, C. Sgt. 14413277, C/*, POW 11B, CN-912
Symonds, P. S/Sgt. E/11, RAR, CN-239

## T

Taitt, A. Capt. 1 Wing/HQ, RAR, CN-*
Tallentire, W.L. Capt. 135502, A/18, F/L, CN-421
Tapping, G.B. Sgt. 7394973, D/13, F/L , CN-462
Tarbitten, J.W. S/Sgt. 7363554, F/*, POW 12A, CN-*
Tarrant, H.A.P. S/Sgt. 2336298, F/*, KIA, CN-*
Tayler, C.C. Lieut. 174387, A/1, KIA, CN-140
Taylor, J.D. Sgt. 1447250, D/*, KIA Apel, CN-*
Taylor, R. Sgt. 2079667, D/*, RAR, CN-1014
Taylor, E.R. Sgt. 2928549, B/*, POW *, CN-127
Taylor, B.J. Sgt. 4462557, B/*, RAR, CN-135
Taylor, A.C. S/Sgt. 118290, E/*, RAR, CN-287
Taylor, B.S. Sgt. 4617191, C/*, RAR, CN-356
Taylor, J.B. S/Sgt. 2092974, C/*, RAR, CN-356
Taylor, J.W.B. S/Sgt. 4536864, G/10, RA , CN-998
Taylor, C. Sgt. 2579189, D/13, RAR, CN-*
Taylor, H.C. S/Sgt. 2058361, F/16, KIA, CN-*
Taylor, F.W. Sgt. 2193360, F/16, KIA, CN-265
Taylor, R.K. Sgt. 552484, D/5, RAR, CN-791
Taylorson, T.W. Lieut. 299372, C/6, RAR, CN-910
Taziker, J. Sgt. 12088321, C/*, POW 7A, CN-355
Telfer, R.D. Lieut. 151828, G/10, RAR, CN-1005
Thackeray, C.L. S/Sgt. 57484, B/19, POW 12A, CN-337
Thomas, E.J. Capt. 233883, F/15, KIA, CN-*
Thomas, L.R. Sgt. 1442239, G/9, F/L-POW 8C, CN-1001
Thompson, J.M. Sgt. 14423893, B/3, POW 12A, CN-*
Thompson, A. S/Sgt. 1435268, C/*, RAR, CN-369
Thompson, Sgt. C/*, RAR , CN-902
Thompson, G. S/Sgt. 3320254, D/8, POW 11B, CN-*
Thompson, D. Sgt. 2576545, G/9, KIA, CN-*
Thomson, J.W.R. Sgt. 866624, F/16, KIA, CN-*
Thomson, J.J. S/Sgt. 3194205, B/19, POW *, CN-344
Thomson, W. S/Sgt. 1986016, B/20, POW 9C, CN-297
Thorndale, D.P. Sgt. 6204928, F/*, POW 11B, CN-*
Thorne, L. Sgt. 6847559, C/*, RAR, CN-907
Thornton, H. S/Sgt. 6982007, E/11, POW *, CN-268
Thorpe, E. S/Sgt. 2579239, A/*, Nijm
Tigar, J. S/Sgt. 928083, F/*, RAR, CN-*
Tilley, R.F. S/Sgt. 552600, E/11, RAR, CN-274
Tillings, R.S. S/Sgt. 924710, C/*, RAR, CN-915
Tobin, M. S/Sgt. 7596863, F/14, POW 4B, CN-*
Toler, T.I.J. Maj. 47712, B/HQ, RAR, CN-291
Tomblin, B.A. Sgt. 14259326, E/11, POW L3, CN-220
Tomlin, F. S/Sgt. G/24, RAR, CN-*
Tomlinson, K. Sgt. 14312071, D/*, POW *, CN-*
Tomlinson, E.B.E. Sgt. 2364380, B/3, KIA, CN-861
Tomson, J.H. Lieut. 293508, E/*, RAR, CN-270
Tonks, J. Sgt. 1533350, D/*, POW *, CN-*
Topp, J. Sgt. 2890154, E/11, RAR, CN-286
Toseland, P. Sgt. 5511598, B/19, KIA Apel, CN-346

Toulton, Sgt. E/*, RAR, CN-290
Townend, N. S/Sgt. 892940, D/13, RAR, CN-*
Travis-Davison, K. Sgt. 1779501, G/10, POW 12A, CN-139
Treble, S/Sgt. C/*, RAR, CN-378
Treherne, D.A.A. Lieut. 95365, F/16, POW O9A/H, CN-*
Trueman, S. Sgt. 3531498, E/*, RAR, CN-*
Trueman, A. Sgt. 101997, G/9, POW L3, CN-*
Tuck-Brown, W. Sgt. 860001, D/13, RAR, CN-*
Turl, J. Sgt. 5186048, E/*, KIA, CN-*
Turnbull, L.W. S/Sgt. 4343733, F/*, RAR, CN-*
Turner, A. Sgt. F/*, RAR, CN-*
Turner, A.G.C. Lieut. 235670, A/1, Nijm, CN-*
Turner, S.G.S. Sgt. 77962, G/10, POW 8C, CN-*
Turner, D.N.S. Lieut. 300756, E/11, RAR, CN-235
Twiggs, C.W. S/Sgt. 103586, B/4, RAR, CN-132
Twine, N. Sgt. 5338944, F/16, RAR, CN-*
Tyler, P.J. Sgt. 1449919, D/5, POW 11B, CN-*

## U

Urquhart, J.A. S/Sgt. 5185152, F/*, POW DL, CN-*
Urquhart, J.W. Lieut. 304465, A/*, Nijm, CN-*

## V

Venables, G.W.C. Sgt. 5773041, A/*, POW 11B, CN-123
Vickers, R.E. S/Sgt. 1086734, G/24, POW 11B, CN-*
Vincent, B.A.F. S/Sgt. 14422936, E/*, RAR, CN-*
Vivian, Sgt. C/*, RAR, CN-378
Voller, G.F. S/Sgt. 2599591, B/19, POW 11B, CN-339

## W

Wade, R.S. S/Sgt. 6969360, E/25, POW 11B, CN-852
Wade, V.H. S/Sgt. D/*, RAR, CN-*
Wadsworth, L. S/Sgt. 1146581, E/*, KIA, CN-*
Walchli, R.O. Capt. 153528, G/24, RAR, CN-*
Waldron, A. S/Sgt. 2596687, 2 Wing/HQ, RAR, CN-*
Walford, P.J. S/Sgt. 927648, E/11, RAR, CN-235
Walker, F.S. S/Sgt. 6205771, C/*, POW 11B, CN-363
Walker, H. Sgt. 957301, B/4, KIA Apel, CN-*
Wallace, D.B. S/Sgt. 920678, F/15, KIA, CN-*
Wallwork, J.H. S/Sgt. 903986, C/*, RAR, CN-358
Walmsley, W. Sgt. 124598, F/16, RAR, CN-*
Walsh, H.J. Sgt. 14421175, F/16, POW *, CN-*
Walters, J. Sgt. 5989587, F/14, KIA, CN-*
Walton, L. Sgt. 4747549, F/14, POW 11B, CN-*
Walton, N.H. Sgt. 5443079, B/19, RAR, CN-313
Ward, D.E.W. Sgt. 1878308, C/*, POW 12A, CN-368
Ward, R.J. S/Sgt. 961033, F/14, POW 11B, CN-*
Ward, E.L. Sgt. F/16, RAR, CN-183
Waring, P. S/Sgt. C/6, RAR, CN-320
Wastell, W.H. S/Sgt. 2041969, G/24, POW 11B, CN-*
Waterhouse, A. Sgt. 7617473, G/*, KIA Apel, CN-*
Waterhouse, C.E. S/Sgt. 2043042, B/3, POW 12A, CN-875
Waterman, K. Sgt. 4611630, D/13, F/L, CN-457
Watkins, H. S/Sgt. 3660659, E/11, POW *, CN-275
Watkinson, P.H. S/Sgt. 6085068, G/24?, POW 11B, CN-*
Watkinson, C.R. S/Sgt. 809931, B/3, F/L-POW L7, CN-878

Watson, F.C. Sgt. 2082989, A/*, POW 13C, CN-*
Watson, L.F. S/Sgt. 938652, D/*, KIA, CN-*
Watson, C.G. Sgt. 1591231, A/2, POW DL, CN-*
Watt, A.E. Sgt. 5883482, D/5, POW *, CN-*
Watt, R.W. S/Sgt. 3606888, B/20, POW 11B, CN-311
Watt, W. W.O.II, S.S.M. 3246740, B/HQ, RAR, CN-302
Watts, M.N. Sgt. 554563, F/14, POW 11B, CN-209
Webb, W.A. Sgt. 1450029, G/*, POW 11B, CN-*
Webb, H.F. S/Sgt. 917709, E/*, POW 9C, CN-798
Webbley, W.E.B. Sgt. 873399, B/19, POW 11B, CN-338
Wedgbury, E.C. S/Sgt. 906943, F/14, RAR, CN-189
Weeden, L.L. S/Sgt. 2080390, F/14, RAR, CN-190
Wellard, L.E. Sgt. B/19, RAR, CN-310
Wells, J. Sgt. 2040180, D/13, RAR, CN-*
Wells, W.J. S/Sgt. 3326544, F/16, RAR, CN-*
Wells, R.A. S/Sgt. 5500477, F/16, POW *, CN-762
West, R.W. S/Sgt. 926508, F/*, KIA Apel, CN-*
West, J. Sgt. 2329894, C/*, KIA, CN-124
West, E.L. Sgt. 2048513, C/*, KIA, CN-369
West, L.D. S/Sgt. 912765, B/19, POW 11B, CN-345
Wetherall, J.A.B. Sgt. 14414511, F/16, POW 344, CN-*
Wethey, A. S/Sgt. 2889519, G/10, RAR, CN-1004
Whale, R. S/Sgt. 5825452, B/4, RAR, CN-*
Whawell, J.W. Sgt. 6203718, E/*, POW 11B, CN-*
Wheatey, J. Sgt. 2060393, A/1, RAR, CN-*
Wheldon, R.A. S/Sgt. 3715219, D/22, POW DL, CN-*
Whippy, J.W. Sgt. 2044661, D/8, POW *, CN-1025
White, K.J. Sgt. 1891554, F/*, POW 7A, CN-*
White, R.E. S/Sgt. 952832, D/*, KIA, CN-*
White, D.A. S/Sgt. 421356, C/*, KIA, CN-318
White, A. S/Sgt. 5957181, C/*, KIA, CN-913
White, A.C. S/Sgt. 3064882, C/7, POW 11B, CN-905
White, F.H. W.O.II, S.S.M. 5500999, G/HQ, RAR, CN-519
Whitehead, J. Sgt. 3528646, D/13, F/L, CN-478
Whitehouse, N.K. Sgt. 6211502, A/*, F/L-KIA, CN-126
Whitfield, B.J. Sgt. 14375665, F/*, POW 11B, CN-*
Whitmore, F.W. Sgt. 1529509, F/*, POW 12A, CN-*
Whyborn, P.E. Sgt. 5734403, B/19, KIA, CN-334
Wicks, M.W. S/Sgt. 4977604, C/*, RAR, CN-361
Wilce, S.G. Sgt. 88191, F/*, POW 8C, CN-769
Wilcox, R. Sgt. 323350, G/9, RAR, CN-*
Wild, J.R.N. Sgt. G/24, RAR, CN-*
Wilkinson, S.A. S/Sgt. 186344, D/13, KIA, CN-*
Williams, J.F. Sgt. 3858326, E/*, POW *, CN-*
Williams, L.E. Sgt. 2737860, D/*, KIA, CN-*
Williams, N.D. Sgt. 1137632, D/*, KIA, CN-*
Williams, A.R. Sgt. 5384257, F/16, RAR, CN-*
Williams, C. Sgt. 7962313, F/16, POW Frei, CN-*
Williams, A.M. Sgt. 4208939, F/HQ, POW 12A, CN-166
Williamson, D. Sgt. 14579389, E/*, POW 11B, CN-*
Williamson, K.R. Sgt. 6852441, F/*, RAR, CN-*
Williamson, Sgt. B/20, RAR, CN-304
Wilmot, T.J. S/Sgt. 6092888, G/24, POW 9C, CN-*
Wilmot, H.F.T. S/Sgt. 7016404, B/3, RAR, CN-864
Wilson, R. G. Sgt. E/*, RAR, CN-*
Wilson, R.J. Sgt. 7366948, D/*, POW DL, CN-*
Wilson, J.L. Sgt. 1675968, E/*, F/L-POW *, CN-283
Wilson, J.A. Sgt. 3247627, C/*, POW 12A, CN-321
Wilson, A. S/Sgt. 1495536, B/4, RAR, CN-*

Wilson, J. Sgt. 854737, C/X, Nijm, CN-488
Wilson, P. S/Sgt. 6405428, C/X, Nijm, CN-489
Wilton, D.C. Sgt. 5676468, A/*, KIA, CN-*
Windle, J. Sgt. 4616543, C/*, POW 11B, CN-367
Winkworth, C.W. Sgt. 5110811, C/*, KIA, CN-318
Winsper, L. S/Sgt. 7884906, B/3, KIA Apel, CN-890
Winter, R F S/Sgt. 14388562, 2 Wing/HQ, RAR, CN-163
Wisebad, J. Sgt. 6846961, D/*, KIA, CN-*
Withington, T. Sgt. 828381, F/*, KIA, CN-*
Withnall, P.B. S/Sgt. 2332442, G/10, POW 12A, CN-139
Woltag, H. Sgt. C/6, RAR, CN-376
Wood, H. Sgt. 889368, E/*, KIA, CN-128
Wood, P.W. Lieut. C/*, RAR, CN-131
Wood, E.R. Sgt. A/2, F/L, CN-974
Woodcock, G. Sgt. 476311, B/4, RAR, CN-*
Woodcock, R. Sgt. 4541770, E/HQ, POW 11B, CN-219
Woodrow, E.W. S/Sgt. 917835, D/8, KIA, CN-1025
Woods, R.O. S/Sgt. 847224, B/3, KIA, CN-868
Woodward, J. Sgt. 902949, C/*, RAR, CN-*
Workman, H.A. S/Sgt. 7395098, B/3, RAR, CN-135
Worthington, B.G. Sgt. 6461913, D/*, KIA, CN-*
Worthington, L. S/Sgt. 13028948, B/4, RAR, CN-*
Wrenn, J. Sgt. 4975623, C/*, RAR, CN-*
Wright, J.W. Sgt. 10576699, F/*, RAR, CN-*
Wright, N.D. S/Sgt. 2615497, E/*, POW 11B, CN-*
Wright, P.D. Sgt. 6898592, B/*, POW *, CN-*
Wright, W.C. Sgt. 5188672, E/*, POW 11B, CN-*
Wright, G. Sgt. D/*, F/L, CN-152
Wright, G. Sgt. 78851, F/16, POW 11B, CN-*
Wright, J.R. S/Sgt. 857031, B/3, KIA, CN-877
Wright, L. S/Sgt. 1890104, C/6, RAR, CN-325
Wright, J. S/Sgt. 951021, G/9, KIA, CN-*
Wyatt, D. Sgt. 5393017, G/9, KIA, CN-*

# Y

Yates, A.G. Sgt. 2622753, E/*, KIA, CN-*
Yeatman, F.J. S/Sgt. 927243, G/9, KIA, CN-*
Young, L. S/Sgt. 6103389, F/14, RAR, CN-200
Young, K.W. Sgt. 7955475, F/16, POW 11B, CN-*
Young, A. S/Sgt. G/9, RAR, CN-*

# Appendix 12

*Glider Pilot Regiment Decorations and Awards –*
*Operation MARKET*

## DISTINGUISHED SERVICE ORDER (DSO):

Lieutenant M.D.K. Dauncey (9 Flight, 'G' Squadron)

During the action at Arnhem from 20th to 25th September 1944, Lieutenant Dauncey was in command of a party of men defending the guns of the Airlanding Light Regiment, RA at Oosterbeek. The position was continually attacked by superior forces of enemy tanks and infantry. On three occasions the enemy overran the sector necessitating a counter attack. Lieutenant Dauncey, on his own initiative, organised and led each sortie with such determination that the positions were regained with heavy loss to the enemy. In the face of heavy small arms and mortar fire he personally attacked machine-gun posts, showing remarkable coolness and complete disregard for his own personal safety. During these attacks he was wounded on three occasions but refused to be evacuated from the area.

On 24th September a more determined attack was made by the enemy using tanks and S.P. guns. Lieutenant Dauncey, whilst leading his men in a further counter attack, was wounded again – losing the sight of one eye. In spite of pain, and handicap of defective vision, he continued to lead his men in a fearless manner thus recapturing the lost ground and inflicting heavy loss to the enemy. On 25th September the position was subjected to intense fire from an enemy S.P gun. The houses were set on fire and an order was received to withdraw. By now no anti-tank weapons were available and there was imminent danger of the enemy S.P gun penetrating the gun positions. Realising this fact, Lieutenant Dauncey, who had remained alone, assaulted the enemy vehicle single-handed with gammon bombs. By his action the critical situation was averted but Lieutenant Dauncey received further injuries which resulted in his capture by the enemy. The high morale of the men, who had been drawn from many units, was undoubtedly due to the fine example of this officer. Had the enemy broken through this sector, the gun positions would have become untenable and thus unable to support the Airborne Division.

Lieutenant Dauncey's indomitable courage, initiative, coolness and selfless devotion to duty, in spite of his wounds, was in keeping with the highest traditions of the service.

## MILITARY CROSS (MC):

Major F.A.S. Murray (OC 'F' Squadron)

During the whole of the time at Arnhem from 17th to 25th September 1944 Major Murray conducted himself with the greatest gallantry and handled his squadron with great skill in a series of most difficult situations, during one of which he was wounded in the throat. He, however, continued to lead his men in an immediate counter attack on the enemy who had penetrated his area and repulsed them and restored his positions. Only then did he consent to have his wound dressed. He was evacuated to an enemy held hospital but having had his injuries attended to, succeeded in regaining the Divisional perimeter and in so doing had to penetrate the enemy lines; this he succeeded in doing although quite unarmed and in broad daylight. Throughout, Major Murray has shown a wonderful spirit of unselfish devotion to duty and has been an inspiration to the whole unit. It was largely due to his efforts that the line in his sector remained intact to the end.

## DISTINGUISHED CONDUCT MEDAL (DCM):
Sergeant R.F. Tilley ('E' Squadron)

During the operations near Arnhem this NCO was attached to the KOSBs and distinguished himself throughout by his personal gallantry, initiative and unflagging cheerfulness under the most trying conditions. On 20th September, when the MO and part of his staff were captured, Sgt Tilley attached himself to the RAP and did sterling work in attending to the comfort and moral well being of the wounded, many of whom he himself brought in under fire. When the RAP was hit and set on fire he saved several lives by his coolness in organising the evacuation of the wounded. Later when the medical staff was reinforced and when casualties had decimated battalion HQ, he voluntarily assumed the duties of RSM. In this capacity he maintained the supply of ammunition making numerous hazardous journeys to forward positions to do so. When rations ran out he organised a central kitchen from which he produced out of the products of the country, a hot meal for every man daily. In addition to these activities, he volunteered whenever there was dangerous work to be done and was constantly on anti-sniper patrols in and about the battalion area. On one of these on 23rd September, he discovered an enemy post on which he immediately organised and led an attack as a result of which six enemy were captured and many killed. This NCO's enthusiasm, complete disregard for his personal safety and confident bearing had a most marked effect on all ranks of the battalion and his conduct throughout the battle was in accordance with the highest traditions of the British Army.

## BRITISH EMPIRE MEDAL (BEM):
Staff Sergeant S.F. Johnstone (2 Flight, 'A' Squadron)

On Operation MARKET on Sept 18th, S/Sgt Johnstone took charge of 20 other glider pilots from 'A' Squadron who were without an officer. Throughout the operation he led them on many successful patrols and in the final withdrawal to the river. He showed great resourcefulness, courage and cheerfulness and although leading men of equal rank, his leadership was never doubted.

## DISTINGUISHED FLYING CROSS (DFC):
Major J.F.B. Blatch (2i/c, 2 Wing)

Major Blatch took off on 17th September 1944 from Broadwell, but owing to very bad weather was compelled to land in England; this he succeeded in doing safely. The next day he again took off in his glider and over Holland the tug aircraft was hit by flak and Major Blatch's glider had the whole of one aileron shot away, thereby causing him to force land; this he succeeded in doing successfully just inside the British lines near the Albert Canal. Major Blatch then succeeded in contacting HQ Airborne Forces at Nijmegen and made determined efforts to rejoin the Wing in the Arnhem area, but failed to do so. Had it not been for his flying skill, it is certain that the load he was carrying in his glider, which included senior officers, would have suffered serious injury. (Events carried out away from Arnhem.)

Major S.C. Griffiths (OC 'A' Squadron)

Major Griffiths has shown outstanding qualities as a glider pilot and leader. His courage and enthusiasm throughout previous glider training have been an inspiration to all. He has led his squadron with success both in operations by day and by night. In his recent landings in Holland he led his squadron fearlessly and calmly with the result that an important HQ was landed safely, within a few yards of the German frontier. The success of this operation was mainly due to the example set by Major Griffiths who showed a complete disregard for his own safety.

Having landed his load he led his squadron in ground operations and was a continuous example of courage and initiative for over one week.

### Major T.I.J. Toler (OC 'B' Squadron)

Major Toler has been an example of courage and inspiration to his command. He showed complete disregard for his own safety when training his squadron in glider landings. It was completely due to Major Toler's example, leadership and courage that his squadron landed successfully at Arnhem, although faced with flak in the air and shell fire on the ground. During the ground operations he was a constant example of courage and was highly commended by all those who served under him.

### Captain C.B. Dodwell (OC 12 Flight, 'E' Squadron)

Captain Dodwell has taken part in two airborne operations, the D-Day Normandy landing and Arnhem. On the first occasion he landed in total darkness and at Arnhem in daylight. On each occasion his flying was excellent and his example of cool courage and cheerfulness under most difficult conditions was an inspiration to his men.

### Lieutenant G.R.I.M. Stokes ('C' Squadron)

This officer was flying a glider that was heavily hit by flak some 20 minutes before landing. Lt Stokes and his second pilot were both severely wounded, but Lt Stokes continued to fly the glider to the landing zone. He made an excellent landing in spite of opposition from the ground and saw his passengers safely out of the aircraft before becoming unconscious as a result of his wounds. Lt Stokes throughout showed a splendid spirit of determination and self sacrifice and was an inspiration to his passengers.

### MILITARY MEDAL (MM):

#### WO II (SSM) I.J. Blackwood ('F' Squadron)

This Warrant Officer has been a member of the regiment for over 3 years and as Squadron Sergeant Major has shown excellent organizing ability. He took part in the invasion of Sicily and piloted a glider to Arnhem. Throughout the battle of Arnhem he displayed exemplary bravery, devotion to duty and disregard for is own safety. During every enemy attack SSM Blackwood was to be seen cheering on his men, and his personality and contempt for danger was mainly responsible for his section remaining intact. He was wounded in the face and hands but refused to leave his squadron and was wounded a third time and taken prisoner. He has now been repatriated.

### Staff Sergeant D.B. Wallace ('F' Squadron)

The citation for this NCO could not be traced.

### Staff Sergeant E.J. Holloway (10 Flight, 'G' Squadron)

During the period 19th to 25th September Staff Sergeant Holloway commanded a Section in a house in the area of Oosterbeek. He showed great courage in patrol work. When the enemy launched their first big attack against the gun positions he kept up an effective fire with a Bren gun throughout the time the house was being demolished by a self-propelled gun at point blank range. By remaining at his post he was largely responsible for breaking up the enemy attack. His complete disregard for his personal safety saved what might have been a serious break-through by the enemy.

Sergeant L.E. Hagen (22 Flight, 'D' Squadron)

Throughout the action at Arnhem, 19th to 25th September 1944, Sergeant Haig showed outstanding leadership and example to the men. He volunteered continuously for patrolling and after hard fighting each day carried ammunition through enemy fire during the hours of darkness. In spite of being injured whilst firing a Bren gun he refused to leave his post. At all times he was a fine example by his complete disregard for his personal safety. He instilled great confidence to the other ranks and was in large measure responsible for keeping the enemy away from the positions held.

### BAR TO THE DISTINGUISHED FLYING MEDAL (DFM):

Staff Sergeant H.N. Andrews DFM (11 Flight, 'E' Squadron)

Arnhem 17th to 25th September 1944. This NCO has taken part in three airborne operations and on each occasion has displayed outstanding skill and courage in getting his glider down safely and his load into action. At Arnhem he not only landed successfully but fought throughout with the greatest gallantry and dash, and was an inspiring example to his comrades.

### DISTINGUISHED FLYING MEDAL (DFM):

Staff Sergeant R.R. Calder ('E' Squadron)

This NCO has taken part in three airborne operations and on each occasion has displayed great skill and determination in landing his glider safely and getting his load into action at once. His flying skill and general conduct have been exemplary.

Staff Sergeant A.V. Dance (11 Flight, 'E' Squadron)

This NCO has taken part in three airborne operations and on each occasion has landed his glider safely and got his load into action. In each action he has displayed marked flying skill often under most difficult conditions. His determination and gallantry have been an inspiration to his fellow glider pilots.

Staff Sergeant R.G. Douglas ('E' Squadron)

Arnhem 17th to 25th September 1944. This NCO has taken part in three airborne operations and on each occasion has displayed skill and determination to land his glider in the right places and to get his loads into action, with the least possible delay.

Staff Sergeant S.G. Isaacs ('E' Squadron)

This NCO has taken part in three airborne operations, Sicily, D-Day and Arnhem. On each occasion he has shown the most skilful ability as a pilot and has landed his load safely in the correct place. His determination and coolness under difficult conditions has at all times been most conspicuous.

Staff Sergeant W. Mather ('F' Squadron)

This NCO was first pilot of Glider No. 822. On the approach to the landing zone his glider was hit by anti-aircraft fire and Staff Sergeant Mather lost practically all control over his tail surfaces. Despite this, he stayed on tow until he was in a position to land on the LZ. He then released and attempted to land; he still had very little control over the tail surfaces but by his skill and determination he effected a good crash landing. Staff Sergeant Mather and his second pilot were both injured together with one of their passengers. The remainder of his passengers, however, unloaded his glider and were enabled to join their unit and partake in the operation. Action took place at Arnhem on 18th September 1944.

Staff Sergeant J.A. Rye (Squadron unknown)

Arnhem 17th to 25th September 1944. This NCO has taken part in three airborne operations and on each occasion has displayed skill and courage in getting his glider down safely and his load into action.

Staff Sergeant G.F. Stremes ('F' Squadron)

This NCO flew Glider Tactical No. 769. When approaching the LZ his machine was hit by AA fire and the control surfaces damaged. The pressure bottles in the cockpit burst and Sergeant Wice, the second pilot, was seriously injured. Brakes and flaps were rendered useless. Despite this, however, Staff Sergeant Stremes landed his glider in the correct area, saving the lives of his passengers, but causing serious injury to himself. Action took place at Arnhem on 18th September 1944.

Staff Sergeant C.W. Twiggs (4 Flight, 'B' Squadron)

Arnhem 17th to 25th September 1944. The Horsa glider which Staff Sergeant Twiggs was piloting was badly damaged by flak whilst flying over Holland; in spite of this he managed to control the aircraft and under the most difficult and hazardous conditions flew on and successfully landed his load on the LZ. Through his determination and skill he set a fine example to all pilots and inspired great confidence in his passengers.

Staff Sergeant C.R. Watkinson (3 Flight, 'B' Squadron)

During flight on Operation MARKET 18 September 1944 total aileron control of the Horsa glider which Staff Sergeant Watkinson was piloting completely failed on approaching the Dutch coast, but in spite of enemy flak and the fact that the glider was swinging violently from side to side the glider pilot and the tug aircraft captain, through superhuman efforts, managed to control the combination for a distance of 40 miles towards the LZ until finally through great strain the rope parted. Then with calm judgement and great skill Staff Sergeant Watkinson managed to force land the glider without causing injury to passengers. It was entirely through the skill, courage and cool determination of this pilot that he overcame the most hazardous conditions and avoided a fatal crash, at the same time being successful in landing his load intact within reach of our own troops.

## MENTIONED IN DESPATCHES (MID)

Major K.J.S. Andrews (HQ GPR)
Captain C.T. Mills (OC 11 Flight, 'E' Squadron)
Captain F.J.T. Neale (2 i/c 'B' Squadron)
Captain T.A. Plowman (2 i/c 'F' Squadron)
Captain CF4 G.A.F. Pare (HQ 1 Wing)
Lieutenant P.J. Brazier (25 Flight, 'E' Squadron)
Lieutenant C.C. Tayler (1 Flight, 'A' Squadron)
Staff Sergeant J.E.P. Naden ('F' Squadron)
Staff Sergeant E. Phillips ('F' Squadron)
Sergeant M.I. Gwinn ('G' Squadron)
Sergeant P.J.D. Mahoney (16 Flight, 'F' Squadron)
Sergeant J.R. Mann ('G' Squadron)

## DUTCH BRONZE LION

Major R.S. Croot (OC 'G' Squadron)
WO1 (RSM) M.J. Briody (HQ 2 Wing)

## DUTCH BRONZE CROSS

Captain M.T. Corrie (OC 9 Flight, 'G' Squadron)
Sergeant W.H. Swift ('E' Squadron)

## US SILVER STAR

Major B.H.P. Jackson (OC 'E' Squadron)

## US BRONZE STAR

Lieutenant K.F. Strathern (IO 'D' Squadron)
WO II (SSM) W. Watt ('B' Squadron)

# Select Bibliography

PUBLISHED SOURCES

Airborne Museum Hartenstein, *Harvest of Ten Years*, Arnhem, 1988.

Andrews, Staff Sergeant, A., *So you wanted to Fly, Eh?* Burnaby, B.C. ISTE 1997.

Baynes, J., *Urquhart of Arnhem*, Dover, Brassey's, 1993.

Blackwell, Albert, *Diary of a Red Devil*, Solihull, Helion & Company Ltd, 2005.

Buist, Reinders & Maassen, G., *RAF At Arnhem*, Dodewaard, NL, Friends of ABM, 2005.

Carling, Hugh, *Not Many of Us Left*, J & KH Publishing, 1997.

Chatterton, G., Brigadier, *Wings of Pegasus*, Battery Press, 1962.

Eastwood, S., Gray C. & Green, A., *When Dragons Flew,* Peterborough, Silverlink, 1994.

Essame, Major General H., *43rd Wessex Div at War* 1944-45, London, Clowes & Sons, 1952.

Fairley, J., *Remember Arnhem*, Glasgow, Bell & Bain,1978.

Fullick, R., *'Shan' Hackett*, Barnsley, Pen and Sword Ltd, 2003.

Gibson, Staff Sergeant R.P., *Nine Days*, Ilfracombe, Arthur Stockwell Ltd, 1956.

Harclerode, P., *Arnhem: A Tragedy of Errors*, London, Caxton Publishing, 2000.

Hagen, Sergeant L., *Arnhem Lift*, Barnsley, Pen & Sword, 2001.

Kershaw, Robert, *It Never Snows in September*, Hersham, Ian Allan Publishing, 2005.

Lloyd, A., *The Gliders*, London, Arrow Books, 1982.

Margry, K., *Op Market Garden Then and Now*, London, Battle of Britain Ltd, 2002.

Middlebrook, M., *Arnhem 1944*, London,Viking, 1994.

Miller, Staff Sergeant V., *Nothing is Impossible,* Bury St Edmunds, Spellmount Ltd, 1994.

Montgomery, Field Marshal B.L., *Memoirs*, Barnsley, Pen & Sword Books Ltd, 2005.

Morrison, Alexander, *Silent Invader*, Airlife Publishing, 1999.

Otway, Lieutenant Colonel T.B.H., *Airborne Forces*, London, IWM, 1990.

Powell, Colonel G., *The Devil's Birthday*, Barnsley, Pen & Sword Ltd, 1984.

Ryan, C., *A Bridge Too Far*, Aylesbury, Coronet, 1974.

Saunders, Major T., *The Island: Nijmegen to Arnhem*, Barnsley, Pen & Sword Ltd, 2002.

Seth, R., *Lion with Blue Wings*, London, Gollancz Ltd, 1956.

Sims, Private J., *Arnhem Spearhead*, London, IWM, 1978.

Smith, C., *The History of The Glider Pilot Regiment*, Barnsley, Pen & Sword Ltd, 1992.

Sigmond, R., *Off at Last*, Wageningen, GSC (NL), 2009.

Steer, Brigadier F., *Arnhem: Landing Grounds & Oosterbeek*, Barnsley, Pen & Sword Ltd, 2002.

*The Eagle*, vol. 1, No. 1 to vol. 12, No. 2.

Toler, Ian & Toler, Celia, *Gliding into War*, Warrington, Horseshoe Publications, 1998.

Urquhart, Major General R.E., *Arnhem*, Barnsley, Pen & Sword Ltd, 2003.

Waddy, Lieutenant Colonel J., *A Tour of the Arnhem Battlefields*, Barnsley, Pen & Sword, 2001.

Waldron, Alec, *From Pacifist to Glider Pilot*, Woodfield Publishing, 2000.

Watkins, G.J.B., *From Normandy to the Weser*, Dorchester, The Keep Museum, 2006.

Wiggan, Richard, *Operation Freshman*, William Kimber & Co., 1986.

Wilkinson, Major P., *The Gunners at Arnhem*, Northampton, Spurwing Publishing, 1999.

## UNPUBLISHED SOURCES

Diary of Padre Pare, Chaplain No. 1 Wing GPR.

Holcroft, W., Staff Sergeant, 'No Medals for Lt Pickwood', 1945.

## MUSEUMS & ARCHIVES

Airborne Forces Museum, Duxford.

Airborne Museum Hartenstein, Oosterbeek.

Bundesarchiv, Koblenz.

Gelders Archif, Arnhem.

Imperial War Museum, London.

Museum of Army Flying, Middle Wallop.

The Polish Institute and Sikorski Museum, London.

## THE NATIONAL ARCHIVES

War Diaries and Field Returns, Glider Pilot Regiment

| | |
|---|---|
| WO 171/1230 | HQ Comd Glider Pilots |
| WO 171/1231 | A, D & G Squadron |
| WO 171/1232 | B Squadron |
| WO 171/1234 | 1 Wing |
| WO 171/1235 | 2 Wing, C, E & F Squadron |

### Miscellaneous Glider Pilot Regiment

Air 27/1647 /1652 /2162 Glider Raid Reports

Air 27/1576 Form B Glider

Air 37/1217 and WO 171/1323 Abortive Sorties

WO 361/636 & 638 Casualty Lists

### Operational Record Books RAF

Air 27/437 /1154 /1167 /1433 /1574 /1644 /1645 /1648 /1649 /1654 /1876 /1972 /2041 /2046 /2134 /2159

Air 29/443 /444 /445 Air Sea Rescue

### Escape reports

WO 208/3324 /3327 /3335 /3351 /3352

### War Diaries

| | |
|---|---|
| Air 37/1217 | Log GSOI (Air) Eastcote |
| WO 171/393 | 1st Airborne Division |
| WO 171/1248 | 21st Independent Parachute Company |
| WO 171/406 | 1st Squadron Reconnaissance Corps |
| WO 171/957 | 1st Airlanding Anti-Tank Battery, RA |
| WO 171/958 | 2nd Airlanding Anti-Tank Battery, RA |
| WO 171/964 | 1st Airlanding Forward Observation Unit, RA |
| WO 171/1016 | 1st Airlanding Light Regiment, RA |
| WO 171/592 | 1st Parachute Brigade |
| WO 171/1236 | 1st Parachute Battalion |
| WO 171/1237 | 2nd Parachute Battalion |
| WO 171/1238 | 3rd Parachute Battalion |
| WO 171/1509 | 1 Para Squadron, RE |
| WO 171/594 | 4th Parachute Brigade |
| WO 171/1243 | 10th Parachute Battalion |
| WO 171/1244 | 11th Parachute Battalion |
| WO 171/1247 | 156th Parachute Battalion |
| WO 171/1511 | 4 Para Squadron, RE |
| WO 171/589 | 1st Airlanding Brigade |
| WO 171/ | 1st Battalion, Border Regiment |
| WO 171/1375 | 2nd Battalion, South Staffordshire Regiment |
| WO 171/1324 | 7th Battalion, King's Own Scottish Borderers |
| WO 171/1513 | 9 Field Coy, RE |
| WO 171/1609 | 261 Field Park Coy, RE |
| WO 171/480 | 43rd (Wessex) Division |
| WO 171/1059 | 64 Medium Regiment, RA |

# Index